SATHER

ETHNIC GROUPS OF MAINLAND SOUTHEAST ASIA

FRANK M. LEBAR, GERALD C. HICKEY,
JOHN K. MUSGRAVE

Contributing Authors:

ROBBINS BURLING

ROBERT DENTAN

R. E. DOWNS

MAY EBIHARA

LUCIEN M. HANKS, JR.

JANE RICHARDSON HANKS

ANNA P. McCORMACK

MONI NAG

WILLIAM A. SMALLEY

HUMAN RELATIONS AREA FILES PRESS

New Haven

Compilation and publication of this volume has been financed in part by grants G13018, G21843, and GN-157 from the National Science Foundation.

DEDICATION

This book is dedicated to John F. Embree, pioneer worker in the systematization of Southeast Asian ethnography.

PREFACE

In writing a preface to the present volume, the authors might well quote Major H. R. Davies, who in 1909 prefaced his own volume on the ethnography of Yunnan and neighboring regions with this remark: "It can be asserted with confidence that nothing has been written on this subject that does not contain errors. The present attempt will doubtless be found equally open to such criticism." While it is true that the literature on almost any area contains errors of fact and interpretation, judicious selection, compilation, and organization of such data is often a useful first step in furthering and encouraging more up-to-date field work. This kind of systematic assessment of available information on the peoples of mainland Southeast Asia—including the culturally-related regions of southern China—has remained largely undone. John F. Embree and William L. Thomas, Jr. published in 1950 a preliminary volume that attempted something of the kind for northern Southeast Asia. The coverage is, however, limited, the book has long been out of print, and much new field work has since been accomplished. Had he lived, John Embree would undoubtedly have continued this line of investigation, enlarging and updating subsequent revisions of the original work. In a very real sense, then, the present volume owes much to the labors of Embree and others of Yale's Southeast Asia Studies program. A second, and more immediate, source of inspiration has been George P. Murdock who, while Professor of Anthropology at Yale, conceived the idea of an outline of Southeast Asian cultures similar to his previously-published volumes on South America and Africa. In 1960 a grant was obtained from the National Science Foundation for the compilation and publication of such a book by the Human Relations Area Files— the work to be done by Frank M. LeBar with the collaboration of George P. Murdock and Wu-chi Liu. Both Murdock and Liu were subsequently called to the University of Pittsburgh, and LeBar, as senior author, then continued the writing in collaboration with Gerald C. Hickey and John K. Musgrave. In addition, outside contributions were invited from individual fieldworkers—particularly those with new and hitherto unpublished data. The summary format used in the present volume is largely Murdock's contribution, although the scope of the over-all work and the extent and detail of coverage depart somewhat from his original conception. • Considerable thought has been given by the authors to the problem of the identification of units for purposes of ethnographic description and to the subsequent organization of descriptive summaries for presentation in book form. After much casting about, it was agreed that language, although admittedly not always in agreement with the realities of cultural identification and cultural dynamics, nevertheless offered the only consistent and complete basis for the selection and arrangement of units. E. R. Leach, writing on the peoples of the Kachin Hills area of Burma, rightly points out the incorrectness of always assuming that the people who speak a particular language form a unique unit with a particular culture, i.e. a "tribe" or "race." Leach demonstrates very well how in a relatively small area in northern Burma common social and political structures crosscut the conventional, linguistically-derived concepts of tribe and tribal culture. Nevertheless, Leach himself, as soon as his discussion leads him outside the confines of his definition of Kachin culture, uses the very terminology he decries earlier; thus we find him discussing *the* Lakher, *the* Hkamti Shans, *the* Atsi, Lashi kinship, etc. And this, of course, is the crux of the problem. Until Leach or someone continues his type of analysis beyond the Kachin Hills, we are left with the conventional tribal units and subunits—defined in most cases largely on the basis of linguistic criteria, and adopted almost without exception throughout the existing literature. • Similarly, the order or arrangement of groups for presentation could be based on criteria such as location within a particular country or geographical region, type of economy, relative altitude, etc. In all such criteria, however, there are implicit serious drawbacks —inadequate data for a consistent and exhaustive classification, overlapping leading to repetition, and the like. The authors have attempted a compromise in this situation; the over-all order of presentation is in terms of major language stocks and divisions within these; and within this general framework they have attempted to distinguish between lowland and upland groups—a distinction reflecting also to some extent the type of economy. A similar arrangement has been followed with respect to the ethnolinguistic map at the back of the book. • The area included within the present volume considerably exceeds that covered by Embree and Thomas in 1950. It includes some 28 degrees of latitude—from Malaya north to the Nosu country of southern Szechwan. Its westward extension includes the Garo, a Tibeto-Burman-speaking people of Assam; eastward, it includes the peoples of Hainan Island and the middle Hsi Chiang drainage in eastern Kwangsi province of southern China. Ethnologically speaking, northern Southeast Asia does not stop at the China border; centuries of migrations, trade, and political relationships link the peoples of Burma, Thailand, Laos, and Vietnam with the southern provinces of China—Yunnan, Kweichow, Kwangsi, and Kwangtung. This entire region, which might be termed greater mainland Southeast Asia, forms an integrated whole for purposes of the study of racial and linguistic history, ethnic distributions, and cultural evolution. Adequate understanding of the past history and present relationships of speakers of Tai dialects, for example, can only be had by considering them in the perspective of this broader regional concept. The importance of India and the Hinduization of the early Mon and Khmer states cannot, of course, be overlooked in any consideration of cultural evolution in Southeast Asia. However, preoccupation with the sometimes spectacular results of early Indian influence can lead to an underestimation of the great significance of China and the Han Chinese for the present ethnological picture of mainland Southeast Asia. Particularly is this true if one considers the total ethnic make-up of the area—the tribal groups in the uplands as well as the developed civilizations of the river valleys—and if one's perspective is extended backward in time to the early dynastic periods of Chinese history and beyond to a consideration of a southern China—northern Southeast Asia neolithic. Viewed in this manner, China's influence has perhaps been less in terms of the more obvious traits of art, architecture, and governmental structure, and more in the nature of subtle, centuries-old currents of ethnic history—the ebb and flow of diverse ethnic strains and the widespread distribution of very basic cultural traits. Over the centuries the sociopolitical evolution of China has affected the course of events, the movements of peoples, and the ethnic complexion of Southeast Asia—a relationship that continues to operate down to the present time. **Technical notes.** In general, groups are called by the name used most frequently in the literature, e.g. Kachins rather than Jinghpaw. Each cultural summary is prefaced by a list of synonyms for the name of the group, wherever such are reported. Only generic-type synonyms are listed. All names, including variant spellings, names of local or restricted usage, sub-group names, etc., are included in an index at the back of the book, where each is keyed to the relevant group name as it appears in the table of contents. Pluralization of names in general follows popular usage as reflected in the literature. To aid in the location of ethnic groups by country, each of the groups summarized is listed at the back of the book under the political entity within which it is most numerous. • The summaries are, with obvious exceptions, written in the present tense. In each case, however, the reader should consult the historical section and also refer to the publication dates included in the documentation, in order to form his own judgment of the contemporaneousness of the data. • A special effort has been made to document each summary section, and often each paragraph, as fully as possible. References pertaining to an immediately preceding sentence or paragraph are enclosed in parentheses; those encompassing an entire section or several sentences or paragraphs are enclosed in brackets. Those sources used for a particular summary are listed alphabetically in the bibliography section at the end of the summary as well as in the complete bibliography at the back of the book. • Diacritical marks indicative of an author's transcription of native words, such as kin terms, have in general been omitted; the reader wishing to do so can easily find the relevant reference in the bibliography and proceed from there to consult a particular author's phonetic system. Anthropological terms for kin groups and descent rules have generally been reported as the original author uses them; where reference is made to G. P. Murdock's terminology the reader should consult his *Social Structure,* New York, 1949. • The authors of individual contributions are indicated by name in the table of contents, opposite the names of groups on which they have written summaries. The remaining groups have been covered by the three principal authors: In general Musgrave has assumed responsibility for groups in the Burma area, Hickey for groups in the area of what was formerly French Indochina, and LeBar for groups in southern China, Thailand, and Malaya. • Musgrave's contributions include the Burmese, Chins, Kachins, Mons, and Palaungs. • Summaries on the following groups were written by Hickey: Alak, Ataouat, Bahnar, Bih, Black Tai, Bout, Brao, Bru, Cao, Chams (Cambodia), Chams (Vietnam), Cheng, Chong, Chrau, Churu, Cua, Duane, Halang, Halang Doan, Hre, Hroy, Jarai, Jeh, Kalo, Kasseng, Katang, Katu, Kayong, Khua, Kil, Krung, Kui, Lang Ya, Lat, Laya, Lolo (Indochina), Loven, Ma, Man (Indochina), May, Menam, Meo (Indochina), Mnong, Monom, Muong, Ngeh, Ngung Bo, Nha Heun, Nhang, Noang, Noar, Nop, Nung, Oy, Pacoh, Pa-y, Pear, Phuong, Pru, P'u Noi, Raglai, Rai, Red Tai, Rengao, Rhadé, Rien, Ruc, Sach, Saoch, Sapuan, Sayan, Sedang, Sek, So, Sop, Sork, Sou, Souei, Sre, Stieng, Tau-Oi,

Thap, The, Tho, T'ou Lao, Tring, Trung-cha, Ven, Vietnamese, and White Tai. ● Those groups summarized by LeBar include the Achang, Ahom, Akha, Chaobon, Chinese, Chuang, Chung-chia, Haw, Hkamti Shans, Hpon, Jakun, Kadu, Kelao, Khorat Tai, Khün, Lahu, Lamet, Laotian Tai, Laqua, Lati, Lawa, Li, Lisu, Lolo, Lolo (Kweichow), Lolo (Yunnan), Lü, Lutzu, Meo (Thailand), "Miao" (Hainan), Miao (South China), Minchia, Moken, Nakhi, Neua, Nosu, Nüa, Pak Tai, Panthay, Phuan, Phuthai, Semang, Shans (Burmese), Shans (Chinese), T'in, Tung-chia, Wa, Woni, Yao (Lingnan), Yao (Thailand), Yuan, and Yumbri. In addition, LeBar, as senior author, has been responsible for the over-all arrangement of the book, the drafting of introductory sections, arrangement of the bibliography, and preparation of the two indices. **Acknowledgments.** The contributing authors—Robbins Burling, Robert Dentan, R. E. Downs, May Ebihara, Lucien M. Hanks, Jr., Jane Richardson Hanks, Anna P. McCormack, Moni Nag, and William A. Smalley—have given generously of their time as well as their specialized knowledge, and their considerable contribution to this book is hereby gratefully recognized. George P. Murdock and Wu-chi Liu aided greatly in the preparation of the present volume, particularly in the early stages of planning and discussion. George Devereux contributed unpublished data on the Sedang and checked the Sedang manuscript. Unpublished information on the Chams of Vietnam and the Lue of Thailand was made available by Rufus S. Hendon of Columbia University and Michael Moerman of the American University School of International Service. Miss Sylvia Lombard, Overseas Missionary Fellowship, Chiengrai, contributed notes on the Yao of northern Thailand and checked information in the field. Demographic information on urban populations was kindly furnished by Norton S. Ginsburg of the University of Chicago; Irene B. Taeuber of the Office of Population Research, Princeton University, helped with advice and data from the Chinese People's Republic census, as did William Carr of Alexandria, Virginia. The following individuals kindly checked draft manuscripts: Charles S. Brant of the University of Alberta, Edmonton (Burmese Shans), Michael Moerman (Lü), Robert Dentan of New York (Jakun and Moken), Joel M. Halpern of Brandeis University (Laotian Tai), Pierre Lafont of the Ecole Française d'Extrême-Orient (Lü, Black Tai, White Tai, Nhang, etc.), and Georges Condominas of the Centre de Documentation sur l'Asie de Sud-Est (Mnong). In addition, professors Lafont and Condominas contributed material from unpublished field notes and aided in the location of various groups in Vietnam and Laos. Rev. Gordon Smith, World Wide Evangelization Crusade, Tourane, and David D. Thomas, University of North Dakota Summer Institute of Linguistics, Wycliffe Group, Saigon, checked locations of groups in the central and southern highlands of Vietnam. Robert Dentan kindly furnished a sketch map of the ethnic groups of Malaya, as did Rev. Don Rulison, Overseas Missionary Fellowship, Chiengmai, for portions of northern Thailand. William J. Klausner, Asia Foundation, Bangkok, James W. Hamilton, University of Michigan, Robert B. Textor, Harvard University, and William A. Smalley, Thailand Bible House, Bangkok, checked the location of groups in parts of western and northeastern Thailand. Huynh Sanh Thong, Southeast Asia Studies, Yale University, gave assistance with the Vietnamese sources; Chester Natunewicz of Yale University assisted with the Russian sources, as did Timothy J. O'Leary of the Human Relations Area Files staff. Hesung Koh, Mary Rouse, and Wu-chi Liu aided at various times in the handling of Chinese and Japanese language materials. An unpublished manuscript on the T'in of northern Thailand was kindly furnished by Rev. Garland Bare, Churches of Christ Mission, Nan province. Inez deBeauclair of the Academia Sinica, Taiwan, generously furnished advice and information on the Miao and Yao groups of southern China, and John F. Brohm, Institute of International Education, Bangkok, provided demographic and other information on various groups in northern Thailand. The Southeast Asia Studies program, Yale University, aided in the publication of the ethnolinguistic map, and the program director, Karl J. Pelzer, and members of his staff advised on mapping problems at various times. To all these individuals the authors owe a special debt of gratitude. Special thanks are due, also, to Peter J. Wilson and John F. Plummer, who aided in the preparation of first drafts of a number of the summaries. Editorial assistance has been cheerfully and competently rendered by Adrienne Suddard, Lorna Bissell, Elizabeth Swift, and Irene Thamel. To Frank W. Moore, Timothy O'Leary, Michael Lazna, Gladys Page, Josephine DePonte, Helen Reed, and other members of the Human Relations Area Files staff, the authors are grateful for advice and assistance in various stages of manuscript preparation. The assistance of the National Science Foundation, in support of the research and publication of this book, is hereby gratefully acknowledged.

New Haven, Connecticut
May 1964

A NOTE ABOUT THE MAP

A fold-out map in two sheets, designed to accompany the text, is included in a pocket at the back of the book. The map covers an area equivalent to that of the text, with the exception of a portion of northern Kwangtung, including the Ju Yüan–Linshan region. It is keyed to the arrangement of groups within the body of the text, the primary criterion being language. In this respect the classification largely follows that of Greenberg (1953). Linguistic affiliation within major divisions and subdivisions is indicated by the color key, as well as by number; ethnic group names are printed on the map in capital letters in the approximate area of location. Areas of marked ethnic mixture, as along the border regions between major groups, are indicated by the substitution of dots for solid colors. Where subgroup names are reasonably well-known and accurately located, these have been indicated. All of the major groups summarized in the text are included on the map. ● Ethnic mapping is at best a thankless task—perhaps more so in a region such as Southeast Asia than in some other parts of the world. In reality, there are few fixed "tribal" boundaries that can conveniently be shown on a map, most areas of Southeast Asia being highly mixed from an ethnic point of view. Furthermore, the conventional map cannot indicate the vertical distribution of peoples, so important in the mountainous regions; and swidden farmers, in particular, are frequently migratory, so that ethnic boundaries are at best only indicative of the actual situation. In recognition of these facts, only the approximate location of groups is shown—ethnic boundaries have been intentionally omitted. The map should perhaps best be viewed as a whole, in order to grasp the over-all distribution of peoples and their spatial interrelationships in this part of the world. ● The important published ethnolinguistic maps for greater mainland Southeast Asia are the *Carte ethnolinguistique de l'Indochine,* prepared under the direction of the Ecole Française d'Extrême-Orient and published in Hanoi by the Service Géographique de l'Indochine in 1949; a map of northern Southeast Asia, extending south as far as 17° N. and including groups immediately across the border in China, published by Embree and Thomas of Yale's Southeast Asia Studies program in 1950; and, more recently, the two maps, one on China and one on Southeast Asia, published in Moscow by the N. N. Miklukho-Maklay Ethnographic Institute (Bruk 1959a, 1959b). The Embree-Thomas map relies heavily on the French map, plus older sources such as the *Linguistic Survey of India* (Grierson 1903-28) and various gazetteers and censuses published by the colonial government of India in the period 1900-30. The Russian map for Southeast Asia, in turn, relies on the *Carte ethnolinguistique,* Grierson, and other standard sources, and contains little if any new information. The Bruk map for China, however, has incorporated the results of Russian surveys, together with the results of censuses and mapping surveys undertaken by the Chinese People's Republic since 1949. The China portion of the map accompanying the present volume relies heavily, therefore, on Bruk (1959a). Additional sources of information for China have been Wiens (1954), Davies (1909: end map), Its (1960: 8), Stübel (1937: end map), Rock (1947: end maps), and, for provincial boundaries and the location of autonomous nationality areas, the atlas published by the United States Central Intelligence Agency (1959). For the complex border areas of China with northern Southeast Asia, in addition to the Bruk maps, the following have proved helpful: Grierson (1903-28: vols. 2 and 3), *Carte ethnolinguistique de l'Indochine* (1949), Embree and Thomas (1950: end map), and Rose and Coggin Brown (1911: Plate 9). The Burma portion of the map relies to a considerable extent on Bruk (1959b), with additions based on Embree and Thomas, the 1931 *Census of India,* the *Imperial Gazetteer of India* (1908), and the report of the Union of Burma, *Karen Special Enquiry Commission* (1951). The mapping of northern Thailand is mainly based on Young (1961), supplemented and corrected somewhat by sketch maps and personal information obtained from Rev. Don Rulison and William A. Smalley. The distribution of Karen speakers in northern and western Thailand is based on Bruk (1959b), Young (1961), and personal information from James W. Hamilton. The remainder of Thailand relies primarily on Bruk (1959b), Credner (1935a: facing p. 144), and Seidenfaden (1958: facing p. 89), with some changes in the northeastern portion based on comments by Robert B. Textor, William A. Smalley, and William J. Klausner. General sources for Indochina, in addition to the *Carte ethnolinguistique de l'Indochine*, include the NNCDT (1959) for Vietnam, and Hoffet (1933) for central Vietnam and southern Laos. For the location of highland groups in southern Vietnam, Dam Bo (1950), Phillips (1962), and Smith (1959) proved especially useful. The following were utilized for the mapping of specific groups in the Indochina area: for the Muong, Cuisinier (1948: 22); for the Red Tai, Robert (1941: map 3); for the Rhadé, Maurice and Proux (1954: facing p. 149) and Jouin (1949: 133); for the Mnong, Huard and Maurice (1939: 28-30) and Condominas (1957: frontispiece map); for the Sre, Boulbet (1957: 108); and for the Samre, Baradat (1941: 4). In addition, Pierre Lafont personally advised on the location of groups in northern Laos and Vietnam, as did Georges Condominas for Mnong groups in southern Vietnam. The Rev. Gordon Smith and David D. Thomas contributed information on the location of groups in the Vietnamese central and southern highlands. The Malaya portion of the map relies heavily on a sketch map prepared by Robert Dentan (1962), working from unpublished materials in the Kuala Lumpur office of the Department of Aborigines, Federation of Malaya. Additional sources for Malaya have been Schebesta (1952: facing p. 182), Noone (1936: end map), and Skeat and Blagden (1906, 2, facing p. 386). The mapping of areas of concentrated Chinese settlement within Malaya is based primarily on population maps in Ginsburg and Roberts (1958: 58, 59, 132). Two recent linguistic publications by Pinnow (1959) and Salzner (1960) were utilized in checking the location of Mon-Khmer and Malayo-Polynesian-speaking groups, respectively.

TABLE OF CONTENTS

PART III. TAI-KADAI

PART IV. MALAYO-POLYNESIAN

PART I. SINO-TIBETAN

SINITIC

ACCORDING TO 1953 CENSUS FIGURES for mainland China, the Han total over 554 million. They do not, however, constitute a homogeneous population; the figure does not, for example, include some 3.5 million Moslem Chinese—the Hui or Hwei. Physical type and culture vary in different parts of China, and there are at least nine major dialects of spoken Chinese. Only two of these are important in southern China —southwestern Mandarin in the Yunnan-Kweichow area and Cantonese in Kwangtung-Kwangsi (Hu et al. 1960). ● Native Chinese speakers in Yunnan and Kwangsi number more than 24 million. Adding to this figure the more than 10 million overseas Chinese on mainland Southeast Asia, it is evident that Sinitic is the largest single language stock within the area under consideration in the present volume. It is closely rivaled, however, by Tai, with a total of some 30 million speakers. If, as has been the traditional view, Chinese and Tai are considered to be related within a Sino-Tibetan macrofamily of languages, then speakers of Sino-Tibetan languages account for well over 60 per cent of the total population of greater mainland Southeast Asia, including the culturally related provinces of Yunnan and Kwangsi in southern China.

CHINESE

ORIENTATION. Chinese peasant farmers have for centuries been settling within the tribal areas of southern and southwestern China. This "march to the tropics" of the Han has been documented by Wiens (1954). Today they are found over practically the whole of the area except in low-lying malarious valleys, such as those in extreme southwestern Yunnan, or inaccessible mountain retreats, such as the heart of the Taliang Shan in southern Szechwan. Sinicization—both acculturation and actual physical assimilation—of non-Han peoples has been extensive, and original distinctions have become blurred, reduced in many instances to differences in language and minor social usages (Wiens 1954; Coon, in preface to Mickey 1947). Practically everywhere in South China the Han are settled on the plains and along fertile river valleys, with the non-Han populations occupying the less desirable land in the foothills or on higher mountain slopes. Exceptions occur, however, as in southwestern Yunnan, where Tai-speaking Lü occupy fertile river basins considerably below Chinese hill farmers (Wissmann 1943). Han Chinese penetration has also occurred all across northern Southeast Asia, where despite a generally mountainous terrain discouraging to wholesale immigration,

Chinese hill farmers are present in small numbers. The Han influx here has, however, more often been in the form of itinerant merchants and caravan traders, as witness the extensive caravan traffic to and from Yunnan recorded by late nineteenth-century observers of Zimmé (Chiengmai) town in north Thailand. Incursions into northern Indochina of Chinese refugees turned brigands were especially troublesome in the years following the Moslem rebellions in the 1850s (Le Boulanger 1931). ● More recent has been the entry of the overseas Chinese, estimated at ten to fifteen million, into the major ports, cities, and surrounding areas throughout Southeast Asia (cf. Purcell 1951). In Thailand, Chinese immigration is of long standing, and here the definition of "Chinese" at times presents difficulties (Coughlin 1960). In countries such as Malaya the influx has been more recent and cultural separateness is more pronounced (Ginsburg and Roberts 1958). Overseas Chinese are concentrated in the major cities and towns, but they can also contribute to an ethnically mixed farming population, as along the western coast of Malaya (Dobby 1955). Generally the urban Chinese have engaged in trade and commerce, their dominant role as middlemen in the rice economy of Thailand being a case in point (Blanchard 1958). The numbers of Chinese are particularly striking in the large port cities: In 1947, Singapore (city) was 79 per cent Chinese, and the population of Bangkok has been estimated to be almost one-half Chinese. ● Southeast Asia has for centuries experienced the periodic repercussions of political events in China, and at times, as with Vietnam, has actually come under Chinese control (cf. Coedès 1944). Contemporary pressures of China into Laos and Vietnam would thus appear to be a continuation of a long-established pattern.

BIBLIOGRAPHY. Blanchard 1958; Coedès 1944; Coughlin 1960; Dobby 1955; Ginsburg and Roberts 1958; Le Boulanger 1931; Mickey 1947; Purcell 1951; Wiens 1954; Wissmann 1943.

PANTHAY

Synonyms. *Ho, Hui, Hui-tze, Hwei,*
Pang-hse, Panthe, Pathee

ORIENTATION. **Identification.** The well-known Moslem Chinese muleteers of the Burma–China frontier area are known locally by the Burmese term Panthay (Panthe, Pathee). They are called Pang-hse by the Shans (Scott and Hardiman 1900: 606-13). In China, Mohammedan Chinese are called Hui (Hui-tze, Hwei). In northern Thailand, according to Embree and Thomas (1950: 48), they are called Ho. **Location.** There are an estimated 3,500,000 Moslem Chinese in all of China, located chiefly in the north and northwest. There are Moslem Chinese settlements in Yunnan in the Tengyueh area, and scattered settlements in Burma in the Wa States–Kengtung area. [Scott and Hardiman 1900: 606-13; Embree and Thomas 1950: 48-49.] **Linguistic affiliation.** Sinitic. **Demography.** Bruk (1960: 24) lists 217,000 Hwei in Yunnan and 10,000 in Kwangsi. Because of their itinerant habits, it is difficult to estimate the number of Panthay in Burma; in 1931 there were said to be slightly over 1,100 (Embree and Thomas 1950: 48). **History and cultural relations.** The Hwei of China, according to Bruk (1960: 23-24), are probably of mixed origin, some being descendants of Persian, Arabic, and Central Asian Moslems who migrated to China in the thirteenth and fourteenth centuries and became Chinese; others deriving from Chinese who, in areas such as extreme northwestern China, adopted Islam from their neighbors. Bruk adds that the Hwei seldom live together with other Chinese, but form separate communities or quarters within cities. The Panthay of Burma are chiefly known as muleteers on the trade routes. They are excellent caravan drivers, carrying goods as far as Rangoon and Moulmein. They are mostly engaged in trade, and cultivate only just enough to supply their immediate needs. Much of the domestic work is carried on by slaves or by hired servants. [Scott and Hardiman 1900: 606-13.]

BIBLIOGRAPHY. Bruk 1960; Embree and Thomas 1950; Scott and Hardiman 1900.

HAW

Synonym. *Ho*

ORIENTATION. **Identification and location.** Chinese, mainly Yunnanese, hill farmers and traders resident in northern Thailand and Laos are known locally by the Tai term Haw or Ho (Young 1961: 110; Sisawat 1952: 272; Le Boulanger 1931: 236). Likewise the Lü term for Chinese hill farmers in the Sip Song Panna is Ho (Wissmann 1943: 5, 19). **Linguistic affiliation.** Sinitic. **Demography.** Scattered communities in Thailand number at most 650 persons (Young 1961: 111). **Cultural relations.** Those in Thailand, with their relatively advanced agricultural techniques and methods of animal husbandry, are said by Young (1961: 111) to be greatly admired by other hill peoples such as the Lahu and Lisu. Their example, therefore, may be of considerable importance should they continue to settle in these areas.

BIBLIOGRAPHY. Le Boulanger 1931; Sisawat 1952; Wissmann 1943; Young 1961.

TIBETO-BURMAN

TIBETO-BURMAN SPEAKERS in greater Southeast Asia number in the neighborhood of 19 million. They occur in relatively large concentrations in western and northern Burma, and are widely scattered in Yunnan and along the China-Burma border south into Thailand and northern Indochina. With the exception of the Burmese, they are predominantly upland dry-field farmers, integrated to varying degrees into the economic and social systems of the dominant people around them. Relatively little is known of the languages and cultures of the Tibeto-Burman-speaking groups in China and their position relative to the more adequately described Kachins, Burmese, Chins, and Nagas. Shafer (1955) places the majority of those languages classified as Tibeto-Burman in the present volume within a Burmic division of Sino-Tibetan. Lolo, Lahu, Lisu, and Akha—which Davies (1909) classed together as a Lolo group within Tibeto-Burman—are also classed together by Shafer, as part of a Lolo branch of a Burmish section of his Burmic languages. These four groups appear to be closely related both linguistically and culturally, and in fact Lin (1944: 47) writes that the Lolo consist of five groups: the Lolo proper, the Woni, the Lisu, the Lahu, and the Akha. They have in common a segmented (patrilineal) lineage system and the division of the totality of, e.g., the Akha, into (usually seven or nine) major named "tribes" (major lineage divisions). A similar structure is also found among the Kachins and the Nakhi. Frequently these divisions are explained by an origin legend including a postdeluge motif (and in some cases, e.g. Lisu, brother-sister incest). ● Peoples such as the Lolo are widely scattered and in Yunnan, for example, tend to live with members of other groups in an ethnic complex dominated by the Han Chinese. The description by Chiang (1948a) of the situation in Kunming county helps to clarify the problems of ethnic and tribal identity and of the dynamics of culture change in an area such as southwestern China. The Lolo live in some 200 villages, mainly in the northern and western parts of the county. Speakers of Lolo do not, however, occupy a single block of territory; rather their villages are interspersed with those of other groups such as the Miao, Tai, Minchia, and Han. Despite strong Han acculturative and assimilative influences (in the form of a Han administrative system, Han schools, Chinese as a lingua franca, Han domination of trade within the area, and intermarriage with Han women), each village continues to maintain its ethnic identity. Many villages continue the custom of refusing to allow other races or tribes to move in, and the indigenous language tends to be spoken within the village even though most villagers know Chinese. ● One might well speak of village-level ethnicity in an area such as that described by Chiang; identification is with the village, and the dividing line between one group and another is often based on difference in language. Under such circumstances the traditional concept of tribe in any kind of territorial or political sense is misleading. These observations are similar to those made by Leach with respect to the Kachin Hills area of Burma. As phrased by Leach (1954: 290), the only "continuing unit of political structure is the village [and] peculiarity of language serves to uphold the continuing unity of the village community in the face of rapid shifts of power in the external political world." Going a step further, Chiang's data are suggestive of what might be called "Kunming county ritual culture" analogous to that found by Leach in the Kachin Hills, i.e. a common language of mutual values and concepts relative to political power, correct status behavior, and the status ranking of different languages. Some of the significant factors are: common participation in the Han political-administrative system; a system of land tenure and landlordism that may include Han landlords over Lolo tenants, and Lolo landlords, in turn, over Miao tenants; the tendency of certain villages to specialize in performing services and supplying the needs of both Han and non-Han; and participation in a common religious culture made up of elements from both Han and non-Han sources. The Lolo *hsi-po* serves both Lolo and Chinese clients, for example. Lolo, Miao, Tai, and Han hold common beliefs regarding the potency of Tai practitioners of *fang-tai* and *ku* poisoning, and annual festivals and religious gatherings are attended by Han and non-Han alike.

EASTERN UPLAND GROUPS

LUTZU

Synonyms. *Anu, Lutze, Noutze, Noutzu, Nu, Nusu, Nutsu, Nutzu*

ORIENTATION. **Identification.** The small population of Tibeto-Burman speakers in the upper Salween valley, between the Lisu country to the south and Tibet to the north, call themselves Nusu, Nu, or Anu. They are known to the Chinese as Lutzu (Lutze) or Nutzu (Nutsu, Noutzu, Noutze, etc.), terms meaning "people of the Salween," and occasionally used in a generic sense to include the Lisu as well as the group specifically known as Lutzu. [Bruk 1960: 29; Rock 1947: 330-35; Ward 1912: 584; Siguret 1937: 167-68.] D'Orléans (1898: 260-62) describes what he regards as a closely-related group in extreme northern Burma just west of the Salween, called by the Chinese, Kiu-tse. He adds that they are called Khanung by the Hkamti Shans—given on English maps as Nung. Embree and Thomas (1950: 145) and Rock (1947: 338-39), giving the name as K'iu-tzu (Chiu-tzu), say essentially the same thing, adding that the K'iu-tzu (or Nung) are hired by the Lutzu to plow and plant their crops. Leach, in discussing the Nung within the Kachin Hills area of Burma, states that they resemble the Jinghpaw closely in most aspects of culture other than their language, which appears more closely related to Tibetan. He makes no mention of their relationship, if any, to the Lutzu (Leach 1954: 45, 59). **Location.** The upper Salween valley in extreme northwestern Yunnan and in Tsha-rong district in southeastern Tibet, between 27° 30′ and 28° 30′ N. and 98° 20′ and 98° 50′ E. Here the Salween valley opens out into broader reaches, and the "wild Lisu are replaced by a more tractable folk, the real Lutzu" (Rose and Coggin Brown 1911: 256). They are usually divided into two groups—the northern or Black Lutzu of the arid valley region in Tsha-rong, and the southern Lutzu of the more moist regions of the Salween in northwestern Yunnan. [Rock 1947: 275-76, 330; Ward 1912: 589; Siguret 1937: 168.] **Linguistic affiliation.** Tibeto-Burman. The southern Lutzu are nonliterate, but among those in the north a very few have knowledge of Tibetan writing. [Bruk 1960: 25; Rock 1947: 330; Siguret 1937: 173.] **Demography.** Siguret (1937: 168), using Chinese sources, reports about 10,000 southern Lutzu and some 6,000 northern Lutzu. Bruk (1960: 19), quoting 1953 Communist census figures, gives a total of 13,000. **History and cultural relations.** Both Ward (1912: 588) and Siguret (1937: 175-76) oppose the theory that the Lutzu migrated southward along the Salween together with other Tibeto-Burman-speaking tribes. Ward suggests that because of their short stature, their head carrying straps, their crossbows (which he identifies as jungle weapons), their gourd and bamboo utensils, and their rope bridges, they are a jungle people who migrated from west to east. ● The Lutzu are effectively confined to the Salween valley and the lower slopes of the mountains separating its tributaries; on the higher slopes, as well as to the south, are the warlike Black Lisu, while to the north are the frequently hostile Tibetans. The latter have greatly influenced the northern Lutzu, who have the two-storied Tibetan house with flat roof, wear Tibetan waist sashes, sometimes use Tibetan writing, and have an economy more approaching that of Tibetans than Lisu. In the past the southern Lutzu have been politically dominated by the Nakhi, or by the Chinese indirectly through the Nakhi. More recently Chinese political domination has been more direct (cf. Wiens 1954: 327). There has long been contact with a few Europeans through a Catholic mission at the Lutzu village of Bahang. [Rock 1947: 330-35, 339; Ward 1912: 586-89; Siguret 1937: 168-69, 175-76; d'Orléans 1898: 260-62.]

SETTLEMENT PATTERN AND HOUSING. **Settlement pattern.** Villages are usually located on bluffs overlooking the Salween; they are small and the houses are widely scattered in a haphazard pattern. [Siguret 1937: 586; Rock 1947: 330; Ward 1924: 139.] **Housing.** Except for the Tibetan-style architecture in the north, houses are built of roughly dovetailed pine logs. A ridge pole supports crossbeams which rest directly on two walls. The roof consists of large wooden shingles often kept in place by rocks. The gable ends are left open or are partially filled in with bunches of dry bracken. There is no chimney. Inside are one or two rooms. Often the house is built on piles or against a slope so that the space underneath can be used for cattle and for pigpens and chicken coops (Ward 1912: 586; Rock 1947: Plate 189). Rock (1947: 334-35), citing Chinese historical sources, mentions houses with bamboo roofs and plaited bamboo walls.

ECONOMY. **Agriculture.** The Lutzu, like the Lisu, are primarily shifting agriculturists. Crops include buckwheat, maize, white potatoes, beans, barley, millet, wheat, rice, tobacco, gourds, and hemp. Rock, citing Chinese historical sources, also mentions yams and taro. [Rock 1947: 334-35; Ward 1912: 586; Wiens 1954: 327.] **Fishing and hunting.** Fishing is accomplished by drifting downstream in a canoe, sweeping under the water a V-shaped net supported between two long bamboo poles. Hunting for large and small game and birds is done with the crossbow and sometimes with firearms. [Ward 1912: 586, 589; Siguret 1937: 172.] **Domestic animals.** Herding is a prominent activity. Cattle are important, each family owning one or two head. They also keep sheep, pigs, a few horses, and chickens. When agricultural labor is suspended during winter and spring, the uncultivated fields become pastures for sheep and cattle brought down from the uplands. [Siguret 1937: 168-69.] **Food** and stimulants. The staple is maize, supplemented by barley, wheat, buckwheat, and rice. They also eat wild animals and plants. Most foods are boiled, and salt is used sparingly. Large quantities of grain liquor and beer are consumed. The liquor, drunk warm, has a pea-soup consistency and, according to Ward, is more nourishing than inebriating. In winter men and women sit around the fire for hours drinking from bamboo cups and smoking tobacco in long pipes. [Ward 1912: 586-87; Siguret 1937: 168; Rock 1947: 334-35.] **Industrial arts.** Drinking vessels are made from bamboo and gourds. The Lutzu also make rope bridges and dugout canoes, and weave hemp cloth. [Rock 1947: 334; Ward 1912: 586, 588-89.] **Trade.** The area was opened to Chinese merchants some 50 years ago. The Lutzu barter opium and skins for salt, tobacco, iron kettles and plows, alcohol, and cloth. Salt, strictly controlled by the Chinese, is in great demand. [Siguret 1937: 173; Wiens 1954: 327.] **Division of labor.** Both men and women work at agriculture. The men also hunt and trade, and the women look after the children and weave cloth. [Ward 1912: 586; Siguret 1937: 168; Rock 1947: Plate 189.]

KIN GROUPS. The major kin group is the nuclear family (Siguret 1937: 170).

MARRIAGE AND FAMILY. Siguret quotes a Chinese author on the inconsistencies of the Lutzu system of courtship and marriage. It seems to have elements of strict Chinese regulation on the one hand, and of prenuptial intercourse and easy divorce on the other. [Siguret 1937: 171-72.] **Mode.** Siguret (1937: 171) reports two kinds of marriage. In one, the girl, when still young, goes to live in the family of her future husband. In the other, a couple decide on marriage themselves and then ask the parents to arrange the betrothal. Cattle, liquor, clothes, utensils, and other gifts are presented to the bride's family at the time of betrothal, and feasting goes on for several days at the time of the marriage. [Siguret 1937: 170-72.] **Form.** Monogamy is usual, although concubinage is occasionally found among the southern Lutzu (Siguret 1937: 170). **Residence.** Residence is neolocal (Siguret 1937: 171). **Domestic unit.** The domestic unit is the nuclear family. Upon marriage a couple set up their own household (Siguret 1937: 170). **Divorce.** If a couple are not in accord they have the liberty of divorce, which is frequent and easy (Siguret 1937: 171-72).

SOCIOPOLITICAL ORGANIZATION. **Political organization.** The Lutzu customarily acknowledge the authority of the Nakhi (or, through them, the Chinese) at Weihsi. Actually, rule from Weihsi has often been suspended because of warfare and poor communications. The actual ruler is the village headman, who occupies himself with local affairs and settles disputes. [Siguret 1937: 169.] **Social stratification.** Ac-

cording to Siguret (1937: 172), there is little or no stratification. On the other hand, Wiens (1954: 327), citing Chinese sources, reports remnants of slavery; children of slaves remain slaves, and class differences between masters and slaves are marked. **Warfare.** Although they have knives, crossbows, and firearms, the Lutzu are generally regarded as peaceful and are preyed upon by their neighbors (Siguret 1937: 172; Rock 1947: 333-34).

RELIGION. Religion is a modified form of Lamaism grafted to a much older animism, according to Ward (1912: 587). Priest-exorcists seem to be the main practitioners, although certain rites are carried out by individuals (Siguret 1937: 172, 174).

BIBLIOGRAPHY. Bruk 1960; Embree and Thomas 1950; Leach 1954; d'Orléans 1898; Rock 1947; Rose and Coggin Brown 1911; Siguret 1937; Ward 1912, 1924; Wiens 1954.

NAKHI

Synonyms. *Lühsi, Lükhi, Moso, Nachri, Nahsi, Nashi, Nazo, Wuman*

ORIENTATION. **Identification.** The name Nakhi (*na*, black; *khi*, man) was probably given these people by earlier inhabitants of their present area of occupation, referring either to their relatively dark complexions or to the fact that they formerly lived in black tents. Those in the area of Likiang, the capital city of the old Nakhi kingdom, call themselves Nakhi (Nahsi). The Chinese term Moso, used as a synonym in much of the literature, is felt to be derogatory and is therefore resented by the Nakhi. Whether the ancient Moso of the Chinese annals are identical with the Nakhi remains a moot question, according to Rock. The same author regards the present-day Moso, living in the Yungning area to the northeast of the Nakhi, as a related people; they do not, however, possess a written language. The Likiang Nakhi call these people Lükhi (Lühsi). ● The Nakhi also call themselves Nazo, meaning "the sons of Na," and Nashi. They are sometimes referred to as Nachri (cf. d'Orléans 1898: 210-15). Wuman, an old Chinese term meaning "black people" or "black barbarians," is sometimes applied both to Nakhi and Lolo. Under the Chinese People's Republic they are called Na-hsi and their territory has been designated the Li-chiang Na-hsi Autonomous Hsien. [Embree and Thomas 1950: 151-53; Wu 1945: 28; Rock 1947: 65; 1952a: 2-3; 1963: 11.] **Location.** The Nakhi territory extends from 26° to 29° N. and from 98° 30′ to 102° E. The majority are in northwestern Yunnan province, within the loop of the Yangtze river north of Likiang. They extend westward as far as the Mekong, north to the

Tibetan border, and east into southwestern Szechwan. Tibetan villages are interspersed with those of the Nakhi in parts of this area; to the west and southwest are Lutzu and Lisu tribesmen, and some 30 miles to the south are the Minchia. Chinese influence has remained minimal until relatively recently; Chinese settlers have been few, barred by the mountainous terrain and the deep gorge of the Yangtze which encircles much of the Nakhi homeland. [Fitzgerald 1941: 12; Cordier 1908: 663-65; Rock 1947: 4; 1963: 9; Bacot 1913: 3-7; T'ao 1936: 130-31.] **Geography.** The Nakhi inhabit an area of high mountain ranges and deep river gorges. The climate varies, depending on altitude. Likiang, at 8,200 feet, has a moderate, temperate climate with a summer rainy season. Oak, pine, spruce, and hemlock forests cover much of the area. The fauna includes deer, leopards, bears, foxes, rats, porcupines, wildcats, wild dogs, pheasant, ducks, and other fowl. [Rock 1963: 15.] **Linguistic affiliation.** The language is Tibeto-Burman, closely resembling Lolo. An indigenous script contains both pictographic and syllabic characters. The latter, according to Rock, was primarily brought from Tibet. The former the Nakhi developed *in situ*. Manuscript books preserve ancient tribal legends and rituals of Bon shamanism. Largely mnemonic in character, the writings are chanted only by the priests, *dto-mba*. Although many Nakhi can speak some Chinese, literacy in Chinese in the Likiang district was less than 5 per cent in 1933. [Rock 1935; 1936b; 1947: 181; 1952a: 17-20; 1963: 42-44; Bacot 1913: 27-28, 64-67.] **Demography.** In 1933 there were an estimated 132,582 Nakhi in the Likiang district (Rock 1947: 173). Wu (1945: 28) reports 150,000 to 160,000. Bruk (1960: 19), using 1953 Communist census figures, gives a total Nakhi population of 143,000. **History.** Rock, reasoning from the evidence of indigenous manuscript accounts, Chinese historical records, and comparative ethnology, believes that the Nakhi have been in their present area for upward of 2,000 years, having migrated from an original homeland in northeastern Tibet where they were a branch of the Ch'iang. Originally a nomadic, herding people living in felt tents, they were evicted by the Chinese and forced to move southward. During their migrations they became hunters, but when they reached the area of present-day Likiang they settled on the lands of an autochthonous agricultural population and themselves became tillers of the soil. By 1000 A.D. they had largely replaced or absorbed the earlier inhabitants. The period 1600-1650 marked the height of the Nakhi kingdom, famous for its warriors. The Likiang area came under Chinese influence during the Mongol dynasty, and in 1390 the surname Mu was granted the indigenous line of rulers. These continued to rule under the *t'u-ssu* system until the 1700s, when the area was nationalized and Han magistrates were appointed from Kunming. During the Republic the ruling families lost much of their remaining land

and political power. The last Nakhi prince, of the 33rd generation, was reportedly executed by the Communists. [Rock 1963: 11ff.] **Cultural relations.** Historically the Nakhi evidence close cultural ties to Tibet, especially with respect to religion, writing, and certain aspects of economy. The Minchia, to the south, have long been a source of supply for trade goods such as pottery. More recently the Nakhi have come under Chinese influence, particularly in the area of Likiang city. Eastward, in the area of Yungning, and to the north, in southern Chungtien district, there was prior to World War II considerably less evidence of Chinese administrative controls (Wiens 1954: 323-24). Contact with Europeans has been through Catholic and Protestant Pentecostal missions in the predominantly' Chinese town of Weihsi, and a weather strip and emergency landing field established during World War II. According to Goullart (1957: 236-59), Likiang was infiltrated and taken over by the Communists in mid-1949, after an earlier attempt by military force had been repulsed by a combined force of Nakhi and Tibetans. [Rock 1947: 45-46, 66-69, 180-81, 191-93, 274.]

SETTLEMENT PATTERN AND HOUSING. **Settlement pattern.** Settlements are nestled in narrow valleys, ravines, and small alluvial basins, or built on terraces above river gorges. Altitudes generally range between 6,000 and 10,000 feet, although Nakhi villages do occur above 10,000 feet. Terraced fields supported by rock walls surround most settlements. [Rock 1947: 171-200 passim.] **Housing.** Houses in Likiang city are built on the Chinese model with brick and tamped earth walls, tiled roofs, and upturned gables. Those in the rural villages are of (mud) brick and stone, built directly on the ground with earthen floors. They have wooden superstructures and rough plank roofs held down by stones. Tall wooden racks for drying grain and turnips are interspersed among the houses. [Rock 1947: 399 passim.]

ECONOMY. The subsistence economy reflects the historical origins and migrations of the Nakhi people. Although they are for the most part sedentary agriculturists, herding on alpine meadows is of almost equal importance, especially in mountain areas. Hunting, once a major source of food, still provides a portion of the diet. Trade is particularly well developed in the Likiang area. **Agriculture.** Major crops are wheat, maize, barley, buckwheat, potatoes, and turnips. The latter are particularly important. Oats are raised but are of minor importance. Vegetables include peas, lentils, peppers, beans, cabbage, parsley, cucumbers, and eggplant. Walnut, peach, persimmon, and other fruit and nut trees are raised. Opium poppies, formerly an important cash crop, declined in importance following the suppression of poppy cultivation in the 1930s. Along the deeper river valleys, where the growing season is sufficiently long and warm, cotton, tobacco, and rice are grown. [Rock 1947: 40-41 passim.] Most crops depend on rainfall rather than irrigation because the fields occupy terraced hill and mountain slopes and limestone plateau surfaces, with numerous sink holes and little surface drainage. Planting and harvesting are done collectively, each family supplying labor proportionate to the amount of land it holds. [Wu 1945: 31.] Fields are plowed with oxen. Nakhi manuscript accounts mention the use of wooden flails, braided bamboo containers for winnowing grain, and stone mortars with wood pestles for husking grain. [Rock 1963: 21.] **Fishing and hunting.** Hunting was formerly a major source of food, according to Rock. Manuscript accounts mention the use of the bow and arrow, traps, and dogs. Hunting is still done to some extent, and deer, muskdeer, stag, blue sheep, goral, and serow are taken for food. Foxes, small panda, lynx, wildcats, leopards, and weasels are hunted for their skins. [Rock 1963: 23.] **Domestic animals.** Manuscript accounts mention horses, cattle, yak, sheep, chickens, and dogs, as well as the construction of beehives (Rock 1963: 23, 25). Cattle, goats, yak, and sheep are pastured on alpine meadows. The herds are extremely important for the subsistence of villages in mountain areas. The animals spend spring and summer on the upland under the care of shepherds and are returned to the village when cold weather comes. In the warm valley areas, pigs and chickens are raised. [Rock 1947: 3; Wu 1945: 31.] **Food and stimulants.** The diet varies according to climate and also to the degree of sinicization. Peasant farmers in the mountainous areas remote from Chinese influence live largely on roasted barley meal, unleavened wheat bread, turnips, nuts, yak butter, and tea. As in Tibet, the butter is taken, together with salt, in tea. The dry, flat bread is baked in ashes. Mutton is eaten occasionally and the meat from game is cooked in soups and stews. In other areas, e.g. in and around Likiang, the Nakhi diet may resemble that of the Chinese, consisting of rice, chicken, pork, and vegetables. The latter include cabbage, parsley, beans, cucumbers, and eggplant. Cooking oil is expressed from walnuts, rape, and hemp. Manuscript sources mention pickled fish and vegetables. A special food is boneless, meatless pig, called *bu-cher*. The skin, with the fat attached, is salted, sewn together, and stored for a number of years. Nakhi chiefs keep immense numbers of such skins. They may be used as mattresses, and when desired as food the skin is cut into strips and dropped into boiling water long enough to soften it without melting the fat. Liquor is made by steaming grain and fermenting the resulting mash with the aid of an alpine plant. Opium is smoked but there are few cases of addiction; according to Rock, the Nakhi only grew opium under pressure from the Chinese. [Rock 1947: 413-14 passim; 1963: 21-22; Bacot 1913: 10.] **Industrial arts.** Manuscript accounts mention locally-made utensils of wood. The Nakhi appear to have had no knowledge of pottery, obtaining what pottery they did use from the Minchia. Women wove hemp cloth and made felt from sheep's wool. Armor and weapons of leather and iron were formerly in use, but whether these were made locally or obtained from the Minchia is unclear. [Rock 1955: 26-30; 1963: 22-23.] **Trade.** The people rarely leave their homeland. Exceptions are the muleteers who travel as far as Tali and Kunming, and the few Nakhi traders who formerly made twice-yearly trips to Lhasa. During the years of the opium trade, caravans carried raw opium to Szechwan. Domestic trade is carried on in local and regional markets. At daily markets in Likiang, Nakhi and other tribesmen exchange local products for imports such as salt and Chinese tea. In more isolated areas barter is still common; in more urban and sinicized areas Chinese currency is used. Women do most of the trading, both in markets and shops. Observers comment on the remarkable freedom and economic independence accorded women in Nakhi society. [Rock 1963: 18; Wu 1945: 31-32; Goullart 1957: 24, 94-96.] **Division of labor.** Women do most of the work, except plowing and hunting. Men sometimes play nursemaid while the women work. In many families the chief economic producers are women. **Land tenure.** There is some tenancy in the more fertile and accessible areas but large landowners are now rare. The average family is estimated to need from 1.5 to 3.0 acres in order to maintain itself. In the mountains most people work their own land. [Wu 1945: 32.]

KIN GROUPS. The Nakhi of Likiang area belong to a number of [patrilineal] clans, descended from four original clans established by four sons of a legendary postflood ancestor. These four took the names: Ho, Ma, Yu, and Ssu. Clans today include Gv-har, Gv-ndza and Pu-dtv (belonging to the Ssu clan), and Gv-ho (including the line of native rulers, known to be descendants of the Yu clan). The ancient Nakhi had no family names; the ruling family was granted the Chinese name Mu in 1390, and at this time peasants took the name of Ho. The related Lükhi (Lühsi) of the Yungning area have different family names. [Rock 1963: 20.] According to Wu (1945: 29-30), a clan head arbitrates disputes, especially those concerned with the division of family property. Most clans have some common property on which sacrificial ceremonies to heaven are held. Rock (1952b: 16-17) adds that the clans differ with respect to the dates on which they perform these ceremonies. ● Lo (1944-45) describes a genealogical patronymic linkage system common to Burmese, Nakhi, Lolo, and Akha, whereby the last one or two syllables of the father's name are repeated in the first part of the son's name. The system appears to be more common among ruling families.

MARRIAGE AND FAMILY. **Mode.** Except in the more remote areas, marriages are arranged by the parents through go-betweens, following Chinese custom. Largely Taoist ceremonies mark most marriages today, although there was formerly an indigenous ceremony in which the *dto-mba,* or priest, tied the string of the family life god to a man and his bride. The many suicides among Nakhi are attributed by observers to incompatibility of indigenous premarital intercourse with the Chinese system of early betrothals and arranged marriages. Young men who have formed romantic attachments often commit double suicide with their sweethearts. Manuscripts, chanted for the propitiation of suicides, paint the afterlife of a love suicide in the most rosy colors and thus, according to Rock, provide a great inducement to suicide. [Rock 1963: 31-32; Fitzgerald 1941:75; Goullart 1957: 181, 182.] **Form.** Monogamy is common, although polygyny is, or was, permissible (Rock 1963: 31). **Extension of incest taboos.** Only people of close blood relationship and living in the same area consider themselves members of the same clan or surname group. There is no prohibition against marriage within the same surname, provided the couple do not live in the same immediate area. [Wu 1945: 30.] **Residence.** Patrilocal residence, either within or near the house of the parents, is general among the Nakhi of Likiang area. **Domestic unit.** The patrilocal extended (stem) household is found in more remote areas, whereby one son is designated heir apparent and continues to live with his parents after his marriage. **Inheritance.** Strictly within the male line. If there is no son, a married daughter's husband may join the family as an adopted heir. In cities and towns, inheritance tends to conform to Chinese custom. [Wu 1945: 29.] **Divorce.** Easy and inexpensive in more remote areas uninfluenced by the Chinese. Concubinage occurs only among wealthy acculturated Nakhi.

SOCIOPOLITICAL ORGANIZATION. Hereditary ruling lines exist in both Likiang and Yungning. The Likiang line, bearing the family name Mu, has been in the area for 33 generations. The history of the Nakhi kingdom, which seems to have reached its height in the seventeenth century, is contained in Chinese annals as well as indigenous manuscripts; these, however, concern themselves solely with biographies of rulers and their military exploits. Nevertheless it seems clear that the Nakhi rulers sorely taxed the peasants within their domains in order to contribute money, supplies, and manpower to the Chinese in return for titles and honors from the imperial court. [Rock 1947: 45-171; 1963: 25.] According to Wu (1945: 30-31), the political unit is the fortified village, in charge of a headman. The headmen within an area are usually related to the hereditary ruling family, e.g. the Mu in the Likiang area. **Warfare.** The Nakhi have for centuries fought both in local bands and in Chinese armies against brigands, Tibetan raiders, and others. Estimates of the Nakhi as warriors differ. According to Wu (1945: 30), they prefer bows and arrows to modern arms and are weak defensively; whereas according to Goullart (1957: 96) they are brave, loyal soldiers, long the mainstay of Yunnan provincial armies. Manuscript accounts mention a variety of weapons and armor, including swords, bows and arrows (but not crossbows), a clawlike weapon of iron fixed to a wooden staff, bamboo shields, segmented iron helmets, and laminated hide cuirasses. [Rock 1955: 26-30; 1963: 27.]

RELIGION. **Major religions.** Few Nakhi are strong adherents of any major religion, although there have been attempts to establish Christianity and Buddhism. Lamaism, the Tibetan offshoot of Mahayana Buddhism, numbers some adherents, among whom it is mixed with pre-Buddhist paganism. The number of Nakhi lamas has, however, been decreasing for years. Both Red and Yellow (reformed) sects are represented —the lamas among the latter, however, being almost all Tibetans. Religious beliefs and practices also evidence Taoist, Chinese Buddhist, and Confucian influences. [Rock 1947: 201-11; 1952a: 1-20; 1963: 36-45; Bacot 1913: 14-26; Goullart 1957: 100.] **Indigenous religion.** The Bon shamanism of pre-Buddhist Tibet long ago diffused to the Nakhi, among whom it is still maintained in much of its original form. The continuation of these ancient beliefs and practices is due in great part to an extensive literature written in pictographic script and preserved by hereditary priests, *dto-mba,* who for some one thousand years—until the first decades of the twentieth century—directed the lives of villagers. [Rock 1963: 36-45.] **Supernaturals.** The great gods of the Nakhi are represented in the sacred texts. There are innumerable spirits, *nagas,* including those of sky, earth, mountains, rivers, trees, rocks, cliffs, and other natural objects. In addition, the Nakhi recognize over 500 demons. [Rock 1935; 1947: 269; 1952a: 8; 1963: 39.] **Practitioners.** Religious specialists include priest-exorcists (*dto-mba*), shamans (*llu-bu*), lamas, Taoist priests sometimes utilized at marriages, and Chinese Buddhist priests employed at funerals. The *dto-mba,* priests of the Bon cult, were formerly found in every village, although within the past few decades they have virtually ceased to function in the Likiang area. The office, including the sacred manuscript texts which preserve the ancient tribal legends and Bon rituals, is inherited within the male line. The texts are only partially written in syllabic characters, the remainder being in pictographs which serve a mnemonic function; the priest chants the text largely from memory, as learned from his father (Rock 1952b: 10). The *dto-mba* perform a great variety of ceremonies at most of which they chant the appropriate litany—inviting the gods to be present, or cursing demons to make them harmless. They formerly wore large felt or bamboo hats and long dark blue cloaks when professionally engaged. When evicting demons, the *dto-mba* fight sham battles with them—dancing in pairs while gyrating and slashing the air with their swords and carrying their Bon gongs. They perform divination by a variety of methods—consulting the sacred manuscripts, tying cords, burning the shoulder blades of sheep and interpreting the cracks produced thereby, burning chicken bones, etc. A *dto-mba* can be engaged to sorcerize an enemy by praying him to death —preparing a straw image of the victim and chanting over it for up to seven days. [Rock 1936a; 1963: 36-38; Goullart 1957: 179-92.] The *llu-bu,* according to Rock (1963: 36-38), have nothing to do either historically or in practice with the *dto-mba.* They cannot chant the indigenous script and are ignorant of the ceremonies performed by *dto-mba.* They were formerly women, but are now always men—frequently individuals inclined to mental imbalance and nervous disorder. They suffer from hallucinations and illusions and become shamans by being possessed by a spirit. When excited, they are insensible to pain, holding red hot plowshares between their teeth, and dipping their hands into burning oil. In practice, the *llu-bu* chant in a peculiar wailing tone, manipulating objects such as swords and gongs, and sometimes beating a large drum. They specialize in exorcising demons and performing séances in which they put clients in touch with long dead ancestors. **Ceremonies.** Rock has recorded a great many Bon rituals in detail, including those for worshiping nature, curing illness, assuring the prosperity of the family and the increase of herds, propitiating mountain and tutelary spirits, performing marriages, conducting funerals, inviting the ancestors, prolonging life, evicting demons, purification and elimination from sins, and propitiation of suicides. The *dto-mba* selects the appropriate ritual text after consulting the divinatory manuscripts to determine the spirit causing the trouble. Many of the Bon ceremonies include blood sacrifice, and are conducted at an altar in a grove of trees outside the village. The major ceremony, Muan Bpo, or the "Sacrifice to Heaven," is carried out twice yearly, or oftener, depending on clan affiliation. [Rock 1947: 191-200; 1952a: 4-5, 25-30; 1963: 44.] **Illness and medicine.** Illness is caused when demons or evil spirits take up their abode in man or beast. In serious cases a *dto-mba* is called in to exorcise the offending spirit. [Rock 1952a: 8-10.] Wu (1945: 15-16) describes belief in *ku* poisoning, i.e. illness due to snake *ku,* centipede *ku,* and the like, magically introduced into the food of a victim by *ku* poisoners, mostly women. **Soul, death, and afterlife.** Ancient and elaborate funeral ceremonies and cremation of the dead are still carried out in isolated areas; otherwise, the Nakhi have adopted burial and the use of Chinese Buddhist priests at funeral ceremonies. Manuscript accounts mention elaborate funerary rites performed periodically by an entire village, at which time the bones of cremated bodies were collected, placed in small bags, and deposited in caves or interred on a mound. [Rock 1955; 1963: 33; Goullart 1957: 179-80.]

BIBLIOGRAPHY. Bacot 1913; Bruk 1960; Cordier 1908; Embree and Thomas 1950; Fitzgerald 1941; Goullart 1957; Lo 1944-45; d'Orléans 1898; Rock 1935, 1936a, 1936b, 1947, 1952a, 1952b, 1955, 1963; T'ao 1936; Wiens 1954; Wu 1945.

MINCHIA

Synonyms. *Ber Dser, Ber Wa Dser, LaBhu, Minchia-tzu, Pai, Pai-jen, Pai-man, Per-nu-tuu, Per-tsu, Petsen, Pe-tso, Petsu, Shua Ber Ni*

ORIENTATION. **Identification.** Minchia (families of the people), Minchia-tzu (sons of the families of the people), and Pai-jen (white people) are all names of Chinese origin. Minchia names for themselves include Shua Ber Ni, Ber Dser, Ber Wa Dser, Per-tsu, Per-nu-tuu, Pe-tso, Petsu, and Petsen. Their neighbors to the north, the Nakhi, call them LaBhu. [Davies 1909: 372; Fitzgerald 1941: 12, 13.] **Location.** In western Yunnan between 25° 30′ and 26° 40′ N. and 99° 10′ and 100° 20′ E., north of the Burma Road between the Mekong and Yangtze rivers. The main concentration is in the plain of Tali east of Erh Hai lake; lesser concentrations are in the valley of the Erh river, along the eastern shore of the lake, and in the valley of the Yang Bi river west of the lake. Some smaller separated groups are found in the Kunming plain, in the Ho Ching region to the north of Erh Hai, and in scattered colonies near the Mekong river. [Fitzgerald 1941: 1; Wiens 1954: 319ff.] **Geography.** The Tali plain is just north of the tropics, at an altitude of about 6,000 feet. The altitude modifies the summer heat, and the subtropical position results in warm, sunny winters. **Linguistic affiliation.** The exact linguistic position of Minchia is as yet unclear. It was considered by earlier writers to be a Mon-Khmer language with strong Sinitic and Tibeto-Burman influences with respect to both vocabulary and grammar. Others (cf. Chiang 1948a: 25 ff.), possibly reasoning from the fact that these people inhabit the area of the ancient kingdom of Nanchao —supposed to have been a nation of Tai speakers— have regarded Minchia as basically a Tai language. Credner (1935b: 8-9), on the basis of vocabulary studies, found no evidence for a Tai relationship, however. Greenberg (1953: 283) finds that even when obvious Chinese borrowings are accounted for, the language still shows a fundamental affinity to Chinese, and therefore tentatively classifies it as Sinitic. Bruk (1960: 31), presumably following modern Chinese usage, classifies the Minchia (called Pai by the

Chinese People's Republic) as speakers of a Tibeto-Burman language related to the Lolo group. ● Despite many Chinese loan words, the language is unintelligible to ordinary Chinese. More than half the vocabulary and grammar are unlike Chinese, many words being partly polysyllabic. Most Minchia are nonliterate, and such literacy as exists is in Chinese. However, most speak Chinese and also maintain their own language. [Fitzgerald 1941: 13, 15-20.] **Demography.** Bruk (1960: 19), using 1953 Communist census figures, gives a total of 567,000. **History and cultural relations.** Unlike other non-Han peoples of northern Yunnan, the Minchia are old inhabitants of the area. They are not dispersed among other population groups, and they have not been displaced by Chinese rice farmers. They themselves have been rice farmers in the area at least as far back as the seventh and eighth centuries A.D., when Tali was a capital in the kingdom of Nanchao (Fitzgerald 1941: 21-22). If they are an old branch of the Tai, as Fitzgerald thought, they have no sense of kinship with Tai groups today. Credner (1935b: 11) theorizes that Nanchao was an expression of Tai dominance of a basically non-Tai population. ● Nanchao was conquered by Kublai Khan in the mid-thirteenth century, and has been a part of China ever since. The result has been the gradual penetration of Chinese culture, especially in dress, architecture, and village plans. The main break in the steady sinicization of the area came in 1855, when the Moslem population of the Tali district rose up against their non-Moslem neighbors—resulting in 20 years of confusion and bloodshed. ● Because their centers of population are surrounded by hill country, the Minchia have relatively few contacts with the Szechwanese on the east or the Nakhi to the north. Most contact is with the Chinese, particularly along the southern border of the Tali plain. According to Fitzgerald, they do not feel themselves an oppressed people and have had no great desire to distinguish themselves from the Chinese. ● There is also contact with Lisu and Miao villagers who come to fortnightly Minchia markets and spring and autumn fairs, with Tibetans through caravan trade, and with Burmese, both through trade and because of the Minchia who work in the jade mines of northern Burma during the winter. Until World War II, contact with Europeans was limited to travelers and missionaries. The main impact of the missionaries was to set the standard of living for the small wealthy class. Poverty, inaccessibility, and the lack of an export to replace the opium which was banned in the 1930s have made conditions unfavorable to rapid cultural change. [Embree and Thomas 1950: 148-49; Fitzgerald 1941: 11-14, 188-90, 210-26; Hsu 1943: 2.]

SETTLEMENT PATTERN AND HOUSING. **Settlement pattern.** The Minchia cultivate good rice lands in the Tali plain and nearby river valleys. Only rarely do they dwell on the nearby mountains. To free as much land as possible for rice cultivation, they build their houses in clusters on the poorer land near the lake, or on lower mountain slopes. [Fitzgerald 1941: 8, 43.] **Housing.** Houses are built on the typical Chinese courtyard plan, but are usually two-storied. Other distinctive features are the black and white arabesque patterns on the end walls, which are thought to show Moslem influence, and the small pointed windows in the end and back walls. [Fitzgerald 1941: 47.]

ECONOMY. **Agriculture.** Although they are found mainly in the Tali basin at about 6,000 feet, some are located as high as 7,500 feet in the surrounding hills. It is thus possible, according to Credner, to speak of plains Minchia and hill Minchia. Among the former, wet rice is the main crop, along with barley, wheat, millet, and beans, and it is possible to grow both summer and winter crops. The hill Minchia grow barley, buckwheat, oats, and beans, and only summer crops are possible (Credner 1935b: 10-11). Other crops, particularly among the plains Minchia, include tobacco, carrots, onions, taro, turnips, artichokes, peas, long beans, potatoes, corn, sorghum, apricots, tea, and cabbages. They also grow hemp for string, pulse for lamp oil, and indigo for blue dye. On the eastern shore of Erh Hai are highly productive pear, peach, and citrus orchards. Opium was an important cash crop from early in the nineteenth century until its suppression in 1937. [Fitzgerald 1941: 7, 48; Hsu 1943: 4; Buck 1937.] **Fishing and hunting.** The potentialities of fishing in Erh Hai are fully realized. Along the shallow shores fishing is done with tame cormorants; in deeper water nets are used. Fish are kept alive in a barrel or tank until they are brought to market, where they are in great demand. Most net fishing is done by families from those eastern shore villages that have little or no rice land. They live permanently on their boats, but often own village property as well. [Fitzgerald 1941: 42-43.] Game is scarce in the intensively cultivated plains area, although there are pheasant, hares, partridge, wild goats, deer, wolves, leopards, and possibly tigers on the wooded slopes of the mountains west of Erh Hai. According to Fitzgerald (1941: 39), the Minchia have little aptitude for hunting. **Gathering.** Many kinds of wild fruit grow in the mountains west of Erh Hai but no attempt is made to cultivate them or gather them for sale (Fitzgerald 1941: 42, 186). **Domestic animals.** Villagers at the base of the mountains graze small flocks of sheep, cattle, and goats on the lower slopes. Many families also keep a few pigs and chickens. Water buffalo and oxen are used for plowing. Unlike the Chinese, who think milk and milk products unfit for human consumption, the Minchia milk their cows and make two kinds of cheese. The quality of wool is poor, and the flocks are not large enough to produce an appreciable amount. Little mutton is consumed (Fitzgerald 1941: 39, 41; Buck 1937). **Food and stimulants.** Except for the consumption of milk and milk products, the kinds and use of food and stimulants are much the same as among the Chinese (Hsu 1943: 6, 7). **Industrial arts.** Boats are large and well built, the details of their construction suggesting a long and independent development. Tsang Shan, a large mountain west of Erh Hai, is famous for its marble, and Minchia laborers are employed in this industry. The men are known throughout Yunnan as masons and carpenters and are employed in the cities by wealthy Nakhi and Chinese (Goullart 1957: 128-31). The extraction of sulphur and its sale for medicine employ still other Minchia. Cottage industries include embroidery, needlework, furniture carving, and leatherwork. **Trade.** According to Fitzgerald (1941: 32, 44), external trade is unimportant. Hsu, however, believes that external trade is a major activity (Hsu 1943: 10), and Goullart (1957: 128-31) mentions that Minchia men are regularly engaged in running caravans from Likiang down to Tali. The suppression of opium in 1937 took away the main cash crop and trade item, and most people now live largely on their own produce. Direct barter of rice for commodities is common. Rents are paid in rice, and rice land is both the chief investment of the wealthy and the principal source of revenue for the government. Most villages have no shops. To make purchases a villager goes to Tali or to one of the markets held every sixth day in a few of the larger villages and towns. There are also large fortnightly fairs in Tali. [Fitzgerald 1941: 23, 43-44.] **Division of labor.** Men do the heavy work of plowing, but otherwise men and women do the same field work. Women weed, cultivate, transplant, assist the men at harvesting, and carry produce to market and sell it. [Fitzgerald 1941: 157-58.] **Land tenure.** Most rice land is in private ownership. Ideally, married sons live in the parental home and work the land held by the father. Actually, the land is usually divided among the sons when the parents die (Fitzgerald 1941: 57-58).

KIN GROUPS. Although they are politically and militarily Chinese, and the Chinese language is replacing Minchia, the social organization and kinship system are largely indigenous. The village, not the kin group, is the fundamental social unit above the extended family. No matter what surname they bear, people in the same village revere a common ancestor (*ber dser*), the reputed founder of the village. [Fitzgerald 1941: 78.]

MARRIAGE AND FAMILY. Both Fitzgerald and Goullart mention the freedom accorded young girls, who attend the markets and there engage in buying and selling produce quite on their own. Goullart also calls attention to the coquettish nature of the Minchia girls. Despite this apparent freedom, however, the Minchia follow the Chinese custom of regarding premarital intercourse as a crime punishable by imprisonment for a man and drastic family action for a woman. [Fitzgerald 1941: 157-58; Goullart 1957: 128-31.] **Mode.** Marriage is arranged by the parents through a marriage broker known to both families. Bride and groom never meet before the marriage and it is considered bad taste for families to negotiate directly. **Form.** Monogamy is the general rule. If a couple fall in love without an arrangement being made by the parents, the usual custom is for the man to abduct the girl and bring her to his home. After some wrangling, an arrangement is usually worked out between the families whereby the man may be forced to take his betrothed as his first wife and the girl he loves as his concubine. [Fitzgerald 1941: 78, 158.] **Extension of incest taboos.** Village exogamy is not practiced. Minchia not only marry members of families with the same surname but also paternal cousins of the same generation (Fitzgerald 1941: 86-87). **Residence.** Residence is initially patrilocal, but after the death of the parents, the sons usually divide the property and set up separate establishments. **Domestic unit.** The patrilocal extended family is still the most common domestic unit. **Divorce, separation, and concubinage.** Divorce is difficult for both men and women, and is avoided if possible because of the scandal, which results in hostility and sometimes ostracism. The easiest solution is for a man to take a concubine in addition to his wife, but few individuals can afford this. Even among the rich there are few concubines except in exceptional cases—as when a wife is barren. Among peasants, a nephew or cousin of a younger generation is adopted if a wife is barren. [Fitzgerald 1941: 148-70; Hsu 1943: 3.]

SOCIOPOLITICAL ORGANIZATION. **Political organization.** The political organization is completely Chinese (Fitzgerald 1941: 74-75, 90-92). **Social stratification.** Social stratification depends largely on wealth, which is based on landownership. Large landowners make up the highest social class within a community; somewhat lower on the scale are those who own and work their own land; tenants and laborers are placed in the lowest social class (Fitzgerald 1941: 92). **Warfare.** Since the days of Kublai Khan, connection with warfare has been largely through recruitment in various provincial and national Chinese armies. The Chinese army has always been one of the main channels through which Chinese civilization has penetrated the Minchia area.

RELIGION. **Major religions.** Local deities and ancestral spirits are venerated along with Buddhist and Taoist gods. **Indigenous religion.** Ancestor worship, little different from that of the Chinese, is the main religious concern. Whether those aspects of ancestor worship that differ slightly from current Chinese practice reflect indigenous religion or merely an earlier Chinese influence has not been determined. **Supernaturals.** Buddhist Bodhisattvas and Taoist deities, together with local gods and ancestral spirits are all called *ser* (supernatural beings). A distinction is made between *ser* and the ghosts of deceased people, called *gur*. **Practitioners.** Buddhist priests are sometimes called in to recite sutras at a funeral or when there is sickness in a household. Otherwise, ancestor worship is conducted at home by the head of the family. **Ceremonies.** The two main ceremonies honor the ancestors. The Shu Pao (Burning the Bundles) ceremony consists of burning cardboard boxes which are covered with colored paper and made to resemble books. The name, birth and death dates, and age at death of one deceased ancestor are inscribed on each book. The head of the household reads each inscription, and then hands the book to one of the assembled children to burn on a nearby fire. The second major ceremony in honor of the ancestors, differing slightly from Chinese Buddhist practice, is held at the lunar new year. **Illness and medicine.** For sicknesses which are due to possession by an evil spirit or a demon, hereditary exorcists are called in to dance and chant secret formulas to control the ghosts and evil spirits. [Fitzgerald 1941: 128-29, 138-39.] **Soul, death, and afterlife.** The Minchia generally follow Buddhist belief in regard to the soul, death, and afterlife. Tombs are elaborate and distinctive. A cylindrical monument with a rounded top and an arched front of granite is fitted over a false tomb chamber of marble, which covers the actual grave. The arch and marble slabs are elaborately carved with dragons, horses, and, more recently, flags. [Fitzgerald 1941: 93.]

BIBLIOGRAPHY. Bruk 1960; Buck 1937; Chiang 1948a; Credner 1935b; Davies 1909; Embree and Thomas 1950; Fitzgerald 1941; Goullart 1957; Greenberg 1953; Hsu 1943; Wiens 1954.

KACHINS

Synonyms. *Chingpaw, Jinghpaw, Kakhieng, Singhpo, Theinbaw*

ORIENTATION. **Identification.** Kachin, a term of uncertain origin, is applied particularly to the people who call themselves Jinghpaw (other spellings, Chingpaw and Singhpo), speakers of one language of limited dialectical variation. Kachin is also applied to a larger group which includes the Jinghpaw as well as the Atsi, Lashi, and Maru, smaller ethnic groups in the area. Kachin will be used here for the Jinghpaw, since the sources usually, though not always explicitly, describe the latter. Indeed most of the sources—Carrapiett, Gilhodes, Hanson, and Leach—appear to have described the Jinghpaw of the same rather limited

area—the southeast corner of the Kachin State and the adjoining northern part of the Shan State—who represent only about one-fifth of the total Jinghpaw population. There is little information on the Atsi, Lashi, and Maru, whose culture seems to be very similar to that of the Jinghpaw and for whom the Kachin (Jinghpaw) language serves as a lingua franca. [Hanson 1913: 30; Leach 1954: 3, 41-61.] **Location.** The Kachin State of Burma, with some extension eastward into southwestern Yunnan province of China, southward into the Shan State of Burma, and northwest into northeastern Assam. The approximate boundaries of Kachin territory are 96° and 99° E. and 23° and 28° N. The Kachins in the Kachin State tend to live in the eastern and central portions; the Atsi, Lashi, and Maru are found for the most part along the China-Burma frontier. **Geography.** Rough mountainous country cut by narrow valleys, the mountains paralleling each other in a north-south direction. At the apex of Burma (rather outside the area of Kachin settlement) the peaks are over 15,000 feet above sea level; in the southern portions of the Kachin area the highest elevations are about 4,000 feet; and the important towns of Kachin State—Myitkyina and Bhamo on the Irrawaddy—are less than 1,000 feet. A northern wall of mountains protects the land to the south so that freezing temperatures are rare in the valleys. Rainfall, as in the rest of Burma, is of monsoon distribution; but even in the winter months there is some rainfall so that the forests remain green and wild food plants can be gathered, although staple crops cannot be grown. Summer rainfall ranges from 75 to over 100 inches. [Huke 1956b: 674-77.] **Linguistic affiliation.** Kachins, Atsi, Lashi, and Maru are all members of the Tibeto-Burman group, but whereas Atsi, Lashi, and Maru are, relatively speaking, close to Burmese, Kachin is only remotely related to Burmese and the other three languages, the close nonlinguistic connections of Kachin, Atsi, Lashi, and Maru notwithstanding. There is some evidence to the effect that Kachin is divided into dialects, but systematic information is lacking. [Cf. Shafer 1955: 103-04.] **Demography.** The most recent Burma census listing the Kachins recorded slightly over 150,000 in enumerated areas, and contemporary estimates for the unenumerated areas totaled another 100,000. In 1931 Kachins constituted about half the population of the territory now in the Kachin State and a quarter more of all Kachins lived in the northern margin of the Shan State. On the basis of observations in the early 1950s, Huke estimated a Kachin population of between 350,000 and 450,000, to which must be added a few thousand in Assam and several thousand in Yunnan. [Huke 1956b: 669.] **History and cultural relations.** Kachin history before the beginning of the nineteenth century is hardly more than speculation. Tradition suggests an origin somewhere to the north of their present location, and there is some support for this in its concurrence with the direction of other migrations in mainland Southeast Asia as recorded in Western sources of the last century. Aside from their contact with small groups like the Atsi, Lashi, Maru, Nung, Lisu, and so on, the Kachins appear to have had most intensive relations with the Tai-speaking Shans of Burma. In certain localities various degrees of assimilation to Shan culture are found. An unsystematic examination of the Kachin lexicon shows that borrowings from Shan are more numerous than those from Burmese and Chinese, the other two major contact languages. [Hanson 1913: 24, 29; Leach 1954: passim.] The fact that most of our knowledge of Kachins is based on accounts by people from the Bhamo-Namhkam area reflects the intensity of contacts here with Christian missionaries (American Protestant and European Catholic) who have been active in Bhamo since the end of the nineteenth century. Only later were missions established to the southeast in the Kachin areas of the Shan State, and considerably later in the north toward Myitkyina and beyond. The most effective administration and military control was also in this part of the Kachin State and in the southwestern portion of the State along the railway opened to Myitkyina in 1899. The so-called Triangle, stretching north from Myitkyina between the two branches of the Irrawaddy, was not brought under effective control until just before the Japanese invasion of 1942. Several hundred men were recruited for the army in World War I, almost half from the east and south of Bhamo. [Enriquez 1923: map.]

SETTLEMENT PATTERN AND HOUSING. **Settlement pattern.** In recent years the Kachins have begun living in valley bottoms, but their villages were traditionally on ridge tops or the upper portions of slopes. Because of constant warfare, villages were large and remote from each other; peace has brought a reduction in settlement population size and a dispersal of dwellings. Water supply often but not always decides locations, and some settlements on elevations may be some distance from their water supply. ● Most villages are entered through a sacred grove marked by prayer posts with representations of boons desired from the spirits (such as grain, weapons, and household goods), and by shrines to the spirits, especially the earth spirit. Here the community sacrifices are held. The choicest site is likely to be occupied by the chief's house. There are no public buildings; the main structures are houses and granaries. [Carrapiett 1929: 9-10; Gilhodes 1922: 148, 168-69; Hanson 1913: 38-40; Huke 1956b: 700-01; Leach 1954: 114-15.] **Housing.** The house is rectangular, about 30 feet wide, somewhat longer (occasionally as much as 100 feet), and raised 3 or 4 feet off the ground on posts. Posts and beams are of wood; flooring, external walls, and internal partitions are of woven bamboo; and the roof usually of grass. Small

animals are sheltered under the house; larger animals stalled under a projecting gable at the front. A number of household tasks, such as weaving, rice pounding, etc. also take place under the gable. Inside, the house is divided lengthwise by a partial partition, the left side being subdivided into a succession of apartments each with a hearth, the right being left open as a storage, cooking, and entertaining area. At the end of the large room is a space sacred to the household spirits and to any ancestral spirits not successfully seen off to the land of the dead. In front of the house are altars to spirits, and large posts, customarily X-shaped, to which cattle are bound for sacrifice. There is little internal decoration of houses; the exterior in front may have crude carvings or horns and antlers. Furnishings are limited: traditionally mats, containers, and blankets, and nowadays stools and low tables. [Carrapiett 1929: 10, 12-14; Gilhodes 1922: 159-68; Hanson 1913: 40-43; Huke 1956b: 701-02; Leach 1954: 108-11.]

ECONOMY. Based upon the farming of field crops, with hunting, gathering, animal husbandry, and specialization in manufactures all relatively less important than agriculture. Trade, whether in farm produce or the products of other economic activity, plays a minor role. Most communities, in fact most households, are self-sufficient units of production and consumption, except for a few items. Farming is the way of life for all Kachins, including the chiefs; there is no full-time occupational specialization. **Agriculture.** The basic crop is rice grown by swidden farming on forested hillsides. The burned-over swidden is cultivated with a short-handled, heavy hoe. The rice seed is planted with a planting stick, and the crop reaped with a sickle or knife. [Hanson 1913: 71 ff.] Swiddens are also used for maize, sesame, millet, tobacco, and a number of species of the pumpkin family. Some vegetables and fruits are planted in gardens in house yards, and cotton and opium poppies are also raised. [Carrapiett 1929: 9, 11; Hanson 1913: 73-74.] In a few localities, especially near Shan or Chinese settlements, the Kachins have adopted wet-rice cultivation on valley floors (Hanson 1913: 73). The farming year for rice begins in February and March with the cutting of the swiddens, the burning and planting occur just before the onset of the southwest monsoon in June, and harvesting comes in October. The grain is threshed by the treading of buffalo, and put in storage by December. [Hanson 1913: 71-73.] Swidden farming is not very complex technologically: rudimentary tools are used, and no animal power is employed except for threshing. The Kachins usually do not use a swidden for more than three years in succession, but the rotation of fields does not require the shifting of settlements; one village moved only once in 40 years and then a mere three-quarters of a mile away. [Huke 1954: passim; 1956b: 702-74.] **Fishing and hunting.** Fishing with traps and poison is popular, but there seems to have been no elaboration of this activity nor any great dependence upon it. Hunting is common during the cold season from December to February and is done with traps, snares, deadfalls, pellet bows, and guns (Carrapiett 1929: 10-11; Hanson 1913: 37, 77). **Domestic animals.** Cattle, buffalo, pigs, dogs, and fowl are bred for sacrifices, but not for meat or milk. Pigs are fed prepared food in the evenings by the women but allowed to forage during the day, and in so doing act as scavengers in the villages. [Carrapiett 1929: 10-11, 69.] **Food and stimulants.** Boiled rice with an accompanying dish of stew made from vegetables and, occasionally, meat or fish, is eaten three times a day. Tastes in animal foods are eclectic, the only pronounced aversions being cats, horses, dogs, monkeys, sheep, and goats. Tobacco is usually chewed, and betel, also chewed, is common. Opium is now fairly widespread, although it is said to have been introduced only in the last century or so. Rice is made into a beer by fermentation, into a spirit by distillation, and into a sort of malted mash taken at times of such heavy work as swidden preparation and house raising. These liquors are accompaniments of hospitality and sacrifices. [Carrapiett 1929: 10-11, 70; Gilhodes 1922: 151 ff.; Hanson 1913: 55-56, 74, 137.] **Industrial arts.** Iron hoes and machetes abound, but smiths seem to be neither numerous nor important, most hardware being obtained from Chinese or Shans. Pottery is used although it is not reported to be a Kachin product. Baskets, cases, trays, mats, and house walls are woven from bamboo, grasses, and rattan. Cordage appears to be unimportant, perhaps because of the considerable use of bamboo splints. Woodworking is undeveloped; religious carvings appear rather crude. Textile weaving seems to be the most elaborated craft, done by women during the cold season on a belt loom with locally grown and processed cotton thread. Some of the textiles are also embroidered. [Hanson 1913: 76, 78-81.] **Trade.** Information on trade is limited, especially in respect to volume. Salt is largely obtained from the Burmese, although it was formerly produced from local sources. Iron and iron pots are bought from the Chinese. Cloth, distilled liquor, tobacco, and opium, though all produced locally, may also be imported. The Kachins have no markets, visiting nearby Shan, Burmese, and Chinese trading centers instead. [Carrapiett 1929: 9, 11; Gilhodes 1922: 151-56; Hanson 1913: 73, 75-76, 80, 87, 152.] **Division of labor.** Men clear and burn the swidden fields, hunt, and assume most political and religious roles. Women have full responsibility for the crops—weeding, harvesting, transporting, threshing, and either preparing the crops as food or marketing any surplus. They also fetch water, collect firewood, and prepare the cotton from field to cloth, making their clothing from their own cloth but their husbands' from bought cloth. Women also do the brewing. [Carrapiett 1929: 5-6, 15; Hanson 1913: 73, 77-79.] **Land tenure.** Forest land around a village and the products of it are free to all in the village; there is no personal property in swidden land. The chief of a village has the right to dispose of the land to those wishing to use it, and may not refuse land to a member of the village community. Membership in the village is apparently at the sole discretion of the chief. A villager, so long as he cultivates a field, has the right to the use of it. The assignment of plots as the swidden cycle moves from abandoned field to old fallow or new forest land is in the hands of the chief and the elders. Where wet-rice cultivation in permanent fields has been introduced, the individual retains greater though not absolute control, and can pass his wet fields on to heirs in the male line or sell to another villager with permission of the chief. No land can be sold to an outsider. [Hanson 1913: 64-65, 68; Leach 1954: 155-59.]

KIN GROUPS. **Descent.** Descent is traced in the male line. **Kin groups.** The superior kin group is the sib, a unilinear (patrilinear) group descended putatively from a remote ancestor. An exhaustive treatment of Kachin sibs does not exist. The most common presentation of them is in terms of five chiefly sibs, which in order of ideal precedence are the Marip, Lahtaw, Lahpai, Nhkum, and Maran, to which list may be added a small number of variable groups. The sibs in turn are divided into lineages and further subdivisions of these. The span, or number of generations which can be recited, varies from lineage to lineage, and indeed may vary from locality to locality for the five major chiefly sibs. ● Ideally the sibs are exogamous; in practice, they are probably not exogamous, and the longer the lineage span, the more relaxed are the rules of lineage exogamy, so that rigid exogamy is likely to be associated only with the most subordinate fraction of a lineage. Many older sources speak of the sibs, especially the five chiefly ones, as tribes, and even treat them as coordinate with linguistic groups like the Atsi, Lashi, and Maru. This confusion seems to have originated in the facts that the chiefly sibs frequently are concentrated in certain areas and that a village would be assigned to the sib of its chief. [Cf. Hanson 1913: 24-26, 220.] Although there is little information on the sib or lineage composition of specific villages, it is unlikely that clan communities are common among the Kachins (cf. Leach 1954: 68, 116). By marriage, a woman does not acquire membership in her husband's sib (Carrapiett 1929: 36; Gilhodes 1922: 141, 196, 208). **Kin terminology.** The terms given below are from Gilhodes (1922: 199-202) and Leach

(1954: 304-08). The cousin terminology corresponds to Murdock's Omaha type:

Fa, FaBr	*wa*
Mo, MoSi	*nu*
FaSi	*moi*
MoBr	*tsa*
ElBr	*hpu*
ElSi	*na*
YoBr, YoSi	*nau*
FaBrSo, MoSiSo	*hpu nau*
FaBrDa, MoSiDa	*na nau*
FaSiSo, MoBrSo	*hkau* [FaSiElSo, *hku* (wsp); FaSiYoSo, *rat* (wsp)]
FaSiDa	*hkri* [*ning* (wsp)]
MoBrElDa	*rat* [MoBrDa, *ning* (wsp)]
MoBrYoDa	*nam*

MARRIAGE AND FAMILY. Traditional Kachin culture tolerates premarital sexual relations. The front apartment of a house is the *nla dap* where adolescents gather in the evening for singing, recitation of poetry, and, finally, lovemaking. Such relations do not ordinarily lead to permanent and recognized unions. Illegitimacy is not lightly regarded. The girl who becomes pregnant will have less chance to marry well, whereas she who does not is sought after as if virginal. To father an illegitimate child is a wrong against the girl's family and must be repaid by marriage or payment of a fine, the latter solution frequently being preferred. [Gilhodes 1922: 209-11; Hanson 1913: 179; Leach 1954: 136-40.] **Mode.** Parents play a considerable role in the choice of mates for their children. For a son they review the eligible maternal cross cousins and, having made a choice, turn the negotiations over to go-betweens. The bride price, often the occasion for prolonged discussions, is provided by the bridegroom's father and his local sibmates, and in addition the new husband after marriage must often perform various chores for his father-in-law for one or two years. The payment of the bride price may extend over a period of time. In partial exchange, the members of the bride's family give a dowry and pay certain wedding costs. [Carrapiett 1929: 28, 32-35; Gilhodes 1922: 211-12, 221; Hanson 1913: 179-86.] **Form.** Polygyny is permitted, and some chiefs are reported to have had a number of wives, including Shan and Burmese women, but there is no information on the frequency of the practice; presumably costs of plural marriage would make monogamy the norm. Some polygynous marriages arise from the obligation of a man to assume the responsibility for his brother's widow. [Gilhodes 1922: 225; Hanson 1913: 180.] **Extension of incest taboos.** Sib exogamy theoretically bars a man from marriage as well as from informal sex relations with any woman in his own patrilineal sib. The preferred marriage is with a mother's brother's

daughter or with a daughter of any man of Ego's mother's sib. A further prescription, at least for the chiefly class, among whose five sibs there is an institutionalized circular exchange, is the *dama-mayu* relation. Thus the sibs in the column on the left below take wives from those in the column on the right:

dama		*mayu*
Marip	from	Maran
Maran	"	Nhkum
Nhkum	"	Lahpai
Lahpai	"	Lahtaw
Lahtaw	"	Marip

[Carrapiett 1929: 32, 36, 70; Gilhodes 1922: 207-08; Hanson 1913: 181-82; Leach 1954: 136-40.] **Residence and domestic unit.** The Kachin house is not usually a dwelling for several households. Each new family, except that of the younger son, customarily has its own dwelling. Before slavery was abolished, slave families may have shared the master's house. The ideal rule of residence is patrilocal in the community of the husband's father, but matrilocal marriages are reported to be common. [Gilhodes 1922: 168, 221; Leach 1954: 83, 109, 167-72.] **Inheritance.** Usually the youngest son inherits his father's house. The movable property of the father is distributed by gift during his lifetime to daughters as dowry and to older sons as they also marry and leave the household. Unless a child leaves the family, no distribution of property seems to be made. In return for the inheritance of the house, the youngest son supports his parents and pays most of the costs of their funerals. In case a man dies childless or without sons, his property passes to his brothers or to their sons. When an elder son moves into his own house, a ceremony takes place in which the protection of the ancestral spirits is sought for the new house. [Gilhodes 1922: 80-82.] **Divorce.** Divorce is permitted and involves a resettlement of the economic arrangements made for the marriage. If divorce is by mutual consent, the two parties return the dowry and bride price. If the husband is at fault, he forfeits the bride price; if the wife, her family loses the dowry. [Carrapiett 1929: viii, 35-37; Gilhodes 1922: 222; Hanson 1913: 57.]

SOCIOPOLITICAL ORGANIZATION. **Political organization.** Prior to the creation of a Kachin State in 1947, there was no central state or political authority encompassing all Kachins. The people were divided into a number of groups each with its own territory under the control and leadership of a chief, *duwa*. The size of the groups and territories varied considerably from a few villages to as many as a hundred. Although the status of chief was hereditary in the male line and from father to youngest son, and although the chief was a member of one of the chiefly sibs, the chief was not necessarily an autocrat. His power was usually exercised in concert with a council of elders. His actual powers seem to have depended largely upon the vigor of his own personality. An energetic commoner could sometimes create for himself the role of front man for the chief, a role sufficiently formalized to have a name, *bawmung*. [Carrapiett 1929: 25; Gilhodes 1922: 280; Hanson 1913: 61-63, 76-85; Leach 1954: 124, 188.] The chief had no large source of customary income from the villagers, who were therefore liable to certain forms of corvée, e.g. for preparing his swiddens and harvesting his crops. He had the right to the thigh of all large sacrifices, hence the epithet, "thigh-eating chief." Most of his income probably came from exactions in the form of tolls and tribute on foreigners, i.e. the Shan valley dwellers and Shan and Chinese merchants. On the other hand, the office of chief involved certain liabilities: the worship of certain spirits entailing expensive sacrifices could be performed only by the chief. [Carrapiett 1929: 25-26; Hanson 1913: 64; Leach 1954: 135.] The other formal political status in Kachin society was that of elder. He was an older man and in some cases the head of his sib in the community. The elders, who, with the chief, formed a council, customarily determined the sites of swidden fields for the coming season and rendered judgments in disputes. The chief seems seldom to have acted contrary to the consensus of the council. [Carrapiett 1929: 27-29; Hanson 1913: 64.] **Social stratification.** In the Kachin view, communities are organized in either of two forms, *gumsa* or *gumlao*. In brief, *gumsa* social organization is aristocratic and stratified; *gumlao* is democratic and egalitarian. With each type are associated various patterns of authority, marriage, and religion. A detailed, analytical study of the two modes of social structure is given in Leach (1954: passim). Society is divided into two major classes, chiefs and commoners. Formerly there was also a class of slaves and in some places even a fourth class of descendants of free men and slave women. In areas under British administration, slavery was gradually abolished (as late as 1926 in the Hukawng valley). Slaves acquired their status through capture in war, debt, and legal penalties. They are reported to have been fairly well treated. Information is lacking on the relative size of the chiefly and commoner (and the former slave) populations, although chiefs are said to have been few in number. [Gilhodes 1922: 142; Hanson 1913: 71-72; Leach 1954: 299-303.] Chiefs are wealthier than most commoners, from whom they have the rights to certain dues. Their houses are likely to be larger and of better quality, their genealogies are longer, their ghosts inhabit a separate realm in the afterworld, only they can make sacrifices to certain important spirits, and they perhaps belong to separate sibs. The chiefly celebration of rites like weddings and funerals is also more elaborate than among commoners. As a rule there is no intermarriage between commoners and chiefs, but some members of chiefly families from time to time fail to maintain their status, and gradually their descendants slip into the commoner class. The sources occasionally allude to wealthy commoners, but their relations to the chiefs in terms of prestige, influence, and power are not described. [Gilhodes 1922: 142.] **Warfare.** Warfare, which was suppressed upon the extension of British rule to Upper Burma after 1886, was chiefly in the nature of guerrilla war, raids, and ambushes. Head taking and ritual cannibalism seem occasionally to have been features of Kachin warfare, though not prominent. [Hanson 1913: 84-86.]

RELIGION. Catholic and Protestant missionaries have been at work since the last half of the nineteenth century, and in recent years there has been some Burmese Buddhist evangelization. But most Kachins are still probably adherents of traditional religious beliefs and practices, frequently and misleadingly called animism in popular publications. **Supernaturals.** The supernatural world is largely personal, two classes of spirits being prominent. First are the ancestral spirits. This class includes the major deities, those who have names and are common to all Kachins—remote ancestors of the chiefs and commoners in general. Minor deities, like the household guardian spirits, are the more immediate ancestors of the living. All these are concerned to some degree with the welfare of their descendants in this world. Their attitude is generally benevolent or neutral. Their malevolent activities are provoked by their imagined neglect by the living, who must approach them as they would superiors in this world, through gifts, sacrifices, and the proper forms of speech. [Hanson 1913: 150-58.] Spirits of the second class are those who seem to represent or embody the indeterminate and frustrating incidents of human existence. Of these there are two subgroups. First are those spirits whose attitude toward men is almost wholly hostile and who are responsible for such untoward events as bad luck of hunters and fishermen, death in childbirth, and fatal accidents. People who die as a result of these causes become spirits of the same class. They are not rendered the respect shown to one's living seniors or to the ancestral spirits. Second are the *maraw*, who seem to represent chance in a general way; operating in the realm of the dead they frustrate the presumed good will of the ancestral spirits toward the living who have properly approached them for a boon. [Hanson 1913: 158-59.] The Kachins also believe in the existence of a demiurge or creator, but he is little concerned with human affairs and is rarely turned to for help. Kachin spirits have no bearing on morals or ethics. [Gilhodes 1922: 5, 19, 100; Hanson 1913: 168-69.] **Practitioners.** Relations with the supernatural are maintained through nonhereditary specialists whose training, status, and reputation may vary widely from individual to individual. First are the seers, of two kinds, the shamans (or mediums) and the diviners. The shaman is believed to be able in a trance to put himself in contact with the spirits either by traveling to their abode or by being possessed by a spirit who speaks through him. The status of shaman is not in theory attained by training, for the power to become a shaman comes in some mysterious manner. The diviner employs a variety of techniques, and the results are interpreted as indicating courses of action. Divination is a learned skill, and the diviner lacks the prestige of the shaman; the decisions in regard to which he is consulted are of less importance than those referred to the latter. Girls are said to practice a kind of divination, without the aid of a specialist, in the course of which they invoke the moon, which is thought of as a girl. The Kachins also believe in omens, customary interpretations of natural phenomena. Shamans and diviners are not conceived as having power in the human world, but since they are able to indicate courses of action, they probably hold informal positions of influence within the village. [Carrapiett 1929: 20-23, 26-27, 53-54, 69; Gilhodes 1922: 114-21; Hanson 1913: 131-38; Leach 1954: 192-94.] A second series of ranked specialists are the priests and their assistants. (Occupying one of these statuses is compatible with being a seer; indeed, a priest is often a diviner, and there is no prohibition against one of these specialists also fulfilling the secular role of elder or chief.) These statuses are also achieved by training, but only that of priest requires any lengthy apprenticeship. The priest's chief task is to offer sacrifices to the spirits with appropriate invocations. Most of his training consists in learning prayers and formulas, some of which are quite long, in a special, obsolescent style of speech. The priest is recompensed with a part of the sacrifice. He has two assistants: one, the *hkinjawng*, a sort of ritual butcher, cuts up the sacrifices and prepares the flesh for the spirits, the chief, religious dignitaries, and the common people; the other, the *hpunlum*, is the actual slaughterer of the victims but, since this is not an exacting job, any male Kachin, even one without special training, may occasionally do it. Both assistants also receive portions of the sacrifice. [Carrapiett 1929: 21-29; Gilhodes 1922: 112-18; Hanson 1913: 153-54; Leach 1954: 190-92.] Of the preceding specialized roles, women may exercise only that of shaman (Gilhodes 1922: 118). An additional specialized status is that of *jaiwa*. Although older sources regard this as a religious status, their descriptions support the term "saga-teller" used by Leach. Certain rites are accompanied by lengthy recitations of traditional cosmogony and history, of which the saga-teller is the repository. Despite his being involved in some of the ceremonies, the *jaiwa* does not seem to be a "high-priest." Considerable study is required for achievement of this status.

[Carrapiett 1929: 31; Gilhodes 1922: 113-14; Hanson 1913: 94, 109, 152-53; Leach 1954: 190, 277.] **Ceremonies.** The chief method for dealing with the supernatural is propitiation with offerings and prayers. Anything may be offered to the spirits, but the chief sacrifice is a flesh offering. The larger animals—buffalo and cattle—are the most important and are given to important spirits or at important crises, if the donor can afford them. Pigs and chickens are of less value. • A number of critical times, whether recurrent or unique emergencies, are marked by periods of cessation or reduction of ordinary activities, e.g. a number of ceremonies during the farming season. (The chief plays a role in these, which he does not do in the emergencies of illness or the crises of an individual's career.) The first takes place just before the sowing of the year's swidden fields. In the sacred grove offerings are made to the spirit of the earth, some being made in the presence of only the priests and chief. This important occasion is followed by a four-day sabbath. One family is then chosen by divination to begin the sowing. Another two-day sabbath follows, with offerings. When the grain is half grown a second, somewhat less important, ceremony—again headed by the chief—takes place. A series of other sabbaths of fewer days accompanied by various magical acts follow—when the grain is ready for reaping, during the threshing, and at the carrying home of the grain. [Gilhodes 1922: 122-24; Hanson 1913: 154-67.] **Illness and medicine.** The supernatural and its specialists are intimately involved in curing. The first step is consultation of one of the seers to determine the spirit to be approached and the best method for doing this. Then the priest is called in to deal with the spirits. One source says that curing is the most common occasion for approaching the supernatural. [Gilhodes 1922: 134, 286-89; Hanson 1913: 167.] Illness is sometimes attributed to witches, i.e. people who have been possessed by evil spirits, although the person so possessed may be unaware of his condition. Spirit possession of this kind is regarded as both hereditary and communicable to one's spouse. Evidence on the fate of witches is contradictory: on the one hand the condition is described as being incurable, with enslavement or death as the consequence; on the other, an attempt may be made to secure a confession from the possessing spirit, after which exorcism is undertaken. [Carrapiett 1929: 73; Gilhodes 1922: 293-96; Hanson 1913: 140-47.] There are also references to sorcery, the employment of a priest to enlist the aid of a spirit to cause harm, usually disease, to another (Gilhodes 1922: 293). **Soul, death, and afterlife.** Cause of death is not clearly described. One explanation is that the soul is sustained by a cord held by the creator and broken by the gnawing of spirits. Another is that spirits entice the soul away, whereupon death ensues. [Gilhodes 1922: 134, 231; Hanson 1913: 231.] Burial takes place within about a week after death, during which time a number of things are done to remove the deceased from the world of the living and to place his spirit in a sort of limbo from which it is later recalled. For example, the corpse is washed with motions the reverse of those used by the living, and in dressing the corpse significant items such as the machete and pouch are put on also in reversed positions. In addition the priest makes an offering to the deceased and tells him that he is dead, admonishing him to sever relations with the living. A symbol of the transition from the living to the dead is an artificial bamboo clump erected in front of the house of the deceased which remains there until the final send-off. The second portion of the funeral may be postponed for as long as a year while resources to cover the expenses are accumulated. When the time arrives, the bamboo clump is dismantled, and another structure, of branches, is placed over the grave. The priest removes the bamboo bedstead on which the spirit of the deceased has been staying, recalls the spirit from limbo, and in a long address traces the route the spirit must follow to the land of the dead. Virtually the last acts are certain attempts to divine whether the spirit has in fact departed. If it has not, a new spirit must be cared for at the household altar, which is brought back into the house, having been removed at the time of death. [Hanson 1913: 194-209.]

BIBLIOGRAPHY. Carrapiett 1929; Enriquez 1923; Gilhodes 1922; Hanson 1913; Huke 1954, 1956b; Leach 1954; Shafer 1955.

ACHANG

Synonyms. *Maingtha, Ngachang, Mönghsa*

ORIENTATION. **Identification.** The people call themselves Ngachang, and are called Achang by the Chinese. The term Maingtha is the Burmese rendering of the Tai (Shan) Mönghsa, meaning the "people of the two Hsa states." [Scott and Hardiman 1900: 390.] **Location.** Along the upper Burma–Yunnan border, in the Chinese Shan States area. More specifically, the two small Shan states of Hohsa and Lahsa in the valley of a southern tributary of the Taiping river just east of the Burma frontier. The area is known to the Shans of Burma as Mönghsa. The Achang are also found as seasonal laborers throughout much of northern Burma. [Scott and Hardiman 1900: 390; Leach 1954: 58.] **Linguistic affiliation.** The language appears to be basically a Tibeto-Burman (Atsi) dialect, mixed with Shan Tai (Leach 1954: 29). Shafer (1955: 103) places Achang, along with Maru, Lashi, Hpon, and Atsi, within a Burmic division of Sino-Tibetan. **Demography.** Bruk (1960: 19) records 18,000 Achang in Yunnan province. **History and cul-**

tural relations. Earlier sources, e.g. Davies (1909), speculate that the Achang are Atsi who moved east and came under the influence of the Shans in Mönghsa. They form the commoner population of Mönghsa, where they are integrated into a distinctly Shan political system. They are nominally Buddhist, and for all intents and purposes are culturally Shan. Some Achang recognize kinship with Atsi Kachins in the vicinity. [Leach 1954: 29, 58.] Davies (1909: 395ff.) adds that the relatively small area of Mönghsa, by virtue of its elevation, has attracted a considerable population of Chinese rice farmers. Possibly because of this strain on the agricultural resources, large numbers of Achang go regularly for some months in the winter to the Burmese Shan States as carpenters and blacksmiths.

BIBLIOGRAPHY. Bruk 1960; Davies 1909; Leach 1954; Scott and Hardiman 1900; Shafer 1955.

HPON

Synonym. *Phon*

ORIENTATION. **Identification and location.** A small group of shifting agriculturists of mixed cultural and linguistic affiliations living on the Irrawaddy between Bhamo and Sinbo in northern Burma, at about 24° 30′ N. Scott and Hardiman report two divisions, based on dialect variations: the Hpon Hpye or Möng Ti Hpons, and the Hpon Samong or Möng Wan Hpons. Their fields, located on the hills, are moved from time to time. They do some fishing and also work in the timber industry. They are reported to be rapidly becoming similar in culture and language to the Shans who surround them on all sides, and most of them are nominally Buddhists. [Leach 1954: 30; Scott and Hardiman 1900: 567-68.] **Linguistic affiliation.** Tibeto-Burman. Leach (1954: 30, 45) tentatively classifies Hpon as basically a Maru dialect, but with some Burmese influence. Shafer (1955: 103) places Hpon, along with Maru, Lashi, Achang, and Atsi, within a Burmic division of Sino-Tibetan. **Demography.** There were less than 1,000 surviving Hpon speakers in 1931.

BIBLIOGRAPHY. Leach 1954; Scott and Hardiman 1900; Shafer 1955.

KADU

Synonyms. *Kudo, Mawteik, Puteik, Sak*

ORIENTATION. **Identification and location.** A small group of wet-rice agriculturists of mixed cultural and linguistic affiliations located in northern Burma between 24° and 24° 30′ N., chiefly in the Katha district near the Assam frontier east of Manipur. They are called Kadu or Kudo by the Burmese, Puteik by the Kachins, and Mawteik by the Shans. They call themselves Sak. Villages are located on spurs of hills just above the valley floor. Glutinous rice is grown on irrigated terraces, and some tea and cotton is also grown. Through intermarriage they are becoming Burmese in culture, and practically all Kadu are nominally, at least, Buddhists. Many of them work for Burmese lumbering firms as elephant drivers and wood cutters. [Leach 1954: 30, 45; Scott and Hardiman 1900: 569-75; Embree and Thomas 1950: 28.] **Linguistic affiliation.** Tibeto-Burman. Leach (1954: 30) classifies Kadu as mainly Jinghpaw, with a heavy admixture of Tai and Assamese. **Demography.** Approximately 40,000 (Leach 1954: 45).

BIBLIOGRAPHY. Embree and Thomas 1950; Leach 1954; Scott and Hardiman 1900.

LOLO

Synonyms. *Hei-I, Hei Ku T'ou, I, I-chia, Leisu, Lo-kuei, Man-chia, Man-tzu, Mosu, Neisu, Nesu, Ngosu, No, Norsu, Nosu, Pei-I, Pei Ku T'ou, Yi*

ORIENTATION. **Identification and location.** Davies (1909: 337) advanced the idea of a Lolo group of Tibeto-Burman languages, including Lolo (Neisu or Ngosu), Lisu, Lahu, and Woni (including Akha). Of these, the Lolo speakers are by far the most widespread and the most numerous, and together with the Miao they are the most mobile of all non-Han peoples in Southwest China. At present they are found throughout most of the mountainous areas of Yunnan, extending north into southwestern Szechwan, east into western Kweichow, and south into northern Indochina. Their homeland for some hundreds of years, and the area where they have continued longest as an independent ethnic group, has been within the Taliang Shan (Cold Mountains) of southwestern Szechwan. Here the Independent Lolo or Nosu have intrigued the imagination of travelers and ethnologists since they were first "discovered" by the West about the turn of the century. Here was a "blood-proud caste of nobility . . . who fought, rode, herded horses, and ruled . . . a stratum of underlings and slaves" (Wiens 1954: 94). The tall physique and Caucasoid-like features of the nobility, their sacred books written in a pictographic script, their felt cloaks, their herding, and their use of cremation have been the subject of much ethnological speculation. The Lolo have been known to the Chinese under various names for nearly 2,000 years. Throughout this time they have been located in the Yunnan-Szechwan area (Feng and Shryock 1938:

103-05). ● The word Lolo has its origin in a Chinese transcription dating from Yuan dynasty times, but its etymology is obscure (Feng and Shryock 1938: 103-05). Lolo has long been employed by missionaries and travelers, but it is only occasionally used by the people themselves, and the Chinese are more likely to use terms such as I (Yi), I-chia, Man-tzu, or Man-chia (all carrying the connotation of "Southwestern Barbarian"). The official Communist term is now I (Yi). The term Lo-kuei is a derogatory nickname of recent origin. The people call themselves variously Nosu, Mosu, Ngosu, Nesu, Neisu, No, or Leisu. Nosu (sometimes Norsu) is current among the Lolo of Taliang Shan, and also in nearby Kweichow province. Terms such as Hei Ku T'ou (Black Bones) and Pei Ku T'ou (White Bones), or Hei-I and Pei-I, refer to the stratification of classic Lolo society into two endogamous castes—an aristocratic landowning elite, the Black Bones, and their serfs, the White Bones. In addition, the literature contains frequent mention of Lolo "tribes" such as the Meng-hua Lolo south of Tali, the Pu-la of the Red river area of southern Yunnan, and the Xa Pho Lolo in the Bao Ha area of northwestern Tonkin (cf. Davies 1909: 389ff.; Henry 1903: 102-07; Carey 1899: 384; Abadie 1924: 185; Liétard 1909, 1913). In many cases, according to Feng and Shryock (1938), these names designate some characteristic of dress, occupation, location, or even the name of a particular ruling family. **Demography.** Estimates of the total number of Lolo (exclusive of Lahu, Lisu, etc.) have varied from the 1,000,000 of Feng and Shryock (1938: 103) to the recent Chinese Communist figure of 3,000,000 (cited in Bruk 1960: 19). Of these, well over one-half are in Yunnan province. The numbers of Lolo speakers outside China are negligible; those in Vietnam and Laos number between 10,000 and 15,000. **Cultural relations and history.** South of the "heartland" area of Szechwan, the classic Lolo physique becomes less noticeable until in southern Yunnan these features are seen only occasionally. Culturally, too, Lolo speakers in Yunnan and Kweichow are more like the Han Chinese. Cook (1936: 70-71) points out that there are actually two kinds of White Lolo—one category, consisting of serfs subject to Black Bone masters, are limited in their distribution and less numerous than the many thousands of Pei-I (White Lolo) who may still hold allegiance to the Black Bone nobility even though they are subject to Chinese authority. These Pei-I (Pai-I) are the acculturated Lolo speakers of much of Yunnan and Kweichow. They tend to adopt Chinese dress, observe Chinese religious festivals, and take on Chinese surnames. Davies mentioned a half century ago that the Lolo of Yunnan are in the process of absorption by the Chinese. Winnington (1959) records the manner in which this process is now being extended to the Independent Lolo under the auspices of the Chinese People's Republic. ● The problem of the origin of the Lolo remains unsolved. As Feng and Shryock point out (1938: 124-27), language would seem to point to Tibet, and Eickstedt (1944: 191-92), judging from a variety of evidence, thinks that they originally came from the East Tibetan mountain lands to the north and west. The seemingly Caucasoid physical features may point to a connection with Iranian or Indo-Afghan types farther west (cf. Stevenson 1932: 606-07). The use of felt, herding, and the lack of pottery, according to Feng and Shryock, point toward the Mongols and related peoples to the north; whereas other traits, such as barefootedness and the use of poison arrows, point to the south. It is certain that the Black Lolo (Nosu) of Szechwan are a highly inbred population of relatively pure stock, distinctly non-Oriental in appearance, and possessing a combination of distinctive cultural traits which set them apart from most other peoples in Southwest China. Feng and Shryock (1938: 107) and Stevenson (1932: 607) suggest that the marked physical differences between Black and White Lolo may be accounted for on the theory that the former represent a conquering group of relatively pure stock, whereas the latter represent differing stocks which were subjugated and on whom the conquerors imposed their language. In Yunnan, due to decimation by the Chinese, the Black Lolo have largely retired northward, and the majority of those called Lolo in the province today are White Lolo—remnants of a former stratification that must have been similar to that now found in Szechwan. Only a few of the old ruling families remain, accepting office under a new elite, the Chinese. ● Used as an ethnic term, other than to denote a linguistic relationship, Lolo is unsatisfactory—including as it does people of what appear to be markedly different racial stock and sociocultural position. At best, the term indicates a commonality among the people so designated, arising from historical circumstances rather than common ethnic origins. The unique position in this conglomerate of the Black Bone Nosu of the Taliang Shan should be recognized whenever the term is used.

BIBLIOGRAPHY. Abadie 1924; Bruk 1960; Carey 1899; Cook 1936; Davies 1909; Eickstedt 1944; Feng and Shryock 1938; Henry 1903; Liétard 1909, 1913; Stevenson 1932; Wiens 1954; Winnington 1959.

NOSU

Synonyms. *Neisu, Nesu, Ngosu, No, Norsu*

ORIENTATION. **Identification.** The Independent Black Lolo, the landowning nobility of the mountains in southwestern Szechwan province, call themselves Nosu (Neisu, Norsu). Firsthand accounts of the unsinicized Nosu of the Taliang Shan are rare, with that by d'Ollone (1912) still one of the best available. Lin (1961), although a professionally-trained observer, is less satisfactory, since he fails at times to distinguish his data on the relatively unsinicized Nosu of the Taliang Shan from those on the more sinicized groups in the Hsiaoliang Shan. ● Many observers have remarked on the occurrence of Caucasian (Aryan) features among the Nosu, calling attention to their tall stature, oval faces, aquiline noses, and horizontal eyes (deBeauclair 1956: 259). Lin (1961: 97) says, however, that the Nosu are basically Mongoloid, calling attention especially to their Mongoloid eye fold. **Location.** Mainly in the Taliang Shan and Hsiaoliang Shan of southwestern Szechwan (the Liangshan I Autonomous Chou), approximately 28° N. and 103° E. This is a mountainous area some 300 miles long by 200 miles wide. The Black Bone (Nosu) aristocracy is also represented in the population of extreme western Kweichow and northern Yunnan, as well as in the Ninglang I Autonomous Hsien in southwestern Szechwan, north of Likiang city. **Geography.** The Taliang Shan is a mountain fastness penetrated by only a few passes. The rugged topography is broken by plains which are often the seat of Lolo villages. The climate is temperate but the winters rigorous. Fauna include tigers, leopards, bears, wild boar, and foxes. **Linguistic affiliation.** Usually classed as Tibeto-Burman, related to Lahu, Akha, and Lisu. The Nosu have a pictographic script preserved in the form of sacred manuscripts or scriptures which can be read by only a few individuals (cf. Feng and Shryock 1938: 104). Judging by what d'Ollone has to say, it appears that in 1906 the Nosu knew little or no Chinese (1912: 105-06). **Demography.** Lin (1961: 11) estimated the Lolo-speaking population in the Liangshan area at 200,000. According to deBeauclair (1956: 265-66), the Communists place this figure at 500,000. The Lolo of Ninglang I Autonomous Hsien, numbering 56,000, account for only about one-half the population of that district, the rest being made up of Chinese, Lisu, Nakhi, etc. (Winnington 1959: 29). All sources agree that the Black Lolo or Nosu account for only a small percentage of the total Lolo-speaking populations in these areas, the majority being White Lolo and slaves. **History and cultural relations.** Lin (1961: 1-25) documents the history of Nosu resistance to the steady encroachment of Han Chinese agricultural settlers. According to Feng and Shryock (1938: 120), the Liangshan (or at least the eastern portion) was not brought under any kind of effective control until about 1900. Institutionalized trade relations have, however, apparently existed for a long time, partly due to the fact that the Han have a monopoly on salt, which the Nosu need both for their animals and their own consumption. These trading arrangements are well documented by d'Ollone (1912). ● The Chinese Communists designated the Liangshan an Autonomous Chou in 1951, and have been attempting since that time to penetrate the area by exploiting the dissatisfactions of the White Lolo serfs and slaves. Schools and clinics have been established, and the Communists have devised a romanized script for the Lolo language. The story of Communist penetration into Ninglang county area west of the Taliang Shan is recorded by Winnington (1959).

SETTLEMENT PATTERN AND HOUSING. **Settlement pattern.** Villages range in size from only a few houses to as many as 40 or 50. Since the normal domestic unit is the nuclear family, the maximum village population is probably 250 to 300 persons. Villages are located on slopes or at the edge of an intermontane plain. The houses are somewhat dispersed. [Lin 1961: 28.] **Housing.** The nobility live in houses of roughhewn planks. Those which form the roof are held in place by large stones. The houses tend to be drafty and cold in the winter. The interior is usually divided into a main cooking and living area and a sleeping or storage space in the rear. Furnishings are sparse and crude. The hearth is fitted with a large flat stone for cooking. The houses of the less affluent White Lolo are more often made with mud walls and thatched roofs. Black Lolo chieftains usually surround their houses with wooden fences or earthen walls. A fortified tower may be located next to the house. Animals are quartered in pens or enclosures within the outer walls. ● D'Ollone (1912: 57) remarks that the "true home of the Lolo is his cloak," referring to the great felt cloaks worn by all Nosu, and to their ability to wrap themselves in these cloaks and go to sleep no matter where they may be. [Lin 1961: 59-60; d'Ollone 1912: 56-57.]

ECONOMY. The subsistence economy is a mixture of agriculture and animal husbandry, with agriculture the main source of food. The Nosu nobility disdain working in the fields, but do not mind taking personal care of their herds. The Nosu are mainly interested in warfare and horsemanship. They enjoy hunting, although game supplies a relatively small portion of the diet. They are not interested in an agricultural surplus, and large herds of cattle and sheep are common only among the wealthy. **Agriculture.** Dryland farming is the rule except for a very few irrigated paddy fields in areas of strong Chinese influence. Swiddens on the mountain slopes planted to buckwheat seem most characteristic of the unsinicized Nosu. The fields are burned off and used for several seasons, after which they are abandoned (Lin 1961: 87-89). D'Ollone (1912: 65) also reports that the forests are cleared in order to get open pasture for herds and flocks, and that there are as a consequence few trees in the true Nosu country. According to Lin, the Nosu also have more permanent fields on the plains near the villages where they plant corn. These fields are plowed and fertilized with cattle manure.

They are rotated, according to Lin, so that corn alternates with such crops as wheat, peas, and beans. It is not clear, however, whether fields of this type are characteristic of the whole Nosu country or only the more sinicized eastern portion. D'Ollone (1912) mentions oats, barley, buckwheat, and potatoes, but makes no mention of corn. In recent years some Nosu have begun to cultivate opium, primarily as an export commodity in exchange for silver and guns. **Hunting.** By individuals or in groups, using guns, poisoned arrows, spears, knives, nets, stones, and traps. Dogs are used to chase and corner the quarry. Animals taken include deer, roebuck, wild boar, tigers, leopards, bears, and foxes. [Lin 1961: 91.] **Domestic animals.** Sheep and goats are most numerous, but the Nosu also raise pigs, cattle, and horses. The latter are a small, agile strain used only for riding. They are unshod. Sheep are kept in a pen within the courtyard in winter; corrals are often built on the pasture lands in summer. The herds are watched day and night by slaves, although the Nosu nobility are not averse to caring for their animals on occasion. During the winter, animals may be fed on grass cut in the fall. Although salt is scarce, the Nosu give their animals salt water once or twice a month. Shearing is done three times a year, and is a popular social occasion. Castration and selective breeding are known and practiced. [Lin 1961: 90-91.] **Food and stimulants.** D'Ollone (1912: 93) describes the Nosu diet as consisting mainly of unleavened buckwheat cakes, supplemented by potatoes, which he says are very common. Salt, rice, and meat he describes as luxuries. He saw no vegetables, nor did he see the Nosu making any use of milk or milk products. According to Lin (1961: 62-63), the diet consists mainly of unleavened corn or buckwheat cakes, supplemented with sour vegetable soup. Boiled potatoes or bean curd with green vegetables may be added for luxury meals. Beef, pork, mutton, and poultry may be eaten, but mostly by the nobility, and then only on special occasions. Alcoholic beverages are made locally from corn or grain. To consume them, the drinkers sit around a common jar, each equipped with a long bamboo tube. Tobacco is smoked by men, women, and children, using stone pipes with bamboo stems. **Industrial arts.** Bamboo baskets are used for storage purposes. Bowls, cups, spoons, ladles, and wine jars are made of wood. Pottery and ironware are imported from the Chinese. The Lolo weave their own rough hempen fabrics and also make their all-purpose capes of hand-matted felt or woven wool. [Lin 1961: 91-92.] **Trade.** The Nosu barter among themselves and with Chinese merchants. They import salt, oil, needles, pottery, metalware, guns, and cloth, and export domestic animals and agricultural and forest products. Silver coins and bars are often used as a medium of exchange. The Nosu go down from their mountains to the Chinese market towns, and Chinese traders also visit Nosu settlements, but only by the established routes along which they traditionally enjoy the protection of local chieftains. [Lin 1961: 93ff.] **Division of labor.** Larger animals, such as cattle and sheep, are cared for by men, mostly slaves. Slave women look after the pigs and poultry, do the cooking, and carry firewood and water. Male and female slaves work side by side in the fields. Noblewomen enjoy a relatively high status in Nosu society, and spend much of their time directing the work of the household slaves. Warfare, hunting, horsemanship, and magic are the domain of the male nobility. [Lin 1961: 62-63, 85.] **Land tenure.** Land is controlled by the clans. Pastures, streams, hunting grounds, and forests may be used freely by clan members. Arable land is considered the property of noble families; it can be inherited but cannot be alienated, since it must remain within the clan. The amount of land a family works depends in large part on the number of slaves it owns. White Lolo serfs are sometimes given land by their Nosu masters, and in return they must deliver a stipulated amount of produce. Such land can be passed on by inheritance, but if a serf moves away, dies without heir, or commits a serious offense, the land can be taken back by its original donor. Each village claims an area within the larger clan territory, with boundaries which are known to all. [Lin 1961: 86-87.]

KIN GROUPS. **Descent.** Patrilineal. **Kin groups.** Exogamous patrilineal clans. Residence is patrilocal, and the clan usually occupies a definite territory, forming a clan village or several villages adjacent to each other. Clans and lineages are named, but they do not constitute surname groups as among the Chinese. The Nosu employ a patronymic linkage system in naming, whereby the first element in a son's name is the last element in that of his father (cf. Lo 1944-45). Clan leadership is assumed mainly on the basis of personal qualities, especially bravery and ability in warfare. [Lin 1946: 86-87; 1961: 26-39.] **Kin terminology.** The Nosu kinship system is descriptive both in respect to parents' generation and to cross cousins. Elder parallel cousins are equated with elder siblings, younger parallel cousins with younger siblings (Lin 1946: 96-100):

Fa	*a be*
Mo	*a mo*
FaBr	*pu (pi) o*
FaSi	*a ber*
MoBr	*o gni*
MoSi	*mo gni*
Br	*vi o*
YoBr	*i i*
ElSi	*vi mo*
YoSi	*gni mo*
FaElBrSo, MoElSiSo	*vi o*
FaElBrDa, MoElSiDa	*vi mo*
FaYoBrSo, MoYoSiSo	*i i*
FaYoBrDa, MoYoSiDa	*gni mo*
FaSiSo	*a ber zin*
MoBrSo	*o gni zin*
MoBrDa	*o gni a mi*

MARRIAGE AND FAMILY. **Mode.** Courting is done mainly at festivals, when relatives from different clans come together. Singing sessions after dark are the most popular medium of courtship. Premarital sexual unions occur, particularly between cross cousins. Once the priest, *pi-mu*, has determined that the marriage will be an auspicious one, the details are arranged by a go-between. The groom's family pays a bride price consisting of silver, horses, and sheep. Among the nobility much of this bride price is obtained by levies imposed on White Lolo serfs attached to the groom's family. The wedding date, determined by the *pi-mu*, is marked by the ceremonial escort of the bride to the groom's parents' home, where she is received and then escorted back to her parental home. Here she remains until she becomes pregnant. This "staying at home" period is one of sexual freedom for the girl, particularly with respect to male cross cousins. She is also visited by the groom during this period, but her first child may not necessarily be his. The couple do not establish a separate household until the first pregnancy. At this time, the couple receive the girl's dowry consisting of silver, slaves, and animals, which is considered to be her share of the family inheritance. [Lin 1961: 78-81; Winnington 1959: 41-47.] **Form.** Nosu marriages are usually monogamous. Polygyny is allowed, but occurs only among the wealthy. The lack of a male heir, a desire for an ostentatious display of wealth, and a wish to form influential alliances with other families are some of the reasons for taking a second wife. [Lin 1961: 76-77.] **Extension of incest taboos.** The Nosu practice class endogamy and clan exogamy. Marriage is forbidden with all female cousins descended from males of Ego's own clan, as well as with Ego's MoSiDa. The preferred marriage is with a cross cousin, either MoBrDa or FaSiDa. [Lin 1946: 92-94; 1961: 71-72.] **Residence.** Following the first pregnancy, the couple establish a new household near that of the groom's family. [Lin 1961: 69.] **Domestic unit.** The nuclear family household is the normal pattern. In the case of a polygynous marriage, separate households are established for each wife. **Inheritance.** Movable property is inherited by both sons and daughters. Male slaves go to the sons, while female slaves go to the daughters. The daughters also share in the family inheritance through their marriage dowries. Land, however, always goes to the sons, and the youngest son also receives the family homestead. [Lin 1946: 90; 1961: 96.] **Divorce.** Divorce is possible, but rare after the birth of a child. If initiated by the wife, her family must return twice the amount of the bride price; if by the husband, the wife's family keeps the bride price and asks for additional compensation and a formal apology. [Lin 1961: 82-83.] **Secondary marriage.** The levirate is universally practiced (Lin 1946: 91).

SOCIOPOLITICAL ORGANIZATION. **Political organization.** Leadership in Nosu society may be inherited, but its real basis is in personal ability, particularly personal bravery and skill in warfare. A leader is expected to adjudicate differences among his followers, apprehend and punish wrongdoers in his territory, and protect travelers who have been given safe-conduct. There is no permanent political organization above the level of the clan. An able son may succeed his father as clan chief; otherwise a new leader will emerge by winning the tacit recognition of the community (Lin 1961: 26-29). Since the White Lolo are in the majority, their approval is often important. D'Ollone (1912: 64ff.) speaks of powerful leaders among the nobility, calling them princes, *nzemo*. Such a leader, often but not necessarily a clan head, controls an area as a kind of suzerain, acknowledged by the clans within his territory; the clans, however, continue to have their own clan chiefs and to manage their affairs through councils composed of the heads of powerful clan families. D'Ollone managed to get around in the Taliang Shan by enlisting the support of such a prince, who could guarantee his safe passage through most of the clan lands within his area of influence. ● The determination of guilt by ordeal is current among the Nosu. Methods include retrieving an egg from a pan of boiling water. If the suspect removes the egg without scalding his hand he is judged innocent. Such trials are presided over by a priest, *pi-mu*, and are used in cases involving accusations between two clan members (Lin 1961: 136-37). **Social stratification.** Lolo society in the Liangshan is stratified into three groups: Black Bones, White Bones, and slaves. The Black Bone Nosu constitute a strictly endogamous caste at the top of the hierarchy; there is considerable mobility, both upward and downward, between the other two classes. The latter are practically all of Han Chinese origin, with a sprinkling of neighboring non-Han peoples such as Hsifan and Nakhi—captives taken in warfare and in raids on the surrounding lowlands. Of the total population, roughly 10 per cent are Black Bones, 20 per cent slaves, and 70 per cent White Bones (Lin 1961: 104). ● The Black Bone nobility do little manual labor. They are obligated to protect their subjects (bondsmen and slaves) and to settle disputes among them. In return, they demand absolute respect and loyalty. A White Lolo must dismount and stand aside whenever he meets a Black Lolo on the road. Prestige among the nobility is measured by personal qualities and the amassing of lands and subjects. ● The White Lolo are mostly second or third generation descendants of Han Chinese slaves who have obtained a measure

of freedom through faithful service and who have been assimilated into Nosu culture. They are attached as bondsmen to noble Black Bone families, who grant them arable land for their own support. They pay rent on such land, and in addition are subject to levies of goods and money to defray the costs of marriages, funerals, etc. among the nobility. They are also liable to military duty and other services if called upon. An energetic White Lolo can become wealthy and can exercise a measure of influence in his own community, but he can never become a member of the nobility. Furthermore, he can be reduced to the status of slave if he allows himself to be captured in a clan feud or goes into debt slavery. White Lolo bondsmen may buy and own slaves, but they cannot enslave one another. They are divided into exogamous surname groups with names such as Ts'ai, Yang, and Po. Most of the craftsmen and priests in Nosu society come from the White Lolo class. ● The slave class includes both household slaves and "separates." They have no rights, and can be sold, exchanged, killed, or given away by their masters. They are regarded by the Nosu nobility as wealth, along with horses and sheep. A wealthy family may own well over 100 slaves, some of whom will be given to a son at his marriage and others to a daughter as part of her dowry. Slaves of long standing are not ill-treated, but those newly captured are put through a period of extremely harsh treatment. It is possible for slaves to accumulate savings and to buy their way into the status of bondsmen, but this change is more often a gradual process during which their owners grant them land and other privileges generally reserved for the White Lolo class. [Lin 1961: 97-110; Winnington 1959: 28-41.] **Warfare.** The Black Bone Nosu have a well-deserved reputation as fighters, both against the Chinese and in their incessant interclan feuds. All sources comment on the Nosu preoccupation with warfare and on the prestige accorded bravery and skill in horsemanship and with weapons. Nosu clans are quick to feud over real or imagined insults. A clan is responsible for the actions of its members and for avenging wrongs or insults committed by another clan. A feud can be forestalled by payment of gifts or blood money, but more often it results in warfare. If war is decided upon at a meeting of the heads of families, a wooden tally is sent by messenger to notify all members of the clan of the designated gathering place. Weapons include spears, swords, poisoned arrows, stones, and firearms. In the old days, warriors carried leather shields and donned a battle dress of silk, decorated with small gold and silver pieces designed to display the wearer's wealth. In recent years, however, the use of firearms and the consequent disappearance of hand-to-hand combat has made the wearing of bright battle dress unfashionable. ● Prior to the battle, a *pi-mu* divines the probable outcome. If the signs are unlucky, the leader may attempt to negotiate a settlement, sometimes through the intervention of a female peacemaker, dressed in her finest, who stands in front of the opposing forces. The battle is fought by young men, who commit themselves by oath to fight bravely. Ambushes, concerted charges, and hit-and-run attacks are familiar tactics. An unwritten code prohibits attacking an enemy before dawn. The outcome of the battle is often decided within a few hours. The defeated side frequently retires into the territory of a neutral clan. The victors invade the enemy territory and carry away all the goods and people they can find. ● After subtracting funeral expenses and other costs, the booty is divided among the members of the victorious clan. Captured Black Lolos almost never surrender. They are either killed by their captors or commit suicide. Captured bondsmen and slaves are enslaved by the victors. The killing of women and priests is taboo. A Black Lolo woman is usually held for ransom. The death of a Black Lolo in captivity results in the continuance of the clan feud for generations. The defeated clan may migrate en masse to a distant locality, put themselves under the protection of another clan, or sue for peace. An influential Black Lolo who is the mutual friend or relative of both sides is invited to be the mediator. The most important question is the compensation to be paid for the dead and wounded on both sides. A successful negotiation is sealed by a ritual oath conducted by a *pi-mu*. An ox is killed, and its skin stretched over a wooden frame. The *pi-mu* recites scriptures while the representatives of both sides walk under the skin. A chicken is then killed and its blood mixed with wine. The oath takers drink the wine and vow to keep the covenant. This kind of oath is also a part of other solemn occasions such as treaties of amnesty with the Chinese. [Lin 1961: 111-23.]

RELIGION. **Supernaturals.** There is a strong belief in the efficacy of amulets and charms such as lamb's wool and tiger's whiskers. The personal effects of a deceased ancestor are thought to be imbued with a spiritual power and must be handled carefully. There is a particular concern with evil spirits and ghosts, e.g. ghosts of persons who have died under unusual circumstances such as hanging or murder. A variety of exorcistic and avoidance rituals reflect the belief that such ghosts can cause sickness, misfortune, and death. Earth, sky, sun, and moon are thought to have spirits also, but the Nosu do not particularly concern themselves with these spirits except in their rain-making rituals. [Lin 1961: 124-37.] **Practitioners.** There are two categories of native practitioners, both drawn primarily from the White Lolo stratum. The male priest-exorcist, *pi-mu*, is found in almost every village. He acquires his skill through instruction, usually from his father or a close male relative. Chief among such skills is the ability

to read and interpret the sacred manuscripts written in Lolo script. These are handed down within families and include texts on ancestral legends, fortune telling, divination, invocation, exorcism, and praying for rain. Magico-religious recitations from the scriptures are employed at festivals, for sickness, and for purposes of fortune telling. When reciting scriptures and conducting sacrificial ceremonies, the *pi-mu* functions as priest-exorcist. Divination is also usually the task of the *pi-mu;* methods include examining the cracks in the burned shoulder bone of a sheep or the mottling on the rib of a pig. In egg divination, which is also popular, the *pi-mu* observes the pattern made by breaking the yolk. The *pi-mu* is also employed as a sorcerer by individuals, families, or clans. He may make a straw figure or write a victim's name on a piece of wood; these objects are then pointed toward an enemy, or secreted near or within his house. An individual who suspects that he is a victim may in turn employ a *pi-mu* to locate the hidden agent. ● Male or female *su-nieh* specialize in curing illness. A person takes on this status when the spirit of a deceased *su-nieh* manifests itself in his or her body resulting in temporary mental derangement. The *su-nieh* do not know the Lolo script and make no use of sacred scriptures. [Lin 1961: 126-29, 132-33.] **Ceremonies.** There is little evidence of Buddhism or of the Buddhist ceremonial calendar. An annual new year festival is the occasion of major social gatherings, with feasting and drinking and animal sacrifices conducted by the *pi-mu*. The periodic soul-delivery ceremonies for deceased relatives are occasions for major clan gatherings, and are also presided over by the *pi-mu*. [Lin 1961: 65-66, 133-36.] **Illness and medicine.** Birth ordinarily takes place in the home, attended by female relatives. In poor families a woman may resume work after three days rest. In some localities, however, the woman is considered unclean, and may not leave the house for upwards of a month. ● Although some diseases are attributed to drinking cold water or to sexual overindulgence, most illnesses are thought to be caused by evil spirits or sorcery. A *su-nieh* may be called in, or even a *pi-mu*, who works with an assistant or disciple, reciting scripture, manipulating objects such as a straw figure and a bell, and sacrificing a goat or chicken. The *su-nieh* puts on a shamanistic type of performance, chanting and beating a sheepskin drum while he whirls and dances with shaking body before the patient. [Lin 1961: 126-28, 130-31.] **Soul, death, and afterlife.** There is a belief in multiple souls which embark on separate careers after death. One keeps watch at the grave, while another, according to Lin (1961: 132-33), is eventually reincarnated as a human being or other form of life. Soul-loss may be a cause of illness, in which event a *pi-mu* must recall the errant soul to the patient's body. Anyone who wishes to place a curse on an enemy obtains portions of his hair or fingernails for the purpose. ● The Nosu cremate their dead, a task nowadays performed by the very poor or aged among the White Lolo. The corpse, washed and dressed, may remain in the house five or six days. The day of the funeral and the cremating ground to be used are both selected by the *pi-mu*. The corpse is borne to the cremating ground on a litter of bamboo and wood (formerly wrapped in a cowhide or horsehide, according to some sources). The *pi-mu* officiates along the way, describing the route to the soul of the deceased and pleading with it not to haunt the living. The litter bearing the corpse is burned on a wooden platform. The personal belongings of the deceased are warmed over the fire and returned to the family. The ashes are buried, and the spot marked with stones and some wine and food. Alternatively, the ashes may be scattered in the forest. ● At the time of the funeral, the *pi-mu* is invited to construct for the soul of the deceased a spirit tablet or spirit house, consisting of a slip of bamboo wound about with lamb's wool and cotton thread and bound within two halves of wood. The tablet is given to the family of the deceased and is installed behind the hearth. Periodically, as at the annual new year festival, sacrificial offerings are made to the ancestral spirit residing within the tablet. After the lapse of a year—sometimes longer—the deceased's clan is called together for a soul-delivery ceremony. For a wealthy family, this may involve heavy expense, and last up to ten or twelve days. The *pi-mu* conducts the complicated ceremonies, placing sticks in the ground according to patterns prescribed in the Lolo scriptures. The spirit tablet is then removed to a cave high in the mountains where the tablets of other deceased clan members are kept. No further ceremonies are held. [Lin 1961: 132-36.]

BIBLIOGRAPHY. DeBeauclair 1956; Feng and Shryock 1938; Lin 1946, 1961; Lo 1944-45; d'Ollone 1912; Winnington 1959.

KWEICHOW LOLO

Synonyms. *I-chia, Nosu*

ORIENTATION. **Identification.** Lolo speakers are relatively recent arrivals in western Kweichow. Their situation is described by Clarke (1911: 112ff.), who says that "two days to the north [of Anshun] begin the estates and residences of the large No-su landholders, which stretch away as far as Chaotung, Yunnan, one hundred and fifty miles distant as the crow flies." According to deBeauclair (1956: 264-65), there are approximately 100,000 Lolo speakers in extreme western Kweichow province, mainly in the Weining-Chaotung area. According to Winnington (1959: 16), contact is maintained with their independent relatives in Szechwan. He adds that the Nosu of Kweichow sometimes bring back brides from across the Yangtze.

● The Lolo in this area subsist on maize, buckwheat, and potatoes; the rough climate does not permit rice cultivation on the slopes (deBeauclair 1956: 271). According to Clarke (1911: 112ff.), they call themselves Nosu, but are generally called I-chia by the Chinese and Miao. They are divided into Black and White, distinguishing landowners from their tenants and slaves. The terms White Bones and Black Bones are heard only in the Independent Lolo country to the west. Clarke reported that the Black Nosu own much of the land, although they themselves are not numerous. Their tenants are mainly Miao. The Nosu lairds (Clarke's term) are left alone by the Chinese as long as they pay taxes and do not make trouble. Tenant disputes are settled on the spot by the laird, but the lairds themselves continually resort to the Chinese courts in their own disputes over land. They all speak Chinese, and employ Chinese tutors for their children. The Nosu lairds marry within their own class, seeking through such unions to enlarge and consolidate their estates. Many have Chinese and Miao women as concubines. The laird has practically feudal power over his tenants; he can demand levies on the occasion of a wedding, and his tenants are expected to fight for him in his disputes with other lairds. Most lairds own at least a few slaves; on occasion they purchase children from poor Han families and marry them to their Miao tenants.

BIBLIOGRAPHY. DeBeauclair 1956; Clarke 1911; Winnington 1959.

YUNNAN LOLO

ORIENTATION. **Identification.** Villages of Lolo speakers are found throughout most of the mountainous areas of Yunnan, located above the plains dwellers—the Chinese and the Tai. Except where they are in intimate contact with centers of Han Chinese population, as in Kunming county, they practice dry farming on the lower mountain slopes, raising chiefly rice, corn, buckwheat, and wheat. Animal husbandry is of less importance than among the Independent Lolo of Szechwan, and hunting and fishing are secondary. In general they dislike the term Lolo, chiefly because they seek to identify with the Han and resent any term that implies a non-Han origin. ● The Lolo of southern Yunnan, in the region of Mengtse and Szemao, have been described by missionaries and travelers; these accounts mention the characteristic women's headdress, the sacred texts in the Lolo script, and the preoccupation with ghosts—all traits that identify these southern Lolo with those farther north in Szechwan. On the other hand, their "opening the way" ceremonies at death, grave burial, and exogamous surname groups point to Chinese acculturation (Carey 1899: 384; d'Orléans 1898: 60-62; Henry 1903: 97-98, 102-07). ● The situation of the

Lolo in Kunming county—an area of heavy Chinese acculturation—is described by Chiang (1948a). According to Wissmann (1943: 14), the Lolo were the inhabitants, even before the Han, of the whole of the Yunnanese central highland triangle. Responding to the climate and agricultural potential, the Han have since settled in large numbers in this area, and the Lolo, Miao, and other tribesmen have been driven back into the surrounding mountains and hills. According to Chiang (1948a: 11, 17), the material culture and farming methods of the Kunming county Lolo, although "somewhat primitive," are similar to those of the Han. According to Chiang (1948a: 25ff.), their religious practices feature professional priest-exorcists trained to read sacred books in the Lolo language. The books are passed down from generation to generation in certain families, of which there were six in Kunming county in the late 1930s. The practitioners, *hsi-po*, owe their power to the ownership of these books and the ability to read them at least to some extent. Due to the encroachment of Chinese religion and the gradual disappearance of the books into the hands of collectors and museums, however, the *hsi-po* were declining in prestige, and only one could be called a full-time specialist. The books, in the form of ritual incantations, are read on such occasions as funerals, natural disasters, illnesses, and to determine auspicious dates. The *hsi-po* performs before an altar in his home, dressed in a bamboo rain hat and a woolen blanket or cloak, and holding a bell and an iron sword in his hands. Chiang emphasizes that these evidences of indigenous religion are minor compared to the extent to which the Lolo have adopted Chinese religious forms and edifices. There are Buddhist and Taoist temples in almost every village; and the associated rites and sacrifices, although they may be conducted by a non-Han dressed as a monk or priest, are entirely Han in character. Chiang adds that a Han Buddhist or Taoist priest is called in on all important ceremonial occasions.

BIBLIOGRAPHY. Carey 1899; Chiang 1948a; Henry 1903; d'Orléans 1898; Wissmann 1943.

WONI

Synonyms. *Hani, Houni*

ORIENTATION. **Identification.** Woni (Houni) is a generic term for a number of groups in southern Yunnan and northern Indochina speaking dialects related to Lolo. According to deBeauclair (1956: 269), those in Yunnan number some 138,000. Davies (1909: 337) includes the Woni dialects in his Lolo group of Tibeto-Burman languages. Woni "tribes" most often mentioned are Kado (Katu), Mahei (Mahe), Pudu (Putu), Kutsung, and Sansu (cf. Wissmann 1943; Davies 1909; Henry 1903). Davies and Henry would include the Ak'a (Akha) among these Woni groups.
● Woni are found in the area of southern Yunnan between the Red river and the headwaters of the Black river. Their greatest concentration is in the region of Talang, where, according to Davies (1909: 393), the Putu, Pio, and Katu form a cultural unit speaking mutually intelligible dialects. They are frequently described as "swarthy" and "inferior" in physique and appearance to the Lolo. D'Orléans (1898: 43-44) characterized them as "muscular and dark, with straight noses . . . hardy but independent mountaineers, not very amenable to Chinese supremacy." The same source mentions such traits as bride price, polygyny, ancestor worship, and grave burial. All sources agree that the Lolo script is unknown among the Woni.

BIBLIOGRAPHY. DeBeauclair 1956; Davies 1909; Henry 1903; d'Orléans 1898; Wissmann 1943.

INDOCHINA LOLO

Synonyms. *Fou-La, Ho, Houo-Ni, Penti, Piao, Pou, P'ou La, Xa Pho*

ORIENTATION. **Identification.** Lolo speakers in northern Vietnam and Laos are known under a variety of names: Lafont (1961) lists Pou (Piao, Penti), Fou-La, and Xa Pho; Lunet de Lajonquière (1906: 322-23) lists Fou-La (P'ou La), Pen Ti, Ho, and Houo-Ni; the NNCDT (1959: 241) lists Xa Khao, Xa Cau, Xa Xip, Xa Pho, and Xa Kha as subgroups speaking a Sino-Tibetan language presumably related to Lolo. Lafont adds that Houo-Ni, while generally considered to be the name of a Lolo-related group, is in northern Phong Saly province in Laos and among some Tai groups in northern Vietnam used for all Lolo speakers. The terms White Lolo and Black Lolo are also used (Le 1955: 49), and Lafont adds that these denote caste or class differences. **Location.** Lolo speakers are found in the northern Vietnamese areas of Lai Chau, Lao Kay, and Yen Bay at elevations above 1,500 meters (Le 1955: 49). There are several hundred Fou-La in the vicinity of Hoang Su Phi, Muong Khuong, and Ba Xat in northern Vietnam, and some 3,000–4,000 Xa Pho Lolo on the right bank of the Red river in the areas of Bao Ha and Coc Leu (Abadie 1924: 182, 185). Pen Ti Lolo are located mainly in the area of Yen Minh in the Bao Lac circle (Lunet de Lajonquière 1906: 339). **Demography.** The 1925 population estimate of the Lolo was 12,000 to 13,000 (Abadie 1924: 22), and more recently Le (1955: 49) gives a figure of 12,000. The NNCDT (1959: 242) places the Lolo population in Vietnam at 2,138. This figure, however, omits some 18,000 members of Xa groups which were counted as Lolo by Abadie and others. Observers are in agreement that the Lolo who have entered Indochina have lost much of their cultural identity, merging with those other groups—Meo, Tho, Man, Black Tai—with whom they happen to be in closest contact.

SETTLEMENT PATTERN AND HOUSING. According to Lafont (1961), houses are characteristically constructed on the ground. According to Lunet de Lajonquière (1906: 326) and Abadie (1924: 177), however, houses on piling do occur in those villages practicing wet-rice agriculture. Where shifting agriculture is predominant, houses are built on low earthern mounds, with thatched roofs and walls of corn stalks.

ECONOMY. Most Lolo speakers in Indochina practice swidden agriculture on the slopes; some, however, maintain paddy fields in the lower areas of the river valleys. Maize and rice are the staple crops, but tobacco and opium poppies are also grown. Kitchen gardens and fruit groves produce greens, cucumbers, kidney beans, peas, pumpkins, eggplant, plums, guavas, pears, grapefruit, and chestnuts. Domestic animals include cattle, buffalo, horses, and poultry. Bees are kept for their honey, which is traded. Hunting is of little importance. Some of the Lolo produce earthenware cooking pots. They do weaving and dyeing, and know how to distill alcohol. Honey and other products are traded to Chinese merchants for cloth, and the Lolo also do some trading with neighboring Meo groups. Where they have paddy fields, the Lolo have family ownership. Either the swiddens are communally owned, or the family that clears a swidden is considered to have usufruct rights. [Lunet de Lajonquière 1906: 325-31; Abadie 1924: 178-79.]

MARRIAGE AND FAMILY. The male initiates courtship. Gifts are exchanged, and a bride price is set. The marriage is marked by a nocturnal feast. There is no ritual. After the marriage feast, the bride and groom live together for a short period, after which she returns to her parental home. The husband has visiting privileges until she becomes pregnant, after which they establish their own household. Polygyny is allowed but rarely practiced. Land and family property are divided among the male children. In the absence of male offspring, one-half of the property goes to the widow, and the other half to the brothers and male nephews of the deceased. Male children are frequently adopted. [Lunet de Lajonquière 1906: 329-32; Abadie 1924: 179-81.]

SOCIOPOLITICAL ORGANIZATION. The Lolo in northern Vietnam are too dispersed to have their own political enclaves. The village is under the direction of a *siao phay*, and in most instances there is no higher political office. Some Lolo live in areas where the Meo are politically dominant, but for the most part they are found in areas dominated by Tai-speaking groups. [Abadie 1924: 179.]

RELIGION. Lolo speakers in northern Vietnam have adopted some religious beliefs of neighboring Meo, Man, and Tai. They believe in evil spirits, and practice an ancestor cult. The altars found in each house are simply arranged, with figures representing deceased members of the family made from orchid stems and paper. There are sorcerers who verbally transmit their techniques to their eldest sons. After death, the corpse is kept in the house for three days. Close kin visit the grave, where they keep a vigil fire burning for nine days if the deceased was male, eight if female. In some cases the bones are exhumed after three years and reburied in a special container. [Lunet de Lajonquière 1906: 330-31; Abadie 1924: 180-81.]

BIBLIOGRAPHY. Abadie 1924; Lafont 1961; Le 1955; Lunet de Lajonquière 1906; NNCDT 1959.

LISU

Synonyms. *Li-hsaw, Li-shaw, Lisaw, Liso, Lu-tzu, Yaoyen, Yaw-yen, Yawyin, Yeh-jen*

ORIENTATION. **Identification.** The people generally call themselves Lisu. They are known to the Chinese as Liso, Lisaw, Li-hsaw, or Li-shaw. Those in the upper Salween are sometimes called by the Chinese Lu-tzu ("Salween-men") or Yeh-jen ("wild people"). According to Ward (1921: 294-95), the latter term has given rise to Kachin terms for Lisu such as Yawyin, Yaw-yen, and Yaoyen, and the Lisu in Burma frequently appear under those names in accounts by British authors (cf. Rose and Coggin Brown 1911). Tai speakers in northern Thailand have adopted the Chinese terms Lisaw or Li-shaw to refer to the Lisu in this area. • Terms such as Pai or Pe (White) Lisu, Hua or Hwa (Flowery or Variegated) Lisu, and He (Black or Independent) Lisu are Chinese designations expressive of differences in dress, dialect, and degree of sinicization among the Lisu-speaking populations within China. Prior to World War I the area of the upper Salween was largely outside effective Chinese administrative control. Here, between 26° 30′ and 27° 30′ N., the Black Lisu have retained a fierce independence, raiding Chinese caravans and feuding among themselves. In an area of this kind practically the only effective measure which can be used by the Chinese is the strict control of salt imports, since salt is in great demand among the hill tribes (Wiens 1954: 327). • Moving south from the Black Lisu area, toward Tengyueh and the Northern Shan States, the heavily sinicized "tame" Lisu are more in evidence. The colorful multilayered clothing of the women accounts for the Chinese appellation "Flowery" or "Variegated." Hemp clothing gives way to cotton, and houses tend to be built directly on the ground. These "southern" Lisu (the Yawyin and Lisaw of Burma and Thailand) identify with China to the east, whereas the Independent Lisu claim their original homeland to be to the north, in the direction of Tibet. Lisu have entered Thailand only during the last 50 years. [Rose and Coggin Brown 1911: 255, 257, 268; Scott and Hardiman 1900: 587-88; Metford 1935: 135-43; Davies 1909: 391; Young 1961: 34-35.] **Location.** The main concentration is in western Yunnan, between 26° and 28° N. Here, in an area bounded on the east by the Salween–Mekong watershed and on the west by the Nmai Hka, Lisu speakers form the main population. They have spread eastward along the Yunnan–Szechwan border as far as Tingchou north of Kunming, and westward as far as Myitkyina. Migrations southward have carried the Lisu as far as Chiengmai (Chiengdao and Mae Taeng districts) and Chiengrai provinces in northern Thailand. Scattered communities occur in both the Northern and Southern Shan States. [Embree and Thomas 1950: 35; Rose and Coggin Brown 1911: 257; Credner 1935a: 172.] **Geography.** The Lisu prefer rugged upland topography near the tops of mountain ranges, from which they exploit the steep valley slopes below. **Linguistic affiliation.** Davies (1909: 391) identified Lisu as one of the "Lolo group" of Tibeto-Burman languages, closely allied to Lahu and Akha. Most authors have followed this classification (cf. Young 1961). Rose and Coggin Brown (1911: 251) state that the vocabulary is remarkably similar among all Lisu groups; Leach (1954: 45) says that there are several regionally distinct dialects. Indigenous writing is denied by most authorities (cf. Young 1961), although Seidenfaden (1958: 127) mentions a kind of hieroglyphic writing employed by Lisu medicine men. There is also a missionary-devised script. Lisu men usually know several languages, e.g. those in northern Thailand are likely to be fluent in Lahu, Yunnanese, Shan, Lao (Yuan), and Akha. **Demography.** The Lisu in China are said by Bruk (1960: 19) to number 317,000, according to the 1953 Chinese People's Republic census. Embree and Thomas (1950: 35) estimated the total of Lisu in Burma at about 30,000, but Leach (1954: 309) reports some 15,000 in the Burmese Kachin Hills area alone. An up-to-date and fairly accurate figure for the Lisu in Thailand is the 17,300 reported by Young (1961: 34). The total number of Lisu speakers thus probably exceeds 400,000. **History and cultural relations.** Young (1961: 1, 34) suggests that the Lisu are of "Lo-Lo extraction" and that their origins ultimately lie to the northwest of Yunnan. He adds that they show a strong Tibetan influence. There has been considerable contact with Chinese, particularly south of Tengyueh, with resultant acculturation. Lisu intermarry with Chinese, and it is not unusual to find a Chinese merchant settled in a Lisu village, married to a local woman. Wiens (1954: 325-27) and Metford (1935: 135-43) both mention cases of permanent villages and paddy-rice farming among acculturated Lisu in China. Contact with other groups, e.g. for purposes of trade, is not infrequent; Embree and Thomas (1950: 35-36) mention that the Lisu in Burma frequently attend markets at Mogok, Kyatpyen, and Katha, and that some Lisu have reportedly worked as coolies in Palaung tea plantations. The nature of intergroup relations in the ethnically complex area of upper Burma is indicated by Leach (1954: 59) as follows: "Along the whole eastern frontier of the Kachin hills area there are small pockets of Lisu speakers. Such communities are usually in political relation with neighboring Kachin groups with whom they intermarry. For purposes of such a marriage Lisu clans are, by a fiction, identified with Kachin clans and lineages so that the Kachin kinship network is extended to embrace these Lisu speakers." Observers have characterized the Lisu as a "fine" people—robust, independent of spirit, and excellent warriors. Lisu battalions fought in Mesopotamia during World War I. Missionary work has been limited mainly to the southern Lisu, in Burma, China, and Thailand.

SETTLEMENT PATTERN AND HOUSING. **Settlement pattern.** With the exception of some of the heavily sinicized Lisu of Yunnan, villages are located high up on ridge and mountain tops, at elevations ranging from 5,000 to 9,000 feet. The Lisu choose inaccessible spots which can be easily defended, hidden away among thickets of fir and dwarf bamboo. Villages in Thailand average 37 houses (maximum about 100 houses) and 12 persons per house. According to Seidenfaden (1958: 128), the Lisu tend to remain in the same area for a period of 40-50 years. **Housing.** Houses are built either on piles or directly on the ground. Piles (split-level dwellings) appear to be more prevalent among the northern Independent Lisu. Farther south, houses built directly on the ground with earth floors are seen, probably as a result of Chinese influence. Pile dwellings are found as far south as Chiengmai, however. Houses are of the low, thatched-roof variety, divided into two or more rooms if possible. Animals are quartered under the house or in separate pens. [Rose and Coggin Brown 1911: 251, 260; Young 1961: 35.]

ECONOMY. Swidden agriculture and hunting are both important sources of food. Gathering, except for a few products such as wild honey, appears to be less important. The Lisu keep a variety of domestic animals, although with the exception of pigs and chickens these contribute little to the food supply. **Agriculture.** Credner (1935a: 172-73) points out the adaptability of Lisu agriculture to varied environmental conditions: in the heavily dissected upland areas of the Yunnan border region the Lisu are able to raise irrigated rice on artificial terraces in tropical valley bottoms; higher up they plant swiddens to crops such as maize, mountain rice, barley, and millet;

and at still higher altitudes buckwheat is the chief crop. According to Credner, as the Lisu move south into Thailand, rice and maize become the chief crops. Additional crops include beans, yams, sweet potatoes, melons, gourds, chard, peppers, tobacco, cotton, and hemp. Opium poppies are raised by most Lisu; in Thailand, according to Young (1961: 39), the Lisu rank next to the Meo as opium producers. **Hunting.** Except among the heavily acculturated Lisu of Yunnan, hunting is an important economic activity, avidly pursued by all able-bodied males. The crossbow (with poisoned arrows) and the large sword knife, *dah,* are the chief weapons; guns, including a few locally manufactured muzzle-loaders, are used by those who can afford them. Snares and decoys are occasionally used. Animals taken include bears, deer, panthers, boar, foxes, squirrels, and birds. [Rose and Coggin Brown 1911: 251-54; d'Orléans 1898: 227-30; Young 1961: 40.] **Domestic animals.** Most Lisu groups keep at least some goats, pigs, ponies, chickens, and dogs, and occasionally sheep and cattle. Only pigs and chickens are eaten. The Lisu of Thailand are reported to be great hog keepers; these animals are fed twice daily by the women—probably, as among the Meo and Yao, on a cooked mash of maize and other ingredients. [Rose and Coggin Brown 1911: 251-54; Young 1961: 39; Sisawat 1952: 610ff.] **Food and stimulants.** Among the northern Lisu the diet is primarily one of buckwheat cakes and porridge, supplemented with vegetable soup to which chicken or eggs may be added. The southern Lisu eat mainly steamed rice (nonglutinous according to Sisawat 1952: 610) served in a kind of curry with vegetables such as chard. Meat, in the form of pork, chicken, wild fowl, and game, is relatively rare except among those Lisu who keep many pigs and make frequent animal sacrifices. Wild honey, where available, is an important adjunct to the diet. The Lisu in Burma and Thailand, at least, chew betel. Tobacco smoking is characteristic of most if not all Lisu. Although they produce a great deal of opium, they are not normally addicted unless in close contact with the Chinese; opium addiction among older Lisu men in northern Thailand reportedly runs about 6 per cent. Alcoholic beverages, made from maize or millet, are consumed in large quantities. [Ward 1921: 121-22; Rose and Coggin Brown 1911: 251-54; Young 1961: 39.] **Industrial arts.** Bamboo work, basketry, weaving, and blacksmithing. **Trade.** Groups of Lisu not infrequently make trips to lowland markets where they sell such items as opium, peppers, firewood, herbs, and smoked meat. According to Embree and Thomas (1950: 36), Lisu have acted as middlemen in trade between the Yunnanese and tribes across the border in Burma.

KIN GROUPS. Ch'en (1947) reports on the nature of clan names and clan origins among a group of Lisu speakers in southern Szechwan recently moved from across the border in Yunnan. The Lisu explain the origin of these clans, and their arrangement in a kind of dual organization, by a deluge legend involving brother-sister incest; this, together with other evidence, leads the author to regard the Lisu clan system as indigenous. The names for these clans [which appear to be patrilineal surname groups] are Chinese, and according to Ch'en have been adopted by the Lisu. Rose and Coggin Brown (1911: 268) list a number of Lisu clan names which, although they do not correspond directly with those given by Ch'en, refer in most cases, as his do, to names of animals, plants, and forest products.

MARRIAGE AND FAMILY. Institutionalized courtship, premarital sexual freedom, and free choice of marriage partners are reported for the southern Lisu of the Shan State–Tengyueh–Chiengrai area. Among these Lisu a go-between normally negotiates a bride price which is paid in cash. A man may sometimes agree to bride service to help pay off the bride price, in which case he lives matrilocally for a time. An eldest married son may be expected to live patrilocally in the same household with his father; residence in the case of other sons may vary, but appears to be ultimately patrilocal in independent households adjacent to the parental household. Either party may initiate divorce. Small children normally remain with the mother in cases of separation. [Rose and Coggin Brown 1911: 262-64; Young 1961: 41; Sisawat 1952: 638-40.]

SOCIOPOLITICAL ORGANIZATION. **Political organization.** The Black Lisu of the upper Salween have traditionally been independent of Chinese or other outside control. Hereditary chiefs normally exercise control over several adjacent villages. Lisu chiefs in this and other areas function (with or without the help of village elders) in judging crimes and in imposing a system of set fines, graduated according to the seriousness of the offense. In the Tengyueh–Burmese Shan State portion of the Salween valley, Lisu villages are normally subject to a local Shan or Chinese *saohpa,* and are politically integrated under his jurisdiction within a *muong.* [Rose and Coggin Brown 1911: 264-65; Leach 1954: 51ff.; Young 1961: 43.] **Social stratification.** Rose and Coggin Brown (1911: 263) cite reports to the effect that the Black Lisu enslave male captives, using them as agricultural laborers. These captives are, however, allowed to marry Lisu women, and the children of such marriages are free. Class-stratified villages of Lisu speakers are reported by Leach for the area east of the Kachin Hills (Leach 1954: 52).

RELIGION. Young (1961: 36) describes the Lisu as animists with an emphasis on ancestor worship and exorcism. There appear to be few Buddhist elements in Lisu religious behavior, although ritual and paraphernalia in some cases are reminiscent of Chinese Taoism. **Supernaturals.** Include jungle spirits, earth spirits, wind spirits, village (guardian) spirits, a lord of heaven, a lightning demon, and spirits of fields and crops. Malevolent spirits of the demoniac variety cause various illnesses. Small altars are located along the paths leading to and from the village; here the Lisu place sacrificial food offerings to the spirits. An altar shelf opposite the door of the house serves for sacrifices in honor of the ancestral spirits. **Practitioners.** A village practitioner ("sorcerer," "religious leader," or "spirit doctor") conducts exorcistic rituals with candles, incense, swords, rice, wine, blood, etc. In treating an illness, he may work himself into a state of spirit possession by chanting and shaking his body. Walking on hot coals may also be part of such a session (Sisawat 1952: 634). More often he is called upon to ward off misfortune or illness by attaching cotton threads to the neck and wrists of a client; amulets, on which he has breathed or expectorated, may be attached to the threads. According to Rose and Coggin Brown (1911: 265-66), "any man or boy who is willing to learn the priestly language may act as intermediary in the appeals and sacrifices to the spirit world." Young (1961: 36) mentions that the Lisu religious leaders, *maw-pi*, do not exercise the influential role they sometimes play among the neighboring Lahu in northern Thailand. **Ceremonies.** An annual spring festival, lasting from four to six days, is the high point of the Lisu year; one day during this period is reserved especially for honoring the ancestors, with sacrifices of pigs and visits to the graves of the recently departed. This is a time of much drinking and merrymaking; it is a prime occasion for boys to go on courting expeditions to neighboring villages (Young 1961: 41). In cases of serious illness within a village, the entire populace contributes to a sacrificial ceremony to the village spirit, which is accompanied by a feast for all (Sisawat 1952: 655-56). **Birth.** Older women assist at the birth of a child. The mother and child must not leave the house for 30 days; the mother is attended by friends, and is not allowed to work (Rose and Coggin Brown 1911: 260-61). **Death.** Both the northern and southern Lisu inter the body in a grave in the forest. Burial is made in a wooden coffin, to the accompaniment of loud wailing and firing of guns. The grave is marked, and relatives continue to visit the site annually for a period of three years. In the south, at least, a well-to-do family will keep the body of the deceased in the home for several days before burial. [Rose and Coggin Brown 1911: 260-61; Sisawat 1952: 664-68.]

BIBLIOGRAPHY. Bruk 1960; Ch'en 1947; Credner 1935a; Davies 1909; Embree and Thomas 1950; Leach 1954; Metford 1935; d'Orléans 1898; Rose and Coggin Brown 1911; Scott and Hardiman 1900; Seidenfaden 1958; Sisawat 1952; Ward 1921; Wiens 1954; Young 1961.

LAHU

Synonyms. *Lohei, Muhso, Musso, Mussuh*

ORIENTATION. **Identification.** The people call themselves Lahu, to which they suffix various qualifiers. The Lahu Na (Black, Great, or Independent Lahu) have been established for some time in southwestern Yunnan and northeastern Burma, from where they have migrated more recently into northwestern Laos and northern Thailand. The Lahu Nyi (Southern Lahu), an offshoot of the Lahu Na, are found in Burma and are the most numerous of the Lahu groups in Thailand. The Lahu Shi (Yellow Lahu) live primarily in Yunnan and Burma, but are also found in small numbers in Thailand. The Lahu Shehleh emigrated to Thailand from Yunnan about 40 years ago. The various Lahu groups in Thailand (at least) differ somewhat in dialect, but only the Lahu Shi are unintelligible to other Lahu. There are relatively minor differences also in details of dress and religious observances, and in the degree to which the different groups affiliate with their counterparts in Burma. ● The Chinese refer to the Lahu as Lohei, or by the Tai term Mussuh (Muhso, Musso) meaning "hunter." Tai speakers refer to the Lahu Na as Mussuh Dam (Black Mussuh) and to the Lahu Shi as Mussuh Kwi or Mussuh Luang (Yellow Mussuh). The Lahu Nyi resent the name Mussuh Daeng (Red Mussuh), as being a rude usage of the term "red" or "raw." The Lahu may also be known locally by clan names, e.g. the Lahu Shi of Thailand are of the Ba Kio and Ba Lan clans (Lahu Shi Ba Kio or Ba Kio). ● The Lahu are a proud people, inclined to be quarrelsome if they feel that they have been insulted. Their way of life leaves little place for the timid or physically unfit; they live by strict codes of behavior which if broken can result in summary execution. Until recently they managed to retain their autonomy in the mountain lands of southwestern Yunnan, where they gained a reputation as able fighters against the encroachments of the Han Chinese. [Young 1961: 12-33; Embree and Thomas 1950: 34; Wiens 1954: 316.] **Location.** The main concentrations of Lahu are along both sides of the Yunnan–Burma border between 22° and 24° N., and extending southward in Burma to include much of Kengtung state. This is an area bounded roughly on the west by the Salween and on the east by the Mekong. In northern Thailand the Lahu are found mainly in Chiengmai, Maehongsorn, and Chiengrai provinces, and as far south in Tak province as 17° N. Some are also found across the border in Laos, in Nam Tha province. **Linguistic affiliation.** Lahu is a Tibeto-Burman language, monosyllabic with three tonal variations. It has similarities with Akha and Lisu, and is sometimes classed with these as "southern Lolo." Linguistic borrowings from Chinese, Burmese, and Tai reflect the migration history of the Lahu. Lahu Na men usually speak some Burmese, and a few are literate in a romanized script devised by the American Baptist Mission. The Lahu are not inclined to learn the languages of other hill tribes with whom they are in contact; rather it is these others who usually learn Lahu. [Young 1961: 14.] **Demography.** Bruk (1960: 19) gives a 1953 figure of 139,000 Lahu Na and Lahu Shi in Yunnan. Embree and Thomas (1950: 33), citing figures supplied by Harold Young, give a total of 66,000 Lahu in Burma. According to Young (1961), there are some 15,000 Lahu in Thailand in 119 known villages. The number of Lahu in the Haut Mekong region of Laos has been estimated at 2,000 (Izikowitz 1951: 21). The total of Lahu speakers is thus probably well over 200,000. **History and cultural relations.** Scott and Hardiman (1900: 583-86) said that the Lahu probably came originally from somewhere in or near Tibet. The Lahu themselves say that they came to their present areas from farther north, and that they have moved southward under pressure from the Chinese. Young (1961: 20-25) feels that the Lahu, Lisu, and Akha may have a common Lolo origin. Rose and Coggin Brown (1911: 269) also subscribe to this theory, regarding the Lahu as having settled in small numbers among "older, more primitive races" by right of conquest, losing thereby many characteristic northern Lolo physical features, while retaining much of their original language. Scott and Hardiman (1900: 576-77, 583-86) refer to a seventeenth–eighteenth century independent Lahu "kingdom" ruled by 36 *fu* or religious-secular leaders, located along the present Burma–China border between the Wa States on the west and Szemao on the east. As late as the 1880s and '90s the Lahu in this area were offering effective military resistance to Chinese expeditionary forces. ● The Lahu of present-day Thailand generally avoid contact with plains people. They do, however, come down from their mountain villages for salt, and they are visited by itinerant buyers of opium, jungle products, and peppers. Their contacts with other hill peoples, particularly Lisu, Akha, and Yao, are frequent, but there is little intermarriage. They dislike the Chinese and have little to do with the Meo. The Thailand Lahu Nyi and Na maintain contacts in Burma; in the late 1950s some returned to Burma, where a *pawku* (religious leader) had proclaimed himself a "man-god" and was attempting to incite his followers to a "holy warpath" (Young 1961: 20-25).

SETTLEMENT PATTERN AND HOUSING. **Settlement pattern.** Villages are usually located above 4,000 feet, on flat ridge tops just below the summits of higher ranges, often at some distance from a source of water. Villages in northern Thailand average between 15 and 20 houses and between 120 and 160 persons per village. The maximum village population is about 350. The houses in a village are clustered around that of the chief or headman (Young 1961:

16). **Housing.** Houses in northern Thailand are generally of bamboo construction, on piles, with thatched gable roofs. An open porch is reached by log steps. Animals are tethered beneath the house at night (Young 1961: 16). According to Embree and Thomas (1950: 33), the houses of the northern Lahu (Wa States area) tend to be more substantial.

ECONOMY. The Lahu rely mainly on swidden agriculture for their food supply. Whenever possible, however, the men spend much of their time hunting. In Burma and Thailand, wild game and jungle produce contribute significantly to the diet. Domestic animals are raised for food and sacrifice, but apparently the Lahu do not keep as many hogs as the Lisu and some other hill peoples. Some cash income is derived from the sale of opium and other products, but the Lahu are not known for establishing trade relationships with other groups. **Agriculture.** According to Scott and Hardiman (1900: 581-83), the Lahu will attempt wet-rice cultivation where possible, but such opportunities are rare. Swiddens are used for about three years and then abandoned; if they are to be used again they are fallowed for about 10 to 15 years. In northern Thailand a family will clear about 20 *rai* of new land in a three-year period (Young 1961: 18-20). In the south the staple crops are dry rice and maize. Side crops include melons, pumpkins, beans of the genus *Cajanus*, millet, yams, potatoes, cucumbers, bananas, and mustard. The main commercial crops are opium and peppers. Buckwheat tends to replace rice as a staple crop in the northern part of the Lahu area. **Hunting.** Although many hill peoples are avid hunters, the Lahu have the reputation as huntsmen par excellence. Among the Thailand Lahu, hunting provides not only a considerable portion of the diet but also cash income from the sale of dried meat. The title of "supreme hunter" among these Lahu is avidly coveted by all able-bodied men. The crossbow with poisoned arrow is the prime weapon, although guns are used when available. The Kengtung Lahu are reported to make use also of group methods involving beaters and dogs. [Young 1961: 18-20; Telford 1937: 135-36.] **Domestic animals.** Among the Thailand Lahu the main domesticated animals are swine and chickens. Some villages have ponies and mules for transport, and there are a few cattle. Hogs are occasionally fed rice bran or crushed corn, but the Lahu are more casual in their attitude toward animal husbandry than are, for example, the Lisu and Meo. [Young 1961: 18-20.] **Industrial arts.** In Kengtung a village blacksmith makes axes, swords, knives, and hoes for his fellow villagers; they in turn till his fields. Women spin and weave cotton cloth. [Telford 1937: 113.] **Trade.** There is little trade with other hill tribes. In northern Thailand the Lahu go down to the plains to trade dried meat and peppers for salt. They are visited by opium traders. [Young 1961: 21.]

KIN GROUPS. Young refers to the "clans" of the Thailand Lahu, and mentions specifically that the Lahu Shi are of the Ba Kio and Ba Lan clans (1961: 30). Telford (1937: 90) lists seven named "subdivisions" of the Kengtung Lahu Na (e.g. Na Pehn, La Lau, Hpu, Kaleh). For the Lahu Shi he lists four named divisions (e.g. Balang, Banceu). [It is probable that these are patrilineal surname groups, as among the Akha and Lisu.]

MARRIAGE AND FAMILY. **Mode.** Among the Thailand Lahu, the annual celebration of the Chinese New Year affords the traditional opportunity for courtship, and most marriages result from contacts made at this time. The young men do a great deal of visiting to other villages during these periods of institutionalized courtship. Boys and girls camp out separately beside large fires, and engage in antiphonal singing of love songs. Once the choice of a partner is made, a go-between makes the necessary arrangements. A period of premarital sexual activity invariably precedes the marriage. [Young 1961: 22-23.] In both Thailand and Burma, a man must ideally perform bride service (for three years, according to Young). In practice, it is possible to forego some or all of the bride service by the payment of a cash bride price (300 to 1,000 *baht* in Thailand). A wedding ceremony conducted by a village priest or elder is reported for the Kengtung (Burma) Lahu. [Young 1961: 22-23; Telford 1937: 96, 119.] **Form.** The Lahu in Burma and Thailand are almost always monogamous. The Lahu Shehleh, relatively recent immigrants to Thailand from Yunnan, do allow polygyny, but it is restricted in practice to a few chiefs and elders. [Young 1961: 22-23; Telford 1937: 119.] **Residence.** Following an initial period of bride service (if present), a man establishes his own home or returns to his father's house with his wife (Young 1961: 23). **Domestic unit.** Northern Thailand households average eight persons each (Young 1961: 16). It is probable therefore that in this area the Lahu are characterized by [patrilocal] stem families as the normal domestic unit. **Inheritance.** According to Telford (1937: 148), male and female members of the family get an equal share of the inheritance. **Divorce.** Among the Lahu Shi in northern Thailand divorces are not infrequent (Young 1961: 32).

SOCIOPOLITICAL ORGANIZATION. **Political organization.** Many of the more remote villages in Burma and Thailand have little contact with Shan or Siamese officialdom. The village chief (with or without the help of a council of elders) functions as the final authority in most matters. The Lahu do, however, at times bring disputes to a *saohpa's* court; they are fond of litigation, and engage in considerable shouting and mutual accusations. The status of *pawku* (religious leader or priest-shaman) is an important one in most Lahu villages; even a chief's orders are subject to veto by the *pawku* on religious grounds. Occasionally *pawku* become powerful religio-political figures with influence over a wide area. The village chief and *pawku* may also be one and the same person. ● Individuals termed *po* (warrior) may act as sheriffs appointed by a village chief to carry out his orders and (on occasion) to administer capital punishment. Justice, in most cases administered by the chief, consists usually of monetary fines graduated according to the seriousness of the offense. More serious or difficult cases may be decided by ordeal or by divination, with penalties ranging from the loss of a hand to death. Persons accused of possessing an evil spirit may be banished from the village. Village solidarity is strong, and the individual villager takes few actions without the consent of village leaders. Missionaries have noted that whereas individual Lahu seldom convert to Christianity, an entire village may do so if the chief so decides. [Young 1961: 24-25; Telford 1937: 95, 146-47.] As reported by Scott and Hardiman (1900: 583-86), the Lahu on the Burma–China border were formerly organized as a "kingdom," under religious-secular leaders, *fu*, who in turn were subject to a limited number of higher authorities. **Warfare.** Telford (1937: 142-43) reports on Lahu traditions of warfare, mainly against the Chinese. Decisions regarding warfare were made by the chiefs and seers, after resorting first to divination. Chiefs customarily allied themselves in war by a sort of blood covenant. Telford cites incidents during fighting between Lahu and British troops in which the former have believed themselves invulnerable while wearing charms, amulets, and other magical paraphernalia.

RELIGION. Young (1961: 14-16) terms the Lahu "theistic animists," adding that their theism is unique among the hill tribes of Thailand. In contrast to most of their neighbors in the mountains of Burma and Thailand, the Lahu show little evidence of a developed ancestor worship. Scott and Hardiman (1900: 583-86) see evidences of Tibetan lamaism, and add that there is much about the Lahu customs to suggest that they were at one time Buddhists or heavily influenced by Buddhism. The relative sophistication of Lahu religious culture may account in part for their attraction to quasi-religious sects and movements such as those promulgated on occasion by their *pawku*. ● The American Baptist Mission has worked among the Lahu of Burma, and claimed in 1950 over 28,000 converts in that country and in northern Thailand. The 1931 census listed 3,635 Christian Lahu in Burma (Embree and Thomas 1950: 33), and a recent estimate places the number of Christian Lahu in Thailand at about 200 (Young 1961: 14). **Supernaturals.** The Lahu believe in a great many good and evil spirits, *ne*. Among the former are village and house spirits, protective and guardian in nature but inclined to be capricious. Among the latter are the whirlwind spirit and the lightning spirit, sources of illness and misfortune. Some greatly feared spirits or "demons" can enter a man, transforming him into a kind of werewolf. In addition, the Lahu by all accounts possess the concept of a "father god" or "supreme being," called G'uisha by the Kengtung Lahu, who have village temples dedicated to this deity. [Young 1961: 14-16; Telford 1937: 158-59, 170.] **Practitioners.** Large communities, as in Kengtung, usually contain three male religious specialists: a *pawku* (religious leader, village priest); a *mawpa* (seer or shaman); and a *shepa* (medicine man). These different functions frequently overlap, however, and in smaller communities, as among the Lahu Shi of Thailand, the priest and shaman may be combined. In Kengtung the *pawku* leads the people in sacrifices and ceremonies in honor of G'uisha in the village temple, and also participates in marriage ceremonies. A *mawpa* is thought to have occult powers which enable him to discern spirits causing illness, to exorcise evil spirits and demons, to divine, and to practice both black and white magic. He can cause sharp objects to enter the body of a victim, and because of his abilities as magician and sorcerer he is a man to be feared. The medicine man, or *shepa*, possesses both a materia medica and supernatural healing abilities. ● The *pawku* is always a powerful figure within the village. His opinions and interpretations of events, reinforced by supernatural sanctions, frequently override those of the village chief. Decisions affecting the village are rarely taken until the *pawku*, by divination and recourse to magic, has determined the correct line of action. Those *pawku* who also acquire reputations as powerful magicians and sorcerers may extend their influence over wide areas. Recent examples include a *pawku* in Kengtung who claims to have the "magic hammer," "magic rope," and "magic knife" with which to kill all enemies, a claim which has attracted some Thailand Lahu to return to Burma. [Young 1961: 14-16, 31; Telford 1937: 170ff.] **Ceremonies.** Among the Thailand Lahu each house contains an altar where the head of the household (among the Na and Nyi) burns beeswax and joss sticks to the guardian spirits. Each village contains what Young (1961: 16) calls a "nat house," in which only the village chief or the *pawku* may conduct sacrificial ceremonies. For the Kengtung Lahu, Telford (1937: 171-73) mentions a village "temple" within a sacred temple compound; here the *pawku* lights candles and incense while chanting to the accompaniment of gongs and drums. Both the Thailand and Burma Lahu annually celebrate the Chinese New Year with four days of feasting, dancing, and mutual gifts of glutinous rice cakes. Young people wash the elders' hands to obtain their blessings, but there are no ancestral cult observances. Dancing, accompanied by drinking, may be a community-wide affair. According to Telford (1937: 126), the Lahu believe that dancing exorcises evil spirits from the village. Young reports that among the Lahu Na and Nyi in Thailand the young people periodically engage in "purification dances." Exorcistic rituals usually include the sacrifice of a chicken or pig, and the ceremonial manipulation of blood, water, eggs, and the like. Divination is done with both egg yolks and chicken bones. Amulets and charms are popular; a *pawku* may tie threads to a villager's wrists, with appropriate incantations, to ward off evil spirits. **Illness and medicine.** The Lahu recognize natural causes of illness or death, such as the consumption of poisonous food. More commonly they ascribe illness to supernatural causes, including soul loss, the "bite" of malevolent or offended spirits, black magic or sorcery, and spirit (or demon) possession. In the latter case the victim at first becomes violent, speaking in tongues, and later enters a trancelike state during which he is insensitive to pain. Violent exorcistic methods are prescribed to rid the person of the spirit possessing him. There is in addition the belief that some person in the community may be the unknowing "owner" of such a spirit, and thus the indirect cause of illness in others; individuals so accused may be hounded and banished from the village (Telford 1937: 162). In cases of illnesses thought to be due to sorcery, the medicine man first seeks the aid of supernatural powers by burning candles and reciting incantations. He then most generally "bites out" the offending object, e.g. a sharp bone, which he locates with supernatural aid (Telford 1937: 196-97). **Birth.** At birth the woman assumes a kneeling position, pulling on a rope suspended from above. She is assisted by her husband and a midwife (Telford 1937: 100). **Soul, death, and afterlife.** Among the Kengtung Lahu the corpse is laid out with a candle at its head. A *pawku* intones a death chant, part of which consists of "showing the way" to the soul of the deceased. A pig is killed and offered to the soul as food for its journey. Both Young (1961: 25) and Telford (1937: 203) report that the body is interred in a grave at some distance from the village. Scott and Hardiman (1900: 586), however, state that cremation is the rule among the Chinese Lahu.

BIBLIOGRAPHY. Bruk 1960; Embree and Thomas 1950; Izikowitz 1951; Rose and Coggin Brown 1911; Scott and Hardiman 1900; Telford 1937; Wiens 1954; Young 1961.

AKHA

Synonyms. *Ekaw, Hani, Kaw, Kha Ko, Ko, Woni*

ORIENTATION. **Identification.** Akha is said to be the term by which the people refer to themselves. In British (Burmese) areas the Akha are often termed

Kaw or Ekaw. The terms Ko or Kha Ko are used by the Siamese and by Lao and French speakers of northern Indochina. The Chinese Woni (Hani), referring to various southern Lolo (Tibeto-Burman) speakers of southern Yunnan, sometimes includes the Akha of that area (Embree and Thomas 1950; Bruk 1960). There are locally named subgroups or subdivisions of Akha, e.g. Puli, Tyitso, Akhö, Nu-Quay, Jen G'we, Hteu La (Telford 1937; Bernatzik 1947; Roux and Tran 1954; Izikowitz 1943). The Akha are said to be divided into seven (or, according to some sources, nine) such groups; according to Scott and Hardiman (1900: 598), these represent the descendants of seven (or nine) brothers from whom all the Akha derive. **Location.** Akha are found in considerable numbers in southern Yunnan, primarily in the area of the Sip Song Panna. From here they have recently migrated south, particularly into eastern Kengtung state in Burma, into northern and northwestern Laos, particularly south and west of Phong Saly, and to a lesser extent into extreme northern Thailand, in Chiengrai province. Akha have been in northern Thailand for about 20 years. **Linguistic affiliation.** A Tibeto-Burman language, related to Lahu and Lisu. These three, together with various other languages of the Yunnan-Burma border area (Nakhi and Minchia), are classed by some Chinese sources with Lolo as the Yi branch of Tibeto-Burman (cf. Hu et al. 1960: 98; Bruk 1960: 30). The Akha have no native script of their own, although in Burma there are missionary-devised scripts. Young (1961: 2) points out that the Akha of northern Thailand are remarkable linguists, many of the men speaking Yunnanese, Lahu, and Shan. **Demography.** The Akha in the Kengtung area of Burma were estimated in 1931 at slightly over 40,000 (Bernatzik 1947: 456). Halpern (1961b: 52), citing Chinese sources of about 1938, gives a figure of 48,700 for Yunnan. For Laos, a figure of 4,500 is given by Roux and Tran (1954: 153). Young (1961: 2) estimates some 25,000 Akha in northern Thailand. These figures total slightly over 100,000 for the entire area occupied by Akha speakers. It is likely, however, that this estimate is low; the Akha are often located far from administrative centers, so that government estimates mean little. In Thailand, where government estimates ran to "a few thousand," Young, an experienced observer with firsthand knowledge, estimates over 25,000. **History and cultural relations.** The Akha believe their original homeland to have been southern Yunnan. Their legendary history speaks of seven brothers, from whom all Akha are descended, and there are said to be seven divisions, differing somewhat with respect to dress and dialect. ● The Akha in Yunnan are said to mix freely with the Chinese. Chinese men of the poorer class occasionally marry Akha women, and mixed Chinese-Akha villages are reported. [Scott and Hardiman 1900: 588-95.] The Yunnan Akha grow a great deal of opium which they trade or sell to the Chinese. Bernatzik (1947: 383ff.) maintains that

some villages in northern Thailand are virtually on a cash economy basis, selling opium to Chinese traders in return for food and other necessities. According to Young (1961: 8), the Akha of northern Thailand have relatively little contact with lowlanders, preferring to do their trading with itinerant merchants who visit their villages periodically. They remain, according to Young, one of the least contacted tribes in the area. The relations of the Akha with the dominant groups around them occasionally involve them in debt slavery. They may in addition be drafted as fighting troops or for heavy labor. This has been the case in the Shan state of Kengtung (Scott and Hardiman 1900: 588-95). Intervillage disputes among the Akha of northern Thailand may, if serious enough, be taken to the nearest Lao or Shan chief for settlement (Bernatzik 1947: 47).

SETTLEMENT PATTERN AND HOUSING. **Settlement pattern.** Villages are characteristically placed just below the crest of a secondary ridge, on fairly steep terrain. They are generally found above 3,500–4,000 feet, but not as high as the Meo and Lahu. Bernatzik (1947: 284-87) describes the Akha villages of northern Thailand as located in an area of secondary forest growth or high grassland growing over abandoned swiddens. The soil is a barren red loam —dry and dusty in the dry season—and the villages are more or less in the open, exposed to the direct rays of the sun. Wissmann (1943: 18) describes much the same situation for the Akha of the Sip Song Panna area of southern Yunnan. Their fields are located above and below the village, with the area below likely to consist of tall savanna grass through which the Akha make broad paths. ● Villages are not fortified or fenced, and are not laid out in any particular pattern. The chief's house is likely to form the center of village life, and there may be a village smithy. Well-marked paths or trails lead from one village to another; where the path enters the village, gates or archways are set up which figure prominently in Akha religious beliefs and sacrifices. These gates are reported by most observers (Telford 1937; Young 1961; Bernatzik 1947; Scott and Hardiman 1900). Sisawat (1952: 492-93) adds that in northern Thailand a *lok kho* gate, bearing an eight-pointed star device to represent the eight powerful spirits of sky, land, forest, etc., is erected each year. According to this author, it is possible to tell the age of a village by the number of these gates. Beside the gates are male and female (copulating) fertility figures carved in the round. The gates are considered sacred, and are the sites of frequent religious ceremonies and sacrificial offerings. ● According to Young (1961: 2), the average Akha village of northern Thailand has 30 or more houses. With 9.5 persons per house, the village population averages about 300. Young adds, however, that villages may have as many as 50 or more houses. Roux (1924: 376) encountered in northern Laos villages of 40-50 houses. Bernatzik (1947: 284-87) comments on the relatively large size of Akha villages in northern Thailand, and says that villages may contain up to 200 houses, with an average of 10 to 20 persons per house. Wissmann (1943: 18) says that Akha villages in southern Yunnan are large and populous. ● The Akha change their village sites on an average of once every five to ten years. Normally, according to Bernatzik (1947: 284), they do not move more than one day's march. Wissmann (1943: 18) says that villages usually move to another spot within the "widespread territory that belongs to the village." Villages are sometimes moved because of soil depletion, but more often because of epidemic sickness attributed to the malevolence or displeasure of local spirits. **Housing.** Houses are very often, but not always, raised above the ground on short piles. Houses built on a steep slope have at least the front portion on piles (cf. Wissmann 1943: 18; Young 1961: 2; Roux 1924: 386-87). Walls are of bamboo or, occasionally, of wood, and roofs are of thatch. The inside is usually partitioned off into working and sleeping quarters. Storage houses for grain are also raised on piles. Bernatzik (1947: 287-88) describes an extended family compound surrounded by a crude wood and bamboo fence for northern Thailand. For Laos, Roux (1924: 386-87) reports two compartments within the house, one for a man, his wife, and their unmarried children, and the other for his married sons and their families.

ECONOMY. Primarily swidden agriculturists. Hunting is not as important as it is among the Lahu. Fishing is a subsidiary activity. Collecting is probably more important as a source of food than is generally recognized, and is specifically stated so for the Akha of Thailand (Young 1961: 7). The Akha in Yunnan, particularly, but also in parts of Thailand and Burma, obtain some cash income through the sale of raw opium and livestock to Chinese, Shan, and Lao. Bernatzik (1947: 385) reports villages in northern Thailand which have gone over almost completely to a cash economy, selling opium and buying food and other goods in return. **Agriculture.** Food crops include rice, maize, millet, buckwheat, sugar cane, peppers, vegetables, yams, beans, melons, and bananas. Tobacco, tea, poppies, and some cotton are also raised. Bernatzik describes Akha swiddens in Thailand as irregular in shape, covering an area of from one to three hectares. Rice fields are planted two years in succession and then fallowed for a number of years. Crops are mixed in the same field, except that poppies and tobacco are planted separately (1947: 363). Wissmann (1943: 19) reports occasional wet-rice fields among the Yunnan Akha, located in valleys below their villages. Fields may be several hours distant from the village. Men sometimes stay in field huts, and prior to the harvest watchers remain in these huts to guard against wild animals and birds. **Fishing and hunting.** Fishing makes use of lines, hooks, and weirs. According to Bernatzik (1947: 353), the Akha do not use poison to take fish. The crossbow is the main weapon, used mostly for small game. The Akha know how to use muskets, but do not own many. Group methods, with beaters and dogs, are popular. **Domestic animals.** Pigs and chickens are important as a source of food and for sacrifices. Dogs are eaten by the Thailand Akha (Young 1961: 7-8). Cattle, buffalo, and horses are raised by some Akha, often for sale to lowlanders. **Food and stimulants.** Rice, maize, vegetables, and beans are the staple foods. According to Sisawat (1952: 490), the rice is exclusively of a nonglutinous variety. Rice may be mixed with vegetables in a kind of soup, or eaten with peppers dipped in salt. Meat is used occasionally. Rice is steamed, and boiling and frying are the other main techniques of food preparation. The Akha make much use of spicy sauces and of sour (pickled) vegetables. Young (1961: 7) emphasizes the importance of jungle roots, maggots, grubs, and larvae in the Akha diet. Tobacco is smoked in pipes by both sexes, young and old. Tea is a popular beverage. Betel chewing is rare and not indigenous among the Akha. They make no beer, but do distill alcohol, usually from a rice base. [Bernatzik 1947: 383.] **Industrial arts.** The Akha work in wood, bamboo, and basketry. They do some blacksmithing, but little work in silver, buying most of their silver ornaments from the Lao and Shan. Women spend much time spinning and weaving cotton cloth and making fancy embroidered costumes. Bark cloth is made from a kind of tree bast (Bernatzik 1947: 418). The Akha have a reed mouth organ similar in shape and manufacture to those of the Lahu and Lisu. **Trade.** The Akha are not avid traders, and in general shun contact with lowlanders. Much of their opium trade is negotiated with itinerant merchants. **Land tenure.** According to Bernatzik (1947: 242), unworked land is considered public domain. Heads of extended families have title to property in movables as well as tilled fields (see also Roux 1924: 384-85). Wissmann (1943: 18) mentions that for the Akha in Yunnan there are village-owned territories within which village migrations ordinarily take place.

KIN GROUPS. **Descent.** According to Bernatzik (1947: 30-31), descent among the Akha of northern Thailand is defined in the male line. Telford (1937: 149) indicates much the same situation for Kengtung when he remarks that children are always considered as related to the father's family line and to the ancestral spirits of the paternal household. **Kin groups.** Bernatzik's data (1947: 30-31, 110) indicate that the north Thailand Akha, like the Meo in the same area, are characterized by patrilineal surname groups [patrisibs and patrilineages]. It is possible that the various named subdivisions of Akha (Puli, Nu-Quay, Jen G'we, etc.), sometimes called "tribes" in the literature, are composed of localized lineage segments of patrisibs. At the village level, at least, the patrilineage is probably exogamous in fact as well as in theory. Bernatzik is clear on the point that the economically important corporate kin group is not the sib or lineage in its larger sense, but rather the patrilocal extended household. Whether the situation as described by Bernatzik for the Thailand Akha obtains in other areas is difficult to judge from the available literature. **Kin terminology.** Bernatzik (1947: facing p. 34) gives the following kin terms for the Akha in northern Thailand:

Fa	ada
Mo	ama
FaElBr	ao
FaYoBr	ayo
FaSi	ako
MoElBr	au
MoYoBr	aso
MoElSi	amo
MoYoSi	yao
YoBr	ani
ElBr	budo
YoSi	duma
ElSi	yami ayu
FaBrSo	zye
FaBrDa	anum
FaSiSo	yao
FaSiDa	yama
MoBrSo	ago
MoBrDa	yama
MoSiSo	atsa
MoSiDa	atsa

MARRIAGE AND FAMILY. Premarital sexual freedom is reported for the Akha of northern Thailand and Burma. Institutionalized public courting, including antiphonal singing, is a characteristic of most Akha groups. Sisawat (1952: 520, 584-85), speaking of northern Thailand, describes a special courting ground at the edge of the village that is frequented by young people in the evening. According to this same author, adolescent girls must submit to a middle-aged widower, selected for the role by the village elders, before they attain marriageable status. This individual, also mentioned by Young (1961: 8) under the title *aw shaw*, instructs the girls in the art of love-making and intercourse. According to Sisawat, a similar role is performed vis-à-vis boys by a widow, called *mida*, also selected by the elders. If the woman so selected refuses, which is sometimes the case, she may be expelled from the village. **Mode.** Elopement occurs among the Akha in Burma, Thailand, and Laos. It is reported as the preferred mode among the Nu-Quay subgroup in northern Laos (Roux and Tran 1954: 178). Marriages may also require the consent of the families concerned, and in some areas go-betweens are used. Exchange of gifts is common, but

a bride price as such appears to be rare; it is, however, mentioned specifically for one subgroup in northern Laos. [Telford 1937: 121ff.; Bernatzik 1947: 105-06; Roux 1924: 393-403.] **Form.** Polygyny is reported for the Akha in Burma, Thailand, and Laos. It appears to be fairly common in some of these areas, although specific information is lacking. **Extension of incest taboos.** Bernatzik's data (1947: 110) indicate that the Thailand Akha have surname groups which in theory prohibit marriage between Ego and a patrilineal relative up to and including those three generations removed. Bernatzik adds that two family heads in a given enclave may by mutual agreement declare their respective families unrelated, thus making marriage permissible. This is sometimes done in cases where neighboring enclaves become so far removed that contact is difficult or impossible to maintain. **Residence.** Residence among all Akha groups appears to be initially and permanently patrilocal (Telford 1937: 96; Young 1961: 8; Bernatzik 1947: 30; Roux and Tran 1954: 166-67). **Domestic unit.** The patrilocal extended household is found among most, if not all, Akha groups. Bernatzik (1947: 30-31) says for northern Thailand that married sons continue to live in the parental household (which may contain up to 20 or more persons) until about the age of 30, when they set up independent households adjacent to that of the parents. Young's figure of an average of 9.5 persons per household tends to confirm this observation (1961: 2). Roux and Tran (1954: 166-67) describe an extended family household under one roof for the Akha of Laos; whereas in Kengtung state, according to Telford (1937: 96), married sons set up households adjacent to that of their parents. **Inheritance.** In northern Thailand, according to Bernatzik (1947: 247), the eldest son inherits the house. All other property is divided equally among all the sons. Among the Kha Ko of Laos a wife assumes title to all family property on the death of her husband; when she dies all children share equally, except that a horse is always passed on to the eldest son (Roux 1924: 285). **Divorce.** Among the Kaw of Burma divorce is easy for either sex upon the payment of a fine by the initiating party. In all cases the children go with the father (Telford 1937: 96). The same is true among the Akha of northern Thailand (Bernatzik 1947: 114).

SOCIOPOLITICAL ORGANIZATION. Village chiefs are in some cases, as in northern Thailand, hereditary in the male line. In northern Laos, however, the village chief and his deputy are selected by the villagers from among the well-to-do. These officials function in a judicial capacity, assisted in some cases, as among the Kha Ko, by a council of village notables. Telford (1937: 148-49) reports a rather complex system of fines, paid either in money or in kind, according to the type of crime. Payment of fines is also reported for northern Laos (Roux and Tran 1954: 162-

63). ● Roux (1924: 382-84) and Roux and Tran (1954: 162-63) report a supreme chief among the Kha Ko of northern Laos. Whereas he was considered chief of all the Kha Ko, and represented Kha Ko village headmen in negotiations with French authorities, his authority was most effective among the Nu-Quay subgroup. It is not clear whether this office was a creation of the French; nothing of the sort is reported for other Akha groups. Bernatzik (1947: 47) says that in northern Thailand Akha village chiefs usually resort to the nearest Lao or Shan official to settle serious intervillage disputes. **Warfare.** Bernatzik (1947: 392-93) writes that the weapons of the north Thailand Akha are the crossbow with poisoned arrows, and guns. The latter they buy from Shan and Lao lowlanders; although they know how to make gunpowder they usually buy it. Bernatzik says that the Akha fight only in small groups under their village chiefs, and remarks that they lack the organizing ability of the Thailand Meo.

RELIGION. Akha religion is basically animistic in content, with a strong emphasis on the cult of the ancestors. **Supernaturals.** Spirits, including ancestral spirits, are called *ne*. Some *ne* are malevolent and cause illnesses; others are associated with familiar objects such as trees. There are guardian spirits, or *ne*, of the house and of the village. The family *ne* or *mitsa*, i.e. the ancestral spirits, are given particular prominence; they are represented among the Kha Ko by a basket kept in the house, and among the Akha of northern Thailand by a sacred post within the house. Among the Kha Ko, these ancestral spirits are reckoned back three ascending generations. Telford (1937: 114-15) mentions the care taken to avoid offending the rice spirit during the growing season. **Practitioners.** Most villages contain at least one part-time male religious practitioner. At times, as among the Kha Ko, one person combines the function of village priest and village shaman; in other cases, as in northern Thailand, priestly and shamanistic functions are handled by two different individuals. Bernatzik (1947: 199-201), referring to northern Thailand, says that the ordinary practitioner is elected from among any villagers who have shown supernatural powers, and that this office may coincide at times with that of village chief. The shamans function as leaders of periodic village-wide exorcistic ceremonies. The position of *tumo*, or greater shaman, is hereditary. The *tumo* are in communication with good as well as evil spirits. Their reputations as practitioners of black magic make them greatly feared, and a *tumo* may hold power over several villages in his territory. According to Telford (1937: 180-81), what he calls priests among the Kaw of Burma divine the spirit causing an illness or misfortune and also conduct animal sacrifices and exorcistic rituals. Similar functions are ascribed to what Roux (1924: 388-93) calls sorcerers among the Kha Ko of Laos. Female practitioners among the Akha of both Burma and northern Thailand specialize in causing and curing illness. In Burma, according to Telford (1937: 124, 180-81), the woman projects her soul into the spirit world for the purpose of determining which spirit is causing a particular illness. **Ceremonies.** Divination is frequently resorted to in cases of illness, misfortune, or before an important undertaking. Eggs, animal livers, and chickens are all used in divination. The spitting out of rice grains is also a common divinatory practice. Animal sacrifice (pigs, fowl, and occasionally larger animals such as buffalo) is widespread, and may be carried out at family ancestral altars as well as at frequent village-wide ceremonies. ● Telford (1937) emphasizes the importance among the Akha of ceremonies associated with village welfare; on the occasions of such ceremonies, which may last for several days, the entire village may be declared taboo to outsiders. An annual swinging ceremony is mentioned for the Akha of Burma (Telford 1937: 127-28), northern Thailand (Bernatzik 1947: 173-75), and northern Laos (Roux and Tran 1954: 211). According to Telford, villagers take turns swinging during a three-day period which is accompanied by animal sacrifices and other rituals designed to rid the village of evil spirits. A similar type of annual ceremony involves the ritual renewing of the sacred gates set up on the path just outside the village (Telford 1937: 109; Bernatzik 1947: 173-75; Young 1961: 3). According to Bernatzik, carved male and female fertility figures are associated with these village gates. Telford (1937: 109) reports nine recurrent days or religious periods in the Akha ceremonial calendar. One of the most important of these appears to be the annual new year festival, which lasts from three to four days, and is celebrated among most, if not all, Akha groups. Sacrifices to the ancestors are accompanied by general festivities, including courting, drinking, and feasting. This is one of the times when youths travel to neighboring villages for choosing and courting prospective marriage partners. **Illness and medicine.** Soul loss is one cause of illness, according to the Akha of Burma and Thailand. Illness is, however, usually attributed to malevolent or offended spirits, *ne*. The usual recourse is to a practitioner who diagnoses the spirit responsible and recommends or carries out an exorcistic ritual. Bernatzik (1947: 50ff.) says that the Akha have relatively little knowledge of drugs or herbs; the therapeutic use of opium and bloodletting has probably been borrowed from the Chinese. Telford (1937: 164ff.) records seizures of an epileptic nature which are attributed to spirit possession; these are treated by violent exorcistic measures. **Soul, death, and afterlife.** The Kha Ko of Laos believe that each human is composed of two elements—*song-la*, a collection of three spirits, and *yo go*, the body. The departure of one spirit may cause illness, which worsens when another spirit departs. The departure of all three results in death. Kha Ko funeral rituals are complicated and require the participation of the sorcerer. There are prescribed animal sacrifices. The corpse may be kept in the house 50 or 60 days, and periodically it is offered food. The Kha Ko bury their dead (Roux 1924: 408-18). In Burma, according to Telford (1937: 205-06), the body of a well-to-do person may be kept for months until the time for a large ceremony and sacrifice. Ordinarily, burial occurs one to six days after death. Those dying violent or unusual deaths are buried at once in the jungle. Otherwise, the corpse is buried in a wooden coffin, sometimes in a village cemetery, more often at a spot outside the village determined by divination. The grave is marked with stones. A graveside ceremony with animal sacrifice is carried out on the first anniversary of death (Sisawat 1952: 608).

BIBLIOGRAPHY. Bernatzik 1947; Bruk 1960; Embree and Thomas 1950; Halpern 1961b; Hu et al. 1960; Izikowitz 1943; Roux 1924; Roux and Tran 1954; Scott and Hardiman 1900; Sisawat 1952; Telford 1937; Wissmann 1943; Young 1961.

CENTRAL LOWLAND GROUPS

BURMESE [1]

Synonyms. *Bama, Burman, Hamea, Kawl, Man, Myanma, Myen, Payaw, Phama, Vai*

ORIENTATION. **Identification.** In their spoken language the Burmese call themselves Bama but the literary term, attested from 1190 A.D., is Myanma (written Mranma). They are known by a variety of names among neighboring groups: Phama (Siamese); Hamea (Mons); Man (Shans); Payaw (Sgaw Karens); Myen (Kachins); Kawl (central Chins); and Vai (northern Chins). Two names are current in English—Burman and Burmese—usage being variable. [Luce 1959c: 53; McFarland 1941: 579; Shorto 1962: 42; Cushing 1914: 479; Carpenter 1875: 192; Hanson 1954: 448; Lehman 1963: 29.] **Location.** The area of Burmese settlement includes Huke's Central Belt (the valleys of the Irrawaddy, Sittang, and Chindwin from the Andaman Sea to about 24° or 25° N.), and the coasts of Arakan and of the Tenasserim panhandle. In the Central Belt south of about 18° N. and in Tenasserim there are fairly large minorities of Mons and Karens, and in the northern end of the Belt, approximately above 24°, Burmese settlement of the lowlands is shared with Shans. The center of the most undiluted Burmese settlement is still, after a thousand years, near 22° N. and 96° E. In two

locations in East Pakistan—in the Chittagong Hills (approximately 22° 30′ N. and 92° E.) and in Bakarganj (approximately the same latitude at 91° 30′ E.)—are populations of Burmese-speaking Buddhists, totaling perhaps 100,000, who are descendants of people who immigrated from Arakan about the beginning of the nineteenth century. Those in Chittagong call themselves Morma (also written Marma) but are locally known as Mogh (also Magh and Mugh). [Huke 1956a: 73.] **Geography.** The area of Burmese settlement both in the Central Belt and along the margins of the Arakan and Tenasserim coasts is lowland, and the whole area is under the monsoon regime. The annual temperature range is slight. Although annual rainfall in Arakan and much of Tenasserim exceeds 200 inches and is over 100 inches in most of the delta, the historic home of the Burmese is considerably drier, much of the area having less than 40 inches of rain. Here agriculture depends upon irrigation by canals and utilization of river banks and islands. [Huke 1956a: 70-81.] **Linguistic affiliation.** In his review and reordering of the Sino-Tibetan languages, Shafer sets up a Burmic division, one of the sections of which, Burmish, has a Burma branch. The Burma branch is composed of Northern and Southern units. Burmese, Arakanese, Tavoyan, Taungyo, Intha, Danu, and Yaw are assigned to the Southern unit; Hpon, Achang, Maru, Lashi, and Atsi to the Northern unit. There is so little acceptable information on most of these languages—with the exception of Burmese and one or two of the Northern unit—that it is not possible to say more about them. [Shafer 1955: 103.] It should be noted that Arakanese, which has variant dialects, is spoken in Arakan, and Tavoyan in Tenasserim, by people who are here referred to as Burmese, for their culture is largely that of the speakers of standard Burmese. The Taungyo, Intha, and Danu in the southwestern corner of the Shan State (approximately 20° to 21° N., just west of 97° E.) are very inadequately known, but appear to be much influenced by the Shans in culture and speech. The Yaw, living just north of 21° N. and east of 94° E., are rapidly becoming Burmanized. Ranging along the Burma–China border north of 24° N. are the Maru, Lashi, and Atsi, who appear to be largely Kachin in culture. The Hpon have settled along the Irrawaddy in the vicinity of Bhamo (just northeast of 24° N. and 97° E.). The Achang (or Mönghsa, Burmese pronunciation, Maingtha) live in China near 25° N. and 98° E., and extend into northern Burma. **Demography.** The most recent reliable information is the census of 1931, at which time speakers of Burmese and of the dialects of Arakan and Tenasserim were a fraction under 9,651,000. Assuming an average growth rate per decade of 11.4 per cent (an average of Huke's decennial rates for 1921-51 of 11, 12.2, and 11.1 per cent) speakers of Burmese, Arakanese, and Tavoyan in 1961 would be about 13,342,000. [India 1931-34:

---

[1] This section, written by John Musgrave, draws heavily on the author's field notes and on notes of interviews with Burmese in the United States over a number of years.

11, Pt. I, p. 198; Huke 1956a: 92.] **History and cultural relations.** There are references to the Burmese from about the end of the first millennium A.D., but Luce believes that they appeared in Burma, in the area immediately south of Mandalay, in the latter half of the ninth century, expanding southwest, south, and north in the next two centuries. Luce contends that the Burmese entered this nuclear area from the Shan plateau to the east, migrating there earlier from South China, and finding the plateau occupied by the Mons, among other peoples. Some Mons continued to dwell there and it was from them in the next two centuries that the Burmese received a degree of Indianization (often called Hinduization), including Buddhism and writing. (Traditionally this Indianization is dated from a Burmese attack on Thaton in the second half of the eleventh century.) ● The history of Burma from the middle of the eleventh century to the middle of the nineteenth century is essentially that of a succession of dynasties and states in central Burma, where control was most firmly established and institutionalized. From time to time the Burmese kings extended their conquests and temporary rule west into Assam, Manipur, and Chittagong of present-day India and Pakistan or east into Siam and Laos. Now and again the Burmese were invaded, usually from the east or northeast, by Shans, Mongols, Chinese, or Siamese. Early in the second millennium A.D. the Burmese reached into Arakan and down into Tenasserim, but historical details for these coasts are even sketchier than those for central Burma. During much of this time Arakan was independent, though Burmese, and under considerable influence from Bengal. ● Lower Burma, south of 19° N., was for centuries the stage for power struggles between the Burmese and the Mons. In the second half of the eighteenth century the Burmese finally dealt a fatal blow to the Mon state, but for much of the next hundred years they continued merely to administer the area. Only with the British occupation of lower Burma after 1852—Arakan and Tenasserim had been occupied in 1826—do the Burmese appear to have begun in earnest the settlement of the deltas of the Irrawaddy and Sittang, spurred by the growth of the international rice trade. The independent Burmese state, once again confined to its historic home, survived until 1885, when the British gained control. For 60 years all of Burma was under British rule, most of it as a province of India. Then in 1948, after a brief period of Japanese control, Burma again became independent, and for the first time the country was unified under a coastal capital. [Cady 1958; Furnivall 1948; Harvey 1925; Luce 1959d.] The Burmese have been in contact with Europeans—chiefly Portuguese, French, and British—since the sixteenth century, and have experienced an influx of Chinese and, especially, Indian immigrants in the nineteenth and twentieth centuries. There have been borrowings in language, food, dress, implements, and so on from all these contacts, but probably the greatest foreign influence has been that of India in the early Christian era, including the introduction of writing and a fund of texts, an organized, philosophical religion, a cosmology, a theory of statecraft, a substantial architecture and art, and more theoretical medical practices.

SETTLEMENT PATTERN AND HOUSING. **Settlement pattern.** Most Burmese live in compact villages, the two most common types being the linear village along a watercourse or road and the nuclear village among fields off a main road. In either case village land consists of the area devoted to houses, sometimes called garden land, the (rice) fields proper, the land of the monastery and associated buildings, waste land, and the cemetery. The monastery is sometimes a quite unpretentious structure inhabited by only one monk. Almost every village has in addition a rest house and a pagoda, the latter a plastered brick structure nominally housing a religious relic. Small spirit houses are lodged under trees. Village shops are usually portions of dwelling houses. **Housing.** Houses are rectangular and are usually constructed with a wooden framework. The gabled roof is covered with a leaf or grass thatch. Walls and floors in more substantial structures are of planks, but many of the houses in villages and poorer towns have walls and flooring of plaited bamboo. There is usually a front and back veranda, the former, commonly under the same roof with the house, serving as a place to receive guests, relax, or carry on household chores. The rear veranda is reserved for food preparation and the washing of clothes. Houses are raised above the ground, from a foot or two to head height. The interior is basically one room, subdivided by bamboo walls the height of the eaves. There may be a partial second floor, similar to a large balcony, but on no occasion is a woman supposed to be over a man's head. Furnishings are relatively simple, and include a low eating table, a variety of containers, bedding, a shelf containing an image of the Buddha, and sometimes a spirit shrine.

ECONOMY. The fundamental importance of agriculture, either for subsistence or market production, remains unaffected by the introduction of foreign investment capital, which has been directed toward the extractive industries and manufacturing. The traditional agriculture patterns continue to exert a major influence on the society. **Agriculture.** Rice is grown everywhere in wet fields watered by rain—or, in the dry zone of central Burma, by irrigation. The fields are prepared by plowing and harrowing, with implements drawn by bullocks or buffalo. In the delta, nurseries and transplanting (both by hand and with the aid of a sort of dibble) are common. The rice is reaped with a sickle, leaving considerable stubble in the field, into which the cattle are turned. Threshing is accomplished by the treading of cattle. The grain is winnowed by tossing in a tray or by shaking from a tray mounted on a platform. A number of varieties of ordinary rice are grown, the basic types being distinguished by their maturation date. Farmers usually cultivate a small amount of glutinous rice for special purposes. The Burmese raise a large number of vegetables and fruits, such as cucurbits, legumes, tubers, tomatoes, eggplant, onions, garlic, chilies, bananas, mangoes, and citrus fruit. These may be grown in house plots, where trees providing edible fruits and leaves are also planted, or in fields after the rice harvest, where they are watered from wells. In the dry zone there is considerable specialization in crops adapted to the area, such as cotton, tobacco, pulse, chilies, onions, sesame, maize, and millet. Tenasserim has also specialized in various tree crops, coconuts, durians, and mangosteens. Near towns there is specialized market gardening of vegetables and flowers. **Fishing and hunting.** Fish—fresh, salted, dried, or in the processed forms of fish paste and fish sauce—is the most important animal food in the Burmese diet, and hardly any meal is eaten without some amount, however small. Fishing by farmers in streams, ponds, and rice fields is common, but much fish, fresh as well as preserved and processed, is bought. Fish are caught by hook and line, a variety of nets (some used by women), portable and fixed traps, floating tidal traps, weirs, and impounding. Hunting is insignificant both as a source of food and as sport. The chief game are various kinds of deer, pigs, and birds, which are shot with guns or caught in snares and traps. **Gathering.** Many plants in the diet are gathered either in forest and field or from trees and shrubs planted in house plots but otherwise untended. **Domestic animals.** The most common are cattle and buffalo, kept almost solely for drawing carts and field implements. The raising of fowl, ducks, and pigs is limited by a reluctance, probably Buddhist in origin, to kill them or to sell to butchers. Near towns and cities horses are kept to pull carriages. **Food and stimulants.** There are two almost identical meals a day—at about nine in the morning and five in the evening—in which the basic dish is boiled rice. This is accompanied by a vegetable soup of fish or meat stock, one or more "curries"—actually vegetable stews occasionally enriched with fish or meat—raw vegetable salad, and condiments such as chilies and fish paste. Boiling and frying in sesame or peanut oil are the usual methods of preparation. The common meats are pork and chicken. Most of the fish is from fresh tidal waters, as there seems to be a general aversion to deep-sea fish. Dairy products are virtually never eaten, and eggs seldom. Glutinous rice is taken at harvesting time as a hearty meal for the workers or is used in the making of a great variety of confections. During the day the average person will eat several snacks of cakes or peanuts, or of hot dishes such as noodles and sauce, all obtainable from small shops or hawkers in villages and markets. Cigarettes and several traditional types of cigars are smoked by both sexes from late childhood. Betel leaf and betel nut are common stimulants, and visitors in villages will usually be offered betel nut and tea. Alcoholic drinks are fermented from the juice of varieties of palm and distilled from rice. The use of opium is rare. **Industrial arts.** Most villages have a blacksmith and a carpenter. The former, who may also be a cartwright, makes and repairs the heavy all-purpose Burmese knife, *da*, as well as other smaller implements. Many crafts, such as oil pressing, the making of thatch, mats, and matting for house walls and floors, basketry, sewing, wood cutting, charcoal burning, and the making of confections and fermented rice vermicelli, may be either full-time specialties or the part-time activities of farmers and their women. Some villages specialize in pottery, lacquerware, umbrella making, weaving (though most cloth today is the product of domestic or foreign mechanical industry), fishing, and fish processing. Some crafts are more likely to be full-time occupations of relatively small groups of people: gold and silver working (including gold beating), brass and bronze founding, masonry and brick making, stone carving, painting, gem working, and various forms of woodworking such as sawing, turning, joinery, and the making of tools, carts, and boats. With the exception of the drawing of petroleum from wells in central Burma and some stone quarrying and lime burning, mineral extraction and processing is unimportant among the Burmese. **Trade.** As a consequence of the occupational and regional specialization in agriculture, fish processing, and craft manufacturing, trade is an important part of the Burmese economy. In addition to domestic trade, there has been for centuries external trade between the Burmese and the surrounding peoples in what is now political Burma, as well as with Chinese, Indians, Siamese, Cambodians, Lao, Malays, and so on. Trade is carried on at markets in villages and towns, at occasional fairs at pagoda festivals, and by itinerant merchants. The latter include those, largely professional, who travel about accumulating farm produce for shipment to brokers and retailers in the larger villages and towns and who make the round of villages distributing cooking oil, fish products, cloth, etc. There is also the hawker, usually a woman, who sells in her own or neighboring villages items bought in the market or prepared by herself. Women are prominent in the retail trade in markets, although trade is by no means handled exclusively by them. A woman's trading is often a subsidiary occupation within her household role. Foreign imports and the initial stages of internal distribution have been in the hands of Indians, Chinese, and Europeans with overseas connections. Similarly, foreigners have been prominent in the accumulation and initial processing of domestic produce for export; Indians, Chinese, and Europeans engaged in rice milling and the rice trade, timber, and mineral extraction and processing. It is probable, however, that the trade in most traditional produce and manufactured goods consumed by the Burmese has remained in Burmese hands. **Division of labor.** Men prepare land for planting and sow rice. Women transplant seedlings. Both men and women reap grain. Threshing is a man's job, and winnowing is done by both women (from a tray) and men (from a scaffold). Making of cloth and clothing is primarily women's work, as well as washing and food preparation (both for home consumption and for sale), although men share in preparing food for ceremonial occasions. Workers in metal, stone, or wood are invariably men, but pottery, basketry, plaiting, the fashioning of lacquerware, and umbrella making may be done by either sex. Trade, both itinerant and in the markets, is shared by men and women. Transportation of goods by boat and cart is primarily a male occupation. **Land tenure.** Details of traditional land ownership are not complete. Land held on the basis of service to the court was family owned and transmissible by inheritance. Such land could be leased and sold, subject apparently to possible loss of the land if service obligations were not fulfilled. Continued cultivation of newly cleared land gave title. Since British rule there has been ownership of land subject to payment of a tax. [Cady 1958: 29, 31, 36, 49, 158.]

KIN GROUPS. **Descent.** Bilateral (there are no family names). **Kin terminology:**

	(Cornyn romanization)	(Conventional romanization)
Fa	ahpei	ahpe
Mo	amei	ame
FaElBr	ba. ji:	bagyi
FaYoBr	ba. dwei:	badwe
MoElBr	u: ji:	ugyi
MoYoBr	u: lei:	ule
FaElSi	ayi: ji:	ayigyi
FaYoSi	ayi: lei:	ayile
MoElSi	ji: do	gyidaw
MoYoSi	dwei: lei:	dwele
ElBr	akou	ako
YoBr (m.s.)	nyi	nyi
YoBr (w.s.)	maun	maung
ElSi	ama.	ama
YoSi (m.s.)	hnama.	hnama
YoSi (w.s.)	nyi-ma.	nyima

Cousins are called by the appropriate sibling term.

MARRIAGE AND FAMILY. **Mode.** On the whole, Burmese young people have considerable initiative in choice of a marriage partner. Most people of the same village know each other, and acquaintances between young people of different villages are facilitated by meeting in markets and at various ceremonial occasions, religious and secular. Chaperoned courtship in the evening in girls' houses is also permitted. Arrangements for marriage in the village can either be made directly between the parents or with the assistance of informal go-betweens. (Among the well-to-do of cities or provincial towns, more initiative may lie with the parents, who are anxious to make matches advantageous to wealth and status. In such cases more formal go-betweens are enlisted.) Since the essential element in a Burmese marriage is known and regular cohabitation, marriages by elopement are by no means uncommon. In most cases such marriages later receive parental approval and may be solemnized by a wedding in the usual manner. Weddings vary in elaborateness of the ceremony and in scale of expense. In the simplest form the couple place their hands together in the presence of village worthies and the families. More elaborate ceremonies involve the presence of a person in the role of "Brahman," who delivers a homily to the couple. **Form.** Polygyny has always been permitted among the Burmese, but most men usually have only one wife at any one time. [Mi Mi Khaing 1946: 123; Scott 1910: 59.] **Extension of incest taboos.** A man may not marry his mother, daughter, sister or half sister, aunt, grandmother, or granddaughter. (Under the monarchy a king often married his half sister.) There is no institutionalized preferential marriage. [Scott 1910: 59.] **Residence.** Residence immediately after marriage is often reported as matrilocal, but after an initial period of residence with a spouse's parents, Burmese households are neolocal. The only numerical information on this point suggests that initial residence may be ambilocal. [Associates for International Research 1956: C69-70; Scott 1910: 59.] **Domestic unit.** Though normally the nuclear family, the domestic unit often includes one or more other members, such as a younger sibling, widowed parent, maiden aunt, or dependent nephew or niece of one of the parents. Wealthier families may have even more dependent relatives, up to several degrees of relationship removed, who are in fact higher status servants. [Mi Mi Khaing 1946: 19-20.] **Inheritance.** Property is inherited equally by all children, but the estate is usually not divided until both parents have died (Mi Mi Khaing 1946: 123). **Divorce.** Permitted and not at all uncommon. In its simplest form it is the reverse of marriage, i.e. suspension of cohabitation. More formally it may receive express sanction by village elders.

SOCIOPOLITICAL ORGANIZATION. **Traditional structure.** Under the monarchy the king had absolute power, which he exercised centrally through a court composed of both royal princes and commoners. Local administration was in the hands of provincial governors and their subordinates. The offices of the court and provincial officials were not hereditary and the occupants were subject to removal upon the death of the king. (There was no established royal succession; under the last dynasty, half the kings succeeded their predecessors as brothers, half as sons.) Until near the end of the monarchy, the population was broadly divided into two classes, those who occupied royal lands and owed service to the court, including liability to the standing, professional army, and those who paid taxes and were subject as needed to conscription in the army. The former class, largely confined to central Burma, was organized into service units, whose members were subordinate, regardless of residence, to the service unit headman, who was in turn responsible to the provincial governor. The second class, larger and apparently predominant in lower Burma, was controlled by headmen under a special minister at the court. In both cases the office of headman was hereditary. There is some doubt whether many Burmese as such belonged to the second category. The headman and provincial governors retained a portion of the revenue collected in behalf of the court. In addition to royalty and the class of commoners just described, there was a heterogeneous class of the unfree, consisting of pagoda slaves (originally war prisoners or criminals), those afflicted with deformities or loathesome diseases, executioners, gravediggers, and others. **Contemporary structure.** As the British successively took over the territories of the Burmese state (in 1826, 1852, and 1885) the royal administration was territorially restricted and ultimately extinguished, royalty as a stratum of society disappeared, and the legal basis for the unfree stratum was removed. British administration varied in place and time until toward the end of the nineteenth century when the form, still retained by independent Burma, was established. Villages or groups of villages were made the basic unit of administration under appointed headmen whose main functions were the collection of revenue and the maintenance of order. Between the headmen and the governor were successive echelons of officials. At first many of the newly appointed headmen were former hereditary headmen, but subsequent appointments included more and more men with no inherited relation to the people in their charge. Present-day independent Burmese society, the successor to the class of commoners in the old society, is therefore essentially classless. In the towns, status is achieved by occupational advancement in government service, the professions, and business enterprise, and is marked by the wealth and power accompanying that advancement. In post-monarchical society Western education and the command of English have been the most potent means for upward mobility. In rural Burma superior status is linked with being senior, literate, a native or old resident of one's village, male, pious by Buddhist standards, and economically successful. [Associates for International Research 1956: C24-46; Brohm, Brant, and Jackim 1956: 105-22; Cady 1958: 22, 27-38, 90, 103, 142-43; Furnivall 1948: 37, 74-77.] **Warfare.**

Under the monarchy the Burmese engaged sporadically in war with their neighbors. The armed forces of the colonial regime tended to ignore the Burmese and were composed of British, Indians, and, from among the peoples of Burma, Chins and Kachins. The independent republican forces continue to draw upon the minority groups of the country, but Burmese now form a large proportion of the troops and officers. Since independence, the armed forces of Burma have not been involved in foreign wars, but there have been constant skirmishes against domestic rebels, mostly Burmese and Karens, and against Chinese military squatters in the Shan State.

RELIGION. It has been well argued that for most Burmese their religion is what may be called Burmese religion. Examined analytically or especially historically, as has been the convention, it is possible to conceive of this religion as a mingling of elements received from India early in the first millennium A.D. (conventionally called Buddhism) and residual elements (called animism). If Buddhism can be defined as those beliefs and practices supported by the canonical texts derived from India, then the residual animism is composed of elements heterogeneous in origin, some being Indian but not Buddhist, some coming from the Near East, but most no doubt being the modern forms of beliefs and practices proper to the Burmese before their Indianization. Although there are Burmese who are aware of the history of Buddhism, most are not accustomed to a historical-analytical framework, and for them their religious folkways are a whole. [Brohm 1963.] **Major religion.** Theravada, or Hinayana, Buddhism can be regarded as the major religion of the Burmese in terms of its acceptance by all but a very small number of the members of the culture and its character as one of the organized, philosophically elaborated, and enduring world religions. Its material manifestations are the canonical books of Indian origin and their affiliated commentaries by Indians, Sinhalese, and Burmese; the structures of monastery (and ordination hall and library) and pagoda to be seen in virtually every village; and the monks, members of the order. Every Burmese male who is not a Moslem or a Christian becomes a novice sometime during his life, usually for only a week to several months as a boy of five to fifteen in connection with the Buddhist lent. A significant number of men are ordained as monks for extended periods or for life, and it is relatively common for men to seek increased merit by temporary abandonment of family and occupation for a period as a monk. The monks live a celibate life of study and meditation, abstaining from secular activities and leaving the monastery only to go on pilgrimages, to travel to another place of study, or to make the daily round for alms from the villagers. The avowed purpose of the monks is primarily to enhance their own spiritual character as a means of hastening liberation from the cycle of reincarnation, but they also have an important village role, giving instruction in the Buddhist texts and formulas, guiding the boy novices whose stay in the monastery is a source of religious merit for both themselves and their parents, acting as intermediaries with the supernatural, participating in family rituals, etc. In return the villagers supply rice and other food daily, maintain the Buddhist buildings, and periodically contribute clothing and other basic necessities. The order in the strict sense is open only to men over 20 years of age. All monks ex officio are of higher status than laymen; within the order status is a matter of seniority of membership and achievement, i.e. learning and, less definable, sanctity. In addition to the monastic order there is a sisterhood, of inferior status, composed of celibate women and girls, and there are unorganized individual male ascetics; all of these wear distinctive dress and are dependent upon the charity of laymen. The standing and influence of these minor classes of religious people is negligible in comparison with that of the monks. **Indigenous religion and supernaturals.** It cannot be doubted that for many Burmese the Buddha is a supernatural being, though this is not strictly in accord with the ideology of Theravada Buddhism. Spirits of the dead, i.e. ghosts, especially of those persons who died in childbirth, from dread diseases, or in accidents, or who were murdered, must also be considered. There is a general class of spirits called *nats*, the best known being the 37 *nats*, a heterogeneous group including some Burmese historical and legendary personages and at least one member of the Indian *deva* class of supernaturals. Some are tutelary spirits attached to the house, to such regions as tidewater Burma, or to families or individuals, as in the case of spirit dancers, the so-called spirit wives. In addition ogres and various other monsters people the supernatural world of the Burmese. **Practitioners.** Insofar as monks perform rites such as the recitation of the *paritta*, a text sanctioned by Buddhism for the exorcism of disease and disaster, and the recitation of Buddhist texts at funerals, they may be regarded as dealing with the supernatural. A prominent class of practitioner is the spirit dancer, usually a woman, but also possibly a man (who may be a transvestite). Like a shaman, the spirit dancer is possessed by a spirit whose dress and regalia she wears while dancing, sometimes under the influence of alcohol. Some of the spirit dances are more or less regular occasions of homage to one or more spirits, some are for curing or prognostication. Other practitioners include astrologers, several kinds of medical specialists, masters of white and black magic (the upper and lower ways), witches, and those aspiring to become *zawgyi*. A *zawgyi* is one who either by alchemical methods or cabalistic calculations has acquired a superhuman body and achieved eternal youth so that he will survive until the appearance of the next Buddha. Monks

may be, without Buddhist justification, astrologers, and some dabble in alchemy for the same reasons as the *zawgyi*. [Htin Aung 1962.] **Ceremonies.** The major annual ceremonies are the new year's celebration in mid-April, commonly called the Water Festival; Thadingyut, marking the end of lent at the full moon of the seventh Burmese month, about mid-October; Dammasetkya, initiating lent at the full moon of the fourth month, mid-July; Buddha Day, the day of the Buddha's birth, enlightenment, and death, the full moon of the second month, mid-May; Tazaungdaing, the full moon of the eighth month, when clothing and other gifts are presented to monks; and the full moon of Tabaung, the twelfth month, February or March, a sort of harvest festival. Also annual but with dates varying according to locality are pagoda festivals—most occurring in the months January to March—at which staple foods, clothing, and monastic equipment are given to the monks. The chief ceremonies of the individual life cycle are the initiatory rite—entering the novitiate (for a boy) or piercing the ears for ear studs (for a girl)—the wedding, and the funeral. **Illness and medicine.** Western medical notions and practices, familiar in varying degrees to Burmese for over a century, compete with traditional beliefs and methods. In the past most Burmese medicine was physic and there was very little practice of surgery. Today illness is still apt to be attributed to various seminaturalistic causes such as an imbalance of the elements of the human constitution, to the magical injection by a witch of a foreign substance into the body, or to malign influences or possession. Both laymen and medical specialists have a repertoire of household remedies. The medical specialists are divided broadly into two categories, the notions of each being partly formalized in texts: the dietists, who seek a proper balance of the elements by regulating the diet; and the druggists, who dispense a variety of medicines mostly in the form of pills. Various experts in magical methods are called upon to deal with foreign intrusions, possession, and maleficent influences. [Scott 1910: 417-20.] **Soul, death, and afterlife.** Popularly the soul is conceived of as a butterfly, which during sleep can leave the body of its own volition. A person dying of normal, natural causes is reborn in some being appropriate to the amount of merit accumulated by the deceased during his lifetime. Those who die a "green" death (accidental or violent) apparently do not move on in the chain of being, but linger on earth as malevolent ghosts. Such persons are buried as soon as possible and with little ceremony. In other cases, the corpse is laid out in grave clothes on a temporary bier. While the bier and coffin are being made and preparations for the funeral going forward a wake is held at which guests are entertained. On the day of the funeral a procession of monks, mourners, and friends accompanies the coffin to the cemetery. The monks recite the appropriate formulas and receive offerings, water is poured upon the ground to indicate that the deceased and all creatures are to share the merit of the gifts to the monks, the body is buried, and the butterfly soul is told to be off. Burial is now general, although a century or so ago cremation was perhaps more common. The funerals of monks, ending in cremation, are generally arranged at a considerable interval after death and are very elaborate, partaking of the nature of a fete. [Ferrars and Ferrars 1901: 193-99; Scott 1910: 583-601.]

BIBLIOGRAPHY. Associates for International Research 1956; Brohm 1963; Brohm, Brant, and Jackim 1956; Cady 1958; Carpenter 1875; Cushing 1914; Ferrars and Ferrars 1901; Furnivall 1948; Hanson 1954; Harvey 1925; Htin Aung 1962; Huke 1956a; India 1931-34; Lehman 1963; Luce 1959c, 1959d; McFarland 1941; Mi Mi Khaing 1946; Scott 1910; Shafer 1955; Shorto 1962.

WESTERN UPLAND GROUPS

NAGAS[2]

ORIENTATION. **Identification.** The term Naga refers to a number of Indo-Mongoloid tribes inhabiting the mountainous region of the India–Burma frontier. The names of the principal tribes of the group on the Indian side are: Konyak, Ao, Sema, Chakhesang, Angami, Lhota, Sangtam, Yimchungr, Chang, Khienmungan, Phom, Zeliang, Rengma, Mao, Maram, and Kabui. Some of these names have been adopted quite recently as a result of new affiliations, and are consequently unknown to anthropology. For example, the Chakhesang are a combination of a few southern Angami, Sangtam, and Rengma groups, and the Zeliang are a mixture of the Zemi (Kacha Naga), Liangmai, and others (Elwin 1961: 5). The derivation of the word Naga is not clear. One author has explained it as meaning "hillman," derived from the Sanskrit *naga*, mountain. Another derives it from the word *nok*, or "people," which is its meaning in a few Tibeto-Burman languages (Hutton 1921a: 5). Until recently the tribes referred to as Naga by the plainsmen of Assam and other outsiders did not use the name, but called themselves by their distinct tribal names. Today, however, these tribes are more united and like to refer to themselves as Naga. ● It is difficult to establish criteria by which Nagas can be distinguished from neighboring peoples in Assam and

Burma. Hutton (1922: xvi) considers Naga a useful term to denote the tribes living in a particular geographical area, but Elwin (1961: 5) says that "there is an atmosphere, a spirit, in a Naga which is unmistakable," and that it is shared by the tribes known as Naga. Although there are physical, linguistic, and cultural variations among the various Naga tribes, they do exhibit a general similarity with respect to certain beliefs and economic practices. **Location.** Most of the Nagas inhabit the region now known as Nagaland, a newly created Indian state of 6,366 square miles in the mountainous territory between Burma and the Brahmaputra valley of Assam. There are a few groups in Burma, namely, the Htangan, Pyengoo, Haimi, and Rangpan. The Manipur State of India is the home of a few groups, namely the Mao, Maram, Kabui, Quoireng, Chiru, and Marring. The region inhabited by Nagas extends roughly between 24° and 27° 30′ N. and between 94° and 95° E., except for an extension to 93° E. in Manipur State. **Geography.** Most villages stand at 3,000–4,000 feet above sea level, and the highest peak rises to 9,890 feet. The main concentration of the population is at the higher elevations. The foothills toward the plains are unhealthy and thinly populated. Rainfall averages 70 to 100 inches per year. There are many rivers and streams, and a great deal of forest still exists in spite of the devastating effect of shifting cultivation. Wild game, such as elephants, buffalo, tigers, leopards, and bears are rare nowadays. The hornbill is the most treasured bird in Nagaland because of its use in decoration and magic. [Elwin 1961: 4.] **Linguistic affiliation.** The Nagas are characterized by numerous linguistic and dialectical variations. A single tribe may have several different dialects, each quite distinct from the others, and two different dialects may prevail in the same village. The Ao tribe is divided into two parts, based on the two different dialects used: Chongli and Mongsen. People speaking these two dialects, which are "so distinct that they might almost be called different languages," live side by side in many Ao villages (Hutton 1921a: 372). That there are some common elements in the languages and dialects of the Naga tribes is indicated by the fact that Grierson, who conducted a linguistic survey of India (1903-28), classified them as the Naga group of the Tibeto-Burman subfamily of the Sino-Tibetan family. A recent reclassification places the majority in a Burmic division, and a small minority in a Baric division, of the Sino-Tibetan family (Elwin 1961: 12). Because of this linguistic variation and because of their contact with the Assamese-speaking people living in the plains, the Nagas have adopted a broken form of Assamese as their lingua franca. They have no script of their own. Some believe that a supreme being gave them writings on skins, but that a dog ate the skins, since which time they have not been able to write (Mills 1937: 286). **Demography.** Elwin (1961: 5) gives the following population estimates of

---

[2] Moni Nag, the contributor of this section, is a member of the Anthropological Survey of India. He emphasizes that his data pertain chiefly to the Naga tribes of the newly created Indian state of Nagaland. The relatively few Nagas living in Burma and Manipur State are, however, named, and their population figures given where available.

tribes in Nagaland: Konyak (Naked Naga)—63,000; Ao—50,000; Sema—48,000; Chakhesang—31,000; Angami—30,000; Lhota—23,500; Sangtam—20,700; Yimchungr—17,500; Chang—17,000; Khienmungan—17,000; Phom—13,000; Zeliang—5,250; Rengma—5,000; mixed tribes—5,000. The total population of Nagaland, according to Elwin's estimate, is a little over 357,000, which includes 2,400 Kuki in the hills and a mixed community of 8,600 at Dimapur. The total population of Nagaland, as found in the 1961 census of India, is 369,200, which is not very different from Elwin's estimate. The population estimates for the different Naga tribes as given above may, therefore, be accepted as roughly correct for 1961. There were 800 inhabited villages in Nagaland in 1961. Population figures for the Naga tribes of Burma are unavailable. Recent population figures for the Nagas of Manipur State are also unavailable, but 1931 estimates are as follows: Kabui—18,800; Mao—16,700; Marring—4,200; Maram—2,500; Quoireng—552. **History and cultural relations.** The region inhabited by the Naga tribes has been the scene of a series of immigrations from the northeast, northwest, and south. The people from the plains of Assam and Burma have been pushed up into this region. The Nagas exhibit traces of physical and cultural elements found in the Austric race of Kol-Annam or Mon-Khmer type, in Bodo and Tai peoples, and also in the Igorot and other Philippine tribes (Hutton 1922: xxxviii). Traditions and legends indicate the courses of some of these migrations. ● For hundreds of years Nagas have fought among themselves. At the beginning of the thirteenth century the Shan (Tai) chief Sukhapa subjugated the Nagas and treated them very badly. Their relationship with the Tai-speaking Ahom kings of Assam was characterized by both hostility and friendliness. The Ahom kings regarded. the Nagas as subjects and granted land and retainers to their chiefs. The chiefs formerly paid taxes in the form of slaves, elephant tusks, and hand-woven cloth. In the sixteenth and seventeenth centuries there were a number of clashes between Nagas and Ahom. ● The British occupation of Assam in 1826 did not mean complete subjugation of the Naga tribes. Throughout the nineteenth century there were constant raids on the plains of Assam as well as intervillage feuds associated with headhunting. In 1832-33 the king of Manipur marched through the Naga territory. He continued to exercise authority over a portion of that territory for some years, and subsequently the Nagas established trade relations with Manipur. Effective British administration was established in 1881, and intervillage raids and head-hunting quickly came to an end in the administered area. The recent formation of the state of Nagaland is the result of administrative changes which took place after India attained independence in 1946. [Elwin 1961: 18-26.]

SETTLEMENT PATTERN AND HOUSING. Settlement pattern. Villages are characteristically situated on the summit of a hill or on a spur running off from a high range, some 3,000–4,000 feet above sea level. This type of location was formerly necessary for defense, and for the same reason the villages were surrounded by stone walls, palisades, dikes, or fences of thorn. The Nagas generally practice shifting cultivation, but their villages are permanent. The average village population, according to the 1961 census, is 438. There are, however, large variations in size. Mills (1937: 46) reports the number of houses in 12 villages of the Western Rengma as follows: 257, 8, 55, 89, 74, 125, 22, 27, 377, 118, 178, and 52. Ao villages are situated quite far apart, and some are reported to contain 300–700 houses (Ao 1953: 70). ● Naga villages usually contain two or three divisions known as *khels*, an Assamese term denoting a body of men. Although the division of villages into *khels* is purely geographical, the members of a particular language or clan, or a group of later immigrants will usually live together or predominate in a single *khel* (Mills 1926: 82; 1937: 56). There is usually an open space between *khels* which serves as a fire line. ● The Ao and Lhota arrange their houses in regular streets along a ridge top. The houses in the villages of other Naga tribes are less regularly arranged. In Ao villages there are rows of houses behind those flanking the main street. Houses usually face the top of the ridge, and are so close together that their eaves touch one another (Mills 1926: 80-84; Hutton 1921a: 372). **Housing.** Roofs are usually of thatching grass or palm leaves, and walls and floors of bamboo matting. Wooden posts are used by some tribes. The Angami, Sema, and other tribes to the south build their houses on the ground, while the Ao and other northern groups build on a bamboo platform or *machan*. The Lhota make a compromise between the two, building on a *machan* but covering the floor with earth (Hutton 1922: xxx). Houses are usually fairly large. An average Ao house measures 25 feet by 14 feet. It consists of a small front room and a large main room. Houses vary little in size; variations are confined to the front of the house and the decoration of the roof, which reflect the status of the owner. Some have high gables projecting in front, others have crossed wooden horns. ● Men's houses are known as *morungs* and are the finest and most ornate buildings in Naga villages. Usually each *khel* within a village possesses one *morung*, which serves mainly as a men's club and as a sleeping place for unmarried boys of the *khel*. Boys begin to sleep here when they are six or seven years of age. Formerly the *morung* was the social center of the village, and the age groups associated with it formed natural labor teams for all public works. The spread of Christianity has caused a decline in the importance of this institution in Naga life. [Fürer-Haimendorf 1946: 51-52; Mills 1937: 49-50.]

ECONOMY. Primarily dependent on agriculture. Herding, hunting, and fishing, although practiced by most tribes, play minor roles in the economy. Gathering is even less significant. Some Nagas are employed in the tea plantations of Assam and in government service, but cash income from these sources and from trade has little appreciable effect on the economy. **Agriculture.** Mostly swidden agriculture, locally known as *jhum*. Rice cultivation on elaborate terraces is found only among the Angami, although some other tribes, such as the Rengma, and certain groups in Manipur have learned the art from the Angami and have occasional terraced, irrigated rice fields. Some groups, such as the Konyak, Sangtam, and Chang are ignorant of wet cultivation. [Mills 1935: 131, 143-45.] The Angami, Lhota, Rengma, and Sema are careful in sowing the seed, but the Ao, Chang, and Konyak scatter it broadcast (Elwin 1961: 6). Most groups reap with a reaping hook, but the Sema use the hand only (Hutton 1922: xxviii). The Angami use a flat-bladed spade or hoe, a wooden mattock, an iron sickle, and other agricultural implements (Hutton 1921a: 79). ● Rice is the staple crop for most tribes. Taro was probably the staple crop originally, but is at present important only among the Konyak, although a considerable amount is still grown by the Western Rengma. Millet and Job's-tears are staple crops in villages situated in high altitudes. Maize is cultivated by some tribes. Chilies are common in all Naga villages. Cotton is usually grown in low-lying villages. Other popular crops are beans, sweet potatoes, pumpkins, tobacco, and pan (the leaves of which are eaten along with betel nuts). **Fishing and hunting.** Except for the Lhota, the Nagas are not keen fishermen. Traps and nets are used. Poisoning, using the juice of a creeper, is the most important method among the Lhota (Mills 1922: 70). All Nagas enjoy hunting, both as a sport and as a source of meat. Tigers, leopards, and wild boar are hunted with guns and spears, aided by dogs. Deer hunting is very popular. Formerly elephants were taken in pitfalls, but this practice has been forbidden by the government. Traps are used for small animals, and snares for catching birds. **Domestic animals.** A species of cattle (*Bos frontalis*) called mithan is an important domestic animal in all villages, although they are not found in large numbers. They represent a form of wealth, and are used chiefly for ceremonial purposes. The common cow is also present and its meat is eaten. The Nagas usually do not milk their cows. Pigs abound in every village, and serve to keep them free from rubbish and refuse. Pork is indispensable at any feast. Goats and fowl are found in many villages. Dogs are used for hunting and their meat is also eaten. Bees are kept in some villages. **Food and stimulants.** Rice is the staple. Millet and Job's-tears are also important in the higher and colder ranges. Chilies are an indispensable item in the diet. The Nagas prefer beef and pork, but eat almost all kinds of meat and some fish. The diet includes vegetables, especially young bamboo shoots. Dried fish imported from the plains is considered a delicacy. The favorite drink is rice beer, although beer made from millet and Job's-tears is also consumed in many places. Nowadays Nagas drink tea, and some even drink milk. Cheap cigarettes are very popular. Betel nut with pan leaves and lime is chewed in the villages near the plains. [Mills 1922: 81-82.] **Industrial arts.** Naga textiles, famous for their variety of color and design, are generally woven by women on a single-heddle tension loom. Weaving is the most important industry. In many villages home-grown cotton is used for spinning, but threads are also imported from the plains of Burma and Assam. Dyeing is done locally. Basketry is also an important industry. The Nagas make ornaments out of cane, shell, ivory, bone, and horn. Khonoma, an Angami village, is famous for its cane armlets and gauntlets, and has almost complete control over trade in shells and beads. Some are experts at making pottery, including cooking pots and pipe bowls. Blacksmiths make *daos* (large all-purpose knives), spearheads, and axes out of iron purchased from lowlanders in the form of cheap spades. [Hutton 1921a: 62-65.] Not all Naga tribes are good woodworkers, but some of them like the Ao and the Western Rengma, are expert carvers. Their *morungs* are decorated with wooden carvings. Their large xylophonelike drums, which are made by hollowing out huge logs, are striking specimens of Ao handiwork (Mills 1926: 76). **Trade.** For centuries the Nagas have remained isolated due to poor communications and the rugged nature of their habitat. As a result of this isolation and also because of intertribal and intervillage feuds, trade has played a minor role in the economy. Such trading activities as did exist in the past have been increasing at a rapid rate since the opening up of new communications during and after World War II. Pan leaves, cotton, and chilies are sold to the plainsmen of Assam in return for salt, dried fish, and clothing. Some Naga tribes obtain salt and thread from Burma, and they also trade among themselves for such items as cane armlets, cowrie shells, ceremonial spears, *daos*, dao handles, pigs, and cattle. In recent years the Nagas have acquired from the plains many novelties, such as blouses, lipsticks, celluloid combs, brass and aluminum pots, and electric torches. [Elwin 1961: 15-16.] **Division of labor.** Both men and women take part in agricultural activities. Felling of trees for preparing the swiddens is usually done by young men. Sowing, weeding, and reaping are done by both men and women. Among the Konyak, taro is planted by women (Fürer-Haimendorf 1946: 81). Hunting is done by the men, but both men and women fish. Weaving is done exclusively by women, and basketry by men. Trading activities are carried on by both sexes (Hutton 1921a: 167-68). **Land tenure.** There are in general four types of landed property: (1) private land (2) clan land (3) *morung* land, and (4) village land. Most of the cultivable land and all building sites are privately owned, whereas the uncultivable land usually belongs to the village. All terraced land is privately owned. *Morung* land is held by the *morung* for gathering timber and grass, for building or repairing the *morung*, and also for the cultivation of food for *morung* feasts. [Das 1954: 13; Fürer-Haimendorf 1946: 87.] There are some variations in this pattern, however. Among the Sema, most of the land is privately owned. Among the Nagas of Manipur, swidden land is individually owned but cannot be transferred by sale, mortgage, or gift. Among the Western Rengma, there is no *morung* land, but there is a considerable amount of land common to clans. Among the Eastern Rengma, the *khels* own some land.

KIN GROUPS. **Descent.** Descent is defined in the male line. Some authors have cited customs which suggest the former existence of matrilineal descent (cf. Kapadia 1950). **Kin groups.** Exogamous patrilineal clans function in the selection of marriage partners and in various other social and economic activities. Among many Naga tribes, the clans possess common land for cultivation. The clan is responsible for the misdemeanors of any of its members. Clan solidarity is ordinarily greater than *khel* solidarity. Sometimes a village is inhabited exclusively by one clan, but usually more than one is present. Clans are not rigid groups, tending to split up into what Hutton (1921a: 110-15) calls kindreds [patrilineages]. As a result, clan exogamy is not strictly adhered to, and the kindreds [patrilineages] become the real exogamous groups. No traces of totemism have been found except in a very few clans among the Lhota, Ao, and Sema (Hutton 1921a: 390-92). Moities are absent, but phratries are reported (Mills 1926: 30-32). **Kin terminology.** The following kin terms are from Hutton (1921a: 132-34) for the Angami, Mills (1922: 93) for the Lhota, Mills (1926: 172-74) for the Ao, and Hutton (1921b: 139-43) for the Sema:

	Angami (Khonoma)	Lhota (Northern)	Ao (Chongli)	Sema
Fa	po	opo	tobu	....
Mo	zo	oyo	tetsu	aza
FaElBr	apo	oporamo	tobutambu	....
FaYoBr	nyie	oporo	tobutanubu	....
FaSi	nye	onnoramo (El) onnoro (Yo)		ani
MoBr	mi	omo	....	angu
MoSi	zo	tetsutanzu (El) tetsutanuzu (Yo)	....	aza
ElBr	dzereo	ota	titi	amu
YoBr	siezeo	onyuro	tonu	atukuzu
ElSi	dzerepfu	ota	tuyi	afu
YoSi	siezepfu	oyilo	tonu	achefu
FaBrSo	....	ota (El) onyuro (Yo)	....	atukuzu (Yo)
FaSiSo	chu	orrho	....	atikeshiu
FaBrDa	....	ota (El) oyilo (Yo)	....	afu (El) achefu (Yo)

	Angami (Khonoma)	Lhota (Northern)	Ao (Chongli)	Sema
FaSiDa	chupfu	orrhovo	....	atikeshiu
MoBrSo	....	omo	....	....
MoBrDa	....	oyonunghowo	....	aza
MoSiSo	....	....	titi (El) tonu (Yo)	....
MoSiDa	....	....	tuyi (El) tonu (Yo)	

MARRIAGE AND FAMILY. Premarital sexual relations are generally tolerated. Unmarried boys and girls work together in the rice fields for long hours, and get sufficient opportunities there for lovemaking. Although there are no dormitories for unmarried girls in Naga villages as there are for unmarried boys, there are some houses in the villages where the unmarried girls sleep in groups. Among some tribes, men are admitted to these "dormitories." The Nagas generally follow the same incest taboos in premarital relations as in the case of marriage. [Hutton 1921a: 169-70.] **Mode.** Boys and girls generally have freedom of choice in marriage. Parents do not resort to force if they do not like a choice of mate, but they may resort occasionally to a good deal of persuasion (Hutton 1921a: 168). Elopement is rare. The custom of paying a bride price is common, and may be paid in both cash and kind. Among the Angami it is quite nominal—a few chickens, a couple of pigs, a spear, and occasionally 20–100 rupees in cash. Among the Sema and Lhota it is higher, but it can be paid in installments (Hutton 1921a: 168). Among some Naga tribes, such as the Lhota, the groom does some service also for his father-in-law (Mills 1922: 88). **Form.** Monogamy is the usual rule, but polygyny is practiced by the Eastern Rengma, Lhota, and Sema. Among the Eastern Rengma it is reported to be quite frequent (Mills 1937: 213). **Extension of incest taboos.** Clan exogamy is the general rule (Mills 1922: 87). Among the Lhota a man may not marry the following women even if they are eligible in other ways: (1) his mother's sister's daughter (2) his own sister's daughter, and (3) his father's sister's daughter, although he can marry his mother's brother's daughter (Mills 1922: 95). There is a mild prejudice among a section of the Angami against marrying first cousins on the mother's side, even though it is permitted by the rules of exogamy. This has been cited as an illustration of the possible existence of a former matrilineal system among the Angami (Hutton 1921a: 399). **Residence.** Usually patrilocal, near the husband's male patrilineal kinsmen. In some tribes, such as the Rengma, the son brings his wife to his father's house after marriage and builds another house after the next harvest (Mills 1937: 143). Occasionally a son lives with his wife in his parents' house after marriage but has a separate hearth. **Domestic unit.** Usually of the nuclear type, with some variations. Hutton (1921a: 55) describes the typical Angami household as consisting of a man and his wife with two or three children, plus a widowed parent and a younger unmarried brother. **Inheritance.**

47

Inheritance of property is patrilineal. Failing sons or grandsons, brothers, brothers' sons, and first cousins may inherit. A widow is entitled to maintenance from her husband's property until her remarriage or death. Ornaments usually go from mother to daughter. The sons share the landed property equally, but on the death of the father the youngest son inherits the remaining property, including the house. [Hutton 1921a: 135-37; Mills 1922: 98-99; 1937: 143-44.] **Divorce.** Divorce or separation is fairly easy and common. Even temperamental incompatibility is sufficient reason for divorce among some Naga groups (Hutton 1921a: 168).

SOCIOPOLITICAL ORGANIZATION. **Political organization.** Until recently, the Nagas lacked any political or legal institutions transcending the level of the village. Village-level institutions vary from near-dictatorship to extreme democracy. Konyak villages are run by very powerful chiefs, *ang*, autocrats who are considered to be of divine origin, and who have enormous prestige (Mills 1935: 146). Angami, Lhota, and Rengma villages tend to be more democratic (Elwin 1961: 7). Among the Angami, village chiefs (hereditary in some villages) have always existed, but without much authority. Before the establishment of courts under British rule, small disputes were settled by a council of village elders. Interclan or inter-village murders or disputes often led to war. Questions regarding customs are always referred to the old men of the clans (Hutton 1921a: 143-50). Before the advent of British rule, the position of the village chief among the Western Rengma was hereditary in the clan but not in the family. The most suitable man in the leading family of the clan was made village chief. The Eastern Rengma do not remember ever having had hereditary chieftains. Their villages have always been run by the most influential men. This system still works satisfactorily, and very few disputes are even now brought to court (Mills 1937: 140). In former times Lhota villages had chiefs, but the position was not hereditary. Their villages are now managed by an informal council of old men and women of influence, with a headman selected by the government. In villages where the *khels* are large, the leading men of the *khels* tend to manage *khel* affairs (Mills 1922: 45). Ao villages are run by councils of elders representing the heads of lineages. Generally there are two councils in an Ao village—a Mongsen council and a Chongli council. Each has from 25 to 80 members. The chairman's post is hereditary within a single clan. Should an accused person not abide by the decision of one of the councils, the matter is referred to its chairman (Ao 1953: 71). The Sema have a system of hereditary chiefs who derive their power from a monopoly on land. The Chang and Sangtam also have village chiefs, but they are less powerful than those of the Sema (Hutton 1921a: 379; 1922: xxxiii; Mills 1935: 144). **Social stratification.** The Nagas generally lack social groups with graded status, although particular clans in some tribes may have higher status than others. Among the Konyak, the Ang clan has the highest status, and the village chiefs are always from this clan. A Konyak chief's daughter can be married only to a man from the family of another chief (Fürer-Haimendorf 1946: 96). Among the Ao, the Pongen clan is generally recognized as *doyen*, and the village chiefs are usually from this clan (Ao 1953: 71). The prestige of an individual can be increased by collecting trophies in fighting and headhunting expeditions, and also by giving feasts of merit. A man's status is reflected in the way he decorates his house (Fürer-Haimendorf 1946: 52; Mills 1926: 83). **Warfare.** The Naga tribes are notorious for warfare and headhunting. There have been constant interclan, intervillage, and sometimes intertribal feuds, and until the advent of British rule, they used also to raid the Assam plainsmen. The Nagas fight mostly with spears and shields, but some had guns even before the coming of the British. Headhunting was an essential feature of feuds and wars. Its importance was due in part to the belief in the soul-matter or vital essence residing in the human head. It was believed that a village could acquire new and vital energy by acquiring heads from outside (Elwin 1961: 12). The Rengma say that enemies' heads caused their crops to flourish and the number of men and animals to increase (Mills 1937: 161). The Angami sometimes had recourse to headhunting to propitiate evil spirits. Headhunting also gave prestige to the men, who found it difficult to get girls for marriage if they could not bring home heads (Hutton 1921a: 158-65). Government policy has long suppressed headhunting, but Fürer-Haimendorf (1946: 47) cites cases of headhunting among the Konyak even in 1936. Some authors report that the suppression of headhunting among the Nagas has caused them to lose their former virility and keenness (Mills 1935: 147-49).

RELIGION. There is no Hindu influence among the Nagas. There are some Christian converts, particularly among the Ao. Their religion can generally be termed animism. **Supernaturals.** The Nagas believe in the existence of many minor deities, ghosts, and spirits, but without idolatry. Some have vague ideas about a supreme being. The Ao are reported to believe in such a being whom they style *lichaba ali yang raba sangram*—the *deo* who has created the earth (Majumdar 1925). There are many animistic beliefs, particularly as regards stones. An animal or a particular tree may be regarded as an embodied spirit which must not be injured (Hutton 1921a: 180). Offerings are made to all deities and spirits which may influence the events of daily life. The Rengma are reported to make offerings also to the souls of their ancestors (Mills 1937: 164). **Practitioners.** Most villages have priests, usually hereditary, who conduct all magico-religious functions, and who also act as the repository of the genealogical and historical traditions of the villages and clans. They also list and announce the dates of public religious ceremonies. Some villages have a separate category of priests who perform religious functions that are personal in nature (Hutton 1921a: 187-97). The Rengma are reported to have no priests at all (Mills 1937: 164). **Ceremonies.** Almost all religious ceremonies are designed to protect and increase crops. Naga religion, however, is more negative than positive. Avoidance of forbidden acts on particular days is very important. The most important religious ceremony is an individual or village *genna,* during which work and contact with the outside world are avoided. Besides *gennas* associated with agricultural operations, such as sowing and harvesting, others have to do with hunting and house building. *Gennas* may also be held to ensure the health of the community, or friendship between different clans. Some ceremonies are accompanied by dancing and singing. [Hutton 1921a: 195-210.] **Illness and medicine.** Illness is thought to be caused by evil spirits. A medicine man is called to placate these spirits by sacrificing pigs or fowl, or to extract from the patient's body bits of earth, wood, or hair put there by evil spirits (Mills 1922: 79; 1926: 149). The Nagas have some knowledge of herbal medicines, which they apply in cases of wounds and other diseases (Mills 1937: 116-18). The belief among the Angami that neglect of washing causes illness is responsible for their marked habits of personal cleanliness. Angami dwellings, on the other hand, are filthier than those of other tribes (Hutton 1922: xxxv). **Soul, death, and afterlife.** The concept of an afterlife varies from tribe to tribe, with a general agreement that the soul does not perish at death. The Lhota, Chang, and some of the Sema think that there is a narrow path through which the soul goes to paradise. Some believe that the soul takes the form of various insects, especially butterflies. Since some Angami think that souls are not entirely cut off from their former existence, a dead man's drinking horn is frequently left hanging in its usual place (Hutton 1921a: 185-86). Some Nagas say that good souls go to a pleasant place toward the sunrise; whereas bad souls go to a less pleasant place toward the sunset (Elwin 1961: 10). ● The Nagas usually bury their dead, but other methods such as exposure and desiccation have traditionally been practiced. Some Tangkhul and Rengma build small houses over the graves for the ghosts to inhabit, and place little ladders up to them. The Lhota, Sangtam, and Sema build thatched roofs over the graves, which may suggest that they formerly exposed the bodies in the miniature houses. Those among the Ao who have turned Christian also build thatched roofs over the graves similar to those which the unconverted Ao put over bodies exposed on platforms. The Konyak and Phom expose their dead on a platform usu-ally consisting of a bamboo shelf thatched over like a house and covered at the ends. The head is later separated from the decomposed body and brought to the house, where it is treated with some ceremony. The Khienmungan practice what is called desiccation. Dead bodies are smoked for two months over a fire and retained in a wooden coffin until the next sowing, when they are broken up. The bones are then placed in an earthen pot and put at the back of the family granary. [Hutton 1922: xxiv-xxv.]

BIBLIOGRAPHY. Ao 1953; Das 1954; Elwin 1961; Fürer-Haimendorf 1946; Grierson 1903-28; Hutton 1921a, 1921b, 1922; Kapadia 1950; Majumdar 1925; Mills 1922, 1926, 1935, 1937.

CHINS

Synonyms. *Cuci, Khyang, Khyeng, Kookie, Kuki*

ORIENTATION. **Identification.** Although Chin speakers as a whole have no single name for themselves, many groups use what appear to be variant forms of one word, *zo* (*yo, sho*), as in Laizo, Mizo, Hyou, Ashö. *Zo,* according to Lehman, has the meaning of "uncivilized," contrasting with *vai,* "civilized," and, by implication, Burmese. The English name is derived from Burmese *chin,* written *khyang.* This word, meaning "friend," according to Luce, and probably referring to the Chins, is recorded either as Khyang or Khlang from the thirteenth century A.D. Khyang is still current in Arakan and Chittagong for some of the Chins there. The older English form Khyeng is obviously related to Khyang and Chin. In English, the name Chin is customarily applied to these people when they are discussed within the context of Burma. The earliest British contact occurred, however, from the direction of India, and within this context they were called Kookie or Cuci, earlier forms of what is today written Kuki. From these two names has arisen the combination Kuki-Chin. Kuki remains the most common general term for these people in India and East Pakistan, and at this general level it is equivalent to Chin. **Classifications.** The Meithei, the dominant population of the Indian state of Manipur, are usually excluded from classifications of Chins because they alone before Western contact were adherents of a major religion and had writing and a supravillage political organization. Among the Chins of the Chin and Lushai hills of Burma and India, there is a dichotomy of Mar versus Pawi. The Mar, whose men wear their hair in a chignon, include the Lushai (in India) and the related Hualngo, together with the Kamhau and Siyin of the northern Chin Special Division of Burma. The Pawi, wearing their hair in a frontal topknot, include a number of groups in Burma just south of the Mar. Shakespear tends to contrast

Pawi with Lushai and to equate it with "Chin." Scott speaks of wild and tame Chins in the Burmese Chin Hills, divided at approximately 22° N., the tame being the more southerly groups. Lehman's data suggest, however, that when measured by adherence to a traditional, less acculturated life, the tame Chins are the wilder. Lehman also divides the Chins of the Special Division into northern and southern groups, at about 21° 45′ N., but on somewhat different grounds than those employed by Scott. The present chapter follows Lehman's use of the terms northern and southern Chins. **Group names.** The Chins present particularly difficult problems with respect to group identification and synonymy. There is still a considerable ignorance of Chin languages and dialects and their relationships. A few groups, including some of the most insignificant in a numerical sense, have received extensive ethnographic treatment, but many are still inadequately reported. The nature of political and social structures among Chins has meant that names appearing in the literature and in censuses do not always refer to comparable units. Some, for example, may be names of settlements or kin groups within a named linguistic group—which may explain the appearance and disappearance of names from census to census. There are, finally, the twin problems always present in ethnography, one that the name first established in general usage is often a foreign rather than a native name, the other that various foreigners have written the same name in different ways. ● The Meithei, known to the Assamese as Mekle, and to the Burmese as Kathè, are often called Manipuri. In addition to its general meaning of Indian Chins, Kuki applies in a more limited sense to the hill Chins of Manipur and Assam north of the Lushai Hills. The Kukis are often divided into Old and New Kukis, a distinction based upon sequence of appearance in their present areas of settlement, the Old Kuki groups having appeared about a half century earlier than the New. Old Kuki is closer to the languages of the Chins south of the Special Division, while New Kuki resembles those of the northern and central parts of the Division. New Kukis are also called Thados, for whom the Meithei name is said to be Kongjai or Khongshai. The latter is also reported as the Arakanese name for Lakher. None of the Old Kuki groups are numerically significant, but several (Aimol, Chawte or Chote, Kom, Purum, Vaiphei or Waiphei) have been the subject of modern field ethnographies or of theoretical studies. Other Old Kuki groups are the Anal, Biete (Bete, Biate), Chiru, Kolhen (Kolhreng, Kolren, Koireng), Hrangkhol, Hallam, Lamgang, and Hmar (Mhar, Khawtlang, Khotlang). Khawtlang is also reported as a name for the Thados or New Kukis. ● South of the Kuki groups are the Lushai or Lushei, the latter originally the name of a sib speaking a dialect called Dulien. The sib name, misspelled Lushai, has been retained as a general term for various peoples dominated and influenced by the Lushei. At present they seem to favor the name Mizo. ● South of the Lushai are the Lakher (a Lushai name), called Magha by Lehman and Mara by Luce. West of the Lakher are the Khumi (Khami), and to the south of them, the Khyang. ● The 1931 census lists 44 named Chin groups. Starting from the north of the Chin Special Division just south of Manipur, the more important groups are: Sokte (Suhte, also called Kamhau or Kamhow), Siyin (own name Sizang), Tashon (Burmese pronunciation of the native Tlashun, for which Haka Chin is Suntla, whence Sunkhla—kl is an early attempt to represent a lateral consonant, as indicated by the forms Klangklang, Tlangtlang, and Lehman's Thlantlaang), Zahau (Yahow), Zanniat (Zahnyet, Zannet), Laizao (Laizo, Falam, Fahlam), Lai (Haka, Baungshe), Khualshim (Kwelshim), Ngawn (Ngorn), Ashö (plains Chins of the Irrawaddy lowlands), and Saingbaung. In 1943 Stevenson, with local counsel, coined the name Shimhrin as a general name for the culturally very close Zahau, Laizo, Khuangli, and Sunkhla. [Lehman 1963; Löffler 1959; Luce 1959b; Scott 1921: 109; Shakespear 1912; Shaw 1929.] **Location.** Chins occupy much of the area of western Burma and the eastern margins of Pakistan and India south of about 25° 30′ N. They extend southward in the Arakan Range to about 18° N. A number also live in Burma's Irrawaddy valley from about 18° to 20° N. [Lehman 1963: 6; Shaw 1929: 3-12.] **Geography.** With the exception of the valley of Manipur, the Chin homeland is mountainous terrain. Ridges, oriented mostly north–south, fall away at the southern extremity of the Arakan Range. Although the mountains rise to 9,000 feet, Chin settlements are generally found between 3,000 and 7,000 feet. Climate is tropical monsoon. The valleys are warm, with lush vegetation, but the steep slopes on which the Chins live are relatively cool, with mixed evergreen and deciduous forests and alpine flora at the highest altitudes. Rainfall in the northern Chin Hills averages 55 inches, increasing to 100 inches farther south. **Linguistic affiliation.** The Chin languages are Tibeto-Burman. Grierson placed them in a Kuki-Chin group composed of two subgroups, Meithei and Chin, the latter composed of northern, central, Old Kuki, and southern groups. Shafer largely follows Grierson, although he ignores for linguistic purposes the distinction formerly made between Chins and Nagas, including most of the "Naga" languages in his Kukish section of the Burmic division. It may be that the generally accepted cultural watershed at about 25° 30′ N. is not applicable to language classification. [Shafer 1955; Shakespear 1912: 225; Grierson 1903-28: 1, Pt. I, 72-73.] **Demography.** According to the Indian census of 1951, Chin speakers in India numbered some 821,000 in Assam, Manipur, and Tripura. Of these about 500,000 were Meithei, 166,000 Lushai, and the remainder members of various smaller groups of so-called Kukis. Pakistan's Chins have been estimated at about 35,000. Burma's Chins, as recorded in the 1931 census, numbered about 344,000, 53 per cent of whom lived in the territory of the present Chin Special Division. These figures yield a total of 1,200,000 Chin speakers, approximately 42 per cent of whom are probably Meithei. Of the groups listed in the 1931 census, "unspecified" Chins in the Irrawaddy valley (probably mostly plains Chins) numbered 55,000, the Khami of northern Arakan and the southern Chin Special Division 31,000, the Haka of the central part of the Division 24,000, the Chinbok of the southern part 20,000, and the Kamhau in the northern part 20,000; the remaining groups were much smaller in population. Similarly, in India, most groups listed in the 1951 census were less than 3,000 in number; exceptions were 36,000 "unspecified" Kukis, mostly in Manipur, and 20,000 Thados. [India 1931-34: *11*, Pt. I, 198; India (Republic) 1952-57: *12*, Pt. IIA, 76-87; Luce 1959b: 24-25.] **History and cultural relations.** Luce believes that the Chins may have been in the lowlands of Burma east of the Chin Division from about the middle of the first millennium A.D. Their subsequent westward movement into the mountains was the result of fighting between Burmese and Shans in the early sixteenth century. Luce finds no evidence in the early inscriptions of fighting between Burmese and Chins; except for what was probably peaceful trading for slaves, the Burmese did not ascend the valley of the Chindwin, the "hole of the Chins." Hinduism was introduced into the valley of Manipur at the beginning of the eighteenth century, resulting in the creation of a Hinduized state among a Chin people. ● Genealogies of the pagan mountain Chins are believed to extend tradition back to the beginning of the seventeenth century, but the hill Chins came into contact with Westerners, and enter firm chronology, only about 1780. These relations developed only slowly, and largely as the consequence of Chin raids on British areas of interest in eastern Bengal and (later) Arakan. With the annexation of the Burmese kingdom in 1885, the British met the Chins in full force. During the 1890s they mounted expeditions into the Chin Hills from Burma, from Arakan and Bengal, and from Assam. Armed resistance on the part of the Chins continued as late as 1918. Civil administration, followed by schools and labor and military recruiting, was extended gradually; in the southern Lushai Hills it was achieved only on the eve of the Second World War, and in the south of the Chin Division not until after the War. British and American Protestant missionaries began work on both sides of the Bengal–Burma frontier at the end of the nineteenth century. After independence in 1948, Burma established the Chin Special Division, comprising the former Chin Hills District and Arakan and Pakokku Hill Tracts. ● The Chins have for a long time been in contact with and under the influence of Burmese and Indians (chiefly Bengalis and Assamese). Indian influence

has been greatest among the Meithei, and through them it has extended to smaller Chin groups around Manipur. Burmese influence has been strong not only within the boundaries of contemporary Burma but also in the Indian and Pakistani Chin lands west of the Chin Division. [Hodson 1908: 11, 47; Lehman 1963; Luce 1959b: 25-26; Stevenson 1943: table, p. 12.]

SETTLEMENT PATTERN AND HOUSING. **Settlement pattern.** Some Chin groups locate their villages on hilltops or spurs; others prefer sites high on the slopes of a ridge but below its summit. Settlements range from the large concentrated villages of the Lushai to scattered, isolated houses among the hill Chins of Manipur. Formerly the hill Chins surrounded their villages with stockades, with blockhouses at the gates. ● Meithei villages, built along river banks, are straggling collections of houses, each within its own enclosure. The capital, Imphal (meaning "house collection"), is less a town than a group of villages around the royal enclosure. The northern Chins rarely move their settlements, which are customarily located about seven miles apart. The largest village in the south central subdivision of Haka contains 300 houses. Southern Chin villages are somewhat farther apart and less permanent. There is an open space for communal sacrifices, and near it are the chief's house and the houses of the council members and wealthy villagers. Lushai villages of 400 to 500 houses were not uncommon at the end of the nineteenth century, although they have declined in size since then. They are commonly divided into wards, or clan barrios, each with its own bachelors' house. A polygynous Lushai chief establishes his wives' houses at various places about the settlement, each being the center of a ward. [Lehman 1963: 68-72, 81, 87-88, 91; Parry 1932: 60-63; Shakespear 1912: 21-27, 33, 36.] **Housing.** The walls of Meithei houses are of reed plastered with earth and cow dung. Roofs are of grass thatch. All work except cooking is done on a large veranda, and here the family also spends its leisure time. There are no interior partitions, and no windows. Southern Chins use only bamboo and rattan in house construction, although elsewhere houses with plank floors and walls may occur. Roofs are generally of grass thatch. Chin houses, with the exception of those in the far north of the Division, are raised above the ground on posts. The floor plan varies among the different groups, but basically it consists of a veranda, a main room where cooking is done, and a back room which may be used for courting. Each section is equipped with a hearth. Furnishings include baskets (some covered), trays, chicken coops, cooking pots, agricultural implements, and equipment for preparing thread and cloth. [Hodson 1908: 25-27; Lehman 1963: 43, 178; Parry 1932: 62-73.]

ECONOMY. Hill Chins have depended for centuries upon external societies for certain products, notably iron, salt, and prestige goods. Recent decades have seen the development of even greater dependence (cf. Lehman 1963: 103, passim). As Lehman points out, the hill Chins now have in effect two economies, an internal, local, subsistence economy based on agriculture, and an external one based on trade with lowland peoples. **Agriculture.** The major crop of the Meithei is rice, one crop a year raised in irrigated fields prepared by a plow drawn by bullocks or buffalo. Among the northern Chins of Burma, maize grown in swidden fields is the chief crop; among the southern Chins, Lushai, and Lakher of India, it is rice cultivated in swiddens. Some hill Chins do, however, raise wet rice in valley bottoms. The northern subsidiary grain crops are millet, consumed mostly at feasts, and rice. The Lushai grow maize and millet in addition to rice. Swiddens also produce legumes, cucurbits, sugar cane, yams, taro, spices and condiments, cotton, and tobacco. Bananas, onions, garlic, chilies, and indigo are grown in kitchen gardens. The Meithei, who grow most of these, also cultivate the poppy, as well as a great variety of tropical and temperate fruits. ● Chin swiddens are usually within seven miles of the village. They are cleared during the cold season, burned off in March and April, tilled with a hoe, and sown with a dibble. From three to six acres are worked by each household. The best fields among the northern Chins are used for three or four years, with a fallow of seven to nine. Poorer fields are cultivated for a year and may then be allowed as long as 40 years to recover. The southern groups use a swidden for one year with a 12-year fallow. [Hodson 1908: 40-44; Lehman 1963: 47-64; Parry 1932: 75-82; Shakespear 1912: 22, 31-33.] **Fishing and hunting.** As strict Hindus, the Meithei are supposed neither to fish nor hunt. Hill Chins appear to be avid fishermen, both individually and in groups. Fish are caught in traps and nets, with spears, by weirs, and in poisoned water behind dams. (The Lushai are said to know 16 fish poisons.) An important cooperative activity among some groups is the erection and maintenance of communal fish weirs where the men stay in a special house. ● Although game is not everywhere important in the diet, hunting is a popular sport and plays a significant role in Chin ceremonial activity. Chins hunt alone (seldom with dogs), and in parties, using guns, bows, and, for birds and squirrels, pellet bows. Other hunting implements are snares, traps, deadfalls, and pitfalls. A great variety of animals is hunted, but the elephant, rhinoceros, and gaur are no longer found in Chin territory. By many Chin groups the larger felines are treated as a class apart, and the killing of one is celebrated in a manner similar to that for killing a human enemy. [Hodson 1908: 44-47; Lehman 1963: 10, 182-83; Parry 1932: 136-63; Shakespear 1912: 33-40.] **Gathering.** There is little mention of gathering, but it is no doubt a means of supplementing the diet with wild leaves, shoots, and tubers. It also provides

beeswax and stick-lac for export. [Lehman 1963: 53, 166; Parry 1932: 84.] **Domestic animals.** The chief animals are cattle, mithan (used only for sacrifices), swine, dogs, goats, and fowl. The Meithei have long had the water buffalo, which has appeared in the Chin Hills only since the Second World War. Cattle are said to have reached the Lakher, at the southernmost extremity of the Lushai Hills, after the First World War. [Lehman 1963: 48; Parry 1932: 164-67; Shakespear 1912: 18, 21, 31-32.] **Food and stimulants.** The staple is a boiled grain, in some areas with oil added, accompanied by vegetable stews, fish, or, less often, meat. (The Meithei are supposed not to eat meat, but fish is permitted.) Almost all flesh is eaten, including insects, mollusks, and reptiles, but not felines. When the staple grain is scarce, as just before the harvest, much use is made of yams, wild tubers, and other vegetables. Three meals a day seem to be general. Stimulants include tobacco and alcoholic grain liquor, both fermented and distilled. The Meithei are forbidden to use alcohol, and are said not to use opium or marijuana; tobacco and betel, however, are used very generally. [Hodson 1908: 33, 44, 48; Parry 1932: 4, 84-93; Shakespear 1912: 18, 36-37; Stevenson 1943: 194.] **Industrial arts.** Among the hill Chins, locally grown cotton is ginned, spun, woven on a belt loom, and dyed. Pottery is made by the mallet and anvil technique. There is ironworking (repair and making simple tools from imported iron), working of bell metal (usually by simple casting), and brass founding by the cire-perdue process. A great variety of baskets, trays, sieves, mats, and matting, as well as rain clothes are made from bamboo and rattan. Cordage is made from some plants. Wood products include house parts, mortars and pestles, drums, and cotton processing implements. Lacquer is used primarily to decorate objects. There is no leather working. ● Meithei crafts are more varied. Cloth is made on the true loom, and there is elaborate carpentry, turning of wood and ivory, working in precious metals, and lock making. [Hodson 1908: 22, 27-33; Lehman 1963: 160-65; Parry 1932: 35-53, 94-136; Shakespear 1912: 9, 28-31.] **Trade.** The degree of importance of trade for a specific hill Chin group tends to vary with its accessibility to other groups and to outside markets such as those of the Burmese, Indians, or Meithei. Among the more remote groups, such as those of the south of the Chin Special Division, extensive trade in shops is only now appearing. Elsewhere in the hills, although there has long been occupational specialization by both individuals and communities, trade in a great variety of goods, including Western manufactures received through Burma, is a phenomenon of the British period. ● Traditionally the only person approaching full-time nonagricultural specialization was the blacksmith. Some hill villages specialized in metal work, pottery, mats, or cotton gins, although for the workers these were only part-time activities. There were no markets; goods moved through the medium of itinerant traders, transfers of bride wealth, or plunder in warfare. It is difficult to discern how trade with the neighboring civilizations was balanced before the British occupation. Commodity exports seem to have been few, limited to such things as beeswax and stick-lac. Presumably much was simply seized in raids. With the coming of the British, wages from road work, portering, and soldiering have facilitated a peacefully balanced trade. The importance of trade for all hill Chins, and the absence of a completely subsistence economy, is measured by the fact that all metal goods ultimately depend upon imported supplies. In addition, except for mithan and some cloth, all the items so important in ritual giving are imports. In Manipur there are markets along the roads and also in Imphal, the capital. [Hodson 1908: 23, 27; Lehman 1963: 157-69; Parry 1932: 34-55, 65, 81-82, 89, 93-94, 105-08, 130, 163; Shakespear 1912: 17, 31.] **Division of labor.** According to Lehman, men and women among the hill Chins participate about equally in most tasks, except that only men hunt, do blacksmithing, and cut swiddens. Certain tendencies in the division of labor are, however, noticeable. Women pound and winnow rice, fetch water and firewood, and make pottery. Men build houses, make baskets, and trade in markets outside the Chin area. Both sexes weed the swiddens and harvest crops, and both sexes cook, although the daily preparation of food is mostly women's work. Among some groups men are forbidden to weave; among others both sexes weave. Meithei women weave and do most of the trading in locally produced goods. [Hodson 1908: 23; Lehman 1963: 128; Parry 1932: 73-74; Shakespear 1912: 9, 17, 27, 29-30.] **Land tenure.** Northern Chin aristocratic households have fairly extensive land holdings, and the bulk of the population works rented land. In one village of 300 households, 15 held all the land. Landholders in theory rent to anyone, although in practice preference is often given to bondsmen, friends, and followers. Land thus rented can be inherited in part by the heir of the renter. Among southern Chins, the sib usually owns the village and farmlands, but effective control over house sites and swidden land is in the hands of lineages and their segments, usually individual households. In general, any available house site may be taken by a person wanting to build. Households claim traditionally demarcated swidden plots. These may be sold, rented, or inherited. Hodson writes that among the Meithei the raja of Manipur in theory had absolute rights over all land, but that this was not supported by investigation. Rather, nonarable land was communal and joint property, while cultivated fields were owned by individuals, in severalty. [Hodson 1908: 85-87; Lehman 1963: 74-79, 88, 151.]

KIN GROUPS.
Descent. Patrilineal (Lehman 1963: 88; Stevenson 1943: 18). **Kin groups.** The Chins have patrisibs and patrilineages. Among the northern Chins, lineages are ranked according to the rank of the mother; in the south this is not the case. Lineages of shorter line are localized, either in one or two villages or in one ward of a larger village composed of wards. These localized lineages are usually named. Sibs—including one, the royal line—and lineages are also found among the Meithei. [Hodson 1908: 73; Lehman 1963: 88-95, 107-16; Parry 1932: 231-36.] **Kin terminology.** The following Haka terms are given by Lehman (1963: 137). Additional information from Lorrain and Savidge (1898: 164, 213) is asterisked:

Fa, FaBr	*pa*
Mo, MoSi	*nu*
FaSi	*ni*
MoBr, MoBrSo	*pu*
MoBrDa*	*pi**
FaSiSo, FaSiCh*	*tu*
ElSb, parallel cousin of same sex	*u*
YoSb, parallel cousin of same sex	*nau*
Sb, parallel cousin of opposite sex	*far* (m.s.), *tar* (w.s.)

MARRIAGE AND FAMILY.
Mode. Lakher and Lushai marriages are usually arranged by the parents. Bride price is general throughout the hill Chin area. Among northern aristocrats and wealthy commoners, a large bride price is only the first of a series of gifts to the girl's family and her real or classificatory uncle (mother's brother). According to Lehman, it is really a payment for the right to ally oneself with one's wife's family. However, the families of both spouses share the cost of the wedding and the wife's family presents gifts to the couple. There is virtually no bride service. [Lehman 1963: 87, 100-01, 121-25; Shakespear 1912: 82-83; Parry 1932: 292.] **Form.** Most Chin men are monogamous; while polygyny is generally permitted (Stevenson says that it is frowned on by some northern Chin groups), it is largely a practice of the aristocrats and wealthy commoners. There are classes of major and minor wives. A major wife must be the daughter of a major wife, and of a sib equal in rank or superior to that of her husband. She shares in certain household sacrifices with her husband, and a full bride price is paid for her. Among the Meithei the raja, at least, is polygynous. [Hodson 1908: 76; Lehman 1963: 108-11; Parry 1932: 250; Shakespear 1912: 22-23; Stevenson 1943: 19.] **Extension of incest taboos.** Chins may not marry children, parents, parents' siblings, siblings, half-siblings (although the Lakher reportedly permit marriage of children of the same mother by different fathers), immediate parallel cousins, or close agnatic collaterals. The unit of exogamy is a major segment of a sib, thus permitting sib endogamy. Many, perhaps most, hill Chin groups prefer marriage with a real

or classificatory mother's brother's daughter. Among the Haka, central northern Chins, few such marriages actually occur, however. Small villages consisting of virtually a single ward tend to be exogamous; larger communities are more likely to be endogamous. In one large village checked by Stevenson, endogamous unions accounted for 81 per cent of 165 marriages. Meithei evidence is not wholly clear. There are exogamous sibs, some of which do not intermarry. Hodson's statement that a man might not marry a woman of his mother's sib represents a departure from hill Chin practice. [Hodson 1908: 75-76; Lehman 1963: 88-100, 116-23, 135; Parry 1932: 293-95; Shakespear 1912: 50; Stevenson 1943: 19-20.] **Residence.** Ultimately neolocal for all but the heir to the house, usually the youngest son, to whom falls the responsibility for care of aged parents. Lehman reports that a man builds his own house soon after marriage. Among the Lakher he is reported to do this upon the birth of the first child. Stevenson's statement that residence is patrilocal probably refers to temporary residence of newly married sons. [Lehman 1963: 121-22; Parry 1932: 69; Stevenson 1943: 18.] **Domestic unit.** According to Stevenson, the normal household unit is the nuclear family, with perhaps a recently married son in temporary patrilocal residence. Parry reports an average Lakher family of about five persons, larger units being found where a married son has not yet built his own house. [Stevenson 1943: 19; Parry 1932: 69.] **Inheritance.** The usual heir among the Meithei is the youngest son, the older sons receiving settlements while the father is still alive. Among the hill Chins, sons inherit their father's property, but the choice of son varies from village to village; in some, inheritance is by primogeniture, in others, by ultimogeniture, elsewhere by a combination of the two. Inheritance of the father's house is commonly by ultimogeniture. Among the northern Chins, if there are sons by major wives, those by minor wives may not inherit except as they receive a settlement in their father's lifetime. [Hodson 1908: 76-77; Lehman 1963: 75-80, 109-10, 129; Parry 1932: 285-87; Shakespear 1912: 54.] **Divorce.** Reported to be easy, upon the initiative of either spouse. [Lehman 1963: 101, 109; Parry 1932: 29; Shakespear 1912: 52.]

SOCIOPOLITICAL ORGANIZATION. **Political organization.** The Meithei, alone of all Chin-speaking peoples, have a traditional state. The organization of Manipur, headed by a raja, seems to have been intimately connected with the military, and to have had a feudallike structure based upon personal service rather than upon territorial entities. Formal political institutions at the village level are largely absent among Burma's southern Chins. The wards within a village may in fact be at war with one another, and there are no regular village-wide political offices. There is usually one person in each settlement or ward who acts informally as leader in calling meet-

ings of lineage heads and household elders for judicial purposes and to make decisions concerning the cycle of agricultural work. Some northern Chins have chiefs and village headmen, others are governed by village councils and elected headmen. According to Lehman, the office of headman is hereditary in aristocratic sibs, and a chief is essentially a headman whose power in his own village derives from his connections and landholdings beyond his village. To the groups within the area of a chief's power, Lehman applies the term "realm." Realms cut across ethnic and linguistic lines and are generally unstable, subject as they are to the fortunes of war and intrigue. [Hodson 1908: 58-63; Lehman 1963: 89-90, 139-55; Parry 1932: 63-64, 70, 81, 88-89, 239-55; Shakespear 1912: 11, 22-26, 43-46.] **Social stratification.** Individual households among the southern Chins achieve differential status by the performance of ungraded feasts of merit. In the north, sibs are stratified into aristocratic and commoner. Although the distinction is fairly well-defined, both upward and downward mobility do occur. A wealthy commoner household may achieve aristocratic status by repeated marriages into higher ranked lineages. It cannot, however, thereby inherit the office of headman or chief. Similarly, an aristocratic son of a minor wife and his descendants may sink in the social system. Of two sets of children of equal paternal rank, those whose mother's rank is higher rank higher in the social system. The two ranks in traditional Chin society below the rank of commoner—bondsmen and slaves—were both abolished by the British. Slaves were war captives and their descendants. Bondsmen were in positions of debt and dependence vis-à-vis wealthy and powerful persons, brought about by the acceptance of food in time of emergency, money for the payment of ransoms or fines, or asylum from vengeful enemies. The Meithei apparently still have slaves, as well as a class of debtor-bondsmen. [Hodson 1908: 90; Lehman 1963: 74, 90, 108-21; Parry 1932: 222-27, 233, 245-56.] **Warfare.** Some hill Chins, e.g. the Lakher, seem to have been headhunters, regarding human heads as one of the motives for warfare. This was not true of most Chin groups, however, although heads were on occasion taken as an aftermath of a raid. The chief aims of Chin warfare seem to have been booty, slaves, and revenge. Wars were not prosecuted with any great vigor, although they sometimes continued for several years. Ambushes and raids, usually just before daylight, were favored and losses were generally slight. When first contacted by the British, Chin settlements were engaged in almost constant fighting among themselves and in raids on lowland Indians and Burmese. Although the Meithei had an organized military force, their conduct of warfare is believed to have been not much different from that of the hill Chins. [Hodson 1908: 93; Lehman 1963: 90, 186, 218-19; Parry 1932: 5-8, 63, 202-08; Shakespear 1912: 56-60.]

RELIGION. Major religions.

RELIGION. Major religions. The Meithei are Vaishnavite Hindus in the same sense, apparently, in which other Indianized peoples of Southeast Asia are Buddhists, i.e. it is possible historically to see in the popular religion elements of Hindu origin mingled with non-Hindu and presumably inherited pagan elements. Until now, Burmese Buddhism has failed significantly to attract hill Chins. Christianity has fared somewhat better. Large numbers of Lushai are Christian, but only slightly over one-fifth of the Chins in Burma are Christian, according to Lehman's estimate. In some areas, however, entire villages have been converted. Nativistic movements have appeared, for example the Pauchinhau, mentioned by Stevenson. [Hodson 1908: 103; Lehman 1963: 186, 219-20; Stevenson 1943: 199.] **Indigenous religion and supernaturals.** The indigenous religion is characterized by belief in a variety of spirits. There is an otiose creator, below whom is a spirit, or perhaps a class of spirits, who have human characteristics and are concerned with mankind. Another large class of spirits, sometimes termed malevolent, are said by Lehman to be regarded as capricious rather than malicious. Not all of these are known by name. Souls of the living and ghosts of the dead are called by the same word. There are local spirits, field spirits, house spirits, spirits concerned with village welfare, etc. Some are responsible for good fortune among men; others cause illness and misfortune. [Lehman 1963: 172-77; Shakespear 1912: 61-68; Stevenson 1943: 21.] **Practitioners.** The Meithei have shamans, apparently mostly women, who are mainly concerned with illness but also have something to do with rain. Heads of sibs are also priests in charge of annual ceremonies honoring the eponymous ancestor. The raja is considered the high priest of the entire country, but his priestly functions are exercised infrequently. Among the hill Chins, shamans, mostly women, determine while possessed the cause and cure of illness. They do not, however, conduct the curing sacrifice. Their status comes upon them involuntarily; they are not highly regarded even though they are socially necessary. Among some groups hereditary priests receive a portion of the sacrifice and are given an amount of agricultural labor each year by their fellow villagers. In return they conduct sacrifices on behalf of the entire community. In still other cases priests are appointed by a chief. These may also be seers, who determine the required sacrifice by feeling the patient's pulse, and also conduct the sacrificial ceremony. [Hodson 1908: 95, 109-10; Lehman 1963: 89, 175; Shakespear 1912: 46, 80-81, 110-11; Stevenson 1943: 20-21, 37, 83-84.] **Ceremonies.** The Meithei celebrate not only Vaishnavite, but also other Hindu festivals such as Dussera and Holi. What is apparently a non-Hindu ceremony takes place in mid-April, when a "name-giver," nominated by the shamans, is chosen for the ensuing year. Upon him will be the sins of the people, and his luck influences them all. The central act of hill Chin ceremonies is the sacrifice, the chief means of establishing relations with the supernatural. The sacrifice—usually a fowl or pig, or at the greater ceremonies, a mithan —is accompanied by ritual recitations, feasting, and sometimes dancing. Reasons for sacrificing include curing, maintenance of the game supply, and ensuring status in the afterlife. [Shakespear 1912; Stevenson 1943; Hodson 1908: 103-06; Lehman 1963: 179-82.] **Illness and medicine.** According to the Meithei, illness is the result of possession by a spirit. The shaman is the curer, employing some empirical knowledge. Hill Chins too attribute illness to malevolent spirits. Medical remedies are much less important than sacrifices. [Hodson 1908: 109, 151; Lehman 1963: 207; Parry 1932: 169; Shakespear 1912: 67.] **Soul, death, and afterlife.** Meithei funeral rites, including cremation, are Hindu, and are conducted by Brahmans. Some hill Chins conceive of the afterlife as a plain of heaven and a village of the dead. All ghosts go to the village of the dead. Admission to the plain of heaven is based upon achievements in feasts of merit and celebration during the deceased's lifetime; rank attained in life is maintained by the ghost. Some Chins cremate, but most seem to dispose of the dead by burial in a cemetery outside the village. Chin villages contain memorials to the dead, stone platforms and stone or wooden posts upon which the deceased's achievements in hunting and sacrifices are recorded. Those who die by accident, in childbirth, from dread disease, or by violence receive less ceremonious treatment and are buried apart. [Hodson 1908: 116-17; Lehman 1963: 183-93; Shakespear 1912: 84-86; Stevenson 1943: 21-22.]

BIBLIOGRAPHY. Grierson 1903-28; Hodson 1908; India 1931-34; India (Republic) 1952-57; Lehman 1963; Löffler 1959; Lorrain and Savidge 1898; Luce 1959b; Parry 1932; Scott 1921; Shafer 1955; Shakespear 1912; Shaw 1929; Stevenson 1943.

GAROS[3]

Synonyms. *A'chik, Mande*

ORIENTATION. Identification and location. The Garos, who also call themselves Mande (man) or A'chik (hill slope), are concentrated in the Garo Hills District, south and east of the bend of the Brahmaputra river (25°–26° N., 90°–91° E.). A few are also found in the neighboring districts of Assam, and in the Mymensing district of East Pakistan. Their hills generally range between 1,000 and 3,000 feet

[3] The author of this contribution, Robbins Burling, has based his summary of Garo culture on field work carried out in the Garo Hills between 1954 and 1956. He has written a monograph on the Garos (Burling 1963), which contains a four-page bibliography of works on Garo ethnography.

in elevation, and form the western extremity of the Shillong plateau. They are surrounded on all sides by the low-lying plains of Bengal and Assam, except on the east, where the District adjoins the Khasi Hills. **Neighbors and subgroups.** A few Nepalis have settled in the hills, and villages of "plains tribes"— Rabhas and Kacharis on the north, Koches and Hajongs on the west, as well as Bengalis and Assamese —are found on the borders. Otherwise Garo villages are little interspersed with those of other people. The Garos recognize a number of subgroups, based upon location, dialect, and a few minor cultural differences. The Abengs occupy the western third of the District, the Matchi and Dual are found in the center and east center respectively, and the Chisak and Akawe are located to the north. The Ruga are found in the south center, the Gara and Ganching east of the Ruga, and the Atong in the southeastern corner. Except for the Atong, differences among these subgroups are far less than those between the Garos and surrounding peoples. The Atong language, however, although it also belongs to the Bodo subgroup of Tibeto-Burman, is not mutually intelligible with Garo. **Geography.** The District is hilly, with only a few river valleys flat enough to permit wet-rice cultivation. It has a typical monsoon climate, with about 140 inches of rain each year, most of which falls between June and October. Since almost all the land is periodically cultivated, the characteristic vegetation is scrub forest. Monkeys, gibbons, jungle fowl, deer, bears, and elephants abound. **Linguistic and racial affiliation.** The Garos are distinguished both by language and by race from their neighbors in the surrounding plains. Racially they are quite Mongoloid, and their language belongs to the Bodo subgroup of Tibeto-Burman. **Demography.** The Garos total about 300,000. **History.** The Garos have long had market and headhunting relations with the surrounding plains people, but they were substantially independent until the British conquered the District in 1867. Since that time their hills have formed a district within Assam, first under the British and more recently as part of independent India. Since conquest, the Garos have been proselytized by Baptists and Roman Catholics, and at least a third now profess Christianity, the majority of whom are Baptists.

SETTLEMENT PATTERN AND HOUSING. **Villages.** The Garos live in clustered and essentially permanent villages of from 10 to 50 or 60 houses. Their land stretches out on all sides, and the boundaries between the territories of neighboring villages are carefully recognized. Traditional villages have a bachelors' house where the unmarried boys sleep, and Christian villages usually have a church. **Houses.** Rectangular, from 25 to 80 feet long, but rarely more than 15 feet wide. Floors and walls are of split bamboo, hung on a bamboo frame which rests upon wooden posts. The roof is gabled, and made of

thatch. All houses have a large central room for cooking, entertaining, and general use. The larger houses also have a sleeping room partitioned off in the rear, and a separate room for cattle in the front. Most have separate granaries, small pigsties, and woodsheds. Each family builds a smaller and temporary house in its fields.

ECONOMY. **Agriculture.** A new section of the village land is distributed among the households of the village each year. Traditionally, almost all subsistence is derived from the swidden cultivation of these fields. The primary staple is dry rice supplemented by millet, and to a lesser extent by maize, manioc, and taro. Squash, large-pod beans, sorrel, bananas, papaya, gourds, and many other vegetables are grown in smaller amounts. Cotton, chili peppers, ginger, and in some places oranges, areca nuts, and pineapples are important cash crops. Beer is brewed in considerable quantities from rice or other grain. Men clear the forest and burn their patches in March or April. Men and women plant immediately, and both share in the cultivation and harvest. Fields are usually used for two years and then abandoned. In a few low, wet areas, paddy rice has been grown in recent decades. **Fishing, hunting, and gathering.** Nets, poison, and traps are used for fishing. Occasionally a jungle fowl or deer is shot. Bamboo shoots and a few other wild crops supplement agriculture to a small degree. **Animal husbandry.** Cattle, pigs, and chickens are kept, to be eaten following an animal sacrifice. **Crafts.** The Garos continue to plait their traditional and beautiful bamboo baskets, but the weaving, metal work, and pottery making which were formerly practiced are now virtually lost. Dugout canoes are built only in the southeastern part of the District. **Markets.** Market places are now distributed along all the roads in the District, and a weekly market is held at each. Cash crops are carried from the village to market and sold to traders from the plains. Other traders sell cloth, pottery, iron blades for tools, dried fish, salt, tobacco, and knickknacks. Garos would feel completely helpless without these markets.

KIN GROUPS. **Descent and consanguineal kin groups.** Every Garo is a member of one of five named exogamous matrilineal phratries, but two of these are limited to a small area and a third to less than half the District. Each of the larger phratries is divided into dozens of named matrilineal sibs, most of which are restricted to one section of the Hills. Each village typically includes members of up to a halfdozen sibs. The sibs are in turn divided into unnamed lineages. **Localized kin groups.** Each village is built around either one or two matrilineal lineages. Most of the women of these lineages (together with their husbands) live in the village, and a few of the men (with their wives) live there as well. One household ..is always considered the most senior of the lineage, in that all the other households of the lineage are believed to have branched out from it when the non-heiress daughters left to marry. The man of the senior household is also considered the main village headman. His duties, however, are primarily ceremonial rather than directive. **Kinship terminology.** Broadly speaking, kinship terminology is bifurcate merging.

MARRIAGE AND FAMILY. **Marriage.** Each married couple chooses one daughter (often but not always the youngest) as "heiress" (*nokna*), and arranges her marriage with one of her father's classificatory sister's sons. This man, the "heir" (*nokrom*), moves into the household of his wife and participates in all its activities. The heir and heiress are obliged to care for the girl's parents when they grow old, and they inherit all the property of the older couple. A couple with no daughters must adopt a younger matrilineal lineage mate of the wife, usually her sister's daughter, as heiress. All other girls may choose their own husbands so long as they observe phratry exogamy; and soon after marriage they set up a new and separate household, usually in the girl's village, but occasionally in the boy's. The household of the heir and heiress is always considered senior to those of other daughters. The girl or her family is expected to choose the husband, and marriage is by bridegroom capture. The boy may not know of an impending proposal until he is forcefully captured by the girl's male relatives, although he has the right to decline the match. No gifts or bride service accompany marriage, but gifts are made to a man's original household at the time of his death. **Domestic unit.** The household consists of a stem family, including at most a married couple together with one married daughter and her husband, and the unmarried children of both couples. **Divorce and remarriage.** Anyone may demand a divorce, but the matrilineal kinsmen of the instigator (whether husband or wife) must pay a compensation to the kinsmen of the abandoned spouse. Those who have been divorced or widowed usually remarry, although a younger girl is considered more desirable than a woman who has had children. Unless such a woman marries an older man, her new husband is always promised her daughter as a second wife. If she has no daughter a younger lineage mate is adopted. Thus a man may be simultaneously married to a mother and her daughter, virtually the only form of Garo polygyny.

SOCIOPOLITICAL ORGANIZATION. **Traditional authorities.** Wealthy men are respected, and their informal guidance in village matters is accepted by others. In family affairs such as divorce, inheritance, or disputes over adultery, the older men of the lineage are expected to discipline younger members. In any public trial, a guilty person is punished by his lineage seniors, but lineage members are also expected to contribute to any monetary compensation he may incur. If in pre-British times any institutions surpassed the village, none have survived. **Imposed authority.** The British instituted a system of local magistrates, each with jurisdiction over 20 or more villages. Today these men preside at all but the pettiest of trials. They are expected to make decisions in accordance with Garo custom, and they must rely upon the lineage to carry out their judgments, but their decisions are backed by the power of the government, and may be appealed to the district courts. The British established a district government, administered by a deputy commissioner. This office still continues, but since independence it has been supplemented by an elected district council with jurisdiction over customary law and other local matters. **Warfare and headhunting.** Before the British conquest, the Garos enthusiastically took each other's heads and sometimes those of neighboring plains people as well, but headhunting has been gone for almost a century.

RELIGION. **Supernaturals.** The Garo world is populated by innumerable and invisible spirits who live in the jungle, along roads, and in streams, and who may cause disease by biting people. The more august gods who created the world and have jurisdiction over agriculture must be supplicated at periodic festivals. **Practitioners.** All Garo men (except Christians) can perform some sacrifices to cure disease. Some men are more skilled than others, but no one specializes predominantly in curing. The headman of the village performs periodic village rituals. **Major ceremonies.** Village-wide ceremonies and festivals are held after cutting the jungle, after burning the fields, before planting rice, at several times during the growing season, and at the time of the harvest. Ceremonies include an animal sacrifice, which is followed by feasting, dancing, the drinking of rice beer, and the beating of gongs and drums. **Treatment of disease.** Illness must be cured by encouraging the departure of the spirit who caused it. For this, animals are sacrificed, and blood, rice, and rice beer are offered at a specially-built altar. More rarely, herbs are collected from the jungle and administered as medicine. Quinine, penicillin, and other modern medicines are becoming increasingly popular. **Soul, death, and afterlife.** After death the body is cremated and the soul journeys to an afterworld. Eventually, however, the soul is expected to be reborn into this world. Souls of people who die unnatural deaths may haunt those still living.

BIBLIOGRAPHY. Burling 1963.

KAREN

KAREN SPEAKERS, TOTALING CLOSE TO one and a half million, are, next to the Miao and Lolo, the largest of the so-called "hill tribes" within the area covered by the present volume. The linguistic position of the Karen languages is still somewhat uncertain. In a recent classification of Sino-Tibetan, Shafer (1955) places Karen within a separate major division (Karenic), indicating a rather distant relationship to those languages usually classified as Tibeto-Burman—Jinghpaw, Chin, Moso, Lolo, Lisu, etc.—most of which are placed by Shafer within a separate Burmic division. Others, e.g. Luce (1959a), apparently see a closer relationship to the Tibeto-Burman group of languages.

KARENS

Synonyms. *Kareang, Kariang, Karieng, Kayin, Yang*

ORIENTATION. **Identification.** The English word Karen and its equivalents in Burmese, Siamese, and Shan refer to a number of populations in Burma and Thailand speaking fairly closely related yet different languages. The many names in the literature are due to at least three factors: (1) Populations of Karen speakers differ not only linguistically but also with respect to religion, economy, and such obvious criteria as details of dress. (2) Many small groups are known mainly from turn-of-the-century sources which are inadequate, incomplete, and studded with synonyms often of uncertain reference in a variety of transcriptions. (3) Burmese, Siamese, Shan, and to a lesser extent English all apply the term Karen or its equivalent to small groups of Mon-Khmer speakers located in the Shan State, who are quite different linguistically yet show a general cultural similarity to Karens. Thus in Shan the Yang Lam (Black Yang) and Yang Hsek, linguistically close to the Mon-Khmer-speaking Wa, are called by the Tai generic term for Karens, Yang. On the other hand, groups known in Shan as the Yang Leng (Red Yang) and Yang Hpök (White Yang) are, linguistically speaking, Karens. ● The major Karen groups are the Sgaw (who call themselves Kanyaw), the Pwo, the Pa-O, and the Kayah. The Burmese generic term, equivalent to the English word Karen, is Kayin. Like Karen, it refers in practice mainly to the two large plains-dwelling groups, Sgaw and Pwo. The Burmese usually refer to the Pa-O as Taungthu (as a common noun meaning "hillman"), and originally referred to the Kayah as Kayin-ni (Red Karen), whence the English Karen-ni or Red Karens. Since 1948 the desire of the Burmese and Kayah to distinguish the latter from other Karens, and the associated implications of rebellion, has led

to the use in Burmese of Kaya, usually romanized as Kayah or sometimes as Kayar. The Burmese distinguish between Sgaw and Pwo by the names Bama Kayin (Burmese Karen) and Talaing Kayin (Mon Karen). The Mons know the Karens as Kareang and make a distinction between Sgaw and Pwo similar to that made in Burmese. The Shans, when referring to the Karens, use the Tai generic term, Yang. This term is also commonly used by the Siamese, along with Kariang (Karieng). For the Pa-O the Shans have borrowed the Burmese name, Taungthu, pronouncing it Tong-su. Judging by Young's account, Siamese discrimination is uncertain; they are reported to call all their Karens by the term Yang Daeng (Red Karens) and at the same time to use Yang Khao (White Karens) for the Sgaw. [Cushing 1914: 526; Jones 1961: 61; McFarland 1941: 81-82 s.v. *kariang*; Shorto 1962: 70; Young 1961: 92, 101, 105.] **Minor groups.** Luce recently offered a classification of most of the Karen languages listed in the census of 1931: Paku (close to Sgaw); Western Bwe, consisting of Blimaw (apparently the Brek of the census and the Bre of J. G. Scott) and Geba (the Karenbyu, or White Karens, of the census); Padaung; Gek'o (written Gheko in the census and elsewhere); and Yinbaw. For Luce, the Kayah are Eastern Bwe, written Bghai or Bghe by some authors. The census lists three groups which are not considered by Luce: Monnepwa (Mawnepgha), Zayein, and Talaing-Kalasi, and enters two additional groups as mere names without figures, Wewaw and Mopwa (Mopgha). Some older classifications divide the Karens into two groups, the White (lowland Sgaw and Pwo) and the Red (all remaining Karens). Additional names scattered in the literature include: Kekaungdu (self-reference of the Padaung, according to J. G. Scott), Keku (presumably Luce's Gek'o), Lakü (self-reference of the Brek, according to J. G. Scott), Manö (a Brek group), Manu-Manaw (Burmese for the Brek), Yangtalai (Shan for the Burmese Yintale), Sawngtung (known to the Burmese as Gaungto), Sin-

sin, Kawnsawng, Mepu, and Mepauk. The census of 1911 also lists Karennet (Kayin-net or Black Karens in Burmese). Information on many of these names is entirely inadequate for purposes of identification. All refer to minor groups, none of which in 1931 exceeded 17,000 in population. They inhabit the Kayah State, the northern Karen State, the Shan state of Loi Long, and the adjoining part of Burma proper. [India 1912: 9, Pt. I, 206, 214, 275-76; Luce 1959a: 3-4; Scott 1932.] **Location.** Karens are found in Burma in the Irrawaddy and Sittang valleys from the coast to about 19° N., and in the entire length of Tenasserim from 10° N. up through the hills along the Thailand border into the Shan plateau as far as 21° N. The majority are in the central Irrawaddy delta and in the northern end of Tenasserim at the head of the Gulf of Martaban. In Thailand they occur along the Burma border from about 12° N., extending north and east to the Mekong, approximately 20° 30′ N. The greatest concentration is along the western boundary south of 20° N. [Musgrave 1956; Young 1961: 92, 101, 105.] **Geography.** Karen settlements occur in three distinct physiographic regions: the low, relatively flat plains of the Irrawaddy, Sittang, and Salween deltas and the coast of Tenasserim; the Pegu range, a hilly region of steep slopes and narrow valleys lying between the Irrawaddy and Sittang south of 19° N.; and the Shan upland which in the north (in the Shan State) is a rolling plateau averaging 3,000 feet, and in the south (in the Kayah and Karen States and in interior Tenasserim), a country of narrow valleys separated by long parallel hills running from north to south. The climate is tropical monsoon, precipitation ranging from over 100 inches in the central Irrawaddy delta to over 200 inches in Tenasserim. In the southwestern Shan State rainfall is less than 80 inches annually. The deltas are largely covered by ricelands, whereas the Pegu range and the Tenasserim and Karen State hills are forested. The Pa-O area in the southern Shan State is more open forest and downland. [Huke 1956a: 70-81.] **Linguistic affiliation.** Although the Karen group of languages is usually placed within the Sino-Tibetan stock, its position therein has remained in doubt. Shafer (1955: 107-08) would assign them to a Karenic division of Sino-Tibetan. A recent judgment by Luce is that Karen is most closely affiliated with the Tibeto-Burman languages, although there are a number of words in the basic vocabulary of as yet undetermined origin. Much work remains to be done on the relationships among Karen languages, but it now seems clear that Pwo and Pa-O form one subgroup, and Sgaw and some of the languages of the eastern hills another. [Luce 1959a; Jones 1961: passim.] **Demography.** Young's recent estimates for Thailand yield a calculation of about 72,000 Karens, almost three-quarters of them Sgaw, the rest mostly Pwo. The census of 1931 remains the most recent reliable source for the number of Karens in Burma. At that time there were slightly over 1,340,000 speakers of Karen languages. Of these, about 500,000 were Sgaw, 473,000 Pwo, 223,000 Pa-O, and 32,000 Kayah. The Pwo, largely plains dwellers, were concentrated in the Irrawaddy delta and northern Tenasserim. The Sgaw were more widely and evenly distributed, throughout the Irrawaddy delta area, Tenasserim, the Pegu range between the Irrawaddy and Sittang, and the eastern hills. The Pa-O were in the southwestern portion of what is now the Shan State, as well as east of the Gulf of Martaban in Tenasserim. The Kayah State was the homeland of most of the Kayah. [Young 1961; Musgrave 1956.] **History and cultural relations.** Karen history prior to the nineteenth century is largely a matter of conjecture. The word Karyan (possibly Karen) occurs in an inscription near Pagan of about 1238 A.D. The word Cakraw, which Luce is tempted to identify with the modern name Sgaw, appears at about the same period. If the Cakraw were Karens, then they were in central Burma as early as the thirteenth century. Beginning in the early nineteenth century, the Karens became known through British colonial records and accounts by travelers and missionaries. The activities of the latter, begun in Tenasserim after 1825 and later extended to the delta and the eastern hills, included the opening of schools, creation of writing systems for Sgaw, Pwo, and some other languages, and publishing. There gradually arose a Karen elite of teachers, doctors, clergy, and lower-grade officials, and with it some notion of Karen nationality in the European sense. The outstanding political events in Karen life since Burma's independence in 1948 have been the reconstitution of the old Karen-ni states as the Kayah State, the relative prominence of a number of Karens in the civil war which began in 1948 and is not yet wholly liquidated, and the formation in 1952 of a Karen State along the Thailand border between 15° and 20° N. The Karen State, set up in response to Karen demands, includes townships with Karen majorities, although the state itself is inhabited by a minority of the Karens in Burma. ● Although discussions of Karen history tend to emphasize the importance of acculturation due to missionary activity, the majority of Karens seem to have been subject to considerable Burmese and Shan influence. In 1931, for example, almost three-quarters of the concentrated Karen population in the deltas of the Irrawaddy, Sittang, and Salween were speakers of Burmese, and the majority were Buddhists. It is a reasonable assumption that the culture of the Buddhist Pwo and Sgaw in these plains areas is similar to that of their Burmese and Mon neighbors. [Cady 1956; Luce 1959a; Musgrave 1956: 561-62.]

SETTLEMENT PATTERN AND HOUSING. **Settlement pattern.** Karens live in compact villages. These were formerly surrounded by stockades, a pattern still practiced in some places. The main structures are houses and granaries, although the latter are sometimes located along trails at some distance from the village. Young reports an average of 25 houses for Karen settlements in Thailand, a figure which also approximates the number of families reported for hill Karen villages in Burma. [Marshall 1922: 56, 82, 159; Young 1961: 95, 101.] **Housing.** Plains Karens live in Burmese-style houses. The houses of valley villages in Thailand are quite substantial, set on wooden posts, with plank floors and walls. Hilltop houses are less substantial, with bamboo the preferred material. Roofs in both cases are of grass or leaf thatch. The traditional dwelling of the hill Karens of Burma, still not wholly replaced, is the longhouse. Here an entire settlement of 20 to 30 households occupies a single structure composed of apartments opening on a central corridor, each with its veranda on the outer side. In addition to family quarters, each longhouse is equipped with a *blaw*, a combination bachelors' room and room for guests. A longhouse is customarily rebuilt annually in a different location. All Karen houses, whether in Burma or Thailand, are raised above the ground, the longhouses to a height of five or six feet. [Marshall 1922: 56-65; Young 1961: 94-95.]

ECONOMY. **Agriculture.** The majority of Karens, i.e. those dwelling in the plains, are wet-rice agriculturists. Rice culture presumably differs little from that of the Burmese and Mons. Karens of the forested hills practice swidden agriculture, each village claiming a recognized area within which the individual farmer selects his plot—partly by means of divination. Rice is harvested in October and November and after threshing is stored in granaries. Swiddens are also planted to legumes, cucurbits, yams, sweet potatoes, peppers, chilies, and cotton. Valley bottom lands produce tobacco, bananas, citrus and other fruits, and sugar cane. [Marshall 1922: 75-95.] **Fishing and hunting.** The plains Karens fish in ways similar to those of their Burmese neighbors. In the hills fishing gear includes nets, baskets, traps, jars, weirs, hook and line, spears, and poison. Hunting, although carried on primarily for food, is also a favorite pastime. Most popular are group drives in which game is enmeshed in nets and dispatched with spears and crossbows. Hunters also pursue game individually, sometimes accompanied by dogs that are specially bred and trained. Animals most commonly taken are deer and wild pigs, although the total list includes a wide variety of birds and animals, the latter ranging from rabbits to elephants. Weapons include guns, blow guns, crossbows, spears, snares, birdlime, spring traps, box traps, and pitfalls. [Marshall 1922: 96-107.] **Gathering.** Herbs, leaves, and wild fruits are sought for food. Stick-lac, honey, beeswax, cardamoms, and ivory are among the products gathered for trading purposes. [Marshall 1922: 86.] **Domestic animals.** Practically all hill Karens keep pigs, dogs, and fowl.

In addition the Paku specialize in raising cattle as pack animals, and the Kayah breed horses. Karens are noted for their ability to handle elephants, which they catch and train themselves; most mahouts in Burma are Karens. Those of the plains Karens who are Buddhists keep cattle and buffalo; Christians also keep pigs, since they have no objection to slaughtering these animals. [Marshall 1922: 64-65, 86-87.] **Food and stimulants.** The main dish is boiled rice, eaten with boiled vegetables or with a kind of curry—a meat stew with some oil and spices. Meat and fish may also be roasted or baked in a pit. Fried food is reportedly popular among plainsmen. In addition to such foods as pork, venison, duck, and pigeon, the Karens are reliably reported to eat a wide variety of mammals, birds, fish, mollusks, and insects, thus bearing out the Burmese notion that the Karens are indiscriminant eaters. Glutinous rice, steamed or boiled, is eaten on special occasions or as a confection. Dairy products are not consumed. Beverages include tea, fermented alcoholic drinks made from ordinary and glutinous rice as well as the juice from certain varieties of palms, and a distilled drink prepared from rice. Betel is widely used, and tobacco is smoked in pipes and as cigars from an early age by both sexes. Some use of opium by men is reported for Thailand, and its use by men is also cited in the late nineteenth century in territory north of the present Karen State. [Fea 1896: 314; Marshall 1922: 66-74; Young 1961: 97.] **Industrial arts.** Cotton is ginned, whipped, spun on a wheel, dyed, and woven at home. Hill Karens use a belt loom, but those on the plains use the Burmese fixed frame loom. Mats and baskets are made from rattan and bamboo, and baskets may be rendered watertight with gum and lacquer. Earthenware cooking and eating utensils are apparently obtained in markets. [Marshall 1922: 67, 70, 108-14.] **Trade.** Hill Karens have never been noted as traders. Traditionally, however, they have traded or sold to the Burmese and Mons cotton cloth, forest products, game, and the flesh of domestic animals in exchange for rice, pottery, salt, and fish paste. Recent information on the Karens of Thailand emphasizes the importance of trade in the economy of Karen communities, even in respect to food. Trade is carried on mainly by itinerant Burmese and Shan merchants and, in some areas, by Indians and Chinese. In addition, hill Karens frequent markets in Burmese, Shan, and Siamese towns. Bronze drums, obtained from the Shans, are said to be highly valued among the Karens. [Marshall 1922: 115-26; Young 1961: 97-98.] **Division of labor.** Men hunt, plow, build houses, cut timber, and make mats and baskets. Women fetch water and firewood, prepare rice for cooking, prepare alcoholic drinks, raise cotton, spin, and weave. Sowing, reaping, threshing, winnowing, and fishing may be done by either sex. Although women do most of the cooking, men also assist. [Marshall 1922: passim.] **Land tenure.** Land in the hills appears to be primarily the property of the village community, the members being free to use what they need provided only that they select plots within swiddens designated by the village chief and elders. [Marshall 1922: 76, 129.]

KIN GROUPS.

Descent. Probably bilateral. **Kin groups.** Marshall (1922: 254-61) describes a group of matrilineally-related persons participating in certain feasts for ancestral spirits. The leader is the oldest living female of the line; all of her female and male descendants are expected to attend, lest they be thought malicious. No person not matrilineally related may participate. **Kin terminology.** The following Sgaw terms are reported by Marshall (1922: 135):

Fa	*pa*	
Mo	*mo*	
PaBr	*hpa hti*	
PaSi	*mü ga*	
ElSb	*weh*	(Sex is indicated by suffixing *hpo hkwa* for males and *hpo mü* for females.)
YoSb	*pü*	
Cousin	*t'hkwa*	(*Weh* and *pü* are often used for cousins related through PaSb who are older or younger, respectively, than Pa.)

MARRIAGE AND FAMILY.

Mode. Young people meet on occasions such as weddings and funerals, and a young man will normally suggest a girl to his parents. Having obtained parental approval, arrangements are made by a go-between. Small gifts are given by the bridegroom to male relatives of the bride, and the marriage is solemnized at a wedding feast. [Marshall 1922: 134, 139, 176-92; Young 1961: 99.] **Form.** Monogamous marriages are the rule (Marshall 1922: 134). **Extension of incest taboos.** There appear to be no preferential marriages. It is said that while marriage of first cousins is rare, that of second and third cousins is not. Whether both spouses are members of the same village is a matter of indifference, but the linguistic or dialect groups tend to be endogamous. [Marshall 1922: 176; Young 1961: 99, 104, 107.] **Residence.** Usually matrilocal (Marshall 1922: 190). **Domestic unit.** The normal domestic unit is the nuclear family, which among the hill Karens occupies an apartment in a longhouse. **Inheritance.** Property tends to be shared equally among all the children, a slightly larger portion going to the eldest. During her lifetime, a widow retains control of the property, but this control ends upon her remarriage. [Marshall 1922: 150.] **Divorce.** Permitted upon payment of a penalty to the divorced spouse. May be initiated by either partner. [Marshall 1922: 148, 191-92.] **Concubinage.** Unrecognized and unformalized sexual liaisons occur (Marshall 1922: 134).

SOCIOPOLITICAL ORGANIZATION.

Political organization. Most Karens have lived for years under the nominal authority of other peoples: Burmese, Mons, Shans, Siamese, or British. The degree of effective control by such overlords has varied considerably and is even today quite limited in some areas. In the southwestern Shan State and the Kayah State, where Shan culture is influential, there have been states modeled on Shan political organization but headed by rulers of Karen ancestry. The important political unit among all Karens, however, is the village, headed by a chief with the assistance of a council of elders. Chieftainship is hereditary in the male lineal or collateral line. In the event that an heir is lacking, the elders elect a new chief. A chief who displeases too many of his villagers may be deserted by the dissatisfied, who emigrate to found a new settlement. The chiefly role requires leadership in certain religious rites, and the chief's approval was formerly necessary for the conduct of an armed raid. Chief and elders together have certain judicial functions. The virtual autonomy of Karen village communities appears to have been limited somewhat by the institution of ritual brotherhood. As reported in the mid-nineteenth century, formal bonds were thereby created between men in different communities, assuring hospitality when traveling and intelligence when planning raids. [Marshall 1922: 127-29, 137, 143; Scott 1921: 481-93.] **Social stratification.** Wealth and age are the determinants of status within Karen communities. Occupation is of little importance, since all are agriculturists, including the chief, who receives no form of tribute. Wealth is counted mainly in horned cattle and bronze drums, but it is unclear how these are accumulated. Slaves, captives taken in raids on villages of Karens and other peoples, existed in pre-British days. Many were redeemed by their own people, others were sold to Shans, Burmese, and other Karens. Those kept in the villages of their captors were treated as household members and ultimately assimilated into the community. [Marshall 1922: 129-30, 141-42.] **Warfare.** Intervillage raids were common before British intervention. They were chiefly affairs of private vengeance sanctioned by the community. The aggrieved party, having obtained the chief's approval, organized (but did not necessarily lead) a party of volunteers. The latter often (but not always) disclaimed the rights of their families to indemnity in case of death. The raid was undertaken before dawn. The inhabitants of the offender's village were either killed or captured, according to the orders of the organizer of the foray. Plunder was shared among the raiders or used as indemnity for the slain. Such raids did not necessarily result in long-lasting feuds; they were usually followed by a peacemaking ceremony and negotiations by the losing village to redeem its captured. Equipment included spears, swords, guns, and shields. Trophies were taken from the slain, but it is not certain that the Karens were ever headhunters. [Marshall 1922: 152-60.]

RELIGION. **Major religions.** Returns from the 1931 census (India 1931-34: *11*, Pt. II, 244) indicate that three decades ago the majority of Karens in Burma were Buddhists. Among the three major Karen groups, the percentages of Buddhists were: Sgaw, 67 per cent; Pwo, 93 per cent; and Pa-O, almost 100 per cent. One-quarter of the Sgaw were Christian (largely Baptist) and 8 per cent were pagans. The only predominantly pagan Karens were the Kayah. The numerically small groups in the hills between the Sittang and the Siamese border were predominantly Christian (Baptist, Roman Catholic, and Anglican). Pwo and Sgaw Buddhists follow the Burmese tradition, while the Pa-O are closer to the Buddhism of the Shans. According to Young (1961: 93-94, 101, 106), most Karens in Thailand are probably Buddhist, with small numbers of pagans and Christians. **Indigenous religion.** Marshall describes Karen indigenous religion as ethnic or tribal in character, centering on belief in spirits and impersonal power, and employing practices of supplication, propitiation, and manipulation. Organized religious movements inspired by prophets and apparently of a nativistic character have been reported among various Karen groups since the first European contact. These have been syncretistic, combining in various degrees indigenous, Buddhist, and Christian elements. [Marshall 1922: 210-11, 264-65.] **Supernaturals.** There is no wholly precise and systematic account of Karen supernaturals. Belief in an otiose creator has inspired a certain messianic content in Karen religion, with the result that the early missionaries and their Karen colleagues were greatly concerned with problems of diffusion of religious notions from the Mediterranean. This was enhanced by the name of the creator, Yawa, suggesting Yahweh. Supernaturals include local or nature deities with human characteristics, who exercise some control over human events, and ghosts of those who died of disease or violence, or by accident, or who had lived evil lives. Certain ancestral spirits are important in the functioning of matrilineages. There is, finally, a class of heterogeneous spirits, largely malevolent. [Marshall 1922: 210-33.] **Practitioners.** Religious practitioners with ascribed status include the village chief, who leads in the propitiation of local and nature spirits, and the eldest woman in a matrilineal kin group, who presides at ritual offerings to the ancestral spirits. Those with achieved status include the shaman-sorcerer and the medical practitioner. The former practices divination when possessed by a spirit, conducts certain ceremonies, and may engage in maleficent magic. The latter uses drugs and magic to treat illness. [Marshall 1922: 234-61, 270, 274-75.] **Ceremonies.** Various stages in the agricultural cycle are marked by propitiatory rites. Birth and death require appropriate ceremonies, and virtually all therapy requires ritual approaches to the supernatural. Ceremonies conducted for the welfare of the entire community tend to be cyclical and fixed. **Illness and medicine.** The ultimate cause of illness, accident, and death is spiritual. These untoward occurrences result from attacks by spirits upon the vital principle, absence of the vital principle from the body, or victory of a seven-fold spirit which is in constant struggle with the personality. Remedies of vegetable and animal origin are used, but the greatest therapeutic reliance is placed upon rites intended to remove the influence of maleficent spirits or to recover an errant or seduced vital principle and fix it in its proper body. [Marshall 1922: 193, 218-21, 234-47, 270, 275-78.] **Soul, death, and afterlife.** There appear to be at least four concepts of the soul: (1) The *tha*, a sort of conscience, is said to have a personality which persists after death. (2) The living body is thought to be animated by a vital principle, existing before birth and surviving after death. It can leave the body, causing illness or death, and it can, as a ghost, assume the form of its proper body or possess the body of another. (3) The sevenfold *kala* is a lifelong inhabitant of the human body, yet seeks to cause its death. Animals and inanimate objects are also possessed of *kala*, or perhaps by emanations of their owner's *kala*, since at death a person's possessions are destroyed to remove his *kala* from the village. (4) The *so*, or personality, is not well described except that it is in opposition to the seven-fold *kala*. The Karens have a vague notion of a localized afterlife, the destination of the *kala*, provided death was not caused by accident, violence, or dread disease. Eventually the *kala* is reincarnated. ● Disposal of the dead is by burial in a mat or coffin, and associated funeral rites are mainly to ensure that the deceased's *kala* will absent itself from the community of the living. The corpse is taken out of the house through a special opening. On returning from the burial ground, the villagers erect obstacles so that the deceased's *kala* cannot follow. [Marshall 1922: 193-209, 218-22.]

BIBLIOGRAPHY. Cady 1956; Cushing 1914; Fea 1896; Huke 1956a; India 1912, 1931-34; Jones 1961; Luce 1959a; McFarland 1941; Marshall 1922; Musgrave 1956; Scott 1921, 1932; Shafer 1955; Shorto 1962; Young 1961.

MIAO-YAO

IN A RECENT STATEMENT on the linguistic position of Miao and Yao, Downer (1961) says that Yao constitutes a clearly differentiated branch of the Miao-Yao language family. The close connection of the two is, however, apparent. Downer emphasizes that no affiliation of Miao-Yao with Tibeto-Burman, Chinese, Tai, or Mon-Khmer languages has as yet been convincingly demonstrated. Some linguists, e.g. Greenberg, class Miao-Yao tentatively as a separate branch of Sino-Tibetan. **Miao.** There has been much speculation, but little factual information, concerning the origins, history, and ancient migrations of the Miao (cf. Savina 1930). The name itself has been given a variety of interpretations; according to Ruey, it means, literally, "rice-shoot." In northern Southeast Asia Miao speakers are called Meo, which, according to Embree and Thomas, is derived from the Vietnamese term Man Meo. The term Man, in turn, was used in early Chinese dynastic histories to refer to all non-Han peoples (except Tai) in southern China; its later, narrower meaning has encompassed only peoples now called Yao. The total of all Miao speakers is probably in the neighborhood of 2,700,000, including a Chinese People's Republic 1953 census figure of 2,500,000 for China, an estimate for Indochina of about 100,000 (although Communist North Vietnamese figures are much higher), and a conservative estimate of 45,000 for Thailand. Although not the most numerous, the Miao (Meo) are the most widespread of all the non-Chinese minority groups originating in southern China. They are found today not only in Kweichow and neighboring provinces, but also in North Vietnam, Laos, and northern Thailand. They have a long history of migration under pressure from the Chinese; the rate of such migratory movement is suggested by Credner's estimate of 380 kilometers in forty years for the southward movement of Miao in western Thailand (1935a: 139-40). They are now practically everywhere broken up into isolated, swidden-farming groups hidden away in the more remote mountain valleys and hillsides. Fragmentation plus a wide variety of contacts with other groups may account for statements such as that of Eberhard that there is no uniform Miao culture—that it is rather a mixture or aggregate of Tai, Yao, Lolo, Chinese, etc. (cited in deBeauclair 1960: 165-67). In effect the various Miao populations in southern China and northern Southeast Asia exist as small cultural islands, surrounded by peoples of other ethnic background—most noticeably the lowland wet-rice-growing Chinese and Tai. If, as Bernatzik contends, the Miao live in the mountains because they are unable to acclimate to lower altitudes, such isolation has helped to maintain their cultural identity, since if they were to come down into the lowlands to live they would soon undergo cultural absorption at the hands of the Tai and Chinese (Bernatzik 1947: 501-02). • The Miao were apparently recognized by the Chinese as an ethnically distinct people early in the pre-Han period, when they appeared on the lower middle Yangtze. Increasing in number and attracted by the greater fertility of the Yellow river valley, they began moving northward. With the expansion of the Han Chinese southward, the Miao retreated into the area of Kwangtung-Hunan-Kwangsi, and finally into Kweichow —where they were first reported in early Yuan dynasty times. [Wu and Ch'en 1942: 1-2; deBeauclair 1960: 129; Wiens 1954: 88-91.] For the past five or six hundred years the Miao of Hunan-Kweichow have been under constant pressure from the Chinese. Miao uprisings have been frequent, e.g. those against the Manchus in 1735-40, 1795-1806, and 1854-71. The last of the independent Miao disappeared about 1870. However, as late as 1941-43 the Kuomintang government was forbidding the use of the Miao language, and suppressing the wearing of Miao costume (Gjessing 1956: 47). Despite centuries of oppression and disruption, the Miao continue to demonstrate a love of independence and an ability to organize for military action. Epic tales are handed down, perpetuated by traditional singers, of uprisings against the Chinese and of Miao heroism in battle. Most observers agree that the Miao are remarkable among all the hill tribes of Southeast Asia for their strong sense of independence, demonstrated organizational ability, enterprise and initiative, and adaptability. In Thailand they are among the most advanced and prosperous of all the hill tribes, and in Laos the Meo of the Xieng Khouang area have attained a measure of political recognition under their leader, Touby Lyfoung. **Yao.** Fortune regards the Yao (known in Indochina as Man) as remnants of a less civilized branch of the same stock from which the Chinese also sprang. The Chinese sources examined by Wiens generally agree that the Yao are among the original inhabitants of the south China area, apparently originating in the mountainous east coast provinces and subsequently spreading west and south. The total of recognized Yao speakers is probably in the neighborhood of 800,000, including a figure of 660,000 in mainland China according to the 1953 Chinese People's Republic census, an estimated 125,000 in Vietnam and Laos, some 10,000 in northern Thailand, and 6,000 "Miao" on Hainan who are now recognized as very probably speakers of Yao dialects. According to Fortune, all that is known historically is that the Yao were driven south from what is now Hunan province in the twelfth and early thirteenth centuries, retreating into the mountains that fringe the basin of the Hsi Chiang. Subsequently the Yao have been dispersed widely in southern China, Hainan, Indochina, and northern Thailand. These widely dispersed groups have developed along different lines, depending on external influences. At various times and places the Yao have been in contact with Hakka Chinese, Cantonese, northern Chinese immigrants into Kwangsi and Yunnan, as well as Miao, Lolo, and Tai peoples. Their wide dispersal has meant also that they have been subjected to differences in climate and vegetation. Thus there are Yao in Kwangtung who are permanently settled wet-rice agriculturists living in a kind of symbiotic relationship with surrounding Han Chinese lowlanders, whereas in northern Southeast Asia most Yao are migratory swidden farmers who by and large remain at relatively high altitudes. This widespread fragmentation of Yao groups, with accompanying differences in historical contacts and environmental influences and the resultant cultural variation, accounts for the fact that since early times Chinese chronicles and gazetteers have reported a great number of named Yao "tribes," and that in Vietnam and Laos, likewise, there are a great many tribal names recorded in the literature. ● Despite their dispersal over large areas of southern China and northern Southeast Asia, the Yao have retained a considerable degree of linguistic homogeneity. Ling and Ruey (1947), for example, mention the marked cultural and linguistic similarity between the Yao of Kwangsi and the Yao (or Man) of northern Vietnam. Downer (1961), in a similar vein, remarks that the Yao (Man) speech of northern Laos seems almost identical with that of the P'anku Yao of Kwangsi.

MIAO

SOUTH CHINA MIAO

Synonyms. *Hmong, Hmu, Hmung*

ORIENTATION. **Identification.** Miao speakers generally call themselves Hmong, Hmung, or Hmu, followed by a descriptive or identifying term, e.g. Hmong Ntsu, Magpie Miao (Ruey 1960: 143; Clarke 1911: 23). The word *miao* is of Chinese origin, and, according to Ruey, means "rice shoot." Although not used, and even disliked, by the people concerned, Miao has a long history of Chinese usage. In post-Han times, it referred in a general sense to "southern barbarians" or tribes people, but by the Sung dynasty it had acquired a more specific connotation. ● The Chinese further distinguish a great many varieties of Miao speakers according to peculiarities of dress, hair style, occupation, etc., e.g. the Western Miao, the Pointed Miao, the Upside-down Miao, the Shrimp Miao, and the Steep Slope Miao (cf. Lin 1940: 282-83). The better-known varieties of Miao are, however, relatively few: He or Hei (Black) Miao, Hua (Flowery) Miao, Pe or Pei (White) Miao, Hung (Red) Miao, and Ch'ing (Blue) Miao. Dialectical differences and minor variations in dress and other customs serve to mark off smaller groups and subvarieties, e.g. the Ta Hua (Great Flowery) Miao, the Short-skirt Black Miao, the Magpie Miao (probably a subdivision of the White Miao), and the Cowrie Shell Miao. Only a small percentage of the many subvarieties of Miao in South China—estimated at 70 or 80 in all—have been studied and described. **Location.** Miao speakers in South China are found mainly in Kweichow province, but also in some adjacent areas of Hunan, Szechwan, Kwangsi, and Yunnan. The so-called Hainanese Miao, on Hainan Island, are probably Yao. ● The Red Miao are concentrated along the border area of western Hunan–eastern Kweichow. In Hunan they center in the districts of Feng Huang, Kan Ch'eng, and Yung Sui, an area of some 40 by 100 miles which has been declared an Autonomous Chou by the Chinese People's Republic. Southeastern Kweichow, in particular Chienho and Lushan districts, is the homeland of the Black Miao, although they have in recent decades also been migrating into northern Kwangsi and parts of southwestern Kweichow. Most Blue Miao are located in central Kweichow, in particular around Kweiyang city. The White Miao are found chiefly in central and southern Kweichow, and also in southern Szechwan, where they are known as Ch'uan Miao. Like the White Miao, the Flowery Miao are great migrants who, though based in western Kweichow, can be found scattered throughout eastern and southern Yunnan, northern Tonkin, much of Laos, and northern Thailand. [Cf. Ling and Ruey 1947: 22ff.; Wiens 1954: 278-79.] Only the Red Miao in western Hunan show any real degree of concentration. Elsewhere the Miao are relatively scattered and mixed—so that in many instances Flowery Miao villages adjoin those of White Miao or of Tai speakers or Han Chinese. **Geography.** The heartland of the Miao in South China lies in the area of the Kweichow plateau and its extension into adjacent areas of Yunnan, Szechwan, Hunan, and Kwangsi. Averaging 4,000 feet above sea level, extremely cut up and precipitous, and with a wild and sparsely-settled landscape, Kweichow is the most impoverished province in all of South China. Only in the central basins around Kweiyang and in scattered river basins to the east is extensive wet-rice agriculture possible. A temperate monsoon climate prevails a good part of the year. The fauna of the area includes deer, bears, tigers, and wild boar. [Wiens 1954: 16-18; Mickey 1947: 3-5.] **Linguistic affiliation.** Miao dialects have been variously classified as Mon-Khmer (Austroasiatic), Tai, Sinitic "Independent," and so on. Greenberg (1953: 282-83) classes Miao and Yao together as a separate branch of Sino-Tibetan. Miao is a tonal, monosyllabic language, differing somewhat from Chinese in word order and phonetics. Many words in Miao are obvious Chinese loan words. [Cf. Savina 1930: 1-111; deBeauclair 1956: 303.] The major dialects, e.g. Black, Flowery, etc., are said to be mutually unintelligible, so that Chinese or a Tai dialect frequently serves as a lingua franca (deBeauclair 1960: 128). Most Miao men, at least, are able to speak some Chinese. Within a major dialect group such as the Flowery Miao, the various subgroups, e.g. Great and Little Flowery Miao, are presumably mutually intelligible (cf. Clarke 1911: 16ff.). There is no indigenous Miao writing, and until recently the language was written only in missionary-devised scripts. The Chinese People's Republic (Institute of Linguistics of the Academy of Sciences) began collecting and analyzing Miao vocabularies in 1951, and by 1955 three Latinized alphabets had been devised—representative of western Hunan, southeastern Kweichow, and western Kweichow (Its 1960: 105-06). **Demography.** The total of Miao speakers in South China, based on 1953 Chinese People's Republic census figures, is 2,500,000. Of this total, Kweichow has 1,425,-000; Hunan 378,000; Yunnan 360,000; Kwangsi 204,000; and Szechwan 84,000 (Bruk 1960: 32). Earlier estimates are lower, as illustrated by a 1939 figure of 548,000 for the total of Miao in Kweichow province (Wiens 1954: 278-79). According to Its (1960: 113), over 70 per cent of the Kweichow Miao reside in the southern and southeastern part of the province, where the CPR has created two autonomous regions. **Cul-**

tural relations. The most potent acculturative force in Miao history has undoubtedly been the Chinese—both through the steady encroachment of Chinese peasant farmers and the more dramatic policies and programs of successive imperial dynasties and governments. In the traditional hierarchy of southern frontier society under the Manchu and Republican governments, the Miao ranked near the bottom, looked down upon and exploited by Chinese and Lolo landlords, and regarded as inferior by the Tai-speaking Chung-chia—themselves largely second-class citizens. Only the Long-skirt Black Miao, centering in Huang-p'ing district of southeastern Kweichow, were relatively well off—some even landlords in their own right. The generally despised and exploited condition of the Miao may have contributed to their rather widespread acceptance of Christianity in the late nineteenth and early twentieth centuries. In western Kweichow, among the White and Flowery Miao, the Christian missions met with considerable success. Miao villages everywhere participate in the market days and trade fairs characteristic of the area, where they come into frequent contact with Chinese merchants and with members of other ethnic minorities. Intermarriage with these other groups, including the Chinese, has been relatively infrequent, however. ● According to Chinese Communist sources, the Miao of Szechwan and Kweichow formed revolutionary bases during the military campaigns of the late 1940s, and many Miao are said to have joined the ranks of the Communist party. Miao cadres were thus on hand to assist in the Chinese People's Republic's reforms of the 1950s. These reforms have concentrated on education, elimination of the landowner class, and the establishment of cooperatives and state industrial enterprises such as electric power and lumbering. Textbooks have been published in a Latinized Miao orthography. In 1954 the Communists claimed that among the nationalities of Kweichow, 47,000 Communist party members were united through some 4,600 local party organizations, representing 70 per cent of all the villages in the province (Its 1960: 88-89).

SETTLEMENT PATTERN AND HOUSING. **Settlement pattern.** Villages are located at some distance from centers of Chinese settlement, characteristically in a remote mountain valley reached only by trails open to foot travelers or pack animals. A village site is usually located on a hillside with fields on surrounding slopes, and often along a stream or river below, necessitating considerable climbing up and down in pursuit of gathering and farming activities. The layout of villages varies. Among the Cowrie Shell near Kweiyang city, a compact village is laid out with more or less regular footpaths or streets, but without walls or palisades. The orientation of the village and the houses within it is in accordance with the Chinese geomantic system of *feng shui*

(Mickey 1947: 8, 14). Among the Magpie Miao of southern Szechwan, the village is a cluster of separate hamlets (Ruey 1960: 144). The Red Miao of northwestern Hunan occupy an area of relatively recent armed conflict between Chinese and Miao, subject to the Chinese military garrison system, which probably helps to explain their pattern of compact walled villages within which a maze of small alleyways separates the closely spaced houses (Ling and Ruey 1947: 33 ff.). ● The average number of inhabitants per village does not appear to be very large, although the range, e.g. among the Sheng, may extend from 3 or 4 households to as many as 100—the equivalent of about 15 to 400–500 inhabitants (deBeauclair 1960: 141). The average appears to be between 50 and 100 persons. **Housing.** Throughout many of the more remote areas of Kweichow, Miao houses are crudely built, and rest directly on the ground. Walls are of bamboo and/or mud, with thatch roofs. Windows are few or lacking entirely. The structure is essentially a single rectangular room with one section screened off for the family's domestic animals. A fire pit in the earthen floor serves for cooking. In economically more advanced areas, as among the Long-skirt Black Miao of southeastern Kweichow, two-story, multiple-room houses of brick and tile construction occur. The family occupies the upper story and domestic animals are housed below (Wu and Ch'en 1942: 8). The Red Miao of northwestern Hunan retain the basic Miao architectural style, but with variations in materials and method of construction, possibly for defense purposes. Stone slabs, in addition to clay and brick, are used for walls, and roofing consists of slate or tile (or pressed bark among the poorer villagers). The rectangular space inside the house is divided by means of pillars into three areas. Animals are housed in an attached shed, which also provides toilet facilities for members of the family. Potatoes and other vegetables are stored in a pit beneath the house (Ling and Ruey 1947: 38-40). The Sheng Miao of southeastern Kweichow provide an example of the ability of the Miao to assimilate alien culture traits and adapt them to their own environment. These Miao, living in a mountainous, heavily timbered area, have apparently adopted a number of culture traits from their lowland Tai-speaking neighbors, including wet-rice cultivation and housing. Here the house is a rectangular wooden structure raised on piles some ten feet above the ground. A veranda runs along one side of the structure, with a wooden staircase leading down to the ground. The house consists of a main room, with a fireplace for cooking purposes, and two or three smaller rooms for sleeping. The roof is of tile or bark. Animals are quartered beneath the house and crops stored in separate granaries (deBeauclair 1960: 143). ● House furnishings, as with most items of material culture among the Miao, are very similar to those in use among the Chinese.

ECONOMY. The Miao rely primarily on agriculture as a source of food. Secondary resources include domesticated animals, hunting, and some fishing. Gathering is probably a more important source of food than is indicated in the literature. **Agriculture.** Primarily mountain-dwelling swidden farmers, although when given the opportunity the Miao can adapt very well to wet-rice agriculture—as in the mountain valleys of central Kweichow province, where they are found in large numbers interspersed with Chinese and Tai-speaking wet-rice agriculturists. Swidden farming occurs in southern Szechwan (Ruey 1960: 144-45), western Kweichow (Clarke 1911: 182), and northwestern Hunan (Ling and Ruey 1947: 55). Crops include maize, buckwheat, millet, barley, kaoliang, and various vegetables. The upland swiddens appear to be supplemented wherever possible by irrigated wet-rice fields, either along river valleys below the village site or in the form of terraced fields on the lower slopes. Terracing may be extensive and elaborate (cf. Betts 1899: 86). Among the Sheng subgroup of the Black Miao of southeastern Kweichow, terraces, supported by stone walls and irrigated with ditches and bamboo pipes, may cover an entire hillside (deBeauclair 1960: 144-46). Where reliance is mainly on swiddens, as in western Kweichow, there may be frequent clearing of new land and rotation of fields, but only infrequent movement of an entire village from one location to another. Lin (1940: 289) quotes from an 1820 Chinese source:

In agriculture the Miao men and women work together. They have more mountain farms than irrigated fields. The farms are seldom suitable for grain. Burning the thorny trees and decomposing plants and exploiting the mountain slopes, they plant sesamum, millet, rice, wheat, beans, calyx grain, and kaoliang. Having cultivated for three or four years, they relinquish the old land and exploit new places because the land becomes poor after intensive cultivation. After lying fallow several years, when the soil is rich again, they continue to cultivate.

Where the Miao do engage in wet-rice agriculture, their methods, techniques, and implements are likely to be similar to those in use among the Chinese. This is well illustrated by the Cowrie Shell just southeast of Kweiyang, who rely primarily on wet rice grown in paddy fields along river valleys, supplemented with winter crops of beans, peas, and wheat, and by kitchen gardens (Mickey 1947: 29ff.). DeBeauclair (1960: 144-46), however, reports the use of a primitive wooden spade and man-drawn plow among the Sheng Miao wet-rice growers in southeastern Kweichow. Those Miao living in the more mountainous parts of the area usually grow opium poppies as a commercial crop, but are reportedly little addicted to the use of the drug. Tobacco and sugar cane are also grown. **Fishing and hunting.** Fishing techniques include the use of nets, hook and line, and poisoning. Some Miao have adopted the Chinese method of growing fish from spawn in irrigated fields, probably the single largest source of fish in the diet (Ling and Ruey 1947: 70; deBeauclair 1960: 148-50). The Miao are known as avid hunters, pursuing this activity as a sport as well as a supplementary source of food. The crossbow with poisoned arrows is a characteristic Miao weapon, although it may be displaced in the more sinicized areas by old muskets of Chinese origin. Other hunting techniques include traps, snares, pits, and surrounds (using men and dogs). Animals sought include deer, bears, tigers, boar, and birds. [Cf. deBeauclair 1960: 148-50.] **Domestic animals.** Cattle, pigs, chickens, cats, and dogs are raised by most Miao. Sheep, goats, and horses are more common in the west near the Tibetan culture area. Water buffalo are kept where feasible and, together with cows, are the principal draft animals. The Sheng Miao of southeastern Kweichow, however, use a man-drawn plow (deBeauclair 1960: 144-46). Bee-keeping is mentioned for the Red Miao of northwestern Hunan (Ling and Ruey 1947: 72). In general, domestic animals serve less as a source of food than as draft and pack animals and, even more important, as a source of animal sacrifices. **Food and stimulants.** Throughout most of the area, including western Kweichow (Clarke 1911: 182), southern Szechwan (Graham 1937a: 20), and northwestern Hunan (Ling and Ruey 1947: 55ff.), maize is the staple food, supplemented by such crops as beans, millet, buckwheat, and potatoes. Only in central and southeastern Kweichow is rice a major food item. In these latter areas the Cowrie Shell, for example, base their diet on nonglutinous rice supplemented by beans, vegetables, chilies, pork, chicken, and fish in a pattern very similar to that of the Chinese (Mickey 1947: 23). The Sheng Miao staple is glutinous rice, a preference apparently learned from previous association with lowland Tai-speaking peoples of southeastern Kweichow and northern Kwangsi. Wu and Ch'en (1942: 8ff.) call attention to the fondness of the Miao for hot peppers and fermented meat dishes, to the frequency of dishes made from sour (pickled) vegetables, to the relative scarcity of meat (as compared with Chinese), and to the extensive use of alcoholic beverages made from rice and corn. **Industrial arts.** Home industries include weaving, dyeing, embroidery, carpentry, and work in bamboo. Individual specialization is rare, although Ruey reports occasional silversmithing and blacksmithing among the Magpie (1960: 145). The Miao make their own cloth and dye it themselves, using home-grown indigo and other dyes. In general, hemp cloth predominates in the western part of the area, cotton cloth in the east (Wu and Ch'en 1942: 8ff.). The White and Flowery Miao of central and western Kweichow make elaborate use of the batik method of resist dyeing, but the technique is not used among most of the

Black Miao groups to the east (deBeauclair 1960: 148). Its (1960: 77-78) mentions the increased economic importance under the present CPR regime of such industries as lumbering and silkworm culture. Embroidery is being encouraged as a cottage industry. **Trade.** Handicrafts, produce, and game are regularly sold or traded at Chinese markets for such products as salt, cloth, and iron. Among the Cowrie Shell Miao of south-central Kweichow, markets in the Chinese *hsien* towns are held every five or six days, serving a variety of ethnic groups (Miao, Chung-chia, etc.) within a five or ten mile radius (Mickey 1947: 41). Its (1960: 78) reports the development under Communist China of wholesale cooperatives in the Miao nationality areas of Kweichow and Hunan. **Division of labor.** Among the Cowrie Shell Miao, who are sinicized wet-rice agriculturists and therefore somewhat atypical as regards their economic institutions, Mickey (1947: 38) reports the division of labor as follows:

Men—butchering, plowing and harrowing, sowing seed, woodworking and housebuilding, contacts with the outside world, and participation in Chinese political and educational systems.

Women—preservation and preparation of food, kitchen gardens, transplanting, weeding, and harvesting rice and other crops (with some help from men in an extremely busy season), gathering firewood, making thread, and sewing clothing.

Both—carrying water, spreading manure, beating grain, going to market, and care of small children.

In general men and women share in the agricultural work. Household chores tend to be women's alone, and hunting to be the specialty of men. **Land tenure.** Throughout much of Kweichow and into adjacent Yunnan, Miao farmers have for many years been tenants on the lands of Chinese, Lolo, and Chung-chia landowners. There is little doubt that the Miao have been economically exploited (cf. Clarke 1911). On the other hand, the Long-skirt Black Miao centering in Huang-p'ing *hsien* in southeastern Kweichow have been in some cases themselves relatively well-to-do landowners (deBeauclair 1960: 130-31); and in a good many instances Miao farmers have worked as tenants on land owned by other Miao, often the descendants of former *t'u-ssu* chieftains appointed to hereditary positions by the Chinese. Where Miao have settled down as permanent wet-rice agriculturists and been assimilated into the Chinese administrative system, as among the Cowrie Shell, farmers may own the land they work (Mickey 1947: 29, 42). In such cases the patrilocal extended family is the corporate land-owning group. ● Its, quoting from Communist Chinese sources, reports that in one sample area, just south of Kweiyang, some 12 per cent of the population owned well over three-quarters of all arable land in the area. The Communists instituted wholesale land reform in Kweichow in late 1954, and by 1956, according to Its' sources, some 90 per cent of all peasant farms in the Ch'ien-tung-nan Autonomous Chou in southeastern Kweichow were incorporated into agricultural cooperatives (Its 1960: 71-72).

KIN GROUPS. **Descent.** The Miao of South China today are practically everywhere patrilineal. **Kin groups.** The situation among the Magpie of southern Szechwan is typical: exogamous patronymic surname groups, with surnames borrowed from the Chinese, can be equated with the patrisib; the localized core of a hamlet, or occasionally of an entire village, made up of families bearing the same surname, is synonymous with the exogamous patriclan; the males of a patrilocal extended family, together with outmarrying females, equal a patrilineage (Ruey 1960: 145-46). A 1943 report by Yang Han-hsien describes the Ta Hua (Great Flowery) Miao of extreme northwestern Kweichow as formerly organized into 12 exogamous [patrilineal] clans. A clan was served by a hereditary priest-leader who officiated at sacrificial rites to a common remembered ancestor, preserved a genealogical record, and settled minor disputes. [As reported in deBeauclair 1960: 185-86; Its 1960: 174.] This type of organization shows many similarities with that of the traditional Han Chinese, and is by all indications a result of cultural borrowing; that this has occurred relatively recently is indicated by Lin Yueh-hwa's translation of an 1840 Chinese source which records an absence of surnames among the Flowery Miao of western Kweichow (Lin 1940: 286). Nor have the Miao taken over the Chinese system in toto: in most instances, for example, they are less strict about surname (sib) exogamy, restricting it in practice to individuals who can trace descent to an actual common ancestor, i.e. to lineage exogamy (cf. deBeauclair 1960: 186-87). ● Ruey suggests that the Miao may have originally had a bilateral type of organization. He bases this hypothesis on such evidence as bilateral characteristics within the kinship system; the retention among the Red Miao, at least, of independent nuclear families; and the tendency, e.g. among the Magpie, to maintain a close association among near kinsmen on both sides—approximating a bilateral kindred (Ruey 1960: 145-46). **Kin terminology.** The kinship system, like the rest of the social organization, appears to reflect the imposition of a unilinear (patrilineal) principle on an older base that by all indications was probably bilateral. Thus within the Magpie kinship system the first ascending generation is bifurcate collateral (different terms for Fa, Mo, FaBr, FaSi, MoBr, MoSi), a feature characteristic of the patrilineal Chinese. On the other hand, for Ego's generation, sibling terms are essentially extended to include all first cousins, a feature normally associated with bilateral societies. Unilineal

influences are noticeable here, too, in that ortho-cousins (FaBr children) are terminologically differentiated from other cousins (Ruey 1960: 147ff.). Adequate information is lacking on the kinship terminology of most other Miao groups of South China. The Red Miao of northwestern Hunan, as reported by Ling and Ruey, do, however, call parents and parents' siblings by separate terms—the bifurcate collateral feature reported above for the Magpie (1947: 455).

MARRIAGE AND FAMILY. **Mode.** Premarital sex freedom and institutionalized courtship appear to have been at one time characteristic of practically all Miao groups in South China. As they become assimilated to Chinese culture, however, the Miao tend to modify these practices or to give them up altogether. [Ling and Ruey 1947: 94; Graham 1937a: 30; Wu and Ch'en 1942: 133, 199; Clarke 1911: 78ff.; Mickey 1947: 49; deBeauclair 1960: 176-77.] Courtship takes place at annual festivals, bazaars, and other public occasions. An institutionalized form of courtship may take place on a hillside outside the village, where young people engage in antiphonal singing and young men serenade their partners on the reed organ. Where the patrilineal name-sib or lineage is synonymous with the local group, as among the Cowrie Shell, this courtship pattern is exogamous, i.e. the girls of a hamlet or village are serenaded by visiting boys from a nearby village. Fine clothes, dancing skills, and clever singing are highly prized attributes in the selection of a mate. Older Chinese sources mention the existence of youth houses located outside the village. These are not reported, however, in the contemporary literature (Ling and Ruey 1947: 94; deBeauclair 1960: 176-77). ● Where the older patterns of premarital freedom and courtship still exist, a go-between is normally engaged by the boy's family once the couple have decided to marry. A bride price is paid, consisting of cattle, goats, sheep, or (more recently) money. The Magpie, for example, pay a substantial bride price of money and cattle (Ruey 1960: 146-47). Among the Red Miao a kind of gift exchange was formerly practiced, consisting of a "bride price" of five or six cattle and a "dowry" of cows, goats, and implements (Ling and Ruey 1947: 94). The more sinicized Miao follow the custom of arranged marriages, with a marriage ceremony conducted by a local (Taoist) priest. **Form.** Marriages are predominantly monogamous, although polygyny appears to be allowed. In one Cowrie Shell village, there were 3 or 4 cases of polygyny out of 32 marriages (Mickey 1947: 19). **Extension of incest taboos.** Theoretically, marriage is prohibited among members of the same surname group. In practice, however, this seems to be limited to individuals descended from the same actual ancestor, i.e. the lineage (Ling and Ruey 1947: 95-96; deBeauclair 1960: 186-87; Ruey 1960: 146-47). Premarital sexual freedom with cross cousins is allowed among a number of South China Miao groups. Asymmetrical patrilateral cross-cousin marriage is specifically reported for the Black Miao (Ling and Ruey 1947: 94) and the Magpie Miao (Ruey 1960: 146-47). Among the former, a FaSiDa must consult her maternal uncle before marriage, and he may demand an indemnity of her father if she marries outside the preferred pattern; on the other hand, if he has no son for her to marry, then her father may seek an indemnity from him. **Residence.** Somewhat variable. Ranges from neolocal in northwestern Hunan (Ling and Ruey 1947: 98) through various degrees of matri- patrilocal among some Kweichow Miao groups, to straight patrilocal among the southern Szechwan Miao (Graham 1937a: 26; Ruey 1960: 145-46). Ruey feels that neolocality among the Red Miao may be associated with an earlier bilateral social organization; he also suggests an earlier bilateral structure with neolocality for the Magpie. Among the Black Miao of southeastern Kweichow, the bride remains with her parents, with periodic visits from her husband, until the first child is born, after which she moves to his home. This is true also of the south-central Kweichow Cowrie Shell, except that change of residence takes place once the girl becomes pregnant (Mickey 1947: 19, 43, 47). With rare exceptions, then, it appears that most Miao in South China today are ultimately patrilocal. **Domestic unit.** The Red Miao of Hunan retain what Ling and Ruey call the old tradition of independent nuclear families (1947: 93). More typical of the South China Miao today, however, are the Cowrie Shell, where extended patrilocal families (sometimes living in adjacent households) slightly exceed the number of nuclear households (Mickey 1947: 16-17). As among the Magpie, extended families tend to be of the minimal or stem type. Once the parents die, these extended households break up into nuclear units which later repeat the cycle. **Inheritance.** Among the more sinicized Miao, the patrilocal extended family functions as a corporate group with respect to land ownership and ownership of animals and nonpersonal property. At the death of the parents, the sons normally divide the family property among themselves. [Mickey 1947: 37, 42; Graham 1937a: 26ff.] **Divorce.** Divorce, including that initiated by the woman, is relatively easy and is said to occur frequently—at least until the first child is born. **Secondary marriage.** In general, both the levirate and sororate are permitted. [Clarke 1911: 78ff.; deBeauclair 1960: 186-87.]

SOCIOPOLITICAL ORGANIZATION. **Political organization.** The variety of Miao groups encountered today, often termed "tribes" in the literature, is probably a result of centuries of oppression and disruption at the hands of the Chinese. It is also possible that some of these distinctions may reflect the existence of former indigenous kin-based political institutions that transcended the village level. Today, however, indigenous political organization above the village level is lacking, and the Miao are integrated into the Chinese political-administrative system. Each village is a separate unit, subject to the local Chinese governmental authority (cf. Mickey 1947: 43-44; Ruey 1960: 146). ● Varieties of Miao, such as the Flowery or Black, cannot be considered tribes in any political sense. Nevertheless these groupings of Miao have in the past organized for purposes of military resistance, e.g. the insurrection of Black Miao in Kweichow in the 1860s. A type of loose tribal formation, primarily kin-based and consistent with a long history of migrations, seems a likely hypothesis. It is probable that such formations were dominated by ephemeral quasi-religious leaders much on the order of the Miao "kings" reported by French researchers for the White and Flowery Miao at the time of their migrations southward to Indochina in the late eighteenth century (deBeauclair 1960: 186). Further information is contained in a 1943 report by Yang Han-hsien, a Ta Hua (Great Flowery) Miao trained in sociology at West China Union University. According to Yang, the Ta Hua had exogamous clans served by hereditary priest-leaders who officiated at sacrificial rites to a common remembered ancestor, preserved genealogical records, and settled minor disputes. The various clans differed somewhat with respect to the details of ancestral ceremonies, such as the type of animal sacrificed and the method of killing it. The obligations of clan membership, including mutual help and attendance at various ceremonies in the life cycle, superseded those of village residence, and clan affiliation continued despite change of residence. [Cited in deBeauclair 1960: 185-86; Its 1960: 87.] A possible kinship basis for such loose "tribal" formations is indicated also in the case of the Cowrie Shell:

> Since they consider themselves descendants of a single ancestor, the Cowrie Shell Miao reckon all other Cowrie Shell Miao their kin, and one finds among them the same degree of unity as among members of a large family distributed over a considerable territory . . . they are simply an aggregation of people who trace their descent from a single ancestor, follow the same or similar customs, and speak a common language (Mickey 1947: 9).

The Cowrie Shell Miao area in south-central Kweichow is roughly 30 to 40 miles square. A somewhat similar case is that of the Ch'uan (White) Miao of southern Szechwan, who are said to be defined in part by the legend of a common female ancestor (Graham 1937a: 56). In these cases there is apparently a feeling of oneness based on the idea of pseudo-sib. Clarke cites cases of Flowery Miao emigrating out of Kweichow into eastern Yunnan and continuing to maintain contacts with their kinsmen at home (1911: 178, 278). Related to this kind of identification is the fact that the various Miao groups rarely intermarry (cf. deBeauclair 1960: 186-87). **Social strati-**

fication. The Miao lack any kind of indigenous stratification. They were, however, formerly involved in the feudal type of landlord-peasant class system characteristic of the frontier areas under pre-Communist Chinese rule. Their role has often been that of tenant farmer, although in a few cases the Miao themselves, usually descendants of former *t'u-ssu* chieftains, have been members of the landlord class. The Chinese introduced the *t'u-ssu* system into Kweichow and the surrounding areas about 1500 A.D. Tribal chieftains, including Miao chieftains, were appointed to hereditary administrative positions, adopting Chinese surnames and entering into a kind of feudatory arrangement with the imperial government on behalf of the tribesmen within their jurisdictions. [DeBeauclair 1960: 130-31; Clarke 1911: 26; Wiens 1954: 214ff.] The old feudal institutions of southern frontier society are now under heavy attack by the Chinese Communists, and the position of the Miao in this area is undoubtedly undergoing change. Miao are reported to be managers of agricultural cooperatives in Kweichow, and delegates to the All-China Assembly of People's Representatives (cf. Its 1960: 88-89).

RELIGION. Religious behavior reflects the centuries of contact in the South China area between the Miao and the Chinese, Tibeto-Burmans, and Tai. Some animistic and magico-religious beliefs and practices, as well as some elements of ancestor worship, appear to be very old in Miao culture, or possibly related to an ancient cultural complex common to both Miao and Chinese; other elements are clearly of Taoist or Buddhist origin; and Lolo (Tibeto-Burman) influences are evident in certain magical feats of healers and exorcists in western Kweichow. ● Propitiation and exorcism, directed at local spirits, demons, and ancestral ghosts, comprise a good portion of Miao religious behavior—up to 90 per cent, according to Ling and Ruey (1947: 128). Religious specialists carry out animal sacrifices and perform various magico-religious acts in connection with most of these activities. Evil and malevolent forces abound, and much energy and time is spent in placating, avoiding, or exorcising them. The Chinese People's Republic is today striking at these ideas, particularly the widespread habit of animal sacrifice, which is labeled both anachronistic and wasteful. The CPR has devoted special attention to introducing scientific medicine as a counteracting force to animal sacrifice (Its 1960: 94). **Supernaturals.** Animistic beliefs are evident in the many food offerings made to spirits of trees, rocks, and so on. Also propitiated are a variety of local deities, household gods, demons, and spirits. Many of these, such as the Jade Emperor, the Lady Buddhas, and the Mouth Odor Ghost, are of Chinese origin (cf. Wu and Ch'en 1942: 27ff.). Ling and Ruey (1947: 129) catalogued some 40 different classes of supernaturals in northwestern Hunan, 16 of which

they identified as Miao, and 24 as Chinese. Ancestor worship and the propitiation of ancestral ghosts is a prominent feature of Miao religion (cf. Its 1960: 98). Offerings to "Lord and Lady No" are characteristic of the Red Miao (Ling and Ruey 1947: 129ff.). These two beings figure in a creation myth common to many Miao groups, wherein the incestuous union of a brother and sister, saved from a universal deluge, results in the peopling of the entire earth or of various Miao clans or surname groups (cf. Clarke 1911: 55ff.). **Practitioners.** Most Miao villages have at least one individual, usually a male, who specializes on a part-time basis in knowledge of the spirit world and in the propitiation and exorcism of malevolent spirits, demons, and ghosts. He may or may not combine with his over-all priestly functions the additional functions of curing, divining, and fortune telling. Curing is often the special province of a female shaman or exorcist. Practitioners employ ritual incantations, animal sacrifice, and the manipulation of a variety of objects—practices which have a distinctly magical connotation and appear to be related to, if not derived from, Chinese Taoism. ● Among the Cowrie Shell, the priests are ordinary men of the village who perform at rites of passage, ancestral sacrifices, and on various ceremonial occasions to ensure good fortune for home and village. They manipulate incense, paper money, bowls of wine and rice, and a sacrificial fowl, while delivering a ritual incantation in Miao (Mickey 1947: 45). The Red Miao village priest operates in much the same way, wearing a special robe and cap and making use of incense, wax, rice, meat, wine, a trumpet, cymbals, paper money, fire, and so on (Ling and Ruey 1947: 128-29). Whereas the Red Miao priest may also engage in healing ceremonies, rain making, and divining, most curing functions among the Cowrie Shell are handled by a female specialist or shamaness (Mickey 1947: 45, 62). The Black Miao of southeastern Kweichow combine these various functions in one person, a part-time village priest or exorcist (Wu and Ch'en 1942: 27-28; deBeauclair 1960: 162); whereas the Flowery Miao of western Kweichow, like the Cowrie Shell, employ a priest, *kwei-shih*, as well as a female shamaness-exorcist, *mi-la* (Ch'en 1942: 89). The southern Szechwan (White) Miao conform to the western Kweichow pattern except that their shamans or exorcists are males endowed with extraordinary or supernatural powers, such as the ability to walk on knives and handle red-hot metal. These attributes, plus the elaborateness and complexity of their incantations and formulas, reflect the influence of Tibeto-Burman cultures farther west (Graham 1937a: 65ff.; deBeauclair 1960: 162). There are indications that Miao priests may also have had in the past secular functions as quasi-religious leaders of loose tribal (kin-based) formations during periods of migration and insurrection (cf. deBeauclair 1960: 185-86). **Ceremonies.** Individual or family-oriented ceremonies include periodic offerings of food and incense at small shrines outside the village and along the road to a variety of local spirits and ancestral ghosts. The more sinicized among the Miao preserve a small shrine within the home for the ancestral tablets. ● Many of the annual ceremonial occasions and religious festivals reflect a strong Han Chinese influence. Most characteristic are the annual flower dances or musical festivals and the periodic buffalo sacrifices. The festivals, which tend to be associated with the Miao agricultural calendar, not only ensure good crops but are also major recreational events. Neighboring villages among the Flowery Miao, for example, may cooperate in putting on a dance festival outside one of the participating villages. Music, dancing, gaiety, and courting may go on for a day or more. Chinese merchants set up their stalls, and racing and buffalo fights serve as added attractions (Wu and Ch'en 1942: 195ff.; Clarke 1911: 63). ● Miao ancestor worship often involves animal sacrifice. The Red Miao, for example, tie a pig to a post, where it is ceremonially slaughtered to the accompaniment of incantations and ritual acts by a village priest (Ling and Ruey 1947: 131ff.). Among the Flowery Miao, a memorial ceremony should ideally be performed on the thirteenth anniversary of death. A straw pavilion is erected on ground outside the village and here the members of the family and friends congregate, together with a *kwei-shih,* village priest. The latter conducts the ritual aspects of the ceremony, while the actual sacrifice is performed by a male descendant of the deceased ancestor. The sacrificial animal is dismembered and cooked on the spot. The body parts are eaten by all family members assembled and the head is placed on the altar within the pavilion (Ch'en 1942: 91). ● The most spectacular of these ancestral ceremonies are the periodic village-wide buffalo sacrifices. According to deBeauclair (1960: 158), such sacrifices in western Kweichow are at present sponsored by individual families following the death of a male member; only in central and eastern Kweichow, among the White and Black Miao, is the killing of buffalo simultaneously carried out by all families of a village every seven or thirteen years. Water buffalo fights may be held in conjunction with these cyclical ancestral ceremonies, or they may be purely recreational events, as among the Tai-speaking Tung of Kweichow. According to deBeauclair (1960: 158), fighting buffalo on the occasion of ancestral sacrifices is limited in Kweichow to the area of Kweiyang and eastward. ● Cyclical, village-wide buffalo fights and sacrificial ceremonies in honor of the ancestors are described by Wu Tsu-lin for the Cowrie Shell south of Kweiyang (quoted by Mickey 1947: 78ff.). The families of a village enter specially selected and fattened bulls in paired contests. Prior to the fighting, the animals are led in procession around the bullfight meadow, accompanied by family representatives, village priests, and musicians. The victorious animals are sacrificed in individual family rites outside the village. The killing is done on an inscribed stone which remains in place as a memorial. The body is cut up and divided among friends and relatives and the horns preserved in the family homestead. These are occasions also for village-wide feasting and for courting and merrymaking among the young people. ● Drum dancing is reported specifically for the Red Miao of Hunan in connection with certain sacrificial ceremonies. Here men and/or women dance around a drum set on crosspieces. Methods of beating the drum are elaborate and varied (Ling and Ruey 1947: 202ff.). DeBeauclair (1960: 152-53) reports the use of bronze drums among the Sheng and certain other Black Miao groups of eastern Kweichow. ● An ordeal or oath-taking ceremony by "eating blood" occurs among the Red Miao. Two individuals engaged in a dispute will, in the presence of a priest, drink a mixture of animal blood and wine following the invocation of a powerful spirit by the priest. The Miao maintain that whoever is at fault in the dispute will immediately die (Ling and Ruey 1947: 152). **Illness and medicine.** Sickness and death are in most instances attributed to supernatural causes—either soul loss or the presence of a malevolent spirit. In the case of the latter, the usual procedure is to identify the offending spirit and exorcise it by means of magical ritual and incantation. Among the Red Miao, identification is made by a female specialist and the exorcistic ritual carried out by a male priest (Ling and Ruey 1947: 129, 194). The Black Miao combine these functions in one person, a village priest, who also officiates at ancestral ceremonies, funerals, and the like. The most usual pattern appears to be that found in central and western Kweichow as well as in southern Szechwan, where curing rites are the specialty of a female exorcist or shamaness. These persons among the Cowrie Shell undergo no special initiation, one woman stating that she received her powers after a serious illness during which she "died" and recovered. The woman goes into a trancelike state, moving her hands and feet in a prescribed fashion to the accompaniment of whistling, hissing, and coughing noises in an attempt to enter into communication with the spirit world. The remainder of the ceremony consists of an exorcistic ritual with Taoist overtones (Mickey 1947: 45, 62). **Insect poisoning.** A kind of witchcraft or sorcery by insect poisoning, *ku,* is reported for the Red Miao (Ling and Ruey 1947: 199ff.), the Black Miao (Clarke 1911: 63), the Flowery Miao (Ch'en 1942: 92), and the Cowrie Shell (Mickey 1947: 61). It was formerly widespread among the Han Chinese, who continue to ascribe to the women of the Miao and other minority groups the ability to harm or influence others through this practice (cf. Feng and Shryock 1935). As reported for the Miao, a woman acquires knowledge of *ku* poisoning as a result of secret training at the hands of a female relative. A variety of poisonous creatures are put together in a jar for a time until only one is left. This is the *ku*, or *ku* spirit, which contains the essence of all the poisons. According to different versions, a powder is made from the *ku* which is secretly put in the food of an intended victim; or the woman, having absorbed the *ku* essence or spirit into her own body, releases it by pointing or shaking her fingers at a victim. It is generally held that a woman must periodically release her poison or she herself will lose her reason, or sicken and die. Symptoms of *ku* poisoning are said to include bodily swelling, stomach cramps, diarrhea, and coma. It is also believed that Miao women use the poison, or the threat of it, to retain a husband or lover. Egg divination is used in some cases to determine whether an illness has been caused by insect poisoning. Antidotes appear to be few, although Feng and Shryock (1935: 15) mention that according to some sources the person so afflicted must resort to the original sorcerer. Persons suspected of being insect poisoners are shunned and occasionally ostracized from their home villages. **Birth.** Both Ling and Ruey (1947: 99) and Mickey (1947: 47ff.) report that childbirth among Miao women is relatively easy. The former maintain that among the Red Miao of Hunan a woman will continue working up to the day of delivery, which may occur unattended while she is still in the fields. The woman is said to maintain an upright position, legs apart and slightly bent while grasping a stationary object, with a lined basket or receptacle on the ground to receive the baby. The mother is back in the fields and working again within three or four days. The Red Miao are said to know of an herb which makes their women strong and able to give birth easily. Mickey, reporting for the Cowrie Shell, confirms this account of the ease of birth, and the fact that a woman is up and doing hard labor within three to five days. **Soul, death, and afterlife.** The Miao have the Chinese concept of three principal souls, as well as their ideas about transmigration and reincarnation. Particularly feared are the souls of persons who have died unnatural deaths, since these linger on earth as malevolent spirits. Much attention is paid therefore to ensuring that the soul gets well started on its journey to the afterlife, and to making sure that no evil influences are present during the period of mourning and burial. ● The funeral ceremonies of the Miao also show much Chinese influence. The body is placed in a wooden coffin in the home for a period of one or two days, during which time it is attended by mourning relatives and also by a village priest. The priest exorcises evil influences by chanting and magically manipulating various objects, and performs an "opening the way" ceremony for the soul. On the second day, a buffalo or other animal may be sacrificed. Burial usually takes place on the third day, preceded by a procession to the village

cemetery where a grave site has previously been selected by geomancy. Postmortuary rites may include visits to the grave for a period of years and the maintenance of an ancestral tablet in the home. [Cf. Mickey 1947: 46, 52 for the Cowrie Shell; Wu and Ch'en 1942: 27 for the Black Miao.] Cremation is practiced only in cases of death by contagious disease. Methods of disposing of the corpse apparently varied much more in the past than they do now. Wu and Ch'en (1942: 11-12) report stone-lined graves and exposure; while deBeauclair (1960: 159-60) mentions cases of live burial among a subgroup of the Black Miao. Among the White (Chu'an) Miao of southern Szechwan, a second burial takes place after an indefinite period; the bones are washed, put in a new coffin, and reburied (Graham 1937a: 57ff.).

BIBLIOGRAPHY. DeBeauclair 1956, 1960; Betts 1899; Bruk 1960; Ch'en 1942; Clarke 1911; Feng and Shryock 1935; Graham 1937a; Greenberg 1953; Its 1960; Lin 1940; Ling and Ruey 1947; Mickey 1947; Ruey 1960; Savina 1930; Wiens 1954; Wu and Ch'en 1942.

INDOCHINA MEO

Synonyms. *Mlao, Mnong*

ORIENTATION. Identification. The Indochina Meo refer to themselves as Mnong or Mlao (Bourotte 1943: 33; Lafont 1961). According to Abadie (1924: 150-51), those in northern Vietnam are divided into five groups, each named for a characteristic of the women's costume: the White Meo, Black Meo, Red Meo, Flowered Meo, and the Mung Cha Meo. A recent source from North Vietnam (NNCDT 1959: 244) also describes five Meo groupings in northern Vietnam, using Vietnamese transcriptions: the Meo Trang (White Meo), Meo Hoa (Flowered Meo), Meo Do (Red Meo), Meo Den (Black Meo), and the Meo Mong Sua. According to Lafont (1961), the Black Meo and White Meo predominate in northern Laos. **Location.** In northern Vietnam the most important concentrations of Meo are along the Chinese frontier between Dong Van and Quan Ba, between Pa Kha and Muong Khuong, and along the right bank of the Red river between Nghia Lo, Van Bu, and Tu Le. On the Black river they are located north of Vau Yen. In the Dong Van and Muong Khoung regions they constitute the majority of the population. [Embree and Thomas 1950: 112.] The Meo in Laos are most heavily concentrated in Xieng Khouang province (Barney 1961: 10-11). **Linguistic affiliation.** The language is predominantly monosyllabic. It contains 53 consonant phonemes, 13 vowel phonemes (9 simple vowels and 4 vowel clusters), and 7 tone phonemes. The Meo of Xieng Khouang in Laos are of two major dialect groups, the Mon Tleu or White Meo, and the Mon Len or Striped Meo. [Smalley 1956: 50.] In northern

Vietnam, the Meo are reported to use *kwan hoa* as their lingua franca in dealing with other groups (Abadie 1924: 152). Lao is the lingua franca in Laos, according to Barney (1961: 45). **Demography.** Savina (1930: 193) estimated the total Meo population of Laos and Vietnam at 200,000, although Roux and Tran (1954: 388) consider this figure much too high. Abadie (1924: 149) reported the Meo in Vietnam at 40,000 and Morechand (1952: 355) later raised it to 60,000. Bourotte (1943: 34) reported 100,000 in all of Indochina, with 40,000 in Vietnam and 60,000 in Laos. Le (1955: 48) also placed the Meo population of Indochina at 100,000. According to Barney (1961: 2), the governor of Xieng Khouang province in Laos estimated the Meo population for that province at 45,000. Lafont (1961) agrees with the 1931 census which lists 60,000 Meo in Laos. The NNCDT (1959: 244) reports the Meo population of Vietnam to be 182,747. **History and cultural relations.** Early in the nineteenth century, the Meo are reported to have begun their large-scale migrations into northern Vietnam. At this time several thousand moved into Vietnam, after devastating large areas of Yunnan province in southern China. They clashed with the Man (Yao) and Tai groups of the Dong Van area, driving them out and occupying their land. Around 1860, the second Meo "invasion" occurred, coincident with the T'ai-ping rebellion in China. Several thousand Meo swept across the upland area of northern Vietnam, reaching the fringes of the delta before the Vietnamese repulsed them. It is said that the heavy, humid climate of the lowland was too much for the Meo, since they were accustomed to higher altitudes. They also are reported to have been terrified of the elephants used by the Vietnamese army. ● Sioung, the semilegendary leader of the Meo, appeared about this time. Gaining prominence for his remarkable physical feats, he led the Meo in combat against the various groups in the Yen Ming and Quan Ba areas. Some of the Man and Nung accepted his leadership, but the Tho fought Sioung and his followers for twelve years. [Abadie 1924: 150, 163; Diguet 1908: 129; Lunet de Lajonquière 1906: 297.] The Meo in Vietnam have been involved in a long series of rebellions against the central government. In 1862 the White Meo led an uprising which was repressed by the Vietnamese, aided by various Tai groups as well as some Meo. In 1919, in an attempt to neutralize the Meo potential for rebellion, the French seized all their firearms. Because of the traditional skill of the Meo at making muskets, this proved to be an ineffective effort. The role of Meo priest-sorcerers in these uprisings has been emphasized by some investigators. [Bonifacy 1919: 24; Grossin 1926: 43.] Migrations into Laos have been largely without conflict. As early as 1850 Meo are reported to have established numerous villages in the mountain area around the city of Luang Prabang, where they cleared the forest to plant maize and poppies. [Le Boulanger

1931: 212.] In northern Laos the town of Xieng Khouang with its market place attracts most of the ethnic groups in the area. The town population includes Vietnamese artisans, Chinese traders, Indian cloth merchants, and a scattering of Westerners. The daily market and the grand festival of the eighth lunar month provide opportunities for visiting Meo to meet other ethnic groups. These contacts have had some effect on Meo society. Some have been drawn into the labor market and others have adopted wet-rice agriculture. Those of the Xieng Khouang area have also been integrated into the national political life of Laos, and have been influenced by the expanding educational facilities in the area. [Barney 1961: 5, 45-50.]

SETTLEMENT PATTERN AND HOUSING. **Settlement pattern.** The Meo prefer higher elevations ranging from 3,000 to 6,000 feet. Despite a traditional pattern of periodic moves in search of new land to clear and cultivate, some settlements have remained in one site for a relatively long time. Morechand (1952: 356) describes one such settlement in Vietnam located in the same place for over a hundred years. Because of their poppy cultivation, the Meo in Laos are more restricted in their selection of village sites. They must seek fresh, arable land and slopes that are relatively less exposed to the sun. A site thus chosen is occupied for five or six years. [Lafont 1960: 186-87.] Morechand (1952: 355), in studying a White Meo canton in northern Vietnam, found that there were no real agglomerations; instead, farmsteads were dispersed. A total population of 676, divided among 133 families in 82 households, yielded an area density of 16 per square kilometer. Barney (1961: 12) reports that in the Xieng Khouang area of Laos, Meo villages average around 8 houses, with some larger villages of around 40 houses. **Housing.** Meo houses in Vietnam are rectangular in shape and built directly on the ground, with walls normally of wattle and a thatched roof. Well-to-do Meo use planks for walls and either tile or wooden shingles on the roof. Windows may be cut into the walls. A main room serves as storage room, granary, and reception room for visitors and also contains the hearth and altar of the ancestors. Usually there are several small sleeping compartments. A stable, constructed of sticks and other available wood, is located nearby, and a kitchen garden and fruit grove are near the house. [Abadie 1924: 157-58; Savina 1930: 184-200; Lunet de Lajonquière 1906: 304-08; Maspéro 1929-30: 244.] In the Xieng Khouang area, Meo houses are constructed entirely of axe-hewn wood. Most have two doors; none have windows. A raised platform serves as a sleeping area. Most houses have two hearths, one for cooking and one which is used during social gatherings. A shrine for the spirits is usually found attached to one wall. Family and personal possessions, which are stored in the main room, include a rice pounder, a husking machine, a corn mill, tools, crossbows, flint-lock guns, utensils for cooking, musical instruments, and saddles. [Barney 1961: 30.]

ECONOMY. **Agriculture.** Maize is the traditional staple, although Gourdon (1931: 92) points out that whenever possible the Meo adopt paddy agriculture. Abadie (1924: 151) reports that some Meo in northern Vietnam have irrigated paddy fields along the slopes and bottoms of upland mountain valleys. Farming them during the daytime, they climb the slopes back to their villages in the evening. In Laos, particularly in the vicinity of Xieng Khouang, some Meo have been engaged in wet-rice agriculture, and some of the White Meo and Striped Meo cultivate upland rice by the swidden method (Lafont 1960: 188; Barney 1961: 24-26). For upland-rice swidden agriculture, the heavy vegetation and trees are cut and allowed to dry. In March, before the rains start, the dried wood is burned. Debris is cleared from the swidden, and the soil is loosened with hoes. After the first rains of late April or May have moistened the soil, the seeds are planted. The Meo are casual about weeding, and they irrigate the swidden only occasionally. When the swidden is located some distance from the village, temporary shelters are erected for the young men who guard the growing crops. • Maize swidden agriculture is similar to that for rice. When the first rains begin, the men make holes with digging sticks, and the women follow, placing animal dung fertilizer and kernels in each hole, after which the soil is pounded with a hoe. At harvest, the maize is stored in the upper parts of the house, away from the animals, where the heat from the fires dries it. Stalks are cut and carried to the house to be used as fuel. The Meo customarily cultivate a maize swidden three years, leaving it to lie fallow for eight to ten years. Secondary crops may be planted in the swidden after the maize harvest. [Abadie 1924: 160; Diguet 1908: 138; Lunet de Lajonquière 1906: 309.] The French have attempted to prevent Meo swidden agriculture on several occasions. In 1912 the *résident* of Xieng Khouang became apprehensive about deforestation, and issued a decree that the Meo would either have to replant areas they had cleared, burned, and cultivated, or leave the province. The Meo agreed to replant, and it is reported that they have continued to do so. [Roux and Tran 1954: 389.] Secondary crops, grown in kitchen gardens and sometimes in the swiddens, include green beans, peas, pumpkins, cucumbers, buckwheat, sorghum, turnips, eggplant, cabbage, squash, and a local grain called *cao lien.* Tobacco and hemp are less common. [Lunet de Lajonquière 1906: 310; Diguet 1908: 138; Abadie 1924: 160; Roux and Tran 1954: 390.] Some of the Meo in the Xieng Khouang area of Laos grow potatoes, of which some are sold to Westerners, but most are fed to livestock. Maize and squash are also fed to livestock in the wet-rice

growing zones, but they are consumed by the family when the rice crop is inadequate. The Meo of Xieng Khouang also cultivate flax for weaving. [Barney 1961: 26-28.] Roux and Tran (1954: 390) report that opium poppies constitute the major cash crop among the Meo. According to Barney (1961: 26-28), each patrilineal residence group in the Xieng Khouang area has its own poppy field. Opium was formerly bartered at the Xieng Khouang market. **Fishing and hunting.** The Meo are skilled hunters. They make their own firearms, which resemble European muskets of the eighteenth century. Diguet (1908: 139) reports that neither hunting nor fishing contributes very much to their sustenance, however. **Domestic animals.** The Meo are celebrated horse breeders. They also raise cattle, buffalo, pigs, goats, chickens, ducks, guinea hens, dogs, and cats. A special breed of white dog is a common household pet. Goat's milk and cow's milk are sometimes consumed among the Meo in Laos, but the eggs obtained from chickens and ducks are usually traded at the local markets. [Lunet de Lajonquière 1906: 311; Abadie 1924: 158; Barney 1961: 28-29.] **Industrial arts.** Meo industry is predominantly familial, although there usually are several specialists in each village. Within the family, the women weave cloth for clothing and coverings. For male garments the cloth is dyed, but for female garb it is elaborately embroidered in intricate and colorful designs. A batik type of design is produced by a cire-perdue (lost wax) method, using beeswax collected in the forest. Silk and needles are purchased from Chinese and Vietnamese merchants in the market towns. [Abadie 1924: 161; Cresson and Jeannin 1944: 435; Barney 1961: 28.] An alcohol made from maize is produced by most Meo families. Village specialists work silver purchased in the market towns into heavy bracelets and collars, intricately designed. In addition to their value as jewelry, they serve as a public display of family wealth. Village specialists also produce farm implements, and Meo armorers make musketlike weapons. Powder is prepared from saltpeter found in mountain caves and sulphur purchased from lowland groups. [Fromaget 1937: 168; Dussault 1924: 41; Grossin 1926: 42-44.] **Trade.** The Meo are active traders. In northern Vietnam along the Chinese border they sell wood for coffins to Chinese merchants (Lunet de Lajonquière 1906: 310-15). In northern Laos, Xieng Khouang and Luang Prabang were until recently the principal markets for Meo opium. In the traditional pattern reported for the Yunnan–Indochina border area, Chinese merchants travel from village to village, purchasing opium from individual farmers. [Roux and Tran 1954: 391; Hickey 1956; Lafont 1961.] **Division of labor.** In the Xieng Khouang area men prepare the fields, care for the crops, and construct the granaries. At harvest time, all able-bodied members of the family participate. Men cut the stalks while women flail, and the men carry the baskets of grain (maize or paddy) to the granaries. Should pack horses be needed to transport grain, they are led by young boys, while the girls help gather grain into baskets. Older members of the family watch the small children and prepare meals. [Barney 1961: 25-26.] In the production of opium, women are more active than men. Men construct the woven rattan or bamboo fences around the poppy fields, while women sow the seed, weed, and cut the bloom to remove the opium fluid. [Barney 1961: 27.] Men construct and maintain the houses and care for the livestock. Boys and older men gather firewood. Women are responsible for preparing and serving food, but at festivals, the young men prepare special rice cakes. [Barney 1961: 30-31.] **Land tenure.** In the Xieng Khouang area, Barney (1961: 31) reports that wherever there is swidden agriculture, the man who clears the land has usufruct. A Meo patrilineal descent group working together may have three or four cleared swiddens planted to upland rice and one planted to opium poppies. A married son may begin work on a field of his own if he can do so without disrupting the division of labor. [Barney 1961: 31.]

KIN GROUPS. **Descent.** Lunet de Lajonquière (1906: 314-18), Diguet (1908: 144), and Abadie (1924: 167-69) report that Meo groups in northern Vietnam have patrilineal kinship systems. Descent is patrilineal, and the father holds title to family property. After his death, the bulk of the property passes to the eldest son, who also receives exclusive right to use the family swiddens. Residence after marriage is either patrilocal or neolocal, but in the vicinity of the paternal house. **Kin groups.** The White Meo of Xieng Khouang in Laos are reported to have exogamous patrilineal clans, each of which has a name and an origin myth. Members trace their descent from a common ancestor. There is prescribed behavior for members of the same clan, and special terms of reference and address. They refer to other members of the clan as *ku to kew ti* (my juniors and seniors). The clans constitute the most important social units among the White Meo, and in some villages a clan is coextensive with the village, so that the head of the clan is also the village headman. Marriage is considered a bond between two clans, and the reciprocal feasting which is integral to the marriage ritual symbolizes this relationship. [Barney 1961: 10-17.] According to White Meo informants in northern Laos, there normally are several clans in each village, each with a leader who is the eldest male of the senior line. Each clan has its own name and origin myth, and ancestors who are contacted in prescribed rituals through the special powers of the clan chief. Children are members of their father's clan, and clans are exogamous. One informant reported that in his village there were four clans. [Hickey 1956.]

MARRIAGE AND FAMILY. **Mode.** The North Vietnam Meo permit their children to select their own mates. The young people gather at periodic "marriage fairs" to display their prowess at handicrafts and games. Courtships start in this festive atmosphere of singing and dancing. When a selection has been made, the boy's parents obtain the services of an intermediary to approach the girl's parents, and an agreement is made concerning the bride price. If the boy is too poor to pay the bride price and the cost of the marriage feast, his parents-in-law usually defray the cost, and the boy is then expected to do service for a two-year period. [Lunet de Lajonquière 1906: 314-18.] According to Barney (1961: 31-33), in the Xieng Khouang area of Laos young people meet at village celebrations such as the lunar new year feast. Villages extend invitations to other villages, and games are organized so that the young people may meet. A ball game is the most common. Boys and girls form two lines, arranged so that those facing are of different clans. A ball is tossed back and forth, and the participants sing to one another. Relationships resulting from the ball game are expected to result in courtships. In courtship, the boy visits the girl's village, where they may initiate a trial marriage. The formal marriage is arranged by an intermediary, usually an elder brother or paternal uncle of the boy. A bride price is agreed upon, and the marriage date is set. A young man is responsible for accumulating his own bride price, although members of the patrilineal residence group may assist. Usually a young man earns it by extra labor or wage labor. Marriage consists of a celebration at the groom's house followed by another ritual at the bride's house. Gifts are exchanged. Residence is patrilocal, and the bride visits her family. [Barney 1961: 13-32; Bourotte 1943: 38-45.] **Form.** In northern Vietnam, the Meo permit polygyny. Usually it is found only among the well-to-do. It is not uncommon for a man to have three or four wives. [Grossin 1926: 49; Bourotte 1943: 45.] Among the Meo of the Xieng Khouang area of Laos, many cases of polygyny result from the levirate. Sororal polygyny is found, but is not common. Well-to-do Meo usually have more than one wife, all living under the same roof, even sharing the same sleeping area. The first wife is considered the head wife. [Barney 1961: 15-16.] **Residence.** In northern Vietnam, residence after marriage is patrilocal or neolocal, but in the vicinity of the paternal house. If the family is poor, however, or there is insufficient land, sons may have to disperse. Young men may reside matrilocally for a service period when they cannot afford a bride price. [Lunet de Lajonquière 1906: 314-18; Abadie 1924: 165; Grossin 1926: 45.] Among the Meo in Laos, residence is temporarily patrilocal. After a child is born, the couple establish their own household near the paternal house, and the son is still under his father's authority. [Barney 1961: 11.] **Domestic unit.** Meo households normally consist of parents and at least one married son and his family. The patrilocal extended family (or minimally, the stem family) is probably common. For Laos (Xieng Khouang area) Barney reports households of up to 35 residents, containing married sons and their families as well as other dependent kin. [Barney 1961: 9-10.] **Inheritance.** In northern Vietnam, Meo family property consists of the house, furnishings, animals, produce from gardens and swiddens, and the swiddens themselves. After the death of the household head, the wife assumes temporary control of family property, and after her death, the eldest son inherits the bulk of the property and exclusive use of the swidden. Other sons receive a small share of the movable property. [Abadie 1924: 167-69; Diguet 1908: 144.] Barney (1961: 31) reports much the same pattern among the Meo in Laos. Unless the widow is elderly, she normally becomes the second wife of her husband's brother, who then becomes guardian of his brother's family property. Bourotte (1943: 38-45), writing of the White Meo in Laos, says that it was traditional for the eldest son to become head of the house on the death of his father, and also to inherit most of the family property with the understanding that he be responsible for all males who chose to remain in the paternal house. Due to Lao influence, however, the White Meo now divide the patrimony evenly among the sons, and the son who remains in the paternal house becomes the head of the family. **Divorce.** Among the North Vietnam Meo, if the wife is proven to have committed adultery, she can be repudiated by her husband, and her parents must return the bride price. [Grossin 1926: 49.] Divorce is possible, but not frequent among the Meo of the Xieng Khouang area of Laos. In cases of marital difficulty, the heads of the patrilineal residence groups may arbitrate, perhaps with the assistance of the district chief. [Barney 1961: 16.]

SOCIOPOLITICAL ORGANIZATION. In northern Vietnam most Meo groups are dispersed, and in most instances the highest political position is that of village chief. In Meo villages populated by members of the same kin group, often the eldest male is automatically the village chief (Diguet 1908: 137). In areas where there are relatively dense groupings of Meo, they have sometimes attained positions of authority recognized by other ethnic groups. In the Dong Van area the Meo have gained political control, and in the Pa Kha area, the *ly truong* (the position above village chief) was at one time Meo (Lunet de Lajonquière 1906: 319). In areas where Tai-speaking groups have been in control, the Meo have been subject to them only in respect to taxes and furnishing labor for corvées (Bonifacy 1919: 26). Diguet (1908: 137) points out that Meo terms for political offices vary from north to south of the Red river. Diguet also contends that some terms refer to military

functions; for example *ma phai* is "keeper of the horse register" and *ping t'eou* is "chief of the troops." ● Since 1954, when the Democratic Republic of North Vietnam was established, the Meo have been politically integrated in the semiautonomous Tai–Meo zone in which they have representation. [Fall 1960: 80-100.] In the Xieng Khouang area of Laos, where there are relatively dense groupings of Meo, their political authority extends beyond the village. Several district chiefs are Meo, and all Meo in the area at the present time recognize Touby Lyfoung as their "paramount chief." The present Lao government also has declared him the official leader of the Xieng Khouang Meo. Meo villages in the Xieng Khouang area enjoy a great deal of autonomy, and consequently most administrative responsibility rests with the headman. When the patrilineal group is coextensive with the village, the head of the group is village headman. When there are several kin groups, the eldest of the kin-group heads assumes the role. The headman must arbitrate disputes, organize village festivals, and supervise public works projects such as opening new trails and maintaining existing ones. If a village moves, the headman organizes the migration. In addition to receiving a small commission from all taxes collected, he also receives gifts from the villagers. Since the organization of the Royal Lao government, the Meo of Xieng Khouang have had representatives in the National Assembly. [Barney 1961: 20-23.]

RELIGION. **Major religions.** Formal Buddhism is not found among the Indochina Meo, although they do venerate some Buddhist deities. Quang Am (Vietnamese name for Quan Yin), the Buddhist Goddess of Mercy, is venerated by some Meo (Diguet 1908: 144; Abadie 1924: 167). **Supernaturals.** The Meo pantheon of spirits is extensive. Among the most important are: To, the spirit of heaven, Ang, spirit of earth, Sien Chen, spirit of the mountain, Lu Shen, spirit of thunder, Long Wan, the spirit of the dragon, and household spirits known collectively as *tsao chen*. The Meo also believe that each human has three souls called *pli* which are reincarnated in the bodies of pregnant women. [Lunet de Lajonquière 1906: 310-15.] The cult of the ancestors is found among the Meo, although it is described as less elaborate than among the Chinese and Vietnamese. Ancestral altars are simple—a table containing a jar of sand in which joss is burned, and two bands of red paper containing invocations in Chinese calligraphy. [Diguet 1908: 144; Abadie 1924: 167.] Among the Meo in Laos, the *tlan*, or spirits, are classified according to their functions. There are *tlan* associated with the elements, fertility, the trails, rice, the hearth, and sleeping quarters. *Tlan* are related to good and bad fortune, and to natural phenomena and unusual events, and they also are believed to affect individual behavior. [Barney 1961: 35-39.] **Practitioners.** Morechand (1955b: 509-58) describes a form of shamanism among the White Meo of northern Vietnam and Laos in which the shaman, male or female, must meet specific requirements and must be initiated. The initiate cannot be too young, and the male must not be of low social status, while the female should have at least two children. These shamans heal illnesses, exorcise evil spirits, and make talismans. Shamanistic rituals are elaborate—characteristically there is a dance, spirit messages, and a trance. ● Shamans among the Meo of Laos are known as *tu ua neng*, and they may either be male or female. They are believed to have *tlan* (spirits) dwelling within them, from whom they receive the power to heal, determine the meaning of signs, protect newly born infants, predict the future, and communicate with the *tlan*. In addition to preparing amulets, they erect altars in houses, in the fields, and along paths. The role of the shaman is not necessarily hereditary, although children of shamans often manifest the presence of *tlan* and assume the métier from a parent. A village may have more than one shaman, each of whom may have specialized functions. All receive fees. [Barney 1961: 35-37.] **Ceremonies.** In addition to ceremonies associated with the cult of the ancestors, there is a feast to mark the new lunar year. The Meo "eat the new year" by killing a pig as an offering to the spirits and the ancestors, and afterward serving it at a large meal. At planting time a chicken and joss sticks are offered to the spirit of the mountain. [Maspéro 1929-30: 244.] **Illness and medicine.** It is commonly believed that evil spirits cause illness, and the Meo also attribute ailments to soul loss. Among the White Meo in Laos, it is believed that should the *pli* (soul) leave the body, the person will fall ill. The shaman is summoned to perform a ritual in which he employs a figure representing the victim. A blood sacrifice is then made to restore the *pli* to the body. [Barney 1961: 39.] There are no food taboos for a pregnant woman, but the husband must observe a vegetable diet, and he also must remain near the house. According to Abadie (1924: 165), both practices are survivals of Meo couvade. If the newborn is male, the placenta is buried before the entrance to the house; if female, it is buried beneath the hearth. Thirty-three days after the birth, the child is named, and friends and kin bring gifts. **Soul, death, and afterlife.** In northern Vietnam, the corpse, dressed in fine clothes, is attached to the wall in the main room of the house where kin, neighbors, and friends have gathered. There is feasting and dancing, and occasionally some food is placed in the deceased's mouth. The grave site is selected by the shaman. The body is carried on a stretcher to the accompaniment of firecrackers and firearms. After burial, the cortege returns to the house to continue feasting. There is no grave cult. [Abadie 1924: 167.] Among the Meo of Laos, there is a belief that after death the soul goes to live in the land of the *tlan* (spirits), and some Meo believe that the soul of the deceased enters the next newborn member of the family. In the Xieng Khouang area the corpse may be placed in a chair during several days of feasting. The corpse is buried outside the house. Each year the [patrilineal] residence group observes a "visit" with their group *tlan* or ancestors. The house is taboo for several days and the family remains in seclusion. [Barney 1961: 34-35.]

BIBLIOGRAPHY. Abadie 1924; Barney 1961; Bonifacy 1919; Bourotte 1943; Cresson and Jeannin 1944; Diguet 1908; Dussault 1924; Embree and Thomas 1950; Fall 1960; Fromaget 1937; Gourdon 1931; Grossin 1926; Hickey 1956; Lafont 1960, 1961; Le 1955; Le Boulanger 1931; Lunet de Lajonquière 1906; Maspéro 1929-30; Morechand 1952, 1955b; NNCDT 1959; Roux and Tran 1954; Savina 1930; Smalley 1956.

THAILAND MEO

Synonyms. *H'moong, Meau, Mong*

ORIENTATION. Identification. Called Meo (Meau) by the Siamese, to which they add terms for "Flowery," "Black," and "Striped" (Meo Dawk, Meo Dam, Meo Lai), referring to differences in dress. The people refer to themselves as H'moong (Mong). Young (1961: 44), following native usage, categorizes the majority of Meo in Thailand as either H'moong Njua (Blue Meo) or H'moong Deaw (White Meo). Bernatzik (1947: 3-4) investigated groups of White and Black Meo in Nan province near the Thailand–Laos border. **Location.** Mainly in Nan, Chiengrai, and Chiengmai provinces of northern Thailand, with scattered settlements as far south as 16° 30′ N. (Young 1961: 46). **Linguistic affiliation.** The Thailand Meo speak dialects related to those of similar groups of Miao speakers in South China. The linguistic position of Miao (and Yao) is as yet unclear. The dialects of the various categories of Thailand Meo are in some instances mutually intelligible, although rather wide differences do exist (Young 1961: 47). Lao is used as a lingua franca, and many of the older men are in addition fluent speakers of Yunnanese. In the Chiengmai area Shan is an important second language. **Demography.** The Meo population of Thailand is given "conservatively" by Young (1961: 46) as 45,600. **History and cultural relations.** The migration of the Meo into Thailand has occurred mainly within the last 50 years. The movement has been generally in a north-south direction, coming from Laos and, secondarily, from Burma. Many of the Meo in northern Thailand are in all probability related to the White Miao of South China, who emigrated in large numbers into Tonkin and northern Laos during the last century. The Meo in their Thailand environment continue to be independent and averse to intermarriage with other ethnic groups. In the vicinity of Chiengmai and other population centers, however, they are frequently seen in the markets, and the younger Meo here have responded to government and mission schooling. In more remote areas, as in the mountains of the Thailand–Laos border, they remain largely self-sufficient, visited occasionally by Chinese traders and venturing themselves only rarely into the plains areas below. [Young 1961: 56; Bernatzik 1947: 109.]

SETTLEMENT PATTERN AND HOUSING. **Settlement pattern.** Villages are rarely located under 3,600 feet, and are generally found above 5,000 feet. The Meo prefer a slope just under the summit of a mountain ridge, near a source of water that can be piped into the village through bamboo troughs. Such sites are generally covered with monsoon forest, which the Meo reduce to low dense bush forest by repeated burning. [Young 1961: 48-49; Bernatzik 1947: 26ff.] Young reports about 35 houses to a village, with an average village population of around 280 (1961: 48-49). Bernatzik reports a lower figure (3 to 13 houses) for Meo villages in the region bordering on Laos (1947: 263). Houses are clustered somewhat irregularly, with the chief's house in the center. There are no village walls or stockades. ● The Meo move their villages on the average of once every 10 to 15 years, due to soil exhaustion, high taxes, epidemics, or the urging of a shaman. Such moves may be made over long distances, involving many days of travel, according to Young (1961: 56), although Bernatzik (1947: 260) reports that the Meo never move a distance greater than one day's march if they can help it. A new village site is pioneered for one harvest season by a few selected families before the entire village moves (Bernatzik 1947: 260). **Housing.** Single-story, rectangular houses are built directly on the ground, surrounded by shallow ditches to drain off rainwater. Walls are of wood and bamboo, and roofs of grass thatching. The space inside may be partitioned off, depending on the size of the family. Furnishings include wooden beds and tables. A fireplace is sunk into the floor of the main room, and there is a Chinese-style earthen stove for cooking mash for the livestock. Separate rice storage bins are built on piles, as are the temporary huts in the rice fields. [Bernatzik 1947: 265.]

ECONOMY. The people are passionate hunters and fishermen, but agriculture is the main source of food. According to Young (1961: 51-52), hunting is regarded more as a sport than a necessity. Normally, collecting achieves importance only after the harvest, but during times of food shortage collecting may contribute significantly to the diet. Young (1961: 51-52) emphasizes that the Meo are among the most advanced and prosperous of the ethnic minorities in Thailand, due in part to their sales of opium and livestock, and in part to a natural business ability and independence of spirit, in which respect they are similar to the Yao. **Agriculture.** Swidden agriculture is practiced almost exclusively. Credner (1935a: 168) comments on the absence of terracing and irrigation, probably due to lack of suitable terrain. Young (1961: 56) cites recent reports that a few Meo in northern Nan province have taken up wet-rice agriculture. The main crop is mountain or dry rice, both glutinous and nonglutinous (Bernatzik 1947: 253). Opium poppies constitute the second most important crop. Other field crops include maize and buckwheat, both of considerably less importance than among the Tonkin Meo. Sugar cane, yams, cucumbers, beans, tobacco, onions, hemp, and some cotton are also raised. The Meo plant crops of varying dates of maturity so that some food is available most of the time (Young 1961: 51-52; see also Bernatzik 1947: 353-62 for detailed data on this point). ● A new field is cleared by the members of an extended family. A large family may clear a considerable area, dividing it into smaller fields of up to three hectares each. Fields are cleared by repeated burning. Seeds are planted by hand, in holes made with a digging stick. A rice field will continue to yield from one to three years, after which it is fallowed to a new growth of forest trees. Poppy fields, however, will produce continuously for up to 20 years. Rice is cut and partly husked in the field, and then stored in special bins near the houses until used. Some vegetables and fruit trees are raised in kitchen gardens. [Bernatzik 1947: 353-62.] Credner points out that the importance of field crops coupled with the Meo's relatively primitive agricultural techniques requires the exploitation of a considerable land area; fields are sometimes many hours distant, and men may remain in temporary field houses for days or weeks at a time (1935a: 169). **Fishing and hunting.** Hooks, hand nets, and weirs are used, but the favorite method of taking fish is by poisoning. The Meo are avid fishermen, but since suitable fishing grounds may be some distance away, fishing supplies a relatively small portion of the diet. [Bernatzik 1947: 352.] Although the Meo are passionate hunters, hunting does not account for very much of their food supply except in the more remote mountain areas. Traps and snares are used, but the chief weapons of the hunt are the flintlock musket and the crossbow with poisoned arrows. The muskets are manufactured and assembled by Meo gunsmiths, using iron obtained from Chinese traders. Elephants, stags, and wild boar are highly prized. Birds and small game are also taken. [Bernatzik 1947: 340-41.] **Domestic animals.** According to Young (1961: 52), the Meo far surpass the other hill tribes in animal husbandry. Animals are well cared for in pens, coops, and corrals. Pigs are fed a specially cooked corn mash once a day. Castration is common, and is performed by specialists. Pigs, dogs, and chickens are found in every village, the former raised for both food and sacrifice. Cattle and ponies are raised wherever the terrain is suitable. Buffalo are less common, and, like cattle and ponies, are often raised for sale to the valley-dwelling Lao and Siamese. [Bernatzik 1947: 365-66.] **Food and stimulants.** Staples are rice, vegetables, and beans, commonly spiced with peppers, chilies, or sour (pickled) vegetables. Meat, when available, may be smoked, salted, or dried in the sun, and is often fried in animal fat. Forest plants, roots, insect larvae, and honey are also consumed, particularly in times of poor harvests. There is considerable variety in the Meo diet, particularly in the methods of preparation. [Bernatzik 1947: 372-77.] Native tobacco is smoked in pipes by both sexes, young and old. Alcohol, distilled from corn mash, is very popular, and is consumed in considerable quantities by both sexes (Bernatzik 1947: 381). Next to rice, the most important crop is the poppy, from which the Meo obtain raw opium and seeds for food. Some villages have virtually a cash economy based on the sale of opium and the purchase of foodstuffs and other necessities. The Meo themselves use opium both as a medicine and a stimulant. It is swallowed, chewed, and smoked —mainly by men (Bernatzik 1947: 383). According to Young (1961: 51), the rate of opium addiction among the Thailand Meo is about 12 per cent. **Industrial arts.** The Meo are skilled in wood and bamboo work, and in basketry. Most villages have a blacksmith who works with a piston bellows on iron bars purchased from Chinese traders. Highly skilled silversmiths make women's jewelry from old silver coins. Hemp and cotton are made into cloth in the home by spinning, weaving, and dyeing. The Meo know the technique of batik (wax) dye. Women are highly skilled in embroidery and appliqué work. [Bernatzik 1947: 124, 130, 403-04, 410-11, 425.] Music is highly developed; the Meo are great singers of improvised poetry, particularly love songs, which are occasionally sung antiphonally. Musical instruments include the reed organ (consisting of some eight bamboo pipes and a vibrating metal or wood reed), the jew's-harp, skin-head drums, and small brass gongs. [Bernatzik 1947: 141-43, 146-48.] **Trade.** There appears to be little economic specialization with the exception of a few part-time trades such as blacksmithing and gunsmithing. Bernatzik reports little internal trade, with the work of specialists confined mainly to the needs of members of their own patrilineages (1947: 423). Young (1961: 54), however, reports a brisk internal trade among the Meo. External trading relations consist of periodic visits to the market towns in the valleys and bartering with itinerant traders (the Chinese, or Haw, from Yunnan, or the Lao from northern Thailand). The Meo are said to be good businessmen in their trading relations with other groups. Bernatzik reports a well-developed pattern of borrowing and lending money, including the use of witnesses, fixed interest charges, and legal

procedures in case of forfeiture (1947: 241). **Division of labor.** The men hunt, make arrow poison, and distill alcohol. They also do most of the carpentry and engage in metal work of various kinds. Women carry firewood and water, spin, sew, cook, and do much of the weeding in the fields. Men and women together work in the fields during planting and harvesting; they go on fishing trips together; and they care for pigs and chickens jointly. Weaving and load carrying may be done by either sex. [Bernatzik 1947: 437ff.] **Land tenure.** Land within the territory of a village (the maximum area of actual or potential economic exploitation) is theoretically the property of the village chief. In practice, cultivated land is worked by members of extended families. The head of each family has the right to allocate and redistribute the plots worked by the various members. [Bernatzik 1947: 239-41.]

KIN GROUPS. According to Bernatzik (1947: 30, 35, 54-55, 111), the Meo are characterized by nonlocalized, exogamous patrisibs or surname groups. A village is usually inhabited by members of one surname group. The land-owning and economically important kin group is not, however, the patrisib, but rather the patrilocal extended family occupying a cluster of adjacent houses. The sibs have no insignia and no chief, and function mainly in regulating marriage and in channeling intervillage visiting and borrowing relationships; there are some indications, however, that they may once have played a role in something approaching a politico-military organization. [Judging from Bernatzik's data, the ordinary Meo village is probably an exogamous clan community composed of a localized (lineage) segment of a patrilineal surname group or patrisib.] **Kin terminology.** The following kin terms are given by Bernatzik (1947: facing page 34):

Fa	tse
Mo	na
FaElBr	ti lou
FaYoBr	nyu ku
FaSi	pu-nya
MoBr	tse tlan
MoElSi	na tay lou
MoYoSi	na tay hloa
ElBr	ti lou
YoBr	nyu ku
ElSi	pu nyan
YoSi	ku moa
Male cousin	mpeu
Female cousin	moa

MARRIAGE AND FAMILY. Mode. Opportunities for courtship occur at festival times, particularly the new year's festival after the harvest, when boys can visit girls in nearby villages. Antiphonal singing of love songs to the accompaniment of a jew's-harp and a reed organ usually leads to sexual familiarity and intercourse. Group courtship patterns are lacking among the Thailand Meo. Couples retire alone to secluded spots outside the village. ● Marriage may be initiated simply by the act of cohabitation and/or announced pregnancy, although in well-to-do families the boy's father usually consults the ancestors as well as the girl's family before setting a date for the wedding. A girl's family rarely goes against her choice of a partner, but a boy's male relatives may attempt to influence his choice by pretending that the ancestors are opposed to the marriage. Where the villages of the couple are far apart, a Chinese trader may be employed as a go-between. A bride price in silver coinage is paid by the members of the groom's family. This sum must be repaid by the girl's family if she later deserts her husband. The bride is escorted to the groom's home by her female relatives, bringing with her a trousseau of blankets, fancy embroidered clothing, and silver ornaments. She is welcomed by the head of the groom's extended family, who sacrifices to the family ancestors and welcomes the new bride into his family and sib. Feasting and drinking, at the expense of the groom's family, may last for two or three days. [Bernatzik 1947: 97-100.] **Form.** Polygynous marriages are allowed, but are in practice limited to village chiefs and older, well-to-do men. The wives of a polygynous marriage share the same quarters and the same bed with their husband. [Bernatzik 1947: 76.] **Extension of incest taboos.** Marriage is theoretically prohibited between persons of the same name [patrilineal surname group exogamy]. In practice, marriage can take place if the relationship is more than three generations removed. [Bernatzik 1947: 110.] **Residence.** Married sons continue to live with their wives in a section of their father's house until they attain majority at age 30. Thereafter they set up an independent household near their father's residence. [Bernatzik 1947: 30-31.] **Domestic unit.** The household unit consists normally of a patrilocal extended [joint] family, including married sons not yet 30 and their families. The oldest male retains authority, including the making of ancestral sacrifices on behalf of all the family members. Large households of up to 30 members may occur, but according to Young (1961: 49) the average number per household is 8. [Bernatzik 1947: 35, 77, 259.] **Inheritance.** At the death of the head of an extended family, the oldest married son still living in the family homestead inherits his father's status, including control of the plots of land cultivated by members of the extended family. When the last of the wives of the original family head dies, all movable property is divided equally among all surviving sons; the original household group is dissolved, with the oldest son retaining rights to the homestead. [Bernatzik 1947: 244-47.] **Divorce.** A widow normally marries her deceased husband's brother. Divorce is said to be rare, in part because of family pressures on both sides to avoid trouble over the bride price (Bernatzik 1947: 111-13).

SOCIOPOLITICAL ORGANIZATION. **Political organization.** The highest level of political integration at the native level is the village. Most village chiefs have been legally installed by Siamese government officials, and in a few cases Meo leaders have been recognized as *kammans,* or circle headmen (Young 1961: 56). A village chief who has gained power and wealth through plural marriages and many offspring may have judiciary functions not only in his own village but also in neighboring ones—particularly if he has also acquired a reputation as a specialist in divination and magic. He is likely to be a repository of tribal lore and technical knowledge, and is expected to offer periodic sacrifices to the ancestors—on behalf of the village and also of his own extended family (Bernatzik 1947: 114-15, 190). ● Bernatzik (1947: 40) mentions the tradition among the Meo of a "king" and a "kingdom" in China, and of repeated battles with the Chinese. The Meo of Thailand believe that a Meo king will rise again among them and lead them to victory. Even more vivid, according to Bernatzik, are their memories of "great chieftains" who had power over 20 or more villages. The Meo on the Laos border claim that their grandfathers were led out of Yunnan to the Thailand–Indochina border by one such chieftain. According to present-day Meo, the territory of a great chieftain was organized primarily for warfare. The chieftain was elected by vote of all arms-bearing men in his jurisdiction, and acted as supreme judicial authority and war leader. He appointed village chiefs within his territory to collect fines and taxes. Important matters were settled by general assemblies, presided over by the great chieftain and attended by village chiefs and heads of families. It was the function of the great chieftain to offer animal sacrifices and invoke the spirits on behalf of the assembly (Bernatzik 1947: 41-44). ● The kinship basis, if any, of the kind of politico-military organization described by Bernatzik is unclear, but it may have rested on some form of nonlocalized kin group such as the sib. Today, according to Bernatzik (1947: 253-59), most disputes within a village are handled by the heads of extended families. If they fail to settle the matter, it is brought before the village chief, who can impose fines and order punishment, and who may resort to divination. Major matters, such as the decision to move to a new location, are decided by a popular assembly of all men able to bear arms. Here the opinions of the village chief and the village shaman bear great weight. **Warfare.** Bernatzik (1947: 394-97) characterized the Meo as fiercely independent and warlike when aroused. According to Bernatzik's informants, all able-bodied men were once liable to military service. In time of war they were called up by the "great chieftain," and organized under a hierarchical system of officers and leaders, with a basic unit of 60 to 100 men. Meo warfare was carried on by small units which would attempt to take all strategic points and passes by means of advance planning and coordination. Ambush was a favorite tactic. Weapons included crossbows, long-handled spears with poisoned points, flexible wooden clubs joined by chain links, two-bladed swords, and a sort of bolas consisting of iron balls attached to the end of a long thin rope. Defensive armor was made by attaching iron plates to pieces of animal hide. Present-day weapons are limited to the crossbow and flintlock muskets. The Meo make their own guns and gunpowder from materials purchased from Chinese traders (Bernatzik 1947: 386-92).

RELIGION. Bernatzik characterized Meo religion as based on belief in ancestors and spirits. Most Meo are animists, according to Young. Only about 100 Meo in Thailand are Christians. **Supernaturals.** In addition to the souls of the ancestors, the Meo believe in a variety of spirits, some of which inhabit trees, rocks, and fields. Others are patron spirits of activities, such as blacksmithing, or teacher-spirits of medicine men and shamans. A guardian dog spirit protects the house and its inhabitants. These spirits and souls live in a spirit world, and look and behave as human beings. There is also a supreme spirit who has no particular form and is present everywhere. Malevolent spirits must be propitiated by animal sacrifices, particularly when they have been inadvertently offended. [Bernatzik 1947: 164-65, 169.] **Practitioners.** Among the Meo there are both male and female shamans. The occupation is not necessarily hereditary—a person may become a shaman involuntarily through being possessed by a spirit, after which he can communicate with his teacher-spirit. In practice, the shaman goes into a trance, stamps his feet, shakes his body, rolls on the ground, and may lapse into an unconscious state. He manipulates swords, rattles, sacrificial animal blood, and spirit money while chanting and reciting incantations. Shamans interpret omens, foretell the future, and exorcise evil spirits, but they do not engage in black magic or sorcery. When not engaged as shamans, they function as ordinary members of society. [Bernatzik 1947: 176-80.] The shaman's political role, if any, is unclear, but it is known that a village chief may at the same time be a recognized shaman with a wide reputation in divination and exorcism. The chances for such an individual to extend his political control in times of crisis would seem considerable. ● Heads of families and ordinary citizens may carry out ancestral sacrifices and make hunting magic. The Meo believe strongly in the interpretation of dreams and omens and in the efficacy of divination, activities which may be carried out either by shamans or by other individuals, including the village chief. **Ceremonies and ritual.** The most important annual ceremony is the new year's festival, which begins in December after the harvest. Animal sacrifices to the souls of the ancestors and to other spirits occupy the first day, after which there may be several days of drinking, visiting, courting, and general merriment and relaxation. Animal sacrifices, which make up a good portion of Meo ritual behavior, are made by heads of families and others on a variety of occasions. Small altars are set up in the homes, in the fields, and along paths outside the village. The Meo characteristically do not sacrifice cattle, horses, or buffalo, but prefer pigs and chickens instead. Divination is practiced with the aid of chicken bones or with cracked bamboo sticks. [Bernatzik 1947: 193, 204-07.] **Illness and medicine.** Illness may be caused either by angry spirits or soul loss. Black magic does not cause sickness or death among the Thailand Meo (Bernatzik 1947: 180). Shamans carry out rituals designed to exorcise evil spirits causing illness; other specialists may administer herbs and medicines, but only after the guilty spirit has been discovered through divination. The Meo have an extensive pharmacopoeia, and also make much use of Chinese medicines which they obtain from traders. They are skilled in obstetrics and bonesetting. [Bernatzik 1947: 235-37.] **Birth.** Takes place in the house with the husband assisting. The Meo try to prolong confinement of the mother after delivery as long as possible, in the case of prosperous families up to 30 days (Bernatzik 1947: 49). **Soul, death, and afterlife.** The Meo believe in the existence of three souls (Young 1961: 47). After death, a person's soul is reborn in the next child born into the sib. When a village migrates, the souls of the ancestors not yet reborn are ceremonially informed of the move and migrate with the group. [Bernatzik 1947: 160.] The corpse is washed, dressed in new clothes, and laid out in the home for one or two days while immediate relatives keep vigil. The body is borne to a grave in the woods in a wooden coffin. The funeral procession is attended by members of the deceased's sib. Much care is taken to "show the right road" to the departing soul, and a priest-shaman functions to exorcise evil spirits during the period between death and burial. After burial an animal sacrifice is made, and some of the food offered the soul of the deceased. Additional sacrifices and ceremonials are carried out for three days following burial, and are followed by a festival of the dead one year after burial. [Bernatzik 1947: 115-19; Young 1961: 47-48.]

BIBLIOGRAPHY. Bernatzik 1947; Credner 1935a; Young 1961.

YAO

LINGNAN YAO

Synonyms. *Kim Mien, Kim Mun, Yu Mien*

ORIENTATION. Identification and location. The Lingnan region (Kwangtung–Kwangsi) has long been a center of dispersal for the Yao of Yunnan and northern Southeast Asia, and Kwangsi at present contains more Yao than any other Chinese province. Yao settlements are mainly concentrated in a series of mountainous backwater areas—ethnic islands surrounded by Chinese culture. In Kwangtung these are the Yao Shan or Yao hills in the northwestern part of the province. In the area of the upper North river, just north of Ju Yüan, the Yao inhabit a mountainous retreat designated by the Communists as the Shao-pien Yao Autonomous Hsien. This area, described by Leuschner (1911), P'ang (1932), and Stübel (1938), is one of rugged topography, relatively inaccessible to Chinese traders and officials. The Yao there appear to be somewhat less subject to Han influence than those farther west in the less rugged area of Linshan. The latter area is designated by the Communists as the Lien-shan Chuang and Yao Nationalities Autonomous Hsien, and has been described by Fortune (1939). In Kwangsi, major concentrations of Yao occur in a series of hill areas across the south-central portion of the province. Wang (1936) studied Hua-lan Yao settlements in the vicinity of the Ta Yao Shan (Great Yao mountains) near Hsiang Hsien in eastern Kwangsi. For Kwangsi, Wist (1938: 80) lists numerous subgroup names of Chinese origin, such as the Pan Yao, Chai-shan Yao, Cheng Yao, Lan-tien (Indigo) Yao, and Hua-lan (Flower Basket) Yao. The Yao groups refer to themselves by such names as Kim Mien, Kim Mun, and Yu Mien. **Linguistic affiliation.** Linguistic position uncertain, but frequently classified with Miao as Sino-Tibetan. **Demography.** Bruk (1960: 32), using 1953 census figures, gives 469,000 Yao in Kwangsi and 41,000 in Kwangtung.

SETTLEMENT PATTERN AND HOUSING. Settlement pattern. Yao villages in the mountains north of Ju Yüan average some 125 persons, with the maximum number about 400 (Stübel 1938: 359-62). Villages are located on mountain slopes, with the houses arranged in rows, parallel to the face of the slope. Fields may be some distance away, in which case small field houses are used during part of the year. Settlements are connected by narrow footpaths. In the less mountainous area near Linshan, Fortune (1939: 366-67) found villages with as many as 1,200 inhabitants. Fortune's data indicate that here villages may be divided into sections or wards inhabited by different *fong* [patrilineages]. Wang (1936: 33) found an average of 138 persons in the five villages

she surveyed in the Kwangsi Ta Yao Shan. **Housing.** Stübel (1938: 359-62) reports one-story, rectangular structures, with gable roofs, built directly on the ground. Walls are of air-dried brick, and roofs are covered with bark shingles (or, more recently, tiles). The interior is divided into two or three rooms, with earthen floors. P'ang (1932: 477-78) adds that poorer families may build houses with wood or bamboo frames plastered with mud. Secondary buildings include outhouses, pigsties, cow sheds, and granaries. Stübel describes the latter as made entirely of wood and raised above the ground on piles. Three or four are sometimes built in a row, with a common roof. House furnishings are simple, consisting of a clay oven, a wooden sleeping platform, and a few wooden stools and benches. Wist (1938: 86) adds that the water supply is frequently conducted into the house by means of a bamboo trough running from a nearby stream.

ECONOMY. The Yao of the Lingnan area appear to be relatively permanently settled agriculturists. Permanency is, however, probably more assured in an area such as Linshan than in the rougher terrain of the Yao hills north of Ju Yüan. The Yao in both Kwangtung and Kwangsi spend the major portion of their time in agriculture. They trade or sell their excess produce, along with timber and forest products, to the Chinese in return for manufactured goods and even some foods, such as rice, which they cannot grow in sufficient quantity for their own use. Industrial arts are relatively little developed. **Agriculture.** Dry-field farming on slopes is characteristic, but wet rice is grown whenever possible, either on terraces or along valley bottoms. Wang (1936: 19-20), describing the situation in the Ta Yao Shan area of Kwangsi, mentions both wet-rice agriculture, with terracing, along the rivers, and slash-and-burn farming at higher altitudes. The latter method, she says, is more prevalent. Stübel (1938: 262-63) describes the preparation of swiddens by burning. Swiddens, planted to mountain rice, sweet potatoes, maize, various millets, and taro, are cultivated for an average of three years, after which they are fallowed for ten to twelve years. In addition to dry fields, terraces up to several hundred meters long are constructed along the slopes. Rain water is distributed by an extensive system of ditches. According to Stübel (1938: 262-63), methods of cultivating wet rice on irrigated terraces are the same as among the Chinese, and include the use of a plow pulled by a cow or an ox. [P'ang 1932: 478-79; Wist 1938: 95-96.] Small kitchen gardens supply a variety of vegetables. Fortune (1939: 409) mentions both lowland wet-rice farming and cultivation of slopes and terraces to produce maize, taro, beans, cotton, sesame, wheat, chilies, potatoes, spinach, lettuce, mustard, cabbage, pumpkins, and winter squash. ● Stübel (1938: 380) also describes the Yao of Chihing (Shih-hsing) county in extreme northeastern Kwangtung near the Kiangsi border. Here he found only dry-field farming, using the hoe, but coupled with a regulated rotation system with forestation. The first year after burning, a swidden is used mainly for mountain rice and maize; the second year for sweet potatoes; and the third year for taro. Simultaneous with the first planting, seedlings of various economically important trees are put in the ground. At the end of three years, these are large enough to discourage further growth of weeds and grasses. The swidden is thereafter fallowed for 18 or 19 years until the trees are large enough to be cut for timber. The importance of arboriculture in the Yao economy is mentioned also by Fortune (1939: 410), who says that the Yao sometimes plant cedar and bamboo. **Fishing and hunting.** Neither fishing nor hunting is of much economic importance, although men hunt deer, wild boar, squirrels, and birds as a hobby, sometimes aided by dogs. The universal weapon is the primitive muzzle-loader obtained from the Chinese. Fishing is done occasionally, using either poison or nets. [Stübel 1938: 363; Wist 1938: 100; Fortune 1939: 412.] **Domestic animals.** The Lingnan Yao pay relatively little attention to animal breeding, and the meat of domestic animals does not contribute greatly to the diet. Pigs are kept in pens separate from the houses, but a family ordinarily slaughters only about one pig per year. Chickens are plentiful, and used mainly for blood sacrifice. A variety of red-brown humpbacked cattle is found in most villages, but they are not plentiful and are used chiefly as work animals. Water buffalo are found only at the lower altitudes. Most Yao families keep bees, and trade honey and wax to the Chinese. [Wang 1936: 21; Wist 1938: 99; Stübel 1938: 363; Fortune 1939: 410.] **Food and stimulants.** Rice is the chief foodstuff, usually eaten in a gruel mixed with corn or millet. Sweet potatoes and taro are also important. Wist (1938: 93) lists sweet potatoes rather than rice as the staple food. Wild greens, bamboo shoots, peppers, and a variety of other vegetables are eaten when available. The Yao near Linshan, who are in closer touch with the Chinese, include in their diet sour (pickled) vegetables, peas, bean curd, and, among well-to-do families, pork and chicken. The Yao in the more remote areas consume relatively little meat. They drink mainly water and some tea. Alcoholic beverages distilled from rice or millet are popular, especially at ceremonies and festivals. Tobacco, regarded as less important than alcohol, is smoked in pipes, Chinese fashion. Opium smoking is rare. [Stübel 1938: 353; Wist 1938: 94; P'ang 1932: 492.] **Industrial arts.** Crafts are little developed, since the Yao get most of what they need from the Chinese. Those north of Ju Yüan in Kwangtung do no spinning, weaving, ceramic, or metal work. The wet-rice growing Hua-lan Yao in the Ta Yao Shan of Kwangsi do, however, weave cotton cloth which they dye a deep blue or indigo color. Like the Kwangtung Yao, they lack carpentry and masonry skills, preferring to have such work done by Han artisans. [Wang 1936: 23; Stübel 1938: 364; Fortune 1939: 345; Wist 1938: 101-03.] **Trade.** The Yao go down to lowland Han markets; and in the Linshan area, at least, Chinese traders and middlemen visit the Yao villages and may even live there. In return for guns, salt, cloth, tools, paper, and rice, the Yao supply the Chinese with timber, palm fiber ropes, mushrooms, herbs, indigo, honey, and beeswax. In the Ta Yao Shan area of Kwangsi the Han are expected to get the timber out themselves, since the Yao are unskilled at this work. Trade is for the most part in the hands of the Chinese rather than the Yao. [Stübel 1938: 364; Fortune 1939: 345, 414; Wang 1936: 35; Wist 1938: 101-02.] **Land tenure.** For the Yao of Kwangsi, Wist (1938: 98-99), citing Chinese sources, reports that land throughout the Yao hills is privately owned by permanently settled wet-rice farmers (such as the Hua-lan). This, he says, is a relatively recent development, and due largely to Chinese influence. Only a few Yao groups, notably the Pan and Shan-tze, still practice the old shifting agriculture and rent their lands from the more acculturated Yao such as the Hua-lan.

KIN GROUPS. **Descent.** Patrilineal. **Kin groups.** Wang (1936: 27), Stübel (1938: 365), and Fortune (1939: 348-49) report patrilineal clans [patrisibs] with Chinese surnames. The practical units of social organization are, however, the named patrilineages. In the Linshan area the inhabitants of a village tend to be of the same surname but members of different lineages. The surname groups are not strictly exogamous as are their Chinese equivalents. Exogamy does tend to be followed, however, within the lineage. In the Linshan area the village is normally an endogamous unit (Fortune 1939: 376); Stübel on the other hand reports that marriage outside one's own village is considered favorably (1938: 368-69). Wang (1936: 27) suggests that in the Ta Yao Shan of Kwangsi the village was originally an exogamous clan community; with the decreasing emphasis on surname exogamy, marriages within the village are now more frequent. **Kin terminology.** Yao kin terms distinguish among elder and younger relatives, and kin behavior is marked by respect for age. Paternal male cousins are called brother (elder or younger), but with supplementary terms indicating the distance back to their common ancestor (Fortune 1939: 348-49).

MARRIAGE AND FAMILY. **Mode.** Young people have considerable premarital sexual freedom; Fortune (1939: 381) reports seasonal festivals at which experimentation is expected. Among the less sinicized groups, this is accompanied by freedom of choice as regards marriage partners: a young couple begins living together in a relatively informal relationship which lasts until the birth of the first child; thereafter the groom sends the girl's family a sum of money and the marriage is considered fully valid. According to Wist (1938: 108-11), this mode of marriage is found in its purest form among the Hua-lan, Cheng, and Chai-shan Yao of Kwangsi ● Among some other groups, according to Wist, arranged marriages, using a go-between, have been adopted from the Chinese model. Such marriages involve a bride price of pork and money, the choice of an auspicious day by a magician-priest, and a bridal procession to the groom's home, where the bride pays formal respect to her mother-in-law before the groom's family altar. This is essentially the pattern described by Fortune for the Yao of Linshan (1939: 373ff.), except that the girl's family receives only a gift of food, whereas the girl may bring to the marriage a dowry of land (which must eventually return to her paternal clan). Stübel (1938: 368-69) and P'ang (1932: 479ff.) describe for still other Yao groups in Kwangtung a pattern which combines freedom of choice with the subsequent use of a go-between and bride price. **Form.** Monogamy is the rule. Confirmed reports of polygyny are rare, if not absent altogether. Concubinage, however, seems to be present at least among the well-to-do. [Wist 1938: 111; Stübel 1938: 369-70; Wang 1936: 9.] **Extension of incest taboos.** Surname group exogamy is not strictly adhered to. Stübel (1938: 368-69) reports a prohibition on first-cousin marriage, sometimes restricted to those on the paternal side. Fortune reports a prohibition on first- and second-cousin marriage on either side. Wist (1938: 103) says that intermarriage is permitted among any kinsmen four generations removed. **Residence.** Variable for an initial period of one or two years after marriage, following which the couple usually establishes a separate household in the man's paternal village. An eldest son may, however, establish his family in the same house with his parents to form a stem family household. The institution of the adopted son-in-law, in cases where a son is lacking, requires that the boy reside matrilocally. ● The initial period, which may be ambilocal or even duolocal, is reportedly one of sexual freedom for both man and wife; marriages during this period (which often lasts until the birth of the first child) are brittle, and divorce frequent (Stübel 1938: 369; Fortune 1939: 353-76; Wist 1938: 103). According to Wang (1936: 3-4), the Kwangsi Yao do not really consider a marriage established until the birth of the first child. **Domestic unit.** The independent nuclear family household is the normal pattern today, according to Wist (1938: 103). Stem families of three generations do occur, however, as among the Yao of Kwangsi investigated by Wang. **Inheritance.** Both Stübel (1938: 369-70) and Fortune (1939: 416-17) report the inheritance of family property, including land, by sons and daughters (in the latter case as marriage dowries). They add, however, that sons receive the major share, with the family homestead

always going to a son. Wist, however, cites Chinese sources to the effect that all property, land, and goods are inherited equally by sons, and that daughters inherit nothing (1938: 104). All sources agree that if there are no children a man's nearest paternal relatives inherit. **Divorce.** Wist (1938: 112-13) reports that in areas where free choice in marriage prevails, e.g. among the Hua-lan, Cheng, and Chai-shan Yao of Kwangsi, divorce is easy—either by mutual consent or by payment of compensation by the partner initiating the separation. According to Fortune (1939: 373ff.), children go with the mother, but boys later return to the paternal clan.

SOCIOPOLITICAL ORGANIZATION. **Political organization.** Indigenous political institutions do not extend above the village level. In the mountains north of Ju Yüan in Kwangtung, the adult men of a clan elect one of their number as clan chief (Stübel 1938: 366-67). In villages where several clans are represented, village affairs are in the hands of several clan chiefs, who are responsible for affairs within their own clans and also, acting jointly, for settling cases that concern more than one clan, or the entire village. They judge crimes and impose punishments, which are usually in the form of monetary fines. P'ang (1932: 476) adds that one of the qualifications of the clan chief or village head is that he must have gone through the *tu-shen* ceremony. ● In the Linshan area of Kwangtung, where the Yao are in closer touch with the Chinese, village affairs are handled not only by clan chiefs but also by a number of lesser officials representing the various *fong,* or lineages. Some officials specialize in dealing with the Chinese, others are fire wardens, road supervisors, etc. (Fortune 1939: 363-66). **Social stratification.** Although there are some differences in wealth and amount of land owned by different families, all Yao spend most of their time in agricultural labor. The Yao priests constitute the closest thing to a leisure class. For the Ta Yao Shan of eastern Kwangsi, Wang (1936: 46) and Wist (1938: 98-99) describe a class stratification of sorts whereby settled wet-rice growers along the river valleys own land and exact rent from the Yao who engage in shifting agriculture at higher altitudes. The former regard themselves as the "real Yao," and look down on the swidden farmers, whom they consider to be immigrants. **Warfare.** The Kwangtung Yao have traditions of former battles against the Chinese. Intervillage and interclan disputes still go on, and quarrels and fights over boundaries and cattle or field thefts are frequent. Some disputes approach the stature of clan feuds, and may go on for years. Intervillage warfare is arranged by mutual agreement, usually during the daytime. Muskets are used, and although some killing does occur, most of the hostilities consist of cattle raids, pillage, and taking prisoners for ransom. [Stübel 1938: 366-67; Fortune 1939: 366-68; P'ang 1932: 482.]

RELIGION. Fortune (1939: 347-48) says that Yao religion combines ancestor worship and exorcism of ghosts, the latter for the express purpose of curing illness. These practices he equates with Chinese ancestor worship and popular Taoism respectively. Stübel and P'ang have less to say about ancestor worship, but document the importance of exorcistic ritual. **Supernaturals.** The Yao have the myth of a dog ancestor, P'an-ku. According to Stübel (1938: 371ff.), both the Yao and the Miao in South China have this myth. In the Yao hills north of Ju Yüan he found sacrifices to P'an-ku, although in contemporary Yao culture the dog appears to have no magical significance. Fortune (1939: 358) also mentions the presence of a dog ancestor legend, adding that dog meat is sacred, in the sense that it can only be consumed by a priest and his client in connection with curing rites. ● The Yao believe in a variety of gods and demons, many, such as the god of the door, similar to those found in the Chinese pantheon. The Yao priests maintain a large inventory of supernaturals, such as the lord of creation, the lord of longevity, and the Jade King. [Fortune 1939: 397-98; Chiang 1948b: 247.] Ghosts and spirits are greatly feared, particularly the ghosts of persons who have met unusual or violent deaths. The Yao maintain temples or shrines containing figures of actual or legendary ancestors. Some of these figures are of the founders of surname groups, but most are of people who were murdered, or died from other unnatural causes. In the Linshan area the houses contain wooden figures of family ancestors, and family ancestral rites are held twice each lunar month. [Fortune 1939: 374, 397-98.] **Practitioners.** The institution of the priest-exorcist is an important and characteristic feature of Yao culture. These individuals, males only, are present in most Yao villages. They function primarily in exorcising ghosts and demons in cases of illness, but also conduct village-wide sacrifices to P'an-ku, the dog ancestor, and officiate at funerals, marriages, and naming ceremonies. They are organized into age grades, and recruit their numbers from among village boys, whom they instruct in reading the Taoist classics written in Chinese. These texts, copied in corrupt and almost incomprehensible characters, serve as mnemonic signs for the priests' exorcistic chants and incantations. In addition to the chants, the ritual inventory includes blood sacrifice, the wearing of special garments, and the use of such articles as sacred wooden staffs, sacred brass knives, bells, rattles, and bamboo throwing (divining) sticks. Dancing, sometimes in pairs, is also a characteristic feature. [Fortune 1939: 347-48, 365; Stübel 1938: 373.] **Ceremonies.** Fortune (1939: 381-82) mentions an annual new year festival for the Linshan area, as well as cyclic festivals (every 5, 12, or 15 years) when the figures of clan ancestors are taken from their temples and the young men are instructed in the lore and legends of the Yao.

Wang also mentions cyclic festivals among the Yao of eastern Kwangsi (1936: 40-41). Festivals to honor the ancestors and perpetuate the oral tradition may last up to nine days, and are the occasion for much feasting, drinking, and courting. Major ceremonies are mentioned also by P'ang (1932: 496-97) and Wist (1938: 131) under the names *pai-wang* and *tu-shen*. The latter, lasting seven days and nights, requires prior fasting and the accumulation of large amounts of wine, meat, and other foods to be consumed during the ceremonial period. A person who "goes through" *tu-shen* enhances his status in the community and ensures that his soul will go to heaven when he dies. Every wealthy Yao strives to sponsor a *tu-shen* ceremony once during his lifetime. Both sexes are eligible, but women must first have gone through the lesser *pai-wang* ceremony. The *tu-shen* ceremony requires the presence of a good many priests, and the construction of a high tower. The climax is an "opening heaven's door" ritual, during which the priests lead the participants in walking on the edges of sharp knives imbedded in the ground. The ceremony is sponsored by the participants and their families, who must contribute large amounts of food and wine, both as payment to the officiating priests and for the general feasting. **Illness and medicine.** According to Fortune (1939: 372), a woman who has given birth must remain inside the house for 30 days. This observation is confirmed independently by Wist (1938: 112). During this period she may do no work, although she is required to bathe herself and her baby frequently. ● Because the Yao believe that most illnesses are caused by evil or malevolent ghosts and spirits, most curing rites are reported to be exorcistic in nature. Fortune, however, says that illness is thought to be due to soul loss, and that the function of the priest is to placate the ghost responsible for this condition, thus restoring the patient to health. The curing rituals performed by Yao priests usually involve blood sacrifice (a chicken or in serious cases a pig or cow), and the burning of strips of paper on which the names of offending spirits are written. More elaborate rituals require the construction of bamboo towers, bridges, and like structures, and simultaneous performances by several priests. Manipulation of sacrificial animals, sacred knives, bells, and staffs is accompanied by incantations from the sacred Taoist manuscripts. [Fortune 1939: 402-07.] **Soul, death, and afterlife.** Wist (1938: 113-15) maintains that the indigenous method of disposing of the corpse among the Yao is cremation. The body is placed in a coffin and carried to the cremation grounds, which are some distance from the village. Here the coffin is placed on a heap of stones and covered over with a protective roof of thatch. It is left in this condition for anywhere from three or four months to several years, after which the coffin and its contents are burned and the deceased's ashes placed in an earthen jar and buried in a specially constructed underground chamber lined with stones. Such chambers are sometimes large enough to hold ten or a dozen jars. According to Wist, this method is still used by all Kwangsi Yao except the Pan Yao, who, together with the Yao of Kwangtung, have adopted the Chinese method of grave burial within a wooden coffin. Their grave sites are scattered on wooded slopes near the villages. The procession to the grave is accompanied by exploding gunpowder and burning joss sticks. The grave is visited frequently by relatives. For anyone who has gone through the *tu-shen* ceremony, funeral rites are more elaborate, and include the services of several priests and the sacrifice of a pig or, in the case of a wealthy family, a cow or an ox. Secondary burial, in which the bones are exhumed, cleaned, and reburied, is reported for some villages. [Stübel 1938: 374-77; Fortune 1939: 377-78; P'ang 1932: 504.]

BIBLIOGRAPHY. Bruk 1960; Chiang 1948b; Fortune 1939; Leuschner 1911; P'ang 1932; Stübel 1938; Wang 1936; Wist 1938.

HAINAN "MIAO"

Synonym. *Li-Miao*

ORIENTATION. **Identification.** The shifting agriculturists of the mountains of Hainan, other than the aboriginal Li tribes, have in much of the Chinese literature been termed Miao. They are so called, for example, by Wang (1948) and by the present Communist regime in China, which designates the area as the Hainan Li and Miao Autonomous Chou. Among Western writers, Moninger (1921) also uses the term Miao. In fact, however, these people are in all probability Yao, related to the Yao in nearby Kwangsi and Kwangtung on the mainland. As pointed out by deBeauclair (1956; 1961), the misunderstanding stems from Ming dynasty times, when Yao were brought from Kwangsi to Hainan as auxiliary troops; at that time, and especially during the succeeding Ch'ing dynasty, the aborigines of southwestern China were designated by the generic term Miao. According to deBeauclair, the misnomer has been perpetuated down to the present time. ● The problem of what is Miao and what is Yao, culturally speaking, is complicated by inadequate comparative data and by the long exposure of both groups to Chinese acculturative influences. Such traits as the dog ancestor myth and certain patterns in batik and embroidery are sometimes cited as evidence that the Miao of Hainan are really Yao. Stübel, however, points out the importance of the dog in the mythology of many circumpacific folk, and says that both the Yao and Miao have the myth of the dog ancestor, P'an-ku. On linguistic grounds there seems to be much stronger evidence favoring Yao on Hainan. Wang (1948: 6ff.) says that the language of the Miao on Hainan is almost identical to the dialect of the Lan-tien (Blue Indigo) Yao of northwestern Kwangsi. Savina (1926: 13), writing on languages of Yao (Man) groups in Indochina, remarks that at least one of these Yao dialects is also represented on Hainan, and Meriggi, analyzing the Hainan linguistic material collected by Stübel, remarks that the Miao on Hainan are linguistically the same people whom Savina called "Man" (in Stübel 1937: 309). **Location.** Interspersed with aboriginal Li peoples in southern Hainan, including Paoting, Lotung, and Paisha districts. A detailed distribution has never been worked out, partly because the people are shifting agriculturists. In general they are found in remote, mountainous areas. [Wang 1948: 8-9.] **Linguistic affiliation.** Most probably Yao, closely related to Miao. The two together are often considered as a separate branch of Sino-Tibetan. **Demography.** The total of Yao on Hainan, according to deBeauclair (1956: 254), is 6,000. **History and cultural relations.** Reported to descend from troops, called "crossbow warriors," brought by the Chinese from Kwangsi about 1520 to suppress Li rebellions on Hainan (Wang 1948: 1-4). As latecomers, the "Miao" have been forced to subsist in unproductive areas in the more remote mountainous parts of the island, where they have been little better than tenants of Li and Chinese landlords in the richer lowlands. Sporadic attempts by the mainland Chinese to improve their lot have been resisted by the wealthy Li landowners and by local Chinese merchants and landlords. Chinese, the language of communication and trade throughout the area, has considerable prestige. [Wang 1948: 112ff.]

SETTLEMENT PATTERN AND HOUSING. **Settlement pattern.** Villages are usually located on the lower slopes of a valley between high hills, and near a stream if possible. The number of houses in a village ranges from 6 or 8 up to 40 or 50. The houses are located haphazardly, with paths connecting them. The countryside is precipitous, and villages are connected by steep mountain paths. Cultivated lands, with the exception of vegetable gardens, are located at some distance from the village. Shifting agriculture compels the abandonment of fields after two or three years, and few villages remain in the same location more than ten or twelve years. In villages located at higher elevations, water is frequently piped in bamboo troughs from nearby springs. **Housing.** Houses are single-story rectangular structures with walls of bamboo plastered with mud or covered with woven bamboo screens. Roofs are covered with palm or rattan thatch. Houses are built directly on the ground, with floors of pounded earth. The interior is normally divided into three rooms, with a center room for eating and cooking. Furnishings are few and simply constructed of wood or bamboo. Pig troughs and chicken coops are located beneath the overhanging eaves. Separate storage sheds are located near the houses. [Moninger 1921: 40-44; Wang 1948: 33.]

ECONOMY. Agriculture is the mainstay of the food supply, followed in importance by hunting and gathering, and to a lesser extent by animal husbandry. Fishing is of little economic importance. While there is some trade with the Chinese, the Hainan "Miao" are relatively self-sufficient with respect both to food supply and manufactured goods. **Agriculture.** Practically all agriculture consists of swidden farming on mountain slopes; only a few wealthy families grow paddy rice in irrigated fields. Swiddens are burned for clearing, and the ashes used for fertilizer. The land is worked with a hoe. Mountain rice [glutinous, according to Moninger (1921: 45)] is the chief crop. Maize, beans, sweet potatoes, and a few vegetables are also grown in the fields and kitchen gardens. Swiddens are used continuously for two to three years and then fallowed. When surrounding slopes are used up, the village moves (about once in every twelve years). [Wang 1948: 23-24.] **Fishing and hunting.** Fishing, which is of little importance, is done mainly by poisoning streams. Hunting with dogs is a popular pastime, and contributes some food to the diet. Muzzle loaders, traps, pitfalls, and crossbows with poisoned arrows are used. Bears, wild boar, porcupines, squirrels, and birds are taken. [Moninger 1921: 46-47.] **Gathering.** It is probable that gathering supplies a considerable part of the diet, particularly in times of poor crops. Moninger (1921: 46) mentions palm hearts, roots, leaves, and grubs. **Domestic animals.** Include mountain cattle, pigs, dogs, and chickens. Horses are kept by only a few wealthy families. Most cattle are leased to the Li, with the calves reverting to the original owners. Most animals are left to forage for themselves, although cattle are sometimes penned at night within rude shelters. [Moninger 1921: 46; Wang 1948: 25-26.] **Food and stimulants.** The usual dish is a crude rice gruel. Maize and sweet potatoes are also eaten, but relatively few vegetables. Meat is eaten only on festival occasions. Grubs, roots, and leaves are gathered and eaten, particularly during famine times. Men drink and smoke, but reportedly not to excess. Betel chewing is a favorite pastime. [Moninger 1921: 46-47; Wang 1948: 42ff.] **Industrial arts.** Men work extensively with bamboo and rattan, making baskets, boxes, and furniture. The women are good weavers, and dye the woven cloth a blue or indigo color. The technique makes use of the batik method of resist dyeing, whereby the designs are painted on with a wax brush, the dye applied to the entire piece, and the wax then removed. [Wang 1948: 27-28.] **Trade.** There is little intervillage trading. There are, however, various trade and economic relationships with both the Li and Chinese. Chinese merchants and peddlers visit the mountain villages, and the "Miao" occasionally go down to Li or Chinese market towns. Such visits are infrequent, however, since the markets are some distance away. Bamboo, timber, and other forest products are bartered or sold for such commodities as rice and salt, and cattle are leased to the Li. [Wang 1948: 28-29.] **Land tenure.** Every village has its common land, common pasture, and common cemetery. These village lands are, however, usually bought or rented from Li or Chinese landlords on a contract basis, and the frequent demands of the landlords for new contracts are in part responsible for the migratory tendency of the Hainan "Miao." Each family has rights to a piece of the common village land. Private ownership of land exists among only a few wealthy families. [Wang 1948: 36-41.]

KIN GROUPS. **Descent.** Patrilineal. **Kin groups.** There are patrilineal surname groups, probably going back to the period before the "Miao" were brought to Hainan. Lineages within the surname group keep genealogical records and thus, although frequent migrations tend to disperse a surname over a wide area, those closely related by blood remain conscious of kinship ties. The surnames are in theory exogamous, but in fact marriage is prohibited only in cases of a known close relationship. Occasional villages are composed of members of a single surname, but more often two or three surnames are present. [Wang 1948: 31-33.]

MARRIAGE AND FAMILY. **Mode.** Boys and girls engage in antiphonal singing on the hillsides on the occasion of spring festivals. Premarital sexual relations are permissible, and commonly young people make their own choice of mate, although arranged marriages are not unknown. Once the choice is made, the parents complete the arrangements through a go-between. The betrothal is not set, however, until the horoscopes of the young couple have been matched by a priest. If the bride comes to live with or near the groom's family, as is usually the case, the latter pays a bride price of money, rice, wine, and pork. If, as sometimes happens, the groom is adopted by his parents-in-law and goes to live matrilocally, a dowry is paid by the girl's family. In cases where a family lacks sons, the adopted son-in-law may change his surname and ultimately inherit the property of his parents-in-law. The wedding ceremony may take as long as two days. It includes ceremonial processions back and forth between the homes of the bride and groom. Friends and relatives participate to the accompaniment of much feasting and singing. [Wang 1948: 46-50.] **Form.** Monogamy is the rule. Polygyny and concubinage are unknown except among a very few wealthy families. [Wang

1948: 30-31.] **Extension of incest taboos.** The patrilineal surname groups are in theory exogamous, but in practice marriage is prohibited only among close relatives. **Residence.** Variable, particularly during the early years of marriage (Moninger 1921: 50). According to Wang (1948: 46ff.), the young couple ordinarily reside patrilocally except in the case of an adopted son-in-law. **Domestic unit.** Nuclear family households occur, but the extended family household of three generations is more common (Wang 1948: 30-31). **Inheritance.** Family property is divided equally among the sons at the death of the father. Women do not ordinarily inherit except in the case of a daughter married to an adopted son-in-law. [Wang 1948: 31.]

SOCIOPOLITICAL ORGANIZATION. Political organization. There is no indigenous political structure above the village level. Under the Chinese administrative system, the status of village headman, *chia-chang*, corresponds to the former elective position of village chief. The village chiefs are the repository of native lore and knowledge; they can usually read some Chinese, and may double as magician-priests. [Wang 1948: 33ff.] **Social stratification.** No marked social differences. The role of village headman-priest is one of the few avenues open to power and prestige.

RELIGION. The Hainan "Miao" have a dog ancestor myth, and do not kill dogs or eat dog flesh. They also have a creation myth which includes a deluge and brother-sister incest motifs. They practice *feng-shui* (geomancy) and divination, and their pantheon includes many gods and demons of Chinese (Taoist) origin. **Practitioners.** Village priest-exorcists function at religious festivals, birth, marriage, and death. They usually have some ability to read and write Chinese, and make use in their rituals of corrupted Taoist classics written in Chinese characters. The status of priest is open only to males, and there is an initiation ceremony. Priests may acquire some power and prestige, particularly if they combine with their priestly status the additional positions of village headman and powerful sorcerer. It is believed, for example, that they can cause illness or insanity through sorcery. The active agent in such cases may be the victim's name written on a slip of paper. **Soul, death, and afterlife.** The body of the deceased is borne in a procession to the grave, where it is buried in a coffin. Priests officiate by exorcising evil spirits with swords and incense. Two or three years after death the soul is helped to find its final resting place through a ceremony which may last up to five days and require the services of ten or more priests. It also may require the erection of a wooden platform from which the priests call to the spirit of the deceased. [Wang 1948: 51-70.]

BIBLIOGRAPHY. DeBeauclair 1956, 1961; Moninger 1921; Savina 1926; Stübel 1937; Wang 1948.

INDOCHINA MAN

Synonyms. *Mien, Mun, Yao*

ORIENTATION. **Identification.** According to Lafont (1961), Yao is the Chinese designation for this group. French investigators, most of whom were administrators and military men, called them Man, which term is also used by the Vietnamese. Lafont states that there has been erroneous reporting on subgroups by Lunet de Lajonquière (1906: 255), Le (1955: 46-48), and Abadie (1924: 125). For example, Abadie distinguishes the Man Tien, Xanh-Y, and Son Dau, which are actually subgroups, as separate entities. Furthermore, Lafont claims, the Xanh-Y should be spelled Panh-Y, although Du Perron (1954: 23-42) also refers to them as the Xanh-Y. The following table gives Lafont's (1961) Yao, Tai, Vietnamese, and Chinese designations for the various subgroups in Vietnam and Laos:

Yao	Tai
Kim Mun	Lan Ten
Tsan Sieu Nin	Can Ho
Koa Pe Mun	Can Coa Khao
Kim Mien	Taio Tcha Ine
Tsun Yan	Can Ban
Kun Mien	Man Coc

Vietnamese	Chinese (Kwan Hoa)
Man Lan Dien	Man Lan Tien
Man Quan Coc	Man Tsang Tang
Man Quan Trang	Man Pe Sing
Man Son Dau	Man Siao Pan
(Man Deo Tien)	(Man Pan Y)
Man Son Ti	Man Cao Lan
(Man Son Tu)	
Man Sung	Man Ta Pan

The NNCDT (1959: 244) lists the Man subgroups as: Man Tien, Man Do, Man Quan Chet, Man Son Dau (Man Logang), Man Coc, Man Dai Ban, Man Lan Ten, and Man Quan Trang. According to Arutiunov and Mukhlinov (1961), the subgroup known as the Man Cao Lan is actually a separate Tai-speaking group that properly should be known as Cao Lan. **Location.** The Man are usually located at elevations of 900 to 2,000 feet, and in northern Vietnam are concentrated in the northwest upland area west of Cao Bang along the Chinese border. Abadie (1924: 125-38) reported that the Man Ta Pan, found at higher altitudes than other Man groups, form relatively dense concentrations south of Bao Lac between the Song Gam and the Clear rivers, to the south and southeast of Pa Kha, and on the heights of the right bank of the Red river around Phong Tho. The Man Tien are located closer to the delta of the Red river than are other Man groups, and the Man Quan Trang live at rela-

tively low elevations in the vicinity of Yen Binh Xa, around Luc An Chau, and along the Red river in the Bao Ha area. According to Du Perron (1954: 23-24), the Xanh-Y, who are spread throughout southern China, have concentrated in Vietnam largely in the areas of Mon Cay, Lang Son, and Pho Ba Che. There also are small groupings of Man scattered throughout the upland regions of northern Laos. **Linguistic affiliation.** Greenberg (1953: 282-83) classes Yao and Miao together as a separate branch of Sino-Tibetan. The exchange language of the Man Tien is either Tai or Vietnamese rather than *kwan hoa*, lingua franca of many of the ethnic groups in northern Vietnam and the exchange language of the Man Lan Ten (Abadie 1924: 124, 135). The Xanh-Y usually speak Cantonese in dealing with the Chinese and Tho in northern Vietnam (Du Perron 1954: 24). Arutiunov and Mukhlinov (1961) identify two Yao dialect groups—the Man Quan Trang and the Man Coc. **Demography.** Various population estimates have been made from time to time: 55,000 in Vietnam (Abadie 1924: 107); 89,000 in Indochina (Indochina service de la statistique 1936); 70,000 in Vietnam (Morechand 1952: 356); and 100,000 in the northern Vietnam provinces of Lao Kay, Ha Giang, Yen Bay, Tuyen Quang, and Thai Nguyen (Le 1955: 46-48). A 1940 census recorded 120,000 Man in Vietnam and 5,000 in Laos, figures which Lafont (1961) feels are still accurate. The NNCDT (1959: 244) gives the total Man population in Vietnam as 177,000. Of the sub-groups, estimates have included 8,000 Man Tien, 3,000 Man Quan Trang (Abadie 1924: 134-38), and 5,000 Xanh-Y (Du Perron 1954: 24). **History and cultural relations.** Investigators differ as to the date of the first Yao migrations from southern China into Vietnam and Laos. Abadie (1924: 106) believes they may have begun as early as the thirteenth century, when the Chinese expanded southward, but Gourdon (1931: 87) and Le (1955: 47-48) write that it was during the sixteenth and seventeenth centuries that the first small groups began moving into northern Vietnam and Laos where, because Tai-speaking peoples were already in possession of upland valleys, the Yao settled on the hills and higher elevations. Robequain (1929: 223) claims that Yao movements into Thanh Hoa province of northern Vietnam—their southernmost penetration—began around 1905. ●
Those in central and northern Laos maintain contact with other minority groups as well as with the Lao through trade in the valley market towns (Iwata 1961b: 14-15, 26). In Muong Nang and Muong Long in northern Laos, the Man trade with the Tai Lü and with the Tai Yuan in the vicinity of the Muong Sing–Nam Tha trail (Lafont 1961). In the Vang Vieng area, north of the Laotian capital of Vientiane, the Man employ Chinese calligraphy, which they learned from Chinese teachers of a group known as the Ho or Khon Ho (Lao designation), said to have come to Laos at the time of the T'ai-ping rebellion in south-

ern China (Iwata 1961b: 14). In northern Vietnam, the Man Lan Ten have contact with valley-dwelling Tai-speaking groups, although this contact has not always been peaceful—for example, in 1914, the Man Lan Ten of the Ha Giang region fought the Tai. The Xanh-Y are in contact with the Chinese in Kwangsi and Kwangtung provinces of southern China as well as with the Tho in northern Vietnam (Du Perron 1954: 24).

SETTLEMENT PATTERN AND HOUSING. **Settlement pattern.** In northern Vietnam the Man Lan Ten normally group in villages of 5 or 6 houses, although there are villages of 20 or more houses near the Song Chay. Most Man Quan Trang settlements have around 12 houses. [Abadie 1924: 113-38.] Robequain (1929: 224) describes settlements of 8 to 15 houses in Thanh Hoa province. In the Muong Vang Vieng area of Laos, Man villages vary in size, a few having only 5 to 8 houses, others from 25 to 27. In the vicinity of Luang Prabang, villages may be divided into hamlets, e.g. one village consists of three hamlets of 25, 5, and 10 houses respectively. Some villages in Laos have been located on the same site for relatively long periods: around Vang Vieng are several constructed 15 to 20 years ago and one which has been in the same location for over 50 years (Iwata 1961b: 10). Lafont (1961) notes that the village of Tafeng in Muong Sing has been on its site for more than 25 years. **Housing.** House types vary from group to group and place to place. Man Lan Ten houses are found both on level ground and on slopes with one end supported by piling; Man Quan Trang houses rest on piling; the Man Tien usually borrow the house type of their neighbors, building their houses on the ground if near the Vietnamese, on piling if near the Tai. [Abadie 1924: 135-39.] Robequain (1929: 224) reports houses in Thanh Hoa province constructed on slopes with one end on piling. Xanh-Y houses can be either on piling or on the ground (Du Perron 1954: 34). Thatching is widely used and, in Laos, plank walls and shingled roofs are common. A few even have galvanized iron roofs (Iwata 1961b: 8-9). Should the house be on the ground, the floor is of pounded earth; animals are stabled underneath houses built on piling.

ECONOMY. **Agriculture.** Staple crops are upland rice and/or maize, cultivated in swiddens, maize being more widely cultivated among the Vietnam Man. The Xanh-Y are described as having the least productive agriculture and consequently as relying more heavily on hunting and fishing. [Diguet 1908: 121; Lunet de Lajonquière 1906: 265.] In the Vang Vieng area of Laos the Man cultivate upland rice as the staple and maize for livestock (Iwata 1961b: 10-11). Normally, swiddens are cultivated for three years, followed by fallow periods of at least nine years. Since the village is rarely moved and swiddens may therefore be some distance away, the people construct temporary shelters near the swiddens for the young men who work the fields and guard the crops. [Gourdon 1931: 89; Abadie 1924: 114.] The Man Ta Pan move to the lowlands when possible to cultivate paddy fields but, uncomfortable in the lowland climate, keep their villages at higher elevations, residing near their fields only during the planting season. [Cuisinier 1948: 42; Gourou 1945: 447.] The tool complex includes a long-handled knife for clearing the forest, a hoe to prepare the soil, a digging stick for holes, and a variety of small knives for cutting stalks. • Chassigneux (1929: 44) describes the swidden technique of the Du Cun, a subgroup of the Man Ta Pan, who live at about 2,000 feet in Hoa Lung village on the slope of Nui Ban mountain in northern Vietnam. Having selected a place with few rocks, the Du Cun cut the trees and brush which are then allowed to dry for 15 days before burning. Planting is usually done in the fourth lunar month. Holes are dug 8 inches apart and filled with about 10 seeds each. The growing period varies depending on the amount of rainfall. Fields are cultivated for 3 successive years then allowed to lie fallow for 30 years. In addition to upland rice, the Du Cun use the swiddens for sweet potatoes, beans, pumpkins, ginger, castor beans, and cotton. A slightly different pattern in the Xanh-Y area reflects the scarcity of water there. Upland rice and, if the soil is sufficiently fertile, maize too are planted the first 2 years, after which manioc or taro is planted and new fields cleared for rice and maize. Fields are allowed to lie fallow for 10 to 13 years. [Du Perron 1954: 31-32.] In the Vang Vieng area of Laos, rice and poppy swiddens are located several hours walk from the village; secondary crops are planted between rows of poppies and rice (Iwata 1961b: 10). Other secondary crops cultivated by Man groups in Laos and Vietnam include buckwheat, red peppers, cabbage, onions, bananas, sugar cane, a wide variety of greens, tobacco, and ramie (Robequain 1929: 226; Lafont 1961). **Fishing, hunting, and gathering.** According to Abadie (1924: 118), fishing and hunting supplement the food supply to some extent among all the groups, but only among the Xanh-Y does hunting assume any importance, the animals taken ranging from pigeons and pheasant to stags (Du Perron 1954: 30). The Xanh-Y also gather bamboo shoots, wild mushrooms, and certain nuts used for producing dye (Du Perron 1954: 30-31). **Domestic animals.** Traditionally the Man raised only pigs and chickens, but began to raise buffalo and cattle as draft animals after the adoption of paddy agriculture (Abadie 1924: 118). Those of the Vang Vieng area of central Laos nowadays raise horses, cattle, pigs, chickens, water buffalo, cats, dogs, and geese (Iwata 1961b: 10). **Industrial arts.** In Vietnam, the Man produce their own farm tools, knives, crossbows, and rifles, making the powder for their rifles from locally mined saltpeter,

wood carbon, and sulphur purchased from Chinese and Vietnamese merchants. In both Vietnam and Laos they produce opium, alcohol, and paper, and those in Vietnam are reputed to be particularly able ironworkers with a fondness for jewelry. Bracelets and neckbands are skillfully fashioned from a mixture of silver mined in the upland areas and melted-down French Indochina alloy coins (the Man Tien, literally "money Man," are so called for wearing the old French silver-alloy sapeks as jewelry). The Man dye and weave cloth which is then elaborately embroidered. [Abadie 1924: 120; Du Perron 1954: 30.] In Laos they mine lead and silver, pouring the silver into bamboo measures to make currency for local market use. Iron ingots are brought from Bangkok to make farm tools, utensils, and weapons. [Iwata 1961b: 29-30.] **Trade.** The Xanh-Y in Vietnam take forest products to lowland Chinese and Vietnamese merchants to trade for salt, cloth, tobacco, and manufactured goods for household use (Du Perron 1954: 30-31). In Laos the Man in the vicinity of Vang Vieng trade with Lao merchants, exchanging their farm produce for condensed milk, coffee, and glutinous rice, which they use on ritual occasions but do not cultivate (Iwata 1961b: 13). **Land tenure.** Among the Xanh-Y in Vietnam, private land ownership does not exist: the land a village clears for cultivation is collectively owned (Du Perron 1954: 27).

KIN GROUPS. Descent. Patrilineal in Vietnam, with the father's responsibilities and prerogatives inherited by the eldest son (Abadie 1924: 118). Exogamous common descent groups are mentioned by Lunet de Lajonquière (1906: 241, 262) for the Man Ta Pan in Vietnam, and also by Iwata (1961b: 18) for the Man in Laos. The latter also reports the surnames Chao, Cheng, and Li, pointing out that those with the same surname are *ton sinh* or *ton fi:nh.*

MARRIAGE AND FAMILY. Mode. According to Lafont (1961) and all other investigators, premarital sexual intercourse is permitted. Relations between unmarried Man girls and non-Man males are permitted, and in the vicinity of Nam Tha in northern Laos have developed into prostitution, with older women acting as intermediaries. • In both Vietnam and Laos, a young man is free to select his mate, and his father retains an intermediary to make arrangements. The intermediary consults the couple's horoscopes and, if these are compatible, visits the girl's parents to discuss the bride price. On a second visit, the date for the wedding is set. A boy unable to pay a bride price may reside with the girl's parents, taking her family name while doing service for an agreed length of time. If he should leave or be expelled during that period, he must be compensated for his labor. After the bride price is paid, the wedding ritual, which consists of the couple drinking libations of rice alcohol before the boy's ancestral altar, can take place. [Abadie 1924: 118; Diguet 1908: 123; Du Perron 1954: 26-27; Iwata 1961b: 17, 30.] **Form.** Polygyny is permitted, but usually practiced only by the well-to-do (Abadie 1924: 118; Iwata 1961b: 17). **Residence.** Neolocal residence reported for the Man Lan Ten (Lunet de Lajonquière 1906: 262). Other Man groups in Vietnam have temporary patrilocality lasting up to seven years, after which separate households are established, preferably near the paternal house (Diguet 1908: 123; Abadie 1924: 136). In Vang Vieng, residence is matrilocal for one to two years if the bride's family lives some distance from the groom's village. After that period, the couple return to his village to establish their own household. [Iwata 1961b: 17.] **Inheritance.** Among the Man Tien, the wife inherits from her husband, and on her death the children divide the property, the eldest son receiving the largest share. Among the Man Quan Trang, sons, unmarried daughters, and sons-in-law doing service inherit from the father, the eldest son receiving a double share since he is expected to care for the widow and carry on the cult of the ancestors. [Lunet de Lajonquière 1906: 275; Abadie 1924: 139.]

SOCIOPOLITICAL ORGANIZATION. **Political organization.** Man groupings are too small in most cases to have more than local leaders, but Diguet (1908: 107) reported that Man Ta Pan and Man Tien villages in the Nguyen Binh area of northern Vietnam were under the authority of one chief called the Man Muc or "Man Chief." The Xanh-Y in Vietnam have their own village headmen, but several villages often recognize the leadership of a Quan Man, a local Man leader who acts as liaison between the Man and the Vietnamese—previously French—administration (Du Perron 1954: 26). A similar pattern is reported for northern Laos (Lafont 1961), where in the vicinity of Tafeng in Muong Sing there is a Nai Ban, a Man leader officially recognized by the Lao administration. Some other groupings of villages, in the Nam Tha and Muong Sing areas of northern Laos, also have their own leaders, those of Muong Sing being Tai-speaking Lü. According to Iwata (1961b: 30), the Man of Vang Vieng in Laos continue to believe that there is a Yao nation in Kiukiang (China) with its own emperor.

RELIGION. **Indigenous religion.** The Man share many beliefs and practices with the Chinese and Vietnamese. There is a cult of the ancestors as well as a cult honoring the spirit of the hearth in a manner similar to the Chinese, and the Man celebrate the lunar new year. They also have a pantheon of spirits associated with thunder, clouds, fire, water, earth, sky, rivers, mountains, seas, fields, and so forth—all of which are believed to have an influence on human beings. The Man Lan Ten practice a form of witchcraft designed to bring about the sickness or death of an enemy. [Abadie 1924: 124; Lafont 1961.] **Cere-**monies. The most important rituals are held during the lunar new year period. Veneration of the ancestors is performed at this time much as it is among the Chinese and Vietnamese. In Laos the participants in one type of ritual achieve a trancelike state. [Iwata 1961b: 19-23.] **Practitioners.** The *tsai* communicate with the spirits, and are often the best-educated villagers. Three degrees of priesthood are awarded on the basis of examinations: the lowest, *sip mien*, gives power to exorcise evil spirits; the second, *qua tang*, confers geomantic powers and the right to officiate at funerals; *tu say*, the highest, invests the holder with power over all spirits. [Lunet de Lajonquière 1906: 240; Diguet 1908: 115; Abadie 1924: 122-32; Lafont 1961.] **Funerals.** Funerals usually continue for two or three days after death. The corpse is washed, dressed, and placed in a wooden coffin before the altar of the ancestors. While kin and friends gather, the *tsai* is summoned to lead chants and strike a gong during long vigils by the coffin. The Man Lan Ten either cremate or bury their dead, using a coffin for the latter and collecting the ashes in a jar if the corpse is cremated. The Man Ta Pan cremate their dead and formerly carried the jars containing the ashes on their migrations. This practice has ceased, but they continue to record the place where the ashes were buried. The Man Tien bury their dead, though they still have the expression *pua-se* "to burn bodies." With the exception of the head of the family, who is cremated, the Man Quan Trang bury their dead and abandon the tombs. The Xanh-Y bury their dead and maintain a tomb cult. [Diguet 1908: 125; Abadie 1924: 122-41; Du Perron 1954: 27.]

BIBLIOGRAPHY. Abadie 1924; Arutiunov and Mukhlinov 1961; Chassigneux 1929; Cuisinier 1948; Diguet 1908; Du Perron 1954; Gourdon 1931; Gourou 1945; Greenberg 1953; Indochina service de la statistique 1936; Iwata 1961b; Lafont 1961; Le 1955; Lunet de Lajonquière 1906; Morechand 1952; NNCDT 1959; Robequain 1929.

THAILAND YAO

Synonyms. *Man, Mien, Yu Mien*

ORIENTATION. **Identification.** The Yao of Thailand call themselves Mien, which according to Embree and Thomas (1950: 91) means "men." Lombard (1963) gives Mien or Yu Mien. They are also known as Man, the term for Yao speakers throughout northern Laos, from which area most of the Thailand Yao emigrated as recently as 50 or 60 years ago. **Location.** Although formerly reported as most numerous in northern Nan province, the Thailand Yao are now concentrated in northern and eastern Chiengrai province at altitudes of between 3,000 and 3,500 feet (Young 1961: 57). **Linguistic affiliation.** Related to

Miao. Many similarities to Chinese, but classification uncertain. There is no indigenous script, but some Yao know and use Chinese characters. A few are literate in a romanized script devised by missionaries (Young 1961: 58). **Demography.** Young (1961: 58) gives a total of 10,200 persons in 74 known villages. **History and cultural relations.** Most Thailand Yao have come from the Nam Tha district of Laos in relatively recent years. Some of them say that they originally moved into Laos from Yunnan about 90 years ago. Their villages in Chiengrai province are becoming more permanent, and there are few Yao leaving the province at present. According to Young (1961: 61-64), the Yao have the highest earning ability of any of the hill tribes of northern Thailand. He describes them as industrious and friendly—shrewd businessmen eager to trade and to improve their lot. They have considerable contact with their neighbors, but seldom intermarry with outsiders. Marriage prohibitions are strictly applied to the Yunnanese Chinese, with whom the Yao trade but whom they generally distrust. Since the Yao live at somewhat lower altitudes than the Miao and Lisu, their villages are more easily reached by plains-dwelling traders and missionaries. Although the Yao make alcohol and grow poppies, they are not heavy drinkers, and there are few opium addicts (Young 1961: 63). Both the Yao and Meo engage in the sale of livestock, and they are more firmly committed to a cash economy than most of their neighbors in the northern Thailand hills. Credner (1935a: 171) comments on the similarities between the two groups, and adds that Meo and Yao are able to coexist in one and the same settlement.

SETTLEMENT PATTERN AND HOUSING. **Settlement pattern.** The Yao prefer to locate along stream heads at 3,000 to 3,500 feet. Villages average 15 houses, with about 125 persons. They tend to relocate a village about once every 10 to 15 years, but do not move very far. **Housing.** Houses are large, and, especially among the well-to-do, quite substantially built. They are rectangular in shape, and built directly on the ground. The roof is of thatch, and the walls of bamboo slats or split wood. The interior is partitioned off into two or more sections. [Young 1961: 59; Lombard 1963.]

ECONOMY. Participation in a cash economy through the sale of opium, hogs, and cattle, but they also raise most of their own food crops. Although they do hunt and fish, these activities contribute little to the food supply. **Agriculture.** Dry-field farming of the slash-and-burn type is characteristic. Swiddens are worked with a hoe, and planted mainly to rice, opium poppies, and maize. Garden crops include cotton, tobacco, potatoes, pumpkins, gourds, onions, peas, turnips, ginger, and chilies. **Domestic animals.** The Yao keep large numbers of hogs, mainly for

sale but also for domestic consumption on special occasions. They are skillful breeders, and feed the animals a specially prepared mixture of maize and banana stalks. Other animals include cattle, ponies, chickens, ducks, and, in some areas, buffalo. Livestock is relatively well cared for in stalls and pens. **Food and stimulants.** The diet is mainly one of rice and vegetables, with mustard greens an important ingredient in most dishes. Many foods are cooked in pork fat. Meat, however, is consumed only rarely. The Yao drink a great deal of tea. Alcoholic beverages are made, but are not consumed in large quantities. Tobacco is smoked, but betel chewing is absent. **Industrial arts.** There is some degree of specialization on the part of blacksmiths, silversmiths, and makers of rice paper (the latter learned from Siamese). Yao blacksmiths make excellent hoes, axes, and muzzleloading shotguns. Women are skilled at embroidery. **Trade.** The combination of a cash economy and craft specialization makes for some degree of domestic trade. The Yao are also enthusiastic traders with other groups, including itinerant Yunnanese merchants. **Division of labor.** Men clear the fields, hunt, butcher, build houses, and make traps. Women weed the fields, prepare the food (including rice pounding), gather firewood and wild greens, and care for the animals, mainly hogs. Both sexes participate in planting and harvesting rice. [Young 1961: 61-62; Lombard 1963; Embree and Thomas 1950: 90.]

KIN GROUPS. Exogamous, patrilineal clans (Lombard 1963).

MARRIAGE AND FAMILY. Premarital sexual experimentation is permitted, and young people are expected to choose their own marriage partners, subject to some advice from their elders. The groom's father may act as go-between to arrange the bride price of silver and livestock which, among well-to-do families, may be considerable. Residence is patrilocal except in cases where the groom cannot pay the required bride price. The average household unit is somewhat over 8 persons, and extended families of 15 to 20 persons under one roof are not uncommon. The Yao are generally monogamous, but second spouses are not unknown. [Young 1961: 63; Lombard 1963.]

SOCIOPOLITICAL ORGANIZATION. Village chiefs are selected by elders. Most disputes are handled by the chief and settled by the imposition of fines. There is no special status for warrior or sheriff. Village affairs are usually settled by democratic process through group decisions arrived at by the chief, the elders, and family heads. [Young 1961: 64; Lombard 1963.]

RELIGION. Young (1961: 59) characterizes the Yao as animists who place a good deal of importance on the reverence for ancestors. Less than 200 are converts to Christianity. **Supernaturals.** Considerable attention is paid to evil spirits in exorcistic and propitiatory rites which are carried out on such occasions as harvest or illness. The spirits of dead ancestors are potentially troublesome, and must be appeased. **Practitioners.** The position of priest-exorcist, *mo kung,* is important in Yao society. The *mo kung* are skilled at divining with chicken bones and bamboo sticks, and also at various forms of magic, such as exposure to fire. Their real power, however, lies in their knowledge of incantations taken from books written in corrupt Chinese characters. The sons of wealthy Yao families are given special instruction in this art during their teens so that they may become *mo kung* when they grow up. Yao priests are called in on occasions of illness, and also officiate at various village-wide ceremonies. When exorcising evil spirits they may enter a trancelike state marked by incoherent mumblings and involuntary jerking of parts of the body. Their rituals also include animal sacrifice, burning joss sticks and paper money, and dancing while brandishing knives and other objects. [Lombard 1963.] **Ceremonies.** Boys between 15 and 18 go through a "coming of age" ceremony. Usually male cousins—sons of full brothers—undergo this ceremony together. The ceremony lasts several days, preceded by 15 to 30 days of purification. Each boy is accompanied by and subject to two priests, *mo kung,* who read the "life lamp" of the boy and render incantations to secure good luck and a high position for him in the afterlife. The boys are also at this time instructed in the stories and legends of the Yao. [Lombard 1963.] **Soul, death, and afterlife.** Death is announced by a gunshot. The Yao usually bury their dead in a coffin, but cremation is not unknown. The burial place is selected by a priest, *mo kung,* after consulting the sacred book on burials. Periodic ceremonies are held for the souls of deceased ancestors —ideally one year after death. Lasting three or more days and including incantations by priests and feasting and dancing by participants, the ceremonies cleanse the souls and enable them to ascend into the spirit world. [Lombard 1963.]

BIBLIOGRAPHY. Credner 1935a; Embree and Thomas 1950; Lombard 1963; Young 1961.

PART II. AUSTROASIATIC

MON-KHMER

MON-KHMER-SPEAKING SWIDDEN FARMERS make up the majority of what are sometimes called *montagnards*, a generic term which in Indochina includes such groups as the Bahnar, Mnong, Sedang, and Loven, as well as the Malayo-Polynesian-speaking Jarai, Raglai, and Rhadé. Traditionally, these upland groups have been known by generic, usually pejorative names, meaning "savage" or "slave"—Moi in Vietnam, Pnong or Phnong in Cambodia, and Kha in Laos, Thailand, and eastern Burma. More recently the trend has been toward less pejorative designations: in official parlance the upland peoples in Cambodia are now termed Khmer Loeu, "upland Khmer," while in South Vietnam they have become the Dong Bao Thuong, or "upland compatriots." The North Vietnamese now consider all groups "Vietnamese," referring to the ethnic Vietnamese as Nguoi Kinh, "those of the capital." Terms such as Phuteng (Phouteng), Phuteung, and P'u Ting, meaning "people who live high up," are the Lao polite equivalents of the pejorative Kha. They are sometimes used in Laos and eastern Thailand to refer to groups such as the Khmu, Brao, Sek, etc. Local designations for these groups are numerous and often confusing: Dodd, on a trip from Xieng Khouang to Muong Sai, passing north of Luang Prabang, met representatives of 17 named Kha groups—Kha Kwen, Kha Bit, Kha Chawl, Kha Hok, Kha Kat, etc. (Dodd 1923: 236 ff.). To the south, in the low hills of northeastern Thailand just west of the Mekong, are the Kha Hinhao, Kaleung, Kha Brao, So, and Sek—immigrants from across the Mekong in the mountains of Cammon and Savannakhet provinces in Laos. With a few exceptions, these northern Kha groups are poorly described. • Mon-Khmer speakers have been considered by some linguists to belong to a single Austroasiatic [Austroasian] language stock, although they may be classified more finely under headings such as Mon-Khmer, Palaung-Wa, Khasi, Bahnaric, etc., indicative of differences between, e.g., Khmer and Wa. [Cf. Pinnow 1959; Greenberg 1953; Thomas 1962.] The authors of the present volume have not attempted to arrange these groups linguistically, other than calling them Mon-Khmer and placing them, along with more distantly related groups such as the Vietnamese, Muong, Semang, and Senoi, within a single stock. It has seemed useful, however, to divide them into lowland and upland groups and to further subdivide the latter—by far the more numerous—roughly by geographic location. Northern upland Mon-Khmer speakers, accordingly, include groups extending all across northern Southeast Asia, from North Vietnam (Khua, May, Ruc, Sach), through northern Laos and Thailand (Khmu, Lamet, P'u Noi, T'in, Yumbri), into the Shan State area of Burma (Lawa, Palaungs, Wa), and, in the extreme west, into Assam (Khasis). Central upland Mon-Khmer speakers are located largely in the mountains and upland valleys of central Vietnam and southern Laos, between 14° and 18° N. Southeast upland groups are found primarily in the mountains of South Vietnam, as far west as the valley of the Mekong. Those groups classified as southwest upland are located in the isolated mountain ranges of Cambodia, primarily along the borders with Thailand and Laos. • Mon-Khmer highlanders of the Indochina-Siam area are physically Paleo-Mongoloids, darker complexioned than the Lao and for the most part shorter in stature (Credner 1935a: 154-55). They are generally thought to represent an older stratum, predating the evolution of the modern Siamese, Laotians, and Vietnamese within their present areas of distribution. With the exception of the Yumbri, they rely on shifting agriculture, with rice, usually glutinous, the staple crop. There is a general absence of terracing with a consequent heavy reliance on rainfall. A considerable number supplement their swidden farming with wet-rice agriculture, but where this is not the case, periods of drought can result in near-starvation. The fact that upland Mon-Khmer speakers are generally not found above 3,000 feet helps to explain why these peoples (with the exception of the pagan Wa) are not known as growers of the opium poppy. Their relative nearness to lowlanders has in some instances, as with the Khmu, P'u Noi, Lawa, Chaobon, Loven, Sek, and So, resulted in considerable acculturation and partial physical assimilation. Production of a cash crop (tea among the Palaungs and T'in, coffee among the Loven) can play a role similar to that of opium growing among tribes at higher altitudes. In addition, Kha tribes in many areas furnish labor and domestics to nearby lowlanders. Historically, the contact of these peoples with lowlanders has not always been pleasant. In the period 1860-70 Kha were being taken as slaves by Siamese, Annamese, and Cambodians alike, and as late as 1880 were still much in demand in Phnom Penh, Bangkok, and Kengtung (Colquhoun 1885: 53-54). In more recent years these hill tribes have been subject to a variety of government policies and programs. Following the example of the Chinese People's Republic, the Communist North Vietnamese regime has established autonomous regions within the areas inhabited by its tribal minorities, retaining the traditional *chau* administrative units but placing leadership in the hands of the local populations (Fall 1960: 89-93).

LOWLAND GROUPS

MONS

Synonyms. *Mōn, Mun, Peguan, Talaing, Taleng*

ORIENTATION. **Identification.** Mon is the name these people use for themselves. For centuries they have been known to the Burmese as Talaing, although in recent years the name Mun has also been used. The Siamese call them Mōn, occasionally Taleng. The old English name Peguan is no longer current. [Halliday 1917: 2; McFarland 1941: 357, 629; Shorto 1962: 170.] **Location.** The Mons are found today only in Burma and Thailand. Ninety-seven per cent of those in Burma were in 1931 located in the northern portion of the Tenasserim panhandle, between 15° and 17° N. Scattered villages also occur in an arc at the head of the Gulf of Martaban west to Bassein in the delta of the Irrawaddy. Scattered settlements occur in Thailand mainly between 13° and 15° N., north and south of Bangkok and in the lower valley of the Mae Khlong. A few villages are reported near Lopburi and Khorat, north and northeast of Bangkok. In the nuclear area of settlement in Burma, 73 per cent of the Mon population was in 1931 concentrated in the single district of Amherst; in four townships they averaged 78 per cent of the population, equivalent to 43 per cent of the district as a whole. [India 1931-34: *11*, Pt. I, 190-91; Halliday 1917: 2; Shorto 1962: ix-x.] **Geography.** The Mon homeland is in the deltas of the Irrawaddy, Sittang, and Salween rivers around the Gulf of Martaban. Temperatures are high throughout the year, with little daily variation and only slight seasonal differences. The area has a monsoon climate with a rainy season in summer. Rainfall ranges from about 110 inches in the western delta to about 215 inches on the eastern shore of the Gulf of Martaban [Huke 1956a: 71-80.] **Linguistic affiliation.** Mon is an Austro-asiatic language, placed by Pinnow in what he calls the southeastern, or Mon-Khmer, group of an eastern supergroup including Khmer and the other Austro-asiatic languages of Cambodia, Laos, eastern Thailand, and Vietnam. ● Three Mon dialects are reported for Burma; from north to south, these are: Pegu, Martaban-Moulmein, and Ye. Shorto's recent dictionary is based upon a "central" dialect surrounding Moulmein, to which is related the speech of Pak Lat, south of Bangkok. The majority of adult Mons are probably bilingual, using Burmese as a second language, but it appears that in the central dialect area Mon is the most frequent medium of daily intercourse among Mons. Although there is no Mon state or major urban center, the central Mon dialect is accepted by Mons in Burma as a standard —the result of the use of Mon in the monastic educational system. [Pinnow 1959: 2; Shorto 1962: ix-x.] **Demography.** The most recent estimate of the Mon population in Burma remains the census of 1931, according to which there were 337,000 Mons by race, and 305,000 speakers of Mon. The respective numbers in 1921 were 324,000 and 189,000. In 1921 a speaker of Mon was one using the language in the home; in 1931, one who had learned Mon as his mother tongue. Definite information on the size of the Mon population in Thailand is lacking, but in the early twentieth century it was estimated to be 60,000. [India 1931-34: *11*, Pt. I, 190, Pt. II, 260; Halliday 1917: 1; Pinnow 1959: 2; Shorto 1962: ix-x.] **History and cultural relations.** The history of the Mons prior to about 900 A.D. remains conjectural. During the period of well-recorded history, approximately the last thousand years, the Mons of Burma have been located in the area in which their villages are now found. Their villages in Thailand are largely plantations of the last three or four hundred years; the oldest Mon inscription in Thailand, however, dates from the seventh or eighth century A.D. In 1057 Anawrahta, king of the Burmese in Upper Burma, attacked the Mon city of Thaton, within the present area of Mon settlement, and is supposed to have taken Theravada Buddhism and writing back with him. During most of the succeeding seven centuries there was a Mon state in Lower Burma, stretching from Bassein in the delta eastward to northern Tenasserim, with a fluctuating expansion northward. Mon political independence ended in 1757 with their defeat by the Burmese under Alaungpaya and the final establishment of the Burmese upon the coast. ● The most obvious external influence has been that of India, whence came Buddhism, writing, and other elements of Hinduization. Their bilingualism would indicate that the Mons have been undergoing considerable Burmanization during the past two centuries, or, what is probably more likely, that the two communities have been subject to mutual acculturation—a subtle process as yet little studied in the present context. Even the contemporary, and significant, linguistic acculturation of the Mons may be partly artificial, since it is said that from the end of the Mon kingdom until the first Anglo-Burmese war in 1824 the use of Mon was discouraged by the Burmese, and that from then until 1852 the teaching of Mon in the monasteries was forbidden in Burmese territory. [Halliday 1917: 4-16; India 1912: 9, Pt. I, 208, 277.]

SETTLEMENT PATTERN AND HOUSING. **Settlement pattern.** The Mon village contains houses, granaries, cattle sheds, a monastery which serves also as a school, pagodas, an image house containing images of the Buddha, and a rest house which may serve as a meeting place. Less permanent structures are erected for festivals and ceremonies in fields and gardens at some distance from the houses. [Halliday 1917: 23; Shorto 1962: 93 s. v. *caik*, 109 s. v. *tai*, 153 s. v. *put*, 161 s. v. *phea*, 196 s. v. *sop*.] **Housing.** Mon houses in Burma are similar to those of the Burmese, while in Thailand they tend to conform to Siamese dwellings. Houses are rectangular, with a wooden framework raised above the ground on piles. The gable roof is covered with thatch. Walls and floors are generally of woven bamboo matting; the homes of the well-to-do may contain plank walls and floors. There is a veranda in front, and a kitchen at the back of the house. The main room is often divided, the rear portion being reserved for family and near relatives. Furnishings, including water jars and sleeping mats, are simple; tables and chairs are not common. [Halliday 1917: 22-23, 29-32.]

ECONOMY. Primarily peasant agriculture, with some development of trade and crafts. **Agriculture.** Irrigated rice is the main crop, grown chiefly for subsistence, although a portion is sold. Yams, sweet potatoes, sugar cane, and pineapples are reported grown in gardens, primarily for home consumption, although some people specialize in raising them for sale. En-

tries in Shorto's dictionary suggest that the Mons also raise most of the vegetables and fruits grown by the Burmese. Swiddens, presumably for rice, are reported. Wet rice is cultivated in fields prepared with plows and harrows drawn by buffalo or oxen. Reaping is done with a sickle, and the grain trodden from the straw by cattle. [Halliday 1917: 35-37; Shorto 1962: passim.] **Fishing and hunting.** Fish and fish products are an essential part of the diet. Fish are caught both for home consumption and for sale. Techniques include the use of rod and line, casting nets, traps, poison, and tidal traps hung from stakes. Small fish and shellfish are used for the pressed fermented fish paste so important in the Mon and Burmese diets. ● Hunting is done with snares, traps, deadfalls, guns, crossbows, and pellet bows. The latter are used for birds, whereas smaller game such as monkeys, flying squirrels, flying foxes, pangolins, and pigeons are taken mainly with the crossbow. Guns are used for deer, wild pig, and other large game. [Halliday 1917: 37-42; Shorto 1962: 117 s. v. *tot*.] **Domestic animals.** Include cattle, buffalo, swine, horses, dogs, and poultry. **Food and stimulants.** Boiled rice, the staple, is eaten with vegetable soup or curry. Cooked or raw vegetables are seasoned with pressed fermented fish paste and fish sauce. Fresh fish and meat are eaten when possible, but expenditures for food are small. Glutinous rice, usually steamed, is employed in making confections, and rice is also made into liquor. Tobacco is smoked in the form of cigars. [Halliday 1917: 32-33, 160; Shorto 1962: 42, 149 s. v. *haplu'*, 190 s. v. *palong*.] **Industrial arts.** Subsidiary or part-time crafts include carpentry, wood turning, sawing, working of gold and other metals, tailoring, thatching, brick making, pottery making, weaving, basketry, and mat making. Blacksmithing is usually a full time profession and the better boats are made by specialists. Village specialization in Thailand formerly centered on the making of bricks, thatch, and pottery, including the marketing of these products. With the increasing development of communications and trade, only the coarser pottery wares are now made at home. [Halliday 1917: 33-35, 43, 47-52.] **Division of labor.** Men till the rice fields and presumably clear the swiddens. Pottery, mat making, and weaving are womens' occupations. Much of the basketry is done by old men and young boys as they tend the cattle. [Halliday 1917: 34-37, 43-51.]

KIN GROUPS. **Descent.** Probably bilateral. **Kin groups.** Unreported, with the exception of the patrilineal group concerned with the house spirit, *kalok hoe'* (written form in Halliday: *kalok sni*). This spirit is associated with the southeast post of the house of the eldest living male of a line. On the post is hung a basket containing clothing and gear belonging to the spirit. The owner of the house where this spirit resides and his brothers, together with the wives and children of all of them, are said to be of, or have, one *kalok*. Upon marriage, the sisters of the men are attached to the *kalok* of their husbands. A non-Mon has no *kalok* and neither will his children have one, even though their mother be a Mon. Succession to the head of the *kalok* line is first to sons, then to brothers, finally to brothers' sons. If for any reason a man cannot participate easily in functions of the spirit line, he must make exact replicas of the spirit's clothing and ornaments. [Halliday 1917: 96-100.] **Kin terminology.** Shorto (1962: passim) gives the following kin terms:

Fa	*apa* (or *ta'*)
Mo	*ame* (or *yai*)
PaElBr	*anai*
PaYoBr	*(a)mu*
PaElSi	*i'nai*
PaYoSi	*i'ci* (or *soe*)
ElBr	*kao*
ElSi	*boa*
YoSb	*te'*
Cousin	*kon kao kon te'*
	(*kon*: child, young person)

MARRIAGE AND FAMILY. Mode. Early marriage is general, preceded by a brief period of courtship. Young people have the opportunity to meet at festivals and while girls are weaving at home. Young men also court girls at their houses in the evening. When a courtship is well advanced the boy asks friends to approach the girl's parents. The essential element is the agreement to cohabit, following which the bridegroom may simply move in with the bride and her family. Alternatively a simple ceremony may be held at the bride's home, where, after the gifts of friends have been presented with considerable banter, the couple hold hands. In a somewhat more formal ceremony, vows are taken in the presence of a person of authority and status. Monks may be present but they play no actual role in the proceedings. Elopements are fairly common. [Halliday 1917: 58-61.] **Extension of incest taboos.** Cousins are not given in marriage, but may elope. Patrilateral cousins, however, and others related in the male line should not marry, since they share the same lineage spirit. [Halliday 1917: 61, 100.] **Residence.** Initially matrilocal, for as much as three years. The couple then establishes an independent household. [Halliday 1917: 58, 97.] **Domestic unit.** Probably the nuclear family, except in the case of a couple with recently married daughters living matrilocally. **Divorce.** Permitted, and may apparently be initiated by either party (Halliday 1917: 61).

SOCIOPOLITICAL ORGANIZATION. Political organization. Following the loss of their independent state in 1757, the Mons were first under Burmese rule and later, from 1852 to 1948, under British rule, with a reversion to Burmese administration in the past 15 years. **Social stratification.** There is a word for slave, *doik* (Shorto 1962: 125), but this status was abolished under the British. **Warfare.** During some 200 years of political dependence, except for brief revolts in the later eighteenth and nineteenth centuries, the Mons have shown little aptitude for warfare.

RELIGION. Viewed historically, a major element in Mon religious belief and practice is Theravada, or Hinayana, Buddhism, associated with these people during virtually all of the historic period. The monasteries, monastic organization, and ceremonial calendar of Mon Buddhism are in general similar to those of Burmese and Siamese Buddhism—also of the Hinayana tradition. In practice, Mon monks appear at weddings, but do not participate; they do participate in funerals, and may be called in to recite the *paritta*, an invocation to avert evil. They are also called on for advice, and sometimes act as astrologers. There is a sisterhood of *prea min*, "nuns," inferior in status to the monastic order. [Halliday 1917: 64, 85-86, 89-90; Shorto 1962: 147 s. v. *parat*, 154 s. v. *prea min*.] **Indigenous religion and supernaturals.** Belief in a variety of spirits merges with Buddhist beliefs and practices in everyday life. Not strictly Buddhist in derivation, but part of the Hindu inheritance of Buddhism, are the spirits known as *tewatao* (written form, as in Halliday, *dewatau*), inferior to the major gods In (Indra), and Prem (Brahma). They are associated in some fashion with trees and fields, and are tendered offerings on such occasions as the occupation of a new house (Halliday 1917: 95, 108; Shorto 1962: 113 s. v. *tewatao*). Spirits, with the exception of the *tewatao*, are called by the generic term *kalok*. The *kalok* par excellence is the house spirit, *kalok hoe'*, or simply *kalok*. Others are the *kalok mi' me'* (written form: *kalok mi me*), spirits of the parents, *kalok pea kalok mi'* (written form: *kalok bau kalok mi*), spirit of grandmother and mother, *kalok harai*, spirits living in the ground and causing illness, *kalok tai prai*, spirits of maleficent magical influence, and *kalok daik*, a sea spirit which carries off children. Additional categories of spirits include the *pea cu'* (written form, *bau ju*), local spirits to whom villages erect small house-shaped shrines, the *pea thöng*, spirits of the fields who control rain, *prat* or *phut* (also *kalok*), ghosts, and *pöng hamao* (written form: *pung samū*), souls. Offerings are made to most of the various classes of spirits, and for some, notably the *kalok hoe'* and *pea cu'*, periodic festivals and dances are held. [Halliday 1917: 94-95, 107-09; Shorto 1962: 71 s. v. *kalok*, 136 s. v. *pöng hamao*, 140 s. v. *prat*, 150 s. v. *pea*, 162 s. v. *phut*.] **Practitioners.** Buddhist monks function as intermediaries vis-à-vis the supernatural. Other practitioners are shamans (*tong*, written form: *dong*), doctors (*aca so*), astrologers (*aca paneh*), and witches (*hamui*, written form: *gamuy*). Male and female shamans are consulted frequently on both private and public business, for which they receive a small remuneration. The shaman becomes possessed by a spirit and is then able to give counsel. Shamans also organize and lead spirit dances, perhaps their most important role. Spirit dances are held on such occasions as the annual festival to the *pea cu'*, local tutelary spirit. They may also occur within a family context, to alleviate an illness or calamity or to fulfill a vow made at a time of emergency. In this case the shaman wears the dress of the family spirit and all those associated with this spirit must participate. They too, in addition to the several shamans who may be present, usually experience spirit possession. At these spirit dances, the shamans and those possessed tend to be mostly women. [Halliday 1917: 100-04, 147-60; Shorto 1962: 40 s. v. *haneh*, 44 s. v. *hamui*, 117 s. v. *tong*, 157 s. v. *paneh*, 193 s.v. *so*.]

Ceremonies. The major Buddhist cyclical observances are the days of full moon at the beginning and end of lent (approximately early summer and early autumn); the new year (usually in mid-April); and the annual festival associated with each pagoda. There are in addition periodic festivals and spirit dances associated with indigenous animistic beliefs and practices. **Illness and medicine.** Any person with a knowledge of simple remedies can deal with some illnesses. Doctors work both with formal therapies, which may be recorded in texts, and with various forms of propitiation and exorcism of supernatural influences. One class of therapy rests upon a theory of the balance of four elements and associated dietary prescriptions; the other depends upon medicines, decoctions, and pills made up of pounded ingredients. In the case of supernatural causation, which is probably the most generally held theory of disease among the Mons, a doctor determines which supernatural agency is responsible. If it is a spirit, a shaman will probably put on a spirit dance. If it is determined that a witch has caused the patient to be possessed, a doctor seeks to exorcise the offending spirit by reciting formulas, threats, and commands, and (in some cases) by prodding the patient's body with a piece of ginger. If it is thought that the patient has moved in a direction unpropitious for the day, causing him to be seized by *hanem* (written form: *thanim*), the doctor prescribes the offering to be made (if the patient does not already know the remedy from books). The patient's ruling planet may be singled out as the maleficent agency, in which case an astrologer, working with mathematical calculations to the accompaniment of recited formulas and offerings, determines which planet to propitiate. **Birth.** Immediately after birth, the mother and her baby are bathed and smeared with turmeric. The baby's shoulder and hip joints are then set, since it is believed that they are still not in their proper places. For about three days after delivery the mother rests near a specially made fire while hot stones are applied to her body. [Halliday 1917: 52-56, 108-16; Shorto 1962: 26 s. v. *hanem*,

120 s. v. *tha' hanem*, 140 s. v. *praik kröh haröh toa*.] **Soul, death, and afterlife.** The soul is thought to be a part of the living person. It can absent itself during sleep and is sometimes seen as a butterfly. Most funerals are occasions for considerable expense and entertainment. For about one week after death people gather nightly at the deceased's house, where refreshments are served. On the seventh day a large meal is served. Food is presented to the monks and gifts to the guests. Funeral costs also include the hiring of musicians and construction of a coffin. The dead are usually cremated at the cemetery, where a monk leads the people in the recitation of Buddhist scriptures. The remains of persons who have suffered inauspicious deaths are buried as quickly as possible, e.g. women who have died in childbirth or persons killed by contagious disease or malignant tumors. The most elaborate funerals are held for monks of high status. The corpse may be kept in a coffin for a number of months to permit accumulation of funds for what is not only a cremation but also a festival, with theatricals and sideshows. [Halliday 1917: 62-67, 154.]

BIBLIOGRAPHY. Halliday 1917; Huke 1956a; India 1912, 1931-34; McFarland 1941; Pinnow 1959; Shorto 1962.

KHMER [1]

Synonym: *Cambodian*

ORIENTATION. **Identification.** The term Khmer refers to the ancient as well as the present dominant ethnic population of Cambodia. A national of the country may be called a Cambodian (the ancient Hindu term was Kambuja), although this term also includes groups that may be ethnically distinct from the Khmer. **Location.** The ethnic Khmer extend somewhat beyond the boundaries of Cambodia, particularly into southeastern Thailand and the Mekong delta in South Vietnam. **Geography.** The interior of Cambodia is largely a flat lowland plain, rising to mountain ranges in the southwest, north, and east. Cutting through the country are two important waterways: the Mekong river in the east and the Tonle Sap lake and river in the west. Smaller rivers and streams run off these main drainage systems. Cam-

---

[1] This account of Cambodian (Khmer) peasant culture, contributed by May Ebihara, is based upon field work conducted in 1959 and early 1960 in a Khmer village 30 kilometers southwest of Phnom Penh. Investigation centered in one hamlet, West Village Kong, although most data were checked in the other hamlets as well. The author feels that many aspects of the culture described herein are applicable to the peasantry of the country as a whole, but warns that there may be regional and individual village differences regarding the composition of the community population, economic activities, and details of ceremonials. The author's transcriptions for the most part are of spoken rather than written Khmer.

bodian soils are varied, but in general are said to be sandy and poor in humus, potash, and lime, but extremely rich in phosphate (Zadrozny 1955: 63; Delvert 1961: 90-113). Along the river banks, the low fertility of the soil is alleviated by flooding. In the highlands, forests are the dominant vegetation; while savanna, short grass, and clumps of palm and other trees are characteristic of other areas. The climate is hot and humid, with most rain during the months of May–November. **Linguistic affiliation.** Khmer is a language of the Mon-Khmer family. Villagers speak a colloquial form of Khmer which differs somewhat from the more formal speech of the educated. Special forms of Khmer are used in speaking to and about Buddhist monks and royalty. Some regional dialects exist. **Demography.** The Khmer in Cambodia total some three and one-half million out of a total population estimated at slightly over four million (Steinberg 1959: 28). **History and cultural relations.** The ancestors of the present-day Khmer were probably immigrants into the area, perhaps coming from somewhere to the north or west during protohistoric times. In the early Christian era, the Khmer proper (often identified as part of the Chenla kingdom) shared the mainland Southeast Asian peninsula with the Funanese, Cham, and Mon kingdoms. Chenla gained ascendancy over Funan in the mid-sixth century, and during the ninth century the Khmer kingdom came to be known as Kambujadesa. Influenced by the neighboring high civilizations of India and China, Khmer culture became quite complex. India had the more important effect, leaving marks on many aspects of culture, especially religion (Hinduism and Buddhism). Early chronicles record the rise and fall of various dynasties and empires. Of particular significance and fame is the Angkor or Kambuja period (802-1432 A.D.), which saw the construction of Angkor Wat and its associated complex of monumental structures. [Cf. Briggs 1951; Leclère 1914; Coedès 1944.] After this period, the Khmer went through a time of vacillating and weakening power, harassed by attempted encroachments from the immediately neighboring Siamese and Vietnamese. In 1864 the French were accepted as protectors, and in 1887 Cambodia, Laos, and Vietnam were combined to form the Union of French Indochina. During the French protectorate, the culture of Cambodia remained essentially unaltered by European influences. After World War II the Cambodians pressed for independence from France, which was granted in 1954. The present political structure is that of a constitutional monarchy with the real power vested in a prime minister, assembly, and ministries. ● Khmer villagers reveal some urbanization and Westernization in their material culture and in some attitudes (e.g. the aspirations for and of the younger generation to achieve nonagricultural occupations), but in many other respects, they retain what is basically a "folk" culture, with a conservative morality, a provincial

distrust of unknown villages and other ethnic groups, the practice of traditional ceremonies, and a very limited knowledge of the world outside Cambodia.

SETTLEMENT PATTERN AND HOUSING. **Settlement pattern.** Khmer villages, which have an average population of 300-400 people, are either of a linear type, with houses strung out along a roadway or stream, or of a compact pattern, with a cluster of houses surrounded by fields. In more sparsely populated areas, houses may be dispersed at random, each some distance from the others. Village Kong, a sedentary village of the linear type, is divided into three named hamlets. There are 168 houses in the village, housing a total of 784 people. Houses are built relatively near one another, separated by small kitchen gardens, fruit trees, and other flora. The rice paddies belonging to the village surround it on three sides. Villagers show little desire to emigrate; houses are occasionally moved for pragmatic reasons, but always within the village and for relatively short distances. These findings conflict with those of Delvert (1961: 200), who says that Cambodians are really rather "nomadic." Village Kong has its own Buddhist temple, Wat Kong, which has been in existence for about 60 years. The temple compound contains within its walls the temple proper (*vihiá*); the *salaa* or open hall for gatherings and worship; residences for the monks; a bathing hole; some *chedai* or tomb-monuments; and several small shrines dedicated to animistic spirits (*neak-taa*). **Housing.** The gable-roofed houses are usually rectangular or square in shape, ranging in size from about 12 x 20 feet to 20 x 30 feet. Poorer houses generally have but one room, with perhaps a few partitions of cloth, thatch, or wood. Better dwellings may consist of several rooms. The kitchen is often partitioned off, although some households cook underneath or beside the house. The house is raised on wood or concrete piling which may be from two to eight or more feet in height, the height usually increasing from poorer to better homes. Access to the house is by means of a ladder or wooden stairs, with the doorway usually facing east. The poorest houses are entirely of thatch except for the floors; the better houses are of wood with tile roofs.

ECONOMY. Villages may tentatively be typed on the basis of their primary economic activities: (1) rice-growing villages; (2) river-bank *chamkar* villages, in which fruit and vegetable production may equal or surpass that of rice; (3) fishing villages, most abundant in the Tonle Sap lake area; and (4) a relatively few craft villages specializing in weaving, pottery, or metallurgy. Most villages in Cambodia appear to have mainly subsistence rather than market economies. This impression, which is contrary to that given by some studies, is supported by the findings of the United States Overseas Mission (USOM) Agriculture Department. Cambodia's national economy is based overwhelmingly upon agriculture, with some 80 per cent of the cultivated land devoted to the production of rice for domestic and foreign consumption (cf. Delvert 1958 and 1961; Morizon 1936). ● Village Kong's economy centers around agriculture, i.e. the cultivation of wet rice for subsistence rather than the market. Food resources are supplemented by small gardens, with fishing and gathering of secondary importance. Fish are caught in the paddies and water holes by traps or hooks and line during the rainy season, but do not constitute a substantial proportion of the diet. Crabs, frogs, and sometimes insects are gathered in small quantities. There is no hunting. Cash income may come from part-time specialization (craft or other skills), temporary urban employment, the raising of pigs and/or chickens, and the processing of palm sugar. **Agriculture.** Permanent wet-field cultivation with diked paddies of varying size and irregular shape (usually rectangular with rounded corners). These fields are worked year after year, primarily by the household, but with an exchange of cooperative village labor during the busy periods of transplanting and harvesting. Fertilization may be provided by: (1) placing heaps of dung and/or fish parts and/or rice husks at various points on the paddy; (2) burning heaps of brush or the stubble of last year's growth on the paddy to provide ash; and/or (3) using the cow dung dropped during plowing. There is not much fertilization, nor is the fertilizer distributed evenly over the fields. The major source of water for Village Kong is rain, with no extensive irrigation. Paddies which are near a stream or water hole may be irrigated by scooping water into the fields. The water level in the paddies may be controlled to some extent by letting water flow from one into another through channels cut in the dikes. Village Kong's relative lack of irrigation is typical of most rice villages. River-bank *chamkar* villages are more likely to have irrigated rice fields fed by canals leading inland from the river. ● Agricultural implements include a light metal-tipped wooden plow and a harrow (both pulled by a pair of oxen and guided by one person); a hoe for clearing and maintaining paddies and dikes; a small sickle for harvesting; and a dibble which may be used for transplanting rice where the ground is hard. The necessities of rice cultivation determine to a great extent the rhythm of village life. When the rainy season begins, the dikes are repaired and the fields are cleared of stubble, plowed, harrowed, and sown with rice by the broadcast method. About six weeks later, the rice seedlings are pulled out and transplanted again in orderly fashion to grow for about four to six months, depending on the type of rice. By November or December, the rice has matured and is harvested and threshed by flailing on a wooden board—or it may be trampled by oxen or buffalo in areas of large rice harvests. The rice is winnowed by being shaken in baskets or by means of a simple wooden machine,

and it is then stored in mat bins at home. The yield in Village Kong is not great, averaging perhaps 40–50 bushels per hectare in a good year, sometimes only a half or a third of that amount in poor years. [For the seasonal cycle in *chamkar* agriculture, see Delvert 1961.] **Domestic animals.** Cows and oxen (for plowing), pigs and chickens (to be sold), cats and dogs. In villages near streams or permanent sources of water, the water buffalo may replace oxen as the primary domestic work animal. **Food and stimulants.** Rice is the major crop and the staple food. A variety of different types are grown ("light" rice, "heavy" rice, glutinous rice, etc.). The sugar palm (*Borassus flabillefera*) provides fruit, juice, sugar, and thatching material. This tree is a national symbol, and of great importance to village life. Small gardens and fruit trees provide coconuts, mangoes, bananas, papaya, guava, sapodilla, tamarinds, tangerines, jackfruit, belfruit, grapefruit, citronella, mint, ginger, turmeric, peppers, sweet potatoes, yams, white potatoes, gourds, cucumbers, squash, beans, tomatoes, eggplant, betel, and a number of other flora for which Western names are not known. Any one garden, however, is likely to have only a few things from this list. *Chamkar* villages in particular grow maize, tobacco, and cotton in addition to rice, fruit, and vegetable crops. Double cropping is sometimes practiced. Fish in dried or paste (*prahoc*) form is another staple. Fish sauce, *nuk-mam,* is of less importance. The greater proportion of fish is purchased rather than caught locally. Other foods bought at market include meat in small quantities for special events, various vegetables such as corn and onions not grown locally, and manufactured foods such as vermicelli, pastries, spices, etc. **Industrial arts.** Weaving of cotton or silk sarongs or scarves is done on a part-time basis by the women of some households, using a fairly large loom with a permanent wooden frame. Thread is purchased, although it is sometimes dyed at home. Some men have special skills in carpentry or woodworking, such as the making of musical instruments. Most men possess some knowledge of carpentry. Wicker baskets and containers and mats of woven palm leaf are made by almost everyone. A few families specialize in making cow collars out of lacquered rope and bits of metal. There is no pottery, blacksmithing, or metalworking in Village Kong. Villages which specialize in these crafts supply what products are needed. **Miscellaneous economic pursuits.** Temporary urban employment provides income during the few months before and after the rice harvest, when the fields need little care. During this time, about a third of all adult males in the village go to Phnom Penh to drive bicycle-cabs or work as manual laborers. Processing palm sugar by boiling down the juice of *Borassus flabillefera* was formerly an important economic activity, but because the work is both dangerous and arduous, it is now carried on by only a few very needy families. Pigs and chickens are purchased by some families from Chinese merchants and raised for sale but not for consumption. Other specializations or skills which provide extra income are: lay priest (*achar*), magical practitioner, midwife, barber, musician, and chauffeur. **Trade.** Because rice is used primarily for food, to pay debts, or as a money substitute in making small purchases, there is usually little left to sell on the market. Only about 50 per cent of those families in Village Kong who own a hectare or more of paddy land are able to sell rice in a good year. Villagers customarily sell what surplus rice they have to Cambodian and Chinese rice dealers. These merchants also extend credit, with an interest rate of about 5 per cent a month to be paid in cash or rice. Villagers by and large are not burdened with debt, and relations with the merchants are amicable. The town nearest Village Kong has a permanent market and shops (operated primarily by Chinese or Sino-Cambodians) selling a variety of goods, food, and services. The Kong villagers go there on an average of once a week, and itinerant peddlers selling food or small dry goods come from this town to the village almost every day. Shopping is done in Phnom Penh only for goods which are not available locally. The purchase and sale of labor skills, craft products, and noncraft specializations are generally restricted to the village itself or to neighboring villages. Payment may be in rice, money, and/or fruits, vegetables, cigarettes, incense, etc. **Division of labor.**

	Male	Female
Preparing paddies for planting	yes	yes
Plowing and harrowing paddies	yes	rarely
Pulling seedlings	—	yes
Transplanting	sometimes	yes
Tending paddies	yes	yes
Harvesting rice	yes	mainly
Threshing rice	mainly	yes
Winnowing rice	—	yes
Tending gardens	yes	mainly
Collecting sugar palm juice	yes	—
Making sugar	—	yes
Caring for cattle	mainly	yes
Caring for pigs, chickens	—	yes
Selling and buying rice, pigs, food	possibly	yes
Selling and buying cows, chickens	yes	—
Selling and buying land	yes	yes
Carpentry	yes	—
Weaving	—	yes
Wicker basketry	yes	—
Making mats and bins of thatch	—	yes
Temporary urban employment	yes	possibly
Care of household money	—	yes

Land tenure. The two major types of landed property in Village Kong are: (1) rice paddy land, and (2) land within the village proper which may be used either as house sites or garden sites, or left vacant. Land, like other property, may be held by either males or females in individual ownership, and may be inherited from either father or mother, or purchased. There are no communal lands. Land is partible, and the paddy lands in particular have been parceled through generations of inheritance. There is no form of land rental for money in Village Kong, but there is a limited amount of share cropping in which usufruct of paddy land is given in return for half of the crop. This may be practiced either by people who have more land than they can work themselves, or by individuals who have moved away but still own land in the village. Land may be sold or purchased according to individual needs and desires. It is almost always sold to fellow villagers, although there is no explicit rule about this. Sugar palm and coconut palm trees are subject to bilateral inheritance and may also be purchased or sold. Sugar palms are sometimes rented to those who make palm sugar. Taking the country as a whole, land pressure and population density are not great. Land holdings can range as high as 30 hectares in some areas (Zadrozny 1955: 259), but in many areas a concentrated population and the continued parceling of land has led to holdings of rice paddy land which average less than one hectare per family.

KIN GROUPS. Descent. Bilateral. **Kin groups.** Beyond the family, the only larger kin unit is the personal kindred, i.e. individuals related to Ego through both males and females, the membership of which differs more or less for each person. The boundaries of the kindred are vague, but the core might be considered to include grandparents or grandchildren where present, parents' siblings, first cousins, and children of siblings. Some affinal relatives (usually the spouses of close consanguineal kinsmen such as aunts and uncles, or the kindred of one's own spouse) will generally be included within an individual's personal kindred. The affection felt toward these affinals and the various functions which may be fulfilled by or for them are frequently the same as for consanguineal kin. ● Although distinct groupings of kin descending from common progenitors can be abstracted from the genealogical data of the village, these groupings cannot be considered as corporate entities or nonunilineal descent groups—there is no property held in common, no continuity through time, no real remembrance of common ancestors beyond a few generations, and no union as a group except in partial ad hoc assemblages for ceremonies or labor. Nonetheless, the kindred merits consideration because of the terminological distinction made by the people between kin and nonkin; there are supposed to be much stronger sentiments, loyalty, and obligations toward the former than toward the latter. The intensity of these bonds presumably varies proportionally with the degree of relatedness, although in actuality, personal likes and dislikes lead to the selection of particular kin for the most frequent interaction and deepest sentiment, regardless of the closeness of genealogical relation. Friction among kin is not sanctioned by public opinion, and is further believed to be punished by supernatural beings. **Kin terminology.** Aunt and uncle terminology is lineal, i.e. MoSi=FaSi, distinct from Mo, and MoBr=FaBr, distinct from Fa. Age relative to the connecting parent is distinguished, i.e. Fa or MoElBr is distinct from Fa or MoYoBr; Fa or MoElSi is distinct from the YoSi. Cousin terminology is Eskimo for terms of reference, i.e. cousins are distinguished from siblings, and both cross and parallel cousins are called by the same term. But terms of address are Hawaiian, i.e. both cousins and siblings are addressed on the basis of age relative to oneself as "elder person" (*bóng*) or "younger person" (*phaon*). Degree of cousinship is distinguished in the referential terminology. The term for first cousin is translatable as "same grandmother," that for second cousin translatable as "same great-grandparent," and, by extension of the same method, terms for third cousin and beyond are possible, but rarely used.

Relation	Reference	Address
Father	aupok	au, pok, paa
Mother	mday	may, mday
Aunt older than the connecting parent (i.e. Fa or MoElSi), or wife of uncle older than connecting parent	mday tom (tom=large, big)	tom, om
Aunt younger than connecting parent (i.e. Fa or MoYoSi), or wife of uncle younger than connecting parent	ming or mday ming	ming, sometimes name
Uncle older than connecting parent (i.e. Fa or MoElBr), or husband of aunt older than connecting parent	aupok tom	tom, om
Uncle younger than connecting parent (i.e. Fa or MoYoBr), or husband of aunt younger than connecting parent	puu or miá	puu, sometimes name
Sibling older than Ego	bóng	bóng, or name
Sibling younger than Ego	phaon	phaon, or name
First cousin	bóng-phaon chiidon muy (literally "one grandmother")	bóng if older than Ego; phaon if younger than Ego; or name
Second cousin	bóng-phaon chituát muy (literally "one great-grandparent")	bóng if older than Ego; phaon if younger than Ego; or name

MARRIAGE AND FAMILY. One of the major preoccupations of adolescents is the search for a potential spouse. Premarital sex, however, is not condoned in village morality, and a pregnant bride is a source of great shame to the family. Despite some stated preference for village endogamy as a means of ensuring the selection of a trustworthy spouse, there is in reality a preponderance of village exogamous marriages in Kong—due apparently to the fact that age-mates known since childhood are rarely objects of romantic interest. Most of these exogamous matches, however, occur with neighboring villages within a radius of approximately seven kilometers. Within the household, the husband is the legal head of the family, but the woman's authority is actually almost equal. The wife usually controls the family budget. [Cf. Monod 1931.] **Mode.** Ideally, a young man who has decided upon a particular girl asks his parents to begin marriage arrangements. A go-between is selected by the boy's parents to make inquiries and conduct negotiations with the girl's family, who may or may not accept the marriage proposal. The girl herself has the right of veto if she is opposed to the marriage. In actual practice, it is possible for the parents alone to arrange marriages, with both children acquiescing to parental desires. Upon agreement by both sides, arrangements for the wedding are made and a number of small gifts of betel, fruit, food, clothing, etc. are made by the boy's family. Shortly before the marriage, the fiancé also presents a fairly substantial gift of money, the amount having been decided upon in the betrothal negotiations and averaging about 2,000–5,000 *riels* (approximately $35–$75 at the unofficial exchange rate). This money is used to defray the expenses of the wedding, and any remainder is given to the couple. This money gift has been called "mother's milk price" by some writers, but the villagers of Kong had never heard this term. More small gifts are given by the groom's family at the wedding, and at this time the bride's family reciprocates with a few sarongs and scarves. It was once the custom for the fiancé to "do service" for the girl's family during the period of betrothal, aiding her family in various economic and other activities to prove his worth, but this custom is now dying out, due to the fact that many fiancés come from distant places. **Form.** Although polygyny is legally permissible in Cambodia, it is in fact practiced only by the wealthy. There appears to be some reluctance on the part of village women to allow polygyny, as evidenced in the cases of two village men whose attempts to take second wives were completely aborted by the harangues and agitation of the incumbent wives. **Extension of incest taboos.** Sexual relations and marriage are prohibited between members of the immediate nuclear family (including step-relations) and between aunts–nephews and uncles–nieces. Marriage is permitted and fairly common between cousins of any degree, although there appears to be no particular preference for such. The levirate and sororate are possible but not necessarily preferred. Incest taboos may be extenuated in the case of royalty. One ruler is known to have had a child by an aunt, and stories of brother–sister relations occur in old legends. **Residence.** A nuclear family living in neolocality is considered preferable by young couples. But this preference is achieved in Village Kong only about 50 per cent of the time due to two major reasons: first, the young couple's lack of money to build a new house; and second, the desire of many older couples to have one married child remain in the household to care for them, with the prospect of eventually inheriting the parental house as compensation. In such cases, either the husband's or the wife's home may be chosen, depending on the particular circumstances, e.g. which house has more room, which spouse feels strongly about remaining at home, or whether male or female manpower is most needed or desired by the parents. Although there is no explicit preference for such, matrilocal residence is much more common than patrilocality, probably because women are more loath than men to leave the security of their own houses and villages. Examination of residential histories reveals three main possibilities of residence and resultant kinds of groupings within the developmental cycle of the family: (1) A young couple may establish immediate neo-locality at the outset of marriage, with the family of procreation thus living separate from the families of orientation throughout the marriage. (2) A young couple may live in temporary matri- or patrilocality for a number of years and eventually build a separate home. (3) A young couple may live matri- or patrilocally from the start of their marriage, with the expectation of having the house to themselves after the parents die. In all of these cases, when, in turn, the younger generation marries, most of the children will follow patterns (1) or (2), i.e. of immediate or eventual neolocality, and almost always one child in each household will follow pattern (3). **Domestic unit.** There are two major types of household groupings: (1) the nuclear family, and (2) the larger or stem family, a two- or three-generation unit consisting of parents, their unmarried children, and a married child with spouse and children. Another type of larger family may arise from a nuclear family's inclusion of parental siblings, nephews or nieces, cousins, or grandchildren, who may be orphaned or unmarried and in need of support. • The nuclear family must be considered the primary kin unit in terms of both sentiment and function. Within this group exist the strongest emotional bonds, assurance of aid in the event of trouble, economic cooperation in labor and sharing of produce and income, and contribution as a unit to such things as ceremonial obligations. The larger family has many of these same characteristics, but the nuclear families within it frequently maintain some distinctiveness, e.g. by keeping their finances separate or by using different sections of the house. While it has been said that urban families are primarily nuclear in type (cf. Steinberg 1959: 77), extended families of the stem type are not unknown. Indeed, there are rather strong pressures necessitating this, since property, building materials, and even rent can be very expensive in the cities. Either matrilocal or patrilocal residence may be practiced, although some urbanites state that matrilocality is more prevalent because of the reluctance of parents and daughters to part from one another. Furthermore, it is not at all uncommon for urban dwellers to have relatives reside with them for varying periods of time to shop, work, attend school, or merely visit the city for pleasure. In turn, the urbanites visit the villages fairly frequently, particularly when there are close kinship bonds such as sibling–sibling, parent–child, or grandparent–grandchild relationships. **Inheritance.** Ideally, inheritance is according to shares that are equal in value, if not always in type of goods, for all children. In practice the personal favoritism of parents or individual circumstances frequently dictate unequal inheritance, e.g. giving more to children who have taken special care of the parents, or giving little to a child who has made a prosperous marriage. Land is customarily apportioned out to children as they marry, although other property (jewelry, cattle, house, etc.) is usually not disposed of until death, even though wishes may be made known beforehand by spoken or written will. In case of death intestate, the national court divides all property equally among the children or next in line. If there are no children, property reverts to the deceased's parents, or if they are already dead, to the deceased's siblings, who are expected to sell the property to provide a fine funeral. The only form of joint property is that earned jointly by a married couple. In case of divorce, each spouse retains whatever property was brought to the marriage, and anything gained by common effort is divided equally between them. **Divorce.** Divorce is not common, but it does occur in cases of incompatability, prolonged absence without good reason, failure to provide, or adultery on the part of the wife but not the husband. In case of widowhood, the remaining spouse takes over the household and is free to remarry, a common practice when the widow or widower is still relatively young.

SOCIOPOLITICAL ORGANIZATION. **Political organization: pre-French.** The highest stratum within nineteenth-century Cambodian society was composed of: (1) a divine king, usually hereditary from father to son; (2) a privileged aristocracy made up of relatives of the king, membership in which automatically ceased after five generations; (3) the *baku*, descendants of priestly Brahmans, who were responsible for certain royal ritual functions; and (4) major government officials, graded and ranked, who were selected from among well-educated freemen by the king or other officials. A middle stratum of ordinary commoner freemen, including the agricultural peasantry, small merchants, and artisans, formed the bulk of the population and supported the higher groups through their produce, taxes, and labor. A feudal-like patronage system existed whereby freemen selected protectors who gave them assistance in time of need and were responsible for the collection of their taxes and corvée labor. At the bottom were slaves—temporary in the case of insolvent debtors, permanent in the case of prisoners of war and their descendants; captured tribal peoples; and criminals. The primary territorial divisions under this system were the provinces and the districts, *srok*, the latter rather vaguely defined units. Of significance also were appanages, sometimes comprising several provinces, given to ministers and other high officials. [Leclère 1890; Aymonier 1900.] **Contemporary political institutions.** Each province, *khayt*, is divided into districts, *srok*, subdistricts, *khum*, and finally villages, *phum*. At the village level, the chief is elected from among several candidates, with the runners-up forming an informal village council. A village chief has minor duties such as apprehending petty criminals; his authority in Village Kong is, however, limited. ● The subdistrict chief for Village Kong is elected from among six villages, and is assisted by a secretary and two tax collectors, all local inhabitants. This office is important to the villages, and its duties are varied: collection of taxes; registration of all vital statistics (births, marriages, deaths); apprehension of criminals; adjudication of disputes; issuance of bills of sale for important items of property such as land or cattle; and acting as the major channel through which government orders are passed on to the local level. ● The district political office is located in a town and is referred to for matters which the subdistrict chief cannot handle. The district chief is appointed by the national government, and is assisted by various individuals who form the lowest rung of the impersonal and formal government bureaucracy; villagers do not ordinarily come to this office. ● The provincial administration does not directly affect the village. Beyond it is the national government, a constitutional monarchy with a king who is largely a figurehead ruler and a prime minister who has the real power, assisted by a national assembly and various ministries. The villagers have very little to do with the national government except to pay its taxes, abide by its policies, and hear its propaganda, but they do feel great patriotism for Cambodia and deep respect for the king and prime minister. **Social stratification.** It is possible to delineate several different social strata in Cambodia as a whole, although perhaps only the two extremes of the system are clearly defined for the people themselves. The major "classes" might be described as: (1) The "elite" group, composed of the royal family and related aristocracy plus the highest ranking officials within the government, military, or religious orders. High prestige, wealth, and/or education characterize persons at this level. (2) The "intermediate" group, a residual category for all those not engaged in manual labor: white-collar workers in business and government offices, teachers and other professionals, and lesser ranking monks. This group might be further subdivided into "upper" and "lower" strata depending on relative prestige and prosperity, i.e. the "upper intermediate" might include wealthy businessmen and professionals, moderately

high-ranking officials, etc., as contrasted to the "lower intermediate" of clerks, teachers, small shopkeepers, etc. At the present time there are relatively few Khmer in commercial or professional pursuits as compared to the number of Chinese and Vietnamese. (3) The "lower" group, composed of the rural peasantry and those urban dwellers who perform relatively unskilled tasks such as coolie labor and driving pedicabs. Persons at this level are often not far removed from rural origins. ● Within the village there are no real social classes, although differences of wealth may be recognized and manifested in such things as houses, clothing, and land. In daily life these wealth variances make no difference, nor do they carry any special prestige. Respect and informal authority are acquired by age, religiosity, or special personal qualities. Mobility is possible in this structure. Individuals may rise from the peasantry to the "intermediate" or perhaps even the "elite" group through education and connections. In general, however, the groups maintain integrity and continuity because of the opportunities for education and manipulation of wealth or power inherent in them, i.e. the son of an "elite" has more chance to acquire the training and to exercise the connections necessary for an elite position than does the son of a peasant. **Warfare.** Warfare occupies a prominent position in the ancient history of Cambodia. Military campaigns and conquests waged against the neighboring Chams, Viets, and Siamese were characteristic of the Kambuja period of empire (cf. Briggs 1951). Within the village itself, all able-bodied men from the ages of 20 to 50 years form a sort of local militia (*chivapol*), an adjunct to the police and formal military troops, which may be used to combat banditry, subversive groups, etc.

RELIGION. **Major religions.** Theravada (Hinayana) Buddhism is the national and official religion of Cambodia. The two "sects" of Buddhism in Cambodia, the Thomayyut and Mohanikay, are represented in Village Kong by two temples. While individual families may have more allegiance to one than to the other, most families attend both temples almost equally. The Buddhist precepts exert a fairly strong influence over everyday behavior; attendance at Buddhist ceremonies is high; and three-quarters of all men in West Village Kong have been monks at some point in their lives—for an average period of two years. Buddhist monks are greatly revered, and the local temples serve as educational, moral, and social centers for the community (cf. de Berval 1955). Elements of Hinduism (Brahmanism) are still evident in court ritual and regalia, in some details of life cycle and other ceremonies, and in the recognition of certain deities (*tivoda*) who are ultimately Indian in origin, as well as in Cambodian art, literature, and drama. But Hinduism as a religious system is of no significance to the villagers. **Indigenous religion.** Coexisting peacefully with Buddhism is an ancient folk religion centering around belief in a variety of supernatural beings which include animistic spirits of trees, stones, forests, villages (*neak taa*), ghosts (*kmauit long*), demonlike spirits (*praet*), house guardians (*chmniúng pteah*), ancestral spirits (*meba*), and others. While a few of these beings are benevolent, most of them are harmful or malicious and characteristically cause illness to those who displease them or cross their paths. To placate them, there are charms, shrines, offerings, ceremonies, and magical practitioners who request mercy or repel evil. **Practitioners.** The major types of practitioners are: (1) the *kru*, knowledgeable in magic, with such skills as curing illness, finding lost objects, and making charms (either for invulnerability, as aphrodisiacs, or to prevent illness), whose position and knowledge are usually passed down from father to son; (2) the *tmóp*, a special kind of *kru* who deals in a type of magic which may kill people; and (3) the *arak*, a spirit medium, usually female, who is possessed by spirits, and speaks for them in a ceremony held annually. The *arak* may also perform small ceremonies throughout the year to communicate with spirits. **Ceremonies.** (1) The Cambodian new year (Chol Chnam), mid-April, the biggest ceremony of the year; (2) the anniversary of the birth, enlightenment, and death of Buddha (Visak Bochiá), May; (3) the entrance of the monks into retreat (Chol Vossa), July; (4) the festival to honor the dead (Prachum), September; (5) monks come out of retreat (Cheng Vossa), October; (6) giving of gifts to the monks and the temple (Katún), October; and (7) the anniversary of the last sermon of Buddha (Miák Bochiá), February. All of these ceremonies are celebrated at the Buddhist temple. The villagers take food and other offerings (incense, small amounts of money, etc.) to the monks and the temple, with prayers by the monks. Participation in these ceremonies is not only a means of earning religious merit but also an opportunity for social conviviality, since the festivals draw large crowds from the surrounding countryside. [Cf. Leclère 1917; Porée-Maspero 1950 and 1958.] **Illness and medicine.** Illness and therapy have two aspects: (1) a "scientific" recognition that illnesses are due to physical disorders which may be remedied by Western medicines or by folk medicines made from herbs or other ingredients; and (2) the belief that some illnesses may in addition have underlying "spiritual" or "moral" causes, due to the patient's having offended some spirit or ghost, or to his not having been a devout enough Buddhist. In the latter case, a ceremony with offerings to the animistic beings and/or to Buddha is undertaken. Frequently both medicines and a ceremony will be used for serious illnesses. **Birth.** Aided by female relatives, friends, and a midwife (men and unmarried girls are excluded). For three days after birth, the mother lies upon a wooden slatted bed under which fires are kept burning, because heat is considered salutary. On the third day

after birth, there is a ceremony "to ask forgiveness of the midwife" for having caused her trouble, to present her with small gifts (betel, candles, incense, money, fruits, etc.), and to name the child. There is no set period of prohibited intercourse between husband and wife before and after birth, but it is usually considered wise to abstain for a few months preceding and following birth. **Soul, death, and afterlife.** The concept of a "soul" is rather hazy to the average villager, but there is definite belief in the Buddhist idea of reincarnation. The particular type of reincarnation is determined by the accumulation of merit through good deeds and by adherence to Buddhist commandments in this life. While ordinary villagers do not think of actually attaining *nirvana*, they do hope for an easier position in the next life. Corpses are disposed of by cremation, except in the case of suicides, who are buried. Village funerals are held as soon as possible after death, usually the next morning or as soon as a funeral pyre can be built on some open ground in the village. Monks are invited to come and recite prayers both when death is imminent and before the actual cremation occurs. The corpse is washed, dressed, and prepared with certain accouterments by friends and relatives, put in a coffin, and carried in a procession to the funeral pyre. After the cremation, any remaining bits of bone are placed in an urn to be kept at home or put in a tomb at the temple. Funerals, next to weddings, are the second most elaborate and colorful life cycle ceremonies in village life, with the assemblage of many relatives and friends, constant music, meals for all the guests, and fairly large expenditures of money.

BIBLIOGRAPHY. Aymonier 1900; de Berval 1955; Briggs 1951; Coedès 1944; Delvert 1958, 1961; Leclère 1890, 1914, 1917; Monod 1931; Morizon 1936; Porée-Maspero 1950, 1958; Steinberg 1959; Zadrozny 1955.

NORTHERN UPLAND GROUPS

KHASIS[2]

Synonyms. *Cassia, Cossyah, Kasia, Kassia, Kassya, Kasya, Khasia, Khasiah, Khassi, Khassia, Khosia*

ORIENTATION. **Identification and location.** The term Khasi has often been applied to that entire

---

[2] This account of Khasi culture, contributed by Anna P. McCormack, is based on field work during 1956-58 in the United Khasi–Jaintia Hills District. The author wishes to emphasize that her data are on the upland Khasis who inhabit the center of the District. She gratefully acknowledges support of the field work from the Department of Anthropology of the University of Chicago, the Wenner-Gren Foundation for Anthropological Research, Inc., and the Ford Foundation, for one of its Foreign Area Training Fellowships.

group of matrilineal and Mon-Khmer-speaking people who claim as their ancestral homeland the present-day United Khasi–Jaintia Hills District (within approximately 90° 47′ and 92° 52′ E. and 25° 5′ and 26° 5′ N.). This group includes the Jaintias (also Pnar or Synteng) in the southeast, who differ from the Khasis primarily in their duolocal residence pattern and less virulent forms of sorcery. (The Hadem in eastern Jaintia are a Kuki people.) It also includes the Lyngngams (also spelled Lynngam) in the west, who practice migratory swidden agriculture and certain peculiar funerary rites, and are said by Ehrenfels (1955) to be culturally intermediate between Khasis and Garos. Finally, it includes Bhois, Wars, and upland Khasis, which terms are primarily territorial. Bhoi country is the north-central part of the District, and is culturally complicated by the presence of Mikirs, Lalungs, and Nepalis. War country spans the entire southern length of the District, so that Wars divide into Jaintia Wars and Khasi Wars; of these, the Khasi Wars have traditionally transmitted property to sons as well as to daughters. The upland center of the District is the country of the Khasis proper, those whose culture provides the most useful model for interpreting the variations found elsewhere. [For general reference on all categories of Khasi culture, cf. Costa 1936 and 1937; also Gurdon 1907, especially for data on regional variations.] **Geography.** The District is 5,554 square miles of hilly tableland, intricately dissected by numerous rivers, and marked by significant ecological variation over very short distances. The tablelands step gently downward north from Shillong Peak, which at 6,445 feet is the highest point in the District, and over about 55 miles ease into the Brahmaputra valley where this is some 250 feet above sea level. To the south, the land slopes more steeply downward for about 20 miles, and then drops abruptly, in cliff and steep-slope formations, to the Ganges sea-level delta that begins at its north with Sylhet. The annual southwest monsoons drop torrential rains around Cherrapunji and Mawsynram villages (for Cherrapunji, a record 805 inches in 1861), but then, reaching Shillong 33 miles to the northeast, provide only about 100 inches per year. Rainfall is again greater in Bhoi, which shares the Brahmaputra valley climate. Climate is temperate on the high Shillong plateau, where it seldom freezes and never snows. To the north, climate becomes subtropical, forest is jungly, and fauna abound. The climate to the south is also subtropical. [Cf. Hooker 1891: chap. XXIX.] **Linguistic affiliation.** Khasi is one of the major Mon-Khmer languages, related to Mon, Khmer, Semang-Sakai, Nicobarese, and Palaung-Wa. The major Khasi dialects are Khasi, Jaintia, and Lyngngam, to which Grierson adds War. Further minor variations occur from village to village. The Khasis had no script until 1842, when the roman alphabet was successfully applied to the Cherrapunji dialect of Khasi proper. [Cf. Rabel 1961; Grierson

1903-28: 2; Bareh 1962.] **Demography.** According to the 1951 census of India, the United Khasi–Jaintia Hills District contained 221,982 Khasis and 67,532 Syntengs, Pnars, and Jaintias (India [Republic] 1952-57). These figures, together with those for Khasis enumerated in Cachar (4,005), Mikir and North Cachar Hills (467), Lakhimpur (287), Sibsagar (276), and Darrang (211) districts, and those for Syntengs enumerated in Mikir and North Cachar District (464), yield a total of 295,224 Khasis. **History and cultural relations.** Khasis believe that they had supernatural origin in Khasi Hills (see Gait 1926: 260 for historical evidence, and Rafy 1920: 8-9 for myth, but see also Costa 1958, 1960; Gurdon 1907: 10-11; and Chatterji 1953: 12). Khasi tradition also states that in early times they moved gradually from east to west, from Jaintia toward Khasi Hills, in the practice of swidden agriculture (Gatphoh 1947: 97-98). The salient fact of known Khasi history, which begins generally in the mid-sixteenth century A.D. when there already existed the present-day 25 native Khasi chiefdoms, is the distinctive line of development followed by the separate kingdom of Jaintia. To the north, Jaintia was successively tributary, in part or in whole, to the Kachari kingdom (ca. 1230 A.D.), the Koch kingdom (strongest ca. 1560 A.D.), and the Ahom kingdom (strongest ca. 1700 A.D.) (Shakespear 1914: Map I). To the south, about 1500 A.D., Jaintia extended its rule over a tract of Sylhet, which was populated by Hindus and Muslims, and saw its kings fall thereafter under Brahman influence. In the early 1800s, Jaintia became involved in the fratricidal strife then prevalent in the ruling family of Manipur. In 1835, after the Jaintia king ignored British warnings not to seize British subjects for human sacrifice, Jaintia was punished by the British annexation of the Jaintia parganas in Sylhet. The Jaintia king then voluntarily turned over to the British the hills area of his domain, so that the whole of Jaintia became part of British India and, in 1860, came to be taxed as such, although the Jaintias were otherwise allowed to maintain their traditional system of village government. • By contrast, the remaining Khasi states had few formal external relations until British times. Khasis raided and traded in both the Brahmaputra and Sylhet valleys, but were basically turned inward on their own hills, where warfare between villages and between the states was apparently common. Khasis came into indirect relation with the British in 1765, when Sylhet and its markets became part of British India. In the 1790s, stepped-up Khasi raids into Sylhet caused the British to throw up a deterring line of forts along the foothills. Later, it became necessary to place an embargo on Khasi products in the Sylhet markets. In 1827, the British penetrated into western Khasi Hills by negotiating with the Khasi chief of Nongkhlaw State to build a road through his territory, linking the recently annexed Brahmaputra valley with Calcutta. For three decades thereafter, the British negotiated treaties with all the Khasi states, the last treaty being signed in 1862. It was contracted that the chiefs would be subject to the authority of a resident political agent, whose duties would involve maintaining law and order, judging cases of heinous crimes, approving the popular selection of any new chief, and exercising control over certain categories of natural resources. Khasis were guaranteed noninterference in their customary way of life, and they were not then, nor are they now, taxed. Most Khasis, as opposed to Jaintias, were never an integral part of British India, but they did undergo social change as a result of British presence. To summarize Mills (n.d.): (1) The British introduced the potato, which the Khasis rapidly took up as a cash crop for marketing as far as Calcutta. The intensive specialization exhausted the soil and made for ever-poorer crops. (2) Christian missionaries made large numbers of converts, and there arose the difficult question of whether a Christian should inherit property that traditionally was earmarked for her performance of non-Christian religious rituals. (3) About 1864 the British transferred their headquarters from Cherrapunji to Shillong. When they made Shillong the capital of the entire state of Assam, non-Khasis flocked to it, land values soared, and the concept of private property became increasingly important. Khasis began to marry with members of other ethnic groups, which introduced confusion into traditional social patterns. These problems were exacerbated during World War II, when Shillong and its environs enjoyed enormous economic prosperity. One notable aftermath of this affluence has been the accelerated enrollments in schools and colleges. Hundreds of Khasis now have the B.A., M.A., and even the Ph.D. degree. ● With the Independence of India in 1947, and under the Sixth Schedule of the Constitution of India (which was drafted by a Khasi), the United Khasi–Jaintia Hills District became a Part B, or Autonomous, Tribal Area, to be governed by a District Council composed largely of Khasis and Jaintias, and responsible not to the Legislature of Assam, but to the Governor of Assam as agent of the President of India. The native-state system and the chiefs still exist, and the District Council finds it difficult to effect legislation which is neither offensive to regional custom nor a simple blueprint of ill-fitting all-India legislation. The major political schism at this time is between Jaintias, who are accustomed to centralized authority and taxation, and Khasis, who resist the notion of taxation to support the work of a central District Council. [Cf. Gait 1926; Aitchison 1931; Bhuyan 1949; Morris 1910.]

SETTLEMENT PATTERN AND HOUSING. **Settlement pattern.** Khasis live sedentarily in named, nucleated, and unplanned villages which are situated just below hill summits to avoid strong winds but still be defensible, and which usually include a de-

pendable water supply. Villages are about two to five miles apart, and have no boundary markers. In the past, villages contained semipublic buildings and grounds: the home of the village priest (also the home of a chief if he resided in that village), the village marketplace, and tree groves, cremation grounds, or other awesome spots that were believed to be inhabited by supernatural beings. Villages today may have also one or more Christian churches, government social welfare buildings, and schools. Formerly, villages were entered through a guarded gateway; this is no longer the case, and paths feed into villages from all directions. Often several villages are nucleated into one large unit, named and also described as a "village." These were once defense units, but were so uncohesive otherwise that institutionalized rivalry obtained among the component villages. Now, they have been integrated through the agency of all-village public services, especially schools. **Housing.** The traditional Khasi house is entered through a door at the rounded end of a U-shaped ground plan, and is about 20 feet at widest extent; it is about 30 feet deep, and is elliptical or hogback in profile. Its walls are of stone blocks cemented with mud. The roof of grass thatch, supported by a bamboo frame, overhangs the walls on their outside, down to about three feet above the ground. The house is divided into two parts: the front one-third is on the ground level, floored either with stone blocks or tamped earth, and is used for storage of occupational instruments and as a shelter for poultry. The rear two-thirds is raised four feet on piles of stone blocks to a platform of planks, and is partitioned into six rooms, comprising a kitchen, areas for storage of food and water, and sleeping quarters. Furniture is minimal, and the house is totally undecorated. There are no windows, and no smoke vents. A house generally has a companion shed, walled of wood and grass matting and thatched with grass. This serves as a pigsty, but it may be partitioned also to house cows, and it may have a loft for fuel storage. Compounds often contain garden plots, and are fenced around with stone or bamboo and mud. Nowadays, the traditional house has given way to Western-style bungalows of wood and tin, especially in and around Shillong. [Cf. Mukherjee et al. 1941.]

ECONOMY. The Khasi economy is a market economy based on agriculture, and most Khasis are primary producers, sellers, middlemen, and/or providers of services in connection with markets. Khasis are often multioccupational: they produce goods for partial subsistence, and also play some part in trade. **Agriculture.** On the Shillong plateau, the major field crops are potatoes, maize, millets, and dry rice, still produced mostly through swidden farming, with a two- to three-year period of fallow, but increasingly through continuous use of a single field with the aid of manure and chemical fertilizers. Both level land and hillsides are cultivated by the same hand techniques: 3 × 6-foot patches are fashioned with walkways between, sods are overturned within the patches and allowed to dry, the sods are burned slowly and the ashes spread over the soil, and finally the seed is sown, either broadcast or sunk with the aid of the typical Khasi hoe. The coldest part of the upland enjoys a two-crop year, and Khasis often double crop as well. Paddy has long been found in the lowlands, in parts of Jaintia and Bhoi, the only places where the plow is found. Nowadays paddy is more and more seen in the uplands, together with a simple terracing and irrigation technology. Many upland Khasis have house gardens in which they raise a wide variety of vegetables, including pumpkins, cabbage, radishes, sweet potatoes, eggplant, and many others. Important crops in Bhoi country are paddy rice, lac, caoutchouc, cotton, bananas, and pineapples; in War, they are betel nut, pan leaf, oranges, and sugar cane. **Fishing and hunting.** Fishing is done by poisoning streams, but this is a subsistence activity only in the southern foothills. Hunting was formerly by bow and arrow or by traps, including spring guns and pitfalls, but was always primarily a sport. [Cf. Stegmiller 1925.] **Gathering.** Khasis once gathered about 150 species of wild plants, most of them for food, but some for medicine. Thrifty villagers still gather food plants, but there is no real dependence on gathering. Medicinal plants continue to be very important. **Domestic animals.** Fowl, goats, pigs, and cattle are bred both for meat and sacrifice. Milk was formerly not utilized, but is now so popular that specialists keep herds of milch cows. Pigs are used as village scavengers, but some also receive prepared food. Cattle and goats forage freely in the fields during the winter, but are herded by a communally hired herdsboy during the agricultural season. Most households keep chickens, primarily for their eggs, and a few keep ducks. A few horses are also seen. Dogs are pariahs, except for hunting dogs. Cats are popular. **Food and stimulants.** The staple food of Khasis is boiled rice, together with the dried fish which is imported from Sylhet. Boiled beef, pork, and chicken are relished, but beyond the means of most. Meals are taken twice a day, in the morning and evening, although farmers also take a midday meal in the field, and others may take tea and cold sweet potatoes or rice bread. Certain foods are taboo to certain sibs. Stimulants are extremely common, especially betel nut, which is often accompanied by a bit of tobacco. Tobacco is also smoked as cigarettes and in hookah and other pipes. Every village has one or more household taverns, where distilled rice whisky is cooked and sold by the glass and by the bottle. Imported opium had spread widely in the malarious Bhoi country, but controls instituted in the 1940s have been fairly successful. All stimulants were once taken by men, women, and children, but Christian influence has eradicated or driven underground the consumption by women and children. **Industrial arts.** The only industrial arts traditionally practiced in all households were a rudimentary carpentry and a simple utilitarian basketry. Other arts were few, and were practiced as village specialties: the washing and smelting of iron ore and the forging of hoes, daos, knives, swords, and cooking pots (upland Khasis); the spinning of cotton thread (Mynso village, Jaintia); the dyeing of cotton thread and the weaving of cloth (Jaintias, Bhois, Lyngngams, Wars); the spinning and weaving of Eri silk (Khyrwang and Nongtung villages, Bhoi and Jaintia); and the hand manufacture, without wheel, of painted earthenware pots (Larnai village, Jaintia). Ironworking and the production of cotton goods have nearly died out through the competition of machine-made goods. Carpentry has greatly improved. An innovation of major importance is the sewing and tailoring, on sewing machines, of ready-made garments for both sexes. [Cf. Darrah 1896; C., W. 1832.] **Trade.** Khasi villages normally contain a number of household shops operated by women. Every Khasi also lives within walking distance of several village markets that are held on successive days of the eight-day week. The limits of market intercourse for the members of any particular village can be roughly distinguished by their naming the days of their week, which are called after the active markets. The exception is the huge market at Shillong, much of which is active daily, and which serves as a magnet for Khasis from all over the hills. The traditional barter has given way to currency in all markets. The small ones contain at least some local farm produce, plus other essentials like betel nut, and the food and tea stalls which serve as centers of social intercourse. The big markets contain not only regional produce and manufactures but also products from distant parts of the hills, brought for sale by traveling middlemen. There is also substantial trade, from the hills to the valleys, in potatoes, pears, hides, lac, cotton, caoutchouc, the wood of the sal tree, Eri silk thread, limestone, coal, ivory, bay leaf, betel nut, pan leaves, bananas, sugar cane, oranges, til, turmeric, and chilies. From the plains to the hills, there is trade in dried fish, paddy rice, salt, cooking oil, kerosene, matches, tea, sugar, wheat flour, machine-made cloth, shoes, metal pots, crockery, porcelain objects, coral beads, silver, and gold. Markets are important not only as economic institutions but also as centers for recreation (including archery competitions), courtship, reaffirmation of kinship ties with distant relatives, and the dissemination of information of all kinds. [Cf. Stegmiller 1924a.] **Division of labor.** Men do the heavy work, such as clearing and burning the swidden fields, caring for cattle and goats and driving them to market, butchering and selling large cuts of beef and pork, carpentry and mining, and driving and laboring on motor vehicles. They also tailor men's clothing, operate the large Khasi business establishments in Shillong, and provide all civic and religious leadership. Women care for children and for the home, do the marketing, and sell dried fish, betel nut, lime, fruits, and rice breads at markets. Other tasks can be performed by either sex. **Land tenure.** Land was formerly divided into sib land and public domain. Sib land was corporately held in perpetuity, and was inalienable except by the unanimous consent of all members of the sib. The public domain was subject to usufructuary right by anyone who kept the land regularly under habitation or cultivation, with a lapse of no more than three years. Most villages grew up on public domain, and then reckoned all land inhabited or under cultivation by a village member as village land. Forests were public, except for sacred groves possessed by villages or lineage groups, and everyone was free to gather branches for fuel. Wastelands and streams were also public. By now, most public domain and village land, together with its forest cover, has been pre-empted as private property and is being rented and sold as such. Sib lands remain intact, unless the sibs agree to rent, lease, or sell. [Cf. Cantlie 1934.]

KIN GROUPS. **Descent.** Descent is matrilineal, and the Khasi is a member exclusively of his own matrilineage from birth to death. Adoption, which is very rare, is only within the matrilineage. **Kin groups.** The maximal matrilineage is the sib; this is a named, widely dispersed, strictly exogamous, lineage group, which claims but cannot trace its origin from a single ancestress. Sibs used to meet as corporate groups from time to time. Some sibs are linked with others in large amorphous groups that are unnamed and are defined solely by exogamy. Such a group is composed of two or more sibs, the ancestresses of which are claimed to have been either real sisters or dear friends who out of affection declared that thenceforth their descendants would be as consanguineals. The origin and function of sib-linkage is now unknown, and today the members of a sib will often disagree on whether or not their sib is linked with another. • The minimal matrilineage is the local descent group, or *iing*. This is the largest kin group that normally rallies at life crises. It is said that the *iing* formerly spanned six generations; today, it encompasses only four. If an *iing* grows to more than four generations in a single village, it segments. New houses are located at some distance from the old and the *iing* soon forgets exactly how to trace genealogical connection, except for which segment descended from a youngest sister. The term *iing* may also be applied to an extended family, an elementary family, and a house. The elementary family is the basic domestic unit in Khasi society. In any village there are likely to be one or two households which stand as sole local representatives of the lineage of the female household head. Such a household is known as an

iing from the time it consists of an elementary family until it grows to a local descent group four generations deep. [Cf. Chattopadhyay 1941.] **Kin terminology.** The terms of address given below are also terms of reference except where otherwise indicated, and are uniform for male and female speakers. They were collected in an upland Khasi village near Shillong (cf. Ehrenfels 1953 for some regional variants).

Fa	*pa*
Mo	*mei*
FaElBr	*pasan*
FaYoBr	*pakhynnah*
FaSi	*kha*
Fa youngest Si	*khaduh*
MoElSi	*meisan*
MoYoSi	*meinah*
Mo youngest Si	*meiduh*
MoElBr	*mama, kni*
MoYoBr	*bah* (ref.: *kni*)
ElBr	*bah khynnah*
Eldest Br	*kong bah*
YoBr	*bah deng*
Youngest Br	*bah duh*
ElSi	*deng*
Eldest Si	*lud, kong*
YoSi	*lud nah, lud rit*
Youngest Si	*khatduh*
MoSiSo, MoSiDa	*para* (ref.: *para ar kmie*)
FaBrSo, FaBrDa	*para* (ref.: *parakha*)
MoBrSo, MoBrDa, FaSiSo, FaSiDa	*bakha*

MARRIAGE AND FAMILY. **Mode.** According to the traditional courtship pattern, a group of young male relatives and friends made nightly visits to the house of some virgin girl in another village, appraising her through banter while she and her parents appraised them, and staying the night to avoid the dark walk home. Marriage was according to the wishes of the parents after negotiation by a go-between from the boy's side. Girls might be 15, and boys 17, years of age. Girls have now acquired freedom of movement through attending school, however. Premarital sexual play is common, and young people choose their own spouses when the girl is about 19 and the boy 21. The most common mode of marriage is elopement, for Christians and non-Christians alike, but some Christians marry in church, and some Khasis still marry according to the traditional ceremony or some variation on it. There are no preferred or prescribed marriage types, nor is there a bride price or dowry. **Form.** Monogamy is the ideal for all. **Extension of incest taboos.** Sibs are exogamous. Other prohibited marriage partners are real and classificatory FaSi and FaBr, FaBrCh, FaMo, and FaMoMo. The MoBrWi is also prohibited. Roy says that the MoBrCh but not the FaSiCh is prohibited (1897: 2), but Gurdon says that the MoBrCh is eligible after the death of MoBr, and that FaSiCh is eligible after the death of Fa (1907: 78). Nowadays both types of marriage occur, whether the linking relative is living or dead. **Residence.** Residence is either duolocal or matrilocal under the roof of the wife's mother until the birth of one or two children. For a man married to a youngest daughter, it then continues to be matrilocal. For men married to other daughters, it becomes uxorilocal; there have also always been cases of virilocal residence, and it is now common to find neolocal residence in Shillong. For non-Christian Jaintias, it is duolocal throughout the marriage. **Domestic unit.** The domestic unit is the elementary family, though for a youngest daughter it may temporarily include also her aged mother, aged father, unmarried siblings, or divorced or widowed brothers. **Inheritance.** Traditionally, after the Khasi mother had helped each of her daughters to build and supply a house when each one married and had children, her only real obligation to help them economically was ended. Everything she possessed, excepting certain personalty that was destroyed in her cremation, was inherited by her youngest daughter. Failing daughters, a woman's property reverted to her next youngest sister's daughter. Today, this pattern is often modified by putting more property into the hands of older daughters and even sons. [Cf. Cantlie 1934; Becker 1924.] **Divorce.** A woman may effect numerous and usually brief separations from her husband by simply closing the door of her house to him, whereupon he returns to the house of his mother or youngest sister. Divorce, however, must be initiated by mutual consent. Divorce is very common, even though women resist it because they do not wish to lose a provider, and men because they do not wish to lose their children. Formerly it was accomplished by a simple ritual in the presence of witnesses, followed by public announcement by a town crier. Now, the witnesses and the public announcement have been dispensed with, and evidence for divorce consists only in the word of the parties concerned.

SOCIOPOLITICAL ORGANIZATION. **Political organization.** The basic unit of political organization is the village, which is composed of one or more dominant local descent groups plus several others. Village government is by an assembly of all resident adult males, under the informal chairmanship of a headman elected by them from among their number. The membership of any immigrant household into a village is defined by the participation of the household's males in this assembly. Sustained membership in a village is voluntary. Khasi chiefdoms probably arose out of voluntary associations of villages, which occasionally transferred allegiance from one chief to

another. In other words, a state is not a fixed territorial entity. In the early twentieth century, the most populous of the 25 chiefdoms, Khyrim, contained 36,833 persons occupying 7,859 houses in 372 villages, and the least populous, Nonglwai, contained 246 persons occupying 53 houses in 3 villages. Fifteen of the chiefdoms were headed by a *syiem* (chief), three by a *lyngdoh* (priest), six by a sirdar, and one by a *wahadadar*. These leaders all had executive and judicial functions, but a chief's authority was limited in that he had to obtain the approval of his executive council before acting. The other leaders were subject to a similar limitation. A chief maintained a small police force. His major sources of revenue were market tolls, fines, and, more recently, income from licenses to distill rice whisky. Succession to a ruling role in the larger states traditionally involved election by members of a lineage that had a hereditary right to elect, from among members of a lineage that had the hereditary right to rule. In British times, the elective basis was broadened, differentially in the various states, even to the point of popular elections. [Cf. Aitchison 1931; Lyngdoh 1952.] **Social stratification.** The three classes of lineage are the nobles, the commoners, and the slaves or servants. This stratification applies only to the recruitment to office in the native-state system, for there is no hypergamy, and in a village assembly everyone has equal voice. The noble lineages have the hereditary right to fill from among their male members roles such as village or state priest, councilor to a chief, or elector of a chief. The few lineages which today are remembered as slave or servant lineages had the inherited obligation to render special services to a chief's household. There is no Khasi term for "commoner." Every lineage other than a noble or a slave lineage is a commoner lineage, and the commoner lineages are in the majority. **Warfare.** Warfare was suppressed by the British, and little is known for certain about its traditional forms. The tactics which confronted the British were the ambush and the guerrilla raid. Traditional goals included taking heads from other Khasis and capturing women from the valleys.

RELIGION. **Major and indigenous religions.** A Welsh Calvinistic Methodist missionary penetrated into Cherrapunji in 1832, and the work that he began continues to this day. His society, which has since become the Welsh Presbyterian Foreign Mission, introduced writing, village primary schools, a high school, a theological seminary, and a hospital. Competing missionaries followed, and by 1914 some Shillong Khasis were puzzling over the tenets not only of traditional Hinduism and Islam but also of the Buddhists, Brahmo Samaj, Arya Samaj, and Unitarians (Roy 1914). By the 1920s, missionaries of the Church of God and the Seventh Day Adventists were also active, and in that decade one U Kyrhai, a Khasi convert to Presbyterianism, left that church and founded a unique sect that blends something of himself with something of mystical Hinduism and Christianity. The competitors who most seriously threatened the dominance of the Welsh Presbyterians were the Roman Catholic missionaries who arrived in Shillong about 1890. Catholics have since opened a number of high schools, colleges, convents, and orphanages. They also established a technical school, and are now constructing a seminary. At the present time, one estimate is that there are about 100,000 Presbyterians and 80,000 Roman Catholics among Khasis. Members of other Christian sects are comparatively few; adherents to Hinduism and Islam are fewer still, comprised chiefly of Khasi women married to Hindu or Muslim men; U Kyrhai's sect is dying out; and the balance of Khasis are, according to their own term, "Khasi" in religion. [Cf. Lyngdoh 1937; Morris 1910; Ropmay 1940; Singh 1950; Pugh 1951.] **Supernaturals.** The great deities are two, an unnamed masculine God (U Blei) and an unnamed feminine Goddess (Ka Blei Nongsynshar Nonghukum). God created the earth, and in the beginning instructed man in cultivation techniques and also laid down the framework of a moral order that should guide his every move if he wished to join God in heaven after death. This framework was then filled in by the first ancestors, who are therefore the authorities on the subject and are semideified as Ka Iawbei (the mother), U Thawlang (the father), and U Suidñia (the mother's brother). Very early, Goddess undertook to keep account of the numbers of human beings on earth, and this role was so important, relating as it did to the health and the multiplication of the people, that she became of major importance in the Khasi pantheon. When sin beset human society, God activated automatic punishments in the form of natural calamities, and man finally decided that some animal should go and intercede with God on behalf of humans. The cock went, agreed to take upon himself the burden of human sin, and received instruction in the correct divinatory and sacrificial techniques for which he would be one of the main objects of the knife. Again, over a period of time, it was the ancestors who perfected these techniques. Now, God is regarded as powerful and merciful, but passive. His punishments have their own impetus, and the expression of His mercy is solidified in ritual. Goddess is more vaguely conceived, but is much closer to the individual. [But cf. Ehrenfels 1950, who conceives of one double-sexed, great deity among Khasis.] Regarding ancestors, it is never clear from prayers whether supplication is to generalized semideities or to particular first ancestors of a Khasi's own matrilineage, and such a distinction seems not to matter. There are three other categories of minor deities: those who protect places (such as villages, groves, or springs),

household deities, and measles and smallpox deities. Deities of the first two categories are simply aspects of the high God or Goddess. ● The earth is peopled with two great orders of land demons and water demons who cause all undesirable, unnatural, and otherwise inexplicable events, acting either on their own or as instruments in the hands of sorcerers. Apart from omens, both in nature and in dreams, Khasis attach supernatural significance also to mystic numbers, and to the colors white, black, and red. They hold especially important folk beliefs regarding betel nut, paddy rice, gold and silver, and clothing. **Practitioners.** The two classes of religious practitioners are the village or state priests and the sacrificers. Both are male. They use the same divinatory techniques of reading broken eggshells and the entrails of cocks, and they both sacrifice cocks, hens, goats, pigs, and cattle. Their skills are not taught to them so much as picked up by observation and confirmed by demonstrations of efficacy. A priest is elected from among the men of his sib to direct his skills to the public good until he dies, and his rewards are institutionalized and come from the village or the state. A sacrificer acts for private persons or kin groups, on call, and is rewarded by them personally with gifts in cash or in kind. The sacrificer is called upon to explain and then to ritually remedy every variety of misfortune, especially illness, though his powers are nowadays regarded with ambivalence, and he is widely expected to become a sorcerer sooner or later. ● There are two major types of sorcerer. One is the ritual specialist or sacrificer who secretly turns his skills from good to evil, manipulating demons to injure a person or kin group, and acting always for himself alone out of considerations of jealousy or revenge. The other is normally a leading citizen, a woman who is so wealthy and successful that it is believed that she must keep a *thlen*, i.e. a creature which will bring her prosperity as long as she feeds it periodically with human blood. To provide this blood, the men of her household, or other males whom she bewitches with a special whisky, will indiscriminately murder anyone except a member of her matrilineage. The Jaintias have an analogue to the *thlen* in their *taro*, except that the ultimate result is death from illness rather than murder. Minor witchcraft can be perpetrated by poison keepers or persons with an evil eye, who are often women. **Ceremonies.** The important traditional ceremonies were the life-crisis rituals relating to pregnancy and childbirth, the naming of a child, and death. Lesser ceremonies related to marriage and divorce, and to housebuilding. All these rituals were addressed primarily to the ancestors, and they are still performed in modified form by many Khasis. Other rituals, which were performed by groups such as villages, sibs, local descent groups, or households, were addressed to the unnamed aspects of the high

God or Goddess, deities regarded as helpful in bringing prosperity, producing fertility, and so on. Rituals of this kind are no longer practiced, except for the Bedingkhlam ceremony designed to protect the Jaintia village of Jowai. Finally, the state religion of many chiefdoms was expressed in one great ceremony per year which was intended to secure ancestral blessing for a chief and his lineage, and, through this, for the entire chiefdom. The notable example, still practiced, is the Pomblang Syiem of Khyrim chiefdom. [Cf. Lyngdoh 1937; 1946; Stegmiller 1924b; Becker 1909.] **Illness and medicine.** In time of illness, a Khasi calls in a sacrificer, and possibly also a medicine man. The medicine man is an ordinary individual who has hit upon some herbal remedy for one or more ailments, who has become famous enough to be sought out and rewarded in cash, and who jealously guards the formula of his medicine until it dies with him. He and his patients tend to regard him as specially blessed. **Soul, death, and afterlife.** The universe is comprised of a heaven, the earth, and the air between. Heaven is where the souls of deceased mortals live in eternal peace, grouped sib by sib. The earth and all nature were created by God, and everything that God created has its own individual soul. There is no other great earth deity, for it was God who created the earth. The air is inhabited by the wandering souls of those dead for whom full death rites were not performed. A Khasi's potentiality for enjoying an afterlife in heaven with his ancestors depends on his receiving proper death rites at the hands of his sib mates. First, his body is cremated by his children, notably his youngest daughter, and his bones are collected and deposited temporarily in a small stone receptacle. All work stops in the village while everyone participates in the funeral. Once every several years, an entire sib gathers to witness the transfer of the bones of recently deceased sib mates from their temporary receptacles to the great sib cairn that is in the keeping of the youngest daughter, descended from the sib ancestress through a line of youngest daughters. This final ceremony covers five days, and is elaborate and expensive, but when an individual's bones are finally resting with those of his antecedents in the cairn, it is understood that his soul is finally in heaven, "eating betel nut in the house of God."

BIBLIOGRAPHY. Aitchison 1931; Bareh 1962; Becker 1909, 1924; Bhuyan 1949; C., W. 1832; Cantlie 1934; Chatterji 1953; Chattopadhyay 1941; Costa 1936, 1937, 1958, 1960; Darrah 1896; Ehrenfels 1950, 1953, 1955; Gait 1926; Gatphoh 1947; Grierson 1903-28; Gurdon 1907; Hooker 1891; India (Republic) 1952-57; Lyngdoh 1937, 1946, 1952; Mills n.d.; Morris 1910; Mukherjee et al. 1941; Pugh 1951; Rabel 1961; Rafy 1920; Ropmay 1940; Roy 1897; Roy 1914; Shakespear 1914; Singh 1950; Stegmiller 1924a, 1924b, 1925.

KHMU [3]

Synonyms. *Kha Khmu, Kha Mou, Khamu, Khamuk, Mou*

ORIENTATION. **Identification.** Khmu? is a morphophonemic spelling of which the phonemic base is *kûmhmu?*, with *ûm* morphophonemically predictable on the basis of rules outlined in Smalley (1961: 16). The word either means "people" (as opposed to animals, rice, etc.) or is applied to a group of people by that name who speak the same language or share the same culture (as opposed to *jê?* "non-Khmu?"). Khamuk is the term used in Thailand, e.g. by the Tai in Chiengmai. Seidenfaden (1958) also uses it. Halpern (1957) uses Khamu. Kha is a Lao word, a generic term for any of the Austroasiatic [Austroasian] peoples of Laos, corresponding to Vietnamese Moi. Its central meaning is that of "slave," and it is therefore pejorative. The Lao refer to the Khmu? as Khmu?, Kha, or Kha Khmu. Roux and Tran (1954) use Tsa Khmu?; according to them, Tsa is the Black Tai equivalent of the Lao term Kha. The same authors (1954: 297) add that the Khmu? were also called Tsa Muong Sing by the Black Tai, after the area where they were concentrated in the north. French maps sometimes bear the term Mou or Kha Mou, resulting from a false etymology. Hearing *kûmhmu?* pronounced by the Lao as *khamu* or *khamu?*, a false analogy was made with the Kha Lamet, Kha Hok, etc. The real Lao analogy, as indicated above, is Kha Khmu?. Terms such as Phouteng, Phou Teng, or P'u Ting are different spellings of a Lao expression meaning roughly "people who live high up," referring to the fact that the Khmu? are a hill people. This is a polite expression covering the same peoples as the pejorative Kha. ● Each of the several subdivisions of the Khmu? has its own name. The generic term for a subgrouping of this kind is *tmôôy*. It is used in combination with the name of a specific subgrouping to give terms like

---

[3] This account of Khmu culture, contributed by William A. Smalley, is based primarily on linguistic field work in Luang Prabang during 1951-53. Additional sources of information include a brief visit to Luang Prabang in 1961, several brief encounters with Khmu (and discussions with others who had contact with Khmu) in Thailand, and the scanty literature on these people. The author points out that most of his knowledge of Khmu culture is derived from conversations with informants and analysis of Khmu texts. His intended residence in a Khmu village for the purpose of studying the culture at first hand was not possible due to unsettled conditions in Laos. With the exception of his introductory discussion of names and synonyms, the author's spelling of Khmu? has been changed to Khmu for typographical convenience. Other typographic changes from the author's morphophonemic spelling of Khmu terms are as follows: *ê* and *ô* are used for "open e" and "open o" respectively; *û* and *â* are used for high central and mid-central vowels respectively; and *ny* and *ng* are used for alveopalatal and velar nasals respectively.

tmôôy rôôk, "the *rôôk* subgroup." It is also used in the sense of "stranger" or "unfamiliar." There are dialect differences among the *tmôôy,* and some are considered more "backwoods" than others. The Tmôôy Rôôk are one of the larger Khmu? subgroups. The Lao, who have no initial /r/, call them Hok or Kha Hok. They are often listed as a separate group from the Khmu?, but the latter count them as one of their subgroupings. The Khmu? of the Luang Prabang area look down on the Rôôk as being backwoods and unacculturated (to Lao culture). The Tmôôy Ksak are an unusual group living in the range of hills above Xieng Ngeun, to the southeast of Luang Prabang. This group is regarded by the Khmu? as a cognate group; it has Khmu? culture, but the language is Lao with its own particular accent. The Ksak have completely switched from Khmu? to Lao in the last two generations. In addition to the fact that they have taken on Lao speech, the Ksak are notable for the fact that the Lao use them in important ceremonies in Luang Prabang, when special attention must be paid to the spirits. The Tmôôy Mee are the most numerous subgroup in the Luang Prabang area. The term Tmôôy Lûû refers to two different Khmu? dialect groups, one in the Muong Sai area of Laos, another in Nan province near Pua, in Thailand. Izikowitz (1951: 24) mentions the Khuen, saying that they are "identical with the Khmu?, the difference being only that the Khuen have adopted Buddhism." **Location.** The Khmu are without doubt the largest so-called Kha group in northern Laos, and the only important one in Luang Prabang and Xieng Khouang provinces. There are Khmu in Sayaboury, Nam Tha, and Phong Saly provinces as well. In Thailand they are found mostly in northern Nan province, near the Thailand–Laos border. **Linguistic affiliation.** Haudricourt (1953: 122; 1962: 410) classifies the Khmu language as being in the Palaung-Wa family. Izikowitz (1951: 20-21) considers Palaung-Wa a subgrouping within Mon-Khmer, and considers Khmu to be a member of it. Greenberg (1953: 280) sides with Schmidt in considering Palaung–Wa and Mon-Khmer as parallel groups within an Austroasiatic stock, rather than subsuming the one in the other. The writer has made no systematic study of the problem, but his impression is that Khmu is more like the Mon-Khmer languages of South Vietnam than like Lamet (Izikowitz 1951) or Lawa (brief personal contact in Thailand), at least in basic vocabulary. This was also Greenberg's impression in personal communication to the writer. Details of language relationships in this area remain vague. Of the general fact that Khmu is in some way included within Austroasiatic there can be no doubt. **Demography.** The Khmu look like other Mon-Khmer-speaking peoples. On the average, they are darker than the Lao, sometimes quite dark. A few have wavy hair, and there is reported to be a strain of red hair in some Khmu communities along the Lao border in northern Thailand. ● Estimates of Khmu population in northern Laos vary enormously (cf. the population tables reproduced in Halpern 1961b), but the total would seem to be in the neighborhood of 100,000. Young (1961: 76) reports 3,300 Kha Mu in northern Thailand, with many more scattered throughout the country who have "become Tai." **History and cultural relations.** The Mon-Khmer-speaking Kha preceded the Tai-speaking Lao in the area of northern Laos. The Lao consider the Khmu their "older brothers" in this respect. The origin legend of the gourd (LeBar and Suddard 1960: 8) is shared by the Lao and Khmu with minor variations. ● One Khmu legend describes the ancestor of the Ksak as the older brother of the original king of Luang Prabang. The two brothers set out to find a place to found the city of Luang Prabang, the Ksak in a brass canoe, and the king in a leather one. The Ksak arrived first, and planted a marker to stake out the city. When the king arrived, he placed his marker on the top of the tree, and an argument followed over who got there first. The king won by insisting that his marker was higher, and therefore must have been first. The Ksak had to go off and live on the mountain, and the king took over the city. This theme of being tricked and deprived of their rights is a common one in Khmu texts. ● The Lao believe that the Khmu have power over the spirits of the area, and the Ksak are by tradition brought to the Lao court as magico-religious specialists. They take part in annual court ceremonies, and it was the Khmu who purified the royal palace in Luang Prabang after it was built and before the king took occupancy. ● The significance of the Khmu role in the court of Luang Prabang, and in Buddhist ceremonies involving the spirits, is heightened with the realization that they played the same role in the ancient kingdom of Nan in Thailand. According to a prince of the former kingdom of Nan, the old records show that even there the Khmu were believed to have control of the spirits. They are still considered the most powerful practitioners within the Nan area. Seidenfaden reports that the Lawa had a similar function in the ancient kingdom of Chiengmai (Seidenfaden 1958: 119). **Acculturation.** The Khmu of the Luang Prabang area are heavily acculturated toward Lao life. Most Khmu around Luang Prabang know Lao, some know it well, and a very few are literate in Lao. With the exception of the Ksak, however, they maintain their own language among themselves. Those Khmu who "become Lao" also adopt Buddhism. Others may spend time in a Buddhist *wat* in order to learn to read Lao, but without becoming Buddhists or giving up their Khmu identity. Izikowitz (1951: 24) reports a group of Buddhist Khmu in Nam Tha. ● The Khmu of the Luang Prabang area feel and act inferior to all other groups. In northern Thailand this is also true, except that the T'in and Yumbri are even lower in the social order. The Khmu of this area show apathy and cultural disintegration, and very little zest for life. The ancient symbols of prestige—gongs, jars, and buffalo—are gone, or nearly gone in the case of the buffalo, for few Khmu can afford them. The Khmu described by Roux and Tran, and others referred to by Izikowitz, on the other hand, do not seem as apathetic. Those in the Xieng Khouang area also seem more vigorous and prosperous. Part of the reason for Khmu apathy is economic. They are desperately poor. They have also been the traditional slaves of the Lao, with little political recourse. When the king's free-roving elephants tear down their barns to eat their grain there is little they can do effectively. ● The Khmu are ripe for a messianic movement. Some have found a measure of reintegration in Christianity. Others look for the return of their traditional culture hero, Cŭang, who gave them their culture in the first place, and now waits in a cave in the north with all kinds of modern material goods—refrigerators, airplanes, etc.—for the Khmu. Although this movement was not apparent in 1951-53, it is reported by Halpern (1960: 63; 1961e: 144), and in 1961 the writer found it in Thailand, where it was associated with Communist propaganda in the minds of many Khmu, but taken seriously by others. Halpern reports that in the Luang Prabang area some Khmu stopped making rice fields to make sacrifices which would induce Cŭang to come to them. ● Thousands of fully assimilated Lao are probably of Khmu descent. Passing takes place constantly, as does intermarriage. For centuries, mixed families have lived in Lao communities and grown up Lao. The only way to get out of the class of "slaves" and "savages" is to pass into Lao culture. On the other hand, in spite of all the acculturation which goes on, habit, fear, the spirits, and tradition keep the Khmu a distinct group.

SETTLEMENT PATTERN AND HOUSING. **Settlement pattern.** The houses and barns of a Khmu village are built fairly close together, often on the mountainside. The earth is scraped clear of vegetation, and one of the few places where deep erosion can be seen in Laos is in these villages. Sometimes several small hamlets some distance apart may be under the same headman. If the site is a good one, and if there is no calamity to make people fear it, the village is not moved with any great frequency. There are no distinctive community structures in Khmu villages in the Luang Prabang area, except for some Christian villages which have simple churches. **Housing.** Khmu houses are similar to those of the country Lao, but much poorer. Whenever possible they are built on piles, but the poorest are built on the ground. Characteristically they are entirely of bamboo except for the piles and for crossbeams and some of the supports of the floor and roof, which may be of wood. The roof is most typically of thatch, although split bamboo is used by the more prosperous. Houses range in size from an estimated 8 feet x

10 feet to 20 feet x 30 feet. The gable roof has a fairly steep pitch, extending out over the walls about 2 feet to 3 feet for protection. The space underneath the house is used to store firewood, bamboo, and large objects. In the rare case of an acculturated Khmu household with women who weave, the loom is under the house. Animal pens are often under the house, or buffalo may be tethered there. The rafters of the house provide a storage area for baskets of dried foods, extra traps, seed rice, and valuables. ● The furnishings of the house are very simple. In addition to the hearth, there is a shelf for the *hrooy gaang* or house spirit; a shelf over the fire for drying food and bamboo for arrows; sleeping mats, which are rolled up in the daytime and spread out at night; a few utensils such as basins, pots, and water containers (often of bamboo); and perhaps an old suitcase for extra clothing. Prosperous families may have kapok bed pads, mosquito nets, and a greater variety of tools, clothes, and utensils. Many Khmu live in small huts in the rice fields for several months after the rice has begun to sprout and until the harvested grain has been carried to the barns, both to save the long walk from village to fields, and to protect the fields from animal and bird marauders. The field hut is often built off the ground for better visibility, but is usually little more than a platform with a roof.

ECONOMY. Agriculture is the main source of food, supplemented by gathering, hunting, trapping, and fishing. Some Khmu keep a few domestic animals, but these are used for sacrifices more often than for food. **Agriculture.** Rice is the staple. There are many varieties, all of them glutinous. Other crops include corn, bananas, sugar cane, cucumbers, beans, chilies, scallions, water cress, cabbage, eggplant, tobacco, and occasionally cotton, flax, and opium. Many of the fruits and vegetables are raised in small garden plots maintained in or near the village. Swidden farming is the prevalent form of rice cultivation, although some of the more acculturated Khmu in suitable locations have prepared wet-rice fields. ● In the Luang Prabang area there are serious problems in finding enough swidden fields. The Khmu realize the necessity of a long fallowing period, but in the Luang Prabang area fallowing is no longer than seven or eight years, and sometimes it is necessary to make a field sooner than that. A field is used for two or three years, often with only nonrice crops toward the end. Corn, beans, gourds, cucumbers, and a variety of other plants are planted in the swiddens along with the rice. ● There is a definite system of rotation of the fields. Decisions as to which fields are to be used in a given year are made on the basis of convenience, omens, the length of time in fallowing, and consultation with the spirits. Although the swidden fields are not legally owned by anyone, the last village to use a field is considered to have rights over it. A person using a field over which he does not have rights must pay a fine. The fine set by tradition is now so small, in the face of inflation, that some prefer to pay it rather than forego using the field. Among village members the swidden plots are assigned by group decision of the headman and elders. • Because of the rotation system, the Khmu do not move their villages widely. They may move a short distance because of some calamity, anger of the spirits, or personal grudge, but they do not range like the Meo. The Khmu say that the Meo move because of their different system of cultivating swiddens, by which they normally do not return to the same fields. • The principal implements used in swidden agriculture are the machete for clearing the fields prior to burning, the iron-pointed digging stick, the hoe, and the knife used in harvesting (which may also be done without any instrument). Baskets are used to transport the grain. Winnowing utilizes large fans of woven bamboo strips. These tools do not differ from those of the Lao. • Permanent wet-rice cultivation techniques, where they are used, are borrowed from the Lao. Many Khmu work for Lao farmers from time to time as hired laborers, and can easily learn the necessary techniques. The barriers to a wider spread of permanent field cultivation include cost (many Khmu do not have the buffalo needed), initial labor (it is less work to make a swidden than to make a permanent field), yield (a swidden will initially produce more, acre for acre), taste, and tradition. Fertilizer is not used in wet-rice fields except for the chance fertilization of grazing animals. The water used is rain water or water from mountain streams, lacking the heavy sediment of topsoil which would enrich the fields. If it were not for the amount of territory needed to support a population by swidden agriculture, the Khmu would probably be right in feeling that they are better off with swiddens. **Fishing and hunting.** The Khmu fish by netting, by trapping, by damming water and poisoning it, or by catching fish with the hands. They hunt with crossbows or, for the prosperous, with flintlock guns. For trapping, they use deadfalls, nooses, spear traps, and a host of ingenious devices identical with or similar to those reported in Izikowitz (1951: 183-94). Fishing and hunting exploit nearly the whole of the available fauna, large and small (a notable exception being a person's totem animal, which is taboo). In the Luang Prabang area large game is scarce, which is one of the many reasons for the impoverished state of the Khmu there. **Gathering.** The number of foods gathered in the jungle is bewildering. Scores of leaves, roots, shoots, etc. are eaten, including bamboo shoots, honey, and mushrooms. **Domestic animals.** The most common domesticated animals are chickens, ducks, pigs, and dogs. Buffalo are the most valued, but few Khmu can afford them. Goats are sometimes found, as are cats. Chickens, pigs, dogs, and especially buffalo are important for sacrifices. **Industrial arts.** The Khmu show great skill in weaving baskets, trays, and

stools of thin strips of bamboo and rattan. Another skill, less characteristic of the Luang Prabang area than of the north, is making net bags. The Luang Prabang Khmu do very little blacksmithing, except to repair tools. Silk or cotton weaving is not characteristic of the Khmu, but a few of the more acculturated women have learned to weave. **Trade.** Halpern (1957: 4-9; 1958: 69-74) reports the institution of the *lam*, usually a Lao who serves as an intermediary between the Khmu and the outside world of traders and government. Halpern's contention that the Khmu will desert a dishonest *lam* is questionable, however. The Khmu have traditionally feared to cross the Lao. They still complain that when they come into market with produce the Lao through whose villages they pass will sometimes take what they want with little or no payment. To the Khmu, who have no effective redress, the *lam* would be a powerful figure, and few would dare to cross a powerful Lao, nor could they do it with impunity. In the Luang Prabang area today the principal Khmu trading takes place through barter in the village, primarily with traveling traders who are usually Ho (Chinese); by taking goods to Luang Prabang; and by trading with neighboring villagers. Items bartered or sold in the Luang Prabang market include firewood, charcoal, banana leaves, bamboo shoots, rattan, honey, beeswax, tubers, roots, edible greens, materials for medicine, sugar cane, bananas, betel leaf, scallions, chilies, cucumbers, corn, baskets, stools, mats, trays, and brooms. • Although the Khmu in the Luang Prabang area do not usually have a rice surplus, those from farther away may be more fortunate. They carry the rice over the mountains to the nearest river, where they build a bamboo raft some 20′ x 8′ by tying bundles of bamboo together and covering them with a platform of woven bamboo and mats. Covered with a bamboo-leaf or mat awning, the rice is transported downstream on this raft and sold in Luang Prabang. Forest produce and manufactured items are sometimes brought down as well. When all is sold, and when the Khmu have bought what they want to take back with them, they walk home, a walk of from eight days to two or three weeks. Outlying Khmu also trade lac, benzoin, oranges, and even occasionally opium, none of which are common immediately around Luang Prabang. • A traditional source of Khmu income is wage labor for Lao, Chinese, Meo, and more recently French and Americans. The Lao have considered the Khmu subject to corvée labor, but have also hired them regularly to do agricultural work and other coolie labor. When agricultural duties back home are not pressing, the Khmu come from some distances to the Lao villages and into Luang Prabang to work in gardens, to carry water, and to work on roads. The small amount of cash which the Khmu raise and the goods which they barter are used to obtain salt, clothing, cloth, tools, utensils, blankets, and (very rarely) prestige luxury goods. They may also purchase animals for sacrifice. **Division of labor.** A rigid division is not always maintained, but the following lists are approximate:

Men	Women	Both
clearing forest	planting seed	weeding
hunting	splitting firewood	harvesting
trapping	fetching water	carrying
basket making	gathering	cooking (men
iron work	milling rice	are consid-
gathering firewood	washing clothes	ered better)
making charcoal	feeding animals	fishing
trade involving	cleaning house	shaman
men's produce	trade involving	
and long travel	women's produce	
distant travel	making alcohol	
headman	ginning cotton	
	(rare)	
	weaving (rare)	

"Carrying" is listed as an occupation of both men and women, but there is a difference in the mode of carrying. Women normally carry heavy loads in baskets on the back, supported by a strap going around the forehead. The weight therefore hangs down on the head and neck. There may be additional supports around the shoulders. Men do not like to be seen by outsiders carrying in this fashion. They carry in the Lao manner, with baskets suspended from the two ends of a pole over the shoulder, or hanging in a bag from the shoulder.

KIN GROUPS. **Descent.** Patrilineal. **Kin groups.** Exogamic patrilineages are totemic (cf. Izikowitz 1951: 85ff.). Penalty for touching the totem animal or plant is that the offender will automatically be burned by the touch. Penalty for killing or eating the animal is to have the teeth fall out and to die young. Each totem has a different origin myth, often based around some kind of incident in which the ancestor of the lineage was killed under circumstances associated with the totem. Lineage names in the Luang Prabang area include three different tiger lineages, four bird totems, one plant totem, and two other animal totems. Patrilineage and cross-cousin marriage are not so rigidly structured as to produce universal patrilocal residence or rigid inheritance of property within the lineage. The property of a mother goes to her children. There appears to be a tendency among fellow lineage members to congregate in the same village; on the other hand more than one lineage is often found in a single village. **Kin terminology.** The significant terminology for consanguines in Ego's generation and in that of his parents is given below (terms of reference, male speaking).

Si, FaSiDa, MoSiDa,	
Wi of any *siaʔ*, WiFaSiDa,	
WiMoSiDa	*kûn* (or *môôk*)
SiHu, Hu of any *kûn*, FaSiSo	*siaʔ* (or *prhaa*)
ElBr, WiElSi	*taay*
ElBrWi, WiElSi, MoBrElDa	*pâây*

YoBr, WiYoSi, MoBrYoDa	*hêêm*
YoBrWi, WiYoSi	*maʔ hêêm*
WiBr, MoBrSo	*ʔeem*
MoBrSoWi, MoBrWi	*maʔ ʔeem*
FaSi	*maʔ kûn*
FaSiHu	*yong kuuny*
FaElBr, MoElSiHu	*yong deeng*
FaElBrWi, MoElSi	*maʔ deeng*
FaYoBr, MoYoSiHu	*yong ʔaaw*
FaYoBrWi, MoYoSi	*maʔ ʔaaw*
MoBr	*yong ʔeem*
MoBrWi	*maʔ ʔeem*

MARRIAGE AND FAMILY. **Mode.** Marriage is arranged through the paying of a bride price, feasts, and the drinking of alcohol. It generally involves a period of service by the husband, and the husband's family also provides gifts for the marriage feast, such as alcohol, money, and one or more pigs and chickens. Some people are too poor for this outlay, in which case a man and woman may simply start living together, but a preferable solution is for the groom to move into the bride's father's house more or less permanently, making his labor available to the father-in-law. If the family eventually acquires the needed bride price, the couple may then move out. There are no formal age-grades. A girl from 14 on up may be married; boys are usually a little older. There are no puberty initiations or formal symbols of adulthood. **Form.** Monogamy is the predominant form of marriage. Polygyny, which would probably be more common if the Khmu were not so poor, is sometimes sororal. The first wife calls each of the others "younger sister," while they call her "older sister." **Extension of incest taboos.** Preferred marriage for a man is with his mother's brother's daughter, for a woman her father's sister's son, or in either case any more distant relative going by the same kinship term. Marriage within the father's patrilineage is forbidden, as is marriage with anyone who has been ceremonially included within that patrilineage by participation in an animal sacrifice. In this ceremony, the person making the sacrifice distributes the meat as follows: people classified as *taay*, "older brother," get the forequarters; those classified as *hêêm*, "younger brother," get the hindquarters, *ʔeem*, "wife's brother," or "mother's brother's son," get the sides, and the headman gets the filet. **Residence.** Residence with the wife's family is usual for at least three or four years, at which time a new home may be set up, or the couple may move to live in the home of the husband's parents if it is not crowded. **Domestic unit.** The form of the domestic unit is not fixed beyond the nuclear family. Whether married children live for very long with their parents is largely a matter of convenience. Khmu houses are small, and it is rare for more than three nuclear families to be under one roof. **Inheritance.** If the wife dies while the husband is living in her family home, their belongings and children stay with her parents, and he returns to his parents' home. If she dies after a new home has been set up, the children are more likely to be brought to his parents' home. **Divorce.** Divorce is easy, except for an adultery case, which is decided by the elders. In such a case the wife must repay twice the bride price; the husband pays a fine.

SOCIOPOLITICAL ORGANIZATION. There are no indigenous social or political groupings beyond the village level. Whereas the Khmu are closely tied to their neighbors economically, politically they have no interest outside the village and want to be left alone. Khmu villages are incorporated into the Lao system of civil control, just as are Lao villages. Khmu are headmen of Khmu villages, and report to their superiors, the *tasseng*, along with Lao headmen. The Khmu have no larger political role, except as they are drafted into the army, pay taxes, or vote. In this, however, they are not much different from village Lao. Within the village the headman is chosen by the Lao government. He is usually a prosperous and able Khmu. In the Luang Prabang area at least, he has considerable prestige and authority. The elders sit in informal judgment, and make important group decisions. Even women, however, will speak their piece, and the discussion is general.

RELIGION. Khmu villages are not usually Buddhist, although there are exceptions to this. The Khmu who do become Buddhist usually assimilate to Lao life in other ways as well. Scattered over northern Laos are roughly two thousand Khmu who are evangelical Christians, usually clustered in "Christian villages," but also found in communities of traditional religion (see Smalley 1960: 63ff.). **Supernaturals.** Traditional Khmu religion centers around spirits called *hrooy* (the *phi* of the Lao). Of particular importance are the *hrooy gaang* (house spirit) and *hrooy hôô* (apparently one of the most powerful of the jungle spirits). The *hrooy pôôp* and *hrooy sûû* are particularly feared because they possess people and make them dangerous. The latter flies around in the evening with flames coming from its mouth. The *hrooy pôôp* are constantly being detected, and the people in whom they reside are ostracized from the village. They are greatly feared as the cause of calamity. There are in addition spirits of the village, jungle, mountain, rock, water, sun, and one particularly identified with shamans. [Cf. Roux and Tran 1954: 309ff.] **Practitioners.** The only religious practitioners are priest-shamans, who may be either men or women. They determine which spirit is causing the illness or calamity, and prescribe the necessary sacrifice. Since sickness is a focal point of religious concern, a large part of their function is in curing. In addition they officiate in ceremonies designed to predispose the spirits to give good crops, etc. Ceremonies in honor of the spirits are performed when the house posts are set, at certain points in the rice-growing cycle, and in times of calamity. The Lao recognize the Khmu as magico-religious practitioners par excellence. **Ceremonies.** At important ceremonies, the entrance to or exit from the village becomes taboo for varying periods of time. A special sign made of strips of bamboo indicates that the village is sealed off (see the design in Roux and Tran 1954: 335). The sign also prevents evil spirits from intruding. Should a stranger ignore the sign and come into the village, trouble, sickness, or death will ensue, and indemnity must be paid by the transgressor. The same symbol has much the same meaning to other groups in the area (Izikowitz 1951: 54, 155, 220, 250, 255). **Birth.** Birth takes place in the home, with midwives and members of the family helping. The infant is carried constantly by the mother, and fed whenever it cries. The mother carries the infant or small child in a shawl at her side or on her back, or slung in front, if she is feeding it. The child sleeps in this shawl on the mother's back while she works in the field, gathers in the jungle, or pounds or winnows rice. **Soul, death, and afterlife.** Unlike the Buddhist Lao, the Khmu bury their dead in the jungle. The Khmu fear that the soul of the deceased may return to the village, and the burial party makes elaborate precautions for a roundabout return in order to confuse the ghost. A chicken is split open and the blood used to make protective marks on the knees of all those in the burial party.

BIBLIOGRAPHY. Greenberg 1953; Halpern 1957, 1958, 1960, 1961b, 1961e; Haudricourt 1953, 1962; Izikowitz 1951; LeBar and Suddard 1960; Roux and Tran 1954; Seidenfaden 1958; Smalley 1960, 1961; Young 1961.

KHUA

ORIENTATION. **Location.** The Khua occupy mountain sides in Quang Binh province of northern Vietnam. [Cuisinier 1948: 39-45.] **Linguistic affiliation and demography.** A North Vietnamese source (NNCDT 1959: 246) reports that the Khua are a Mon-Khmer-speaking group numbering 892.

BIBLIOGRAPHY. Cuisinier 1948; NNCDT 1959.

LAMET

Synonyms. *Kha Lamet, Le-Met*

ORIENTATION. **Identification and location.** The Lamet, known to the Lao as Kha Lamet, or sometimes Le-Met, are a relatively small population of hill-dwelling Mon-Khmer speakers located along the Haut Mekong—Luang Prabang boundary in extreme northwestern Laos. This is an area of some 2,000 square kilometers, watered by the Nam Ngao and the Nam Tha, together with their tributaries. There are slight cultural and linguistic differences between the Upper Lamet, in the northeastern part of the area, and the Lower Lamet, in the southwest. [Izikowitz 1951: 20-21, 34-37.] **Geography.** The hills inhabited by the Lamet are covered with thick tropical vegetation, and travel is difficult. The climate is typical monsoon, with well-defined rainy and dry seasons. Fauna include wild pigs, deer, gaur, monkeys, bears, pheasant, and other fowl. [Izikowitz 1951: 34-37.] **Linguistic affiliation.** Mon-Khmer, related to Palaung and Wa. Lamet contains many Tai loan words, and most adult males speak Tai Yuan as a second language. [Izikowitz 1951: 20, 23.] **Demography.** Approximately 5,800, in 103 villages (Izikowitz 1951: 38). **History and cultural relations.** The Lamet area contains villages of Khmu, Lü, Yuan, and Lao; the Lamet are in contact with all these groups, and have borrowed various cultural traits from them. The Upper Lamet, in particular, are in touch with their close cultural relatives, the Khmu, and their young men are frequent visitors to Thailand, where they work for wages in the teak forests. The Lamet say that they and the Khmu are the original inhabitants of the country. [Izikowitz 1951: 19-33.]

SETTLEMENT PATTERN AND HOUSING. **Settlement pattern.** Villages are located on mountain crests, between 1,500 and 4,500 feet. Water is obtained from mountain streams, which characteristically flow at some distance below the village. Village populations range from 10 to 150, with an average of 56. The average number of houses per village is 14. Villages are connected by pathways, and average about two hours walking distance apart. Those of the Lower Lamet are circular in plan, with a street running through the center. The houses are clustered around an open space which contains the communal mens' house. Upper Lamet villages are irregular in shape, with the communal house in an open square and with storage barns and granaries at either end of the village. [Izikowitz 1951: 39-80.] The relatively small size of villages and the abundance of available land make it possible for a group to remain in the same area for a considerable time. When villages are moved, it is usually because of an epidemic or the displeasure of angered spirits. New villages sometimes split off from old ones as a result of quarrels among families. [Izikowitz 1951: 81-84.] **Housing.** Houses are rectangular, with sloping roofs. With the exception of communal houses, they are built on piles. The framework is of wood, the walls and roofs of palm leaf thatch. Houses are not divided into rooms. Those of the Lower Lamet contain a row of sleeping berths, each with its own hearth. Temporary houses are built in the swiddens during the growing season. [Izikowitz 1951: 149-60.]

ECONOMY. The Lamet are almost totally dependent for food on agriculture, supplemented by the gathering of wild roots, shoots, and buds. Fishing and hunting are of secondary importance. Occasionally the Lamet work for wages. They engage in some trade with lowlanders, and buy many of their manufactured necessities from the Lao and Siamese. **Agriculture.** Slash-and-burn type, making no use of animals or of the plow. A swidden is used for only one year and then fallowed for from 12 to 15 years. The swidden group consists of a number of families who cooperate in clearing and cultivating a given area of land. The families in a swidden group should belong to the same clan and be of a comparable age range. An effort is made to maintain this group over the years (Izikowitz 1951: 210-11). Rice, mainly glutinous, is the staple crop. Other grains include eleusine, millet, and Job's-tears. Root crops include taro, manioc, yams, and sweet potatoes. Vegetables, raised mainly in gardens within the villages, include onions, spinach, cucumbers, gourds, beans, and a fragrant grass, citronella. The Lamet also raise red peppers, peanuts, melons, mint, ginger, and tobacco. Tea is semicultivated. Fruits include mangoes, tamarinds, lemons, tangerines, bananas, pomelo, and guava. A few areca palms are grown, but most betel is purchased. [Izikowitz 1951: 206-59.] **Domestic animals.** Include buffalo, zebu, pigs, chickens, and dogs. All are eaten, although only children eat dogs. Buffalo are of most value, and are used chiefly for sacrifices. Bees are kept for their honey and for beeswax, an important item of trade. [Izikowitz 1951: 200-05.] **Food and stimulants.** Rice with dried roasted meat constitutes the everyday food. A soup of vegetables and dried meat, spiced with red peppers, is a favorite. Peppers are an important ingredient in all cooking. Rice, millet, and maize are used for making wine and brandy. Fermented tea leaves are chewed, as is betel, the latter mostly imported. [Izikowitz 1951: 299-302.] **Industrial arts.** The Lamet do no weaving, pottery making, or iron work. They do make hunting traps, and are skilled in the making of baskets and wooden implements and weapons. They also grind and repair metal tools. [Izikowitz 1951: 143-49.] **Trade.** Items of trade include rice, beeswax, wine, brandy, fermented tea balls, powdered deer horn, and dried bears' bladders (the last two used in Chinese pharmacy). These items are traded to the lowland Lao and Siamese for tools, clothing, and pottery. The Lamet obtain their bronze drums from the Karens of northern Thailand. [Izikowitz 1951: 308-14.] **Division of labor.** Women carry rice from the fields, gather wild plants and produce, care for children, and do most of the cooking. Men make all tools and weapons and most of the utensils, hunt and fish, construct houses, and cook meat and certain dishes which include red peppers. Men and women cooperate in clearing, sowing, weeding, and harvesting, with men doing the heavier work. [Izikowitz 1951: 261-68.] **Land tenure.** Individual and family ownership and inheritance of land is unknown. Land is owned by the village, and the territory of the village is open to all its members. Portions of land to be cultivated by a particular family are agreed upon by that family together with other families in the swidden group to which they belong. [Izikowitz 1951: 294-99.]

KIN GROUPS. **Descent.** Patrilineal. **Kin groups.** Exogamous, totemic patriclans [Murdock's patrisibs]. At least two clans should be represented in a village and there is some tendency toward local endogamy. The Lamet say that their clans are found also among the Khmu. [Izikowitz 1951: 90-93.] **Kin terminology.** Izikowitz (1951: 90-93) gives the following terms:

Fa, FaBr	*un*
Mo, MoSi	*ne*
FaSi	*ma*
MoBr	*ta*
FaSiDa, MoBrSo	*ko*
MoBrDa, FaSiSo	*haem*
ElBr, MoSiSo (older than speaker)	*ek*
YoBr, MoSiSo/Da (younger than speaker)	*yu*
ElSi, MoSiDa (older than speaker)	*al*

MARRIAGE AND FAMILY. **Mode.** Premarital sexual experimentation is allowed. Unmarried men past puberty sleep in the communal mens' house; adolescent girls sleep at home, but apart from their parents, which enables them to receive boys at night. There is a substantial bride price (usually partly paid in bride service), with a reciprocal dowry. The former is paid in buffalo, gongs, and (rarely, but most prized of all) bronze drums. The dowry consists of cloth, jewelry, and pottery. Among the Upper Lamet, bride service is limited to three years. [Izikowitz 1951: 98-103.] **Form.** Polygyny is practiced, but is confined to the upper class of wealthy men, *lem.* Sororal polygyny is preferred. The first wife is the chief wife. [Izikowitz 1951: 98-103.] **Extension of incest taboos.** The clan [sib] is exogamous. Marriage with a MoBrDa is allowed, but is forbidden between parallel cousins and with a FaSiDa. [Izikowitz 1951: 93-94.] **Residence.** Matrilocal during the period of bride service, if this is present. Otherwise initially, and for some time thereafter, patrilocal. When a son's family begins to get large, he will ordinarily leave his parental home and establish his own household. [Izikowitz 1951: 98-103.] **Domestic unit.** The patrilocal extended family is the ideal, but the nuclear family household is most common. Polygynous family units are also found. [Izikowitz 1951: 108-09.] **Inheritance.** Land is not inherited. Movable property, principally valuables, is inherited by sons. Exact division is arbitrary according to the will of the father. [Izikowitz 1951: 294-99.] **Divorce.** Divorce occurs with some frequency. Girls go with the mother, boys with the father. [Izikowitz 1951: 93.]

SOCIOPOLITICAL ORGANIZATION. **Political organization.** There is no form of indigenous political organization above the village level. The office of village priest-chief, *xemia,* is usually inherited, but is subject to the approval of the married men of the village. The *xemia* is responsible for carrying out all sacrifices to the village spirits, as well as for supervising the communal house and maintaining order. His jurisdiction does not, however, extend beyond the village to the swidden areas. *Xemia* were generally confirmed in office by the French colonial administration, thereafter acting as tax collectors in addition to their other duties. Although the *xemia* have well-defined duties and responsibilities, power within Lamet villages is largely decentralized, and remains with the heads of house groups and the wealthy men. **Social stratification.** Wealth, reckoned in buffalo, gongs, and bronze drums, is sought by most adult males. Those who acquire it are admitted to a class of wealthy men, termed *lem,* at a feast which marks the occasion. Membership is not hereditary, but because of the high bride price, it is difficult for a poor man to marry the daughter of a *lem* member. The *lem* are of particular importance among the Upper Lamet. Age-grades, secret societies, and slavery are all lacking in Lamet society. [Izikowitz 1951: 112-17.]

RELIGION. Animistic beliefs and practices, together with the cult of the ancestors form the basis of Lamet religion. [Izikowitz 1951: 322ff.] **Supernaturals.** Each house has guardian spirits to whom sacrifices are made. There are village guardian spirits as well as spirits, *mbrong* (sometimes *phi*), of the forest and of crops. The rice soul or spirit is of particular importance. **Practitioners.** In addition to the village priest-chiefs, *xemia,* there are medicine men in most villages. **Ceremonies.** All major economic and social activities are accompanied by sacrifice. Burials and marriages are marked by elaborate feasting and sacrificing to the ancestral spirits. Buffalo, pigs, chickens, and (sometimes) dogs are sacrificed. [Izikowitz 1941: 14-24; 1951: 322-42.] **Illness and medicine.** Illness is brought on by displeased or malevolent spirits. Cure is effected by a medicine man, who first divines the cause and then treats the illness with spells and incantations. **Soul, death, and afterlife.** A person is thought to have two souls, one in the head and one in the knees. Disposal of the dead is by burial in a wooden coffin. The grave site is marked by a stone monument and surrounded by a wooden fence. [Izikowitz 1941: 11-14.]

BIBLIOGRAPHY. Izikowitz 1941, 1951.

LAWA

Synonyms. *Lava, Lavu'a, La-woe-a, Lua, L'ua, Luwa, L'wa*

ORIENTATION. **Identification.** Young (1961) identifies the Lawa (Luwa, L'ua) of northern Thailand with the ancient L'wa mentioned in Siamese chronicles, and feels that they are definitely related to the Wa of Burma. According to Hutchinson (1934: 180), the Lawa call themselves Lavu'a (La-woe-a), whereas they are called Lua by the Tai-speaking Yuan of northern Thailand. Hutchinson adds that Lawa is a Siamese term. Seidenfaden, in an appendix to Hutchinson (1934), points out that the north Thailand Lawa should not be confused with the Chaobon of Khorat province, who are also termed Lawa in Siamese government sources. **Location.** Presently found in Maehongsorn and Chiengmai provinces in northern Thailand, the main concentration being in the Bo Luang plateau area southwest of Chiengmai town. Seidenfaden's map of contemporary and historical Lawa village sites covers an area extending roughly from 98° to 100° E., and from 18° to 20° N. (Hutchinson 1934: facing p. 182). **Geography.** Bo Luang is a flat plateau district some 3,000 feet in altitude, with wide, flat valley passes and relatively little relief (Credner 1935a: 160). **Linguistic affiliation.** Usually included with Palaung and Wa in a Palaung-Wa language group, either subsumed under Mon-Khmer or classed, with Mon-Khmer, as separate but related groups within the Austroasiatic [Austroasian] linguistic stock (cf. Pinnow 1959; Greenberg 1953). Young (1961: 65-68), basing his remarks on firsthand experience with both Wa and Lawa, sees a definite relationship between the two, but feels there can be only a very remote Mon-Khmer influence. The Bo Luang dialect of Lawa is reported to be closer to the "wild" Wa Vu dialect than to that of Kengtung Wa (Embree and Thomas 1950: 81). Most Lawa can also speak some Yuan Tai (northern Siamese), and a few know some Sgaw Karen. **Demography.** Forty-three known villages, totaling 9,000 persons (Young 1961: 68). **History and cultural relations.** When the Mons expanded into northern Siam during the eighth century A.D. they encountered the L'wa, whom they considered savage cousins, i.e. less civilized speakers of a related language. According to tradition, the L'wa were ruled by a powerful chieftain with his capital in the area of present-day Chiengmai. Although they resisted the Mon conquest, the L'wa were gradually reduced in numbers and withdrew to the hills. The present-day Lawa are considered the remnants of the once numerous and powerful L'wa of history. [Seidenfaden's appendix to Hutchinson 1934: 180-82; Young 1961: 67.] On the basis of linguistic and cultural similarities, Young (1961: 65-66) classes the Lawa with the Khmu and T'in as a "Wa-related ethnic group" with origins to the south of their present habitat, and comments on the striking physical similarity of some Lawa types to contemporary Polynesians. ● The Lawa are in contact mainly with Tai-speaking wet-rice farmers, although the degree of acculturation varies widely. In the Bo Luang plateau area and on the plains many Lawa live very much as rural Siamese. Intermarriage in these areas is not uncommon. The residents of more remote Lawa settlements, such as Umpai, west of Bo Luang, reportedly do not speak Tai and have not adopted Buddhism. [Young 1961: 73-74.]

SETTLEMENT PATTERN AND HOUSING. **Settlement pattern.** In areas where they can grow wet rice, the Lawa construct comparatively large and permanent settlements. Their villages on the Bo Luang plateau are built on flat ridges, with paddy fields in the intervening shallow valleys. The largest of these, Bo Luang village, totals 230 houses. The average for all known Lawa villages, according to Young, is 30 houses per village and 7 persons per house, giving an average village population of about 210. In areas influenced by Tai-speaking lowlanders, houses are arranged in orderly rows, each house and its adjoining garden and fruit trees being enclosed within a fence or hedge. In the more remote areas, villages are smaller and less regular. In such areas the greater reliance on swidden agriculture requires that villages be moved every 10 to 15 years. [Young 1961: 68; Hutchinson 1934: 154-56.] **Housing.** Houses are constructed on piles. Acculturated Lawa build walls and floors of sawn boards if possible, and the roof may be of tile. Poorer and less acculturated Lawa use bamboo slats and thatch grass for the roof. The gable-end roof has a characteristically steep pitch, coming down on either side to within a few feet of the ground. There is a veranda, and usually only one room, although separate cubicles may be provided for married sons who live with their parents. Cattle are tethered underneath the house, and there are separate granaries. [Young 1961: 68; Hutchinson 1934: 154-56.]

ECONOMY. For centuries, the Lawa have inhabited the Bo Luang plateau area, where the flat valley passes facilitated the construction of irrigated rice paddies. Buffalo for plow agriculture were purchased with income gained through smelting and forging the iron ore obtained in small mining pits. In this manner the plateau Lawa maintained a balanced economy. [Credner 1935a: 160.] Today mining has declined in importance and the Lawa either work pig iron bought on the market or else buy finished iron implements from lowlanders (Young 1961: 72-73). **Agriculture.** Rice is the main crop, grown chiefly in irrigated paddies, using a buffalo and plow. In the more remote areas, or where land is unsuited to wet-rice culture, rice and chilies are grown in forest clearings. Kitchen gardens produce vegetables, tobacco, and

Indian corn. Opium poppies are raised, but production is limited by poor soil. [Young 1961: 72-73; Hutchinson 1934: 162-64.] **Gathering.** The Lawa swidden farmers in more remote areas also depend to some extent on jungle produce. **Domestic animals.** There are no oxen, but large numbers of buffalo are raised for plowing. Pigs are present but are not plentiful except in acculturated villages. The Lawa formerly kept elephants. **Food and stimulants.** Mainly vegetarians, with nonglutinous rice the staple. Fish is a luxury obtainable only by purchase. Meat of wild or domestic animals is consumed occasionally. Betel chewing is popular among both acculturated and unacculturated Lawa. [Young 1961: 72-73; Hutchinson 1934: 162-64.] **Industrial arts.** The Bo Luang Lawa have traditional rights to open pit mines a day's journey to the northwest. Formerly the entire population migrated to the iron mines during the dry months following the harvest. The ore was transported in baskets to Bo Luang, where it was smelted and forged by Lawa smiths. Both mining and iron-smithing have lost their former importance, since the Lawa can now buy cheap iron implements from the Siamese. [Hutchinson 1934: 164-65; Young 1961: 72-73.]

MARRIAGE AND FAMILY. **Mode.** Hutchinson (1934: 160-61) reports premarital intimacy stopping short of actual intercourse. A boy and girl signify their betrothal by "getting caught" sleeping together in her parents' house. This is followed by payment by the boy's parents of a few rupees for purchase of sacrificial pigs or chickens. **Form.** Monogamy is the invariable rule (Hutchinson 1934: 161). **Extension of incest taboos.** Cousin marriage is forbidden (Hutchinson 1934: 161). **Residence.** A man brings his wife to occupy a cubicle in his parents' house until his younger brother is ready to marry; he then builds his own house (Hutchinson 1934: 161). **Domestic unit.** The residence rules, plus Young's average of seven persons per house (Young 1961: 68), indicate a patrilocal stem family. **Inheritance.** Daughters inherit only if there are no sons (Hutchinson 1934: 161). **Divorce.** May be initiated by the husband or wife. In either case the initiator must pay a monetary fine to his or her spouse. The transaction is supervised by the village headman. [Hutchinson 1934: 161.]

SOCIOPOLITICAL ORGANIZATION. **Political organization.** Among acculturated Lawa the village headman is appointed by a local Siamese official. The Lawa in more remote areas continue to select their own chiefs, usually according to the general will of the people within a given village. In such areas criminals may be dealt with rather drastically; ostracism from the village is a common punishment. [Young 1961: 74.]

RELIGION. **Major religions.** Acculturated Lawa, including those on the Bo Luang plateau, profess Buddhism, but, according to Young (1961: 68), the Lawa are best characterized as animistic Buddhists. There are a few hundred Christian Lawa. **Indigenous religion.** There are house spirits, field or local spirits, and spirits of the iron mines. Many Lawa deities are regarded as disembodied spirits of ancient heroes. A spirit grove adjacent to Bo Luang village contains roughly-made wooden sheds and altars, the site of periodic animal sacrifices. [Hutchinson 1934: 158-60.] **Soul, death, and afterlife.** Cremation, attended by Buddhist priests, is reported by Hutchinson (1934: 160), who says that interment is reserved for victims of violent death or epidemic disease.

BIBLIOGRAPHY. Credner 1935a; Embree and Thomas 1950; Greenberg 1953; Hutchinson 1934; Pinnow 1959; Young 1961.

MAY

ORIENTATION. **Location.** The May occupy mountainsides in Quang Binh province of northern Vietnam. [Cuisinier 1948: 39-45.] **Linguistic affiliation and demography.** NNCDT (1959: 245) reports that the May are Mon-Khmer-speaking people and that they number 904.

SETTLEMENT PATTERN AND HOUSING. Cuisinier (1948: 45) reports that some May are becoming more sedentary, and cites one May settlement that has been located in one place for ten years.

BIBLIOGRAPHY. Cuisinier 1948; NNCDT 1959.

PALAUNGS

Synonyms. *Da-ang, Humai, Kunloi, La-eng, Palong, Ra-ang, Rumai, Ta-ang*

ORIENTATION. **Identification.** The Palaungs call themselves Ta-ang, with several variant forms reported (Da-ang, La-eng, Ra-ang), apparently dialectic. The name Palaung is Burmese but its history remains obscure despite several legendary etymologies. The Shans know them as Palong, apparently from the Burmese form. Kunloi (Kôn-loi), another Shan appellation, merely means "mountaineer." The name Rumai (or Humai), occasionally applied to all Palaungs, is more properly confined to a subgroup. [Cameron 1912: viii; Cushing 1914: 390; Lowis 1906: 2; Milne 1931a: 227; Scott 1921: 134; Scott and Hardiman 1900: 483.] **Location.** Most Palaungs are found in the northwestern corner of the Shan State, in an area comprising the old state of Tawngpeng (Burmese, Taungbaing), with an almost wholly Palaung population and a Palaung prince, and the adjacent states of Hsipaw, North and South Hsenwi, and Möngmit (Burmese, Momeik). Tawngpeng State is at approximately 97° E. and 23° N. Palaungs are also reported as far south in the Shan State as Kengtung, in the southern portion of the Kachin State, and in the southwestern Yunnan province of China. [Milne 1924: 17, 23; Lowis 1906: 1.] **Geography.** The Palaung homeland is a region of ridges up to 6,000 feet above sea level, separated by narrow valleys. There is some open grassland, but most uncultivated land is under forest, with temperate chestnut, oak, and pine at higher elevations. Climate is the monsoon regime common to continental Southeast Asia, with rainy summers and dry winters. [Scott 1921: 269-70; Milne 1924: 8-10.] **Linguistic affiliation.** The relationship of Palaung with a number of other languages of southern Asia has been recognized for many decades. In a recent review of these languages, Pinnow (1959: 1-4) has set up two, or possibly three, supergroups, western and eastern, of an Austroasiatic [Austroasian] family. Palaung is placed in the western subgroup of the northeastern group of the eastern supergroup, this northeastern group being the Palaung-Wa of other writers. Alternatively Pinnow would establish a central supergroup containing a northern group, Khasi, and a southwestern group, Nicobar, in addition to the northeastern or Palaung-Wa group. The linguistic relationships between Palaung and Wa have not been thoroughly examined, but they are apparently not close; the two peoples even when they are in contact deny awareness of any connection (Scott and Hardiman 1900: 493). **Demography.** In 1931 the Palaungs were said to total almost 139,000 (India 1931-34: *11*, Pt. I, 199). **History and cultural relations.** It seems reasonable to assume that Palaung occupation of their present central area preceded Shan and Kachin settlement in the same area. During the nineteenth century the Palaungs, or more strictly, their only political entity, Tawngpeng, were marginal to neighboring Shan principalities and to the Burmese state. Despite former tributary relations with the Burmese court, trade with the Burmese, and evidence of some Burmese loan words, the greatest cultural influence upon the Palaungs appears to have been that of the Shans. The Shan language is the written language of the Palaungs; their few chronicles, largely legendary in character, are written in Shan. Most adult males can speak some Shan and it is a lingua franca not only among Palaung groups with marked dialect differences but also between Palaungs and Shans, Kachins, and smaller groups such as Lisu. [Cameron 1912: vii; Lowis 1906: 7; Milne 1924: 2, 18.]

SETTLEMENT PATTERN AND HOUSING. **Settlement pattern.** Compact villages are located on hilltops, spurs, or ridges between hills. In Möngmit they range in size from two to fifty houses with a mean

of about ten. A main road runs through the village with houses on either side, and more down the slopes. The center contains the monastery, a house for Buddha images, rest house, and market. Settlements were formerly stockaded and closed at night, and some still have gateways on which are written incantations or sentences from Buddhist scriptures—intended to ward off disease. [Cameron 1912: ix; Milne 1924: 201.] Auxiliary structures include granaries, spirit shrines, and, in the tea gardens, houses used during the picking season when virtually the entire village is engaged for days in plucking and processing the leaves. [Cameron 1912: xi; Milne 1924: 229.] **Housing.** From three to six families per house are reported for northern Möngmit just south of the China border, but in the central Palaung area in Tawngpeng one, or at most two, families per house are the norm. Houses are raised on wooden posts, three to twelve feet high, according to the slope of the ground. Frames, floors, external walls, and internal partitions are largely of bamboo; plank walls are found in houses of the well-to-do. The roofs, which extend to within a few feet of the floor, are of grass thatch. Rice is pounded and stock confined within the area beneath the house, which is fenced. Verandas at either end are used, in single-family houses, for entrance and for kitchen tasks; in two-family houses in the central Palaung area, each veranda opens into a separate entrance room. Smaller rooms are used for sleeping and storage; entrance rooms and sleeping rooms are equipped with fireplaces, but are otherwise largely bare of furnishings. Houses vary in length from about 30 to as much as 80 feet. Those of officials or men of authority have distinctive markings in the form of pieces of variously shaped and colored wood on the gables. [Cameron 1912: ix, xi; Milne 1924: 178-80, 183, 187-88.]

ECONOMY. The mainstay of the economy is agriculture; even trade, which is extensive, is in the products of agriculture and stock raising. No data are available to estimate the number of Palaungs engaged in specialized, commercial agriculture, or the proportion of income derived from trade connected with this agricultural specialization. **Agriculture.** It appears likely that Palaungs in most areas practice subsistence agriculture with swidden rice the chief crop. Wet rice is also grown wherever suitable lowland is available. Swiddens are planted with rice, beans, peas, sesame, maize, tobacco, hemp, various cucurbits, yams, and chilies. Kitchen gardens yield pulses, cucurbits, chilies, mustard, onions, tomatoes, eggplant, and sugar cane. Cameron explicitly states that opium is not produced and that neither the betel leaf nor betel nut will grow in the area. Milne, however, mentions the use of betel. Cameron lists sweet limes, guava, papaya, peaches, plums, pineapples, and jackfruit, although Milne says little fruit is grown in Tawngpeng. These apparent contradictions may be related to agricultural specialization. [Cameron 1912: xxvi-xxvii; Milne 1924: 223; Scott 1932: 151.] Palaung agriculture in Tawngpeng, particularly in the vicinity of the chief town, Namhsan, an area whose way of life seems to be taken as the ideal type for the Palaungs, is to a very considerable extent dependent upon the production of tea for export outside the Palaung area. The growing of tea, its preparation, and its transport are all in the hands of Palaungs. Milne (1924: 224) may very well be correct in her assumption that tea culture is a recent innovation, basing her inference on the paucity of rites connected with it; in 1910 its cultivation was said to be just beginning among the Rumai Palaungs north of Tawngpeng (Cameron 1912: xxvi). Fairly rapid changes in the tea economy may account for the discrepancies in information about the scale of enterprise. Scott (writing in 1921, but probably with reference to the 1890s) reports that there were no large plantations worked by capitalists or by the united labor of villagers, but Milne, with respect to about 1910, mentions large and small entrepreneurs, the former employing a good deal of paid labor (Scott 1921: 269-70; Milne 1924: 230). Tea is exported in two forms: dried (the form familiar in the West) and pickled (a fermented form which in Burma at least is eaten with other things as a snack). The processing of both forms is done by the producers in the tea gardens. **Fishing and hunting.** Reported for the northern Palaungs, but apparently unimportant in the central area (Cameron 1912: xxvi, xxxiii, xlii). **Gathering.** Apparently unimportant except for fuel and some vegetables for stews. **Domestic animals.** The Palaungs keep no sheep, goats, or ducks. Cameron, in reference to a marginal area, speaks of pig keeping. Milne, writing of the central Palaungs, emphasizes that animals are not kept for food; cocks are kept for their crowing and fighting but pullets are often turned loose in the forest. Buffalo, cattle, and horses are raised as beasts of burden, the latter for sale to lowland Burma. [Cameron 1912: xxvi; Milne 1924: 36, 193; Scott 1932: 141, 153.] **Food and stimulants.** Diet is predominantly vegetarian, the main dish being steamed rice, accompanied by stews or curries, of cultivated and wild plants—leaves, ferns, and fungi. Despite the normally vegetarian character of the diet, and the fact that only the Rumai subgroup, north of the central area, are said to slaughter animals, the Palaungs do occasionally eat animal products. Milne reports, however, that women neither eat nor cook meat, that when it is prepared, men take care of it. Beef and pork may be obtained from Chinese butchers or from Kachins or Lisu when these latter have made sacrifices, and animals killed by predators may be eaten. In addition, Palaungs eat the flesh of horses, tigers, leopards, bear, and mice, but not that of sheep, goats, dogs, cats, rats, frogs, or snakes. Some fresh water fish and eels are caught for food, and various forms of preserved fish—salted, smoked,

and fermented—are obtained from the Burmese. Eggs are seldom eaten, and milk is not used. [Cameron 1912: xxvii-xxviii; Lowis 1906: 14; Milne 1924: 192-93.] According to Milne, Palaungs are inveterate users of betel, or sometimes of a wild substitute for it. Smoking of pipe tobacco by both sexes is also common, but relatively little opium is used. Tea is said to be a drink for adult men rather than women and children. Alcoholic beverages are known, but information on consumption is contradictory. Lowis says that alcohol is rarely taken; Cameron, that it is drunk at all festivals. [Cameron 1912: xxviii; Lowis 1906: 14; Milne 1924: 192.] **Industrial arts.** Palaungs make baskets, but they also buy them, presumably from Shans. The bags used in plucking tea are made from cloth supplied by Shans. Men's clothing is made from cloth imported into the Palaung area. Some women still weave cloth for their own clothing, but much of the white homespun cotton upon which Palaung women embroider distinctive patterns is woven by Shans. Although some villages have silversmiths, most Palaung jewelry is acquired from Shans. Blacksmiths can make repairs, but, according to Cameron (1912: xxvi), the casting of objects like plowshares calls for the employment of Chinese. Chinese also cut most of the timber. Masonry, carpentry, carving, and painting for such work as pagoda and monastery construction is done by Burmese from the lowlands. Practically no products of Palaung crafts enter trade; trading income is derived from other sources. [Cameron 1912: xxvi, xxviii; Lowis 1906: 12; Milne 1924: 196, 216, 222.] **Trade.** In the hands of the Palaungs themselves and of itinerant Shans, Chinese, Burmese, and Indians, trade is based upon tea, both dry and pickled, and livestock, especially horses. Trade is carried on at markets in Palaung villages, in towns such as Möngmit, Hsenwi, Hsipaw, and Namkham outside the Palaung area, and even as far away as Mandalay and Rangoon. The Palaungs take their tea and livestock to sell in Mandalay or in the neighboring towns, some of which are on the railway. Goods moving into the Palaung Hills are cloth, kerosene, lacquerware, religious objects, betel nut, salt, preserved fish, sugar, canned milk, and biscuits. Palaungs share the handling of this import trade with other groups, although there may be some specialization, such as the supplying of salt and preserved fish by the Shans and Kachins. Most of the trade tea, at least half a century ago, was in pickled form, and moved south to the Burmese and east and north to the Shans of Burma and China. [Cameron 1912: xxvi; Milne 1924: 202, 216, 222, 236.] **Division of labor.** Men plow, tend cattle, build and repair houses, pack and load tea, transplant tea, cook meat dishes, and presumably cut the swiddens. Women fetch water, clean the houses, cook, spin, weave, make clothing, prepare the nurseries for the tea plants, and plant the seed. Both men and women cut and gather firewood and grass for horses; both sexes cut and carry timber for houses. [Cameron 1912: xxvii; Milne 1924: 46, 177, 194, 196, 203-04, 227.]

KIN GROUPS. **Descent.** Uncertain. **Kin groups.** Milne and Cameron mention "clans," but it is doubtful that these are unilinear descent groups. Rather they are named groups comprising, apparently, most of the population of villages in a contiguous area, although on the one hand it is reported that villages of different clans occur side by side, and on the other that members of clans may be widely distributed among villages. The clans are said to differ in respect to dialect and a variety of practices such as marriage rules, courtship and wedding procedures, naming, women's dress, etc. Information on marriage among these groups is contradictory; according to Milne it is unusual, whereas Scott reports that all intermarry freely. Milne, in the title of her monograph, seems to apply the word "clan" to the whole Palaung people, unless she had in mind the group to which most of her material refers, the Samlong of central Tawngpeng. "Clan" is not an entry in her dictionary. [Cameron 1912: v and passim; Lowis 1906: 20 and map; Milne 1924: 18, 57 and passim; 1931a: ii; Scott 1932: 140.] **Kin terminology.** The following terms are reported by Milne (1931a: 349-52 and under appropriate kin terms). The Palaung equivalents of the forms with asterisks occur followed by a special set of terms meaning "first," "second," etc. to indicate relative seniority, with respect to Ego.

Fa, FaYoBr	*kun*	
Mo, *MoYoSi	*ma*	
*FaElBr, MoElSi	*an*	
*MoBr	*pa*	
FaElSi	*vi doh*	
*FaYoSi	*doh*	
*ElSb, PaSbElDa	*vai*	(With suffixes meaning "male" and "female" for siblings.[4])
*YoSb, PaSbYoDa	*va*	
PaSbSo	*vi*	(Also reported PaSbSo, *p're*, and PaSbDa, *hnan*, without reference to seniority.)

MARRIAGE AND FAMILY. Although boys and girls may talk to each other in the tea gardens during harvesting and in groups in the village lanes or at the monastery, courting properly takes place late at night in the entrance rooms of girls' family homes. One daughter at a time is visited by one or more boys, after her parents have gone to sleep. The hostess

---

[4] Child is *kwon* (followed by forms meaning "male" and "female," as for siblings), but when seniority is indicated, for "son" *kwon* is replaced by *vi*, and for "daughter" by *di*, both followed by the special set of terms for seniority mentioned above. For "elder sister" *vai* is replaced by *di*, followed by the same set.

and her callers engage in gossip and repartee in partly conventional form. Sex relations apparently are uncommon. If there should be a child, the rare man who refuses to marry the mother must pay a fine. If a girl will not reveal the father of her child then her father must pay a fine to the elders as an offering to the tiger-spirit haunting the neighborhood. Parents usually do learn the identity of their daughters' visitors and they may praise or criticize them, but more direct interference seems to be frowned upon. Courtship inside the house is characteristic of the central Palaung area and of some other subgroups, but in others the visitors must stand outside the house and carry on their wooing through holes in the floor of the girls' sleeping room. [Cameron 1912: xv-xvii; Milne 1924: 96-127, 191.] **Mode.** An engagement to marry is entered into by a couple without explicitly informing the parents or obtaining their permission. In the central Palaung area and among some subgroups, marriage is by conventional elopement. Among the others, elopement occurs only in cases of disapproval by the girl's parents. Male and female age-mates of the eloping couple accompany them at night to a house of an older male relative of the young man's father, followed by several days of bargaining between the families of the man and the girl, during which time the couple and their party remain in their hide-out. The negotiations are in the hands of two part-time specialists skilled in the necessary traditional rhetoric, involving many Shan and even Pali words. The girl's family expects a sum of money from the man's family the amount of which varies; this is not conceptualized as a bride price but as help toward the wedding meal provided by the bride's family. The wedding is essentially a blessing of the couple by the elders. When the girl is finally surrendered, her parents send with her a dowry of a number of household necessities. [Cameron 1912: xv, xvii; Milne 1924: 97, 104, 116-23, 127-74.] **Form.** Polygyny is permitted, but rare, although half a century ago the head of Tawngpeng State had many wives (Milne 1924: 38, 103). **Extension of incest taboos.** According to Cameron, a man may not marry his brother's or sister's daughter, his father's sister's daughter, or his "aunt" (not specified). There is some indication that preferred marriage is with a mother's brother's daughter. [Cameron 1912: xviii-xx; Milne 1931b: 80.] It would appear from the data in Milne (1924: 134, 138; 1931b: 127) that the village is normally an endogamous unit. Lowis (1906: ii) also refers to an endogamous village. **Residence.** Residence is initially patrilocal, and a widow may either remain in her husband's home or return to her father's (Lowis 1906: 11; Milne 1924: 25, 188). **Domestic unit.** Information is not precise, but the domestic unit is probably the nuclear family, with some semidetached individuals such as an unmarried brother or widowed parent. A son may live patrilocally for a time after marriage. **Divorce.** The possibility of divorce exists but no details are available (Milne 1924: 418; 1931a: 98; 1931b: 98 s.v. *kar-pet*).

SOCIOPOLITICAL ORGANIZATION. **Political organization.**

The Palaungs of Tawngpeng have a state system with a prince (*saohpa*) and a petty court which follows the Shan model. Most other Palaungs are residents of traditional Shan *muong* domains. In both cases the village community appears to have been the primary unit of political organization. In Tawngpeng local administration was carried out by village officials, chosen by the villagers and functioning to some extent independently of the capital at Namhsan. In the neighboring state of Möngmit, subject to a Shan prince, the clans had chiefs who were in charge of the heads of groups of villages, each responsible in turn for the village headmen in their respective areas. Succession to the position of clan chief was usually to the oldest surviving male relative, the actual choice being made by the elders. The choice had to be reported to the *saohpa* of Möngmit. Except where personal influence had rendered them hereditary, the other positions were filled by men chosen by the villagers and confirmed by the clan chief. Village headmen dealt with minor law cases, others were handled by the clan chief. These officials also collected the prince's revenues. ● In the northwestern portion of the Palaung area, in Möngmit State, the Palaungs were obliged to pay tribute to the Kachins owing to lack of protection from the *saohpa*, a fact which may be taken as a measure of the intensity of Shan rule. [Cameron 1912: xxxiii-xxxiv; Lowis 1906: 21-22.] **Social stratification.** Status differentiation according to wealth is reported for the Palaungs of the central, tea-growing area. Servants include those who live with the master's family, receiving food, clothing, and pocket money, but no fixed wages. They reportedly regard as inferior those servants who receive wages but do not enjoy family status. Tea picking for large growers is mentioned as a well-paid occupation for men and girls. Witches, whose power is believed to be hereditary, live in a special section of the village and marry only among themselves. [Milne 1924: 118-19, 203-04, 230, 260.] **Warfare.** Milne refers, without precision, to clans, presumably those in Tawngpeng, fighting among themselves over succession to the office of chief, but otherwise the Palaungs are a peaceful, timid people who seem to have been under considerable pressure from the Kachins at the time of the British occupation of the Shan-Palaung-Kachin areas in 1886. [Cameron 1912: xlii; Milne 1924: 17.]

RELIGION. **Major religions.**

Milne refers to a legend that Theravada Buddhism was introduced into Tawngpeng about 1780 at the instance of the Burmese king, but expresses the opinion, which seems sound, that Buddhism was already known to the Palaungs, since it had been brought to the neigh-boring Shans two or three centuries earlier. Palaung acquaintance with Buddhism has probably relied upon Burmese contacts as well as upon those with the Shans to the east. Two schools are followed: the so-called Burmese, among the northern Palaungs of the upper Shweli valley, and the so-called Yün (Yuan), or Shan, among the others. But the monks of the central area proceed to Burmese monasteries in Mandalay and Rangoon for advanced training, often quite prolonged. Almost every Palaung village has the customary monastery compound. The only cited difference between the Burmese and Yün schools is the existence in the latter of a series of grades among the monks. As a monk progresses upward in this hierarchy, each rise is accompanied by a ceremony of increasing cost, defrayed not only by the monk's relatives but also by a number of godparents. The village monastery is also the traditional school for the few years during which boys receive formal education. [Cameron 1912: xi-xiii; Lowis 1906: 14; Milne 1924: 312-34.] **Supernaturals.** There are two major classes of spirits: the *kar-bu*, in animals and men, which survive death for about a week; and the *kar-nam*, in plants and inanimate objects, which in some cases have human origins. *Kar-bu* of persons suffering violent deaths and those *kar-bu* which do not go off along the road of the dead after the death of their human form become *kar-nam*, the former being especially malevolent. *Kar-nam* which have never had human form are harmless. Some *kar-bu* neither go along the road of the dead nor become *kar-nam*, but become members of another class of spirits, the *pe-aet*, very similar to the European concept of ghosts in their intangibility, vaguely human shapes, and their ability to materialize at will, pass through solids, etc. Each person has two guardian spirits, and there are guardian spirits of the house, the village, roads, tea, growing rice, etc. Additional supernaturals include *pok* (who live upon the dead), ogres, and others, all of whom seem to have Burmese derivation. [Milne 1924: 355-60.] **Practitioners.** Offerings to supernaturals are most frequently made by ordinary people, even in cases of illness, although identification of the spirit causing an illness or misfortune is made by a specialist, the *hsa-ra*—a combination of diviner and medical practitioner. As diviner his advice is sought in such matters as naming a child, choosing a house site, orientating a house, etc. He has knowledge of amulets and incantations, which he sells to those seeking success in love or desiring to bewitch an enemy. He is also likely to be the local tattooer. The *bre*, a witch or wizard, can cause his spirit to possess the body of another. The Palaungs say that they formerly believed in the power of certain people to assume the shape of tigers. ● Attached to the court of the prince of Tawngpeng is an older man, a relative of the prince, known as the *ta pleng* (grandfather, or old man, of the sky) who acts as intermediary for the inhabitants in dealing with the spirits. Annually in September the prince, elders, monks, and people assemble at a great festival. Following a meal for the elders and monks and a recitation of scripture by the latter, all except the elders and monks withdraw. The *ta pleng* and his assistants then summon all the spirits, great and small, to receive the offerings. Other than at this time and occasionally at funerals when they also recite, Palaung monks have no dealings with the supernatural. [Milne 1924: 28, 109-11, 145, 175, 178, 182, 188, 244-50, 263, 346-48.] **Ceremonies.** Major ceremonies are the calendrical ones associated with Buddhism, and, presumably in the central Palaung area surrounding the capital of Tawngpeng, the annual state spirit festival conducted by the *ta pleng*. **Illness and medicine.** Nearly all ills are the work of spirits. According to Buddhist belief, the afflicted person is unable to ward off their influence owing to insufficient accumulation of merit. Some illnesses, especially sudden attacks of insanity, are the consequence of possession by the spirit of another living person, a witch. The affected person or his agents make offerings to the spirit causing the disturbance; if there is doubt about its identity, offerings may be made at a monastery or the building housing the Buddha images. The *hsa-ra* then delivers incantations and administers remedies of plant and animal derivation. A class of women, whom Milne calls merely "wise women," employ massage and charms as cures. Most laymen know many simple remedies which they may use before seeking help from a *hsa-ra*. [Milne 1924: 243-64.] **Birth.** The woman is attended by one or more married friends who have had normal deliveries; her husband may be present. For about 30 days after birth the mother and her child remain in the sleeping room by the fire, which is fed by wood specially collected by the father before the birth. During this period the mother observes dietary rules and is periodically caused to sweat, after which she is massaged, head to foot, by her friends. [Milne 1924: 276-84.] **Soul, death, and afterlife.** The soul, in the sense of the vital principle, is the *kar-bu*, or general animal spirit. Milne's dictionary lists *vin-yin*, the intelligent and immortal part of man; both this term and the concept seem to be Buddhist in origin (1931b: 282). The *kar-bu* is not a unit, but is composed of parts, some of which leave the body during sleep. Varying degrees of amorous infatuation are explained on the basis that different numbers of parts of the soul are involved. The spirit does not pervade the whole body but moves from part to part, some believing that it has a fixed location on each day; thus in wooing, a lover should touch that part of the girl's body where the spirit is that day (Milne 1924: 114-15). At death the *kar-bu* is believed to wander for a period of about seven days, seeking a new mother through whom it may be reincarnated (Milne 1924: 336-42). Palaungs find death horrible, particularly the thought of the *kar-bu's* wandering in search of a mother. ● Ab-

normal deaths include those by violence, lightning, and incidents of childbirth. For these, burial takes place as soon as possible, in an isolated spot in the jungle and without a coffin. Normal deaths, from old age or disease, are treated differently. A monk, or a very old prince, is cremated according to the manner of Burmese monks. Cremation was also possible but not inevitable for other notables such as nuns, clan chiefs, and headmen and their wives, according to Cameron. A deceased layman is buried in an unmarked grave. The body is washed and dressed and carried in a coffin to the village graveyard. Burial takes place the same day, if death has occurred in the night or early morning, otherwise the next day. On the day of death and for a week thereafter, elderly men read Buddhist scriptures in the entrance room of the house, food is taken to the Buddha images near the monastery, and uncooked rice is presented to the monks. On the seventh day more than the usual amount of food is taken to the images by relatives and friends of the deceased, whose spirit is now called upon to depart for the road of the dead and its next life. [Cameron 1912: xxii-xxv; Milne 1924: 285-311.]

BIBLIOGRAPHY. Cameron 1912; Cushing 1914; India 1931-34; Lowis 1906; Milne 1924, 1931a, 1931b; Pinnow 1959; Scott 1921, 1932; Scott and Hardiman 1900.

P'U NOI

Synonym. *Kha P'ai P'u Noi*

ORIENTATION. **Identification.** P'u Noi is a shortened version of the full name, Kha P'ai P'u Noi. According to Roux (1924: 415), the P'u Noi are closely related to the Kha P'ai. **Location.** The P'u Noi live in Phong Saly province of northern Laos, in an area some 30 miles square. They are found in the uplands, in a territory six kilometers north of Phong Saly— bounded on the north by the Ban Kun Num, on the south by the Nam Leng, on the east by the Nam Ou, and on the west by the mountains which separate the upland area of Phong Saly from Ngay Neua, Bun Neua, Muong Yo, and Bun Tay. [Roux 1924: 447-49.] **Linguistic affiliation.** Roux (1924) is unclear on the linguistic position of the P'u Noi. Embree and Thomas (1950: 102-04) classify them with other "Kha" peoples of Laos as Mon-Khmer. Izikowitz (1951: 22), however, says the people he calls Phu-noi (and identifies with the P'u Noi of Roux), speak a Tibeto-Burman language. **Demography.** According to Roux (1924: 446-47), the P'u Noi number some 10,000, scattered among 39 villages. **History and cultural relations.** According to P'u Noi oral history, they previously lived in the vicinity of Vien Phu Kha in the northern Laotian province of Haut Mekong (the district of Muong Sing). They were caught in struggles between the Burmese and Chinese, and later fought the Vietnamese. Eventually they migrated to the Phong Saly area. [Roux 1924: 452-53.]

SETTLEMENT PATTERN AND HOUSING. Settlement pattern.

Most P'u Noi villages contain at least 50 houses. The settlements are divided into two halves —one containing the farmsteads, and the other the granaries. Part of the village is considered permanent, while another part is a temporary residential area for those who are expected to move out when their swiddens are too far removed from the village for them to remain. In the permanent part of the village there are granaries, fruit trees, and a pagoda, and the houses tend to be larger than in the temporary part. Kitchen gardens are located near the houses, and around the village there are specified pasture areas. [Roux 1924: 456-57.] **Housing.** P'u Noi houses are rectangular in shape and are constructed on piling. The frame is wood, the walls and interior partitions are of split bamboo, and the roof is of thatch. There are two entrances to the house. The main room contains the hearth, and there is one bedroom partitioned off from the main room. Entrance to the bedroom is forbidden to outsiders. [Roux 1924: 457-59.]

ECONOMY. Agriculture.

Upland rice is the staple of the P'u Noi, and it is cultivated in swiddens. They cut and burn the forest, and then weed it at planting time in April. Three or four grains are placed in each hole made by a digging stick. Normally the harvest is in October. Maize is an important secondary crop, and every family cultivates some tobacco, which is consumed by the male members of the family. Each family also cultivates some cotton, which is woven into cloth. Other crops include cucumbers, green vegetables, sugar cane, beans, and bamboo. The P'u Noi also raise bees for honey. [Roux 1924: 464.] **Domestic animals.** Buffalo, goats, pigs, chickens, cattle, dogs, and cats. A few well-to-do families breed horses. [Roux 1924: 462-64.] **Food and stimulants.** One curious note in the diet is the consumption of earth. The P'u Noi eat some almost every day, and consider it excellent medicine for diarrhea. [Roux 1924: 461.] **Industrial arts.** Families make their own hoes, sickles, and other tools. Weaving is done in each family. Several villages specialize in jewelry production. [Roux 1924: 464.]

MARRIAGE AND FAMILY. Mode.

The parents of the boy retain the services of an intermediary—a married male—who approaches the girl's parents. If they respond favorably, there are a series of prescribed meetings. On the day of the wedding, the groom and his procession go to the girl's house. When the bride leaves her house she is presented with gifts—among the well-to-do this includes paddy, a buffalo, one head of cattle, some chickens, and a dog. This is followed by the wedding ritual. [Roux 1924: 472-75.] **Form.** Polygyny is permitted, and is practiced by the well-to-do (Roux 1924: 474). **Residence.** According to Roux (1924: 473), it was formerly customary for a young man to do three years of service for his future parents-in-law before the marriage could take place. Residence is now patrilocal for one year, after which a couple has the option to remain or establish a new household. **Inheritance.** When a man dies, his widow may either remain near her parents-in-law or return to her own family. In the former case she has a claim to some of the property her husband possessed at the time of marriage and to all property acquired during marriage. If she returns to her own village or kin group she forfeits any claim to property her husband had at the time of marriage, and the jointly-owned property is divided into three parts, two of which go to the kin of the deceased and the remaining part to the widow. She can remarry with the consent of her parents-in-law, in which case she has no claim to any of her husband's property. The eldest son gets the bulk of his parents' property, and other siblings share the remaining inheritance. An adopted child has equal rights with other children, and the child of a concubine receives half the inheritance of other children. [Roux 1924: 466-67.] **Divorce.** Divorce by either the husband or the wife is possible. If both agree to separate, the family goods are divided into three parts, two of which go to the husband and one to the wife. She also has a right to the animals and other goods she possessed at the time of marriage. If the wife is at fault, however, she loses all claim to any property, including that which she brought into the marriage. [Roux 1924: 474.]

SOCIOPOLITICAL ORGANIZATION.

Each P'u Noi village has a *chao ban* (chief or headman) and a *quan* (deputy), along with several other notables. Several villages are under a chief, and five of these groupings form a *tasseng*. The leaders receive gifts as compensation for their services. Village officials are elected by the villagers, and the chief of each grouping of villages is elected by the village chiefs and notables. [Roux 1924: 465.]

RELIGION.

According to Roux (1924: 486), Buddhism was introduced among the P'u Noi by Tai Lü monks at some unknown date. There are three categories of Buddhist monks:—*thu long* are the chief monks, *thu* are the monks in general, and *phaya* are novices. There are no nuns. Roux notes that their rules are not stringent—they may ride horseback, drink alcohol, eat after midday, and smoke opium. The guardian spirit of the country is one of the most important deities in the P'u Noi pantheon. Rituals honoring this deity include invocations to the spirit of the high mountains and the spirit of the rocks.

When the swidden is being prepared for planting, a special ritual honors the spirit of the village. The spirit of the earth is another important deity. [Roux 1924: 480-86.] **Soul, death, and afterlife.** The corpse is prepared in prescribed fashion, with candles and a bouquet of flowers. Several grains of gold or silver are placed in the mouth. Among the well-to-do, the corpse is kept from two to six days, while among the poor it is buried after a twenty-four hour period. The funeral cortege is formed in a prescribed manner, and after burial in a wooden coffin, a small hut is constructed over the tomb. A woven basket containing rice and a pipe is placed in the hut. A month after the burial, a sorcerer returns to the grave to exorcise evil spirits that may have entered the hut. [Roux 1924: 476-77.]

BIBLIOGRAPHY. Embree and Thomas 1950; Izikowitz 1951; Roux 1924.

RUC

Synonym. *Rôc*

ORIENTATION. **Location.** Quang Binh province of northern Vietnam (Cuisinier 1948: 40-45). **Linguistic affiliation.** Mon-Khmer (NNCDT 1959: 246). **Demography.** Total of 189 persons (NNCDT 1959: 246).

BIBLIOGRAPHY. Cuisinier 1948; NNCDT 1959.

SACH

ORIENTATION. **Identification.** Cuisinier (1948: 39-45) is the only source that reports the Sach as an ethnic group in northern Vietnam, and she notes that they often intermarry with the Nguon Muong.

SETTLEMENT PATTERN AND HOUSING. Sedentary.

BIBLIOGRAPHY. Cuisinier 1948.

T'IN

Synonyms. *Chao Doi, Kha Phai, Kha T'in, Lawa, Phai, Thin*

ORIENTATION. **Identification.** A population of migratory swidden farmers in the northern Laos–Thailand border area. They are called T'in (Thin, Kha T'in) by the Siamese, who also refer to them occasionally as Lawa. In Laos they are called Phai or Kha Phai. Those in Thailand refer to themselves as Chao Doi (Siamese for "mountain people"). [Bare 1961.] **Location.** In the mountains of northern Nan province in northern Thailand, along the headwaters of the Nan river and its tributaries the Wa, Mang, Lae, Kon, Pua, and Quang. Also across the border in Laos, specifically in Sayaboury province. [Bare 1961.] **Linguistic affiliation.** Mon-Khmer. Young comments on the similarities among T'in, Khmu, and Lawa. In Thailand there are two distinct dialect areas corresponding to two mountain ranges extending north–south in Nan province. Most T'in are fluent in Lao and Siamese, but they know none of the languages of the other groups surrounding them. They have no writing of any kind. [Bare 1961; Young 1961: 82.] **Demography.** There are over 120 known T'in villages in Thailand, with an estimated total of between 12,000 and 35,000 inhabitants. The T'in in Laos total between 5,000 and 6,000. [Bare 1961.] **History and cultural relations.** The T'in in Thailand appear to have migrated from Laos within the past 40 to 80 years. They are physically similar to the Khmu, Kha Haw, and other Mon-Khmer hill tribesmen in northern Thailand. Observers have commented on their marginal economy and generally dejected appearance. For the most part they remain in their villages in the hills, having relatively little to do with other groups. There is, however, a tendency among those nearer the lowlands to form permanent settlements, with some wet-rice agriculture. In Thailand, some T'in have adopted Buddhism, and their assimilation by the lowland Siamese is in process. [Young 1961: 85.]

SETTLEMENT PATTERN AND HOUSING. **Settlement pattern.** The T'in settle on the lower mountain ridges and slopes, below the Meo, Lisu, and Lahu. Their villages are found usually between 2,500 and 3,500 feet. In Thailand, villages average 25 houses, with 6 persons per house, giving an average village population of 150. Smaller villages relocate approximately once in ten years, larger villages less frequently. Fairly large T'in villages (averaging 600 to 1,000 persons) are found in Thailand; these are relatively permanent settlements geared to the raising of a single commercial crop, e.g. tea processed and sold in pickled or fermented form. **Housing.** Houses are substantial structures built on piles. Walls and floors are normally of bamboo, although wood is also used. [Young 1961: 81; Bare 1961.]

ECONOMY. The T'in spend much of their time in swidden agriculture although uncertain crop yields force them to rely heavily at times on gathering or on selling forest products or their own labor to lowlanders or other hill tribesmen. In Thailand, they realize some cash income from the sale of pickled tea leaves, rattan mats, and forest products. Salt wells at the headwaters of the Nan river are exploited by a few T'in villages. Some T'in hire themselves out to

Meo and Yao landowners as field laborers; others work as domestics for Siamese government officials or Chinese merchants. In some cases T'in villagers have taken over poppy fields abandoned by the Meo and have entered the opium business. [Bare 1961.] **Agriculture.** Glutinous rice, grown in upland swiddens, is the main crop. Credner (1935a: 154-59), citing data from Laos, emphasizes that T'in agriculture is entirely dependent on rainfall, since it makes no use of terracing, and that as a consequence crop yields are highly uncertain. The T'in have a marginal, if not actually starvation, economy. Fields are burned during March and April and planted in June. Ashes serve as fertilizer. Holes are made with a digging stick and seeds dropped by hand. No agricultural use is made of domestic animals. A field is cleared by four or five households, and worked and harvested cooperatively by the same group. Fields are rarely used for more than two years—generally only one year—after which they are fallowed for about ten years. Frequent shifting of fields means the gradual exhaustion of land within a reasonable distance of a village; thus smaller villages with less available land must relocate. [Credner 1935a: 154-59; Bare 1961.]

MARRIAGE AND FAMILY. **Extension of incest taboos.** Young men hesitate to marry outside the village, which results in numerous first-cousin marriages. **Residence.** Residence after marriage is initially matrilocal, in the same household with the wife's parents. After the birth of several children, the couple normally moves into a new dwelling. **Inheritance.** The house and other important property is inherited by the youngest daughter (Bare 1961). **Divorce.** Divorce is frequent, particularly during the period of matrilocal residence, when the husband may not get on well with his parents-in-law. Few T'in go through life with the same marriage partner.

SOCIOPOLITICAL ORGANIZATION. Major villages have elected headmen, assisted by informally constituted councils of elders. The latter, often men skilled in herb medicine and spirit worship, have a major role in settling disputes and deciding issues affecting the village as a whole. [Bare 1961.]

RELIGION. The T'in are animists whose sorcerers have a considerable reputation among the Meo and Yao. Those who live near the lowland Siamese and Lao have in some cases adopted Buddhism, and there are at least five T'in villages in Thailand which have Buddhist temples. Christian missions have as yet made little headway. [Bare 1961.]

BIBLIOGRAPHY. Bare 1961; Credner 1935a; Young 1961.

W A

Synonyms. *Hai, Hkawa, Hkun Loi, K'a-la, Kawa, K'a-wa, La, Lawa, Loila, Nyo, Tai Loi, Vü, Wü*

ORIENTATION. **Identification.** According to Scott (1896: 139-40) and to Scott and Hardiman (1900: 493), Wa is a generic term of Shan origin, accepted and used by most of the hill tribes so designated. The Burmese refer to Wa in general as Lawa (Scott 1896: 139). The Yunnan Wa are called Hkawa (Kawa, K'a-wa) or K'a-la by the Chinese (Scott and Hardiman 1900: 493; Bruk 1960: 43; deBeauclair 1956: 268). The Shans further distinguish between pagan, unacculturated Wa ("wild" Wa) and acculturated, Buddhist La ("tame" Wa). The pagan "wild" Wa are called Wa Hai by the Shans. They refer to themselves by a variety of names indicative of local dialect and regional divisions: Hsan Htung (Scott 1896: 144), Wü or Vü (Scott and Hardiman 1900: 493), Wa Pwi, Wa Lon (Pitchford 1937: 223), Pato, and Nyo (Embree and Thomas 1950: 54-55). According to Davies (1909), the term La, referring to Buddhist Wa, is heard more often in the territory north of 23° N., including some of the Chinese Shan States, whereas the Buddhist Wa to the south, in Kengtung Shan State, are more usually called Tai Loi. According to Scott and Hardiman (1900: 516), the Shans of Kengtung call all Buddhist hillmen, but especially the Wa, by this term. They add that these Kengtung Wa call themselves Wa Küt, "the Wa who remained," i.e. those who stayed on in Kengtung after its conquest by the Khün Tai. Buddhist Wa in the Southern Shan States area are also called by other names, e.g. Wa Hsap Tai, Hkun Loi, and Loila (Scott 1896: 150; Pitchford 1937: 225). ● There are in addition a great many locally-named populations of Wa or Wa-related speakers scattered throughout the Southern Shan States of Burma and the Sip Song Panna area of extreme southwestern Yunnan. These are in most instances hillmen practicing a combination of swidden and lowland wet-rice agriculture. They are all nominally Buddhists, speaking the local Tai dialect in addition to their own language, and they appear to be in various stages of "becoming Tai." In the Sip Song Panna they are called by such terms as Sam Tuan, Sam Tao, and Sen Chun (Dodd 1923: 61); in Kengtung Shan State there are the En, Sawn, Angku, A-mok, Mong Lwe, and Pyin; and along the Salween, in Manglun Wa State and neighboring areas, are three groups who refer to themselves as Riang (Riang Rioi, Riang Röng): the Yang Hsek, Yang Lam, and Yang Wankun (Scott and Hardiman 1900: 518-20). Pinnow (1959: 4) lists the majority of these languages as subgroups, along with Danaw, in the Palaung-Wa group of the eastern division of Austroasiatic. The Lawa of northern Thailand would also appear to fall in this category, i.e. a remnant population of Wa or Wa-related speakers in varying stages of assimilation by the lowland Tai (Lao or Yuan) of Chiengmai and surrounding areas. **Location.** The true pagan Wa country is a compact mountainous block extending approximately 100 miles north–south along the Salween, and some 50 miles eastward to the watershed between the Salween and Mekong rivers. The cultural center is the area of Lake Nawngkhio, at 22° 54′ N. and 99° 20′ E. (Scott and Hardiman 1900: 495; Pitchford 1937). The true Wa country lies within the so-called Wa States in Burma, historically a disputed area subject to both British and Chinese territorial claims. The pagan or "wild" Wa have remained relatively isolated in their mountain fastness. Their reputation as headhunters has done nothing to lessen this isolation. They are, however, hard workers, and reportedly have a higher population density, larger settlements, more livestock, and larger fields than the "tame" Wa. The latter are generally found associated with dominant Tai-speaking populations; they are usually at least nominally Buddhist, subject to the local *saohpa*. Generally they have abandoned headhunting and the religio-economic complex associated with it (Scott and Hardiman 1900: 511-12). "Tame" Wa are found to the west of the pagan Wa country, along the Salween; southward in Manglun Wa State and Kengtung Shan State; and eastward in Yunnan along the China-Burma border as far north as the Chinese Shan States. A few La are found in scattered settlements north of the Wa States, in the Kachin portion of North Hsenwi (Scott and Hardiman 1900: 516-19). **Geography.** The Wa country is characterized by a series of mountain ranges running north–south and shelving rapidly down to narrow valleys from 2,000 to 5,000 feet deep (Scott 1896: 142). Due to intensive cultivation, particularly of the poppy, there is little forest cover, and Harvey (1957: 126) writes of the "great bare hills" of the Wa country. The Wa construct well-made trails, but these are limited to the higher altitudes. **Linguistic affiliation.** Wa is one of the Wa-Palaung group of languages, related to Mon-Khmer (Pinnow 1959: 4; Scott and Hardiman 1900: 495). Physical isolation and headhunting have contributed to the existence of numerous dialects. The American Baptist Mission has devised a system for writing Wa in roman script (Embree and Thomas 1950: 56). **Demography.** Embree and Thomas, quoting post-1946 population estimates by H. M. Young, arrive at a total of just under 400,000 Wa, including both "wild" and "tame" categories: 324,533 in the Wa States of Burma, 10,000 in Kengtung Shan State, and 58,000 in Yunnan (Embree and Thomas 1950: 54). A recent estimate, based on Chinese Communist census figures, gives 286,000 Wa (Kawa) in Yunnan (Bruk 1960: 20). **History and cultural relations.** The pagan Wa of the northern Wa States massif claim to be autochthonous. Those of Kengtung State, however, cherish legends of having

come from the south and of having resided at one time in the Chiengmai area of northern Thailand (Scott and Hardiman 1900: 495; Young 1961: 65-66). Scott (1896: 139) concluded that the "wild" Wa have been in their present territory for a long time. Here they have successfully resisted outside encroachments. Although they have a well-deserved reputation as headhunters within their own country, they are not known as raiders into lowlander populations as are some warlike hill tribes in the Yunnan-Burma area. ● Following British annexation of Upper Burma in 1885, a British-Chinese Boundary Commission surveyed the Wa States area in the 1890s, but the British did not attempt to administer the area in any real sense of the term. Mining prospects revived interest in the 1920s, and light administration, introduced in 1937, was uninterrupted until 1942. Administrative consolidation was still incomplete in 1948 when Burma gained independence. Headhunting, which appeared to be declining in the late 1930s, may have revived in recent years. [Harvey 1957: 129ff.] The activities of the Chinese Communists, in promoting cooperatives and light industry among the Kawa of Yunnan, are described by Winnington (1959). ● Within the pagan Wa area there are scattered Shan settlements along the Salween and in the valleys. Mohammedan Chinese (Panthay) villages are found in the north, and there are scattered Lahu villages on the higher ridges throughout the area. These intrusive groups are in all cases, however, subordinate to their Wa neighbors. The Panthay and a few Shans are tolerated as middlemen in the opium trade. The Wa are not known as traders or travelers; except for headhunting expeditions, a Wa seldom leaves the range on which he was born. [Scott 1896: 139, 150.]

SETTLEMENT PATTERN AND HOUSING. **Settlement pattern.** "Wild" Wa villages are plainly visible on the higher mountain slopes, often in a hollow sheltered by the crest of a ridge. Sites near streams are avoided, since it is believed that water causes fever; water may, however, be piped into a village by means of bamboo aqueducts. Wa villages are the largest of any hill tribe in the Shan States; few have less than 100 houses and many contain 200 or 300. A village is ordinarily surrounded by an earthen rampart six to eight feet high, covered by an impenetrable thicket of thorn bushes. Further protection is gained by means of a deep ditch, carefully concealed, around the outside perimeter of the rampart. Entrance is through a narrow tunnel, 30 yards or more long, closed at its inner end by a heavy wooden door bolted on the inside. There is no particular arrangement of houses. The headman's house may be somewhat larger than the others, with its gable-end rafters elongated to form a cross, which is sometimes painted or carved. On the outer fringes of the village compound stand separate sheds, on piles, where each household stores its supply of rice liquor. A small wooden shed which serves as a spirit house stands at one end of the village. Inside is a large drum in the form of a hollowed-out tree trunk, which is beaten on ceremonial occasions and is also used for intervillage communication (Pitchford 1937: 226). The spirit house may also contain the bones of sacrificed animals, and near it are kept the newly-taken human heads which will later be placed in a skull grove just outside the village. [Scott 1896: 146-49.] **Housing.** Houses are constructed on piles, up to five or six feet above the ground, and are built in substantial fashion of timber and wattled bamboo. There is no veranda. A bamboo ladder or notched log gives access directly to the main room, containing a hearth and sleeping areas along the sides. Houses are oblong, with gable ends. A heavy thatch roof comes down on all four sides. The house is surrounded by a low fence, inside which stand rows of Y-shaped posts seven to ten feet high, each of which records the owner's sacrifice of a buffalo. The buffalo skulls, with the horns, are piled within the house. Pigs, dogs, and fowl are kept in the space beneath the house although pigs may also be quartered in separate slab houses. [Scott 1896: 146-48.]

ECONOMY. The pagan Wa of the northern and eastern Wa States appear to rely chiefly on dry-field agriculture for food. Domestic animals supply a necessary, but limited, portion of the diet. Fishing and hunting appear to be important, and gathering may contribute more to the food economy than is apparent in the literature. Supplementary foods and other goods are obtained through the sale of opium. **Agriculture.** The Wa hills are largely denuded of vegetation due to continuous and extensive cultivation. Fields are usually either above or below a village; rice, for example, may be planted 3,000 feet or more below a village site. The opium poppy is the chief crop, grown primarily for trade. The chief food crops are beans, maize, buckwheat, legumes of various kinds, and hill rice. The rice is entirely consumed in the production of liquor. [Scott 1896: 148-51.] **Domestic animals.** Among the unacculturated "wild" Wa, domestic animals appear to be limited to pigs, dogs, and fowl. Buffalo, used extensively for sacrifice, are obtained by trade from the lowland Shans (Embree and Thomas 1950: 56). **Food and stimulants.** The diet appears to consist mainly of beans, buckwheat, and the residue from the distillation or fermentation of rice and maize in the production of alcoholic beverages. Rice liquor is made in large quantities and stored in bamboo containers in specially constructed sheds. Dogs, pigs, and chickens also contribute to the diet. Most Wa either smoke or eat some opium. [Scott 1896: 148-51; Scott and Hardiman 1900: 514.] **Industrial arts.** The Wa know how to work iron. Those of the northern Wa States make their own muzzle-loading guns, gunpowder, and lead bullets. Women among at least some Wa groups can weave. [Embree and Thomas 1950: 56.] **Trade.** Relatively little. A few Shans from the "tame" Wa country and a few Mohammedan Panthay go into the Wa hills periodically with salt and other goods in exchange for opium. [Scott 1896: 146.]

KIN GROUPS. According to Scott and Hardiman (1900: 513), the "tame" Wa are divided into five clans, each with a chief: the Hsin Lam, Hsin Leng, Hsin Lai, Hta Mo, and Mot No.

MARRIAGE AND FAMILY. Scott (1896: 152) maintains that wives are purchased with bullocks and other goods. Polygyny is said to be permissible but rare.

SOCIOPOLITICAL ORGANIZATION. **Political organization.** In pagan Wa country village communities are for the most part autonomous and independent of one another. Confederations of three or four villages under a common chief may be formed for mutual defense and mutual respect of heads, but these seldom extend beyond one range of hills. The inhabitants of villages on neighboring hills are regarded as strangers and potential enemies. Each village in a confederation retains its own headman (*kraw*), its own fields, and its own ceremonial feasts. The chief, or *ramang*, of a confederation may receive haunches of buffalo and pig and bamboos of liquor from villages within his territory, and the quarrel of any one village is taken up by the whole confederation under the leadership of the *ramang;* this is, however, the maximum extent of centralized authority recognized by Wa villages. Among the "tame" Wa, villages are smaller and are united in relatively large numbers under paramount chiefs. [Scott 1896: 149; Pitchford 1937: 231; Mitton 1936: 181.] **Social stratification.** Winnington (1959: 132) describes debt slavery among the Wa of southwestern Yunnan. Whether slavery in any form exists in the Burmese Wa States is not clear. **Warfare.** Headhunting among the "wild" Wa is carried out by small parties who may range some distance from the home village. Ambush is preferred to large-scale attack or siege. The latter is, in fact, virtually impossible due to the ramparts, ditches, and other obstructions surrounding each village. The reputation of the Wa for warlikeness and hostility to strangers has discouraged penetration of the Wa States by Burmese, British, and Chinese alike.

RELIGION. **Major religions.** Most "tame" Wa are nominally Buddhists. Although retaining many animistic beliefs and practices, they are not headhunters. Ritual substitution of animal heads for human skulls appears to be common among some "tame" Wa groups. A few thousand Buddhist Wa in the Southern Shan States area have more recently become Christians. **Indigenous religion.** The "wild" Wa have been headhunters at least as recently as 1935. Wa mythology associates headhunting with ancestral deities, the legendary founders of the Wa race. In a more immediate sense, the skulls, which are kept in a grove outside the village, are regarded as a kind of collective insurance against calamities of all kinds, and as an assurance of abundant crops and good health. According to Wa belief, possession of a skull ensures that the ghost of the victim will remain in the vicinity, jealously guarding its territory against the evil spirits that harm crops and bring illness. Heads of strangers, unfamiliar with the local terrain, are preferred, since their ghosts are less likely to wander off. New heads are particularly important in connection with spring planting and the assurance of crops at harvest time. Some divisions of the Wa, the "wet-heads" (Embree and Thomas 1950: 57), kill for heads. Others, the "dry-heads," obtain the heads of the recently dead, such as executed criminals. A headhunting party may travel a considerable distance from its home village, seeking an unattached "tame" Wa, Lahu, or Shan, or a victim from an unrelated or unaffiliated "wild" Wa village. Newly-taken heads are seasoned, i.e. kept until devoid of flesh, within the village, often wrapped in wickerwork baskets slung from tall poles. Later each skull is ceremonially installed in a sacred grove outside the village, a bit of primeval forest wherein skulls are placed in niches cut into stout posts arranged in rows. Most villages in the true headhunting country maintain 10 to 20 skulls in varying stages of decay. The village or villages of a great *ramang* may boast of many more. Cannibalism does not appear to be associated with headhunting among the Wa. [Scott 1896: 140-45.] **Soul, death, and afterlife.** The Wa bury their dead in coffins of wood. Scott and Hardiman (1900: 514) report large barrows or mounds up to 100 yards long and 3 feet high, which are said to be gravesites of early Wa.

BIBLIOGRAPHY. DeBeauclair 1956; Bruk 1960; Davies 1909; Dodd 1923; Embree and Thomas 1950; Harvey 1957; Mitton 1936; Pinnow 1959; Pitchford 1937; Scott 1896; Scott and Hardiman 1900; Winnington 1959; Young 1961.

YUMBRI

Synonyms. *Kha Tong Luang, Ma Ku, Phi Tong Luang*

ORIENTATION. **Identification and location.** The rumored existence of small bands of nomadic gatherers in northern Thailand has intrigued ethnologists and explorers for decades. Two recent firsthand accounts by Bernatzik (1938) and Weaver (1956) have demonstrated beyond doubt that such groups do exist, albeit in extremely small numbers, rapidly ap-

proaching extinction. These people, known to the Tai-speaking Lao and Siamese as **Phi Tong Luang**, or "spirits of the yellow leaves," call themselves Yumbri, "people of the jungle." They are known to the Meo, with whom they are in most frequent contact, as Ma Ku, or "spirits of the jungle." [Bernatzik 1938: 116, 139, 141.] Both Bernatzik and Weaver traveled for brief periods with small bands of these completely nomadic people in the mountains east of the Nan river on the northern Thailand-Laos border. Young (1961), using information supplied mainly by Lahu informants, locates additional Phi Tong Luang in the Doi Vieng Pha mountains north of Muang Prao in Chiengmai province, in the Doi Chang mountains west of Chiengrai, and in Kengtung area of Burma. These groups, however, appear to differ rather significantly from the Phi Tong Luang of Bernatzik (and to a lesser extent, Weaver) with respect to language and certain aspects of culture. Whether it is true, as Young concludes, that the Phi Tong Luang may represent retrogressed peoples from several different tribes, is impossible to judge from the information available. Bernatzik (1938: 142, 180) characterizes them as primitive or Proto-Mongoloids, autochthons once more numerous and widespread, and allied to the early Jakun population of southern Malaya. **Geography.** The Yumbri frequent remote mountain tracts, covered by dense tropical jungle growth. Because of the altitude, extreme temperature variations are common and nights may be uncomfortably cold. **Linguistic affiliation.** Young's Lahu and Meo informants report a variety of Phi Tong Luang dialects with similarities to Lao, Meo, Wa, and Khmu. Pinnow (1959: 4), citing Seidenfaden, who in turn relies on Bernatzik, places Yumbri in an eastern subgroup of Palaung-Wa, together with Khmu and Lamet. Although inadequately known, the language thus appears to be Austroasiatic [Austroasian], related to Mon-Khmer. **Demography.** The Yumbri are fragmented into extremely small, highly nomadic, family bands. Estimates of total population are at best educated guesswork. Bernatzik estimated "several hundred," and Young thinks there may be from 50 to 150 altogether. That the population is declining seems certain; the Yumbri are shot on sight by some of the hill groups, and tigers, disease, and malnutrition take an annual toll. [Young 1961: 89; Bernatzik 1938: 131-85.] **Cultural relations.** Contacts with nearby groups, such as Lao, Khmu, and T'in, are irregular and brief. The T'in reportedly regard the Yumbri as harmful spirits, and therefore shoot them on sight. There is apparently some contact with the Lahu north of Chiengmai, and even some intermarriage with Lahu. According to Bernatzik, the Yumbri of Nan province were in contact mainly with the Meo, visiting Meo villages on a more or less regular basis, in what might be termed a symbiotic relationship. Here it appeared that the extremely impoverished cultural inventory reported by Bernatzik was supplemented to some extent by goods and services obtained through contacts with Meo. Most Yumbri can speak at least some Meo, and there are Meo who can speak Yumbri. [Bernatzik 1938: 113, 141 passim.]

SETTLEMENT PATTERN AND HOUSING. **Settlement pattern.** Small family bands establish campsites consisting of one or more windscreens. Campsites are moved on the average of every three or four days. The Yumbri make no clearings and do little to alter the landscape; therefore their presence is often undetected by nearby groups. The bands generally exploit sparsely inhabited mountain slopes. Since they use only water from certain species of bamboo, their wanderings are not dependent on the location of streams and springs. [Bernatzik 1938: 142-44.] **Housing.** Each nuclear family constructs its own windscreen. A campsite may consist of several such structures, which are crude affairs, quickly made from immediately available materials. A few poles, verticals and horizontals, support a leaf roof, and additional leaves provide some protection around the sides. When the leaves turn yellow the group moves to a new campsite, thus accounting for the appellation "spirits of the yellow leaves." Within the windscreen are one or more earthen fireplaces and beds which are made by placing bamboo cross pieces on short forked sticks and covering with leaves. [Bernatzik 1938: 145, 166.]

ECONOMY. The indigenous food economy described by Bernatzik for the Yumbri of northern Nan province relies almost exclusively on gathering. The Yumbri observed by Weaver evidently rely somewhat more on hunting as a source of food (Weaver 1956: 292), and the Phi Tong Luang of Chiengmai, described by Young's Lahu informants, appear to derive a considerable portion of their food from hunting (Young 1961: 90). In all cases trade provides some additional foods and manufactured objects. **Agriculture.** No cultivation of plants of any description. **Fishing and hunting.** There is no evidence of fishing, and in fact the Yumbri avoid streams, believing them to be inhabited by evil spirits. The Yumbri of northern Nan province do little or no hunting: they have no weapons other than an occasional spear obtained from the Meo, their chief protection against predatory animals being fire; they make no use of traps or pitfalls, other than a few small bird traps; they show no interest in or aptitude for hunting, and fear most of the larger animals. [Bernatzik 1938: 148-49.] **Gathering.** Every moment of the day, with the exception of the time involved in setting up a new campsite, is devoted to gathering food. Women and children remain near the camp during the day, keeping the fire burning and gathering wood and edible herbs and roots in the immediate vicinity. Men usually go off in pairs seeking food. The band moves as a group to a new campsite, gathering food as it goes.

Small domesticated dogs are trained to locate and dig up certain roots and tubers which the people use as food. [Weaver 1956: 292; Bernatzik 1938: 148-49.] **Domestic animals.** The only domesticated animals are dogs, trained in locating and digging out roots and tubers and in catching turtles and lizards. The Yumbri do not eat their dogs. **Food and stimulants.** Bernatzik (1938: 148-49) mentions wild fruits, roots, berries, leaves, bamboo shoots, wild sago palm, wild yams, snails, caterpillars, crabs, lizards, frogs, turtles, mice, rats, squirrels, honey, and birds' eggs. Weaver (1956: 294) indicates that bamboo shoots may constitute a staple during part of the year—otherwise wild yams and other edible roots form the mainstay of the diet. According to Weaver, this basically vegetarian diet is supplemented by the meat from small animals such as porcupines and rodents, and occasionally by a barking deer or wild pig. Meat is roasted over an open fire or boiled in a length of green bamboo. It is usually eaten half raw. Roots, herbs, and shoots are baked in hot coals or boiled in a bamboo container. Occasionally the Yumbri obtain rice by trade or theft. When they can, they season their food with salt, and also make use of wild chilies and peppers. Instead of salt they sometimes substitute soil said to contain salt (Bernatzik 1938: 150). They do not eat blood but are fond of raw bone marrow. Meat may be cooked slightly to preserve it, but it is never salted for this purpose. Both sexes chew tobacco and smoke it in pipes when they can obtain it by barter from the Meo. Betel is used only in isolated instances. Some opium, used chiefly as a medicine, is obtained by barter (Bernatzik 1938: 150). **Industrial arts.** According to Bernatzik, the Yumbri make no pottery or barkcloth, and do no work in bone, shell, stone, or ivory—nor do they work leather or skins in any way. They neither make nor wear any ornaments, and their clothing consists of cast-off remnants obtained from the Meo and Lao. They do work with wood and bamboo to some extent, making such things as windscreens, digging sticks, knives, spears, and bamboo containers. Practically their only other industry is the manufacture of rattan baskets and mats made by a plaiting technique taught to them by the Meo. These articles are traded to the Meo and other groups in return for salt, clothing, and rice. Knives and spears are ordinarily made by the Yumbri themselves from bamboo or wood, although they do obtain an occasional iron spear tip or steel knife blade from the Lao or Meo. [Bernatzik 1938: 132-33, 147, 152.] **Trade.** The Yumbri do not trade among themselves. They carry on direct barter with the Meo, Lao, Yao, T'in, and Khmu, offering wild honey, wax, rattan, firewood, mats, and baskets in return for tobacco, rice, salt, meat, secondhand clothing, knives—and, less frequently, spear points, opium, and alcohol. Barter is usually carried on in the villages of these other groups and it is rare that middlemen—such as Chinese—are involved. There is no mention of so-called "silent trade." [Bernatzik 1938: 153-54.] **Division of labor.** Sexual division of labor and occupational specialization have little meaning in Yumbri culture. Hunting, when it is done at all, is done mainly by men. Otherwise men, women, and children all co-operate in gathering activities and in the preparation of food. **Land tenure.** Traditionally, each band claims a territory which it exploits economically, and within which all vegetation and animal life are regarded as the common property of the band. Individual rights to land and its products are thus unknown. The territory is prohibited to other bands without permission of the owner band; this is always granted unless the entering group has within its membership a sick person. [Bernatzik 1938: 168-69.]

KIN GROUPS. **Descent.** Patrilineal affiliation. A married woman belongs to the family of her father-in-law. [Bernatzik 1938: 166.] **Kin groups.** The basic unit of social organization is the band, consisting of anywhere from three to a dozen members. Often a nuclear family wanders by itself, at least during part of the year. In other cases the composition of the band approaches most nearly that of a patrilocal extended or stem family, e.g. two brothers, their wives and unmarried children, and the married son of one of the brothers, together with his wife. The bands appear to have no regular means of communication, and related bands may wander for days in search of one another. Signs, such as bent leaves, are left at a campsite when a group departs, but these are apparently little used. [Bernatzik 1938: 137-38, 142-43.] **Kin terminology.** Bernatzik (1938: 167-68) gives the following terms for the Yumbri of northern Nan province on the Laos border:

Fa	emum
Mo	emu
FaElBr, MoElBr	ey emum
FaYoBr, MoYoBr	ey kumom
FaElSi, MoElSi	ey uy
FaYoSi, MoYoSi	ey roy
ElBr	ey emu
YoBr	kumom
ElSi	uy
YoSi	roy

MARRIAGE AND FAMILY. **Mode.** According to Bernatzik, both premarital and extramarital intercourse are prohibited. A father arranges for his son's marriage, usually with a girl from another band. If the girl's parents agree to the match, the young man and his father collect fruits, roots, honey, rattan, and wax as a present to them. There is no ceremony; the girl simply joins the band of the groom. In exceptional cases a couple may elope. Bernatzik specifically denies annual gatherings of bands for purposes of courtship and mating. [Bernatzik 1938: 157-58.] **Form.** Exclusively monogamous. **Extension of incest taboos.**

Marriage is prohibited between siblings, uncle and niece, aunt and nephew, and first cousins. First-cousin marriage does occur, however, but only after the couple undergo an ordeal to determine whether the spirits will approve the match. **Residence.** Patrilocal. The girl comes to live with the band of her husband. Within the band, however, each nuclear family maintains its own windscreen. **Domestic unit.** The household unit, i.e. the persons within one windscreen, consists of a man, his wife, and his unmarried children. The band, the normal unit of face-to-face relationship, may be a nuclear family or a patrilocal extended family. **Divorce.** A man can divorce his wife at will, but a woman can leave a man only with his consent. [Bernatzik 1938: 157-58.]

SOCIOPOLITICAL ORGANIZATION. **Political organization.** The leader of a band is always a man, prominent by virtue of age or other qualifications. He has little actual power, however. Matters are settled by mutual consent and discussion, and a family is always free to leave a band if it so desires. Should a leader die, another man assumes his place by informal recognition of his fellows. **Social stratification.** The concept of social stratification is alien to Yumbri culture, according to Bernatzik, who stresses that differential behavior toward others is motivated solely by degree of strangeness. **Warfare.** Most of the Yumbri seen by Bernatzik carried no weapons and showed a striking absence of aggressive behavior of any kind. The Yumbri are timid and difficult to approach except through an intermediary known to them. Their only salvation in the face of aggression is flight, and their chief protection against predatory animals is fire. [Bernatzik 1938: 131, 166.]

RELIGION. **Indigenous religion.** Bernatzik (1938: 170-73) characterizes the Yumbri as animists, with a system of beliefs and practices centering on the concept of souls. According to Bernatzik, they have no altars, no priests or other religious specialists, no magical practices, no charms, and no amulets. They do, however, believe in the power of magicians and medicine men in neighboring tribes, those of the Yao being especially feared. Weaver (1956: 336) generally supports Bernatzik's observations, but reports in addition a kind of spear worship and associated ceremonial. Young's Lahu informants maintained that the Phi Tong Luang known to them have both shamans and amulets as well as sacrifices and dances connected with spear worship (Young 1961: 89). **Supernaturals.** A person's soul can leave his body during sleep—its experiences appearing to the sleeper in his dreams. When death occurs, the soul leaves the body within three or four days. The soul is immortal and may undergo a series of transformations into tigers and other animals. Souls of evil persons may continue to cause illness or misfortune for the living. Spirits, both good and evil, also have souls. Spirits are mortal, and when they die their immortal souls roam the forest. These supernaturals are thought to reside in special trees or in stream beds, and food sacrifices are accordingly made at the feet of certain spirit trees. The Yumbri never eat a food sacrifice, even a pig or other large animal, according to Bernatzik. **Illness and medicine.** Illness is never ascribed to natural causes, but rather to evil spirits and ghosts, or to the magic of the Lao or Yao. The Yumbri believe in the curative value of fire; they expose afflicted parts to heat or smoke, and strew ashes on open wounds. They have no way of dealing with fractures or serious illnesses except through sacrifice or recourse to a Lao medicine man. **Death.** The body is disposed of as quickly as possible following death and a brief sacrificial ritual. At the spot where death occurs, the Yumbri construct a small pile of sticks and branches. The corpse is placed on this crude bier and covered with leaves. Near relatives briefly cower down next to the corpse and weep. They then move on with the rest of the band and the body is abandoned to the forest. [Bernatzik 1938: 158-59.]

BIBLIOGRAPHY. Bernatzik 1938; Pinnow 1959; Weaver 1956; Young 1961.

CENTRAL UPLAND GROUPS

ALAK

ORIENTATION. **Location.** Attopeu province and the vicinity of Thateng in Saravane province in Laos. **Linguistic affiliation.** Mon-Khmer. **Demography.** Lafont (1962b) estimates that the Alak form 50 per cent of approximately 2,500 population in vicinity of Thateng and number about 500 in Attopeu, making the estimated total 1,750.

SETTLEMENT PATTERN AND HOUSING. Circular village centered on a communal house, outside which are several sacrificial posts. The Alak also have longhouses constructed on piling. [Hoffet 1933: 7; Fraisse 1951: 65.] Lafont (1962b) describes a carved buffalo-horn design on communal house roofs.

ECONOMY. Cultivators of upland rice in swiddens and of areca trees, betel vines, and tobacco, which is used by males and females alike. There are weavers of blue-and-red cloth, and some Alak work as wage laborers. [Hoffet 1933: 7; Fraisse 1951: 65; Lafont 1962b.]

SOCIOPOLITICAL ORGANIZATION. The fundamental social unit is the village, under a *pho ban,* headman; the village sorcerer is also an important figure (Hoffet 1933: 7; Fraisse 1951: 65; Lafont 1962b).

RELIGION. Believers in animistic spirits. Buffalo sacrifices are held periodically, and the village sorcerer predicts the future through necromancy. [Hoffet 1933: 7; Fraisse 1951: 65; Lafont 1962b.]

BIBLIOGRAPHY. Fraisse 1951; Hoffet 1933; Lafont 1962b.

ATAOUAT

ORIENTATION. **Location.** The Ataouat massif along the upper Se Kong river in Laos (Hoffet 1933: 23). **Linguistic affiliation.** Mon-Khmer.

SETTLEMENT PATTERN AND HOUSING. Similar to the Katang (Hoffet 1933: 23).

ECONOMY. Cultivators of upland rice in swiddens (Hoffet 1933: 23).

BIBLIOGRAPHY. Hoffet 1933.

BAHNAR

ORIENTATION. **Identification and location.** The Bahnar, identified as a group exclusively by this name, occupy an area of about 4,000 square kilometers in South Vietnam extending from Kontum in the west to Ankhe in the east (Guilleminet 1941: 12-13; Dam Bo 1950: vi). There is some difference of opinion as to the subgroups of the Bahnar. Guilleminet (1941: 12-13; 1952: 7-8) reports the Bahnar Alakong and Bahnar Tolo north and south of Ankhe, the Bahnar Bonom east of Ankhe, the Bahnar Golar in the Pleiku area, four groups known collectively as the Bahnar To Sung in the region east of Pleiku, and to the west the Bahnar Jo Long northeast of Kontum and the Bahnar Kontum in the immediate vicinity of Kontum. Guilleminet also reports such smaller subgroups as the Bahnar Ho Drong of Dakdoa about 30 kilometers southeast of Kontum, the Bahnar Krem north of Ankhe, and the Bahnar Kon Ko De in the vicinity of Ankhe. But the classification by Guilleminet of the Hroy as a mixed Cam (Cham)-Bahnar-Jarai subgroup within the Bahnar conflicts with the conclusion of Thomas (1962: 5) and others that the Hroy constitute a separate group of the Malayo-Polynesian linguistic stock. Similarly, Guilleminet classifies the Rengao as a Bahnar subgroup, though the Rengao are variously regarded by Devereux (1937: 1) as a mixed Sedang-Bahnar group, by Dam Bo (1950: 983) as a separate group, and by Thomas (1962: 5) as a separate but closely related group. **Linguistic affiliation.** Thomas (1962: 5) places the Bahnar language in the Bahnaran group of the Bahnaric subgroup of the Mon-Khmer stock. For ritual occasions there is a special language of obscure origin which has acquired sacred connotations (Guilleminet 1960: 117-43). A written language using a script similar to the Vietnamese romanized script was devised by French Catholic missionaries in Kontum and officially adopted in 1935 (Guilleminet 1941: 13). **Demography.** Three population estimates have been made by Guilleminet in succeeding years: 70,000 (1941: 12); 110,000 (1949: 383); and 80,000 (1952: 7). **History and cultural relations.** The Bahnar have considerable contact with neighboring groups—notably the Jarai, Halang, and Sedang—and intermarriage of smaller subgroups, e.g. the Bahnar Krem and the Bahnar Hroy, with the Cam (Chams) in the Ankhe region has been common. The Bahnar Hroy have also intermarried with the Jarai and many have been absorbed by the Vietnamese. During the colonial period the Bahnar cooperated closely with French missionaries, administrators, and military. [Guilleminet 1941: 12-13.]

SETTLEMENT PATTERN AND HOUSING. Settlement pattern.

One characteristic of village pattern shared by the Bahnar, the Sedang, and some other Mon-Khmer-speaking groups in Vietnam and Laos, is the centrally located communal or bachelors' house, also referred to as the men's house. This relatively large, carefully constructed, often quite elaborate structure rests on piling and has a framework of large logs and beams. Roofs have four sides and are usually stylized in a sweeping slope. At the entrance is a large platform supported by poles, which may be decorated. [Parmentier 1951: 223-24.] **Housing.** Houses are rectangular and as a rule set on piling (Dam Bo 1950: vii). The typical Bahnar house measures 10 to 15 meters by 3 to 4 meters and has an east-west orientation. A ladder to the entrance can be moved into the house to signify that visitors are not allowed. The interior is divided into three rooms for sleeping: the east room for parents and infants; the center room for girls; and the west room for boys and domestics. The center room also serves as a reception room. In the case of plural marriage there is an extra room at the east end for the first wife, and the second wife sleeps at the west end of the house. [Guilleminet 1951-52: 457.]

ECONOMY. Agriculture.

Cultivators of rice in swiddens, which are abandoned after three to five years. Secondary crops include millet, maize, pumpkins, cucumbers, melons, oranges, red peppers, manioc, yams, eggplant, and bananas. **Fishing, hunting, and gathering.** All pursued to supplement diet. Bamboo shoots are an important item. **Taboos.** The Bahnar Kontum may kill dogs but are forbidden to eat dog flesh (Guilleminet 1943b: 369). **Industrial arts.** The Bahnar make their own cooking pots, crossbows, sabers, arrows, tools, and digging sticks (Dam Bo 1950: 980-82; Guilleminet 1951-52: 405-11). **Trade.** The Bahnar belong to a trade network that includes groups to the northwest of their territory (Dam Bo 1950: 976). **Division of labor.** No rigid division of labor. The heavier tasks such as clearing swiddens are performed by the males; fishing and gathering are normally left to the females, but cultivating may be done by either. [Guilleminet 1949: 383-84.] Family rituals may be conducted by either sex. **Specialization.** Among Bahnar specialists are merchants, lawyers, servants, cattle raisers, ferrymen, stringmakers, healers, bonesetters, midwives, wet nurses, gong players, caterers for festivals, and metalworkers, though metalworking declined after the arrival of the French (Guilleminet 1951-52: 522-23).

KIN GROUPS. Descent.

The available literature is confusing. Guilleminet (1952: 18) states that in the last century the chieftainship was passed down through the matrilineal line and also that the Bahnar have the same "clans"—sibs in the Murdock usage—as the Jarai, a matrilineal group. Rules of succession and inheritance, however, suggest that descent is patrilineal or possibly bilateral. **Kin terminology.** The western Bahnar couple address parents-in-law as *met* (uncle) and *yang* (aunt); the eastern Bahnar couple use *ba* (father) and *ma* (mother), but in both areas the couple, following the birth of their first child, address parents-in-law as *bok* (grandfather) and *ya* (grandmother). At the same time the parents-in-law addressing their children shift to the teknonymous "father of [child's name]" or "mother of [child's name]." [Guilleminet 1951-52: 457.]

MARRIAGE AND FAMILY. Form.

Polygyny is practiced, mostly among the wealthy. Consent of first wife necessary. [Guilleminet 1952: 334-65.] **Extension of incest taboos.** It is preferable that cousins do not marry, but possible if prescribed purificatory rituals have been performed (Guilleminet 1951-52: 457). **Residence.** Ambilocal, and the couple must serve an "apprenticeship" period with each set of parents-in-law before the birth of the first child (Guilleminet 1951-52: 457). **Inheritance.** A villager who clears land in the common village territory (*toring*) has title for the period of use. Such title and personal possessions are inherited through the patrilineal line. Property held in common by the household is left to the surviving spouse. [Guilleminet 1951-52: 466-509.] **Divorce.** The husband or wife must sue for divorce before the village tribunal—divorce by mutual consent is not permissible—on such grounds as a serious criminal record unknown to the other party, concubinage, repeated adultery, desertion, cruelty, sexual aberration, or refusal to assist in duties to kinfolk (Guilleminet 1951-52: 476). **Secondary marriage.** The survivor owes fidelity to the deceased and is barred by various customs from remarriage for six months up to three years, depending on circumstances. A special ceremony marks eligibility to remarry. [Guilleminet 1951-52: 477.]

SOCIOPOLITICAL ORGANIZATION. **Village administration.** Each village is governed by a group of elders selected from among the oldest males in the village, who in turn choose the *kra,* village headman (Guilleminet 1949: 383-84; Hickey 1956-58). The *kra,* who holds office with the consent of the villagers, acts as village emissary to the central bureaucracy and is customarily succeeded by his eldest son or, barring this, a younger kinsman (Guilleminet 1952: 224). **Territorial grouping.** The *toring* is the traditional administrative entity, comprising several related villages in a particular geographic area. Land, hunting, and fishing rights are shared by all those residing in the area, and non-*toring* people, or *tomoi,* are regarded as outsiders whether Bahnar or not. [Guilleminet 1949: 383-84.] There are indications that before 1850 the Bahnar were under the hegemony of one or more ruling families but became scattered as dissensions among rival families grew (Guilleminet 1952: 18). **French period.** A political superstructure—canton, district, province—was imposed by the French colonial government. The chief or *résident* was French, but lesser positions could be held by Bahnar, whom the French recruited, wherever possible, from the traditional ruling families of the *toring.* The Bahnar selected their own canton chiefs, and these tended also to come from the same local elite, but the Bahnar make a distinction between the traditional chiefs and the functionaries who emerged under French rule. [Guilleminet 1952: 219-30.] **Social stratification.** Guilleminet (1951-52: 513-15) distinguishes four classes: (1) the freeman, which includes most Bahnar and in which age and wealth ranking are found; (2) the debtors (*dik*); (3) the foreigners (*tomoi*), i.e. non-Bahnar who live in the area but have no rights and, being supposed sources of pollution, are excluded from certain places, particularly streams; and (4) the war prisoners, who are slaves.

RELIGION. **Indigenous religion.** Within a pervasive animism, the Bahnar separate events of the natural order—e.g. the seasons, birth, planting cycles—and anomalous or unexpected events—e.g. sickness, death of the young, accidents, and drought. All unexpected events are attributed to spirits (*yang*) or ghosts (*kiek,* French *mânes*); only the Bahnar among groups in the southern highlands make this distinction between spirits and ghosts. The relationship of the individual (male or female) to the *yang* or *kiek* is personal and direct, resembling a father-son relationship. The *yang* extend protection to those individuals who have personal contractual agreements, which are solemnized with gift offerings according to a prescribed form; the individual is in turn personally accountable to the *yang* for any wrongdoing. A satisfactory contract may be passed on for as many as four descending generations. [Guilleminet 1941: 15-20.] **Practitioners.** What Guilleminet (1941: 17) calls "magicians" have a special role in certain rituals, but the magician (*bo jao*) receives his power by initiation, there being no equivalent in Bahnar society to the hereditary Rhadé, Jarai, or Sedang sorcerers with their esoteric knowledge of prayers and ritual. A special relationship exists between the *bo jao* and the *ya nom,* or female spirit. The term *ya* also denotes a half-human, half-divine creature. Guilleminet cites numerous cases of *ya*—most were people outside the normal village life, e.g. a Vietnamese idiot, or an army deserter; all claimed special powers. The Bahnar also recognize the Sadet of Fire and the Sadet of Water, great sorcerers among the neighboring Jarai. [Guilleminet 1941: 25-33.] **Ritual offerings.** The distinction between spirits and ghosts is maintained in making offerings: for spirits there is a prescribed form, any breach of which may stir their wrath; for ghosts no such formality obtains and substitutions are possible—water in place of alcohol, an egg in place of the sacrificial animal. Spontaneous offerings are customary: a person walking past the grave of a kinsman will probably sprinkle some tobacco from his pipe or drop a few grains of rice there. [Guilleminet 1943a: 261-64.] **Dental filing.** The Jarai dental filing technique has been adopted by the Bahnar. It is considered a bad omen if a tooth breaks in the course of the operation. [Maurice 1941: 136.]

BIBLIOGAPHY. Dam Bo 1950; Devereux 1937; Guilleminet 1941, 1943a, 1943b, 1949, 1951-52, 1952, 1960; Hickey 1956-58; Maurice 1941; Parmentier 1951; Thomas 1962.

BOUT

ORIENTATION. **Identification and location.** The only source that notes their existence (Smith 1959: map) locates the Bout east of Kontum in South Vietnam in an area south of the Monom group. **Linguistic affiliation.** Mon-Khmer.

BIBLIOGRAPHY. Smith 1959.

BRAO

Synonyms. *Lave, Love*

ORIENTATION. **Identification.** Brao is the only name reported by Lafont (1962b) and Hoffet (1933: 1). The group is also sometimes referred to as the Love or the Lave. Bitaro (1952: 9-17) refers to the Krung as a subgroup of the Brao. **Location.** A rather large area extending southerly to Voeun Sai in Cambodia, northerly to the northern part of Attopeu province in Laos, easterly to the area of Dak To, westerly to the banks of the Se Kong river. Preference is for slopes at 400 to 800 meters elevation. Some Brao have emigrated across the Mekong into northeastern

Thailand in recent decades, forsaking their forest mountain uplands for lower-lying flat plateau country (Credner 1935a: 164). **Linguistic affiliation.** Mon-Khmer. **Demography.** The total population figure is unknown, but Lafont reports growth in recent times and estimates the Brao in Attopeu province at 9,000. An estimated 3,000 Brao migrated into Cambodia between 1920 and 1930. [Lafont 1962b.]

SETTLEMENT PATTERN AND HOUSING. The traditionally large villages of the Brao, a response to the need to group for security, have tended since the French administration to fission into two to five or sometimes more villages (e.g. Koklak split into ten). This fissioning, partly attributable to French and subsequent national protection against incursions by the Siamese, also stems from internal dissension. [Lafont 1962b.] The typical village centers on the communal house with other houses arranged like spokes of a wheel, the whole enclosed by a fortification. Villages are occupied by and large only during the dry season, as most of the population lives in shelters near the swiddens from the beginning of the rains to the completion of the harvest. [Hoffet 1933: 8-10; Fraisse 1951: 71.]

ECONOMY. The staple crop is upland rice, cultivated in swiddens usually for two years, and diet is supplemented by fishing. A strict division of labor is maintained between the sexes. The Brao produce pottery. [Hoffet 1933: 8; Bitaro 1952: 9-17; Fraisse 1951: 71.]

KIN GROUPS. The kinship system appears to be bilateral (Lafont 1962b; Hoffet 1933: 8; Fraisse 1951: 71).

MARRIAGE AND FAMILY. Among five subgroups noted by Lafont, there was no regulation of marriage; polygyny is practiced (Lafont 1962b; Hoffet 1933: 8; Fraisse 1951: 71).

BIBLIOGRAPHY. Bitaro 1952; Credner 1935a; Fraisse 1951; Hoffet 1933; Lafont 1962b.

BRU

Synonyms. *Baru, B'ru, Leu*

ORIENTATION. **Identification.** Baru (Smith 1959: map) and B'ru, the Vietnamese spelling; sometimes known as Leu (Thomas 1963). **Location.** Discussing the Kalo, Cadière (1940: 101-07) comments that the Bru are farther north, inland from Quang Tri in central Vietnam. **Linguistic affiliation.** Thomas (1962: 5) identifies the Bru language as the Bruan sub-subgroup in the Katuic subgroup of Mon-Khmer. **Demography.** A North Vietnamese source (NNCDT 1959: 245) reports 855 Bru.

BIBLIOGRAPHY. Cadière 1940; NNCDT 1959; Smith 1959; Thomas 1962, 1963.

CAO

ORIENTATION. **Location.** The high basin of the Song Boung river along the watershed between Laos and Vietnam, west of An Diem (Hoffet 1933: 16). **Linguistic affiliation.** Mon-Khmer.

SETTLEMENT PATTERN AND HOUSING. Villages are enclosed by palisades and usually have a large open space in the center. There are some longhouses, but house length is variable (Hoffet 1933: 16).

ECONOMY. Cultivators of upland rice in swiddens (Hoffet 1933: 16).

BIBLIOGRAPHY. Hoffet 1933.

CHAOBON

Synonyms. *Lawa, Niakuoll*

ORIENTATION. **Identification.** Though the people reportedly refer to themselves as the Niakuoll, the Siamese call the group Chaobon, or "hill people." Another name, Lawa, occurs in some Siamese government sources but is, according to Seidenfaden, erroneously used for this group. [Seidenfaden 1958: 121-22.] **Location.** A few villages in Khorat, Chaiyaphum, and Phetchabun provinces east of the Sak river valley in central Thailand. **Linguistic affiliation.** Mon-Khmer. **Demography.** Slightly over 2,000 Chaobon were reported in the 1920s. Seidenfaden believes that the population was formerly much higher. [Seidenfaden 1958: 121-22.] **History and cultural relations.** Credner (1935a: 164) regards the Chaobon as representative, together with the Kui, of an older cultural stratum, one preceding the coming of the Siamese. Contact with the Siamese has been extensive, and many Chaobon till wet rice and live in permanent settlements much as the Siamese do. A few villages still raise rice and maize in hill clearings. [Seidenfaden 1958: 121-22; Credner 1935a: 164.]

ECONOMY. Cultivators of wet rice; swidden agriculture in a few villages (Seidenfaden 1958: 121-22; Credner 1935a: 164).

RELIGION. Former animistic beliefs and practices have in large measure given way to Buddhism adopted from the Siamese (Seidenfaden 1958: 121-22; Credner 1935a: 164).

BIBLIOGRAPHY. Credner 1935a; Seidenfaden 1958.

CHENG

ORIENTATION. **Location.** The plain between the Se Kong and Se Kamane rivers in Laos (Lafont 1962b). **Linguistic affiliation.** Mon-Khmer. **Cultural relations.** Some association with the Oy (Lafont 1962b).

SETTLEMENT PATTERN AND HOUSING. Settlements form a circle centered on the communal house. People live in longhouses constructed on piling (Lafont 1962b).

ECONOMY. Cultivators of wet rice in paddy fields and of upland rice in swiddens (Lafont 1962b).

BIBLIOGRAPHY. Lafont 1962b.

CUA

Synonym. *Khua*

ORIENTATION. **Identification.** Spelled Khua by the Vietnamese. **Location.** Smith (1959: map) and Phillips (1962: map) locate the Cua east and slightly north of Dak Glei in an area inland and northwest of the coastal city of Quang Ngai in central Vietnam. **Linguistic affiliation.** Thomas (1962: 5) classifies the Cua language as part of the Bahnaran sub-subgroup of the Bahnaric subgroup of Mon-Khmer.

BIBLIOGRAPHY. Phillips 1962; Smith 1959; Thomas 1962.

DUANE

ORIENTATION. **Identification.** The only description (Condominas 1951: 13-38) of this and four other groups —Jeh, Menam, Noar, and Sayan—is inconclusive regarding their classification as distinct groups. **Location.** The valley of the upper Song Tranh river in the Laos-Vietnam border area of the Vietnamese province of Quang Ngai (Condominas 1951: 15). **Linguistic affiliation.** Mon-Khmer. **Cultural relations.** Considerable contact with the Jeh, Menam, Noar, Sayan, and Sedang (Condominas 1951: 13-15).

SETTLEMENT PATTERN AND HOUSING. Close-knit villages surrounded by a fortification (Condominas 1951: 18).

ECONOMY. Economic activities resemble those of the Jeh (Condominas 1951: 20-23).

BIBLIOGRAPHY. Condominas 1951.

HALANG

ORIENTATION. **Location.** Along the Se Son river in Attopeu province of southern Laos and Kontum province of Vietnam (Hoffet 1933: 23). **Linguistic affiliation.** Thomas (1962: 5) places Halang in the Bahnaric subgroup of Mon-Khmer.

SETTLEMENT PATTERN AND HOUSING. The settlements have no particular internal orientation, and there may be more than one communal house. Longhouse construction is sometimes found in communal houses; family dwellings are usually square. [Hoffet 1933: 23.]

ECONOMY. Cultivators of upland rice in swiddens and of maize, an important secondary crop, and tobacco. Some basketry, and one village, Dak Kon, specializes in the production of wooden platters which are sold to the Lao. [Hoffet 1933: 23.]

RELIGION. A large pantheon of animistic spirits. At one time construction of a new communal house was inaugurated with a human sacrifice, the victim being crushed beneath the main pillar. [Hoffet 1933: 33.]

BIBLIOGRAPHY. Hoffet 1933; Thomas 1962.

HALANG DOAN

Synonym. *Duan*

ORIENTATION. **Identification.** Sometimes spelled Halang Duan. Lafont (1962b) thinks this group may properly belong to the Jeh and points out that *halang* means "mixed blood." **Location.** Attopeu province in Laos, the Kasseng plateau, and the left banks of the Se Kamane and Dak Robay rivers are principal areas; smaller groups are found in Kontum province in Vietnam (Lafont 1962b). **Linguistic affiliation.** Mon-Khmer. **Demography.** An estimated 1,000 in Attopeu province (Lafont 1962b).

SETTLEMENT PATTERN AND HOUSING. Fortified villages of longhouses built on piling and grouped in an oval around the communal house (Hoffet 1933: 15).

ECONOMY. Cultivators of upland rice in swiddens. There are a few metalworkers, and there is some trading with neighboring groups. [Lafont 1962b; Hoffet 1933: 15.]

BIBLIOGRAPHY. Hoffet 1933; Lafont 1962b.

HRE

Synonyms. *Da Vach, Davak*

ORIENTATION. **Identification.** Smith (1959: map), Thomas (1962: 6), and Phillips (1962: map) agree in identifying the group as the Hre. Bourotte (1955: frontispiece map) refers to the group as the Da Vach or Davak. **Location.** A mountainous area of central Vietnam, inland from the coastal city of Quang Ngai (Smith 1959: map; Phillips 1962: map). **Linguistic affiliation.** Thomas (1962: 6) places Hre in the Bahnaran subgroup of Mon-Khmer. **Demography.** A South Vietnamese source (NCTXH 1960) reports 27,000 Da Vach (Hre).

BIBLIOGRAPHY. Bourotte 1955; NCTXH 1960; Phillips 1962; Smith 1959; Thomas 1962.

JEH

Synonym. *Die*

ORIENTATION. **Location.** The basin of the Poko, Se Kamane, and Dak Main rivers in southern Laos (Hoffet 1933: 21); and the Vietnamese highlands above the town of Dak Sut near the Lao border in Kontum province. **Linguistic affiliation.** Thomas (1962: 5-6) places the Jeh language in the Bahnaric subgroup of Mon-Khmer. **Demography.** The Jeh population of Laos is not recorded. The NCTXH (1960) reports 7,013 Jeh in Kontum province; the NNCDT (1959: 246) estimates a total of 18,000 Jeh.

SETTLEMENT PATTERN AND HOUSING. Some settlements consist of one or two very extensive longhouses 100 to 200 meters in length. These are constructed on piling, and part of the roof can be raised to provide ventilation and light. A central corridor divides the house and gives access to the family rooms on each side. At the center is a communal room. [Hoffet 1933: 21; Condominas 1951: 19.]

ECONOMY. Cultivators of upland rice in swiddens and secondarily of maize, manioc, pineapples, and tobacco. **Hunting.** Small game supplements the diet. **Trade.** Salt, iron, gongs, brass, cloth, and buffalo have prestigious as well as practical value and form the basis of trade within the group. [Hoffet 1933: 21; Condominas 1951: 20-23.]

MARRIAGE AND FAMILY. Village exogamy is the rule. After a marriage has been arranged there is a four-year waiting period during which the man must present monthly gifts to his fiancée and the two must not be left alone together. A symbolic bride-capture is carried out on the eve of the marriage. Residence is patrilocal after an initial residence in a bridal hut,

which is taboo to all but the bridegroom's mother. [Condominas 1951: 23-24.]

SOCIOPOLITICAL ORGANIZATION. The village is the basic political unit. **Social stratification.** Condominas (1951: 24, 32) reports some differentiation according to wealth, but that age is the more important determinant of status in village society.

RELIGION. A wide range of animistic spirits, with the spirit of the sky and the spirit of the earth important deities. Animal sacrifice is practiced. [Lafont 1962b; Hoffet 1933: 21; Condominas 1951: 33.]

BIBLIOGRAPHY. Condominas 1951; Hoffet 1933; Lafont 1962b; NCTXH 1960; NNCDT 1959; Thomas 1962.

KALO

Synonyms. *Ca Lo, Ka Lo*

ORIENTATION. **Identification and location.** Cadière (1940: 101-07) tentatively identifies the Ka Lo or Ca Lo as a group in the central Vietnamese highlands inland from the coastal city of Quang Tri. They are widespread in the northern upland valleys of Quang Tri province, particularly along the route between Mai Lanh and Rao Quan. Cadière speculates as to whether the Kalo are a separate group or a subgroup of the neighboring Bru. **Linguistic affiliation.** Thomas (1962: 5) classifies Kalo as a Mon-Khmer language, closely related to Bru. Specifically he places it in the Bruan group within the Katuic subgrouping. **Contact.** According to Cadière (1940: 101), the Kalo have considerable contact with the coastal Vietnamese as well as with neighboring groups such as the Katu and Bru.

BIBLIOGRAPHY. Cadière 1940; Thomas 1962.

KASSENG

Synonym. *Kaseng*

ORIENTATION. **Identification.** Kasseng is sometimes spelled Kaseng (Hoffet 1933: 14). **Location.** The higher parts of the plateau between Nam Touei and Nam Ang in Muong Chavane of Saravane province, Laos (Lafont 1962b). **Linguistic affiliation.** The Kasseng speak a language of the Mon-Khmer stock. **Demography.** Lafont (1962b) reports around 4,000 Kasseng.

SETTLEMENT PATTERN AND HOUSING. Villages are usually oval in shape, with the houses arranged around the communal house. The settlements are surrounded by walls. The Kasseng have longhouses constructed on piling. [Hoffet 1933: 14.]

ECONOMY. Swidden agriculture. Crops include upland rice, maize, and tobacco. Many Kasseng weave cloth for trade with neighboring groups, particularly those in the vicinity of Chavane. Some villages produce black lacquered shields covered with tin. [Lafont 1962b; Hoffet 1933: 14.]

BIBLIOGRAPHY. Hoffet 1933; Lafont 1962b.

KATANG

Synonym. *Katteng*

ORIENTATION. **Identification.** Katteng (Hoffet 1933: 19). **Location.** The eastern part of Muong Lao Ngam in the *tasseng* of Kham Thong Noy and the northern part of the *tasseng* of Sene Vang Nhay in southern Laos. (Lafont 1962b). **Linguistic affiliation.** Mon-Khmer.

SETTLEMENT PATTERN AND HOUSING. Villages usually consist of a communal house and from two to five longhouses built on piling, all arranged in a square or triangle (Hoffet 1933: 19).

ECONOMY. Cultivators of rice in both swiddens and irrigated paddy fields. Maize is an important secondary crop, and buffalo are kept as draft animals for paddy cultivation. [Lafont 1962b; Hoffet 1933: 19.]

KIN GROUPS. Hoffet (1933: 19) states that the Katang "are patriarchal with matriarchal vestiges" and cites the fact that female breasts are carved on the plank ladder at the entrance to the longhouse.

BIBLIOGRAPHY. Hoffet 1933; Lafont 1962b.

KATU

Synonyms. *Kato, Ka-Tu*

ORIENTATION. **Identification.** Variant spellings are Ka-Tu and, less commonly, Kato. The word *katu*, meaning "savage," is applied by most of the surrounding groups, but the Katu identify themselves by village, i.e. as *monui* (people) from a specific village. [Le Pichon 1938: 359-61; Hickey 1957.] **Location.** The highland interior of central Vietnam over an area extending from behind the coastal cities of Faifo and Tourane (Danang) in Quang Nam province to the border of southern Laos—particularly on the slopes of the valleys along the Song Giang, the Song Cai, and the Song Boung (Le Pichon 1938: 360-61; Hickey 1957). **Geography.** The Katu area is mountainous, thickly forested, and dissected by river valleys whose slopes tend to be rocky. Climate is very warm and humid. [Le Pichon 1938: 359; Hickey 1957.] **Linguistic**

affiliation. Mon-Khmer. No written language and little, if any, literacy in other languages, i.e. Vietnamese or French (Hickey 1957). **Demography.** The population is estimated variously at 25,000 (Le Pichon 1938: 361) and 20,000 (NNCDT 1959). **History and cultural relations.** Most Katu have little contact with outside groups, the exceptions being those on the edge of the territory and those adjacent to the small Vietnamese settlements along the rivers of the coastal plain. Trading involves some individual contact: a few Vietnamese wood dealers go into the Katu area and a few Katu travel to markets in the coastal towns. [Hickey 1957.]

SETTLEMENT PATTERN AND HOUSING. **Settlement pattern.** The typical village, located on a slope to escape the heavy humidity of the valleys, contains anywhere from five to fifty houses arranged in a circle around the communal house and surrounded by a stockade. In a large open space at the middle of the village stands a carved pole—the sacrificial post to which animals are tied during a ritual sacrifice. [Le Pichon 1938: 369-73; Hickey 1957.] **Housing.** A simple structure of bamboo and wood, set on piling and roofed with thatch, is the usual dwelling. A better house will have a central pillar (*tanal*) supporting the frame and, at the roof edge, poles carved to represent animals, men, or phalli. Communal house construction is similar but more elaborate. [Le Pichon 1938: 369-73; Hickey 1957.]

ECONOMY. **Agriculture.** The staple crops, all cultivated in swiddens, are upland rice, manioc, and maize. The Katu also maintain small kitchen gardens. [Le Pichon 1938: 362-67.] **Hunting.** The bulk of the meat in their diet comes from hunting, at which the Katu are adept. Both traps and crossbows, sometimes with poisoned arrows, are used. [Le Pichon 1938: 367.] **Gathering.** Wild fruit, roots, and edible leaves are collected from the forest (Le Pichon 1938: 367). **Domestic animals.** The Katu raise pigs, buffalo, chickens, and, less commonly, goats. Fresh meat is salted and preserved in bamboo tubes, which are warmed by the fire before the meat is served. [Le Pichon 1938: 367.] **Industrial arts.** Crossbows and traps are made locally and there is some weaving (Le Pichon 1938: 364; Hickey 1957). **Trade.** A trading relationship with the Vietnamese brings the Katu iron for their spears, blankets, pots, and much cloth in exchange for wood, betel leaves, and medicinal roots and bark (Le Pichon 1938: 364; Hickey 1957). **Domestics and contract labor.** Well-to-do Katu sometimes have domestics, usually orphans who work and live with the family. At majority the orphan must be sponsored in marriage by his employer and becomes free to depart, but may, and often does, elect to continue residence with his patron. Another kind of domestic is the poor man and his family, who are paid a fixed amount, perhaps a buffalo each year. [Le Pichon 1938: 378.]

KIN GROUPS. Le Pichon (1938: 378) characterizes the Katu family as a *"régime patriarchat."*

MARRIAGE AND FAMILY. Mode. A boy who has selected a girl informs his father, who obtains the services of an intermediary. Sharing a meal on a day during the full moon, the families discuss the bride price, which usually consists of gongs, pots, jars, buffalo, and cloth. The bride price agreed upon, a sorcerer cuts off the foot of a cock, interpreting from the way the claws contract the disposition of the spirits with regard to the marriage. [Le Pichon 1938: 375-77.] A young villager who has led a blood hunt is considered a desirable husband and is apt to be sought after by girls of his own and neighboring villages. Affairs are common, but if a couple is discovered making love in the forest the boy's family must pay the girl's village a fine, customarily a pig or buffalo to be eaten at a communal house feast. In lieu of the fine, should his family be poor, the boy takes the girl to live with him and accepts an obligation to assist her parents whenever required. A girl who becomes pregnant prior to marriage must go into the forest with the boy for six days while their parents agree on the fine the boy's family must pay the village. [Le Pichon 1938: 376.] **Form.** Polygyny is permitted but rare (Hickey 1957). **Residence.** Patrilocal (Hickey 1957). **Domestic unit.** The extended family forms a household and constitutes the fundamental social and economic unit. Married sons and their families live in the paternal house and the whole household cultivates a swidden in common. [Hickey 1957.] **Inheritance.** The father is head of the household and the owner of all family property, viz. the paddy, the house, jars, gongs, animals, and the use of swiddens. The eldest son inherits the bulk of the family property and the other sons divide the rest. [Le Pichon 1938: 378.] **Divorce.** All of the bride price is returned if the wife is the guilty party, half if the husband. In the case of divorce resulting from adultery by the wife, the bride price is forfeit as above and her partner also is fined one or two buffalo. [Le Pichon 1938: 377.]

SOCIOPOLITICAL ORGANIZATION. Political organization. The headman or chief of a village is selected by the elders and may be replaced by the elders if found guilty of having brought misfortune on the village. The administration of justice is one of the most important functions of the chief and of the elders, who resolve problems related to marriage and divorce or to adultery, murder, and other violations of village custom. Village life centers on the communal house, where the feasts, meetings, and sacrificial rituals are held and where the village men like to gather. The bachelors sleep there, and women are not allowed to enter (Le Pichon 1938: 376-79). **Warfare.** Disputes with other vllages are commonly settled by intervillage warfare and the village also acts as a collectivity in avenging a dishonor or crime against an individual by a person from another village, usually by means of a raiding party. [Le Pichon 1938: 376-79.]

RELIGION. Supernaturals. The communal house functions as a village religious center for the worship of a large pantheon of good and evil spirits and is considered the sacred dwelling place of the souls of ancestors who died a good death, as opposed to the violent or "bad" death of victims of murder, enemy raid, tiger attack, etc. The cult of the dead represents an important element in the religion of the Katu, who believe that while every human being has both a good and a bad soul, only the good soul survives after death. [Le Pichon 1938: 391-405; Hickey 1957.] **Ceremonies.** The Katu burial encompasses a whole series of ritual sacrifices and offerings designed to ensure protection for his kinsmen from the soul of the deceased. Human blood sacrifices are still practiced. The victim, selected by the headman and elders from another village, is kidnaped by a raiding party and carried to the forest to be speared to death. The young men of the raiding party then dip their spears in his blood and, leaving the corpse in the forest, return to the communal house for a ritual sacrifice. [Le Pichon 1938: 391-405; Hickey 1957.] **Tattooing.** Most Katu are tattooed, the usual places being the face, chest, arms, wrists, and above and below the knee. A dancing woman on the forehead and a sun motif on the chest or forehead are the most common; some swastika tattoos are found. [Bezacier 1942: 117-25.]

BIBLIOGRAPHY. Bezacier 1942; Hickey 1957; Le Pichon 1938; NNCDT 1959.

KAYONG

Synonyms. *Ca-Rong, Koyong*

ORIENTATION. Identification. Bourotte (1955: frontispiece map) calls this group Koyong; the Vietnamese spelling is Ca-Rong. **Location.** Northeast of the Sedang area near Kontum, South Vietnam (Smith 1959: map; Phillips 1962: map). **Linguistic affiliation.** Thomas (1962: 6) places Kayong in the Bahnaran subgroup of Mon-Khmer.

BIBLIOGRAPHY. Bourotte 1955; Phillips 1962; Smith 1959; Thomas 1962.

LANG YA

ORIENTATION. Identification. Smith (1959), who has visited the area of Lang Ya several times, is the only source reporting the existence of this group.

Location. Smith (1959) locates them on the southern Laos-Vietnam border, northeast of Dak Glei, and north of the area occupied by the Jeh. **Linguistic affiliation.** Mon-Khmer.

BIBLIOGRAPHY. Smith 1959.

LOVEN

Synonym. *Boloven*

ORIENTATION. **Identification.** Sometimes referred to as the Boloven, which actually means "country of the Loven" (Lafont 1962b). **Location.** The Boloven plateau in southern Laos between Paksane and Thateng, with sizable groupings of Loven in the provinces of Champassak, Saravane, and Attopeu (Lafont 1962b; Fraisse 1951: 55). **Linguistic affiliation.** Mon-Khmer. **Demography.** The exact population figure is not reported. Lafont (1962b) estimates that in Muong Paksong, Champassak province, the Loven number some 6,000, or 90 per cent of the population; in Muong Lao Ngam in Saravane province 10,000 persons, or 50 per cent; and in Muong Tha Teng, also in Saravane, 1,000, or 20 per cent. There also are an estimated 1,000 Loven in Attopeu province, which brings the overall total to 18,000. **Contact.** The Loven have had considerable contact with the Lao, and are considered one of the most acculturated of the so-called Kha groups. They have also had contact with Europeans who established plantations on the Boloven plateau, and with Chinese merchants, to whom they sell their coffee. [Lafont 1962b.]

SETTLEMENT PATTERN AND HOUSING. **Settlement pattern.** Hoffet (1933: 28) describes villages of from seven to twelve houses. Some villages are named for local geographical features, others after the group living there (Fraisse 1951: 55). **Housing.** Rectangular houses constructed on piling (Lafont 1962b).

ECONOMY. **Agriculture.** Cultivators of upland rice in swiddens and a wide variety of secondary crops including maize, red peppers, cardamom, yams, and a number of European vegetables, particularly Irish potatoes which were introduced by the French. Potatoes have become a cash crop, sold primarily to the French military at the Seno airbase. The most important cash crop is coffee, grown in estates by methods learned under the French administration. At the present time the Alak and Ta Hoi (Tau-Oi) work as wage laborers on Loven coffee estates. The produce is transported to Pakse and sold to Chinese merchants. **Industrial arts.** The Loven, though not weavers or metalworkers, are considered skilled woodworkers. [Lafont 1962b; Hoffet 1933: 28; Fraisse 1951: 55.]

MARRIAGE AND FAMILY. Marriage follows mutual consent of parties and their parents. No bride price or dowry is given except in the case of a second marriage, when a bride price is paid to the second wife's parents. Residence after marriage is patrilocal. Both parties must consent to divorce, and the children may live with either parent. [Fraisse 1951: 58-59.]

SOCIOPOLITICAL ORGANIZATION. Each village has a headman (*pho ban*), whose responsibilities include officiating at wedding ceremonies, which he seals with a written document (Fraisse 1951: 58).

RELIGION. A wide range of animistic spirits with, according to Lafont (1962b), increasing acceptance of Buddhism: e.g. in 1960 six of thirty-two Buddhist monks in the Paksong area were Loven. **Funerals.** The coffin is left above ground for fear of offending the deceased's spirit, which will become angered if it is buried. Tombs are elaborately decorated with polychrome wood carvings. [Hoffet 1933: 40-43.]

BIBLIOGRAPHY. Fraisse 1951; Hoffet 1933; Lafont 1962b.

MENAM

ORIENTATION. **Identification.** The only description (Condominas 1951: 13-38) of this and four other groups—Duane, Jeh, Noar, and Sayan—is inconclusive regarding their classification as distinct groups. **Location.** The valley of the upper Song Tranh river in the Laos-Vietnam border area of the Vietnamese province of Quang Ngai (Condominas 1951: 15). **Linguistic affiliation.** Mon-Khmer. **Cultural relations.** Considerable contact with the Jeh, Duane, Sayan, and Noar; some contact with the Sedang (Condominas 1951: 13-15).

SETTLEMENT PATTERN AND HOUSING. Close-knit villages surrounded by a fortification. The houses, described as similar to Sedang houses, are usually oriented around a communal house. The typical Menam house is fairly long, has a bell-shaped roof, and stands on low piling. [Condominas 1951: 18.]

ECONOMY. Cultivators of wet rice in paddy fields and of upland rice in swiddens. Medicinal herbs and cinnamon are collected and traded, primarily with the Duane and Noar. [Condominas 1951: 20-23.]

KIN GROUPS. Menam and Jeh kinship systems are very similar (Condominas 1951: 32).

MARRIAGE AND FAMILY. Marriage practices follow the Jeh pattern (Condominas 1951: 32).

SOCIOPOLITICAL ORGANIZATION. According to Condominas (1951: 24-30), the village with its surrounding territory is the basic political unit.

RELIGION. The religious beliefs of the Menam and Jeh are described by Condominas (1951: 35-38) as being very similar.

BIBLIOGRAPHY. Condominas 1951.

MONOM

Synonym. *Bonom*

ORIENTATION. **Identification.** Often referred to as the Bonom (Huard and Maurice 1939: 29; Smith 1959; Thomas 1962: 6; Bourotte 1955). **Location.** All the above sources agree in locating the Monom to the northeast of Kontum town in Vietnam. **Linguistic affiliation.** Thomas (1962: 6) places Monom in the Bahnaran subgroup of Mon-Khmer.

BIBLIOGRAPHY. Bourotte 1955; Huard and Maurice 1939; Smith 1959; Thomas 1962.

NGEH

Synonym. *Nghe*

ORIENTATION. **Identification.** Also known as the Nghe. Lafont (1962b) refers to a subgroup called the Kieng. **Location.** Primarily in Laos, in the *khong* of Thateng in Saravane province. The Kieng subgroup is found in the *tasseng* of Sene Vang Nhay in the Pakse-Saravane area, with some recent settlements east of Muong Lao Ngam in Saravane province. [Lafont 1962b.] **Linguistic affiliation.** Mon-Khmer. **Demography.** Lafont (1962b) reports some 1,000 Ngeh in the vicinity of Thateng in Saravane province but notes this is only part of the total number of Ngeh.

SETTLEMENT PATTERN AND HOUSING. **Settlement pattern.** Houses are arranged in a circle, and the whole village is enclosed (Hoffet 1933: 10). **Housing.** Longhouses built on piling (Hoffet 1933: 10).

ECONOMY. Cultivators of wet rice in irrigated fields and of upland rice in swiddens. The Ngeh also weave cloth. [Lafont 1962b; Hoffet 1933: 10.]

BIBLIOGRAPHY. Hoffet 1933; Lafont 1962b.

NGUNG BO

ORIENTATION. **Location.** About 20 Ngung Bo villages are found along the banks of the Rao Lao and the upper Se Kong in southern Laos (Hoffet 1933: 20-23). **Linguistic affiliation.** Mon-Khmer.

SETTLEMENT PATTERN AND HOUSING. Houses have a communal room in the center and are long, with family rooms opening on a central corridor; part of the roof opens for ventilation (Hoffet 1933: 2-22).

ECONOMY. Cultivators of paddy in irrigated fields as well as of upland rice in swiddens, and also tobacco. Some buffalo are sold to Vietnamese, and the Ngung Bo produce baskets. [Hoffet 1933: 20-23.]

BIBLIOGRAPHY. Hoffet 1933.

NHA HEUN

Synonyms. *Hoen, Nia Hoen*

ORIENTATION. **Identification.** Lafont (1962b) and Hoffet (1933: 18) identify the Nha Heun, also known as the Nia Hoen or simply Hoen. **Location.** An area in southern Laos, in the eastern part of the Boloven plateau near Saravane and Paksong (Hoffet 1933: 18; Lafont 1962b). **Linguistic affiliation.** Mon-Khmer. **Demography.** Lafont (1962b) estimates 3,000.

SETTLEMENT PATTERN AND HOUSING. Lafont (1962b) notes that Nha Heun are seminomads who have only recently had any permanent settlements. There is no particular orientation to their villages and no communal house (Hoffet 1933: 18). Houses are constructed on piling, with a small platform extending from the front (Hoffet 1933: 18).

ECONOMY. Cultivators of upland rice in swiddens and, from the time of French rule, of coffee plants. Animal husbandry is important and domesticated elephants are used as draft animals. The Nha Heun do not weave cloth, purchasing all they need from the Lao. [Lafont 1962b; Hoffet 1933: 18.]

RELIGION. Belief in a wide range of spirits. Hoffet (1933: 18) reports the practice of witchcraft but also notes increasing Buddhist influence.

BIBLIOGRAPHY. Hoffet 1933; Lafont 1962b.

NOAR

ORIENTATION. **Identification.** The only description (Condominas 1951: 13-38) of this and four other groups—Duane, Jeh, Menam, and Sayan—is inconclusive regarding their classification as distinct groups. **Location.** The valley of the upper Song Tranh river in the Laos-Vietnam border area of the Vietnamese province of Quang Ngai (Condominas 1951: 15). **Linguistic affiliation.** Mon-Khmer. **Cultural relations.** There is apparently considerable contact with the Sedang, Jeh, Sayan, Menam, and Duane (Condominas 1951: 13-15).

SETTLEMENT PATTERN AND HOUSING. Close-knit villages surrounded by a stockade (Condominas 1951: 18).

BIBLIOGRAPHY. Condominas 1951.

OY

Synonym. *Oi*

ORIENTATION. **Location.** Their oral history holds that once the Oy occupied the right bank of the Se Kong in Laos, but the arrival of the Lao forced their migration to the slopes of the Boloven plateau in Attopeu province, where the Oy now occupy an area of roughly 120 square kilometers (Lafont 1962b). **Linguistic affiliation.** Mon-Khmer. **Demography.** According to Lafont (1962b), the Oy once numbered around 20,000, but migration, constant raids by Siamese slave hunters, and a violent smallpox epidemic in 1932 have reduced this total to approximately 4,500.

SETTLEMENT PATTERN AND HOUSING. Villages, which vary considerably in size, have no particular orientation and no communal house (Hoffet 1933: 27; Fraisse 1951: 70). The Oy construct bamboo aqueducts to carry water from springs to their villages. **Housing.** Some Oy construct pentagonal houses on low piling; carved wooden decoration in the form of buffalo horns placed on the edge of the roof is common (Lafont 1962b; Hoffet 1933: 27; Fraisse 1951: 70).

ECONOMY. Wet rice, their staple, is cultivated in paddy fields; upland rice, a supplementary source of food, is cultivated in swiddens. They are also actively engaged in animal husbandry. They do not weave cloth. [Lafont 1962b; Hoffet 1933: 27; Fraisse 1951: 70.]

RELIGION. *Kalam* is the Oy system of well-defined taboos (Hoffet 1933: 27; Fraisse 1951: 70). Buddhist influence is strong and Lafont (1962b) reports some Catholic villages.

BIBLIOGRAPHY. Fraisse 1951; Hoffet 1933; Lafont 1962b.

PACOH

Synonyms. *Khas Pakho, Pokoh*

ORIENTATION. **Identification.** Huard and Maurice (1939: 28) indicate a group in the highlands of central Vietnam called the Khas Pakho. Smith (1959) and Phillips (1962) refer to the same group as Pacoh.

Location. The mountainous area inland from Hue (Smith 1959; Phillips 1962). **Linguistic affiliation.** Thomas (1962: 5) places their language in the Bruan sub-subgroup of the Katuic subgroup within the Mon-Khmer stock.

BIBLIOGRAPHY. Huard and Maurice 1939; Phillips 1962; Smith 1959; Thomas 1962.

PHUONG

ORIENTATION. **Identification.** Phillips (1962: map) is the only source that reports the existence of the Phuong. **Location.** In central Vietnam, south of the Pacoh and inland from the city of Hue. **Linguistic affiliation.** The Phuong language is in the Katuan sub-subgroup of the Katuic subgroup within the Mon-Khmer stock.

BIBLIOGRAPHY. Phillips 1962.

RENGAO

Synonyms. *Reungao, Rongao, Ro-ngao*

ORIENTATION. **Identification.** The name of this group is spelled in a variety of ways—Reungao, Rongao, and more recently, Rengao. There has been some disagreement as to whether the Rengao constitute an ethnic group separate from either the Sedang or the Bahnar. Kemlin (1917: 1-119) treated the "Reungao" as a subgrouping of the Bahnar, as did Guilleminet (1941: 12-13; 1952: 7-8); Devereux (1937: 1) considers the Rengao a mixed Sedang-Bahnar group. Dam Bo (1950: 983) discusses them as separate from the Bahnar, with specific references to the "Rongao." **Location.** In the South Vietnamese highlands, in the region of Kontum. **Linguistic affiliation.** In his linguistic analysis of the Mon-Khmer-speaking groups in the southern Vietnamese highlands, Thomas (1962: 5) lists Rengao separately from Bahnar, but puts both in the Bahnaran group of the Bahnaric subgroup of Mon-Khmer. **Demography.** The NCTXH (1960) reports that there are some 2,933 Rengao; the NNCDT (1959: 247) reports 6,000 Rengao (spelled Ro-ngao in Vietnamese).

SETTLEMENT PATTERN AND HOUSING. Settlements resemble those of the Bahnar, with communal or bachelor houses in the center of the village (Dam Bo 1950: 983).

RELIGION. Kemlin (1917: 1-119) points out that alliances contracted among the Reungao Bahnar between individuals and spirits, whether spirits of plants and animals, or guardian spirits, are internal contracts of one's *ion tau* (interior life, soul). There also are alliances between individuals and between warring villages in the form of blood oaths. Father-son alliances are common. A "milk alliance" results from a hex on parents which affects their young children. In order to avoid the effect on a newborn child, the mother will secure a wet nurse, compensating her with jars. Alliances with spirits tend to be more complicated. There are alliances with a variety of spirits, including the spirits of the elements, the spirit of water, the spirit of rice, the spirit of the mountain, and the spirit of war. Alliances also may be made with spirits associated with certain animals, particularly tigers, wild cats and dogs, elephants, bamboo rats, toads, and a wide range of other animals. Spirits associated with plants, such as the bamboo, various fruits, and the sycamore tree are included in alliances.

BIBLIOGRAPHY. Dam Bo 1950; Devereux 1937; Guilleminet 1941, 1952; Kemlin 1917; NCTXH 1960; NNCDT 1959; Thomas 1962.

SAPUAN

Synonym. *Sapouan*

ORIENTATION. **Location.** Areas along the banks of the Se Kong and the lower Se Kamane in Attopeu province of southern Laos. **Linguistic affiliation.** Mon-Khmer. **Demography.** According to Lafont (1962b), the major grouping of Sapuan, in Attopeu province, numbers 800 to 900. **Cultural relations.** The Sapuan have extensive contact with the Lao and are considered very Laoized. Sapuan men often take Lao wives and reside in Lao villages. [Lafont 1962b.]

SETTLEMENT PATTERN AND HOUSING. **Settlement pattern.** Villages are very loose-knit, consisting of farmsteads scattered amidst the paddy fields, sometimes several hundred meters from one another. There are no communal houses. [Hoffet 1933: 26; Lafont 1962b.] **Housing.** Houses are constructed on relatively high piling.

ECONOMY. Irrigated paddy fields. No swiddens reported. Fishing is an important activity and there is some livestock raising. [Hoffet 1933: 26.]

RELIGION. Hoffet (1933: 26) reports strong Buddhist influence.

BIBLIOGRAPHY. Hoffet 1933; Lafont 1962b.

SAYAN

ORIENTATION. **Identification.** The only description (Condominas 1951: 13-38) of this and four other groups—Duane, Jeh, Menam, and Noar—is inconclu-sive regarding their classification as distinct groups. **Location.** The valley of the upper Song Tranh river in the Laos-Vietnam border area of the Vietnamese province of Quang Ngai (Condominas 1951: 15). **Linguistic affiliation.** Mon-Khmer.

SETTLEMENT PATTERN AND HOUSING. Villages tend to be relatively isolated due to the rough terrain and are defended by surveillance of the trails rather than by stockades. There are no communal houses. [Condominas 1951: 18.]

BIBLIOGRAPHY. Condominas 1951.

SEDANG

Synonyms. *Ha(rh) ndea(ng), Xo-dang*

ORIENTATION. **Identification.** Devereux (1937: 1-2) points out that the French called this group Sedang; their own name for themselves is Ha(rh) ndea(ng). Despite dialect differences, the Sedang consider themselves one ethnic group. Devereux indicates only one subgroup, the Danja, noting that while some investigators consider the Rengao as part of the Sedang, they actually are a mixed Sedang-Bahnar group. The NNCDT (1959: 246) refers to the Sedang (Xo-dang in the Vietnamese transcription) and these subgroups (Vietnamese transcriptions): To-drah, or "those who live in the sparse forest," Kmrang, "those who live in the dense forest," Duong, and Cor (also known as the Ta-Cor). Unlike all other sources, the NNCDT also classifies the Ca-Rong (Kayong), Hre, and Halang as subgroups of Sedang. **Location.** The southern Vietnamese highlands northwest of the town of Kontum. **Linguistic affiliation.** Thomas (1962: 5) places Sedang in the Bahnaran group of the Bahnaric subgroup of the Mon-Khmer stock. He also places Rengao in this group. **Demography.** The NNCDT (1959: 246) estimates the Sedang population at 80,000; the NCTXH (1960) reports 57,376. **Contact.** The Sedang have always had considerable contact with the Bahnar and other neighboring indigenous groups, but they reacted violently to the arrival of the French, openly opposing French pacification efforts in the area during the 1930s (Devereux 1937: 1-3).

SETTLEMENT PATTERN AND HOUSING. **Settlement pattern.** Villages, varying in size from three to twenty or more longhouses, usually center on a larger men's house. In addition to being the ritual center of the village and the place where the unmarried young men sleep, the men's house served as the traditional mobilization center for the defense of the village in times of intervillage warfare. There also is a miniature spirit house designed to house visiting spirits. Prior to French pacification, stockades and bamboo lancets were erected around the villages.

[Hickey 1956-58; Devereux 1961.] **Housing.** Long-houses are built on piling although, where the house site slopes, one side may rest on the ground. All houses have an entrance at either end and a ladder leading to a platform where rice is pounded. A common room at one end of the house contains the house hearth; nuclear families occupy separate compartments. There is a cultural division of the interior between the "upper" and "lower" parts of the house. Thus rice, considered particularly sacred, is cooked only in the "upper" part of the house. The cooked rice may then be carried to the "lower" part. [Devereux 1961.]

ECONOMY. **Agriculture.** The Sedang cultivate upland rice in swiddens, using a swidden for around three years, and also practice paddy cultivation where bottom land is available. Millet is an important secondary crop. Kitchen gardens are common and supply maize, onions, yams, sweet potatoes, and a variety of leafy-green vegetables. [Devereux 1937: 4-7; Hickey 1956-58.]**Fishing and hunting.** The Sedang are avid but intermittent hunters and fishermen, using a variety of techniques, including poisoning (Devereux 1937: 3-7). **Domestic animals.** Water buffalo, pigs, dogs, and chickens (Devereux 1937: 6). **Industrial arts.** Iron, which appeared in the Sedang area relatively late, has a sacred aura, e.g. the smith is believed to have some magical power and the soul of a buffalo killed with an iron spear goes to the gods whereas normally, in the case of a bamboo spear, the buffalo's soul accrues to the soul of the man performing the sacrifice (Devereux 1961). Dam Bo (1950: 947) reports that around 70 villages are engaged in ore extraction. Iron workers produce axes, knives, swords, and other weapons which are either bartered or sold for cash. **Division of labor.** Both males and females participate in agricultural activities: men prepare the fields and make the holes with digging sticks, women plant the seeds, and the whole household group participates in harvest. Females cook, weave, care for the children, and assume responsibility for the domestic animals. Any type of woodworking is exclusively male, as is basketry, and the blacksmiths found in some villages are male. Young boys usually are responsible for the buffalo. [Devereux 1961.] **Land tenure.** Dry-rice land belongs to a household collectively and is cultivated by the household group, both male and female, with each member having some claim to produce. Wet-rice fields, maize fields, and kitchen gardens are owned and cultivated by nuclear families. [Devereux 1937: 6; 1961.]

KIN GROUPS. **Kin groups.** The kinship system of the Sedang is bilateral. In each household there is a house chief, a male whose wife is the female ritual chief of the house. Devereux (1937: 6-8; 1961) describes the family unit as parents and unmarried children. Boys actually live in the bachelors' house but sometimes eat at home. Adoption is practiced, although rarely, and any slaves are considered provisional members of the family. The head of the family is "the more forceful of the spouses." Devereux sees kin groupings of any size as being less important than the village or the household, both of which act as a collectivity in meeting the needs of society though kin, whether consanguineal or affinal, retain a special importance. For example, no kinsman—by blood, marriage, or adoption—may consume flesh from an animal paid by a fellow kinsman as a fine since it would be considered "cannibalism." Similarly, kinsmen cannot fine each other with livestock, which would amount to indirect "cannibalism" since the livestock would presumably be eaten. **Kin terminology.** Devereux (1961) gives the following kin terms:

Fa	pa
Mo	no
FaElBr, FaYoBr	taa
FaElSi	meh
FaYoSi	mie
MoElBr	mie (w.s.), meh (m.s.)
MoYoBr	mie (w.s.), mie (m.s.)
MoElSi	cya, meh
MoYoSi	cya, mie
ElSi	na
ElBr	tao, na
YoSi	a (pronounced as in "raw")
YoBr	a (pronounced as in "father")
Parallel cousins	same as siblings
Cross cousins	mae

MARRIAGE AND FAMILY. **Mode.** According to Devereux, lovemaking short of actual intercourse is permissible and routine during childhood and adolescence. A couple discovered or confessing having intercourse must pay the village the fine of a pig and marriages often result from the decision of a couple to marry rather than cohabit and then pay the fine. Although not sanctioned, homosexuality and bestiality are permitted without punishment. [Devereux 1961.] Marriage negotiations are initiated by the boy through his parents and an intermediary. The parents give a feast during which the promise of marriage is announced and both parties drink from the same jar to symbolize the contract. The marriage feast takes place at the groom's house. [Hickey 1956-58.] **Form.** According to Devereux (1961), both polyandry and polygyny are permissible but are very rarely practiced. The first spouse must approve of the new alliance. **Residence.** Ambilocal. According to Devereux (1937: 6-8), the groom who resides in his bride's house must "buy her mother's milk" so as to have his children suckled in that household, and a woman residing with her husband's family must make the same payment. New members of the household automatically become members of the family, sharing in collective ownership and collective activities. There is a desire on the part of both the woman's and man's households to have them reside there so as to have the extra manpower. A couple leaving the household must make a ritual sacrifice and buy their way out of the unit. **Domestic unit.** The extended kin group occupies the house and some Sedang informants contend that at one time Sedang longhouses held as many as 100 residents. Households of 60 or more persons were not uncommon in the 1930s. At the present time the normal household group is about 20 to 30 people. [Hickey 1956-58.] Regarding the cultural division of the longhouse Devereux (1937: 4-6) states: "Only those of the half of the house nearest to the house chief, *kan hngii,* (big one of the house) and to his wife (*ktyin*) or wives and children live in the half of the house having rice-soul (*mahua phae* or soul of shelled rice) and so only they can cook rice. The rest of the house is fed with rice cooked upon the hearth of the house-chief, and their *mahua pla* reside in the hearth-stones of the house-chief (*muhua pla* or soul of the fireplace). The rice souls of the inhabitants of the other half of the house live in their own family fireplaces." Devereux (1937: 4-5) indicates that while the breaking up of a household into two or more households is often envisaged, sometimes along the lines of the "upper house" or "lower house," it seldom actually happens. **Divorce.** Permitted but rare (Devereux 1961). **Birth.** Birth takes place out of doors with the woman kneeling over a shallow pit, steadying herself by clutching an upright bamboo pole and perhaps being held as well by another woman standing behind her. The umbilical cord is not cut until the afterbirth has been expelled and buried. An infant is not suckled immediately and until it is the Sedang consider it something inanimate which may be killed, as might happen in the case of an illegitimate child. **Child rearing.** Older siblings play a major role in the care of infants, and discipline begins early, sometimes taking harsh forms, e.g. a severe punishment is to rub pepper in the eyes, in the vagina, or under the foreskin of the penis. Children are usually given responsibilities at a very early age: a boy of three or four years of age might watch buffalo; small girls carry water, help with cleaning, and begin to care for younger siblings. There are also games, some involving sex-play, for young children. At six, boys may enter the men's house to sleep every night, returning to their respective longhouses for meals. Homosexuality among unmarried males and females is common. At the men's house, boys are taught the arts of hunting and fighting as well as other skills expected of males. [Devereux 1961.]

SOCIOPOLITICAL ORGANIZATION. **Political organization.** According to Devereux (1937: 3-8), the village is in many respects a more important social unit than the family. Thus a household sacrificing a buffalo is expected to invite the whole village, and the evil effects of a sinful individual act are shared by the village as a whole, which will demand appropriate fines for compensation or rituals for expiation. For example, a couple caught in illicit intercourse must pay a fine to the whole village lest the spirits seek revenge on the community. Refusal to pay his fines or atone for his wrongdoing may result in an individual's being forced to leave the village and live in the forest. Membership in the village is reckoned by those who drink from the same water source. The village headman, *kan pley,* represents the village as a collectivity, officiates at village rituals, and is the leader in war. **Alliances.** Intervillage alliances for trading are common, as are alliances between individuals or groups, the latter type being sealed by drinking from a number of jars tied together. Such alliances are often tantamount to a kin relationship (Devereux 1961). The Sedang also enter into alliances with spirits and animals. **Social stratification.** Devereux (1961) describes the following social structure:

Administrative chief, *tyulang,* a position founded by the French
Village headman, *kan pley*
Household chief, *kan hngii,* and chieftainess, *ktyin*
Male or female shamans, *petyao*
Smiths or iron workers, the only village specialists
War slaves and debt slaves
Animals—on the same continuum but subordinate to men (the Sedang believe men can become animals)
Spirits and ghosts

The household chief's wife, the *ktyin,* is ritual leader for many important household rites as well as a series of ceremonies associated with agriculture. The success of the harvest determines her continuance in the latter role, for the Sedang believe that the *ktyin* has a rice-soul which mystically guarantees good rice crops. A bad harvest is interpreted as a sign that the rice-soul of the *ktyin* has become exhausted. The *ktyin* also apparently serves as distributor of uncooked rice in the household. Devereux, discussing an instance of imminent household fissioning, recorded the complaint of one male in favor of fissioning that the *ktyin* did not give his hearth sufficient rice. **Warfare.** Intervillage alliances are based on trade or war agreements, and in the past villages of an area often banded together to make war on other Sedang villages or villages of neighboring groups. Devereux (1937: 2-3) points out that villages allied to fight French attempts to pacify the area in the early 1930s and would even attack another Sedang village known to favor submission to the French.

RELIGION. **Supernaturals.** The Sedang believe that long ago supernatural beings, i.e. gods, and men were equal, but that in time the gods became more powerful and have since exacted tribute from men by intimidation. Gods die as men do and eventually, through a series of metamorphic reincarnations, both men and gods become the same type of ghost. Gods are invited to rituals but are dispersed when their presence is no longer desired by acts designed to annoy them. The most powerful of Sedang supernatural beings are Grandfather and Grandmother Knda, the creators. The *tara,* or thunder gods are harsh and demanding and are of two kinds—one's own and the enemy's. A-Pia, a female being, is a kind of "mistress of animals" who acts toward animals as the thunder gods do toward humans. A trapped animal is thus considered an animal that somehow misbehaved and as punishment was given to humans. A hunted animal is "robbed" from A-Pia and must be paid for with a sacrificial "fine." ● Ghosts are myriad: ghosts of dead people, dead gods, and ghosts of dead ghosts, as well as a ghost who eats his own liver and one ghost with a swordlike edge on the forearm. Ve Kranah, the ancestors, are venerated as those who set the rules by which human behavior should be guided. [Devereux 1961.] **Practitioners.** Devereux (1937: 1-7) mentions shamans in Sedang villages but gives no details. **Cannibalism and human sacrifice.** According to Devereux (1961), the Sedang practiced ritual cannibalism in connection with human sacrifices until a relatively recent date. A transitional practice was to prick a human or sacrifice an animal tied to a ceremonial pole. As of the 1930s, only animals were sacrificed. **Soul.** The term for soul, *mahua,* is sometimes used synonymously with *khiya* (ghost), according to Devereux (1961). Six days after death, the *mahua* leaves the body. The concept of soul among the Sedang is complex and is found in a variety of contexts. In war the soul of a captive belongs to the spirit who aided the capture.

BIBLIOGRAPHY. Dam Bo 1950; Devereux 1937, 1961; Hickey 1956-58; NCTXH 1960; NNCDT 1959; Thomas 1962.

SEK

Synonym. *Saek*

ORIENTATION. **Identification.** Saek (Fraisse 1950b: 333). **Location.** Same as the So, i.e. both sides of the Mekong river in northeastern Thailand and central Laos. The villages described by Fraisse (1950b: 333-48) are in the vicinity of Thakhek town in the Laotian province of Cammon. **Linguistic affiliation.** Mon-Khmer stock. Many Sek also speak Lao (Fraisse 1950b: 333-34). **Cultural relations.** Considerable contact with the Lao; regarded as a very Laoized group (Fraisse 1950b: 333). The So and Sek intermarry a great deal (Fraisse 1950b: 336).

SETTLEMENT PATTERN AND HOUSING. Settlements are described by Fraisse (1950b: 333-35) as being very similar to Lao, even to having small Buddhist pagodas and Lao names. Close resemblance to Lao houses, according to Fraisse (1950b: 333-37). When a house is newly constructed, village elders are invited to enter and wish the inhabitants prosperity and happiness.

ECONOMY. **Agriculture.** The Sek cultivate wet rice in the Lao fashion, and upland rice by the swidden method, growing in addition a variety of tuber plants, red peppers, and cotton (Fraisse 1950b: 335). In Sek villages there are small groves of jackfruit, mango, tamarind, banana, grapefruit, and lime trees (Fraisse 1950b: 335). **Fishing and hunting.** The Sek fish a great deal, using traps of bamboo as well as lines and hand traps, and also hunt wild boar, panthers, civets, wild cocks, and deer (Fraisse 1950b: 335). **Domestic animals.** Buffalo, pigs, and poultry (Fraisse 1950b: 335). **Industrial arts.** Products of home crafts include cloth, which is also dyed, tools for farming, weapons, and rice alcohol (Fraisse 1950b: 335). **Division of labor.** Men do the laborious tasks associated with the farmstead and farm; women weave, assist with the weeding and harvesting, and care for the household (Fraisse 1950b: 335).

KIN GROUPS. After the birth of the first son, the father is referred to teknonymously. [Fraisse 1950b: 336-37.]

MARRIAGE AND FAMILY. **Mode and form.** In both mode and form Sek marriage closely resembles Lao marriage. On the day of the marriage the groom's family slaughters a buffalo, and the bride's family kills a pig. **Residence.** If the boy brings the bride price on the day of the marriage, the girl immediately goes to reside at his paternal house. If the bride price is not paid, the groom resides with his wife's family until it is paid. **Divorce.** Divorce can take place because of adultery, bad treatment, or laziness on the part of the wife. The children have their choice of remaining with the father or mother. Should either remarry, the procedures are the same as for the first marriage. [Fraisse 1950b: 336.]

RELIGION. **Major religions.** Theravada Buddhism is firmly established among the Sek and there is a pagoda in each Sek village (Fraisse 1950b: 333-35). **Indigenous religion.** The Sek have an ancestor cult which has changed considerably since the advent of Buddhism. There also is a guardian spirit for the village and a spirit for each house. Male spirits are *mang pho,* female spirits *mang mi.* There also is an important ritual offering made to *mang bal,* the guardian spirit of the village, at the commencement of the planting season. *Mang dam* are spirits associated with surroundings, i.e. the mountains, rivers, trees, and so forth. [Fraisse 1950b: 336-37.] **Funerals.** Funeral procedure is similar to the Lao. Among the well-to-do the corpse remains in the house several days, and each night there is a Lao-type "love court" for the young people. There is burial or cremation, but no mourning is observed. [Fraisse 1950b: 336.]

BIBLIOGRAPHY. Fraisse 1950b.

SO

ORIENTATION. **Identification.** So is the only name reported, but Fraisse (1950a: 171-74) also identifies So Trong, So Slouy, So Phong, So Tri, and So Makon subgroups. **Location.** Both sides of the Mekong river, i.e. in Thailand and Laos. The villages described by Fraisse (1950a: 171-85) are in the vicinity of Thakhek town in the Laotian province of Cammon. According to Credner (1935a: 164), both So and Sek have immigrated into northeastern Thailand in recent decades, adjusting to Lao culture and gradually giving up their own language. **Linguistic affiliation.** The So are Mon-Khmer-speaking people and, due to contact with the Siamese and Laotion Tai, speak these Tai dialects (Fraisse 1950a: 175). **Cultural relations.** In addition to their extensive relations with the Siamese and the Lao, the So have contact with other upland groups, notably the Sek, with whom there is considerable intermarriage (Fraisse 1950a: 175).

SETTLEMENT PATTERN AND HOUSING. According to Fraisse (1950a: 174), So settlements are more dispersed than Lao settlements, and very loose-knit. **Housing.** Houses, built on low piling, are similar to Lao houses.

ECONOMY. **Agriculture.** The So cultivate wet rice in paddies, using the same techniques as the Lao, and also upland rice in swiddens. Other crops include maize, manioc, yams, cucumbers, pumpkins, gourds, red peppers, bananas, mangoes, tamarinds, sugar cane, pineapples, lemons, limes, guava, grapefruit, oranges, coconuts, areca nuts, tobacco, and cotton. [Fraisse 1950a: 174-76.] **Fishing and hunting.** Fishing is important and there is some hunting, primarily with the crossbow, of the tigers, gaur, panthers, deer, and wild boar found in the vicinity of the village (Fraisse 1950a: 175-76). **Domestic animals.** Buffalo are raised as draft animals, pigs and poultry for food (Fraisse 1950a: 176). **Industrial arts.** The So weave much of their cloth, make their own baskets and crossbows, and do some blacksmithing (Fraisse 1950a: 176-77). **Trade.** The So barter goods with the Sek as well as with the Siamese and Lao, exchanging produce and animals with the latter two groups for manufactured goods, clothing, and salt (Fraisse 1950a: 176-77). **Division of labor.** Men clear the swiddens, prepare the fields for planting, and construct houses and fences; women weed the fields, aid with the harvest, and do most of the trading (Fraisse 1950a: 176). **Land tenure.** Paddy fields are privately owned, and individual claims for the swiddens are established by a stick

on which some grass has been tied in a unique way for each claimant. [Fraisse 1950a: 176.]

KIN GROUPS. According to Fraisse (1950a: 173), the father has considerable authority in the family.

MARRIAGE AND FAMILY. **Mode and form.** The boy must pay a bride price, and there is a symbolic marriage-by-capture prior to the marriage ritual proper. Monogamy is the most common form of marriage, and there are few cases of polygyny. Residence is patrilocal. Fraisse reports that the nuclear family appears to be the most common domestic unit. [Fraisse 1950a: 172-73.] **Divorce.** Grounds include laziness of the wife in her household duties, cruelty by either spouse, adultery, lack of respect manifest by either spouse for parents-in-law, and mutual consent to separate. Where culpability can be fixed, the children remain with the innocent party. [Fraisse 1950a: 173.]

SOCIOPOLITICAL ORGANIZATION. The village appears to be the most important political unit. Fraisse (1950a: 176-77) mentions some terms such as *pho ban* (similar to the Lao term) to indicate the village headman. The So subgroups appear to be relatively separate from one another. [Fraisse 1950a: 175.]

RELIGION. **Major religions.** Some So adhere to Theravada Buddhism, but these So, being too few to support their own pagodas, attend those of the neighboring Laotian Tai (Fraisse 1950a: 171-72). **Indigenous religion.** According to Fraisse (1950a: 171-73), the cult of the ancestors is predominant and most houses have a small ancestral spirit house close by. Illness is attributed to ancestral spirits, who must be placated by specially prescribed offerings. Those who die of illness are cremated; those who die of old age are buried. In addition there is a guardian spirit in each village and numerous spirits associated with the forces of nature. Ritual offerings for spirits are common, the most prestigious sacrificial animal being the buffalo. [Fraisse 1950a: 175-80.]

BIBLIOGRAPHY. Credner 1935a; Fraisse 1950a.

SORK

ORIENTATION. **Location.** A plain bordering the banks of the Se Kong and the lower Se Kamane in Attopeu province of southern Laos (Lafont 1962b). **Linguistic affiliation.** Mon-Khmer. **Demography.** Lafont (1962b) estimates 500 to 600 Sork. **Cultural relations.** Considerable contact with the Sapuan (Lafont 1962b).

SETTLEMENT PATTERN AND HOUSING. Settlements are dispersed, consisting of farmsteads scattered throughout the paddy fields (Lafont 1962b).

ECONOMY. The Sork have irrigated paddy fields (Lafont 1962b).

BIBLIOGRAPHY. Lafont 1962b.

SOU

Synonym. *Souk*

ORIENTATION. **Identification.** Hoffet (1933: 17) refers to this group as the Souk. **Location.** The plain at the confluence of the Se Kong and Se Kamane rivers in Attopeu province in Laos (Lafont 1962b). **Linguistic affiliation.** Mon-Khmer. **Demography.** Total population is unknown. Lafont (1962b) estimates 1,000 in Attopeu province, commenting further that their birth rate is relatively low and that many died in 1932 and 1944 epidemics. **Cultural relations.** According to Lafont (1962b), the Sou are very Laoized.

SETTLEMENT PATTERN AND HOUSING. Small string settlements along the river banks are usual. Longhouses are constructed on piling. [Hoffet 1933: 17.]

ECONOMY. The Sou cultivate rice in paddy fields and swiddens. Fishing is important, and there is some metalworking. [Hoffet 1933: 17; Lafont 1962b.]

MARRIAGE AND FAMILY. Lafont (1962b) reports that there is no polygyny and that marriages are normally between persons of the same village, indicating some village endogamy.

RELIGION. The Sou believe in a wide range of animistic spirits (Hoffet 1933: 17; Lafont 1962b).

BIBLIOGRAPHY. Hoffet 1933; Lafont 1962b.

SOUEI

ORIENTATION. **Location.** Primarily in Muong Lao Ngam and in the vicinity of Thateng in Saravane province of southern Laos. **Linguistic affiliation.** Mon-Khmer. **Demography.** Lafont (1962b) reports that the Souei constitute 40 per cent of the Muong Lao Ngam population, i.e. about 8,000, and in the *khong* of Thateng number between 500 and 600, or some 10 per cent of the population. **Cultural relations.** The Souei have had considerable contact with the Lao and are regarded as a very Laoized group. In the vicinity of Thateng they are actually considered Lao. [Lafont 1962b; Hoffet 1933: 29.]

SETTLEMENT PATTERN AND HOUSING. Houses are constructed on piling and tend to resemble Lao dwellings (Lafont 1962b).

ECONOMY. Wet rice in irrigated paddy fields and upland rice in swiddens. Trade is conducted with the Lao. [Lafont 1962b.]

RELIGION. Lafont (1962b) notes that the Souei have a syncretic combination of Buddhism and spirit cults, though some villages are now primarily Catholic.

BIBLIOGRAPHY. Hoffet 1933; Lafont 1962b.

TAU-OI

Synonym. *Ta Hoi*

ORIENTATION. **Identification.** Hoffet (1933: 12) and Lafont (1962b) refer to this group as Ta Hoi while Thomas (1962: 6) calls them Tau-Oi. **Location.** The Laotian province of Saravane as well as the mountainous area inland from the Vietnamese coastal city of Quang Tri (Lafont 1962b; Phillips 1962: map). **Linguistic affiliation.** Thomas (1962: 6) classifies Tau-Oi as a language of the Bruan sub-subgrouping of the Katuic subgroup within the Mon-Khmer stock. **Demography.** The NNCDT (1959: 246) reports 6,000; the NCTXH (1960) reports 11,000.

SETTLEMENT PATTERN AND HOUSING. **Settlement pattern.** Villages are usually circular, with the communal house at the center and the other houses arranged like spokes on a wheel, and are fortified (Lafont 1962b). **Housing.** Longhouses constructed on piles (Hoffet 1933: 12).

ECONOMY. Upland rice in swiddens. Fishing is important; there is some basketry; and a few Tau-Oi work as wage laborers. [Hoffet 1933: 12; Lafont 1962b.]

RELIGION. The Tau-Oi believe in a wide range of spirits associated with natural surroundings. Some villages on the Pakse–Paksong route have been converted to Catholicism. [Lafont 1962b.]

BIBLIOGRAPHY. Hoffet 1933; Lafont 1962b; NCTXH 1960; NNCDT 1959; Phillips 1962; Thomas 1962.

THAP

ORIENTATION. **Location.** East of the Cao in the An Diem hinterlands of southern Laos (Hoffet 1933: 28). **Linguistic affiliation.** Mon-Khmer.

SETTLEMENT PATTERN AND HOUSING. There is no particular orientation to Thap settlements; not all villages have communal houses; only some Thap houses are constructed on piling (Hoffet 1933: 28).

ECONOMY. Upland rice in swiddens, with maize an important secondary crop. Betel leaf is collected for sale to the Vietnamese. [Hoffet 1933: 28.]

BIBLIOGRAPHY. Hoffet 1933.

THE

ORIENTATION. **Identification.** Lafont (1962b) feels that the The may properly be a subgroup of the Oy who are still resisting assimilation. **Location.** The slopes of the southeastern area of the Boloven plateau in Attopeu province in southern Laos (Lafont 1962b). **Linguistic affiliation.** Mon-Khmer. **Demography.** Lafont (1962b) reports that there are still around 1,500 The in Attopeu province of southern Laos despite an epidemic in 1944 that reduced the adult population by about 20 per cent.

RELIGION. The The believe in a wide variety of animistic spirits and give a prominent role to sorcerers (Lafont 1962b).

BIBLIOGRAPHY. Lafont 1962b.

VEN

Synonym. *Veh*

ORIENTATION. **Identification.** The group is called Veh by Hoffet (1933: 25). **Location.** East of Honei Vi in southern Laos (Hoffet 1933: 25). **Linguistic affiliation.** Mon-Khmer (Hoffet 1933: 25).

SETTLEMENT PATTERN AND HOUSING. Ven villages, each enclosed by a wall, consist of clusters of farmsteads (Hoffet 1933: 25).

ECONOMY. The Ven cultivate upland rice in swiddens and raise some livestock (Hoffet 1933: 25).

BIBLIOGRAPHY. Hoffet 1933.

SOUTHEAST UPLAND GROUPS

CHRAU

ORIENTATION. **Identification and location.** Bourotte (1955: 5) notes the existence of an ethnic group called the Chrau in the southernmost part of the Annam Cordillera between Phan Thiet and Bien Hoa, northeast of Saigon in South Vietnam. Thomas (1962: 6) further identifies as small groups either closely related or actual subgroups of Chrau—the Ro, Bajieng, Mru, Jre, Buham, Bu-Preng, and Bla. **Linguistic affili-** ation. Thomas (1962: 6) places the Chrau linguistically with the Stiengan group in the Bahnaran subgroup of the Mon-Khmer stock.

BIBLIOGRAPHY. Bourotte 1955; Thomas 1962.

KIL

Synonyms. *Chil, Cil, Mnong Kil*

ORIENTATION. **Identification.** The Kil are sometimes called the Cil or the Chil (Thomas 1962: 6). Huard and Maurice (1939: 29) refer to this group as Mnong Kil, a subgroup of the Mnong. **Location.** Northeast of Dalat, between the Lat and northern Raglai groups, in South Vietnam (Phillips 1962; Queguiner 1943: 395). **Linguistic affiliation.** Thomas (1962: 6) places the Kil in the Koho grouping which is part of the Stiengan subgrouping of the Mon-Khmer stock. **Demography.** The NCTXH (1960) reports 10,837.

ECONOMY. **Agriculture.** The Kil cultivate upland rice by the swidden method, often leasing their land from the neighboring Churu, who prefer bottom land for paddy cultivation (Gourou 1945: 455). **Hunting and gathering.** Both necessary for sustenance (Dam Bo 1950: 1003). **Industrial arts.** The Kil are known as adept basket makers (Dam Bo 1950: 1003).

BIBLIOGRAPHY. Dam Bo 1950; Gourou 1945; Huard and Maurice 1939; NCTXH 1960; Phillips 1962; Queguiner 1943; Thomas 1962.

LAT

ORIENTATION. **Identification and location.** On Queguiner's ethnic map of the Dalat-Djiring area (1943: 395), the Lat are located in the vicinity of Dalat, South Vietnam, as shown also on Bourotte's map (1955). **Linguistic affiliation.** Thomas (1962: 6) places Lat within the Koho group in the Stiengan sub-subgroup of the Bahnaran subgroup within the Mon-Khmer stock. **Demography.** The NNCDT (1959: 246) reports a combined total of 10,000 for the Lat, Nop, Co Don, To-La, and La-Gia.

BIBLIOGRAPHY. Bourotte 1955; NNCDT 1959; Queguiner 1943; Thomas 1962.

LAYA

Synonym. *La-Gia*

ORIENTATION. **Identification.** Thomas (1962: 6) calls this group the Laya, and a North Vietnamese source (NNCDT 1959: 246) calls them the La-Gia

(Vietnamese transcription for Laya). **Location.** South Vietnam, inland from Phan Thiet. **Linguistic affiliation.** Thomas (1962: 6) places Laya within the Koho group, a Stiengan dialect of the Bahnaran subgroup of Mon-Khmer. **Demography.** A North Vietnamese source (NNCDT 1959: 246) reports a collective figure of 10,000 for the Laya (La-Gia), Nop, Co Don, Lat, and To-La.

BIBLIOGRAPHY. NNCDT 1959; Thomas 1962.

MA

Synonym. *Cau Ma*

ORIENTATION. **Identification.** The Ma are sometimes referred to as Cau Ma (Boulbet 1957: 117). The NNCDT (1959: 247) lists as subgroupings the Ma To, Ma Ro, and Ma Sop, which are also known as the Cho To, Cho Ro, and Cho Sop respectively. Phillips (1962) considers the Sop a separate group. **Location.** Both banks of the elbow of the Upper Donnai in South Vietnam, at approximately 11° 50′ N. and 107° 50′ E. The country on the left bank consists of thick forests, high mountains, small valleys, and savanna. Game abounds on the right bank, on the small plateaus and hill crests where vegetation is not as dense. The fertile valley at the bend or elbow of the Upper Donnai is the heart of the Ma country. [Boulbet 1957: 117-24; 1960a: 545-74.] **Linguistic affiliation.** Thomas (1962: 6) classifies Ma in the Koho sub-subgroup of the Stiengan subgroup of Mon-Khmer. **Demography.** The NCTXH (1960) reports 21,490 Ma; the NNCDT (1959: 247) 30,000.

SETTLEMENT PATTERN AND HOUSING. **Settlement pattern.** The form of Ma settlements varies according to the physical surroundings. Usually they are located near water courses. On the left bank of the Upper Donnai the hill-slope villages are comprised of dispersed farmsteads with their swidden fields nearby. On the bottom land along the banks of the Donnai, Ma settlements are clustered, with paddy fields around them. [Boulbet 1957: 120-23.] **Housing.** On the right bank of the Upper Donnai some longhouses are constructed on piling, some rest on the ground. Despite variations, the floor plans are similar. Palm fronds and thatching are used extensively in house construction. [Boulbet 1957: 122.]

ECONOMY. **Agriculture.** Rice is the staple crop among the Ma. In the bottom land along the river banks it is cultivated by the wet-rice method, on the slopes by the swidden technique. [Boulbet 1957: 117-24; 1960a: 546-47.]

KIN GROUPS. According to Boulbet (1957: 154-57), the Ma family is patriarchal. Authority rests with the father, and property is transmitted through the male line. Guilleminet (1952: 98) and Boulbet (1960b: 629) mention the existence of clans, some of which are more powerful than others.

MARRIAGE AND FAMILY. **Mode.** A bride price is paid prior to the marriage, and should either party break the engagement, he or she must pay compensation to the other. **Form.** Polygyny is found among chiefs and the wealthy. The first wife is the senior and must approve of the second and subsequent wives, for whom a bride price must be paid. **Extension of incest taboos.** Patrilateral cross-cousin marriage (father's sister's daughter) is preferred, while matrilateral cross-cousin marriage (mother's brother's daughter) is forbidden. **Residence.** Prescribed postmarriage residence is patrilocal. Exceptions occur when the groom is too poor to pay the bride price and takes up residence with his parents-in-law for a service period. When a poor man marries a girl from a well-to-do family, he may be adopted into that family, and his family receives a dowry. [Boulbet 1957: 150-61.] **Divorce and inheritance.** In the event of divorce, the eldest son remains with the father. On the death of the father, the eldest son inherits prerogatives and property. Should he be too young, a brother of the father or one of the father's male parallel cousins inherits them instead. A widow may return to her paternal family on repayment of part of the bride price. If she remarries, the entire bride price must be repaid. [Boulbet 1957: 154-55.]

SOCIOPOLITICAL ORGANIZATION. Boulbet (1957: 140) tends to agree with Maitre's suggestion that at one time the Ma people were united as one political group, with some hierarchical stratification. At the present time, several villages may be united under the leadership of one chief, and chiefs are drawn from well-to-do families. Prior to the pacification of the Ma in 1937, warfare was endemic. Prisoners of war were made slaves, and female prisoners often were adopted into the family of the captor. There also were bond slaves. [Boulbet 1957: 136-40.]

RELIGION. Like other highland groups, the Ma believe in a pantheon of *yang* or spirits, to which buffalo are offered in sacrificial rituals. At some of these rituals, which last several days, each family is represented by a *pua krong* who acts as intermediary between the family and the *yang*. [Boulbet 1960b: 627-50.]

BIBLIOGRAPHY. Boulbet 1957, 1960a, 1960b; Guilleminet 1952; NCTXH 1960; NNCDT 1959; Phillips 1962; Thomas 1962.

MNONG

Synonyms. *Mnong Gar, Phii Bree*

ORIENTATION. **Identification.** In describing the Mnong Gar, or Phii Bree as they refer to themselves, Condominas (1957: 13-19) mentions other Mnong groups—Mnong Cil, Mnong Rlam, Mnong Prong—and in an earlier work on the Mnong Rlam (1955b: 127-30) referred to the Mnong Kuen and Mnong Dlie Rue. Huard and Maurice (1939: 28-35) list the Mnong Gar, Mnong Kil, Mnong Rlam, Mnong Preh, Mnong Bunor, Mnong Kpreng, Mnong Budong, and Biet. Jouin (1949: 167) reports subgroupings and groupings within them. The Bu Nor are a grouping within the Nong or Dih subgrouping while the Preh are divided into the Preh Rlam, which in turn is divided into the Bu Rung and Dih Brih groups, the Prong or R'but, and the Bu Dong. The Mnong Gar are divided into the Gar Cu and the Rlam. The Mnong Kuen have no subgroups. **Location and contact.** The Mnong are located in the mountainous thickly forested area between the towns of Ban Me Thuot and Dalat in the southern highlands of Vietnam. In the district of Lac, the Mnong Rlam occupy a swampy area in close contact with the Rhadé; the Mnong Bunor and groups in the western part of the area have contact with the Stieng; the Mnong Kil, at high elevations closer to Dalat, have contact with the Raglai to the east. [Jouin 1949: 165-66; Huard and Maurice 1939: 28-35.] **Linguistic affiliation.** Thomas (1962: 6) classifies Mnong (including languages of the Pnong, Biet, Gar, Preh, Rolom, Nong, Bunur, and Rohong subgroupings) in the Stiengan grouping of the Mon-Khmer stock. **Demography.** Jouin (1949: 167) reports 16,496 Mnong; the NCTXH (1960), 15,876; the NNCDT (1959: 247), 40,000.

SETTLEMENT PATTERN AND HOUSING. **Settlement pattern.** Since the topography in the Mnong area varies considerably, the size and form of settlements also vary. Huard and Maurice (1939: 45) describe a Nong village on a valley slope of three longhouses arranged in a triangle, with the immediately adjoining land leveled and planted to tobacco. Condominas (1955b: 127-28) notes that the Mnong Rlam villages, collections of longhouses with attached gardens, closely resemble Rhadé villages though the Mnong Rlam do not orient their houses on a north-south axis. Condominas (1957: 16-19) also describes a Mnong Gar village, Sar Luc, in which nine longhouses, several being forty meters in length, house a population of 146, who collectively cultivate some fruit trees and keep a clearing around the village as a precaution against tigers. Footpaths connect the Mnong villages and log and bamboo suspension bridges are built over ravines and streams (Huard and Maurice 1939: 86-91). **Housing.** Nong houses, varying between 10 and 100 meters in length, have a wood framework, bamboo walls and interior partitions, and thatched roofs which reach almost to the ground. Some variation is discernible among different Mnong groups, e.g. in placement of entrances. The Biet entrance is at one end of the house, the Preh, in the middle of the long side, and some Nong houses have two entrances. ● A house, though customarily constructed on the ground, may have one end on piling if located on a hillside (Huard and Maurice 1939: 49-79). Condominas (1957: 16-21) describes Mnong Gar houses as having rounded ends, a narrow slit in the wall for entrance, and a massive thatched gabled roof reaching to within 60 centimeters of the ground. The interior is divided into compartments, each housing a nuclear, or sometimes polygynous, family with its own hearth. There is a large room at each end of the house, one usually the granary, and pigsties on piling can be found near the house. Mnong Rlam houses, by contrast, are constructed on piling with large log frameworks and a platform extending from the entrance at one end (Condominas 1955b: 129). A variety of temporary shelters for hunting or gathering in the forest are used by the Mnong as well as provisory houses near their swiddens (Huard and Maurice 1939: 50-57).

ECONOMY. **Agriculture.** The Mnong Gar cultivate upland rice, the dietary staple, in swiddens which are chosen by divination and given identifying names, e.g. the village swidden cultivated during Condominas' research was called the Forest of the Stone Spirit Goo. The process of cutting, burning, and cultivating the swidden, used for one year only, is described by the Mnong Gar as "eating the forest." [Condominas 1957: 201-34.] The Mnong Rlam in the district of Lac also practice paddy cultivation, producing two crops annually (Condominas 1955b: 129). Secondary crops include maize, bananas, beans, eggplant, manioc, taro, yams, sugar cane, cucumbers, gourds, oranges, mangoes, limes, papayas, red chili peppers, ginger, and mushrooms, as well as some cotton, indigo, and tobacco. The most common implements are a wooden digging stick, an iron hoe, an ax, an adze, and a chopping knife. [Condominas 1957: 21-24.] The Mnong Rlam use a plow in their paddy cultivation (Condominas 1955b: 128-30). **Domestic animals.** Pigs, dogs, ducks, cats, goats, horses, elephants, and buffalo are raised (Condominas 1955b: 19, 22, 84, 100-14, 147). **Fishing and hunting.** Both activities are important among all Mnong groups, but the Mnong Gar are particularly adept at hunting and have devised numerous techniques for catching river fish (Condominas 1957: 45-53, 180-214). **Gathering.** Important among the Mnong Gar, who collect bamboo shoots, mint, and saffron (Condominas 1957: 22-23). **Industrial arts.** Weaving is an art among most Mnong groups, who cultivate their own cotton for the purpose and make dyes from cultivated as well as wild roots. Weaving techniques vary somewhat from group to group. [Huard and Maurice 1939: 91-113; Condominas 1957: 20-23.] Basketry and iron-working are widespread among all Mnong groups, and villagers make jewelry, including neck pieces and ivory ear plugs, as well as musical instruments for their own use (Huard and Maurice 1939: 124-46; Condominas 1955b: 128-31; 1957: 19-22). The Mnong Gar produce such weapons as crossbows, arrows, lances, and machetes (Condominas 1957: 21, 24-41, 48-52, 63-64). **Trade.** The Mnong Gar trade pigs and poultry for buffalo with the Mnong Rlam and the Mnong Lac, both in the district of Lac, and exchange produce, or cash, for highly valued salt, jars (for producing jar wine or for their own prestige value), and cloth with Chinese and Vietnamese merchants in the highland towns of Dalat and Ban Me Thuot (Condominas 1957: 22). The Mnong Rlam, who do not weave cloth, purchase it from neighboring groups, particularly the Mnong Gar and Rhadé (Condominas 1955b: 130). **Division of labor.** Among the Mnong Gar, swidden clearing, hunting, basketry, and iron-working are male activities. The women plant seeds, gather in the forest, and weave. Both harvesting and fishing are joint activities. [Condominas 1957: 21-22, 28-29, 171-72.]

KIN GROUPS. **Descent.** The Mnong Gar have matri-lineal descent and also matrisibs (*mpool*). The Mnong Rlam also have matrilineal descent (Condominas 1955b: 129). **Kin terminology.** Mnong Gar cousin ter-minology follows the Crow pattern (Condominas 1960: 15-23):

MoYoSi, FaYoSi, FaElSiDa, and all female members of mother's sib younger than mother	*mei eet*
MoElBr, MoElSi, FaElBr, FaElSi	*baap eet*
MoBr, MoSi, FaBr, FaSi, and all members of mother's sib older than mother	*waa*
MoYoBr and all males of mother's sib of same generation and generation younger than mother	*koony*
MoYoBr, MoYoBrDa	*koon koony*
FaYoBr, FaElSiSo, and their sons	*baap eet*

MARRIAGE AND FAMILY. **Mode.** Gifts are ex-changed, the groom's family giving the greater amount. **Form.** Monogamy predominant. Sororal po-lygyny, whereby a man may marry his wife's younger sister, is found but only among the well-to-do. [Condominas 1960: 15-23.] **Extension of incest taboos.** Mnong Gar matrisibs are exogamous and there is pref-erential matrilateral cross-cousin marriage with the mother's younger brother's daughter. **Residence.** Mat-rilocal residence is customary among the Mnong Gar, but patrilocal residence becomes the rule if the bride's family is poor (Condominas 1960: 15-23).

Among the Mnong Rlam the newly married couple live with either parents until the husband con-structs a new house (Condominas 1955b: 129). **Do-mestic unit.** Among both the Mnong Gar and the Mnong Rlam the nuclear family is the domestic unit, living in a compartment of the longhouse allied with other nuclear families by ties of friend-ship and/or kinship. A polygynously married woman may have a separate compartment. The compo-sition of the longhouse does not remain constant and is almost certain to change on the rare occasions when the village is moved. [Condominas 1955b: 129; 1960: 15-23.] **Inheritance.** Rights to use of swiddens are held by the individual nuclear family. On the death of the husband, goods acquired after the mar-riage are divided among the children and the wife or, should she be dead, her family. Property brought to the marriage by the husband is returned to his family. [Condominas 1957: 125, 286-87.]

SOCIOPOLITICAL ORGANIZATION. **Political or-ganization.** The village is the main political unit among the Mnong Gar. The "sacred men in the forest and in the village" are responsible for the dis-tribution of cultivable plots in the swiddens as well as for supervision of land ownership and the perform-ance of the principal rituals, especially those for the spirit of rice. **Social stratification.** Wealth distinctions are important and are measured by the number of buffalo sacrificed by a man. Slavery exists and the son of a slave is born a slave, but it is possible for a slave to gain the status of freeman [Condominas 1957: 22-23, 28, 34-35, 111, 144, 151, 235-36.] **Warfare.** Among the Mnong Gar there is a type of warfare as-sociated with unpaid debts or sorcery which usually takes the form of a raid by a small armed band on another village, ambush in the forest, or nocturnal kidnapping (Condominas 1957: 95, 180, 348, 361-62, 443-44).

RELIGION. **Indigenous religion.** The Mnong Gar be-lieve in a large pantheon of spirits (*yang*) associated with inanimate objects, topographical features, and ancestors. There are paddy spirits, spirits of the soil, water spirits, and spirits associated with fire, forest, stones, sites, paths, the moon, and the sun. There also are hero's spirits and special deities associated with bears, dragons, tigers, and mythical birds. Some spirits are thought to be the cause of illness and other mis-fortune, and there are rituals for all spirits. Each family has its own magic plants for which there are rituals during the planting cycle. **Practitioners.** Sor-cerers (*caak*) play an important role in Mnong Gar so-ciety. **Illness and medicine.** Illness is attributed to both spirits and sorcerers. There are shamans (*njau*) who function as medicine men, effecting cures and officiating at certain rituals. [Condominas 1957: 56, 128, 133, see further citations in Condominas' index un-der *sorcellerie* and *chamane*.] **Ceremonies.** The Mnong have numerous rituals, many of which involve sacrificing animals, particularly buffalo. There are agrarian sacrifices associated with swidden cultivation, sacrifices consecrating goods and individuals, exorcisms, sacrifices to propitiate spirits causing ailments, as well as sacrifices for purification, welcoming, and protection. There also are a series of rituals associated with funerals or more specifically with the preparation of the corpse, the placement of the corpse in the bier with some personal effects, the arrangement of the tomb, and the subsequent abandonment of the tomb. [Condominas 1955b: 127-39; 1957: see index under *les types de sacrifices;* Jouin 1949: 165-204.]

BIBLIOGRAPHY. Condominas 1955b, 1957, 1960; Huard and Maurice 1939; Jouin 1949; NCTXH 1960; NNCDT 1959; Thomas 1962.

NOP

Synonyms. *Noup, To Lop*

ORIENTATION. **Identification.** Sometimes spelled Noup (Dam Bo 1950: 961). According to a North Vietnamese source (NNCDT 1959: 246) they are also known as the To Lop. **Location.** In Queguiner's (1943: 395) and Boulbet's (1957: 1) ethnic maps of the Dalat-Djiring area, the Nop are located southwest of Djiring town in South Vietnam. **Linguistic affiliation.** Thomas (1962: 6) identifies the Nop as one of the Koho, a linguistic cluster of the Stiengan sub-subgrouping of the Bahnaric languages within the Mon-Khmer stock. **Demography.** The NNCDT (1959: 246) lists a combined total of 10,000 for the Nop, Lat, Co Don, To-La, and La-Gia groups.

BIBLIOGRAPHY: Boulbet 1957; Dam Bo 1950; NNCDT 1959; Queguiner 1943; Thomas 1962.

PRU

ORIENTATION. **Identification and linguistic affiliation.** Thomas (1962: 6) reports that the Pru belong to the Koho group of the Stiengan sub-subgrouping in the Bahnaran subgroup within the Mon-Khmer stock. **Location.** On Phillips' map (1962) the Pru are located in South Vietnam south of Djiring town and west of the Nop.

BIBLIOGRAPHY. Phillips 1962; Thomas 1962.

RIEN

Synonym. *Riong*

ORIENTATION. **Identification.** Only Thomas (1962: 6) definitely identifies this group. **Location.** Phillips (1962) places the Rien in South Vietnam southwest of

Dalat near the Sre and the Ma. **Linguistic affiliation.** Thomas (1962: 6) assigns Rien to the Koho group of the Stiengan sub-subgroup of the Bahnaric subgroup within the Mon-Khmer family.

BIBLIOGRAPHY. Phillips 1962; Thomas 1962.

SOP

ORIENTATION. **Identification.** Considered a unique group only by Thomas (1962: 6); classified as a subgroup of the Ma in the NNCDT (1959: 346). **Location.** Bourotte (1955) locates the Sop northwest of Djiring on the Dong Nai river in the southern Vietnamese highlands. **Linguistic affiliation.** Thomas (1962: 6) places Sop in the Koho group of the Stiengan sub-subgroup of the Bahnaran subgroup within the Mon-Khmer stock.

BIBLIOGRAPHY. Bourotte 1955; NNCDT 1959; Thomas 1962.

SRE

Synonym. *Cau Sre*

ORIENTATION. **Identification.** The Sre or Cau Sre are sometimes referred to as part of the Koho, a generic name that includes the Ma B'sre, Ma Blao, Ma Dadong, Nop, and Cau Sre (Queguiner 1943: 396). **Location.** The vicinity of Djiring at the southern end of the Annam Cordillera in South Vietnam (Queguiner 1943: 396). **Linguistic affiliation.** Sre, a Mon-Khmer dialect, closely resembles Kil (Cil) and Mnong (Queguiner 1943: 396). Thomas (1962: 6) places the Sre language in the Koho linguistic grouping within the Stiengan subgrouping of the Mon-Khmer stock. **Demography.** The NNCDT (1959: 247) lists 30,000.

SETTLEMENT PATTERN AND HOUSING. Houses are constructed on low piling with a hip roof of thatch. Length depends on how many members of the extended family are living there, some houses being quite long. There is a platform before the entrance at the end. [Queguiner 1943: 396-97.]

ECONOMY. **Agriculture.** The Sre cultivate wet rice, their staple, in paddy fields on the bottom land of the upland valleys, using a buffalo and plow (Queguiner 1943: 397). Garden cultivation is also common among the Sre, who frighten away predatory birds with a unique device of sticks and reeds (Queguiner 1943: 397).

KIN GROUPS. The Sre kinship system apparently is matrilineal (Queguiner 1943: 392-93).

MARRIAGE AND FAMILY. The girl selects her spouse and holds title to family property. Should the marriage be dissolved, the husband must return to his own family. [Queguiner 1943: 392-93.]

SOCIOPOLITICAL ORGANIZATION. In each village is a body of notables in addition to the "official chiefs" appointed by the administration (Queguiner 1943: 395). According to Dam Bo (1950: 1094) the traditional village headman represents the ancestors and must observe certain food taboos, such as abstaining from fish and alcohol, during prescribed periods.

RELIGION. Dam Bo (1950: 1125) reports that among the Sre there are female as well as male sorcerers.

BIBLIOGRAPHY. Dam Bo 1950; NNCDT 1959; Queguiner 1943; Thomas 1962.

STIENG

Synonym. *Budip*

ORIENTATION. Identification. Gerber (1951: 228) notes that the Stieng, like other highland groups, are erroneously designated as *moi,* a Vietnamese word meaning "savage." According to Thomas (1963) the Stieng are sometimes referred to as Budip. **Location.** A large area in the provinces of Bien Hoa and Thu Dau Mot, to the northwest of Saigon, along the Vietnamese-Cambodia frontier (Gerber 1951: 228). **Linguistic affiliation.** In Thomas' (1962: 6) Stiengan subgrouping of Mon-Khmer stock, the Stieng sub-subgrouping includes Budip, Budeh, Bulach, and Bulo. **Demography.** Gerber (1951: 228) reports around 60,000 Stieng in the Vietnam-Cambodia border area; the NNCDT (1959: 246) reports 20,000 in Vietnam; and the NCTXH (1960) reports 17,162.

ECONOMY. Cultivators of upland rice in swiddens (Hickey 1956-58). The Stieng are also hunters and fishermen with most fishing done in the rainy season and with some use of poison arrows (Dam Bo 1950: 991).

KIN GROUPS. Kin groups. The Stieng family is variously referred to as a *"patriarcat"* (Gerber 1951: 228-30, 258) and a *"famille patriarcale"* (Guilleminet 1952: 98). The father is head of the family; the eldest male is chief of the extended family living in one household.

MARRIAGE AND FAMILY. Mode. The approval of both parties is necessary before marriage arrangements, including payment of a bride price, can be made. When a young man has made his choice, his parents send an intermediary to the girl's parents and the parties meet with witnesses, two older residents who know the marriage customs and the proper incantations for the spirits. The act of marriage consists of tying the wrists of the couple with a cotton string and asking the spirits to bless the union with health, wealth, and numerous offspring. A feast follows to which kin and friends, as well as village notables, are invited. Wealthy families are expected to kill three pigs and offer a number of jars of alcohol, poor families less, perhaps several pigs and only one alcohol jar. [Gerber 1951: 258.] **Bride price.** The payment of a bride price is fixed in Stieng law and Gerber (1951: 258) reports that the bride price must be paid before a newly married couple can establish their own household. Among the wealthy a typical bride price might be: one slave, a "srung" jar, an old iron coupe-coupe (machete), an old iron spear, a "djri" jar, one gong, a silk Cambodian skirt, bowls of varying sizes and materials, bracelets, and necklaces. A large bride price sets a good precedent for, when his daughter marries, a man will ask for the same amount. **Form.** Polygyny is found, the consent of the first wife generally being required, but is rare as the high bride price among the Stieng acts as a deterrent (Gerber 1951: 261). **Extension of incest taboos.** Marriage is prohibited between brothers and sisters, uncles and nieces, or aunts and nephews, and, though not strictly prohibited, marriage between first cousins is to be avoided (Gerber 1951: 261). **Residence.** Patrilocal if the bride price has been paid; matrilocal if not, with the boy under obligation to pay the bride price by working for the girl's family. Such matrilocal residence is normally temporary but can become permanent if the bride price is not paid by the date set originally by both parties. [Gerber 1951: 259-60.] **Inheritance.** Family goods are the property of the husband, providing he has paid the bride price. Upon his death, his adult children divide the heritage and assume responsibility for the widow. If the children are young, and the father has paid the bride price, the widow, under the supervision of her husband's family, assumes control of the property. If the deceased had not paid the bride price, the widow assumes control without supervision—although, when the eldest son reaches majority, he assumes control until his siblings reach majority, and then the property is divided. If both parents die, and the children are minors, control of the property goes to the husband's or the wife's family depending on whether or not the bride price had been paid. Exceptions to these basic rules are noted in Stieng laws. [Gerber 1951: 266-68.] **Divorce.** Though permitted, divorce is not common since the wife's parents must return the value of the bride price except where it is solely the husband who desires the divorce—and this possibility is reduced by the added burden in such cases of specified ritual sacrifices. Other stipulations in divorce are noted in codified Stieng laws. The divorced wife of a man who had not paid the bride price is free to marry whomever she wishes, but if the bride price had been paid the wife, even though divorced, is considered the property of her husband's family. Her second husband must be from her first husband's family, e.g. a younger brother might, with the consent of his own first wife, take the divorcee as his second wife. In such cases the cost of the wedding feast is borne within the family. [Gerber 1951: 261.]

SOCIOPOLITICAL ORGANIZATION. **Political organization.** According to Gerber (1951: 228-29) the Stieng, although referred to as a "tribe," have never had any tribal organization or been under any one ruling authority. The Stieng village could probably best be described as an association of autonomous households which are often interrelated and which have common interests. The tendency of Stieng villages to separate and regroup is at least partly attributable to this loose political structure. Jural authority stems not from the village but from the family, and it is the family that is responsible for any tort on the part of a member and that seeks retribution for any wrong. **Tribunals.** Disputes between families are handled by a traditional hierarchy of village tribunals. A tribunal of the first degree, presided over by the village chief with the assistance of two elderly men versed in local traditional customs, settles cases where punishments are equivalent to two buffalo or less. When the contending parties are from separate villages, the chiefs of both villages must preside. No kin of either party is allowed to sit on the tribunal and, if partiality can be proven, the decision of the tribunal can be negated. A second-degree tribunal has two members selected from among the heads of the households or other older men of good character and known integrity. Cases involving punishments equivalent to more than two buffalo are heard in these second-degree tribunals. [Gerber 1951: 238-39.] **Social stratification.** Slavery exists among the Stieng but a slave is more like a domestic and is treated as a member of the family. The various kinds of slaves include war captives, slaves captured from a family which has refused to honor a debt, and slaves who have been bought outright. The latter are usually children left orphaned whose purchase by kinfolk amounts to adoption. Similarly, in the absence of offspring, a slave may be bought and made a member of the family to perpetuate the line. In the case of debt, sometimes the kin sell the children. [Gerber 1951: 228-29.] There are also temporary slaves, the bond servants who must work for a given period to pay a debt. Because borrowing is common among the Stieng, bond slavery is also common. [Gerber 1951: 228-32.]

RELIGION. **Indigenous religion.** According to Gerber (1951: 227-28), religion among the Stieng, based on belief in a number of spirits, is centered in the family which performs all rituals. **Practitioners.** A *cak* is one guilty of witchcraft—bringing evil to another individual through the intervention of witchcraft. The Stieng believe that the *cak* "eats the liver of the victim" thus causing death. The search for a *cak* is exhaustive. A close kin of the victim and the household heads of the village meet in the woods and after performing a sacrifice with special prayers the group carries out a divination ritual before each house using a bamboo stick and a small weight. When the divination indicates that a particular household harbors the *cak*, the same process is repeated with each adult member of the household. Punishments are severe and often imposed on the entire family. If the *cak* is a male, he may be executed immediately and his children sold into slavery. [Gerber 1951: 232-33.] *Lah cang rai* is a person guilty of bringing the wrath of the spirits on the village, usually by violating some taboo. The guilty party, unlike the *cak*, is known and must make immediate expiatory sacrifices or be guilty of all subsequent misfortune in the village. Punishments for failing to expiate the wrong are severe. [Gerber 1951: 233-34.] **Ceremonies.** About every five years Stieng villages organize harvest rituals to honor the most powerful spirits of the area with sacrifices of ten, twenty, or even sixty buffalo in addition to a number of pigs. All the residents of neighboring villages are invited to participate, and villagers, rich or poor, must contribute to the fete, which thus becomes a cause of debt among villagers without means. [Gerber 1951: 230.] Another ritual sacrifice among the Stieng is designed to placate the spirits angered by some action such as breach of a taboo. Sacrifices range, depending on the nature of the transgression, from a chicken to pigs of various weights or even to a buffalo. If a person dies violently, a completely black dog or a wild goat is sacrificed. Unlike most others, this sacrifice must be performed outside the village in the forest and the flesh consumed outside the house. [Gerber 1951: 236.] **Taboos.** The Stieng laws specify a number of taboos, among them taboos against entering a household or a village. The newly moved village, for example, is taboo for seven days after its reconstruction. Also it is forbidden for seven days to bring in jars of paddy, alcohol, and other specific foods. For the same period of time, food must be cooked under, rather than in, the house and a number of specified foods are forbidden in the house. [Gerber 1951: 257-58.]

BIBLIOGRAPHY. Dam Bo 1950; Gerber 1951; Guilleminet 1952; Hickey 1956-58; NCTXH 1960; NNCDT 1959; Thomas 1962, 1963.

TRING

ORIENTATION. **Location.** In Phillips (1962: map), the Tring are located east of Dalat in South Vietnam. **Linguistic affiliation.** Thomas (1962: 6) places Tring in the Koho group of the Stiengan sub-subgroup in the Bahnaran subgroup within the Mon-Khmer stock.

BIBLIOGRAPHY. Phillips 1962; Thomas 1962.

SOUTHWEST UPLAND GROUPS

CHONG

ORIENTATION. **Identification and location.** Taillard (1942: 43-45) quotes Leclère's theory that the Chong, now largely assimilated into Khmer society, were at one time a widespread group. The Saoch, related to the Chong, are survivals of this group, which at one time extended throughout the Kampot and Kampong Som area, north to Battambang, and into Thailand. Baradat (1941: 2-3) points out that Chong is the name these people use for themselves. Like Taillard, Baradat considers the Chong very closely related to the Pear, and separates the former into the Chong Khnang Phnom in Cambodia and the Chong of Thailand. People calling themselves Chong are today located in the Thailand–Cambodia border area southwest of the Tonle Sap. Some are found in the Cardamom mountains. **Linguistic affiliation.** Mon-Khmer stock (Baradat 1941: 2-3). **Demography.** Baradat (1941: 5-6) reports that the Chong in Thailand number around 2,000.

BIBLIOGRAPHY. Baradat 1941; Taillard 1942.

KUI

Synonyms. *Kuoy, Soai*

ORIENTATION. **Identification, location, and demography.** A Mon-Khmer-speaking population, related to Chaobon, Chong, Pear, etc., located in the hills along both sides of the Thailand–Cambodia border, between 103° E. and 105° E. The majority of the Kui, estimated at over 100,000, are in the Siamese provinces of Surin, Sisaket, Ubon, and Roi Et; those in Cambodia are primarily in the northern Siem Reap–Kampong Thom area. In French language sources on Cambodia, the name appears as Kuoy, while according to Seidenfaden, the Kui are called Soai by the Siamese. [Seidenfaden 1958: 115-16; Zadrozny 1955: 372.] **Linguistic affiliation.** Mon-Khmer. Many Kui speak Lao or Khmer in addition to their own language. **History and cultural relations.** Credner regards the Kui as representative of an older stratum, predating the coming of both Tai and Khmer into the area. There is reportedly much intermarriage with Cambodians. [Credner 1935a: 164; Zadrozny 1955: 372.]

ECONOMY. Although some Kui retain their primitive methods of hoe agriculture, the majority have adopted the permanent wet-rice cultivation of their lowland neighbors. In some areas they have acquired reputations as elephant hunters and iron forgers. [Seidenfaden 1958: 115-16.]

RELIGION. While some Kui have retained their old animistic beliefs, most have adopted the Buddhism of their neighbors. [Seidenfaden 1958: 115-16.]

BIBLIOGRAPHY. Credner 1935a; Seidenfaden 1958; Zadrozny 1955.

PEAR

Synonyms. *Bahr, Pohr, Porr*

ORIENTATION. **Identification.** Baradat (1941: 1-3) considers the Pear part of a larger group that includes the Saoch, also sometimes called the Samre. The Pear are often referred to along with other upland people of Cambodia as the Phnong or Pnong, a generic term. **Location.** Baradat (1941: 1-10) divides the Pear into subgroupings according to location. The Pear of the west are located on the northern slopes of the Cardamom mountains. The Pear of Kampong Thom are located between the Tonle Sap and the Dangrek mountains. The Samre of Siem Reap are intermingled with the Cambodian population and scarcely discernible as a group. All of the Pear groups have considerable contact with the Cambodians. **Linguistic affiliation.** Mon-Khmer, related to Saoch.

SETTLEMENT PATTERN AND HOUSING. **Settlement pattern.** Villages, usually located near water courses, are made up of scattered clusters of farmsteads and range in population from 200 to 1,500 (Baradat 1941: 31). **Housing.** Houses are rectangular and flimsily constructed of bamboo and thatch on piling. They face either east or north. Most houses are divided into two or more rooms. Part of the area beneath the house serves as a pigsty or chicken coop; the remainder is used for storage. Because of the hazards caused by wild animals during part of the year, the Pear at these times favor tree houses. [Baradat 1941: 31-32.]

ECONOMY. The staple crop is upland rice, cultivated by the swidden technique. The main implement is the digging stick. Secondary crops include maize, bananas, millet, sweet potatoes, red peppers, and tobacco. The Pear also gather wild yams, bamboo, and leaves, as well as a variety of shoots. ● Fishing and hunting are important means of supplementing the diet. There are only a few chickens and pigs. Crafts include the production of resin torches, and earthenware cooking pots and storage jars. A group of Pear in the vicinity of Kampong Thom cultivate cotton, which they weave into cloth. Men perform the heavy tasks associated with swidden agriculture, while the women plant. Every able-bodied member of the household assists in the harvesting and in food gathering. The Pear carry on very little trade. [Baradat 1941: 31-38.]

KIN GROUPS. According to Baradat (1941: 70-72), there are three totemic clans among the Pear, each headed by a chief. This office is inherited patrilineally and passes to whichever of his sons the chief considers most fit. These chiefs function primarily in a ritual role—driving away the spirits that cause sickness and other misfortunes.

MARRIAGE AND FAMILY. Marriage usually takes place at an early age—around fifteen years of age. A small ritual bride price is paid by the groom's family. Residence initially is matrilocal until the birth of the first child, after which it is either patrilocal or neolocal. One Pear group is characterized by ambilocal residence (alternately patrilocal and matrilocal for a year at a time). Polygyny is permitted, but is only practiced by the well-to-do. Adultery is not uncommon. [Baradat 1941: 39-46.]

SOCIOPOLITICAL ORGANIZATION. There appears to be no other political leader than the village headman (Baradat 1941: 70).

RELIGION. The Pear have three types of deities. Spirits responsible for creation, fertility, and control of the seasons and the soil make up the first category; evil spirits form another; and spirits embodying desirable human qualities the third. Sorcerers function primarily to control the weather. There are two chief sorcerers—*khvay lin* and *khvay ta*—each assisted by a *khvay cheam*. Their authority derives from that given to one of their ancestors by the Khmer king. [Baradat 1941: 41-54.]

BIBLIOGRAPHY. Baradat 1941.

SAOCH

ORIENTATION. **Identification.** According to Taillard (1942: 15-17), the first mention of the Saoch occurs in an 1830 account of a traveler in Cambodia who described a people with tails which prevented them from sitting down. Menetrier (1926) identifies the Saoch as a separate group. Taillard (1942: 43-45) speculates that the Saoch are a remnant of a larger group also represented by the assimilated Chong. **Location.** During the French period in Cambodia, the Saoch occupied an administrative reserve extend-

ing along the banks of the Kompong Smach to its mouth on the bay of Veal Renh which is equidistant from Kampot and Ream, on the western side of the Elephant Chain (Taillard 1942: 16). **Linguistic affiliation.** Mon-Khmer. **Demography.** Taillard (1942: 15, 17) records a population of 172 and lists two earlier estimates: 75 in 1910 and 100 in 1926. **Cultural relations.** Long considered unfriendly and aloof, the Saoch have been in increasingly close contact with the Khmer, borrowing a great deal from their culture and occasionally taking Khmer wives (Taillard 1942: 36-39).

SETTLEMENT PATTERN AND HOUSING. **Settlement pattern.** Houses invariably have a north-south orientation (Taillard 1942: 35). **Housing.** The very crudely constructed rectangular houses, set on piling, are made of wood (usually bamboo), rattan, straw, and fronds, with thatched roofs and walls (Taillard 1942: 35-36). Some older Cham informants still recall seeing Saoch living in the forest without houses, grouping around fires at night to sleep.

ECONOMY. **Fishing and hunting.** Both are important activities and a wide variety of traps are used; crossbows were common for hunting before their prohibition by the French administration (Taillard 1942: 37-38). **Industrial arts.** Men make their own traps for hunting and fishing, and, until prohibited by the French, also made their own crossbows; women weave mats (Taillard 1942: 37-38). **Trade.** Paddy is sold, and manufactured articles, often Chinese-made, are bought in an exchange with the surrounding Khmer, for whom the Saoch also work as laborers (Taillard 1942: 43-45).

MARRIAGE AND FAMILY. **Mode.** The first overtures come as gifts from the boy's family to the girl's family. Interfamily negotiations follow until the wedding has been arranged. Weddings, celebrated with feasts, are customarily held in the dry season when agricultural activities slow to almost a halt. **Extension of incest taboos.** Females cannot marry outside the ethnic group but males can. A man married to a non-Saoch may not reside in the group with his wife but is expected at her death to return to the group with their children. [Taillard 1942: 39-40.] **Residence.** Patrilocal. The boy's family usually vacates the house for several days following the marriage to give the couple complete privacy. The communal life of the household is resumed with the return of the boy's family. [Taillard 1942: 39-40.] **Divorce.** Divorce is considered against Saoch traditions but separation is possible. A couple wishing to separate is expected to present reasons to the group elders, who usually disapprove and are generally disregarded. Following a separation, the wife returns to her paternal house and the children are divided between the parents. [Taillard 1942: 39-40.]

SOCIOPOLITICAL ORGANIZATION. The Saoch are governed by a council of about ten family chiefs or elders, who fix punishments and fines for any infraction of group law (Taillard 1942: 39-40).

RELIGION. **Indigenous religion.** The Saoch have a vaguely defined cult of the ancestors based on the belief that ancestors watch over their descendants. Another major Saoch cult centers on a stone fetish located in the woods. This stone, known by a Khmer name, is venerated by the burning of joss with incantations in Khmer and by annual rituals during the last month of the Khmer calendar (March-April) in which the sorcerer, reciting prayers in Saoch, makes offerings of rice, meat, and rice alcohol. The Saoch sorcerer is an elderly blind man who lives in isolation with his family; those who wish his services in healing or in making amulets bring him offerings. [Taillard 1942: 41-42.] **Burial.** The body is washed with water and the head anointed with coconut oil. Then, dressed in best clothes, the corpse is placed on a board for one day before burial without ritual in a grave one meter deep. Both earth and plants are replaced and there is no marker or any form of grave cult. [Taillard 1942: 40.]

BIBLIOGRAPHY. Menetrier 1926; Taillard 1942.

VIET-MUONG

THE INCLUSION OF VIETNAMESE (Annamite) and Muong in an Austroasiatic [Austroasian] family of languages was first propounded by Schmidt in 1906. Others, reasoning on the basis of such formal elements as monosyllabism and tonicity, have classified Annamite, along with Tai and Chinese, as basically Sino-Tibetan. Both Greenberg (1953) and Shafer (1955), however, agree with Schmidt's earlier formulation. The historical-cultural position of the Muong vis-à-vis the Vietnamese is still unclear. The former are heavily Vietnamized, and yet, with respect to such things as an entrenched nobility with inalienable right to the land, they resemble most closely the Tho and Black Tai. Such practices may represent a borrowing from Tai-speaking groups, a unique Muong development, or a remnant of an earlier form common to both Vietnamese and Muong—representing, as some think, cultural differentiation from a common genesis (Embree and Thomas 1950).

VIETNAMESE

Synonyms. *Annamese, Nguoi Kinh*

ORIENTATION. **Identification.** The Vietnamese were known during the period of French rule as the Annamese, and their language was referred to in linguistic texts as Annamite. Vietnam was at that time divided into Tonkin, Annam, and Cochinchina, designations which caused some confusion. The people of Annam were also called Annamese, while the people of Tonkin and Cochinchina were called Tonkinese and Cochinchinese respectively. Today in South Vietnam, the official designation is Vietnamese both for the people and the language. However a recent source from North Vietnam (NNCDT 1959: 7) refers to all residents—highland and lowland people alike—as Vietnamese, but distinguishes the lowland people as Nguoi Kinh. **Location.** The Vietnamese are primarily lowland-dwelling people, although small population pockets are found in the highlands of northern and central Vietnam. In a breakdown of the physiographic regions of Indochina, the Vietnamese-occupied areas are well defined. The deltas of Tonkin (Red river delta) and northern Annam are occupied almost exclusively by Vietnamese, as are the deltas of the central coast. In the south-central coastal plain there are some Chams, and while Vietnamese predominate in the delta of the Mekong river, there are also some scattered islands of Khmer populations. [Canada Department of Mines 1953: 1-36.] **Geography.** Fertile alluvial plains occur in the large delta areas of the Mekong and Red rivers. Between is a narrow strip of mountainous plateau bounded on the seaward side by a fertile coastal plain. The lowland, delta, and coastal regions, drained by extensive networks of canals and waterways, produce large quantities of rice. The climate is in general monsoonal and hot and humid, although there are wide variations from north to south and between highland and lowland. The fauna of southern Vietnam includes elephants, tigers, leopards, and wild oxen. Boar, deer, monkeys, and wild fowl also occur. **Linguistic affiliation.** Vietnamese is a tonal language showing some similarity to Tai and containing many words borrowed from Chinese. It is regarded by Greenberg (1953) and others as basically an Austroasiatic [Austroasian] language related to Mon-Khmer. There are slight regional variations in tone and vocabulary. Vietnamese is written in both Chinese characters and in a romanized script. **Demography.** In 1937, the population of Vietnam totaled 18,972,000, with the following breakdown according to region: northern Vietnam—8,700,000, with a density of 75 per square kilometer; central Vietnam —5,656,000, with 38 per square kilometer; and southern Vietnam—4,616,000, with 71 per square kilometer. These figures include the highland (non-Vietnamese) population, and the density figures refer to total areas. [Embree and Thomas 1950: 129.] A more recent source (NNCDT 1959: 7, 240-47) estimates the total population of Vietnam at 25,000,000, of which 63 minority groups account for some 3,298,546, leaving a Vietnamese population of approximately 21,701,454. No regional breakdown is reported. Considerable shifting of population has occurred in recent years. In 1954, over 900,000 refugees, the bulk of whom were Vietnamese, settled in South Vietnam. **History and cultural relations.** Vietnamese history begins in the year 218 B.C., when the emperor Ch'in Huang-ti sent armies to pacify the population in the delta of the Red river. With the exception of relatively brief periods of independence, the Vietnamese continued to be under Chinese domination until 939 A.D. Subsequently the Vietnamese began a southward expansion along the coastal plain of the peninsula, eventually coming into contact and clashing with the indigenous Cham population of what is now central Vietnam. The Chams made territorial concessions, and by 1471 Vietnamese control extended to Qui Nhon. With the final defeat of the Chams in the early seventeenth century, the entire coastal area to the edge of the Mekong delta fell under Vietnamese rule. The scattered Khmer population in the Mekong river delta offered little resistance and by 1780 the Nguyen emperors had annexed the delta to the present border of Cambodia. The arrival of the French in the middle of the nineteenth century marked the beginning of the modern period, culminating in Dien Bien Phu and the division of the country into North and South Vietnam. [Le 1955.]

SETTLEMENT PATTERN AND HOUSING. **Settlement pattern.** Gourou (1936a: 238-43) recognizes a number of distinct settlement patterns in the delta of the Red river. The most common pattern he calls a "relief village," with natural or abandoned levees, hillsides, and beach ridges. Levee settlements tend to be strung along river banks, and often fuse to form one elongated settlement. Hillside settlements may consist of a cluster of farmsteads at the base of a hill. If the hill is low, the settlement may cover most of it. Most villages are surrounded by an earthen wall or bamboo hedge. ● Villages on the coastal plain of central Vietnam are less varied in pattern. Most are small, close-knit clusters of farmsteads, located near a water course. Fishing villages, which predominate in this area, are usually located in a sheltered cove or bay. Morechand (1955a: 315-46) distinguishes two types in the central Vietnamese coastal plain—those in which fishing is the most important economic activity, and others in which non-fishing activities are of almost equal importance. Morechand finds the central coastal village more "open" than northern Vietnamese villages, i.e. not restricted by enclosures, and therefore able to expand easily. He notes that in fishing settlements most buildings, including the *dinh,* face the sea. ● Vietnamese villages in the Mekong river delta are less varied in pattern than those in the Red river delta. String settlements of low density are found along the rivers, canals, and streams, and along many of the major roads. On the flat deltaic plain, most settlements are loose-knit clusters of farmsteads, with some isolated farmsteads scattered in the midst of the paddy fields. [Hickey 1960: 1-30.] Villages are divided into hamlets—*thon* in northern Vietnam, *ap* in southern Vietnam—which form quarters within the village. The internal pattern of northern settlements is often determined by geomantic principles. This fact tends to inhibit canal construction and well digging. [Gourou 1936a: 250-57.] In the center of the village there is usually found a market, a council house, a pagoda, and a *dinh,* or communal temple. Internal communication is primarily by foot. **Paths** interlace the villages, connecting all hamlets and farmsteads. Roads, paths, and a system of water courses connect the villages, except for those in swamp areas or on the fringes of the delta. [Gourou 1936a: 224-68; Hickey 1960: 1-30.] **Village size.** Because of a lack of census material, it is difficult to make definitive statements about the size of Vietnamese villages. In his 1936 study of the Red river delta, Gourou (1936a: 138-71) found an over-all mean density of 430 per square kilometer, ranging from a high of 780 in heavily populated areas to a low of 320. Average village size, however, is unknown, primarily because of the variation of densities in different parts of the delta. In riverain settlements, the density tends to be very high, with villages of from 7,000 to 10,000 inhabitants; while on the fringe of the delta, villages may number only a few hundred. Morechand (1955a: 317) describes two central coastal Vietnamese villages of 1,669 and 2,229 inhabitants, both considerably larger than other settlements of the area, most of which have less than 1,000 inhabitants. Hendry (1959: 1-20), however, in writing about a southern delta village of 3,200 inhabitants, points out that it is smaller than the average village of that particular area (south of Saigon, north of the Mekong river). **Housing.** With the exception of some pile dwellings along the banks of large rivers, Vietnamese houses are constructed on low earthen mounds. Building materials vary according to what is available locally. In northern and central Vietnam, thatching is usually of the local long grass; while in the Mekong delta it is of latania fronds. Houses of the well-to-do are of manufactured materials, with tile roofs and masonry walls. Roof styles vary with the size of the house and, to some extent, the wealth of the owner. Thatched houses usually have saddle or ridge roofs; while well-to-do Vietnamese favor some version of the traditional Chinese-style roof. ● One main room functions as a reception room for visitors, a sanctuary for the altar of the ancestors, and—in a small house—as a sleeping room. In northern Vietnam, a room at the rear serves as the women's room. Rear rooms are usually sleeping rooms, and may also be used for storage. The kitchen is a thatched appendage to the main building. [Gourou 1936b; Hickey 1960: 10-40.] Gourou, in his studies of the Thanh Hoa area, notes nine house types, all similar, but with variations that become more pronounced as one moves southward (Gourou 1936b).

ECONOMY. Agriculture is of first importance, with rice the staple crop. A wide variety of secondary crops are cultivated, some of which can be classified as cash crops. Livestock breeding also is common. Rubber, coffee, tea, and pepper estates are found primarily in southern Vietnam; while coal, iron ore, phosphate, salt, zinc, lead, tin, tungsten, chrome, manganese, antimony, and bauxite are mined in northern Vietnam. The forests are commercially exploited for wood to produce charcoal. Fishing activities are carried on extensively along the coasts and rivers. Manufacturing is by and large restricted to such urban centers as Saigon, Hanoi, and Haiphong. [Canada Department of Mines 1953.] **Agriculture.** Wet rice is the staple crop. Several hundred varieties, including glutinous, are cultivated. Paddy fields are watered by rainfall, inundation, and irrigation. The delta of the Red river is more densely cultivated than the Mekong river delta, with some variation in the planting techniques of the two areas. Planting seasons vary according to climate. A wide variety of secondary crops are cultivated in kitchen gardens and small estates. Large estates, introduced by the French, are a more recent development. Rubber, tea, coffee, and copra plantations are found primarily in southern Vietnam, with large-scale garden agriculture also a relatively recent development around Dalat in the southern highlands. The government of South Vietnam has sponsored planned ramie and jute estates in the southern highlands as a means of resettling refugees and encouraging the economic development of the highland areas. **Paddy agriculture.**

The rice-planting cycle in the Red river delta is divided into two seasons. Tenth-month rice is transplanted in July and harvested in the tenth lunar month, usually December. Fifth-month rice is transplanted in January and harvested in the fifth lunar month, usually June or July. There is some double cropping—quite a bit in the delta of the Mekong river, but less in central Vietnam. Planting in the Mekong river delta usually begins in April or May, depending on the arrival of the rains. The harvest generally begins in mid-September, and lasts until late December. In this area, early or late planting depends on the availability of fresh water. [Gourou 1936a: 400-05; Hendry 1959: 91-128.] The tool complex is the same throughout Vietnam. Plows with iron blades—in southern Vietnam, farmers use a Khmer type of plow in addition to the traditional Vietnamese plow—harrows, winnowing machines, hoes, sickles, and a wide variety of cutting tools. Even in areas with sufficient rainfall to flood the paddy fields, irrigation and drainage systems are used both to guarantee an ample supply of water and to drain the fields when necessary. Canals carry water from the streams and rivers, and small channels carry it to and from the fields. Low dikes are constructed to hold water in the fields, serving also as footpaths and as a means of delimiting ownership. Waterwheels and a variety of scooping techniques are employed to lift water from the canals to the fields. Common threshing methods in the Red river delta are flailing, scraping the ears with a bowl, or drawing them through close-set bamboo sticks. In the Mekong delta area wooden threshing sledges and woven mats are used. The stalks are beaten on the outer edge so that the kernels fall into the mat. Throughout Vietnam, paddy is generally stored in the house. [Gourou 1936a: 387-94; 1945: 300-16; Hendry 1959: 89-142.] In the delta of the Red river, extensive use is made both in fields and gardens of organic fertilizers, including straw ashes, calcined bones, castor oil cakes, sesame cakes, cotton cakes, silkworm excrement, silkworm chrysalises, and soy bean seeds. Buffalo, hog, and cattle manure, as well as night soil and urine are also used as fertilizers. Human waste is collected in the towns and sold to farmers. Residue from the production of castor oil, cottonseed oil, and *nuoc mam* (fish sauce) is also used (Gourou 1936a: 390). Chemical fertilizer is employed more extensively in the Mekong delta than in the north. In some villages, it is used for paddy cultivation, while organic fertilizer is restricted to gardens. [Hendry 1959: 108-13; Gourou 1945: 306-13; Dumont 1935: 185-253.] **Secondary crops.** Fruit groves are commonly found in the rural areas, and every farmstead has a kitchen garden. Some secondary crops are also cultivated in the dried paddy fields, particularly in the Red river delta area. Crops cultivated both in the fields and in family plots include sesame, castor bean, manioc, taro, maize, sugar cane, arrowroot, millet, jute, and tobacco. Some cotton also is grown. Kitchen garden crops include tomatoes, green beans, carrots, peanuts, cauliflower, cabbage, Chinese celery, water celery, cucumbers, kale, onions, and various types of gourds, squash, and melons. Southern Vietnamese gardens grow potatoes and French white beans. Bananas, papaya, and coconuts are the most commonly cultivated fruits. Areca trees are found in some areas, and grapefruit, orange, tangerine, and lemon trees are extensively cultivated in the Mekong river delta. Guava, jackfruit, mangoes, milk apples, tamarinds, peaches, mulberries, and betel nuts are grown throughout the Mekong delta area, and also in the Red river delta, where there are also persimmon and litchi nut trees. [Gourou 1936a: 406-24; 1945: 323-30; Hendry 1959: 143-56; Dumont 1935: 125.] **Fishing.** Among the rural Vietnamese, fishing is almost a universal occupation. Many farmsteads have ponds stocked with fish, and villages are dissected with streams, rivers, and canals. When flooded, paddy fields are also stocked with fish. Small fish, crabs, shrimp, and other crustaceans are found in ponds, streams, and dikes. Fishing may be either essential to subsistence, a means of supplementing the diet, or an important source of income. Fishing specialization is found primarily on the large rivers and along the extensive sea coast. Nets and traps are employed in the streams, canals, and paddy fields. A hemispheric bow net is plunged into the flooded fields or along the edge of a stream or canal, and the catch is removed by hand through a hole at the top. Funnel-shaped rattan traps are set in narrow places to ensnare small fish. Nets of varying shapes and sizes, some with intricate lifting devices, are used in the larger streams and rivers. Water in fields and ponds may be drained, and small nets used to scoop the fish into baskets. [Hendry 1959: 163-67; Gourou 1936a: 430-36; Robequain 1929: 377-404; Claeys 1942: 18-28; Morechand 1955a: 291-354.] According to Gourou (1936a: 442-43), coastal fishing is not highly developed in northern Vietnam. The peasants use relatively crude fishing techniques. Ocean fishing is more important along the coast of central Vietnam, where the variety of fish is great. There are well-defined times for taking different kinds of fish. The variety considered best for the production of *nuoc mam* (a fish sauce used as a condiment throughout Vietnam) is in great abundance from March until the end of May, and from August until the end of September (Langrand 1945: 42-43). Along the coast, there are many styles of fishing boats. Their shapes, modes of construction, materials, types of sails, ornamentation, and other physical features vary from north to south (Paris 1955). **Domestic animals.** Cattle and buffalo are the most common draft animals. Dumont (1935: 140) contends that in the Red river delta area, cross-breeding of cattle with improved strains cannot be attempted, due to unfavorable environmental conditions. Hogs

are raised extensively, and supply the major portion of the meat in the diet of the peasants. Cattle and buffalo are slaughtered only for family or village celebrations. Chickens and ducks are also raised extensively throughout Vietnam. (Dumont 1935: 136-55). In some villages, large flocks of ducks are raised for sale in the village market or in neighboring market towns (Hendry 1959: 167-80; Gourou 1936a: 425-32). **Industrial arts.** Village specialists include carpenters, joiners, masons, and smiths. The role of the specialist generally is hereditary, passed from father to son. In the Red river delta, itinerant artisans and tradesmen set up temporary shops outside the village wall, but this is not the case in the delta of the Mekong, where each village has its own specialists. In southern Vietnam, there are few full-time village specialists, since most of the inhabitants are engaged in agricultural activities. There is little family industry among the southern Vietnamese. In some villages women of lower income groups weave mats and baskets as a part-time activity. [Hickey 1958: 58; Gourou 1936a: 448-531.] In northern Vietnam, groups of families specialize in certain trades and crafts. They tend to be concentrated in a village or group of neighboring villages. There are potters' villages, iron workers' villages, paper makers' villages, cloth weavers' villages, bronze workers' villages, and shoemakers' villages. Many specialize full time; some engage in agricultural activities as well. In the city of Hanoi, the specialists were traditionally located on the same street, which was known by its specialization. Each trade was organized as a *phuong*, comparable to the medieval guild. *Phuong* organization cut across village and urban lines, and included all those of the same specialization. The aim of the *phuong* was to guard techniques, maintain standards of work, fix prices, and provide a marketing cooperative. Within each family, *phuong* techniques were passed from father to son, and each *phuong* maintained a cult to its own guardian spirit. [Hickey 1958: 56-57.] **Trade.** Large-scale commerce and trade is centered in the urban areas of Hanoi, Haiphong, and Saigon. At the village level, there is considerable commercial and trading activity. Throughout Vietnam, commerce is centered in the village market, which is held during the early morning hours. Resident farmers bring their surplus products to sell or exchange for manufactured items. Farmers also bring produce to market towns for exchange or cash sale. In addition to a sizable market, these towns contain shops operated by Chinese, Vietnamese, and sometimes a few Indians, who sell a variety of manufactured goods. Animal markets are also held in some market towns. Itinerant merchants visit villages by vehicle or boat to sell produce, fish, or manufactured articles, particularly pottery. Small village shops sell a wide range of food and articles needed in agricultural activities as well as paper, pencils, and plastic household items. In the Mekong delta, delivery vehicles

—motor scooter transports and bicycles—make periodic deliveries of goods to the village shops. • Commerce in rice is important at the village level. After the harvest, the paddy is moved to the market centers, from which it is transported to urban centers for storage and sale. The Chinese in southern Vietnam have traditionally played the role of middlemen in the rice trade, traveling through delta villages to purchase unharvested paddy, and often making an advance to a farmer in need (Chau 1940: 14-15). In the Mekong delta, money lending is usually done by wealthy villagers or village credit associations rather than outsiders (Hendry 1959: 282-309). In the Red river delta, another important commercial activity is the moving of products from specialist villages to the market centers. [Hickey 1958: 56-58; Gourou 1936a: 539-54.] There is considerable local and regional commerce in most varieties of fish, both fresh and salted. Fresh fish are transported to markets in cities and towns; some are dried and stored; and certain varieties of ocean fish are processed into *nuoc mam.* Fish raised in village pools are sold either in the village or in neighboring towns. [Hendry 1959: 157-67; Gourou 1936a: 433-47; Langrand 1945: 44; Morechand 1955a: 291-354.] **Division of labor.** In southern Vietnamese villages, males engage in carpentry, woodworking, and other specializations, and some women weave baskets and mats. Petty commerce is usually carried on by women, and both men and women keep shops—in most instances a shop is a joint effort. Household responsibilities such as cooking, washing, and carrying water and fuel are female activities; while gardening is done by both males and females. Males do the plowing, harrowing, seeding, uprooting and transporting of seedlings. Irrigating the fields and scattering fertilizer are exclusively male occupations. Both males and females weed the fields, reap the harvest, and thresh. [Hendry 1959: 72-79.] Inland fishing is done by males. Individuals usually engage in field, stream, and pond fishing; while groups of boys using nets and traps are a common sight in most villages (Gourou 1936a: 430-36; Hendry 1959: 163-67). Coastal fishing requires group organization. In northern Vietnam, large boats usually have a crew of eight; smaller boats have five, four, or three, depending on the size of the boat (Gourou 1936a: 500-01). In central Vietnam, crews tend to be larger, and are structured according to specialized ability, with the master fisherman the most experienced sailor in the group. Usually each boat crew has a woman associate whose task it is to sell the fish and keep the accounts (Langrand 1945: 44). • Wage labor is common in agricultural villages. Peasants with little or no land perform seasonal labor for well-to-do villagers, and seek out-of-season employment in the village or in neighboring towns. [Hendry 1959: 46-87; Gourou 1945: 358-59.] Transplanting teams include women of varying ages and young boys, most of whom are from families of the lower economic levels

(Hendry 1959: 104-06). Wage labor is also common in fishing villages, where wealthy boat owners hire crews from among the village specialists (Langrand 1945: 44; Gourou 1936a: 433-47). **Land tenure.** Traditionally, land has been divided into privately-owned land and village-owned land (which also includes most of the pagoda land). The income from *huong hoa,* family land, is used to defray the cost of the rituals and feasting associated with the cult of the ancestors. While title to *huong hoa* is vested in one male member of the family (nuclear or extended), it is considered to be collectively owned by the adult members, and Vietnamese codes favor its inalienability. Prior to World War II, communal land comprised 21 per cent of the total cultivated area in northern Vietnam, 25 per cent in central Vietnam, and 3 per cent in southern Vietnam (Henry 1932: 109). Of the two types of communal land in northern Vietnam—*cong dien* and *cong tho*—the former was inalienable, and its title was held by the village council for the village as a whole. Communal land was periodically allotted to landless villagers. Traditional village land tenure also included cult lands, which belonged to village, Buddhist, or Confucianist cults. [Vu 1939; Hickey 1960: 49-62, 183-98.] Land tenure has undergone some changes since World War II. The Viet Minh movement in 1950 advocated a "land to the tiller" policy, which was implemented in 1953. After the Geneva agreements of 1954, the government of North Vietnam began a land confiscation program which met with resistance among the farmers. Collectivization is the stated goal (Gittinger 1959: 113-26). Private property, communal land, and cult land continue to exist in South Vietnam. As part of an agrarian reform program, however, private ownership has been restricted to 100 hectares. Any land in excess of that must be sold to the government, for resale to tenants. *Huong hoa* land has been restricted to 15 hectares. [Hendry 1959: 21-31.] **Size of holdings.** In the delta of the Mekong, land belongs mostly to large landowners. Small proprietors are more numerous in the zone of mixed crops—near the mouths of the Mekong and the Dong Nai rivers. On the alluviums near the rivers, where horticulture of coconuts and bananas prevails, more parceling of the land takes place. [Gourou 1945: 529-30.] The delta of the Red river is essentially a district of smallholders. Prior to the Indochina War, large holdings were rare; whereas there were thousands of holdings of a few thousand or a few hundred square meters. In Cochinchina large estates predominated: 45 per cent of the paddy fields were part of estates ranging from 50 to several thousand hectares; 42 per cent were in farms of from 5 to 50 hectares; and only 12.5 per cent were small holdings of less than 5 hectares. [Goudal 1938: 17-20.]

KIN GROUPS. **Descent and kin groups.** *Ho* is the patrilineal name-sib, used generally to indicate the

300 family names found among the Vietnamese. In some areas of the Red river delta, where families have been settled for centuries in the same locale, surnames regulate marriage, but the commonly observed rule among the Vietnamese is to permit marriage between those with a common surname if blood relationship can be proven not to exist. • The *toc* is the patrilineal common descent group. It includes all those related through the male line to a common male ancestor in the fifth ascending generation among Vietnamese of northern and central Vietnam, and in the third ascending generation in southern Vietnam. The patrilineage of northern and central Vietnam has retained more of its traditional character than has the southern patrilineage. In the traditional patrilineage, the head is either the eldest male of the senior branch, or the eldest male in the patrilineage. In the rural areas of southern Vietnam, the head is commonly selected by a group of female and male adult members of the *toc*. • The traditional prerogatives and responsibilities of the patrilineage head include holding title to the *huong hoa*, the inalienable family land. He uses the income from the *huong hoa* to defray the costs of rituals and feasting associated with the cult of the ancestors. He also must maintain the *gia pha*, the family genealogy book (usually not found in southern Vietnam), and the family tombs and graves. The head of the patrilineage is a paternal figure, seeing to the welfare of *toc* members, arbitrating their disputes, and counseling them when necessary. Each branch and each nuclear family also has a head, whose role is comparable to that of the patrilineage head. [Hickey 1958: 81-82.] **Kin terminology.** Hickey (1958) gives the following kin terms:

Fa	cha
Mo	me
FaElBr	bac
FaYoBr	chu
FaSi	co
MoBr	cau
MoSi	di
Eldest Br	anh ca
Older Br	anh
Eldest Si	chi ca
Older Si	chi
YoBr	em trai
YoSi	em gai
PElSbSo	anh ho
PElSbDa	chi ho
PYoSbSo	em trai ho
PYoSbDa	em gai ho

The kinship system is patrilineal in form and function. Kin related through the male and female lines are differentiated, and the patrilineage is clearly delineated. Kin terminology is descriptive, and varies somewhat from north to south, as do other features of the kinship system. The syntactical principles of the isolating, monosyllabic Vietnamese language permit an exactness of designation through the use of modifiers. Proximity of kin, generation, and sex, as well as patrilineal and nonpatrilineal kin can be specified by the use of modifiers. There is age-grading of siblings, male kin in the patrilineage, and all collateral kin. Use of nuclear terms rather than modifiers is characteristic of Ego's and the first ascending generation. Sibling terms are extended to collateral kin of Ego's generation, age-graded according to the relative ages of the parents. [Hickey 1958: 75-81.]

MARRIAGE AND FAMILY. **Mode.** Traditionally most Vietnamese marriages were arranged by the parents, and while this continues to be the practice in most cases, it is no longer a rigidly observed rule. Whether arranged by the parents or not, the traditional form of marriage is observed by all Vietnamese except Christians. The boy's parents initiate the negotiations through an intermediary, who makes the first overtures to the girl's parents. Both families must consult their genealogy book to ascertain that no relationship exists. It must also be ascertained that the horoscopes of both parties are compatible. There are several prescribed visits: the first for the parents to meet, and the second to hold an engagement feast and set the bride price. The date of the marriage is set by horoscope. Marriage may not take place during a mourning period. On the day of the wedding, the groom and a procession of his kin and friends go with symbolic gifts to the bride's house, where he kowtows before her ancestral altar. They return to his house, where both kowtow before the groom's ancestral altar and kin to introduce his bride and to symbolize her acceptance of his ancestors and family. [Hickey 1958: 83-87.] **Form.** Polygyny was traditional among the Vietnamese, usually practiced by the well-to-do. Consent of the first wife was necessary for the second wife to live in the same house. Taking concubines has also been a traditional Vietnamese practice. In South Vietnam, both polygyny and concubinage were made illegal by 1958 legislation. [Hickey 1960: 140-54.] **Extension of incest taboos.** Marriage within the patrilineal surname group is permitted if blood relationship can be proven not to exist. **Residence.** For the eldest son, residence after marriage is prescriptively patrilocal, and other sons are expected to settle in the vicinity of the paternal house (Hickey 1958: 83-87). **Inheritance.** Traditionally, only males inherit land. The eldest son, generally considered the successor to the role of family head, inherits the bulk of family land, including the *huong hoa*, inalienable family cult land. Other sons share the remaining land equally. In northern and central Vietnam, the traditional practices continue, but in southern Vietnam inheritance rules are more flexible; females may inherit land, and, in the absence of a will, the children themselves may decide how to divide the patrimony. Traditionally, primogeniture determined inheritance of the paternal house, but in southern Vietnam ultimogeniture is now the rule. [Hickey 1958: 82-83.] **Divorce.** If a bride is not a virgin, the husband has the right to send her back to her parents. He also sends them the ears of a pig, and they are obliged to return the bride price. In 1958, divorce and separation in South Vietnam were declared by government decree to be illegal without government approval. [Hickey 1958: 87.]

SOCIOPOLITICAL ORGANIZATION. **Political organization.** The traditional Vietnamese political organization was modeled on the Chinese imperial system. The emperor, nobles, and high mandarins governed from the capital city, and mandarins occupied the higher administrative positions in local areas. Local administration was fixed in 1419, and larger administrative units were formed along set lines around the end of the fifteenth century (Le 1955: 208-28). With the arrival of the French in the mid-nineteenth century, this system underwent some changes. Southern Vietnam was organized as the French colony of Cochinchina, while northern and central Vietnam became the protectorates of Tonkin and Annam respectively. The traditional system in Cochinchina was replaced by a colonial administration, although some of the mandarin titles were retained. In Tonkin and Annam the mandarin system continued to function and the emperor remained, but ultimate control was in the hands of French administrators. [Le 1955: 380-463.] **Rural administration.** In northern and central Vietnam, several villages comprised a *tong* (a canton in the French administration). Each *tong* had a chief and several assistants. The next higher unit was the *huyen* or *phu,* with inspectors, secretaries, and judicial mandarin positions. The *tinh* (a province in the French administration) was the highest local unit, with a wide range of mandarin positions. [Dao 1938: 108-14; Pasquier 1907: 45.] The colony of Cochinchina was organized along French colonial administrative lines. The large local units were provinces, each with a French *résident,* and the provinces were divided into districts. Cantons were organized in some areas, and below the canton was the village, comprised in many instances of scattered hamlets. Since Independence in 1954, the rural administration of South Vietnam has not changed greatly in structure, although many services and functions and the liaison with the central government have been altered considerably. [Woodruff 1960: 14-33.] ● Traditional rural administration in northern and north-central Vietnam underwent considerable change when the Viet Minh assumed control, and since the establishment of the Democratic Republic of North Vietnam in 1954, many of these changes have been fixed. In 1958, Ho Chi Minh signed a bill promulgating the law on local administration. People's Councils and Administrative Committees were organized for the highland *chau,* the lowland provinces, the cities, and the villages. The People's Councils were responsible for general living conditions, and for supervising the activities of the state in the area. The Administrative Committees were to be responsible for implementing state laws and acting as liaison between central and local authorities. [Fall 1960: 82-83.] **Village level.** There are some variations between the traditional sociopolitical organization of northern and central Vietnamese villages and those of southern Vietnam. In northern and central Vietnam the *xa* (village) has traditionally functioned as an almost autonomous social and economic unit. The *ly truong* was the village headman, elected by a council of notables, usually for five years. Assisted by a secretary and a treasurer, the *ly truong* had the primary responsibility for administration of the village, and also served as liaison with the higher authorities. His administrative responsibilities included education, public works, and village finance, including the collection of taxes. [Gourou 1936a: 263-68.] The most important sociopolitical group in the northern and central villages was the council of notables, whose members were ranked according to age, wealth, and prestige. Their functions depended on their respective places in the council. High notables were in charge of tax assessments, conservation of village archives, and the maintenance of the pagoda. The council and village headman periodically met in the *dinh,* the communal temple. In addition to the traditional grouping of intellectuals, farmers, artisans, and merchants, northern and central Vietnamese villages had hierarchies of at least three ranks: *lao,* including all males over 55 years of age; *quan vien,* the mandarins; and *xa dan,* the village functionaries. At rituals in the *dinh,* each rank had a special place, and ranking also determined position at the feasts that followed the rituals. At buffalo sacrifices, the parts of the sacrificial animal were distributed according to rank. [Gourou 1936a: 263-73; Nguyen 1939: 59-70; Nguyen 1930: 109-20; Pasquier 1907: 45-63; Rouilly 1929: 35-147.] ● Southern Vietnamese village organization differs somewhat from that of northern and central villages. In 1904 French legislation fixed the organization of village councils in Cochinchina. Some traditional titles and functions were changed, and others retained. The *huong ca,* the traditional village chief, was retained, as was the *huong chu,* the deputy chief, while the function of the *huong su* was changed from liaison to legal advisor. The functions of the village councils were again altered by legislation in 1927. Viet Minh control brought about only temporary changes in southern villages. With the restoration of French control, the prewar councils were re-established. In 1953, the southern village councils were completely changed, and both titles and functions were altered. The village chief became the *chu tich,* his assistant the *pho chu tich,* and their functions become more formalized as the village became integrated into the national political structure. The most recent changes in political structure took place in 1956, when the village council was reduced to five members, all appointive rather than elective offices. [Woodruff 1960: 32-72; Rouilly 1929: 36-147.] The ranked hierarchy in southern villages is embodied in the *hoi huong*, or cult committee, whose major responsibility is to maintain the *dinh* (communal temple), and organize the annual rituals. As in northern and central Vietnamese villages, ranking is manifest in the ritual and in the subsequent feasting. [Woodruff 1960: 194-215; Hickey 1960: 62-84.] In coastal villages of central Vietnam there are ranked sociopolitical hierarchies which vary from village to village, like those in northern Vietnam. Morechand (1955a: 315-16) notes in one coastal village a hierarchy which includes seven ranks. **Hamlet level.** The political organization of hamlets is similar in northern, central, and southern Vietnamese villages. Each hamlet has a chief who represents the hamlet residents in the village council. In northern Vietnam, where villages tend to be closely knit, hamlets are separated by a fence or hedge growth. These divisions usually represent a desire for separateness because of political or religious differences. [Hickey 1958: 60-61; Gourou 1936a: 263-66; Woodruff 1960: 67-69.] **Village associations.** *Giap* are the traditional administrative subdivisions of northern Vietnamese villages. The term also applies to male associations in northern villages, which function mainly as mutual aid societies. Lists of members and their families are kept, and a common fund is maintained from which members may borrow. [Dang 1950: 134-35.] *Phuong* are traditional trade guilds in northern villages and towns, organized along lines similar to the medieval trade guilds of Europe. Each *phuong* has its own trade secrets and maintains its own guardian-spirit cult. [Hickey 1958: 56-57.] Other associations, called *hui* or *tontines*, combine mutual aid with some aspects of gambling. [Hendry 1959: 295-308.] The Viet Minh introduced to both North Vietnam and South Vietnam a compulsory association known as the "five-family system." Each group of five families, living in the same locale, has a leader who reports to the hamlet chief on the activities of all members. This system is supposed to serve a variety of functions, from mutual aid and helping with hamlet projects to security. [Hickey 1960: 84-85.] **Social stratification.** The traditional way of ranking the various economic levels in Vietnamese farming communities is as follows: *ban nong* is the poor farmer, *trung nong* the farmer of the middle economic level, and *phu nong* the rich farmer. In the southern Vietnamese village of Khanh Hau, Hendry (1959) found that this three-level ranking includes not only the amount of land owned or rented but also the occupation of nonfarmer, so that it applies both to economic activities and to the general style of life. In his study of a central Vietnamese coastal village in which fishing is the primary occupation, Morechand (1955a:

338-40) notes a traditional breakdown of three economic levels similar to those noted by Hendry. *Ban* are the poor of the village—those without fishing equipment. They comprise the laboring group, taking whatever means of employment they can find. *Tho phu* is the middle group—fishermen with enough equipment to sustain themselves and their families. This category also includes some of the tradesmen and artisans. *Tho* are the well-to-do—those with the means and equipment for relatively large-scale fishing. They also are the entrepreneurs, although the only enterprise available to most of them is the production of *nuoc mam*.

RELIGION. **Major religions.** The traditional roots of Vietnamese formal religious beliefs, practices, and institutions are Chinese, as are most of the popular beliefs and practices (many of which are of the oral tradition). Mahayana Buddhism, Taoism, and Confucianism form the basis of the formal system. Catholicism was introduced in the sixteenth and seventeenth centuries. More recently, several new religious sects—e.g. Hoa Hao and Cao Dai—have emerged in southern Vietnam. Protestantism is a relatively recent introduction, and Protestant missionary efforts in Vietnam have been more intense among the highland groups than among the Vietnamese. **Buddhism.** Mahayana Buddhism was introduced into Vietnam at an early date. Cadière (1958: 2) notes that in the seventh century A.D. it was established in the early Vietnamese kingdom of Giao Chi. Le (1955: 128-219) reports that a Buddhist sect was founded in Giao Chi at the end of the sixth century by Vinitaruci, a southern Indian. Following Vietnamese independence in the tenth century, Buddhism spread throughout northern Vietnam, with the support of the emperors. By the early sixteenth century, Buddhist pagodas were established in the vicinity of Hue in central Vietnam. Pagodas are now found in towns and cities throughout Vietnam. Large pagodas are usually maintained by the state, while smaller ones are either supported by villages or by well-to-do individuals. Most village pagodas have one or two monks, and in larger towns there are larger communities of monks and nuns, but without an organized hierarchy. In recent years, the Buddhist Association of South Vietnam has been established in an attempt to form a fixed hierarchy with set standards for study, training, and examination. [Cadière 1958: 26-32; Hickey 1960: 183-98.] **Taoism.** Although the *Book of Reason and Virtue* is little known among the Vietnamese, many cults, beliefs, and practices find their roots in Taoist philosophy and cosmology. Priest-sorcerers serve cults honoring a complicated pantheon of supernatural beings, animistic beings, and heroes, through exorcistic rites, magical practices, talismans, amulets, and other ritual accouterments, which are all part of the later aberrant type of Taoism. [Cadière 1958: 27-30.] **Confucianism.** Confucius is venerated by the

Vietnamese as a philosopher and a model of the good man. Confucian concepts are deeply rooted in the Vietnamese value system, and cults such as that of the ancestors are sometimes attributed to Confucian principles and the writings of Confucius (Cadière 1958: 25-29). In northern Vietnamese villages, small shrines, *van mieu,* dedicated to Confucius and his disciples, are sometimes described as "temples of literature." In northern Vietnamese villages, rituals associated with the cult of Confucius are held in the *dinh,* with village notables as the officiants. [Nguyen 1930: 114-18.] On an auspicious day in autumn, the emperor formerly presided at an elaborate festival of Confucius at the imperial city of Hue. [Petit 1931: 51-54.] **Catholicism.** In 1533, a royal edict banned the religious ideas taught by a man in the name of Gia To (Jesus) in Red river delta villages. The preacher, named I Ni Knu, is thought to have been Inigo (Ignace). Prior to 1954, the heaviest concentrations of Catholics were found in the Bui Chu and Phat Diem districts of northern Vietnam. In some places the missions organized colonies in which Catholics, under the direction of missionaries, lived in communes, farmed the land, and in some instances established plantations. [Gourou 1936a: 208-10; Robequain 1944: 193-94.] The romanized national language of the Vietnamese, *quoc ngu,* is the work of a French missionary, Fr. Alexandre de Rhodes. **Cao Daism.** Cao Daism is a relatively new religion in Vietnam. Founded in 1925, its aim is to combine the "great religions" of the world, and to incorporate the organizational features, tenets, and deities of the Judeo-Christian tradition with those of Buddhism, Confucianism, Taoism, and Hinduism, together with some aspects of Indian mysticism and the popular beliefs and practices of the Vietnamese-Chinese tradition. Tam Ky, the original sect, was established at the town of Tay Ninh in the western area of the Mekong river delta, near the Cambodian border. A number of divergent sects emerged, each with a "holy see" in the delta. There are eight sects of Cao Daism in southern Vietnam, and while the number of adherents is unrecorded, it is estimated to be relatively high. [Hickey 1960: 200-21; Gobron 1949.] **Indigenous cults.** The cult of the ancestors is observed rigorously by the Vietnamese. All but Christian households have altars dedicated to the ancestors in the main room of the house, which must contain incense burners, candles, offering plates, and tablets on which the pseudonyms of the ancestors are inscribed in Chinese characters. The elaborateness of the altar depends on the affluence of the family. Rituals are held honoring each ancestor on the anniversary of his death, and several rituals are held for the ancestors collectively during the lunar new year period. Responsibility for carrying out these rituals is divided among the adult males of the common descent group and each individual family. The *truong toc,* head of the patrilineal common descent

group, is responsible for rituals honoring the common ancestor, and the eldest male in each segment of the common descent group performs the rituals for the ancestors in that segment. In each individual family (extended household or nuclear family), ritual responsibilities are divided by agreement among the adult males. [Hickey 1960: 164-74; Cadière 1958: 41-44.] **Cult of the guardian spirit of the village.** Traditionally the village guardian spirit, selected by a newly-founded village, was approved by the emperor. There may be one or more guardian spirits for each village, selected from the pantheon of national or local heroes or from among deceased residents of note. In many instances the guardian spirit is the founder of the village. To honor the guardian spirit, the village constructs a communal temple, *dinh.* Custom dictates the architecture and floor plan of the *dinh,* which is used both for rituals and as a meeting room for the villagers. The central room is the sanctuary for the sacred objects and the imperial decree confirming the guardian spirit, and another large room serves as the public part of the *dinh,* the meeting place and scene of village feasts. [Nguyen 1930: 109-11; Hickey 1960: 62-84.] In northern Vietnam, two types of rituals are held in the *dinh;* official rituals honoring Buddha, the guardian spirit, and the spirit of agriculture, and those associated with popular cults, including the cult of abandoned souls and some hero cults. In southern Vietnamese villages, there appears to be a narrower range of cult rituals held in the *dinh.* [Nguyen 1930: 114; Hickey 1960: 62-84; Nguyen 1940: 137-56.] **Animal cults.** In rural communities a complicated set of magico-religious concepts and cults are associated with animals. Some *ma* (ghosts) are identified as animal ghosts, such as the *ma heo* (pig ghost) and *ma meo* (cat ghost). In some areas, animal cries are believed to portend coming events; the cry of the wild goat or deer is believed to herald a change in the weather. If the type of ants known as *dat* build their nest in the riverbank trees, it is a sign that the river will rise to flood levels. There is also a belief in legendary animals, such as the dragonlike *thuong-luong,* the "snake that resembles the eel." The tiger is feared and venerated, and is honored in formal cults. It is a popular animal in Vietnamese legend, and the source of folk medicine (tiger bones and whiskers are used in the preparation of potent medicines). *Con ca voi,* the whale, is also the object of considerable cult veneration, particularly in the coastal villages of central Vietnam. [Cadière 1955: 213-54; Langrand 1945: 80-109.] **Tree and stone cults.** In the vicinity of Hue, tree cults are widespread. Some trees are believed to have supernatural influence, while others are associated with spirits. Various kinds of stone cults are even more popular and more widespread. Like the tree cults, they vary greatly. Dangerous rocks in water courses are objects of ritual, and one general category of sacred stones is called *but,* while another category is used as fetishes. One renowned cult is maintained for the spirit of a large stone at the entrance of the École Professionnelle in Hue. [Cadière 1955: 9-108.] **Cult of the spirit of the soil.** Most Vietnamese families perform rituals to the spirit of the soil on prescribed occasions. When a new house is being constructed, a ritual requesting the spirit's permission to disturb the soil must precede any actual work. Prior to planting, many farmers make small offerings to the spirit of the soil, and at weddings, the bridal couple make offerings and kowtow before an altar dedicated to the spirit of the soil before entering the groom's house. [Hickey 1960: 173-74.] **Secret societies: socioreligious associations.** Coulet (1926) feels that the secret societies active against the French were basically religious. Spirits and deities were honored with offerings, and there was wide use of cabalistic symbols. In the raid on the Saigon prison, the raiders employed Taoist symbols on flags, and also special amulets to protect them from the French bullets. Sorcerers also played a vital role in the secret societies. **Supernaturals.** Collective and individual cults are maintained to a wide variety of supernatural beings. Cadière distinguishes several kinds. *Than,* which he translates as *"génies,"* are found in enormous variety in rural areas. The most common *than* are *than nui,* the spirit of the mountain, *than dat,* the spirit of the land, and *tao than,* one of the three spirits of the hearth. A subgrouping of *than* are the *but,* spirits which are associated with sacred stones. In general, the *than* are beneficent spirits. According to Cadière, *ma* may be translated as *"esprits." Ma* may refer to abandoned human souls, but never to ancestors, and also may refer to the souls of animals. *Ma* are ubiquitous, and while some are harmless, others are malevolent. *Qui* are "demons," not as powerful as the *than,* but generally more feared because of the evil they do. [Cadière 1957: 43-70.] **Practitioners.** *Ong dong* and *ba dong* are the male and female mediums associated with the popular cult of the *chu vi,* the countless spirits associated with the goddess Lieu Hanh and the Vietnamese culture hero, General Tran Hung Dao. The male *ong dong* often appear as transvestites in the ritual ceremonies. Neither *ong dong* nor *ba dong* have an official role in village rituals, but function at the request of individual villagers. *Ba dong* are usually spinsters or widows without children, as the state of being a *ba dong* is considered incompatible with motherhood. The *ong dong,* on the other hand, are usually married men with children. Both *ong dong* and *ba dong* are predestined for their roles. A variety of events or circumstances are thought to be manifestations of latent *ong dong-ba dong* powers. The essence of the cult rituals is communication with the occult, either spirits or the souls of ancestors. [Nguyen 1930: 1-6; Durand 1959.] *Ong thay phap* are the "masters of magic formulae,"

and *ong thay bua* are the "masters of amulets," both of whom function as sorcerers rather than mediums. The metier of the *ong thay phap* is usually passed from father to son. Each receives his powers from a patron deity, and maintains a cult in honor of the deity. *Ong thay phap* may specialize in curing particular types of ailments. They perform their services for a fee, both for individuals and at village rituals. They also make talismans which they sell. [Hickey 1964.] Some *ong thay phap* played important roles in the secret societies in southern Vietnam (Coulet 1926: 25-200). ● *Ong ho* are individuals possessed by the deity Quan De or by its acolytes, Quan Chau and Linh Hau; through the power of these supernatural beings, the *ong ho* can protect individuals and extend the benefits of the deities to them. The *ong ho* make amulets which offer protection against misfortune and epidemic disease. *Ong ho* are generally associated with a particular pagoda. When they are under the influence of the deity, they are obliged to remain in the pagoda and observe food taboos. The deity takes possession of the *ong ho* through a seizure of trembling and convulsive movements accompanied by a trance. [Cadière 1958: 228-40.] ● Geomancy of the Chinese variety has greatly influenced Vietnamese concepts of the physical world and Vietnamese cosmology in general. According to geomantic concepts, position and patterns foster good or evil influences, depending on their orientation to the five elements—water, fire, metal, earth, and wood. The geomancer examines the site of a proposed building to determine the influences of the elements in the area. He interprets physical features as they represent the five elements, and then recommends a position that will combine compatible elements for good effect. ● A number of talismans are believed to have the power to ward off evil influences, and certain "magical obstacles" such as rises, hills, or stones can negate evil influences if they stand between an area of human habitation and such menacing physical features as the bend in a river or trifurcation in a road. [Cadière 1955: 117-70; Gourou 1936a: 345; Tran 1942: 23-24, 146-47.] **Ceremonies.** In connection with the cult of heaven, *nam giao,* an elaborate state sacrifice was held every three years in a special place at Hue. A wide variety of other spirits were also venerated in the ritual, which was renowned for its sumptuousness. Processions of troops, nobles, and mandarins accompanied the emperor to the scene of the ritual. [Cadière 1958: 85-128; de Bertren 1944: 54-61.] Infancy and childhood are marked with a series of rites to protect the child and hasten its healthy development. One month after birth, the child is ritually placed under the protection of the "twelve goddesses of motherhood" (Tran 1942: 273-74). A child may be dedicated to a benevolent protective spirit or to Buddha by means of a ritual at the pagoda. Following the initial rite, the family is obliged to perform prescribed rituals to the guardian deity on the fifth day of the fifth lunar month and the fifteenth day of the seventh lunar month. [Nguyen 1938: 77-79; Cadière 1955: 198-211.] A number of rites are designed to cope with such crises as droughts or epidemics. The cholera spirit ritual is performed by villages which are threatened by or experiencing a cholera epidemic. The cholera spirit is a collective designation for a host of spirits that cause this disease. Rain-making rituals are held in villages during times of drought. [Cadière 1958: 199-212; Lan 1919: 445-50.] **Soul, death, and afterlife.** The corpse is prepared by washing and dressing it in fine clothes. Coins may be placed in the mouth. A number of brief rituals are held, such as giving the deceased a pseudonym, before the relatives and friends gather to express their sorrow. Normally the funeral period is three days, although both large families and well-to-do families prolong the period so that kin from distant places may gather for the burial rituals. "High mourning," observed by parents, husband, and children, lasts for three years in northern and central Vietnam, and for two years in the south. Grandparents, parents' siblings, and wives mourn for one year. Collateral kin are mourned for three months. Vietnamese funeral processions resemble those of the Chinese; relatives and friends in varying degrees of mourning are assigned fixed places behind the catafalque. Well-to-do Vietnamese present the family of the deceased with silk banderoles extolling the qualities of the deceased, which are carried in the procession. Rituals precede the burial. Well-to-do families construct tombs of stone or, more recently, of concrete. A ritual is held for the new ancestor every seven days until the forty-ninth day, when a large ceremony and feast is held in the house of the deceased. On the hundredth day after the burial a rite is held at the tomb, and paper symbols of material objects used in life are burned at the altar of the ancestors as an offering to the deceased. The first anniversary of death is marked with a ritual and feast, and another ritual signals the end of the mourning period. [Hickey 1958: 88-91.]

BIBLIOGRAPHY. De Bertren 1944; Cadière 1955, 1957, 1958; Canada Department of Mines 1953; Chau 1940; Claeys 1942; Coulet 1926; Dang 1950; Dao 1938; Dumont 1935; Durand 1959; Embree and Thomas 1950; Fall 1960; Gittinger 1959; Gobron 1949; Goudal 1938; Gourou 1936a, 1936b, 1945; Greenberg 1953; Hendry 1959; Henry 1932; Hickey 1958, 1960, 1964; Lan 1919; Langrand 1945; Le 1955; Morechand 1955a; Nguyen 1939, 1940; Nguyen 1930, 1938; NNCDT 1959; Paris 1955; Pasquier 1907; Petit 1931; Robequain 1929, 1944; Rouilly 1929; Tran 1942; Vu 1939; Woodruff 1960.

MUONG

Synonyms. *Ao-ta, Mon, Mwal, Mwon, Ngue, Nguoe, Nguon, Nha Lang, Sach, Tho*

ORIENTATION. **Identification.** While the designation Muong is widely used to indicate this group, Cuisinier points out that it is a misnomer, taken from the Tai word *muong*, which is a territorial division. She advocates retaining this designation, however, in view of the fact that the group refers to itself by a variety of names including Mwal, Mwon, Mon, and corruptions of the Vietnamese word *nguoi* (people) such as Nguoe and Ngue. In the vicinity of Vinh, the Vietnamese use the term *muong* to refer to Tai-speaking groups, and refer to the Muong as Nha Lang. Further south, in Quang Binh, they are called Nguon. Cuisinier, when referring to the Muong in these areas, uses the same designations, i.e. Nha Lang and Nguon. [Cuisinier 1948: 22-25.] A North Vietnamese source notes that the Muong in different localities are known by differing names. The Muong of Mai Da are called Ao-ta; those in Quang Binh are known as Nguon or Sach; and in 4th Zone they are called Tho. [NNCDT 1959: 245.] **Location.** The Muong are widely dispersed in northern Vietnam in the highland area on the southwest fringe of the Red river delta. They are found on the eastern slope of the Annam Cordillera from Qui Mong in the north (near the town of Yen Bay) to the Thuong Xuan region in the south. Le (1955: 48-50) reports that the Muong form two large groupings—one in the province of Hoa Binh and the other on the fringes of Thanh Hoa, Song Tay, and Phu Tho. **Linguistic affiliation.** According to Benedict (1942: 576-600), Muong is closely related to Vietnamese. The two languages, Benedict feels, are the northernmost members of the Mon-Khmer stock. Greenberg (1953: 281) recognizes Schmidt's classification of Annamite–Muong together with related Mon-Khmer in an Austroasiatic [Austroasian] stock. **Demography.** In 1931 Gourdon (1931:84) estimated the Muong population at 180,000. The 1936 census placed the Muong at 163,369, with the densest groupings in the vicinities of Hoa Binh, Thanh Hoa, and Phu Tho. Le (1955: 48) reports a total of 260,000; and Cuisinier (1948: 31) gives 250,000. The NNCDT (1959: 245) reports the Muong population at 366,738. **History and cultural relations.** One source (Buttinger 1958: 29) relates the Muong to an Austro-Indonesian stratum which has been largely dispersed or absorbed by other groups who entered Indochina at a later date. Robequain (1929: 110-13) theorizes that the ancestors of the Muong and Vietnamese migrated into northern Vietnam during the same period that Tai-speaking groups were moving southward through the upland valleys. The Vietnamese and Muong formed a relatively homogenous group until the Han conquest of the Red river delta precipitated a sinicization of the population. The resulting divergence is now manifest in the Vietnamese–Muong differentiation. ● Dispersed as they are in some areas, the Muong have had considerable contact with Vietnamese and Tai groups. In the Nghia Lo area the Muong have some contact with Meo and Man who come down to market. The Muong whom Cuisinier refers to as Nguon have contact with the Sach in the Laos border area, and with other groups such as the May and Ruc (or Roc). The Muong also have had considerable contact with the French. [Cuisinier 1948: 40-48; Robequain 1929: 95-131.]

SETTLEMENT PATTERN AND HOUSING. **Settlement pattern.** Settlements are located away from main lines of communication, near rivers. The farmsteads comprising a settlement are accessible by footpath. The house of the *tho lang,* or headman, is usually located in the village center, with the other farmsteads scattered along the river bank or on the slopes of hills. Another important structure in a Muong village is the temple of the spirit of the soil. In the Hoa Binh area and scattered parts of northern Thanh Hoa province, farmsteads are surrounded by enclosures of bamboo, cactus, and other hedge growth. [Cuisinier 1948: 71-75.] **Housing.** Most houses are constructed on piling, with the area below serving as a stable. Size is determined by the owner's wealth or social status. The houses of the elite, in addition to being large, often have common verandas or covered walks connecting them. Walls are of split bamboo or planks, and houses invariably are rectangular. Roofs are of thatch, and the entrance is reached by a veranda that serves as a work area and a place to receive visitors. The interior is divided into several compartments, one of which has a hole in the floor for a latrine. The main room contains the altar of the ancestors, and is a reception room for visitors as well as the room where the family spends most of its time. Usually the hearth is located near a window or door so that the smoke may escape. The hearth is a sacred place. No one may spit in it or approach it while nude, for fear of offending the spirit of the hearth. Granaries are located near the house, and are also on piling. [Cuisinier 1948: 77-90; Robequain 1929: 201-12.]

ECONOMY. **Agriculture.** Agriculture is the predominant economic activity, and nonglutinous wet rice the staple crop, although in some areas, particularly among the Nguon Muong of Quang Binh, rice is cultivated by the swidden method. Glutinous varieties are also cultivated. Terraced fields are common, and irrigation is achieved by digging small channels along the edge of the terrace. These channels are then connected by a system of bamboo tubes by which the flow of water downward may be controlled. In some areas the terraced paddy fields have two crops—the "summer" crop in the fifth lunar month and the "winter" crop in the tenth month. [Cuisinier 1948: 111-13.] For swidden agriculture, the Muong first select a wooded area, and then cut and burn the trees and brush. They usually obtain permission from the administration to burn a given area. Swiddens are cultivated for two or three years, and if irrigation is possible they are transformed into irrigated fields, usually terraced. [Robequain 1929: 165.] The Muong use several kinds of natural fertilizer. Buffalo manure is mixed with hearth ashes to fertilize special crops such as manioc. Ashes also are thinly spread on the paddy fields. Straw is placed at the bases of plants as a compost. Plows of wood or bamboo with iron blades are used in paddy and swidden agriculture, pulled by either cattle or buffalo. A wooden harrow also is used. Several types of sickles, a machete, and various types of cutting knives—a special one for females—are used in the harvesting. [Cuisinier 1948: 114-18.] Maize is an important secondary crop. Other crops include sesame, manioc, white eggplant, tomatoes, *Tetragonia,* papaya, and grapefruit. Some families cultivate kapok trees. Cash crops include castor-bean trees, benzoin, and sticklac. Many Muong families also cultivate cotton. [Cuisinier 1948: 145-46.] **Fishing and hunting.** Fishing is an important means of supplementing the diet, and the Muong use a wide variety of fish traps. Although they enjoy the reputation of being great hunters, the Muong of Thanh Hoa and Hoa Binh do not warrant it, according to Cuisinier. Hunting (usually followed by great feasting) is a leisure-time activity rather than a means of supplementing the food supply. Village males participate in group hunts. Gongs are used to gather men and dogs, and the hunting party then moves into the forest, striking the gongs and beating the brush to scare out the game. The dogs stalk the game, which is then shot by the hunters. A number of Muong use firearms made by specialists and passed down from one generation to another. They also use crossbows. Among the Nguon Muong, crossbow production has ceased, and they must purchase their crossbows from the neighboring May and Ruc. The Muong also employ a variety of game traps made of bamboo, rattan, and other flexible woods. [Cuisinier 1948: 154-80.] **Gathering.** Women sometimes gather wild roots, shoots, and leaves in the forest (Cuisinier 1948: 146). **Domestic animals.** Pigs, cattle, ducks, and chickens are raised for food. Cats and dogs are pets. Buffalo and cattle are common draft animals, and some well-to-do Muong have horses. [Cuisinier 1948: 97-99.] **Industrial arts.** Women weave most of the cloth used in their own garments, but cloth used in men's clothes is usually purchased (Cuisinier 1948: 215). Within the family several different dyes are prepared (Cuisinier 1948: 220-22). Males produce their own crossbows, and game and fish traps. Village specialists occasionally make firearms. There also are carpenters and joiners, and coffin production may be a specialization within the village. Cooking pots are made by specialists, as are farm implements. [Cuisinier 1948: 147 and 214.] **Trade.** Market places are rare in the Muong area. Those found in the larger centers were established by the Vietnamese or more recently by the French. In most Muong villages of 20 or more households, there usually are two or three shops run by Vietnamese specializing in fresh fruits and vegetables of the local area, as well as tobacco, alcohol, and some manufactured goods such as needles, thread, buttons, and matches. [Cuisinier 1948: 330-33.] The Muong in the area of Nghia Lo patronize the market in that town and trade with Tai groups as well as with the Man and Meo. The Nguon Muong of the Vinh region purchase resin and other forest products from the Sach and Ruc, in addition to their crossbows. The Sach purchase monkey pelts from the Nguon Muong, in return for maize, paddy, knives, and sometimes cloth. [Cuisinier 1948: 45.] **Division of labor.** Males prepare the land, including cutting and clearing the swiddens and plowing in wet-rice areas. All members of the family assist in the harvest. Hunting and fishing are male activities, while females carry water and gather plants, herbs, and wood. [Cuisinier 1948: 129-39.] **Land tenure.** The traditional land tenure system was based on the principle of the right of the first cultivator. The man who cleared and cultivated the land gained inalienable title not only to the land cultivated and the site of his farmstead but also to the woods, water courses, and an ill-defined surrounding area. As his family increased, its members gained title to an ever-expanding area. This system resulted in the emergence of a gentry among the Muong—a few families held title to most or all of the land in each local area. Those settling the area at a later date had to obtain permission of the first cultivator or his descendants, and they were also obliged to maintain a cult in honor of the first cultivator. This traditional system has changed over the last several hundred years. The Le emperors sent Vietnamese mandarins into the Muong areas, and Vietnamese influence has slowly resulted in the adoption of the Vietnamese land tenure system. [Cuisinier 1948: 287-93.]

KIN GROUPS. **Descent.** Descent is patrilineal. Males have exclusive right to real property, and the eldest son inherits the bulk of family property. The father has a great deal of authority in the Muong family. **Kin groups.** From information given by Cuisinier (1948: 243-56, 358-61), it appears that the *ho* is a name-sib which regulates marriage, particularly among the *tho lang* elite. Among the *tho lang*, the *ho*, which is also a name-sib among the Vietnamese, appears to have some corporate group functions as well. The most important corporate kin group among the Muong appears to be the patrilineal common descent group, which includes those related through the male line to a common male ancestor in the fifth ascending generation. This group appears to be more functional among the *tho lang*, in that all of its members gather for the rituals honoring the common ancestor; whereas among the peasants, only a small group gathers. ● Cuisinier refers to *familles feodales*, which have food taboos that vary according to region. The Quach family of Lac Son, for example, is forbidden to eat dog; while the Quach family of Kim Boi cannot eat the flesh of white buffalo or marsh hen. The Dinh family of Cao Phong cannot eat monkey; whereas the Dinh family of Luong Son has a taboo against eating panther. [Cuisinier 1948: 211-12.]

MARRIAGE AND FAMILY. **Mode.** Males of the nobility tend to marry early, between the ages of 15 and 20; whereas males of the peasantry usually marry between the ages of 18 and 25. Females, regardless of social status, marry between the ages of 16 and 18. The boy's parents initiate the marriage arrangements once a girl has been chosen, and a peasant boy has considerable freedom of choice. An intermediary visits the girl's parents with symbolic gifts. If the initial overtures meet with approval, the bride price, the length of the engagement, and the date of the marriage are set at a second visit. The amount of the bride price depends on the relative wealth of the boy's family. Length of engagement varies from one to five years among Muong of different areas. The groom is expected to spend a year or two at the house of his parents-in-law before the marriage can be officially consummated. ● The marriage consists of two significant rituals: the first before the altar of the ancestors in the bride's house, signifying her departure from the family, and the second before the groom's ancestral altar, where the bride is accepted into the groom's family. The Muong have the practice of adopting the son-in-law, as a means of giving him part of the inheritance. Some Muong also distinguish between the "transplanting daughter-in-law" and the "harvesting daughter-in-law." In the first instance marriage takes place at the commencement of the transplanting, while the other is celebrated on the last day of the harvest. The bride price in the former is likely to be higher, because the groom's family is gaining an additional agricultural laborer. [Cuisinier 1948: 260-76.] **Form.** Polygyny is permitted, and is customary among the nobility, but peasants rarely practice it. The first wife has a predominant role in the household, and subsequent wives are considered almost the same as concubines. The first wife is also considered to be "mother" of all sons born to the husband. The eldest son of the first wife is considered the eldest son of the family, regardless of prior male births by other wives or concubines. [Cuisinier 1948: 256-59.] **Extension of incest taboos.** The *ho* (patrilineal name-sib) regulates marriage, particularly among the *tho lang*. Cuisinier also reports that it is specifically forbidden to marry "close relatives," i.e. those related through common ancestors of the fourth ascending generation. Some Muong prefer that a mate be selected from another village, and for the nobility the rule is that the first wife must be from another fief. Marriages tend to take place within the same social group, and among the *tho lang* the first wife must be from another *tho lang* family. [Cuisinier 1948: 243-56.] **Residence.** The newly-married couple live with the groom's parents, and during the residence period the girl receives permission from her parents-in-law to establish her own household nearby. [Cuisinier 1948: 256-59.] **Inheritance.** Among peasants the inheritance is not usually divided unless it is considered sufficiently large for all sons to share. Among the nobility, the eldest son of the first wife inherits the prerogatives of the father, the paternal house, and the bulk of the property. If his father is *tho lang* of a fief, he inherits the title. Other sons of the principal wife also may inherit some land. Sons of concubines have no claim to inheritance, although prior to his death, the father may grant them some paddy fields or cash. The eldest son has the responsibility of supporting unmarried females and the widow of the household. [Cuisinier 1948: 280-83.] **Divorce.** A husband may repudiate his wife on a wide variety of pretexts, but not if she is old or without family. Divorce cannot take place during a mourning period, and if the couple has fallen into poverty, divorce is impossible. An unhappy wife has the right to separate from her husband by making an extended visit to her parents, but divorce is rare. [Cuisinier 1948: 276-77.] **Adoption.** Adoption of additional children into a family which already has male heirs is relatively common. A price may be paid, but it is not necessarily prescribed. To adopt a son who will become head of the family is more complicated. The boy must be of the same *ho* as the father, and he cannot be the eldest son in his own family. [Cuisinier 1948: 278-80.]

SOCIOPOLITICAL ORGANIZATION. The traditional Muong sociopolitical organization resembles the Tho and Black Tai systems (cf. Robequain 1929: 142-51), which are characterized by an entrenched nobility and a peasantry with no title to the lands they farm. The elite are descendants of those who first cleared and claimed the land. These first occupants received inalienable title to the land, and after death were deified as the ancestors of the area. In each village, the *tho lang* or headman is of the elite, and claims his title by right of inheritance, as a descendant of the first settler. In most Muong villages the traditional system has been changed as a result of Vietnamese influence. Private ownership of land has been introduced, together with the system of village communal land. The court at Hue also introduced the Vietnamese political and administrative system into the Muong area. ● In Muong villages where the *tho lang* has retained his traditional pre-

rogatives, he is described as having a paternal relationship with the villagers. In times of need he is expected to share his paddy, and traditionally he was obliged to provide a coffin for those unable to afford one. His assistant is the *au po*, who functions as liaison between the *tho lang* and the people. The *au po* is also the *tho lang's* confidant, and he may perform certain rituals for the *tho lang's* family. In most instances the *au po* inherits his position from his father, but in some villages he is appointed by the *tho lang* or named by the notables. Most *au po* also engage in farming. Usually there is no *tho lang* in villages with a majority of Catholic residents, nor in the relatively few villages organized along the lines of the Vietnamese commune. Villages in which a proper male heir is unavailable also have no *tho lang*. ● In areas that have a Vietnamese-instituted village political structure, there are usually the following officials: a *ly truong* (administrative chief), a *pho ly* (deputy administrative chief), a *kai lang, ka sa,* or *ko da* (mayor), and the local *au kwyen, kai com,* or *thu ho* (hamlet chiefs). The *ly truong* is responsible for supervising the local police, for collecting taxes, and for executing orders from higher authorities. In villages where the *tho lang* has retained his role as leader, he has considerable control over the *ly truong*. The *tho lang* may name the candidates for *ly truong* (often from among his kin), and from them the villagers select the *ly truong*. Both the *ly truong* and the *pho ly* are elected for life. Whereas the *ly truong* receives a salary that varies from village to village, the *pho ly* and other minor officials have the use of a certain amount of paddy land as compensation. [Cuisinier 1948: 295-310.]

RELIGION. Supernaturals. The Muong believe in a large pantheon of supernatural beings, many of which are also found in Vietnamese religion of the oral tradition. The spirit of the mountain, the spirit of agriculture, and the spirit of the hearth are honored in communal and familial cults. Individuals maintain a cult of living souls, as well as cults of such spirits as the protectresses of the soul and the protectors of the body. Following group hunts, a ritual offering of game is made to the spirit of the forest, the spirit of the mountain, and either the guardian spirit of wildlife or the spirit of firearms, depending on the region. The cult of the spirit of the soil is carried out in a variety of ways. In the Hoa Binh, Son Tay, Pho Tho, Son La, and Yen Bay areas an altar is dedicated to the spirit of the soil in every house. [Cuisinier 1948: 159-62, 380-414.] Unlike the Vietnamese village guardian spirits, those of the Muong have no imperial document. The number of such spirits varies from village to village. In some villages the guardian spirit is the founder of the village (in addition to being honored as the village ancestor), and often his descendants are elevated to the rank of guardian spirits. Local culture heroes may be guardian spirits, and in some villages new guardian-spirit cults have been formed, absorbing the old ones. Among the Nguon Muong the cult of the guardian spirit has been fused with the cult of the village ancestor in which the original *tho lang* is venerated. [Cuisinier 1948: 365-86.] The Muong practice the cult of the ancestors in a fashion similar to that of the Vietnamese. The altars of the *tho lang* are elaborate, with a carved wooden table, lacquered plaques containing the names of the ancestors, brass candle holders, vases, and offering plates. The altars of the ordinary peasants are simple boards on a stand or attached to the wall. Cult rituals honoring the common ancestor of the kin group are the responsibility of the eldest male of the senior line. The division of cult responsibilities is distributed in similar fashion within the common descent group—the eldest male of each segment and each household has cult responsibilities for his respective ancestors. Rituals honoring the ancestors are held on the anniversaries of their deaths and during the lunar new year period. Rituals consist of kowtowing before the altar—males first, then females. Offerings of food are placed on the altar. Among the *tho lang*, these rituals are under the direction of an officiant, usually the *au po*. [Cuisinier 1948: 340-63.] **Practitioners.** There are diviners, healers, and male and female magicians. Females by and large do not claim the wide range of powers associated with male sorcerers, but the sorceress known as *moi* has an important role in Muong society. Many *moi* remain unmarried, but those who do wed and have children pass their secrets on to their eldest daughters. ● Instruction in the art of sorcery lasts from three to ten years. During the apprentice period the study is general, but after several years specialization is expected, and sorcerers become known for their specializations. *Thay mo* specialize in funeral rituals, while *thay tluong* officiate at most other rituals, and *thay mai* are expert in divination. ● Each Muong sorcerer maintains a cult to the particular spirit who is considered his patron, and makes periodic offerings on an altar in his house. In some areas deceased sorcerers are venerated. All sorcerers receive fees for their services and specified gifts from their pupils. [Cuisinier 1948: 486-98.] **Ceremonies.** Annual rituals are observed by the Muong, either in groups or as individuals. Lunar new year rituals, similar to the Vietnamese *tet* celebrations, are observed by families. A number of taboos are

associated with the new year period. It is forbidden to break the soil for planting for the first three days of the first lunar month. The Muong have adopted the Vietnamese lunar calendar, although they celebrate the new year for a longer period than do the Vietnamese. Rituals honoring the ancestors and family feasts are also associated with the new year celebration, and there is a great deal of intervillage visiting at this time. [Cuisinier 1948: 498-522.] A number of rituals are associated with the agricultural cycle. Traditional ceremonies were held at the time of planting, transplanting, weeding, and harvesting, but planting and weeding rituals have now disappeared in most villages. At the celebration of the lunar new year a special ritual honors the rice spirit. [Cuisinier 1948: 522-61.] **Birth.** When the time for birth approaches, the house is taboo to all strangers. The mother stays in a special place partitioned off from the rest of the house, and a fire is kept burning to purify her. After this taboo period, the birth is announced to the ancestors, and ritual offerings are made on the family altar. The placenta is either hidden in the forest or suspended from a tree. **Death.** The body of the deceased is placed on a bed, where it is bathed and prepared for burial. A *thay mo* is usually summoned to pray over the corpse. Among the nobility it is customary to have the *au po* present at the time of death. He then announces the death before the deceased's house. The death of a *tho lang* is announced by striking a bronze drum. ● Mourning signs are placed around the house, and after the corpse has been ritually placed on the bier, kin and friends gather to offer condolences to the family. The *thay mo* officiates for a period of up to three days. Special robes are worn, and kin wear prescribed mourning garb. On the eve of burial, there is a ritual sacrifice of cattle among the well-to-do, or of a pig among the peasantry. The funeral cortege consists of a catafalque and an orchestra, followed by mourners in prescribed places. On the following day, the mourners return to the grave for additional rituals. The Muong, like the Vietnamese, bring offerings to the grave every fiftieth day for the first two years after burial. [Cuisinier 1948: 443-85.]

BIBLIOGRAPHY. Benedict 1942; Buttinger 1958; Cuisinier 1948; Gourdon 1931; Greenberg 1953; Le 1955; NNCDT 1959; Robequain 1929.

SENOI–SEMANG

SCHMIDT EARLY IDENTIFIED THE Semang-Sakai dialects of the Malay Peninsula as Austroasiatic, related to Mon-Khmer languages farther north in Indochina. Skeat and Blagden, in their monumental study of Malayan aborigines, followed Schmidt's lead; they further identified Semang and Sakai as separate languages, thus setting up the classic trilogy of Semang-Sakai-Jakun that continued to define the dimensions of Malayan ethnography for decades (Skeat and Blagden 1906: 2, 385, 439-62). Racial correlates of these three categories became fixed in popular usage—the woolly-haired Negrito (Semang), the wavy-haired Dravido-Australoid or Veddoid (Sakai), and the straight-haired Proto-Malay (Jakun). As pointed out by Noone (1936), however, language and race in this case do not break down this neatly; there are wavy-haired speakers of Semang dialects, Proto-Malay physical types who speak Senoi, and so on. Modern terminology favors the use of Negrito, Senoi, and Aboriginal Malay in place of the older terms, and Noone, following Malay usage, would reserve Sakai as a general term for all aboriginal groups on the Peninsula (Noone 1936: 1).

SENOI[1]

Synonym. *Sakai*

ORIENTATION. **Identification.** The Senoi fall into the following major groups: the Semai (Central Sakai) in northwestern Pahang and southern Perak; the Temiar (Temer, Northern Sakai, Seroq, Ple) in northern Perak and southern Kelantan; and the Jah Hut and Che Wong (Siwang, Beri Chuba), both just south of the main body of Semai. The little known Mah Meri (Besisi) of the Selangor coast are linguistically related. The Senoi are sometimes described by such Malay terms as Orang Utan, Orang Darat, and Orang Bukit, but these are general names for hill peoples with little or no ethnological value. Sakai, a Malay generic and pejorative name for hill people, is often employed in a specific sense for Senoi. The term Senoi has been used by some writers to mean "Sakai proper," a distinction which is no longer valid. [See Skeat and Blagden 1906, and Williams-Hunt 1952 for compilations of names and synonyms.] **Location.** The Senoi are a predominantly hill people, inhabiting the mountains and foothills of Main Range, the chief mountain unit in the Federation of Malaya. The Temiar are found from Gunong Noring south to Cameron Highlands, while the Semai extend from Cameron Highlands south to the boundary of Negri Sembilan. **Ge-**

ography. Main Range is precipitous, jungle-covered country, much of it inadequately explored. Peaks range up to 7,000 feet and higher. Covering is mainly primary jungle growth alternating with areas of secondary growth, *belukar*. **Linguistic affiliation.** Senoi appears to be closely related to Mon-Khmer languages farther north in Vietnam and Cambodia. There are a great many Malay loan words. Dialect differences among the various Senoi groups are so great that it is frequently difficult for the Senoi from one watershed area to understand those from another. Divisions like that of Williams-Hunt (1952: 23) into northern Senoi (mainly Temiar), central Senoi (mainly Semai), and southeastern Senoi (Jah Hut, Che Wong, and others) oversimplify the actual situation. **Demography.** Recent census estimates by the Department of Aborigines place the number of Semai Senoi at 11,000–15,000; Temiar at 8,000–10,000; Jah Hut at 1,300–1,700; and Che Wong at 180–200. **History and cultural relations.** The Senoi seem to have arrived in Malaya sometime during the period 8,000–2,000 B.C., perhaps from Indochina. Until the nineteenth century A.D., the pacifistic Senoi were harried by Malay raids for slaves and women, which drove them further and further upriver into the inhospitable highlands. Although contact between the two groups was not all hostile, the Senoi remain resentful and distrustful of the Malays, and the Malay term "Sakai" contains a heavy load of contempt. As Malaya moved out of feudalism during the nineteenth century, Senoi communities were able to establish fairly safe trade relations with the outside world, and some communities, notably the more acculturated ones in the west and south, engaged in wage labor. However, the Senoi rarely adopt Islam and there are relatively

---

[1] At the time Robert Dentan contributed this account of Senoi culture he had been resident in the field for 16 months. He feels that his remarks can fairly apply to the Senoi in general unless otherwise specified. His data are based on 13 months with the Semai Senoi and shorter periods with groups such as the Jah Hut and Mah Meri. For comparative data on the Temiar Senoi he has consulted with Iskandar Yusof Carey, Protector of Aborigines, Federation of Malaya.

few cases of Senoi "becoming Malay" in this sense. ● Contact and racial intermixture have occurred most noticeably in the upper Perak and Kelantan river sheds (with nomad Negrito populations), and south of the Jelai river system, where there are populations showing varying degrees of Senoi-Aboriginal Malay mixture (Noone 1936: 29, 52 ff.). The Negritos appear to have had relatively little cultural impact on the Senoi. In the north, where they surround the hill Temiar on three sides, they tend to insulate the latter from the *kampong* Malays downriver. Malay culture has had more noticeable impact on the Senoi, particularly as one moves south into Pahang. ● Although both World Wars left the Senoi relatively undisturbed, the Communist rebellion in the late 1940s and 1950s had cataclysmic effects on their lives. By carrot-and-stick methods, the terrorists were able to enlist the help of some of the jungle people. In response, the government relocated the aborigines where they could be kept under supervision. The first relocation, a purely military affair, resulted in a great loss of property and incredible mortality rates; the Senoi remember it with dread, and would resist any such move in the future. With the establishment of the jungle forts, however, it was possible to let the aborigines return to the jungle. From the Senoi viewpoint, the sole benefit from this period of the Emergency was the establishment of the Department of Aborigines, which has now been vastly expanded, and has taken charge of aboriginal welfare with an enlightened policy.

SETTLEMENT PATTERN AND HOUSING. **Settlement pattern.** The typical Senoi settlement contains 50–200 people, and is strung out along high ground near a river. Most Senoi communities have one longhouse which provides a place for ceremonial activities, and in most places it is supplemented by smaller dwelling units, each of which contains a small extended or nuclear family. Among the hill Temiar in the northern highlands, whole communities may live in a single longhouse (up to 100 feet long, with up to 60 persons), which has compartments for nuclear families and a communal space in the center (Noone 1936: 26). Longhouses decrease in frequency and size as one travels south or west from the Temiar country. In the south, especially where there are neither tigers nor elephants and where a community has used up the nearby land, scattered fieldhouses are common, as a supplement to houses in the village. Most Senoi make fairly permanent clearings (three to eight years in one place), and when they do move it is within a well-defined territory (cf. Noone 1936: 2, 41), called the *sakaq* (from Malay *pusaka*, inheritance). The Che Wong (Siwang) appear to be a seminomadic hunting and gathering group. They have only recently been assimilated into the Senoi pattern, which appears to have spread historically from west to east, absorbing such groups as the Che

Wong in the process. **Housing.** Houses are built on stilts, usually 4 to 12 feet high, but ranging up to 30 feet where tigers are common. Floors are of bamboo slats, walls of bamboo, *attap*, or bark, and roofs are of *attap*. Split-level dwellings are common.

ECONOMY. Subsistence rests primarily on swidden agriculture, supplemented by hunting and fishing. Wild plants, used mostly as medicines or side dishes for manioc and rice, are of minor importance except as a reserve in times of need. The original staple crop was millet, which is still important in remote communities. Within the last two hundred years, maize and manioc have also achieved importance. Hill rice seems not to have come into extensive use until the twentieth century. Manioc is the staple among the Temiar and eastern Semai. It is replaced gradually, to the south and west, by dry rice, which in turn is rapidly being replaced by wet rice among the Jah Hut and Mah Meri. Arboriculture is important from a social as well as an economic standpoint, since inherited trees are an important factor in maintaining a man's loyalty to the *sakaq*, the hereditary area exploited by a group of extended family households. ● Since the Emergency, several of the Senoi groups living near Malay communities have, under the aegis of the Department of Aborigines, taken up wet-rice agriculture, a development which will have far-reaching consequences. At the present, however, only a handful of Senoi farmers plant cash crops (mostly rubber), and few are real peasants. Arboriculture is mostly limited to tending trees already growing, but some bananas are planted. [For a thorough survey of material culture and economic pursuits, see Skeat and Blagden 1906. A large documented collection of Semai artifacts and Jah Hut carvings, made by Robert Dentan, is in the American Museum of Natural History.] **Agriculture.** Most agriculture is slash-and-burn, with the dibble and machete the only tools. The major planting season (for rice and millet) is mid-summer, but there is also an optional spring planting. A man usually clears his own field or *ladang* (Semai-Temiar, *selai*), which is preferably near a river. Relatives and friends help with the main planting, in return for a feast. Ideally, all cultivars of all crops are planted, to ensure that at least some reach maturity. *Lalang* grass is not yet a major problem in most areas, but wild bananas, insects, birds, rodents, and, in some areas, elephants take a heavy toll. Harvesting takes place the year round, depending on the ripening of the crops and the needs of the farmer. Only the rice harvest is marked by a ceremony. Among the less acculturated groups, a complicated series of taboos related to the phases of the moon limits agricultural (and house-building) activities to about three weeks per month. [See Williams-Hunt 1952: 46-50 for details of annual cycle and agricultural methods among the Semai Senoi.] **Fishing and hunting.** Most fish are caught in basket traps. Poisons, weirs, corrals, spears, and hooks are also used. The basic hunting tool is the blowpipe with poisoned dart, although the Semai and the Temiar also use spears. A wide variety of snares, deadfalls, spear traps, and birdlimes, however, provide the bulk of the animal food. A large animal (deer, pig, python, monkey, or civet) may feed an entire community. **Domestic animals.** Any young wild animal (e.g. monitor, boar, kingfisher) that is captured alive is kept as a pet. However, the only truly domesticated animals are, in probable order of acquisition, dogs, chickens, goats, ducks, and cats. The wet-rice groups have water buffalo. Only the chicken is used for food, goats and ducks being raised solely for their cash value. Tiny dogs, mongrelized during the Emergency with larger Malay breeds, are used mainly as watchdogs, and sometimes help in hunting small game. **Food and stimulants.** Staples are rice, maize, and the despised manioc, without one of which a meal is only a snack. Supplementary foods may include pumpkins, onions, taro, peppers, bananas, sweet potatoes, and sugar cane. Collecting provides mushrooms, bamboo shoots, palm leaves, fungi, ferns, snails, land crabs, and turtles. Aboriginal cooking methods include roasting in the embers or cooking in a bamboo; the introduction of metal containers has added stewing, frying, and boiling to Senoi culinary art. The diet is notably high in carbohydrates and low in animal protein. Children are weaned on cigarettes wrapped in leaves, and tobacco has great emotional significance in Senoi life. Old people may chew betel with a wide variety of jungle additives. There are no native alcoholic beverages. **Industrial arts.** The three basic raw materials, in order of importance, are bamboo, rattan, and screwpine (pandanus). Four species of trees provide barkcloth, which is rarely worn nowadays. Basketry is fairly highly developed. Aboriginal pottery and metallurgy are absent. Water transport consists of bamboo rafts, supplemented in the larger rivers by dugouts. **Trade.** Formerly there was silent trade with the Negritos, but within the Senoi group, trading was subsumed under the general economic principle of "from each according to his abilities, to each according to his needs." Jungle produce (rattan, lumber, fruits), goats, chickens, and ducks are sold or exchanged with Malay or Chinese middlemen for metal tools, salt, cloth, tobacco, and sugar. The Jah Hut have recently started under government auspices a highly lucrative trade in sculpture. Noone (1936: 23, 47) mentions that traditionally the relationships of the Temiar with the Malays have been handled by the hereditary office of *mikong*. These individuals are regarded as intermediaries and allies by their Temiar "clients," to whom they make annual distribution of such things as knives and trade goods. The Temiar formerly had two *mikongs*, both descendants of Siamese who had married hill Temiar women. **Division of labor.** The rules governing economic behavior, like those for most aspects of Semai life, are extremely flexible. There are countless individual exceptions, but generally speaking hunting is man's work, basketry woman's; men make traps and hunting implements; women collect agricultural produce and fish with the basket. In most other areas (shamanism, house building, planting) men and women both participate, with one or the other doing most but by no means all of the work. **Land tenure.** A man owns a stretch of land from the time he clears it until the time he stops collecting its produce. Each community, moreover, owns a rigidly defined area of land, *sakaq*, within which in theory only members of that community may set up farms. These hereditary communal lands evoke a strong sense of loyalty which underlies the general Senoi fear that their lands may be alienated from them.

KIN GROUPS. **Descent.** Descent is bilateral, as is inheritance. **Kin groups.** Among the Semai, the nuclear family, for all its lability, is the basic social unit. The extended family and the household, often not easily distinguishable, are of lesser importance. The local group, typically consisting of a village, but sometimes comprising several villages, is a corporate unit holding title to a *sakaq*. A man may change his *sakaq* whenever he wishes, although he retains rights to the trees which he or his ancestors have planted there. Because the *sakaq* group and the village group are more often identical than not, and because of the difficulty of obtaining a spouse within the village, the *sakaq* group tends to be exogamous. The people do not think of the *sakaq* group as a kin group, however, but rather as an alliance for the economic exploitation of the environment. The dry-rice fields belonging to this group (its *selai*; Malay, *ladang*) are tilled by heads of nuclear families. Among the Semai, they are rarely held in common by the extended family. Economic cooperation occurs, but relatives outside the immediate nuclear family expect to be paid in food in return for their labor. Although Noone (1936: 21ff.) calls this *sakaq* group a "kindred," the Senoi kindred spreads through several *sakaq* and does not include affinals. Indeed, a man with a large and powerful kindred may rival the headman as leader of *sakaq* or village activities. Kindreds are most formalized among the western Semai, who have words for both kindred (*jeg*) and ramage (*gu*). ● Because they can travel freely up and down river but have difficulty crossing the mountainous terrain between river basins, the Senoi who inhabit a particular river basin tend to form a loosely defined group which often takes its name from the river. Such a group tends to be endogamous, to develop dialect peculiarities, and to mistrust anyone from another basin area. Members of the group may occasionally cooperate in large fish drives, using poison, but such instances of joint action are rare. These river basin groups are not defined by the Senoi in kin terms; like the *sakaq* groups, they are primarily territorial entities, membership in which is defined on an economic rather than a kinship basis. **Kin terminology.** Kin terms are shown in the accompanying chart, the Temiar terms being taken from Carey (1961: 104-05), and the Che Wong (Siwang) from Needham (1956: 59):

	Temiar	Semai
Fa	boh	abeiq (east)
		apaq (west)
Mo	amboh	amei
FaElBr, MoElBr	akoody	koit
FaElSi, MoElSi	amog	moq
FaYoBr, MoYoBr	anyuq	bah
FaYoSi, MoYoSi	boh wah	waq
Elder sibling or cousin	kelooq	teneq
Younger sibling or cousin	poq	menang

	Jah Hut	Che Wong
Fa	ibiq	bap
Mo	iduq	moi
FaElBr, MoElBr	itai	kesya (kehiaq)
FaElSi, MoElSi	iwe	baha (behah)
FaYoBr, MoYoBr	ibah	bah
FaYoSi, MoYoSi	ideh	deh
Elder sibling or cousin	iem (Br) ium (Si)	to (saudaraq)
Younger sibling or cousin	adiq	adi (saudaraq)

The distinction between patrilateral and matrilateral relations in Mah Meri terms reflects the greater authority of maternal uncles in wedding arrangements among both Mah Meri and western Semai:

	Mah Meri
Fa	uweq
Mo	gadeiq
FaBr, MoBr	ibah
FaSi, MoSi	gomoq
ElBr, FaElSiSo, MoElSiSo	iyeq
ElSi, FaElSiDa, MoElSiDa	gau
YoBr, YoSi, FaYoSiCh, MoYoSiCh	adiq
FaBrCh, MoBrCh, YoSibCh	mon

The Mah Meri may call uncles and aunts "elder/younger parents," but they consider it poor usage. The Senoi "grandchild" term covers two generations, viz. all relatives in the second descending generation plus the children of elder siblings or elder cousins. The Mah Meri further complicate this pattern with their rule that, after man A has a child, both A and his child call A's father "grandfather," although A's father still calls A "child." ● Both Semai and Temiar systems extend up to the sixth ascending generation and down to the third descending one; with the exception of the terms listed above, there is one term for each generation. In the Jah Hut system (and possibly also the Che Wong) the terms for cousins and for younger sibling are of Malay origin, and the sex distinction between elder siblings may also reflect Malay influence. ● Kinship terms are also used in the child-grade system. People who have not yet proven themselves reliable child bearers by having two or three healthy children are called "junior uncle" or "junior aunt." Women past childbearing age are called by a derivative of "grandmother." Children are addressed as "son" or "daughter," but the word for "child" is different from the word for "own child." This child-grade system, reflecting the importance of children in Senoi life, is extremely complicated, especially in regard to the crucial period when one is ready to have a child. Teknonymy must be practiced while children are still young enough to need magical protection, and frequently the teknonym is permanent. ● Except where close consanguinity makes it impossible, the kinship system reflects the autonomy that characterizes Senoi society, and an individual picks his relationship to another. In theory a person can sleep only with his classificatory "spouse's younger sibling," but the frequency of divorce and remarriage allows almost any couple to set up this relationship. If for any reason such a relationship is illogical, a couple may set it up anyway. Mother-in-law avoidance, which diminishes as one goes south, is one of the stricter taboos. Therefore, although a man may refer to his former wife as "wife," keeping the sexual relationship open, he may also call his former mother-in-law by some different term that allows him to associate with her. "Junior uncle" terms are extended to animals. Any food animal (and this means almost any animal) has a "real" name and a euphemism that is used when the animal is eaten, to avoid attracting its ghost's attention—a taboo which reflects a general anxiety about violence. The euphemism is typically "junior uncle so-and-so."

MARRIAGE AND FAMILY. Mode. Marriages among the Temiar and eastern Semai merge almost indistinguishably with casual sexual relationships, although the elders of a village may break up a too casual relationship. The western and southern groups, however, have adopted a simplified version of the Malay ceremony, and here the notion of bride price is widespread, especially for first marriages. Occasionally a man will adopt a girl, raise her, and marry her when she comes of age. Among the Mah Meri, marriage follows the Aboriginal Malay pattern, in which the climax comes as the bride makes seven circuits of a barrow. **Form.** Polygyny occurs in about

4 or 5 per cent of the marriages among all Senoi groups. Polygynous marriages tend to be unstable, since the first wife, who in theory is senior (elder sister) to the others, is often neglected. The western Semai achieve successful polygyny by keeping wives in different villages and spending some time with each. Sororal polygyny occurs in a minority of cases. Fraternal polyandry occurs, although rarely, among the Temiar Senoi (Noone 1936: 35-36). It is unknown among the other groups, although among the eastern Semai, brothers have limited access to each other's wives. **Extension of incest taboos.** Second-cousin marriage is theoretically prohibited, but occurs often enough to warrant the statement that actual practice reflects a taboo on first-cousin marriage. Prescriptive village exogamy seems to be a purely Temiar trait. Because of difficulties of travel, river basins tend to be endogamous, but, if demes were ever present, they were destroyed by relocation during the Emergency. **Residence.** Residence following marriage tends to be somewhat fluid. The general pattern is ambilocal, i.e. the couple goes to live for two or three years with the parents of one, then moves back to the village of the other, and so on, in an attempt to prevent consanguineal ties from disrupting affinal ones. Because of the strength of the former, however, a man and wife may separate for such long periods that it is possible also to speak of duolocal residence. **Domestic unit.** Extended family households are fairly common among all Senoi groups. These vary from the well-defined longhouse groups of the hill Temiar to the more amorphous arrangements which result when families outgrow their living quarters. Nuclear family households predominate among southern and western groups. **Inheritance.** Movable property goes to siblings or children, depending on who needs it most. Close relatives make use of the land, as they did when the owner was alive, and the question of title is not raised, although it is assumed that a surviving spouse has first claim on its produce. Among the western Semai, land or trees acquired after marriage are divided equally among the widow and the husband's relatives. **Divorce.** Long periods of duolocal residence tend to merge by imperceptible degrees into divorce, at which time the offended spouse can demand material recompense for his hurt feelings. Divorce rates are high, reaching a peak among the Temiar and decreasing gradually to the west and south. The children go to whoever wants them enough to pay for them. There is no concubinage, all spouses in a polygynous marriage being of equal rank, but a new wife frequently breaks up an existing marriage.

SOCIOPOLITICAL ORGANIZATION. In ancient days, Senoi government seems to have been carried on by a group of elders. Because of the autonomic nature of Senoi society and the strict taboo against violence, the elders had no effective sanctions at their disposal and ruled solely by verbal persuasion. Verbal facility, thought synonymous with intelligence, was thus the *sine qua non* of leadership, and leaders are still selected on this criterion rather than on economic prowess or generous distribution of wealth. Formerly, it was possible simply to ignore the elders' requests; or, if they badgered and maligned a man too much, he moved to another hereditary area outside their control. ● Increasing contact with the outside world brought a plethora of titles from various languages: e.g. among the Semai, *tandil* (Tamil), *jug kerah* (Aboriginal Malay), *mandur* (Portuguese), *penteriq* (Malay), and *seten* (English, assistant). These ranks were distributed among the elders without any change in role, and there is still little consensus as to who holds what rank. This is less true of the Mah Meri and western Semai, possibly because of their closer association with Aboriginal Malay groups. ● Presumably there was, even in the old days, one man, more glib and charismatic than the other elders, who was *primus inter pares,* although he bore no special title. As contact with non-Senoi peoples increased, one man tended to become spokesman in foreign affairs for the whole hereditary area. Among the Temiar, but not among the Semai, he seems to have had a special title. This authority impressed the government when, during the Emergency, it was necessary to deal intensively with the Senoi, and, partly for administrative purposes, each headman was given the Aboriginal Malay title of *batin* plus a letter of investiture (*surat kuasa*). The office, which had formerly passed by bilateral inheritance to the most capable of the foreign minister's relatives, has now come to be of overriding importance in internal affairs.

RELIGION. The two factors which give Senoi culture its character are their fear of violence and their belief in the autonomy of the individual. These two themes recur in every facet of Senoi life. Children must be shielded by taboos, because they are especially vulnerable to violence, but a parent will himself infringe a taboo to see whether it is applicable in his special case. A parent may threaten a child with violence to make it stop an activity which "brings on" storms; but he will ask a sick child, one who can barely talk, whether he wants a shot of penicillin, because the child must decide his own affairs. Although everyone is terrified of the violence implicit in a storm, the propitiatory rituals to stop it are conducted by individuals, not by the community. In the Senoi worldview, a human being is free, alone, and in almost constant danger. **Supernaturals.** As might be expected in a society where the individual is largely autonomous, religion is formless animism. Most living creatures have detachable "souls." There are two major categories of external spiritual agents, "disease spirits" and "ghosts," but the distinction between the two classes is not hard and fast.

The most readily comprehended spirit world is that of the Jah Hut, as represented in carvings. Common to all Senoi are certain sacred flowers, the dragon, and a coterie of storm gods, the god of thunder being pre-eminent. Islamic ideology (e.g. a high god, a seven-fold heaven, and earth) has been amalgamated to some extent, but the finer points are vague. Although in the 1930s Batak Lutherans converted a number of the western Semai to Christianity, and although there has been some pressure since Independence to Moslemize the aborigines, the Senoi generally maintain their ancient religion. Bahai missionary activities among the Semai are just beginning. **Practitioners.** The Jah Hut, western Semai, and Che Wong name the status of shaman—the Jah Hut use a Proto-Malay (Aboriginal Malay) word—but all Senoi believe that people may be more or less "adept" (*halaaq*). Adeptness usually results from a dream in which the familiar spirit of a recently dead adept gives the dreamer a tune, the style of which varies widely from village to village. **Ceremonies.** Ceremonies generally take place at night in a longhouse. The room is decked with flowers and fragrant leaves. It is a festive occasion, and a good deal of flirting goes on after the fires are quenched at the beginning of the ceremony. The adepts sing their songs, with the audience joining in a choral counterpoint. If the ceremony is for a sick person, the adept whose familiar called the ceremony sucks the sickness out of the patient. If the ceremony is for pregnant women, or to close a mourning period, trials of strength may be performed in the dark by the familiars. The ceremony is held on two or six successive nights. ● The forms of the ceremonies vary widely. The Jah Hut, western Semai, and Mah Meri put diseases into wooden figurines or spirit houses, which are later discarded. The Semai and Temiar dance into trance, and the Mah Meri have masked dances. Aboriginal Malay elements (tree spirits, barrows, etc.) are more important in Mah Meri religion than in that of the other Senoi groups. The only annual ceremony takes place after the rice harvest, combining feasting with a brief religious ceremonial. Evans' description of what he calls "taking the rice soul" (1923: 242-45) applies to the western Semai. **Birth.** Pregnancy is marked by an elaborate set of food taboos imposed on both parents, especially if it is their first or second child. The use of their names is also taboo, and they become "pregnant father" or "pregnant mother." After the birth, the mother and the midwife are restricted for six days to the room where the child was born. The parents become "father/mother of boy/girl." Although the father is relatively unrestricted, the mother is subject to a new (and elaborate) set of food taboos, which gradually drop off as the child matures. Both parents test the applicability of the taboos by sampling bits of tabooed foods to see whether the child gets sick. There is a long postnatal taboo on sexual intercourse, the point of which, according to the

eastern Semai, is to restrict family size so that the children will not suffer neglect. Traditionally, a child's first word was taken as its name (Semai, *möl*), but now that births must be registered, each child usually gets a Malay name at birth. Each child, moreover, gets a name (Semai, *muh*) denoting his birth order. New names are acquired at marriage, on moving to a new place, or whenever someone thinks up an especially witty nickname, with the result that a man may have half a dozen interchangeable names, plus others (e.g. his first name) which he is "ashamed" to mention. **Soul, death, and afterlife.** Even though Senoi society is so undemanding that blind people, mental deficients, and old people can usually fill a productive role, until quite recently those who became totally dependent on others were taken off to a hut in the jungle, given a week's supply of food, and abandoned. Most people, however, die within their community. In some areas, a great adept is "buried" in a tree on his request, but in most cases burial takes place as soon as possible after the person dies. The body is not flexed, nor are graves generally oriented, although the western Semai in theory orient graves east–west. Traditionally, the Senoi abandoned an area in which someone had died, but this custom is slowly dying out. Six days after the burial, a feast is held. Among the eastern Semai the mourning period lasts for a month or two, during which time no one may sing, dance, play musical instruments, or wear make-up. An adept's familiar announces the end of this mourning period, which is celebrated with a six-night ceremony. Despite the use of grave goods and a vague notion of a flower-scented world of the dead, most Senoi, even those who are terrified of ghosts, are extremely skeptical about the afterlife.

BIBLIOGRAPHY. Carey 1961; Evans 1923; Needham 1956; Noone 1936; Skeat and Blagden 1906; Williams-Hunt 1952.

SEMANG

Synonyms. *Mendi, Meni, Menik, Monik, Negrito, Ngo, Ngok, Ngok Pa*

ORIENTATION. **Identification and location.** Until well into the twentieth century, the term Semang was used to refer to the Negroid pygmies of the Malay Peninsula. However, the obscure origin of the word Semang, its use to differentiate western groups of pygmies from eastern pygmies called Pangan, and its use by Malays as a term for other tribes have led to the alternative use of Negrito, "little Negro." [Evans 1937: 19; Noone 1936: 1-9; Brandt 1961: 129.] The Semang refer to themselves as Menik, Meni, Mendi (Skeat and Blagden 1906: *1*, 21), Monik (Evans 1937: 23), and various other terms (Schebesta 1952: 69-95). In Thailand they are called Ngok (Ngo), "frizzy," or

Ngok Pa, "frizzy people" (Evans 1937: 23; Brandt 1961: 129). Malay and Siamese terms such as Orang Bukit and Orang Liar refer in general to mountain, jungle, forest, interior, and hill people. The majority of Semang are in the foothills of the jungle-covered main range of the Malay Peninsula. ● Although there has been some controversy over names and distribution, it is generally agreed that there are six major subdivisions in Malaya, and one in Thailand, ranging between 4° 10′ and 7° 30′ N. and between 99° 50′ and 102° 40′ E. These are primarily territorial units, with some differences in dialect. The seven subdivisions and their present range include the Tonga or Mos (Chong) of the Pattalung-Trang area of southern peninsular Thailand, the Kensiu (Kenseu, Kensieu) of northeastern Kedah, the Kintaq (Kenta, Kintak) of the Kedah-Perak border area, the Jahai (Jehai, Jahay) of northeastern Perak and western Kelantan, the Lanoh (Lano, Sabubn) of north-central Perak, the Mendriq (Menri, Menriq, Menrik) of southeastern Kelantan, and the Bateq (Batok, Batek, Kleb, Tomo, Nogn) of northern Pahang (Schebesta 1952: 85-86; Brandt 1961: 130). The Kensiu, Kintaq, and Jahai overlap slightly into southern Yala province, Thailand. Over the years the southernmost groups have been pushed toward the interior and to the north and northwest. Schebesta first reported the Bateq in central and eastern Pahang (Schebesta 1927: 15-16) and later in northern Pahang (Schebesta 1952: 86). Except for nineteenth century reports of a few Semang near the coast, they have always been described as jungle dwellers. Evans believes, however, that they are not jungle people of the hills and mountains but that they prefer river valleys and even coastal lands (Evans 1937: 11). According to Noone (1936: 52), they are by nature nomadic lowland jungle dwellers, most of them being in a kind of economic symbiosis with lowland Malays; only the Jahai are actually on the ridges of the main range. **Geography.** Climate is tropical with high humidity and heavy rainfall. Rank tropical vegetation is difficult to penetrate, and travel is frequently by water. Fauna include elephants, tigers, deer, wild boar, otters, gibbons, macaques, lemurs, crocodiles, and pythons. **Linguistic affiliation.** The linguistic position of Semang is uncertain. Indications are that the original Semang speech belonged to a separate linguistic family (Credner 1935a: 250), but that it has gradually been submerged in Senoi (affiliated with Mon-Khmer) and Malay loan words (Skeat and Blagden 1906: 2, 462; Schebesta 1927: 94; Williams-Hunt 1952: 22-23; Brandt 1961: 136). The various subdivisions, e.g. Kensiu and Bateq, differ somewhat in dialect, although Schebesta (1927) was able to use Jahai among a number of groups. **Demography.** The difficult terrain and the shyness and nomadic life of the Semang make it almost impossible to obtain an accurate census, and intermarriage and acculturation between the Semang and other groups make ethnic identification difficult (Evans 1937: 14; Williams-Hunt 1952: 9). Despite frequent assertions that the Semang are dying out, every count taken in the last 40 years has placed their number at around 2,000 (Williams-Hunt 1952: 31; Schebesta 1927: 15-16). The Malayan Department of Aborigines now places the number of Semang in Malaya unofficially at between 2,000 and 3,000. Those in Thailand, according to Seidenfaden (1958: 114), number only "about 100." **History and cultural relations.** Their location in the more isolated parts of the peninsula, together with evidence that their range was once greater than it is at present, have led observers to assign a greater antiquity to the Semang than to the other aboriginal groups now inhabiting the peninsula (Evans 1937: 9-13; Schebesta 1927: 16). Always in contact with more populous groups, the Semang have through intermarriage and trade relationships merged physically and culturally with them. This is particularly true of the Senoi, with whom they have had long and friendly contact. Trade with Malays and Chinese is important in the Semang economy, although the Negritos regard them as foreigners in contrast to the Senoi, whom they regard as "human beings" like themselves. [Evans 1937: 9-13; Williams-Hunt 1952: 16-21; Schebesta 1954: 218.] Semang culture seemed to be surviving quite well until the Communist Emergency, but the few reports available during and after that time indicate considerable displacement and acculturation (Williams-Hunt 1952: 34; Schebesta 1954: 66).

SETTLEMENT PATTERN AND HOUSING. **Settlement pattern.** In their aboriginal condition the Semang are nomadic, although each band moves within a well-defined area. For short stays, use is made of natural shelters such as caves, rock overhangs, or groups of trees. When these are unavailable, or when they intend to stay more than a night or two, they build leaf shelters or windscreens, which are placed in a circular or elliptical pattern with their entrances facing an open space in the center. Schebesta reports encampments ranging from 3 to 17 shelters, or from approximately 10 to 55 people. [Schebesta 1927: 14, 27-28, 43-60, 131, 240-43; 1954: 9-10, 16; Skeat and Blagden 1906: 1, 521, 525.] **Housing.** The indigenous shelter is a kind of weatherscreen made by sticking three poles into the ground at an oblique angle, connecting them at their free ends with a horizontal bamboo pole, and then bending this whole framework forward and fastening it to the underbrush with vines. Layers of leaves are interlaced and fastened to the supporting poles. In front, two bamboos are placed obliquely to support the leaf-weighted roof. These can be shifted and the screen raised in sunny weather or lowered against the rain. Occasionally, a number of screens are placed close together so that their tops meet and form a kind of communal tunnel hut, with exits at either end. Tree huts and pile dwellings do occur, but these are copied by the Semang from their neighbors. Furniture includes sleeping platforms made by lashing bamboo poles together. A hearth is usually placed near each sleeping platform. [Schebesta 1927: 51, 59, 128; 1954: 10-12, 25; Skeat and Blagden 1906: *1*, 175-77.]

ECONOMY. In their indigenous state the Semang are nomadic hunters and gatherers who rely primarily on the collection of wild roots and fruits. Forest products are also gathered and traded to Malays and Chinese. At times groups of Semang work for Malays, and at present most groups carry on a very limited agriculture. [Skeat and Blagden 1906: *1*, 228, 341; Schebesta 1927: 273, 278; 1954: 54, 90-93; Evans 1937: 61.] **Agriculture.** Some have learned rudimentary farming and raise small catch crops of rice, sugar cane, cassava, maize, sweet potatoes, bananas, and gourds, but never enough to support permanent settlements. According to Noone (1936: 2), these practices are primarily the result of intermarriage with Senoi or other agricultural groups. **Fishing and hunting.** Although gathering supplies most of the food, fishing and hunting are not neglected. According to Evans, the Semang are not avid fishermen, but they do fish occasionally, using hand and basket nets, rod and line, fish spears, harpoons, and poison. It is possible, according to Schebesta, that the Semang formerly hunted and killed elephants, buffalo, rhinoceros, deer, and wild pigs with the bow and arrow. They have not, however, been able to hunt big game since they abandoned the bow and arrow and spear for the blowgun, borrowed from the Senoi. Small animals—monkeys, bamboo rats, squirrels, porcupines, and flying foxes—are hunted by individuals using the blowgun. Schebesta labels as Malay fairy tales the stories of killing elephants by driving poisoned bamboo splinters into the soles of their feet or trapping rhinoceros in beds of mire. At present the Semang make slight use of snares and traps, although the Senoi use them very successfully. [Skeat and Blagden 1906: *1*, 202, 205; Evans 1937: 58; Schebesta 1954: 95-101, 129-30.] **Gathering.** Women do most of the gathering and supply the bulk of the food. Very little that is edible is overlooked. Among the most important sources of food are jungle roots and tubers, including even the poisonous varieties, which are treated by a variety of ingenious methods. Schebesta (1954: 55-57) identified as foodstuffs 20 varieties of tubers, 10 varieties of rattan roots, 9 kinds of palmaceous plants with edible pith or sprouts, 23 kinds of fruit, and many wild vegetables and shrubs. Bamboo sprouts, edible leaves, fungi, larvae, termites, insects, honey, and mollusks are also eaten. **Domestic animals.** The dog is the only domestic animal present in most camps. It is of little economic use and is not eaten. Cats and chickens are known, but are seen infrequently. Pets are sometimes made of wild pigs, monkeys, and bamboo rats. [Schebesta 1927: 237, 275; 1954: 128-29; Evans 1937: 63.] **Food and stimu-**

lants. Contrary to some reports, the Semang consume neither meat nor vegetables raw. Most food is steamed in a bamboo tube, or roasted on bamboo shafts placed slantwise over the fire. Small animals such as mice and bamboo rats are placed whole in hot ashes. The people live from hand to mouth, and food is seldom stored. Tobacco, obtained from the Malays, is popular (Skeat and Blagden 1906: *1*, 117; Schebesta 1954: 131). Until the 1930s, tobacco was rolled in the form of cigars, with dried pandanus leaf wrappings; by 1939, however, Schebesta found that the cigarette had been universally adopted. Schebesta (1954: 131) found many Semang chewing betel, although not to the same extent as the Senoi. Opium smoking has never been widespread, but there are always a few addicts who learn the habit from the Chinese (Schebesta 1927: 215; Evans 1937: 66-67). Alcoholic beverages are absent. This situation may change, however, as Chinese shops spread into the more isolated areas of Malaya inhabited by the Semang (Schebesta 1954: 132). **Industrial arts.** The techniques of the few smiths found among the Semang are the same as those of the Senoi and Jakun. Unlike other pygmies in Asia and the nearby islands who pound iron into desired shapes, the Semang smith works hot iron and uses the type of piston bellows found throughout Southeast Asia (Schebesta 1954: 150-51). Cooking utensils, musical instruments, blowguns, quivers, darts, basketwork scoops and other kinds of fishing equipment, knives, tobacco carriers, combs, and countless other articles are made of bamboo. Clothing and ornaments are made from the roots, leaves, flowers, bark, and fibers of trees, vines, and herbs. Animal skins are never used for clothing or adornment. [Schebesta 1954: 28.] Metal and cloth articles obtained in trade are increasing in popularity, with consequent loss of some techniques for working bamboo and other jungle products. **Trade.** The importance of trade with neighboring groups is mentioned in the earliest literature. There is, however, little evidence that trade among the Semang groups themselves has ever been important. In their trade relations the Negritos have been dependent in varying degrees on Senoi and Malays, and there is evidence that this dependence is increasing. Williams-Hunt mentions (1952: 58) that they now buy most of their blowguns and quivers from the Senoi. Traditionally, the Negritos have supplied forest products such as rare woods, gums, resins, and rattan, in return for agricultural products from the Senoi and Jakun and tobacco, cloth, and metal tools and weapons from the Malays and Chinese. ● According to Schebesta (1954: 158), stories of "silent trade" between Negritos and Malays, as reported by Skeat and Blagden (1906: *1*, 227-28), are largely legend. The Malays have traditionally monopolized Semang trade to their own advantage; their contempt for the heathen hill tribes, which Schebesta (1954: 157) believes is largely due to their adoption of Islam, prompts the Malays to deal harshly with the Semang. The latter, driven by hunger and a craving for rice, tobacco, and other luxuries, continue to return to the Malay traders despite the ill treatment they receive. In recent years, Chinese traders have taken over much of the trade with the Negritos which was formerly dominated by the Malays (Williams-Hunt 1952: 46). **Division of labor.** The traditional tasks of men include hunting, trapping, making and decorating weapons, and plaiting rattan sacks and baskets; those of women include building shelters, cooking, gathering, some fishing, preparation of bark cloth, and manufacture of leaf bags and baskets. The women, since they do most of the collecting, contribute the major part of the food supply. Among those groups that have adopted limited agriculture, the men do the heavy work of felling logs and clearing fields, while the women help with the lighter work of clearing, sowing, reaping, and winnowing. Division of labor is not always strictly by sex; men and women often help one another, except that women never hunt. [Skeat and Blagden 1906: *1*, 374-75; Evans 1937: 52, 60, 375; Schebesta 1927: 56-58, 75, 224; Brandt 1961: 139.] **Land tenure.** According to Schebesta, every tribe (e.g. Kensiu, Jahai, etc.) has its own territory, in which the foraging areas of the bands or extended family kin groups are found. Bands are free to rove at will and hunt for food within the tribal territory, but they always return to their home territory for the harvest. Here, where the band customarily hunts and gathers, is where the men of the band own *ipoh* poison trees and durian fruit trees, the only immovable property (Schebesta 1954: 229). Beyond this, there is no concept of individual, family, or group land tenure. There is some evidence that the Malays, at least, do not recognize the Semang concept of tree ownership and its significance in defining territorial rights and privileges (Schebesta 1954: 232).

KIN GROUPS. **Descent.** According to Schebesta (1954: 255), patrilocality and patrilineal affiliation prevail, but are greatly weakened by matrilocal and matrilineal tendencies. Murdock (1962: 266), using data from Evans (1937) and Schebesta (1927), infers bilateral descent from the absence of reported ambilineal or unilineal kin groups. Kindreds are also absent or unreported. **Kin groups.** A typical extended family kin group or band is made up of three generations—an old man with his wife, and their sons with their wives and children. Related individuals or nuclear families or relatives of the wives of the camp may join the local group, but this is always a temporary arrangement (Schebesta 1954: 219-20). **Kin terminology.** Schebesta (1927: 114; 1954: 223-24) believes that Semang kin terms cannot simply be called classificatory; father's brothers and mother's sisters, for example are called by additional terms which not only indicate age class but occasionally social position.

Lanoh terms resemble those of the Ple (Temiar) Senoi, with whom they are in close contact. Schebesta reports the following kin terms for the Jahai:

Fa	*ay*
Mo	*bo*
FaElBr	*ay-toi*
MoElBr	*ay-toi*
FaYoBr	*ay-ba*
MoYoBr	*ay-ba*
FaElSi	*bo-toi*
MoElSi	*bo-toi*
FaYoSi	*ma*
MoYoSi	*ma*
ElBr	*pan*
YoBr	*ber*
ElSi	*pan*
YoSi	*ber*

MARRIAGE AND FAMILY. **Mode.** Premarital sexual relations are permitted, although subject to the rule of local group exogamy (Schebesta 1954: 239-40). The young Semang chooses his wife himself. The only exception to this is occasional slight family pressure to consider a girl whose local group or band is already related to his by marriage. There is no formal engagement. When a man has reached an understanding with a girl, he approaches her father. If the father agrees, the prospective groom gives him presents such as a bush knife, cloth, flint, and tobacco, and the marriage is concluded. The young people build a shelter for themselves in the forest, and after a few days alone together return to the camp and participate in daily activities as a married couple. Among groups under Malay influence, a young man often gives the girl's father a small sum of money. A young man with no goods or money may instead render service for his prospective father-in-law. [Skeat and Blagden 1906: 2, 58; Evans 1937: 250; Schebesta 1954: 238-54.] **Form.** Although polygyny is permissible, multiple wives are extremely rare, with almost every case reported being due to some exceptional circumstance (Schebesta 1954: 253-55; Brandt 1961: 150). **Extension of incest taboos.** Only marriage between parents and children and between siblings is prohibited among all the Semang. Otherwise the situation is unclear. Cousin marriage is prohibited only under certain conditions which vary widely among the tribal subdivisions. [Schebesta 1954: 244; Evans 1937: 253.] **Residence.** Although marriage was probably originally patrilocal among all the Semang, and still is among the Jahai, in most groups it is now ambilocal, with patrilocality dominant (Schebesta 1954: 211). A young couple or a family move back and forth between the husband's and the wife's local group, which places the wife's labor at the disposal of the husband's family and vice versa, with no special burden on either group. [Schebesta 1954: 242; Evans 1937: 254.] **Domestic unit.**

Parents and unmarried children usually live under one windscreen. Occasionally several related nuclear families place their shelters so close together that they form a kind of communal dwelling. Each nuclear family, however, maintains its own compartment. Small children always live with their parents; half-grown boys often have their own shelters. Grown or half-grown girls have sleeping areas in their parents' windscreen, but separated by the fire from the parents' sleeping area. [Schebesta 1954: 237.] **Inheritance.** Generally bilateral, with a slight patrilineal bias in some of the tribal subdivisions. *Ipoh* and durian trees, the most important property of the individual Semang, are transferred to another person through inheritance, the method and recipients differing among the various tribes. Among the Jahai, the father distributes his trees to his sons during his lifetime, whereas among the Kintaq, daughters also inherit trees and the wife has the same property rights as the husband, even with respect to trees. Tools, weapons, and other movable property of a deceased person are left to disintegrate in the shelter above the grave. Only iron objects are retained by the deceased's family, because they allegedly harm the dead. [Schebesta 1954: 236.] **Divorce.** Divorce is easy and frequent. Schebesta (1954: 250-51) says that Semang marriages can be regarded as temporary unions. As a rule, a marriage is not terminated until a new one has been agreed upon or is in prospect. The oldest member of the local group supervises the distribution of property. If the husband initiates the divorce, the bridal gifts need not be returned; if the wife initiates it, the gifts are returned. Children may live alternately with either parent's local group. [Schebesta 1954: 250-51; Evans 1937: 254.]

SOCIOPOLITICAL ORGANIZATION. **Political organization.**

The seven tribal subdivisions are territorial and linguistic units, lacking any political function. Each subdivision is made up of completely autonomous local groups or bands. The head of the band is the oldest male if he has leadership ability, or a younger man if one is particularly qualified. The leader enjoys neither material benefits nor emblems of office. He has no executive power, but leads through his own personality. Frequently the priest-shaman, *hala*, is the most important person in the local group. [Schebesta 1954: 225-26; Skeat and Blagden 1906: *1*, 494.] **Social stratification.** There is marked equality and autonomy of the individual in Semang culture (Skeat and Blagden 1906: *1*, 499; Schebesta 1954: 226; Williams-Hunt 1952: 18). **Warfare.** Other than reports of Negrito bowmen with a Siamese army fighting the Malays in the seventeenth century, and an occasional feud, there is no evidence of Semang warring with one another or with non-Semang. Schebesta 1954: 227-28) writes that the psychological attitude of present-day Semang makes them unfit for war. He believes that if they were ever warlike they have by now changed completely.

RELIGION. The Semang do not conceive of their relations with the supernatural in terms of an organized religion. They have a large body of myths and legends, together with a belief in innumerable deities. Investigators have also found concepts which they describe as soul, heaven, and life after death. Schebesta (1957: 4ff.) comments on the extraordinary complexity of their religious beliefs and practices, many of which have been borrowed from neighboring peoples. They may vary considerably from tribe to tribe and even from band to band. **Supernaturals.** The numerous deities known as *orang hidop* are personified natural phenomena symbolized by living animals and plants. These are viewed anthropomorphically, and bear names such as Karei (thunder), Taleg (black hornet), etc. Chief among the *orang hidop* are the celestial pair, Karei, (Kagai, Kaei) and Ta Pedn (Ta Ped'n, Ta Pern, Ple). Although the relationship between them is obscure, it is Schebesta's conclusion that Ta Pedn is generally regarded as the supreme ruler, the lord of the firmament and of earth, but that among some Semang he has been superseded by Karei, the god of thunder. Karei punishes transgressions such as wearing a comb in a thunderstorm, laughing at butterflies, and cohabiting in the daytime. When humans do wrong he slays them directly by lightning or indirectly through animal messengers such as tigers. To appease Karei a blood offering is made by cutting the skin near the shin bone, scraping blood into a bamboo receptacle, mixing with water, and throwing the mixture into the air. [Schebesta 1957: 26-35, 78-95; Skeat and Blagden 1906: *2*, 177-78, 204-05; Brandt 1961: 155.] Ta Pedn rules in a three-layered heaven where many fruit trees grow. Serving Ta Pedn are the *cenoi (chinoi)*, tiny elflike beings whose proper abode is heaven but who also inhabit flowers and other natural objects on earth. They communicate in a *cenoi* language which is also the secret language of Semang shamanism. The *cenoi* are well disposed toward man, and aid in the ripening of durians and other fruits on which the Semang depend for food. [Schebesta 1957: 130-35.] **Practitioners.** The only religious specialist is the *hala*, regarded by Schebesta as a combination of shaman and priest. As shaman, the *hala*, working with the power given him by Ta Pedn and through the agency of the *cenoi* residing in his magic quartz crystal, *cebu*, performs both black and white magic, foretells the future, and cures illnesses. As priest, performing in the *pano* ceremony, he functions as intermediary between the *orang hidop* deities and the people. A man becomes a *hala* by virtue of a dream, or by finding a magic *cebu* stone. The office can also be inherited from father to son (only males among the Semang are *hala*). A young candidate must be initiated and trained by an established *hala*.

Among the Jahai Semang, at least, most candidates go to neighboring Senoi shamans for their training (Schebesta 1957: 126). *Hala* employ a secret or garbled dialect, the language of the *cenoi* spirits. They may become powerful in their own communities, but they are not necessarily feared. A man who has been a great *hala* in his lifetime, with a wide reputation, becomes a tiger after his death, and his corpse is either exposed in a tree or interred in a sitting position with the head exposed above ground. [Schebesta 1957: 123-34, 151ff.] **Ceremonies.** The principal ceremony, performed at irregular intervals, is carried out by a *hala* in a special conical hut, *pano*. While in the hut he is possessed by *cenoi* spirits who arrive one by one; in effect, he becomes *cenoi* during this time. Speaking his special *cenoi* language, he acts as intermediary in a running dialogue between the *cenoi* spirits and the audience seated outside the hut. He also sings special *pano* songs praising the *cenoi*. The purpose of this ceremony, according to Schebesta, is to establish contact with the *cenoi* and enlist their aid in whatever problem is facing the community, e.g. a grave illness. [Schebesta 1957: 138-45.] **Illness and medicine.** The Semang classify many illnesses as due to supernatural causes. In such cases a *hala* may conduct a *pano* ceremony, or he may activate the *cenoi* residing in his magic quartz crystal, *cebu*, by blowing on the stone. *Hala* may also be skilled in conjuring, magic, and sorcery designed to cure or harm another person. Pointing a sharp bamboo sliver at an intended victim and conjuring it to enter his body and kill him is a favorite method of sorcery, much feared by the Malays. Schebesta (1957: 150-51) implies, however, that conjuring and black magic of this kind have largely been borrowed from the Senoi and Malays. As medicine man, the *hala* has an extensive pharmacopoeia of herbal and other remedies, some with helpful qualities. [Schebesta 1954: 170-77, 257-63; 1957: 150-51; Evans 1937: 190-204.] **Soul, death, and afterlife.** Interment in a niche-grave, usually on the day of death, is the most common method of disposing of the dead. The corpse is wrapped in mats, and water is poured in its mouth before burial. A small weatherscreen, containing the personal belongings of the deceased, is erected over the grave. It is commonly believed that the soul leaves the body at death, remains in the vicinity of the corpse for several days, and enters the afterworld on the seventh day. The Semang fear the spirit of the dead and try to discourage it from returning to camp—tree trunks are cut to bar the path, figures are placed near the path to scare the ghost, and the camp where the person died is generally deserted. The soul's long journey takes it to an afterworld in the west which is imagined as a heaven of fruit. Here deceased Semang live a carefree but shadowy existence. [Schebesta 1957: 158-85, 163.]

BIBLIOGRAPHY. Brandt 1961; Credner 1935a; Evans 1937; Murdock 1962; Noone 1936; Schebesta 1927, 1952, 1954, 1957; Seidenfaden 1958; Skeat and Blagden 1906; Williams-Hunt 1952.

PART III. TAI-KADAI

TAI

TAI SPEAKERS, INCLUDING THOSE IN CHINA, number approximately 30 million, making them, next to the Chinese, the largest and most widespread population within the area presently under consideration. Considering the extent of distribution—from 7° to 26° N. and 94° to 110° E.—the various Tai dialects are remarkably homogeneous (Maspéro 1929-30). Historically, as today, these people appear as valley-dwelling wet-rice growers, a fact that gives to the cultures of most Tai-speaking populations a certain uniformity. Cultural differences do exist, however, possibly relating to the recency of influences from dominant traditions such as that of the Han Chinese; thus Ayabe (1961) finds unilineal kin systems predominant from northern Laos as far as Tonkin whereas to the south and west, including the Shans of Burma, bilateral characteristics are more noticeable. Tai-speaking populations also vary somewhat in physical appearance, possibly reflecting assimilation of autochthonous groups, e.g. Khmu, Lawa, and Mons, in areas in which they have settled or conquered (cf. Wiens 1954: 117, citing Eickstedt). The widespread distribution of Tai speakers in Southeast Asia has sometimes been pictured as the end result of a mass migration out of China in response to Han Chinese pressure. More likely, it is the result of a southward and southwestward infiltration of small Tai-speaking ruling and military elites, and the resulting assimilation and Tai-ization of (largely Mon-Khmer-speaking) autochthonous populations of mixed Paleomongolid and Veddid stock (Eickstedt 1940; 1944). The status of the old kingdom of Nanchao as a Tai state and its role in the efflorescence of Tai political enclaves during the twelfth and thirteenth centuries is unclear. Credner's studies in Yunnan cast doubt on the possibility that Nanchao ever had a large Tai-speaking population (Credner 1935b); moreover, as shown by Wiens (1954: 160-61), the Nanchao court was heavily influenced by Han Chinese and the wholesale importation of Han culture. At most, Nanchao appears to have been ruled by a thin stratum of Tai aristocracy. Coedès (1944; 1948) sees the fall of Nanchao in the mid-thirteenth century and the consequent dispossession of Tai ruling elites as important in the formation of Tai states farther south. He attributes much of this development to the example of the Mongol conquest and the subsequent machinations of the Yuan emperors in protecting and consolidating their frontiers with Burma and Cambodia. Leach (1954: 247-48) makes the additional point that many of the *muong* domains of the Shan States appear to have originated as garrison outposts established by the Chinese to protect their trade routes and mining interests in northern Burma. • In retrospect, the well-known propensity of the Tai for forming complex sociopolitical structures may reflect in considerable measure, the historical fortunes of Han Chinese political and military strategy (as well as cultural borrowing from neighboring great traditions such as those of China and Hinduized Cambodia). The Tai, from this point of view, may be seen historically as a people with some assimilative ability and a tendency in the direction of social organization—possibly the result of early concentrated settlement as wet-rice growers in the region of the middle Yangtze and the Chengtu Plain area of Szechwan (cf. Wiens 1954: 295 ff.); subsequent appearance of Tai states and Tai-speaking populations throughout their present area of distribution may be the result less of a simple flight before encroaching Chinese colonization than of the tactical use of Tai military and political elites by the Han. Superimposed on autochthonous populations, these elites have, by virtue of superior breeding power, assimilated and acculturated their indigenous subjects. Large areas have in this manner been Tai-ized, contributing to the present ethnolinguistic map of Southeast Asia (Wiens 1954: 120). The continuing movement of Tai speakers, through the process of village fission, has been recently documented by Izikowitz (1963) and Iwata (1961a);

likewise, the process of assimilation by lowland Tai of indigenous swidden-farming populations continues in parts of Thailand, Laos, and Upper Burma (Hutchinson 1934; Halpern 1958; Leach 1954). ● Names for Tai-speaking groups frequently appear imprecise and even contradictory. In part this is due to the lack of precision within the Tai nomenclature itself, and in part to the fact that the Chinese, French, Siamese, and British may designate the same group by different names. Some names are essentially generic in nature, e.g. the Chinese Pai-i for Tai speakers in southwestern Yunnan, including groups such as the Lü, Nüa, and Chinese Shans, which are usually designated separately. In this case Pai-i (spelled Pa-y) has also been adopted by French writers for a small group of recent Yunnan Tai immigrants into northern Indochina. Others, such as the many names for Tai populations in the middle Mekong area, seem to refer to old political enclaves with which these groups believe themselves to be identified (cf. Moerman 1962). ● Tai speakers as a whole have been classified into major subdivisions according to dialect relationships (cf. Li 1959), geographical location (cf. Seidenfaden 1958), literacy vs. nonliteracy (Dodd 1923), lowland vs. upland (Embree and Thomas 1950), and type of sociopolitical institutions indicative of divergent historical development (cf. Le Boulanger 1931). The subdivisions adopted in the present volume reflect as much as anything the manner in which the bulk of the descriptive ethnographic literature has been organized, e.g. the block of literature on the Tai-speaking peoples of Burma and the Chinese Shan States. Similarly, the large literature on the Siamese Tai and their political evolution within Thailand tends to set these people apart for purposes of descriptive presentation. On the other hand, sociopolitical patterns shared by certain of the lesser known Tai peoples, by virtue, apparently, of a common historical background, have prompted the category, Central Mekong River Groups, and the inclusion of Black and White Tai among related Central Upland Groups rather than with the heavily sinicized Eastern Groups. The central Mekong area, from Luang Prabang north to the Sip Song Panna, and including northern Thailand and easternmost Burma, witnessed in the late twelfth and early thirteenth centuries the development of a series of politically organized petty states which figure in the traditional histories of such modern groups as the Lü, Khün, Yuan, and Laotian Tai. Little is known about these states beyond a recital of inter-*muong* wars and temporary alliances in the face of threats from neighboring powers. It is probable, however, that they were characterized by a semifeudal sociopolitical organization, traces of which are still in evidence among the Lü and Laotian Tai (Coedès 1944: 246). This common sociopolitical complex seems to have encompassed the Black Tai, who are found today primarily in the uplands of northern Laos, and the Sip Song Chau Tai south of the Black river in North Vietnam. The White and Red Tai of North Vietnam appear closely related, if not in some cases identical to, the Black Tai, although in some lowland areas they have been heavily Vietnamized. Other upland groups of northern Laos, such as the Neua and Phuan, likewise appear to share in a cultural heritage centering historically on the middle Mekong. By contrast, the Chuang, Tho, Nhang, etc. of the Kwangsi-Tonkin area show little evidence today of any historical participation in what might be characterized as a middle Mekong cultural tradition. **Lao.** This term is apparently of Siamese origin, referring to Tai speakers to the north and northeast of the central Chao Phraya plain, distinguished by their preference for glutinous rice; by certain differences in the style of their Buddhist architecture, religious script, and terminology; and by an historical tradition common to the various middle Mekong principalities which persisted up to the intervention of the French and Siamese Tai. When the French extended their political control to the banks of the Mekong, they took over this Siamese term for the Tai-speaking inhabitants and adopted the term Laos for the protectorate they created. [McGilvary 1912: 13.] In this sense, the term Lao is practically synonymous with the Tai-speaking population of what was once the old kingdom of Lan Xang, founded by Fa Ngoun in the mid-fourteenth century. The core area of this kingdom was Muong Swa (Luang Prabang). Its political influence was felt throughout the middle Mekong from Champassak in the south to the borders of the Sip Song Panna in the north, and west to the borders of Lan Na (Chiengmai). [Le Boulanger 1931: 44.] The traditional Lao area encompasses much of the Khorat plateau area of northeastern Thailand, as well as modern Laos. There has long been interchange and migration of the ethnic Lao back and forth across the Mekong. Many of the Lao presently in Thailand were brought there from across the Mekong as prisoners of war, some as recently as a hundred years ago. Today there is considerable migration (often temporary) of Thailand Lao laborers to Vientiane, Pakse, and other towns along the Mekong (Halpern 1961c: 14-15). The Lao (Lao Khorat) in northeastern Thailand number approximately 3.5 million (Seidenfaden 1958: 109; Credner 1935a: 176). The most numerous and politically the most important popula-tion group within the greater Lao area is that of the Laotian Tai, i.e. the lowland Lao of Laos. Other named subdivisions reflect present-day political boundaries as well as historical and cultural developments subsequent to the Lan Xang period. In most cases they represent minor dialectal differences, or refer to the place of origin of a displaced population. As these groups become urbanized or assimilated, ter-minological distinctions tend to fade out. Such groups as the Lao Wieng (Wieng-chan), Lao Sau, and Lao Khao (or Phuthai) of northeastern Thailand represent populations only recently removed from across the Mekong in Laos. Some are descendants of prisoners of war deported from Laos over a hundred years ago. [Seidenfaden 1958: 109-13.] In Laos proper, terms such as Phuan, Phuthai, and Neua are ap-plied in the vicinity of Vientiane and Luang Prabang to recent emigrés from the mountain valleys to the east—Tai speakers from areas such as Sam Neua and Xieng Khouang, formerly part of old Lan Xang (Iwata 1961a). Once they settle in the lowlands among the Lao, these people gradually lose their distinctiveness and their old ties, and "become Lao." ● The term Lao (Muong Lao) is frequently extended to include the Tai-speaking population of northern Thailand, in the Chiengmai–Chiengrai–Nan area (cf. LeMay 1926). Locally, however, they are known as Yuan (Yün) or Tai Yuan. This difference in ter-minology accords with the historical distinctiveness of the area as well as its linguistic differentiation from the Lao area to the east. Chiengmai is the seat of old Lan Na, a Tai principality that, except for a brief period, was never subject to Lan Xang and remained free of effective Siamese control until rela-tively late in history. Recent evidence indicates that the Yuan Tai dialect should be considered a separate development from the Lao speech farther east (Brown 1962: 12-17). **Eastern groups.** The Tai-speak-ing peoples of Kweichow, Kwangsi, Kwangtung, southeastern Yunnan, and northern Vietnam are diffi-cult to categorize in any meaningful fashion. Indigenous cultural patterns have been affected by the expansion of strong neighboring traditions—Chinese in the north, Vietnamese in the south. Sinicization has occurred most noticeably in Kwangtung and eastern Kwangsi; in many cases Tai-speaking popula-tions appear to be terminologically differentiated on the basis of minor differences in dialect, peculiarities of dress, or places of origin. That this entire area was once strongly Tai is evidenced by the widespread existence of Tai dialects and of place names of Tai origin. Wiens, using Chinese source materials, esti-mates that 60 per cent of the population of Kwangtung has Chuang (Tai) antecedents (1954: 274). Bruk (1960: 25), using 1953 Chinese census data, puts the total Tai population of Kweichow-Kwangsi-Kwangtung at about nine million. ● Ethnographically, little is known of the area; the variety of ethnic names reflects this difficulty. Chinese terms such as Chuang-chia, Chung-chia, T'o, and T'u-jen have little meaning, ethnologically speaking, since in one instance they may have a generic connotation, and in an-other the sense of purely local usage. Chuang, for example, may mean Tai speakers in a generic sense (Hsü 1939: 75); speakers of Tai dialects in the general area of Kwangsi province (Li 1957); or Tai speakers of Kwangsi province viewed as a nationality group, i.e. the Chinese Communist designation of this area as the Kwangsi-Chuang Autonomous Chou (Bruk 1960: 26). A recent classification of Tai speakers in the South China area, based reportedly on a consideration of language and other ethnic pe-culiarities, groups together on the one hand Chuang-chia and Chung-chia (Pu-yi or Dioi), and on the other Tung and Shui (Bruk 1960: 25 ff.). The same source gives the numbers (in thousands) and distri-bution of these groups as follows:

	Kwangsi	Yunnan	Kweichow	Szechwan	Hunan	Kwangtung	Total
Chuang	6,445	453	14			116	7,028
Chung-chia		14	1,233	1			1,248
Tung	150		439		124		713
Shui	1		133				134

This grouping follows closely the modern linguistic analysis of Tai dialects published thus far by Li Fang-kuei and others. Li (1943; 1957; 1959) has defined the following dialect groups: 1. **Northern Tai dialects.** (a) Chung-chia—the Chinese term for speakers of these dialects in Kweichow. Also known as Dioi, a corrupt rendition of Jui or Yoi, the local term used by speakers themselves. (b) Chuang-chia— the Chinese term for speakers of northern Tai dialects in Kwangsi. 2. **Kam-Sui dialect group.** (a) Kam —a local term for speakers whom the Chinese designate as Tung. Located mainly in southeastern Kweichow. (b) Sui—Chinese, Shui—in Lipo, T'sungchiang, and Jungchiang districts of southeastern Kweichow. Li contends that Kam-Sui separated from an earlier Kam-Tai, before the differentiation of modern Tai dialects such as Chuang and Siamese. 3. **Central Tai dialects.** (a) Tho; (b) Nung. ● The relatively little available ethnographic data are best presented within the framework of the Li–Bruk classification, recognizing that linguistically-derived categories of this kind are not always synonymous with the idea of separate cultures or "tribes." Many of the ethnographic data relevant to the Tai of Lingnan are on related peoples in northern Vietnam and Laos—Nung, Tho, Nhang, Trung-cha, and so on. Authors such as Lunet de Lajonquière (1906), Abadie (1924), and Diguet (1908) were familiar mainly with Indochina south of the China border; therefore their data and their generalizations about the Tai in China are best presented in terms of groups resident mainly in Indochina which, although they may be historically related to the Chuang Tai of Lingnan, nevertheless have been subjected more recently to the acculturative influence of Vietnam. Some of these groups, e.g. the Nung, Nhang, and Trung-cha, are relatively recent arrivals from China. Others, such as the Tho, represent a Tai population long resident in the area and thus subject to heavier Vietnamization. The majority of them are located in the hinterland areas of Tonkin north and west of the Red river delta.

WESTERN GROUPS

AHOM

ORIENTATION. **Identification.** The most westerly extension of Tai speakers was into the historical Ahom kingdom along the upper reaches of the Brahmaputra river in Assam. Their descendants are today completely Hinduized, and only a few of the priests can read the old chronicles written in Tai. **Linguistic affiliation.** Tai, related to Hkamti. **History and cultural relations.** The traditional date of the founding of the Ahom kingdom, with its capital at Rangpur in Sibsagar district, is 1229 A.D. The kingdom, which extended for some 350 miles along the Brahmaputra, from Goalpara in the west to Sadiya in the east, fell at the end of the eighteenth century. ● It is doubtful that the Tai ever entered the area of northern Assam in great numbers; the Ahom kingdom probably represents the extension of power over the local population by a small aristocracy of politically-organized Tai rulers who were related to those already entrenched in the Tai states of northern Burma. Throughout the Ahom period, this relationship seems to have been acknowledged on both sides, and it is evident that the trade routes between Ahom, Hkamti Long, and Mogaung were regularly used. [Harvey 1925: 74, 283; Seidenfaden 1958: 30; Leach 1954: 241.]

BIBLIOGRAPHY. Harvey 1925; Leach 1954; Seidenfaden 1958.

HKAMTI SHANS

ORIENTATION. **Identification.** Those Tai speakers in extreme northern Burma, approximately 27° N. and 97° E., are commonly referred to as Hkamti Shans.

Location. Hkamti Shans are found in the Hkamti Long, an extensive rice plain near the headwaters of the Irrawaddy; in scattered settlements in the Hukawng valley; in the upper Chindwin river valley; and in a few settlements across the border in Assam. Throughout much of this area the Tai element is associated with a more numerous Jinghpaw-speaking population, both of whom participate in a common sociopolitical system. [Leach 1954: 32-35.] **Linguistic affiliation.** Culturally and linguistically close to the Tai of the Burmese Shan State farther south, although by historical accident and geographical position somewhat separated from them. **History and cultural relations.** The Hkamti Shan states of today appear to be the remnants of an earlier northern extension of the old Shan state of Mogaung. In the eighteenth century, Tai power in this area was broken by Burmese armies, the native *saohpas* deposed, and the area ruled directly by the Burmese. Traditions of the former power of Mogaung are still strong. D'Orléans (1898: 307-23) visited the Hkamti Long area in 1895, and his first-hand, if somewhat prejudiced, account is interesting as a historical document. "As far as the eye could reach stretched rice-fields . . . a splendid territory, fertile in soil and abundant in water. The outskirts of the [royal] town were occupied by fenced rectangular gardens, in which chiefly women were hoeing. Between them and the village were rows of small bamboo rice granaries on piles. Passing them we came to . . . a stockade made of wattled bamboos 12 feet high. Once inside [the town] . . . in all directions ran narrow plank causeways a foot or so from the earth, necessary in the rains. The roofs were thatched and sloping, with a conical excrescence at either end, and in the centre a small gable like a bonnet, that allowed light to enter and smoke to escape. At one extremity of the building was an open platform under the eaves. Each dwelling ran from 80 to 130 feet in length, and was erected on piles which formed commodious pens underneath for the livestock. The whole village was arranged on a system of parallels."

BIBLIOGRAPHY. Leach 1954; d'Orléans 1898.

CHINESE SHANS

Synonyms. *Chè, Eastern Shans, Khè, Pai-i, Shan Tayok, Tayok*

ORIENTATION. **Identification.** The people call themselves Tai or Tayok—the latter a possible contraction of Tai Hok Chao, or "Tai from the Six Kingdoms of old Nanchao." Shan Tayok is the Burmese term for them. They are referred to in British sources as Chinese Shans or Eastern Shans, and by Burmese Shans as Chè (Khè). The Chinese include them within the generic term Pai-i, by which they designate Tai speakers in southwestern Yunnan. [Seidenfaden 1958: 21; Leach 1954: 32.] **Location.** The area of the so-called Chinese Shan States along the central–western border of Yunnan, 25° N. and 98° 15′ E., including the areas along the upper courses of the Taiping and Shweli rivers. Many Shans now in Bhamo and Myitkyina districts are immigrants from Yunnan and are classed by the Burmese as Chinese Shans. **Geography.** The Chinese Shan States are an area of wild and rugged topography wherein travel is difficult. The Tai speakers are concentrated in the malaria-infested valleys. [Seidenfaden 1958: 22.] **Linguistic affiliation.** Tai speakers, related linguistically to the Burmese Shans and Tai Lü. **Demography.** The thirteen *muong* domains within the Mangshih–Mengliu administrative area were reported by Chiang (1950: 72-73) to contain 96,000 Pai-i, or 50 per cent of the population; Chingpo (Kachins) numbered 42,000 or 21 per cent; Han Chinese 33,000 or 17 per cent; and "others" 10 per cent of the total. Seidenfaden (1958: 21), using data supplied in Metford (1935), gives a total population of about one-quarter million, mostly Tai but including Achang, Kachin, Lisu, and Palaung hill tribes. **History.** According to Wiens (1954: 301), several of the present-day Chinese Shan States date back to the Koshanpyi, or Nine Shan States, which in turn were the chief components of the Shan kingdom of Pong. The latter is supposed to have included Bhamo and the upper part of the Irrawaddy valley. According to Seidenfaden (1958: 21), the *muong* domains of the Chinese Shan States were once part of Nanchao, and were surrendered when Kublai Khan overran the latter. After achieving independence, coincident with the weakening of the later Mongol dynasty, they were again subdued by the Ming about the middle of the fifteenth century. Chinese officers were appointed hereditary rulers, in most cases taking wives from ruling Shan families. Their descendants are Shan in many respects, although they are proud of their Chinese ancestry (Metford 1935: 190-204). When visited by Metford the *chao fa* (*saohpa*) of Mangshih was living in a *haw* very Chinese in construction, and was serving Chinese food. ● Under the Nationalist Government the Chinese Shan States were part of a Frontier Settlement Administrative Bureau responsible for ten *t'u-ssu* domains (*muong*). Under the Chinese Communists the area has been designated the Te-hung Thai and Ching-p'o Autonomous Chou, with its seat at Luhsi. **Cultural relations.** Chiang (1950) concludes that the Pai-i of the Sip Song Panna and the Chinese Shan States are similar in most respects. The latter, however, are in more intimate contact with Han Chinese, and the nobility are strongly sinicized. Davies (1909: 377 ff.) reports minor differences in dress and dialect between the Chinese Shans and the Lü, and concludes that among the former the religious script and the temple architecture show the influence of Burmese Buddhism. There is much intermarriage with Burmese Shans. Culturally, the Chinese Shan States appear intermediate between Burma to the west and the Yunnanese Tai regions to the south and east (cf. Milne 1910: 136).

SETTLEMENT PATTERN AND HOUSING. The Chinese Shans, like the Lü, live in villages located along streams and rivers. Commoners live in houses raised above the ground on piles. Princely families and dwellers in the larger towns occupy brick houses built directly on the ground—a result of Chinese acculturation.

ECONOMY. Irrigated wet rice is the main crop, grown in basin areas along the major streams. There is some development of industry and trade; Seidenfaden (1958: 21) reports traveling blacksmiths, and jade mining and cutting is important in the area of Tengyueh. Basic features of the land tenure system are similar to those among the Lü, although in the Chinese Shan States the traditional land rights of commoners are less in evidence and the *chao fa* more arbitrary in their administration of *muong* lands. Monetary taxes, grain rent, and other obligations are based directly on the land, with the result that Chinese Shan society appears more feudal in character than that of the Lü.

KIN GROUPS. Leach (1954: 216) says that succession to the throne is governed by patrilineal descent, and that only among chiefly families is agnatic lineage important. The same author concludes that the "royal houses" of the different states are named exogamous patrilineages, with totemic titles. The royal houses of Mengmao, Chanta, and Luchiang, for example, are three separate lineages of the Tiger clan.

MARRIAGE AND FAMILY. In general similar to the Lü. The impact of Chinese civilization is evident in such things as size of the family. The following table (Chiang 1950: 210) shows the average family size in five *muong* domains ranging from the most sinicized (Mangshih) to the least sinicized (Mengmao):

	No. families	Population	Average family size
Mangshih	5,461	27,000	4.80
Nantien	8,000	32,000	4.00
Lungchuan	2,162	7,860	3.60
Chefang	1,260	3,300	2.60
Mengmao	1,500	2,930	2.00

SOCIOPOLITICAL ORGANIZATION. **Political organization.** Chiang (1950) writes that the Chinese Shan States area was composed of thirteen *t'u-ssu* chieftaincies (*muong*). Although theoretically responsible to Chinese officials, the *muong* chiefs or princes (*chao fa*) were in the 1930s relatively independent, both of the Chinese and of one another. As pointed out by Wiens (1954: 308), this situation may have been a temporary one due to the weakness of Chinese political unity and power at the time. As in the Sip Song Panna, a *muong* generally encompasses the area of a low-lying valley plain or basin, averaging 15 to 20 miles in length. **Social stratification.** A marked cleavage exists between the noble and the commoner classes. The nobility are highly sinicized, with a high standard of living, and may even own motor cars. Noble families bear Chinese names, claim Chinese ancestry, and the more sinicized among them maintain ancestral tablets and the ancestral graves. Noble and commoner classes do not intermarry any more than they do in the Sip Song Panna. Noble families are supported by proceeds from taxes, rents, and other obligations imposed on commoners and, in the larger *muong* centers, enjoy an elaborate court life patterned on the Chinese model. Chiang (1950: 101 ff.) emphasizes the autocratic character of the princes, pointing out that in effect each *muong* domain functions as an independent absolutist monarchy on a miniature scale. There is no evidence (at least in modern times) of a paramount ruler or "king." The *muong* courts include titled and graded officials—members of princely or related families—with important administrative functions, as well as appointed officials such as secretary, granary manager, and keeper of the royal horses. A seal keeper, usually the eldest among the prince's brothers, may also function in a quasi-official capacity as a sort of "second ruler." A *muong* court may also have attached to it a Han Chinese teacher and a Chinese clerk, as well as Tai clerks, orderlies, and bodyguards. The court officials are appointed, and there is not, as in the Sip Song Panna, a council of elder statesmen serving as a check on the autocratic tendencies of the *chao fa*. The institution of regent functions much as it does among the Lü. At the local level, villages, in charge of headmen, are grouped in administrative units called *kang*, which are in charge of officials responsible for tax collection and the administration of economic affairs.

RELIGION. **Major religions.** The Chinese Shans are Hinayana Buddhists who lie just on the margin of what Dodd (1923: 76) termed the "Yuan cult area," i.e. that portion of southern Yunnan, southeastern Burma, and northern Thailand which is characterized by a common religious script and common religious terms traceable to the diffusion of Buddhism into the area from the south. In the Chinese Shan States the influences of Burmese Buddhism are evident in the elaborate structure and ornamentation of temples, the presence of pagodas, and the character of the religious script. **Ceremonies.** T'ien (1949) reports a series of life-cycle ceremonies subsumed under the term "Pai cult." The most important of these is "Great Pai," sponsored either by an individual or by a group of several persons. Goods are accumulated (sometimes including a Buddha statue), elaborately displayed, and presented to the village temple. The temple abbot receives the gifts and in turn bestows an honorific title on the giver. The number of times a person has participated in one of these Pai ceremonies, plus the degree to which he impoverishes himself, determines his status within the community. ● Participation in Pai ceremonies also marks a transition point in the lives of adolescents. For this purpose the adolescents of a village, according to T'ien, are organized into youth groups, each under the leadership of a bachelor or spinster (T'ien 1949: 51). For a girl, joining one of these groups and donning skirts signifies her marriageability. The Great Pai ceremony cuts across social class divisions of noble and commoner; both aspire to the honorific titles that can be acquired only by participation in the Great Pai.

BIBLIOGRAPHY. Chiang 1950; Davies 1909; Dodd 1923; Leach 1954; Metford 1935; Milne 1910; Seidenfaden 1958; T'ien 1949; Wiens 1954.

BURMESE SHANS

Synonyms. *Ngiaw, Ngio, Sam*

ORIENTATION. **Identification.** The people call themselves Tai, often adding the name of the village or local group. They are called Shans by the Burmese, a term used also by the British. Those living in the Northern Shan States and in adjacent Chinese Shan States call themselves Tai Yai or Tai Long (Great Tai), referring to their congeners in the Southern Shan States as Tai Taü (Southern Tai). They are known to the Siamese and Lao as Ngio (Ngiaw) and to the Kachins as Sam. [Scott and Hardiman 1900: chap. 6.] **Location.** Shan speakers are found throughout Burma except in the Chin Hills, Arakan, and Tenasserim regions. Their major concentration is in the present Shan State, an area of some 50,000 square miles lying roughly between 20°–24° N. and 96°–101° E. Elsewhere in Burma they are likely to be scattered and strongly Burmanized. In the extreme north the Hkamti Shans, although isolated from the main Shan State area, have retained to some extent their cultural identity and their sense of historical relatedness to the main body of Shans. **Geography.** The Burmese Shans inhabit a large plateau area, averaging 3,000 feet above sea level, intersected by mountain chains running in a general north–south direction. The resulting series of valleys and plains constitutes the nuclei of the various Shan principalities. The area is under the influence of the annual monsoons, with the rainy season occurring during the period July to October. Frost may occur at night during the height of the cool season from December to February. Deciduous and subtropical mixed forests cover the area. Timber, particularly teak, has long been a valuable natural resource. The presence of silver, lead, gold, and rubies has for centuries attracted Chinese, Indian, British, and Burmese merchants and entrepreneurs. [Brant 1956: 622-24; Scott and Hardiman 1900: 274-75.] **Linguistic affiliation.** The Shans are Tai speakers, linguistically related to the Siamese and Lao. Dialect differences are present, e.g. as between the Northern and Southern Shan State areas. The script shows strong Burmese influence. **Demography.** According to the 1931 census, the total of Tai speakers in Burma stood at slightly over one million, the majority being in the Shan State area. Only about one-half of the population of the Shan State consists of Tai speakers, however. Other major groups in the same area are Kachins, Lahu, Akha, Wa, and Palaungs. [Brant 1956: 629.] **History.** The Tai may have entered the region of northern Burma as early as the pre-Christian era, but their influence does not seem to have been felt in any degree until the Nanchao period. The traditional date of the founding of the Tai principality of Mogaung, north of Bhamo, is 1215 A.D. Mogaung, however, seems to have been preceded by earlier petty kingdoms located in the general area of the Shweli river valley, going back as early as the seventh century A.D. Although dates are uncertain, it seems clear that the area of the Northern Shan States saw an early development of a series of semifeudal principalities, and that this political development then spread north to the Hkamti Shan area and northern Assam. In contrast, Tai political exploitation of the Southern Shan States area appears to have occurred relatively late. The actual number of Tai speakers who took part in these early developments may not have been great, consisting of small numbers of politically organized wet-rice growers settled in pockets along the river valleys. The large Shan population of Burma today would then be in part the result of the assimilation of various non-Tai peoples who have gradually lost their original dress and speech and adopted wet-rice agriculture, Tai speech, and Buddhist religion to "become Shan." ● When Nanchao fell to the Mongols in the thirteenth century, Peking established a puppet government in Yunnan. Ensuing warfare with the (Burmese) Pagan dynasty resulted in the collapse of the latter in 1287. The Shans stepped into the resulting power vacuum, and by 1500 most of what is now Burma had become a loose federation of *muong* domains ruled by Shan princes. The sixteenth century saw the resurgence of Burmese power and the gradual extension of Burmese rule over most of the Shan states west of the Salween. Thus by the time the British entered eastern Burma in the late nineteenth century the Shans had been acculturating to Burma for upward of 400 years. The British found the Northern Shan States in a state of chaos; the *saohpas* were fighting among themselves, attempting to shake off Burmese rule, and at the same time fighting a steadily losing battle against encroaching Kachin raids from the north. British rule stabilized the area. By the 1930s many *saohpas* had been educated abroad, plans were underway for the economic exploitation of the area with Shan participation, and some headway had been made toward wiping out the costly feuds and petty rivalries among the princes. ● Today, under independent Burma, some 33 substates constitute the Shan State, which theoretically has autonomy in matters of internal administration, representation in the national legislative body, and its own Shan-staffed civil service. The *saohpas*, although they still enjoy the loyalty of the majority of Shans, have lost much of their old autonomy. Land reform and compulsory education programs are advocated by the Union Government. [Scott and Hardiman 1900: 190-200; Leach 1954: 38-40; Hall 1955: 144 ff.; Brant 1956: 653-65.] **Cultural relations.** The Shans have been in continuous contact with other races and cultural traditions over a long period of time. Historically, the greatest influence has probably been Burmese. The Shans along the western edge of the plateau have been heavily Burmanized, and many can speak Burmese. Members of Shan ruling families have been educated in the Burmese court, and there has been some intermarriage. The British influence was felt principally among the *saohpas*. Chinese merchants and artisans are found in most villages, and intermarriage occurs between members of Burmese and Chinese Shan ruling families. The influence of the Chinese cultural tradition, except in the extreme northeast, is negligible, however, compared with that of Burma (and ultimately, through it, of India). The most frequent contact at the village level with non-Tai peoples occurs with the various hill tribes, e.g. the Kachins and Palaungs. Kachin men enter Shan communities as laborers, taking Shan women as part recompense. Adopting the religion of their wives, they "become Shan." Shan is a lingua franca among Palaung groups with marked dialect differences. Assimilation of hill tribesmen by the lowland-dwelling

Shans is a widely occurring phenomenon which apparently has been going on for a long time. The large southeastern state of Kengtung, across the Salween, has always maintained an existence somewhat apart from the main body of Shans to the west; its orientation and cultural affiliations are more in the direction of the Lü and the Siamese Tai to the east and southeast. [Brant 1956: 628-30; Leach 1954: 218-26.]

SETTLEMENT PATTERN AND HOUSING. **Settlement pattern.** Settlements tend to be permanent. The Shan farmer is tied to his land by political and economic considerations and by a strong sentimental attachment to his own village. Settlements vary in size, but the average rice village probably contains from 200–500 individuals. Villages are located in river valleys or in pockets of level land in the hills, always near water, and frequently in the midst of a bamboo grove. There is no regular arrangement of streets or houses, except that the larger settlements contain a market place or square in the center. The Buddhist temple and the headman's house are usually the most imposing structures—except in those villages or towns which are also the seat of a ruling *saohpa*, in which case his residence, or *haw*, takes precedence. **Housing.** Houses are constructed almost entirely of bamboo, and raised about eight feet above the ground on piles. The gable roof, which slopes down slightly beyond the flooring, is of thatch. There is a veranda reached by a ladder. Inside is a living (public) room, with a fireplace, and beyond, in the back, one or more sleeping rooms. The space underneath may be walled with mats, and is ordinarily used for domestic tasks. Cattle are herded outside the village or tied up near the entrance to the house. Each house is surrounded by a garden. [Milne 1910: 85-105.]

ECONOMY. Primarily settled wet-rice agriculturalists, with garden crops important. Animal husbandry is secondary to agriculture. There is some reliance on gathering. Fish are an important part of the diet, but most fish are apparently obtained in markets. **Agriculture.** The larger alluvial basins are intersected with irrigation canals. Dams and water wheels are also used to divert water to the rice fields (Scott and Hardiman 1900: 275-77). Manure is used. Most rice is grown by transplanting seedlings started in nurseries. Fields are plowed and puddled with a buffalo-drawn plow at the beginning of the monsoon rains. Fields remain flooded until about a month before harvest, which occurs in September or October. The grain is threshed in the field and the paddy stored in large mud-plastered baskets (Milne 1910: 149-53). There is some dry-rice agriculture in the comparatively dry upland areas (Scott and Hardiman 1900: 275-77). In the Hukawng valley area occasional use of irrigated terraces cut out of the mountain side is reported (Leach 1954: 30). Crops include rice, tobacco, cotton, sugar cane, and maize. Garden

vegetables include peas, beans, okra, tomatoes, and cucumbers. Oranges, bananas, melons, and mangoes are cultivated; wild fruits include apples, pears, and papaya. Tea, coffee, and tung are grown as commercial crops in some areas. **Domestic animals.** Cattle are numerous. The Shans also raise horses, water buffalo, pigs, and chickens. [Scott and Hardiman 1900: 275-77.] **Food and stimulants.** Diet consists mainly of rice and vegetables, supplemented with fish, pork, beef, and chicken. Sour (pickled) foods are popular. Snails and frogs are eaten, and the larvae of certain beetles, wasps, and bees are much sought after. Water is the main beverage. Rice liquor is made in a still. Condensation is achieved by placing one earthenware pot inside another, the smaller being filled with cold water (Milne 1910: 176-77). Betel-nut chewing is widespread, and tobacco is smoked. The Shans are not addicted to opium and use it only occasionally for medicinal purposes. [Scott and Hardiman 1900: 327; Milne 1910: 170 ff.] **Industrial arts.** Localized cottage industries include pottery making, sculpture, lacquerware, paper manufacture, silverwork, and cotton cloth manufacture. The Shans in the Lashio–Bhamo area do not work in iron, but rely on itinerant smiths from the Chinese Shan States in Yunnan. [Milne 1910: 150.] **Trade.** The Shans impress the outside observer as a trade-minded people, although trade is conducted on a relatively petty scale (Brant 1956: 638). Shan traders have traditionally moved over most of the area and even made periodic cart caravan trips to the plains of Burma proper. Village markets, attended by Shans, Chinese, Kachins, and Palaungs, are held every fifth day. The various villages within an area hold their markets on different days to avoid conflict. **Division of labor.** Women weave, carry water, gather firewood, pound rice, cook, and go to market. Men build houses, plow fields, and maintain irrigation works. Formerly they engaged in warfare. Men and women work together in transplanting and harvesting rice. Men and boys are responsible for herding cattle and water buffalo. **Land tenure.** Traditionally, the land within a Shan state belonged ultimately to the ruling prince, or *saohpa*. With the founding of a village or the establishment of a separate *muong* (district) within the confines of the state, the *saohpa* designated the limits of the land at its disposal. Village lands were then administered by the village headman. Shan farmers had traditional usufruct rights to the land they worked; these were handed down from generation to generation as long as the land continued in use and the required rent and taxes were paid. Use-right titles of this kind were obtained by clearing and cultivation or by an outright grant in return for services rendered. Land held in this fashion could be mortgaged but not completely alienated, and if the farmer moved outside the state, he lost his rights. [Scott and Hardiman 1900: 326-28; Leach 1954: 215; Milne 1910: 98.]

KIN GROUPS. Leach, speaking of the Shans of the Hukawng valley, reports the absence of any clear-cut kin groups among commoners (1954: 213). Leach also reports bilateral descent (1954: 214), apparently referring simply to the bilateral recognition of kinship ties. Whether there are personal kindreds present here or elsewhere in the Burmese Shan area is not clear. ● Among the nobility there is a decidedly unilineal orientation. Succession to the position of *saohpa* appears in all cases to be governed by patrilineal descent, and patrilineal, rather than matrilineal, descent appears to be a deciding factor in determining an individual's claim to membership in the nobility. Leach (1954: 216) states that the royal houses of the different Shan states are named patrilineages with totemic titles. He records an informant's statement that the various patrilineages are strictly exogamous. The examples he lists are, however, all from within the Chinese Shan States in Yunnan. **Kin terminology.** Kinship terminology appears to follow closely the pattern for neighboring Tai speakers, e.g. the Siamese and Lao (Benedict 1943: 169-72; Cushing 1914):

Mo	*me*
Fa	*po*
FaElBr, MoElBr	*lung*
FaElSi, MoElSi	*pa*
FaYoBr, FaYoSi	*a*
MoYoBr, MoYoSi	*na*
ElBr, ElSi	*pi* plus sex modifier
YoBr, YoSi	*nong* plus sex modifier
Cousins	*pi* and *nong* (based on relative age of kin through whom relationship is traced, e.g. parents' older brother's child is *pi*)

MARRIAGE AND FAMILY. **Mode.** There are relatively few restrictions on premarital sex behavior. Boys, either singly or in groups, court girls by singing love songs and playing on a small Panpipe or reed organ. Choice of a partner, once made, is subject to parental approval, although a couple may elope if the parents object to the match. Normally, a cash bride price is negotiated by a go-between and, after consulting the horoscopes of the young couple, an auspicious day is set for the wedding. The ceremony, witnessed by friends and relatives, takes place at the home of the bride. A village elder officiates by tying a white thread around the wrists of the couple, after which the wedding party removes to the home of the groom's parents, where the latter welcome the bride. Buddhist monks take no part in Shan wedding ceremonies. ● Among the nobility, marriages are likely to be arranged matches for purposes of consolidating political power. A *saohpa's* wives may represent a series of such alliances with ruling families in neighboring states and neighboring countries. Although the nobility is theoretically an endogamous caste, in practice marriages do occur with commoners. **Form.** Marriage among the majority of the population is monogamous. Polygyny occurs mainly among the nobility, the ruling *saohpas* maintaining harems if possible. It is customary, but not obligatory, that a woman marry her deceased husband's brother. **Extension of incest taboos.** A man normally expects to marry a girl from his own village. Since there are no restrictions on marriage between cousins, the local community is to a considerable degree an endogamous group of kinsmen (Leach 1954: 213). **Residence.** A young couple normally set up their own household after marriage, although an only son may continue to live patrilocally after marriage (Milne 1910: 98). **Domestic unit.** The normal household unit is the independent nuclear family with at best a few dependent relatives. **Inheritance.** Inheritance rules are theoretically patterned on the Burmese Buddhist code of *damathat*. Sons, rather than daughters, are favored in the inheritance of property, including land, although daughters do have some rights. Elder sons are favored over their younger brothers. [Leach 1954: 213.] **Divorce.** Divorce is relatively easy. A divorced woman has definite property rights, and a man who divorces a woman without justifiable cause loses thereby his claim to the return of any of the bride price. Young children usually go with the mother. Theoretically divorce conforms to the code of *damathat*. [Scott and Hardiman 1900: 321-26; Milne 1910: 75-85.]

SOCIOPOLITICAL ORGANIZATION. **Political organization.** The Burmese Shans have for centuries lived as settled wet-rice agriculturists. Their secure economic base has permitted the development of trade, small-scale urbanization, and a semiliterate peasantry (Leach 1954: 21). Most of the people live in small endogamous villages. Leadership may be hereditary, but usually it depends more on age and natural capacity. The villages fall within the confines of one or another of a series of feudally organized states, *muong*, ruled by hereditary princes, *saohpa*. Since the sixteenth century the Shan states have been stabilized, first under Burmese and later under British administrative control, and it is difficult to separate out what might have been indigenous Tai sociopolitical patterns from those generated by these outside influences. ● The number of Shan states existing at any one period in history is difficult to determine, partly because of the shifting political fortunes of the *saohpas* themselves and also because of the special administrative arrangements imposed by successive Chinese, Burmese, and British governments. Under the British there were some 15 major states as well as a great many dependencies and minor territorial divisions representative of special political considerations. The four large northern states of Hsenwi, Möngmit, Tawngpeng, and Hsipaw have retained their importance due largely to their mineral and agricultural wealth. The state of Kengtung in the southeast has also figured prominently, but because of its remoteness from centers of Burmese influence and its importance as an opium producer, its orientation has been more in the direction of Thailand than of Burma. ● The political capital of a state is characteristically a town, often of the same name, located in an area of irrigated rice fields. Larger states are divided into feudal dependencies, also called *muong*. At the head of the state is an hereditary prince, *saohpa*, and in charge of each dependency there is a lesser member of the nobility, usually related to the *saohpa*. Scott and Hardiman (1900: 287 ff.) speak, for example, of Hsenwi as being made up of 49 *muong* domains, each in charge of a tributary chieftain. A Shan *saohpa*'s rule is theoretically absolute. He maintains a royal residence, a harem, an entourage of officials and retainers, and a collection of court regalia and paraphernalia patterned on those of Burmese and Siamese royalty. In theory, all land within the state is his by divine right; these lands he grants as fiefdoms to vassal chieftains in return for monetary tribute and military support. Effective political control is maintained in part by marital alignments and in part by a bureaucracy of officials who live off the people by keeping their share of the various taxes and levies. Taxes are now paid in money, although they were traditionally paid in kind on the basis of the number of baskets of paddy seed sown. Special services and corvée labor are due the *saohpa* and other high officials, and males fit for warfare were formerly subject to call at any time. [Scott and Hardiman 1900: 327-29.] **Social stratification.** Shan society is stratified into two main classes, nobility and commoners. There is also a lower class or outcaste group which once included slaves and now consists of fishermen, butchers, and those in other occupations considered unclean by Buddhist standards. The great majority of the population, all those who are engaged in farming, are classed as commoners. Theoretically, marriage does not take place between nobility and commoners, but, as pointed out by Leach (1954: 35), in a bilateral society the nobility tends to be a large and somewhat vaguely defined group, and commoners may marry into the peripheral noble families to ensure noble status for their descendants. **Warfare.** Inter-*muong* warfare of a bloody and fierce nature was formerly common. Petty wars were often set off by disputes over the succession to a throne among the surviving males of a deceased *saohpa*—particularly among the sons of the *saohpa*'s various wives.

RELIGION. **Major religions.** The Shans are predominantly Theravada Buddhists. Their Buddhism, which probably came from Burma, is strongest where Burmese influence has been greatest, e.g. in the west and south of the Shan State area. Young boys attend monastery schools, where they learn to recite a few simple religious texts. At age 10 to 12 they enter the monastery for a short time, serving the monks and learning from them the precepts of Buddhism. Monks are not hierarchically organized; they are, however, divided into sects according to the strictness with which they observe the religious vows. [Milne 1910: 50 ff.] **Indigenous religion.** Along with Buddhism, the Shans hold to a variety of occult beliefs and practices which combine indigenous animism with ancient Brahmanic influences. According to Scott and Hardiman (1900: 320-21), occult beliefs are strongest in the north, where the Shans are "generally admitted to be abler astrologers and more potent tattooers than the Burmans." At about age 14, boys are tattooed by a specialist in the art. The designs, in blue, may appear on the legs, chest, back, or arms. The designs may be regarded as charms, in which case the skill and occult knowledge of the specialist are of utmost importance. Tattooing may also be regarded as a sign of manhood, and it is said that girls ignore as potential marriage partners those boys who have not been tattooed. [Milne 1910: 66-69; Scott and Hardiman 1900: 319-20.] **Practitioners.** Occult specialists interpret dreams, omens, and horoscopes. Divination is carried out by heating a bamboo node until it explodes, and examining the position of the split fibers. Buddhist monks are sometimes credited with occult powers. Persons suspected of the evil eye may be banished from a village. [Milne 1910: 50 ff., 178-84.] **Illness and medicine.** Old people specialize in herb medicines, charms, and spells for curing illness, and many women specialize in massage, using their feet as well as their hands (Milne 1910: 178-85). **Birth and naming.** There are no particular ceremonies at birth. The mother is "roasted," i.e. she stays near a fire for a period of one month, during which time she is not expected to do any housework (Milne 1910: 31-34). At the age of one month the infant is given a ceremonial bath. Guests drop coins and bits of gold into a container of water, which is then used to bathe the baby. At the same time the child is given a baby or pet name which is retained by boys until they are given a monastery name. A system of kin numeratives is used, which, according to Benedict (1945: 34), reflects an ancient diffusion from the Chinese culture area. In this system boys' names are prefixed by *ai*, "eldest," and girls' names by *nang*, "girl." The suffixed numerals are cognates of ancient Chinese forms. The ear lobes of both sexes are pierced during infancy, and the holes enlarged by insertion of increasingly larger objects (Milne 1910: 39). **Soul, death, and afterlife.** Belief in 32 souls or *khwan* is common (Seidenfaden 1958: 44). The majority of Shans inter their dead, using a wooden coffin. Only monks and the well-to-do are cremated. The funeral of an important person may be delayed a week or longer. Normally, the corpse is laid out in the home, where friends and relatives gather. The Shans do not ordinarily grieve at the death of a good old man, since to do so would imply that he had not earned a better life. The procession to the grave, led by monks, is a colorful and noisy affair. The dead are buried in a cemetery outside the village. Graves are not marked permanently, and there is no particular cult of the dead except that they are remembered in annual feasts. Persons who have died prematurely or unnaturally are buried quickly and with little or no ceremony. Avoidance behavior is used, since the ghosts of such persons are held to be malignant. [Milne 1910: 89-95.]

BIBLIOGRAPHY. Benedict 1943, 1945; Brant 1956; Cushing 1914; Hall 1955; Leach 1954; Milne 1910; Scott and Hardiman 1900; Seidenfaden 1958.

SOUTHERN GROUPS

SIAMESE TAI[1]

Synonyms. *Syam, Thai*

ORIENTATION. **Identification.** The word Siamese (also Thai, T'ai, Tai, Syam) has varied references, among them the following: the citizens of the country of Thailand or Siam (as it was called before the revolution of 1932); the people who reside in central and southern Thailand as distinct from the people of northern Thailand (called Yuan or Lanathai) or the people of northern and northeastern Thailand (called Lao); and the people of Thailand who are of Buddhist faith as distinguished from Moslems or other religious groups. Here the word will be used to mean native-born citizens of Thailand, with particular emphasis on rural residents who share Theravada Buddhism, the Tai language, and the predominant national ways of life. ● The Siamese Tai are similar in physique and complexion to peoples of most neighboring countries in southeastern Asia, including Indonesia and the Philippines, and are roughly categorized as Deutero-Malay. Phansomboon (1957) supports the earlier findings by Maneffe and Bézacier (1940) of a closer genetic relationship to the Indonesians than to the Cantonese Chinese. Yet the heterogeneity of physical type reflects a considerable mixture of genetic strains. Tai speakers in northern Thailand are smaller in physique and lighter in skin color than those in the central plain (Andrews 1943; Seidenfaden 1958: 12-13). Andrews proposes that differences in physique have resulted from a more adequate diet in central Thailand than in the north. **Location.** Thailand lies between 5° and 21° N. and 97° and 106° E., varying in elevation from sea level to

2,550 meters at Doi Angkha (Intanon) in the north. **Geography.** The country may be divided into five regions. The mountainous north has narrow valleys of clay and alluvial soils with rivers draining south into the central plain. Central Thailand includes the alluvial plain and the bordering hills that form the valley of the Chao Phraya (Menam) river. The northeast is separated from the central plains by an escarpment, and consists of a plateau of sandy soil draining eastward into the Mekong river. In the southeast, adjoining Cambodia, lies a pocket of hills with red soil, at the crest of which rivers flow east into the Mekong through Cambodia or west into the central plain. The southern region includes the eastern slope of the chain of hills running south along the Kra isthmus, where soils are sandy (Pendleton 1962: 63-82). ● In four of the five regions the monsoon winds bring on a rainy season beginning in May or June and continuing until October or November. The least generous distribution of rain is in the northern and eastern extremes, where problems of water conservation make rice culture difficult. Temperatures fall toward a low in December and January. From February until the beginning of the rainy season temperatures mount to the April highs before the rains begin. In the south a rainy season of September to January alternates with a hot season from February to August (Pendleton 1962: 63-82). ● In terms of both value and quantity of produce, the extraction and refining of tin dominates the few mining enterprises of Thailand. Wolfram, lead, antimony, and iron ores are also extracted in smaller quantities. Development of lignite and petroleum is now proceeding. Salt, gypsum, clay, and marble represent the chief nonmetals currently in production. A variety of other minerals (gold, copper, zircon, titanium, and uranium) are reported, but have not yet been exploited commercially (IBRD 1959: 110, 273, 276; Pendleton 1962: 232-56). **Linguistic affiliation.** Siamese Tai is an isolative and tonal language related to those of Laos and the Shan States. Linguists have not reached an agreement as to whether Tai stands among the Sinitic languages as Wulff (1934) affirms, or in a family of Kadai languages, related to Indonesian, as Benedict (1942) proposes. **Demography.** In 1957 the population of Thailand was estimated as follows (Blanchard et al. 1958: 49):

Siamese	18,585,000
Chinese	3,000,000
Malay	670,000
Cambodian	185,000
Vietnamese	25,000
Indian and Pakistani	60,000
Mon	60,000
Karen	60,000
Westerners	5,000
Others	150,000
Total	22,800,000

---

[1] The authors of this section, Lucien M. Hanks, Jr. of Bennington College and Jane Richardson Hanks, have been associated with the Cornell Thailand Project and have done field work in the village of Bang Chan, Thailand. The authors' use of Thai (Central Thai) has, with their permission, been changed throughout to Siamese to conform with usage in the rest of the volume.

The average population density in 1947 was 35 per square kilometer (Sharp et al. 1956: 63). This figure must be viewed against the fact that the population is concentrated along rivers and their alluvial plains, particularly the Chao Phraya in the center, the Ping in the north, and the Mun and the Chi in the northeast. In roughly 30 per cent of the country density is from 0 to 10 per square kilometer; in another 20 per cent the range is from 11 to 19 (Sharp et al. 1956: Map 7). Population parallels land cultivation patterns. On rice lands, which make up 90 per cent of the cropped area, as of 1947 densities ran up to 154 per square kilometer (Sharp et al. 1956: 64) in an area roughly 200 kilometers up the valley of the Chao Phraya river from Bangkok, and 100 kilometers wide. Comparably high densities occur near Lopburi in the northern part of the central plain and around Chiengmai. Of 15 provinces surrounding Ubon in the northeast, 4 had populations of 48 to 85 per square kilometer; 8 had 30 to 44; and 3 had 12 to 26 (Madge 1955: 12). The nutritional density maps of Zelinsky (1950: 132) support Madge and Sharp in showing that the population pressure on the resources in the northeast is twice that of the central plain, and in the north three times as great because of large mountainous areas. **History and cultural relations.** According to Hall (1955: 750), the chief periods of Siamese history are usually given according to the location of the capital rather than by dynasties: Sukhothai (1238-1347); Ayuthia (1350-1765); Thonburi (1767-82); Bangkok (1782–present). Despite the availability of many chronicles, their questionable validity for purposes of historical reconstruction prior to the Bangkok era passes the main burden to archaeology and epigraphy. ● Some new information is available concerning the time and circumstances of the arrival of Tai-speaking people in Thailand. To the earlier inscriptions, e.g. the Champa inscription of 1050 and the Angkor Wat relief dated 1150, Luce (1958: 124) adds an inscription from Pagan dated 1120 in which "Syam" is mentioned. Gogoi (1956) and Sukhabanij (1956; 1957) find evidence from documentary sources for successive Tai invasions in the north from the Shan States beginning with Payao (ninth or tenth century), Muang Fang (tenth or eleventh century), and leading through "beach-head" states to the establishment of rule at Sukhothai in 1237. On the other hand, Coedès (1948: 318-27) associates the formation of Tai states with the example of the Mongol conquest and the dispossession of Tai chieftains as a result of the fall of Nanchao in southwestern China (1256). He dates the formation of Tai states in the twelfth and thirteenth centuries. This spreading Tai influence has led writers to picture a migration between 800 and 1200 A.D. from a state named Nanchao in southwestern China, sometimes described as an "inundation" (Seidenfaden 1958: 7) and sometimes as a "slow infiltration" (Coedès 1948: 318). Paul Bene-

dict's hypothesis concerning the Kadai family of languages and the blood-type studies of Maneffe and Bézacier, as well as those of Phansomboon, which relate the people of Thailand to those of Indonesia on linguistic and genetic grounds, suggest stability of population. Moreover, Credner (1935b) observed in Yunnan that the Tai-speaking population inhabited valleys with altitudes of less than 1,000 meters, and proposes that Tai speakers probably never occupied much of Nanchao, a considerable portion of which stands above this altitude. He does not deny that certain rulers of Nanchao may have been Tai, but he raises serious doubts concerning the widely-held theory that Nanchao was a state largely populated by Tai speakers (e.g. Carthew 1952). Chinese records of the conquest of Nanchao give further evidence that the local population remained in the area after their defeat, with the exception of certain Shan tribes. The group that settled in Luang Prabang somewhat earlier in the thirteenth century may constitute another exception (Coedès 1948: 319). Such considerations suggest that the Tai-speaking peoples did not migrate into Southeast Asia as tribal or local wholes but only as warrior segments of these groups. In addition to the known water routes, Luce (1958: 128-30) has charted two roads leading into Thailand, one proceeding directly to the Chiengmai region, a second via present-day Laos to northeastern Thailand. ● Since the establishment of Sukhothai in the thirteenth century, Thailand has been a self-governing country. Although periodic tribute missions traveled to China from 1295 onward, China never interceded in the governing of Siam. The Burmese invasions of 1569 and 1765 effectively disrupted internal order, yet the Burmese did not consolidate their gains and hold the country. Under the early Bangkok sovereigns the Siamese re-established the Ayuthian tribute payments from Cambodia, parts of Laos, and four of the Malay states, as well as the principality of Chiengmai which later merged as a part of Thailand. The present territorial limits were reached through negotiations with Britain and France in the late nineteenth century. In 1932 a constitutional form of government with provisions for a king of limited authority and an elected parliament replaced the absolute monarchy. During World War II, Thailand experienced a temporary reduction of sovereignty when it permitted Japan to station troops and conduct war from its territory. ● Since the publication of Ruth Benedict's (1952) sociopsychological observations on the Siamese national character, efforts have been directed toward understanding contemporary Thailand as a unique entity. Until this time, many assumed that the country would develop into an industrial power comparable to those in Europe, and that the duty of persons of good will was to remove the obstacles to this development. Ruth Benedict and the ethnological school of observers advocated study of the social scene to find the inherent direction of movement without regard for theoretical models of development. In keeping with this outlook, Wilson (1959: 59-65) has demonstrated that Western models of government, economy, and social structure do not apply to Thailand. Studies of interest from this point of view include those on political process (Wilson 1959), bureaucracy (Mosel 1957), elections (Wilson and Phillips 1958), education (Hanks 1959), and the Chinese minority (Skinner 1957; Coughlin 1960).

SETTLEMENT PATTERN AND HOUSING. **Settlement pattern.** Sharp et al. state that villages range from 300 to 3,000 persons (1953: 180). Some villages may be spatially distinct, however, while others are only administrative subdivisions in an area of continuous settlement. DeYoung (1955: 8-12) describes two village types: (1) Houses strung ribbonwise along both sides, and fronting on, a waterway or road, with occasional clustering. Unfenced fields stretch to the back. If edging a wide river, any opposing counterparts are separate communities. (2) A cluster of houses more or less circular set among fruit trees, coconut palms, or rice fields, connected to a main thoroughfare by a path or cart road up to a kilometer in length. Pendleton's (1962: 108) island and road (or river) village types, based on aerial photographs, correspond roughly to these two types, both of which occur in the central plains. ● Madge (1955: 20-23) describes northeastern villages as ranging from 300–2,000 people. Cart tracks connect them through stretches of arid rough grass and scrub land, with occasional trees. Set in luxuriant groves of vegetation, each has one or more natural ponds (*nong*) developed from old marshes, which provide dependable water and fish supplies during the long seasons of drought. Schools often lie between two villages. Landless communities of traders, laborers, or charcoal burners form ribbon-hamlets along roads. In the north around Chiengmai, Kingshill (1960) also finds villages stretching along roads. In general, villages in the north are older and more compact than in the central plains. ● To these types can be added another pattern of dispersed settlement, in which each farmer lives on his own land. DeYoung (1955: 11) describes this scattering for the orchard districts south of Bangkok and for the Pasak irrigation district at Rangsit. Where landholdings are large, houses are widely spaced; where inheritance is now fragmenting land ownership, houses are increasingly dotting the scene. ● Prominent features of each village are the temple compound, which is variable in size, and the school. A few shops may be scattered among the houses, especially near the temple and school. Each house must have access to a waterway or road. For most of the year in the central plains, communication is by boat, otherwise by foot. Travel on roads is everywhere supplemented by bicycles, buses, and carts. **Housing.**

Houses are gabled, rectangular, and may be raised above the ground on piles or posts. Kingshill's two types, which depend on level of affluence, hold with minor variations for all Thailand: (1) A sturdy, paneled or clapboard-walled house of teak or mahogany, raised off the ground, with planked floor, a few windows (some with louvered shutters), and a roof of attap palm, tile, or, more recently, of corrugated iron. The traditional gable edging with its carved finials is rarely found on new houses. The wide entry, reached by ladder, is usually protected by a downward extension of the roof to form an earth-floored porch. On one or two sides, under the roof extension, a balustrade substitutes for the wall, providing ventilation (Kaufman 1960: 19). (2) A low-pitched gabled house of bamboo frame, sometimes with wood corner posts, with roof and perhaps a porch thatched with palm or grass, and sides of the same or of woven bamboo or matting. Light is admitted through the one or two doorways, or through a window, or from an area left open around the top of the house wall (Kaufman 1960: 20). Floors are earthen. If the house is raised, piles are usually bamboo, and floors are of woven bamboo or planks. ● An uneven number of rooms, usually three, divides the interior of the wooden houses. The main part of the house opens spaciously. One solidly-walled room with a shuttered window and a well-fitting door provides a quiet spot and a place where valuables can be locked up. The kitchen may be a separate room, sometimes a thatched addition, with clay set in a box of earth to support a stove. ● Thatched houses are not divided into rooms. People sit and sleep on low platforms of boards and cook on a stove on the ground by the door. Both types of houses have a shelf or table altar for the Buddha. They have cupboards, shelves, and jars for storage, including very large jars for collecting rainwater. Bins made of mats and baskets hold the year's supply of paddy, and the rice is stored in jars or chests. In the north and northeast, separate buildings beside the house serve as granaries, while looms and other sorts of manufacture are set up under the house. ● Apart from the house may be an open privy with a bit of thatch on one to three sides for privacy; occasionally a cement slab type is found, but most often none at all, with defecation in field or canal, or through a crack in the floor. Kingshill (1960: 48) notes more substantial sanitary arrangements in the north. Public health programs are continually extending the use of sanitary apparatus. ● In central Thailand where the plain is flooded, mounding up of the house site is essential, with the resulting hole becoming a pond or a passage to the canal for boats. On the mound the threshing floor is situated, if there is space. The house piles rise up from the mound high enough to permit storage under the floor of boats and lumber, and the quartering of draft animals. Outside of the flood areas the same arrangements occur without mounding. Farmers stable animals in separate sheds or lean-tos, or inside or under the house. Houses are occasionally taken down and rebuilt, and materials may be used many times. Thatching must be done about every three years.

ECONOMY. The subsistence economy depends overwhelmingly on agriculture, but practically all rural Siamese also devote time to fishing. Livestock production is potentially important, but at present contributes little as an additional source of food. **Agriculture.** Rice, the principal item of diet, is grown for domestic use in all parts of the country, usually as a single crop, although some areas in the north with dependable water supplies raise a second crop. While shifting dry-rice cultivation has been reported for parts of the north and northeast (Pendleton 1943; DeYoung 1955: 85), wet rice grown in permanent fields predominates. Soil and water conditions determine whether broadcast or transplanting methods are used. The northern and northeastern sections raise glutinous rice; the central plains ordinary rice, mainly for export. Where water must be raised to flood the seed beds, a variety of devices are used, from the water shovel swung manually from a pivot to the *rahad*, an endless belt of paddles which may be powered by hand, windmill, or gasoline motor to push water up a trough. The standard plow of wooden construction with a single metal blade is drawn by bullocks or water buffalo. If harrowing is not done by hoe, the soil is prepared with drags. The crop is harvested by hand. Northerners and northeasterners thresh by beating the sheaves into a large bowl-shaped basket or by flaying on the ground (Kingshill 1960: 35). In central Thailand water buffalo trample the grain from the stalks (Kaufman 1960: 46; Sharp et al. 1953: 136). Winnowing is accomplished by tossing the grain to let the wind blow away the chaff, frequently supplemented in central Thailand with winnowing machines cranked by hand. Siamese farmers also grow a variety of fruits and vegetables (including yams, chilies, cassava, eggplant, and beans). Commercial crops include sugar cane and tobacco, rubber, coconuts, condiments, and cotton. **Domestic animals.** Domestic animals include pigs, chickens, ducks, cattle, and water buffalo. The grasslands of the northeast are particularly suitable for livestock, and many cattle as well as water buffalo are annually driven down for sale in the central plains. **Food and stimulants.** Glutinous and nonglutinous rice are the dietary staples with which vegetables and (less often) meat in small pieces are consumed. Various condiments and sauces further enliven the basic rice dishes. Production of liquors is at present a government monopoly, but distillation in homemade devices has provided alcoholic beverages for many in the past. Tobacco is consumed in the form of homemade cigars and cigarettes, and may also be chewed. Betel chewing remains popular with the older generation. **In-**

dustrial arts. Pendleton (1962: 265) indicates that as of 1947, food processing and the production of textiles and wood products employed the most industrial workers, with mining and ceramics next. Nevertheless, a corps of part-time or seasonal specialists lives in almost every village, e.g. sewing machine operators, blacksmiths, or boat builders, who usually serve only the locality. Madge (1955: 61) reports charcoal, brass, and pottery manufacture for the local markets in the northeast. Ingram (1955: 115-19) emphasizes the persistence of traditional silk and cotton weaving as a home industry in the north and northeast only. For reasons lying deep in history and national character, the Siamese permitted the chief commercial tasks of the market centers to be taken by Chinese immigrants, whose descendants continue to operate rice mills and retail shops, balance ledgers, act as middlemen, and toil as artisans (Skinner 1957: 91-99; Ingram 1955: 209-11). According to the 1947 census for the province in which Bangkok is situated, all occupations except government service, high professional occupations, hairdressers, truck drivers, and domestic servants contain a higher number of ethnic Chinese than Siamese (Skinner 1957: 301-02). The situation in other towns is similar, indicating that the Siamese are by and large the people who farm and who govern. ● The *Dipterocarpus* forests of the highlands have long produced teak and *yang* for lumber, together with wood for fuel and various gums and oils. As exports, wood products and lumber stand fourth in value behind rice, rubber, and tin (IBRD 1959: 269). Commercial ocean fishing is done with large-scale seines and traps. Inland, each household within hailing distance of a body of water fishes for this important source of food with nets, scoops, baskets, spears, and hooks. Programs are developing the home cultivation of fish (Thailand Ministry of Agriculture 1957: 77; IBRD 1959: 84-85). **Trade.** Small stores, peddlers, and local markets are found throughout rural Thailand. Women bring home produce to the markets, where they retail it or supply other merchants. **Division of labor.** Division of labor between the sexes varies from area to area. In the north, women do not plow or harrow fields, although they perform these tasks in central Thailand (Kingshill 1960: 72; Sharp et al. 1953: 92-98). The traditional home tasks are assigned to women, but men also cook, tend babies, wash clothes, and sweep the house. Field work is chiefly a male job, yet during times of heavy work women perform the same tasks with minor exceptions. Both sexes fish, but the throw net and spear are for males. **Land tenure.** Historically, with the Siamese as with neighboring Tai-speaking groups, all land was held by the king, but individuals freely enjoyed usufruct as long as they occupied a tract and paid land taxes. Plots might be sold by the person occupying them, but only land in or near a city, because of its rentability, had market value. In rural sections, where vacant land was ever-present, owners abandoned unused lands rather than pay taxes; thus large estates never grew up. Until the present century land tenure was of little concern in Thailand. ● Today 90 per cent of all farm operators own the land they operate (Thailand Ministry of Agriculture 1953: 71). In the central plains, where renting on a cash or crop basis is most frequent, 75 per cent of the farmers work their own land. This proportion may be decreasing, however. In a village near Bangkok on the central plains less than half the farmers own all of the land they work (Sharp et al. 1953: 147).

KIN GROUPS. **Descent.** The Siamese reckon descent ambilineally, and permit extensive lateral connections by lumping together siblings with cousins and their spouses. The sibling designations refer simply to persons younger or older than Ego; the sex is indicated by additional terms. On the generation above Ego the same tendency may be noted by considering all siblings of the parents as kinsmen. Here, however, younger siblings of mother are distinguished from younger siblings of father. An older brother receives the same designation regardless of the parent's sex. On generations below Ego all except one's own children are described by a single term. In this manner three generation levels of kinsmen extend indefinitely in lateral directions. Such a group appears to fit Murdock's use of the term "kindred." In addition, however, persons may be included who act as kinsmen but lack affinal or consanguineal connections. Addressing any elderly male as "parent's older brother" or an elderly female as "mother" or "mother's mother" is commonplace within the rural scene. These groups, insofar as they are known to each other, are expected to assist at life cycle rites, and also seem to constitute the group for preferred endogamy. A kindred is implied in Kaufman's terms "spatially extended family" and "remotely extended families" (Kaufman 1960: 23, 25). The high frequency of village endogamy reported by Kingshill (1960: 48) as well as by Goldsen and Ralis (1957: 41) further suggests kindred. **Kin groups.** Three types of kindred groupings, often with minimal focus of authority, have been observed: 1. Multihousehold compounds: Siblings' parents and married children, cousins, or co-wives and their children live adjacently in two or more separate houses facing a common area. These groups work cooperatively on common enterprises, using common draft animals and equipment, although the individual households may at the same time conduct their own separate enterprises. Members also assist each other in food preparation, baby tending, lending of money, and construction. The largest observed group of this type contained about 30 persons in 5 households (Cornell 1948-57). As no such groups have been reported for other areas, this type may occur only on the central plains. 2. Hamlet cluster: Houses of kindred stand independently, each with its own compound, but forming a distinguishable group. These hamlets are organized in one of two ways both observed on the central plains (Cornell 1948-57): (a) The households own approximately equal resources, and each household operates its own enterprise, drawing upon the resources of its neighbors on an exchange basis, particularly for labor and house building. Hamlets of this type have also been reported in the north (Kingshill 1960: 28-29, 34, 47-48). Services such as boat building, midwifery, and medicine may be provided on a fee basis. Although the extent of such groups has not been determined, they probably grow as large as 200 or more people. (b) The household of one wealthy person may dominate the hamlet. In return for labor, the leader provides protection, living facilities, clothing, and equipment for personal use. This type of grouping was more frequent under the monarchy, when a prominent official's personal hamlet might reach as many as 400 people. Today such a kindred group is not likely to exceed 100 people, and is more likely to be found in urban centers. Although local government officers summon labor in villages for public works (Kingshill 1960: 83-91), these same officers may exchange labor for their own private undertakings and hence not qualify as leaders of kindred groups. It is likely that the majority of rural hamlets are of the unfocused leadership type. 3. Linked hamlets: Kindred living at a distance may continue to assist each other at life cycle rites, and in addition provide food and shelter for visiting kinsmen, help secure employment or land for a migrating kinsman, and provide residence for children attending school (Kingshill 1960: 21; Cornell 1948-57). **Kin terminology.** The following is an abbreviated list of kin terms from Kingshill (1960: 235-37):

FaFa	*pu*
MoFa	*ta*
FaMo	*ja*
MoMo	*jaj*
Fa	*phau*
Mo	*mae*
So, Da	*lug*
FaElBr, MoElBr	*lung*
FaElSi, MoElSi	*pa*
FaYoBr, FaYoSi	*a*
MoYoBr, MoYoSi	*na*
ElBr, ElSi; child of parent's older sibling	*phi*
YoBr, YoSi; child of parent's younger sibling	*naung*
Grandchild; child of sibling	*lan*

These terms are, with slight differences in phonetic transcription, the same as those listed by Benedict (1943: 169 ff.). In all respects the Siamese system conforms closely to those of the Lao, Lü, and Shans.

MARRIAGE AND FAMILY. **Mode.** Among the well-to-do, marriage negotiations are conducted by a go-between who seeks to balance the contributions in money, land, house, and furnishings which are offered by the two contracting families. The degree of grandeur of the new establishment indicates the wealth and interest of the families concerned. On the day of the marriage the final contributions are tallied by a selected third party. Elaborate nuptial ceremonies end with the formal installation of the bride and groom in their new house. ● Choice of a marriage partner is largely left to the young people themselves, and there are numerous opportunities for courtship. Formal courting to the accompaniment of antiphonal singing and reed-organ playing goes on now only in the north and northeast. The premarital sexual liaisons reported by DeYoung (1955: 62) and Kingshill (1960: 49) as precursors to marriage in the north are not acceptable in the central plains. Elopement, which is most common among less well-to-do couples, is usually followed by family reconciliation and a modest cash gift from the groom to the bride's family. Older couples often enter upon married life by the simple act of coresidence. [Sharp et al. 1956: 199-203; Rajadhon 1954b.] **Form.** Although polygynous marriage has long been part of Siamese culture, particularly among the nobility, most marriages today are monogamous. Second or third spouses are matters of individual arrangement, and consent of the principal wife is sometimes sought. [Kaufman 1960: 28.] **Extension of incest taboos.** Incest rules prohibit marriages within the nuclear family. Cousin marriage, particularly with second cousins, is allowed. Kindred or village endogamy is preferred. [Kaufman 1960: 28; Kingshill 1960: 47.] **Residence.** The nuclear family, established independently on or soon after marriage, is the ideal. In poorer and rural areas the couple usually resides in the house of the bride's family for at least a short period after marriage. Thereafter, residence depends on the opportunities which the couple wishes to exploit to establish themselves. Residence with either the bride's family or the groom's family under the same roof is becoming increasingly common. [Kaufman 1960: 29; Kingshill 1960: 47-48; Janlekha 1955: 37; Hanks and Phillips 1961: 643-47.] **Domestic unit.** The people who cook and eat meals about the same hearth are considered a family. This group not only lives and consumes goods as a unit but conducts joint economic enterprises such as farming. Although hearths with one or two people occur, ordinarily the minimal group is the nuclear family, to which grandparents, grandchildren, aunts and uncles, co-wives, cousins, and spouses of children may be added. Where property of value must be transferred to another generation, the unit may assume the form of a stem family, with succession through ultimogeniture. In rural areas of the northern and central regions, the average number of persons per household is between five and six. Madge, however, reports 6.6 for the northeast. [Kingshill 1960: 50; Kaufman 1960: 17, 66; Madge 1955: 43;

Sharp et al. 1953: 25.] **Inheritance.** Property is divided equally among surviving children, but the child who cares for the parents in their old age (often a younger daughter) ordinarily receives the homestead in addition to his or her normal share of land. Written wills are more frequent in the north, while in the central plains a person makes special bequests in the presence of witnesses on his deathbed (Kingshill 1960: 54; Kaufman 1960: 22). **Divorce.** Separation or divorce is effected by mutual agreement, common property being divided equally. In the central plains the children may accompany either parent, while Kingshill (1960: 48) reports that in the north they remain with the mother.

SOCIOPOLITICAL ORGANIZATION. **Traditional structure.** In old Siam the king, surrounded by a hierarchy of courtiers and sustained by elaborate Brahmanic rites, held absolute power. His many wives and concubines gave birth to a nobility, which included also the descendants of previous kings. Both nobles and commoners took part in the government, administering nearby territories directly from Bangkok, and the more remote ones through vassal princes. Administrative organization was complicated by the fact that ministries shifted frequently in jurisdiction and were organized simultaneously on territorial and functional lines. Officials received revenues collected by their inferiors, from which expenses were deducted. The importance of a given official could be measured by the number of persons under his jurisdiction. ● Below officialdom were the freemen and the slaves, the former consisting mostly of rice farmers subject to taxation, corvée labor, and military service. The slave population included debt slaves, who were entitled to repurchase their freedom, and various nonredeemable slaves such as prisoners of war. Although the social system was stratified and ranked, people moved upward and downward over almost the entire range. Commoners were elevated to privilege through official appointment, and nobles automatically became commoners after five generations of decreasing rank. In 1805 a price was set which prisoners of war might pay to regain their freedom. Entering the priesthood, although not a legal escape from justice or creditors, offered an avenue for persons in distress. ● As in other Tai states, no clear rules of succession governed the kingship, and even though many monarchs designated their own successors, a council of high officials not infrequently disregarded this preference. When the council disagreed, the transition to a new reign was likely to become a period of bloodshed. [Credner 1935a: 331-38, 356; Sharp et al. 1956: 7-11.] **Contemporary structure.** Siamese society today is organized into a hierarchy based on age, occupation, wealth, and residence (Sharp et al. 1956: 181-89; Sharp 1957: 3; Benedict 1952: 4-8). The rural dwellers, who are largely farmers, stand below the artisans,

merchants, and government officials of the city. Because even the king makes obeisance to priests, the clergy may be said to stand as a group above or perhaps apart from society. The factor of sex in the hierarchy is unclear: Benedict (1952: 40-41) speaks of female subordination, while others emphasize the equality between the sexes (DeYoung 1955: 24; Kaufman 1960: 39; Sharp et al. 1956: 212-13). Some doubt has been expressed as to whether or not the contemporary social order of Thailand can be described as a class society. The division of nobility and freemen (and formerly slaves) has been modified by recent observers into occupational classes of government officials, merchants, artisans, unskilled laborers, etc. who live in the capital city, provincial centers, and rural areas. The religious and ethnic minorities occupy adjacent positions in the hierarchy (Sharp et al. 1956: 158-91). Sharp acknowledges the limited applicability of the term "class" to the social scene. Hanks (1962) argues that the built-in social mobility of Siamese society necessitates discarding the class-type model. In its place he suggests that the social order is akin to a military organization wherein people move in and out of fixed positions, each with its own set of duties that contribute to the whole. ●
In rural areas the framework of government knits localities together (cf. Reeve 1951: 40-59). Provinces are subdivided into administrative units of decreasing size as follows: districts (*amphoe*), communes (*tambon*), and villages (*mu*). The district officer (*nai amphoe*) governs an area comparable to a county in the United States. Local agents of the central government provide police, judiciary, health, education, and agriculture services, and take care of tax collection and registration of births, marriages, and deaths. The district government maintains the highways, canals, bridges, schools, and irrigation systems, using paid workers from the area. For special tasks needing additional labor and for communicating with the people of the district, administrative units have been formed with elected headmen (*phujajban*) of hamlets (*muban*) and headmen (*kamnan*) of communes (*tambon*). With the aid of the headmen, district governments have established credit unions, producer cooperatives, and committees for local improvement (Madge 1955: 40-42). Although local leadership may sometimes be assumed by the village and commune headmen, wide differences in their effectiveness have been noted (Sharp et al. 1953: 43-48). Other potential leaders are schoolteachers and priests, who have instituted changes in certain localities (Madge 1955: 29-37; Sharp et al. 1953: 72-75). **Warfare.** In former times recourse to arms generally arose from questions of succession to the throne, misbehavior of a vassal, and contests with neighboring states. During the Khmer empire Siamese warriors served with the Khmer army. In the Sukhothai period the Siamese princes maintained their own armies, and not until well into the Ayuthia period (possibly between 1450–1500) were armed forces integrated into the administrative order under the king. Thereafter a standing army was raised by levy from about half the population to serve several months each year in military exercises and guard duty. In case of war the entire population was open to conscription (Wales 1934: 135-65). The last war using a military force of this kind fought the Shan state of Kengtung during the 1850s. During the late nineteenth century the entire military and naval services were reorganized with the aid of foreign advisers. In 1904 universal military conscription, bolstered by a core of professional soldiers and sailors, brought the armed forces further into line with European practice. Since 1932 military personnel have taken an increasingly active part in politics. Control of the police and air force as well as the army and navy has been a major factor in changes of government (Wilson 1959: 37).

RELIGION. **Major religions.** Sharp et al. (1956: 338-39), drawing on the 1947 census, give the following percentages for the major religions of Thailand: Buddhist 94.00 per cent; Moslem 3.75 per cent; Christian 0.65 per cent; Hindu, Confucian, and animist 1.60 per cent. Probably 90 per cent of all Siamese Buddhists follow the Theravada (Hinayana) doctrine. ●
Buddhism has helped sustain Siamese society certainly since the thirteenth century, and documentary sources suggest its influence among the Tai in Yunnan as early as the fourth century A.D. (Carthew 1952: 8). Its history in Siam has received little attention from scholars. Today, Theravada doctrine underlies the hierarchic social order and is the official state religion. The supreme patriarch is appointed by the king, and the governing body of the national church now holds administrative position under the Ministry of Education (Wells 1960: 7-11). Some indication of the extent of popular devotion may be seen from the fact that there are 21,000 Buddhist temples (DeYoung 1955: Appendix IV) and from Wells' figures on the growth of temple land (1960: 29). In any given area a devoted person may give daily food to the priests in his local temple, attend weekly devotional meetings, contribute to the traditional large-scale festivals, and participate in various other occasional celebrations. To the temples he sends his sons for ordination and his parents for last rites; and he may show his piety further through gifts of money, labor, or produce. Goldsen and Ralis (1957: 48, 54, 55) report that 44 per cent of the sample of a central Siamese community attended a particular festival, that nearly 80 per cent had contributed money or goods to the temple during the past year, and that 85 per cent of the men had been ordained. ● Ordination is for men only. At age 20 or over, many men, formerly all, join the Buddhist priesthood. All who work and underwrite the costs of this lavish ceremony derive religious merit thereby. At the ordination proper the entire chapter of priests and the

assembled kin and guests witness the taking of vows (Kaufman 1960: 123-28). The ordinary minimum period in the priesthood is three months, but many stay longer. A man may spend a lifetime there, or leave and re-enter for shorter stays. Young men below age 20 may enter as novices, with curtailed ceremony and obligations (DeYoung 1955: 118, 126). In the northern temples, there are more novices than priests, unlike central Thailand, where the reverse is true (Kingshill 1960: 102). ● A newly ordained novice or priest is expected to spend considerable time in study and meditation. The ecclesiastic hierarchy encourages study by offering examinations on religious matters, and those who wish to go beyond the elementary stages may enter one of two Buddhist universities in Bangkok (Wells 1960: 16). The head priest at each temple maintains the basic rules of the monastic order. The degree of stringency with which these rules are observed divides the more ascetic Mahanikai orders from the Thammayut orders (Sharp et al. 1956: 360-61). It is assumed that real learning of virtue and the way of the cosmos arises from the individual's own initiative. In his daily life at the temple each novice or priest receives the offerings of food on his morning round, eats only before noon, and chants verses. On the request of any local family, he reads sermons, sings blessings to the assembled laymen in the temple on holidays, receives visitors in his dormitory, or participates in one of the life cycle rites. If he has special skills in healing the sick, occultism, blessing a new house, carpentry, or radio repair, he may be in great demand. Many of these skills are taught in the temple. Except for the three months of Buddhist Lent beginning in July, priests may move about at will, and some make long pilgrimages to sacred shrines. **Supernaturals.** In addition to the Buddhist rites, various supernatural beings commonly play a role in village life. Rajadhon (1954a) and Textor (1960: 176-382, 396-500) list some from the central plains, varying from creatures easily brushed aside to those which may cause death, from ones whose aid is solicited to those who are avoided as malefactors, and from those concerned solely with mankind to those with cosmic roles. Some indication of regional variations may be seen in the fact that harvest rites addressed to the Rice Mother occur more in the south and central plains than in the north (Rajadhon 1955: 56; DeYoung 1955: 141-42; Hanks 1960: 298-300). In parts of the central plains each house has its own guardian spirit (Kaufman 1960: 198); while in the north and northeast, spirits guard neighborhoods or entire villages (Kingshill 1960: 180-81, 184; Madge 1955: 77). Certain beings help insure the success of particular life cycle rites (Wells 1960: 137-39), others the success of a new undertaking (Kaufman 1960: 199; Textor 1960: 501-10). Spirits may possess a person, cure, assist in recovering lost property, or advise on the solution of a family problem (Kaufman 1960: 179; Kingshill 1960: 181; Cornell

1948-57). ● In addition, rites occur which seem to assume no animate beings. Some use the power of command or verbal formulas, which in a love potion may overcome a girl's resistance, or in an amulet protect the wearer from injury (Textor 1960: 61-175). The chanting of ritual verses is thought to produce special essences which may be collected and transferred by contact (Textor 1960: 80-98, 396-411). These essences restore health and give certainty to new undertakings such as marriage. Formulas also exist which reduce a buffalo hide to a small size and send it off on the wind, where it may enter a person to cause sickness. Unusual objects and those associated with unusual events may contain special properties. Through one or more of these means, plus knowledge learned from a special teacher, a person may acquire skills such as telepathic perception, foretelling events, and controlling natural phenomena. **Practitioners.** A variety of exorcists, spirit doctors, diviners, and other intermediaries between man and the spirit world work through sympathetic actions, possession, charms, and incantations. "Old style" doctors and exorcists work with medicinal or magical therapy to cure the sick. Astrologers, formerly mostly Brahmans, are still active. **Ceremonies.** The religious calendar runs as follows: the New Year's Festival in April; the day of birth, enlightenment, and death of Lord Buddha in May; the beginning of Lent in July; the end of Lent in October; and the Festival of Lights in November. These festivals are observed at temples throughout Thailand at times set by the lunar religious calendar. Another fixed feast, celebrated particularly in the northeast, is Magha Puja, which occurs in February. Two additional festivals may be held almost every year: a fair and a ceremonial presentation of robes to the priests. In the central plains, an annual day of offering special food to the priests (Wan Saad) occurs, which seems to have no equivalent in other regions (Sharp et al. 1953: 65; Kaufman 1960: 189). Kingshill (1960: 185) reports for the north a day in October set aside for Indra, and in the central plains a celebration for Mother Earth is reported for February (Sharp et al. 1953: 66), but neither one is reported elsewhere. **Illness and medicine.** Sickness is dealt with on several levels. A person with greater merit from past lives is predisposed to be healthier than a person with less merit, and so recovers more quickly or remains immune. Inimical experiences such as fright or prolonged adversity may cause debilities which, because they are attributed to loss of soul substance (*khwan*), are strengthened by its return. The specific methods of restoring the soul vary from region to region (Kingshill 1960: 188-90; Kaufman 1960: 144, 201-02). A person may also become ill because of being possessed by a hostile spirit, in which case an exorcising doctor must be called (Textor 1960: 279-85). Benevolent spirits, when offended, may cause illness, and here a medium or a person with telepathic powers is needed to determine the best manner of propitiation. A supernatural missile in the body of a person may be extracted by special poultices. On the physiological level, illness occurs because of an imbalance of elements within the body; thus excessive air within the body is cured by giving the patient additional earth through some medicine, and excessive heat by cooling baths (Kaufman 1960: 177-78; Kingshill 1960: 151-57; Sharp et al. 1953: 252-60). For minor complaints people seek out home remedies or medicines purchased in the local markets. For persistent illnesses patients may try a variety of remedies, going from one healer to the next. • Privacy is not sought at parturition. Kin, husband, friends, or a midwife assist. Difficulty in labor is caused by lack of merit in the mother and in the child, by weak winds in the body, or by improper orientation to the cosmic influences of the day. The umbilical cord is cut on a rhizome (*phlaj*) or on a clod of earth with a bamboo knife. Postpartum rest by a fire from 5 to 15 days serves to speed the flow and drying of the birth fluids. The fire-rest is entered and left ceremonially. At its conclusion, the baby, hitherto lying on a tray with auspicious items, is transferred to a cradle. The placenta is then buried in a pot under the stairs or under a tree so as to be inaccessible to spirits and to insure that the child will stay at home. [Kaufman 1960: 140-44.] **Soul, death, and afterlife.** Of all the life cycle rites, the funerary are the most important, for they launch the deceased toward his next existence. His rebirth occurs after a stay in purgatory, the length of which is determined by his sinfulness. The older and more prestigious the deceased, the more lavish the rites. At death the corpse is washed, dressed, and tied with holy cord, then placed in a coffin, with a light by the head. Priests chant at the bier during the night. In the central plains they repeat this every night for seven nights, and periodically during the ensuing year, although poor people curtail these observances. Kin and friends come to keep the bereaved company, for the deceased's ghost is hovering close. On the seventh day the coffin is taken to the morgue at the temple, where it remains until cremation. Rich families with large houses may keep the corpse in a separate room for months or years. The practice also has been noted of removing the flesh from the bones of a corpse after six months and cremating the bones alone (Cornell 1948-57). • Cremation occurs only after the family has had time to muster its resources, a period ranging from a few days to several years. At a ceremonial in its most lavish form, hundreds of formally invited guests, lay and priestly, are entertained with music and theatricals, instructed with sermon, fed, and sent home with gifts. After cremation the bones are collected, and may be kept in an urn. A memorial service is held at the home about four days after cremation. Persons dying violently or prematurely are buried or cremated as soon as possible,

for untimely death creates a malevolent spirit. In the north, cremation follows within a week of death. Burial also occurs, probably more frequently than on the central plains (Kingshill 1960: 164-65). On the day of cremation the relatives attend services at the local temple, and the body is conducted from the house in procession to cremation grounds outside the village. On one or more of the succeeding days, and again after a year, priests may be invited to perform special ceremonies and read sermons to gatherings of relatives (DeYoung 1955: 68-74; Kingshill 1960: 164-78).

BIBLIOGRAPHY. Andrews 1943; Benedict 1942, 1943; Benedict 1952; Blanchard et al. 1958; Carthew 1952; Coedès 1948; Cornell 1948-57; Coughlin 1960; Credner 1935a, 1935b; DeYoung 1955; Gogoi 1956; Goldsen and Ralis 1957; Hall 1955; Hanks 1960; Hanks 1959, 1962; Hanks and Hanks 1963; Hanks and Phillips 1961; IBRD 1959; Ingram 1955; Janlekha 1955; Kaufman 1960; Kingshill 1960; Luce 1958; Madge 1955; Maneffe and Bézacier 1940; Mosel 1957; Pendleton 1943, 1962; Phansomboon 1957; Rajadhon 1954a, 1954b, 1955; Reeve 1951; Seidenfaden 1958; Sharp 1957; Sharp et al. 1953, 1956; Skinner 1957; Sukhabanij 1956, 1957; Textor 1960; Thailand Ministry of Agriculture 1953, 1957; Wales 1934; Wells 1960; Wilson 1959; Wilson and Phillips 1958; Wulff 1934; Zelinsky 1950.

KHORAT TAI

ORIENTATION. Identification. A Siamese term for Tai speakers of the Khorat province area of east–central Thailand. They dress and live like the central Siamese, but speak with some mannerisms. They are said to be the descendants of Siamese soldiers and Khmer women (Seidenfaden 1958: 109-13). They are classed with the central Siamese by Credner (1935a: 137).

BIBLIOGRAPHY. Credner 1935a; Seidenfaden 1958.

PAK TAI

ORIENTATION. Identification. A Siamese term for Tai speakers in extreme southern Thailand, in the provinces of Chumphon and Nakhon-Sithammarat. Estimated population 1,500,000. Said to be mixed with Malay and some Negrito. Speak a patois termed *dambrö*. They are largely paddy farmers and cattle breeders, but also engage in rubber growing and commercial fishing (Seidenfaden 1958: 109-13).

BIBLIOGRAPHY. Seidenfaden 1958.

CENTRAL MEKONG RIVER GROUPS

NÜA

Synonyms. *Nö, Nü*

ORIENTATION. **Identification and location.** The term Tai Nö was used by Davies (1909: 380) for those Tai speakers living in southwestern Yunnan between the Mekong and the Salween, and extending generally from 22° to 25° N. Davies used the term for the literate Buddhist Tai in Yunnan other than the Lü of the Sip Song Panna; according to him the term means northern Tai and is used by these people to distinguish themselves from the Tai of the Burmese Shan States area, whom they call Tai Taü, or Southern Tai. Tai Nö (Nü, Nüa) is also used by both Dodd (1923: 78, 171) and Seidenfaden (1958: 24), but in a somewhat more restricted sense. Whereas for Davies the Tai Nö, whom he also called Chinese Shans, include the Tai of the Chinese Shan States, for Dodd and Seidenfaden the term excludes the latter, whom Seidenfaden calls Tayok. ● The hill tribes in this area are mostly Lahu and Wa, the latter mainly concentrated along the Yunnan–Burma border. **Linguistic affiliation.** Tai speakers, closely related to Lü. **Geography and demography.** The Nüa country, as defined by Dodd and Seidenfaden, extends over some 22,000 square miles and includes a Tai population estimated at 600,000.

SOCIOPOLITICAL ORGANIZATION. The indigenous sociopolitical organization was much the same as that in the Chinese Shan States and the Sip Song Panna, i.e. some 28 quasi-feudal domains, *muong*, centered in low-lying wet-rice basins along streams and rivers. By the mid-1920s, however, most of these *muong* areas were integrated into the local Chinese administrative and economic system, and showed little evidence of ever having been incorporated into a native Tai state of the kind that still existed, in remnant form, in the Sip Song Panna. The indigenous cultural features of the Nüa landscape are probably similar in most respects to those of the Lü.

BIBLIOGRAPHY. Davies 1909; Dodd 1923; Seidenfaden 1958.

LÜ

Synonyms. *Lu, Lue, Pai-i, Shui Pai-i*

ORIENTATION. **Identification.** The people call themselves Lü (Lue, Lu). The term is used by other Tai speakers to refer to the Tai of southern Yunnan—specifically those in the territory of the Sip Song Panna—as well as those who have emigrated into nearby areas of Burma, Thailand, and Laos. The Chinese use Pai-i to refer at times to almost any Tai-speaking group, but most often to the Tai of southwestern Yunnan. The Chinese also refer to the Lü as Shui (Water) Pai-i. **Location.** The Lü homeland, an area traditionally known as the Sip Song Panna (in Chinese, Shih-êrh-pan-na), occupies more than 6,000 square miles in extreme southern Yunnan. Centering on the Mekong, it extends from about 100° to 101° 30′ E. and from about 21° 30 ′ to 22° 30′ N. Lü are found also in Kengtung state in Burma, and in Chiengrai and Nan provinces in Thailand. In Laos they are numerous in western Phong Saly and also in northern and western Haut Mekong; there are in addition Lü villages along the Nam Tha and Nam Beng as well as in the vicinity of Luang Prabang. Groupings of Lü occur in northern Vietnam, in the area of Binh Lu and along the China border just west of the Black river. [Scott and Hardiman 1900: 205-07; Abadie 1924: 98; Lafont 1962b.] **Geography.** The mountains in the Tai Lü area of Yunnan are relatively smooth and low, and there are numerous small plains along the river valleys. The largest, up to 20 miles in length, have become the sites of the various *muong* domains which make up the Sip Song Panna. The climate is in general warm and humid. There is a wet, rainy season from April to October, and a relatively dry season from November through March. Fauna include elephants, leopards, tigers, bears, and deer. Bamboo flourishes in the valley bottoms and is of prime economic importance. Fish are plentiful in the rivers, which are navigable throughout most of the area. [Chiang 1950: 75-80.] **Linguistic affiliation.** The Lü dialect is most closely affiliated with those of other Tai speakers (Yuan, Khün, Nüa) in northern Thailand, Burma, northwestern Laos, and southwestern Yunnan between the Mekong and Salween rivers. Here, in an area roughly 600 miles N–S and 300 miles E–W, is located a relatively homogeneous speech area characterized by common religious terms and a common religious script, the latter based on the ancient Khmer alphabet which Rama Khamheng revised to form the basis for modern Siamese (Dodd 1923: 76; Clarke 1911: 91). The missionaries Dodd and Freeman, working out of the Chiengmai area about the turn of the century, found that outside of this "Yuan cult" area of literate Tai, the most easily understood dialects were those of the illiterate Black and White Tai of Tonkin (although they lacked the abstract religious terms associated with Buddhism and Pali). The Siamese to the south of Chiengmai spoke a dialect "not easily understood by our people . . . [while] west of the Salween [were] the western Shans whose speech differs also through Burman [Buddhist] influence" (Freeman, quoted in Clarke 1911: 91). **Demography.** The Chinese 1953 census gives 17,470,000 as the total population of Yunnan. Halpern (1961b: 53), using post-1953 Russian and Chinese sources, arrives at a non-Han population of about 5,000,000 in Yunnan, or roughly 30 per cent of the total. This figure contrasts with Wissmann's estimate, based on 1935 census figures, of roughly 60 per cent non-Han population (cited in Wiens 1954: 294). Even allowing for discrepancies in reporting, the relative percentages indicate a decrease in the ethnically identifiable non-Han portion of the population over the past two decades, a phenomenon due probably to at least two causes: assimilation by Han Chinese and the emigration south out of Yunnan of such groups as the Tai, Wa, Miao, and Lahu. ● Dodd (1923: 185) estimated 350,000 Lü in Yunnan and an additional 50,000 in Kengtung and Laos. By contrast, Chiang (1950: 70), after several years' residence in the Ch'eli area and a sample house-to-house survey, arrived at a total Tai population of 71,600, or 62 per cent of the Sip Song Panna population. The Han, he said, made up 7 per cent, and the hill tribes and other non-Han peoples the remaining 31 per cent. It is probable that Chiang somewhat underestimated these totals. Chen (1949: 2), citing a 1935 survey, gives 550,000 Pai-i in southern Yunnan, and says that the Pai-i [Lü] in the Sip Song Panna account for 50 to 85 per cent of the population. The Lü in Laos, according to Lafont (1962a: 370), total 16,000, while those in northern Vietnam number somewhat over 1,000 (NNCDT 1959: 242). **History.** The ruling families of the Sip Song Panna maintain traditional histories written in Tai. According to Chiang (1950: 35 ff.), the Ch'eli (Chiengrung or Kenghung) ruling family traces its origin to an ancestor-founder, Patseng, who in 1180 A.D. conquered the kingdom of Lê (Meengle, probably Muong Le) and founded the kingdom of Alopi, which was considerably larger than the present Sip Song Panna, reaching north to the Red river and west to the Salween. ● Although Han penetration of this area predates the Christian era, the southwestern frontier continued to be largely independent until the Mongol conquest of Nanchao in 1253 A.D. The Chinese then established the Ch'eli Pacification Chieftaincy, instituting what was later known as the *t'u-ssu* system of indirect rule. The *t'u-ssu* system continued in effect, with minor changes in number and composition of administrative units, until the period of the Manchus. [See Chen (1949: 8-16) for a summary of pre-nineteenth-century Chinese-Lü relations.] Under Nationalist Chinese control, the Sip Song Panna remained one of the few quasi-independent "tribal" areas in southwestern China. Although under the ultimate control of a Chinese resident magistrate, the local nobility, in the personage of the Ch'eli Hsuan-wei (Tai, *chao fa*), members of his family, and the families of *muong* chieftains, continued to wield considerable authority—largely at the expense of the peasant-farmers within their domains. Chinese peasants, long deterred from entering the area in any number by the low-lying (malarious) plains and river valleys, were apparently just beginning effective penetration prior to the Communist seizure in 1949. Since 1949 the Sip Song Panna has been reorganized as the Hsi-shuang Pan-na Thai Autonomous Chou, with administrative headquarters in Ch'eli. ● Successive Han dynasties have exacted tribute from Chiengrung, but beyond this tribute and the sending of occasional military expeditions, it is doubtful that Chinese claims to suzerainty are any more firmly based than those of Burma or Thailand, both of whom have for brief periods (particularly during the later nineteenth century) exercised nominal or actual authority in the area. Han Chinese civil officials, for example, were apparently unknown in the Sip Song Panna until the 1890s (Carey 1899: 381). **Cultural relations.** Despite exposure to Han Chinese cultural influences, the Sip Song Panna remains one of the least acculturated Tai areas in China, according to Chiang. Although much of the material culture shows Chinese influence, housing and women's clothing are still characteristically Tai. Political organization, especially, and social structure to a somewhat lesser extent, still conform to earlier patterns. Religious behavior reflects the influence of Hinayana (Theravada) Buddhism, and in this respect the Yunnan Lü can be classed with the Tai of Burma, Siam, and Laos rather than those of Kweichow, Kwangsi, and Kwangtung. The Yunnan Lü maintain their closest cultural relations—including intermarriage among noble families —with the closely related Tai of neighboring areas. They are not known as traders or merchants, and do not normally venture far outside their own territory. The Sip Song Panna is known to the Tai as far north in Yunnan as the Yangtze, where it is spoken of as the "glutinous rice country," and regarded as a Tai homeland with which these northerners seek to identify (Dodd 1923: 46). ● The Lü live in the plains, communicate easily, and are politically organized. Contact with hill tribes is chiefly for purposes of trade. Tai Lü, Han Chinese, and hill peoples come together at weekly markets in the larger towns. Hill tribes in the Sip Song Panna, estimated by Chiang (1950: 70) to make up 31 per cent of the population, are chiefly Akha inhabiting the lower mountain slopes —looking down on the lowland Tai clustered in villages along the valley bottoms. Above the Akha are a few Yao tribesmen, and on the highest ranges occasional Lahu villages. Scattered Wa villages are inhabited by Mon-Khmer speakers related to the "wild" Wa farther west in Burma. These Wa, whom the Lü call Tai Loi, are Buddhists, speak Tai in addition to their own language, and practice wet-rice agriculture alongside the Lü. As observed by Dodd in 1910 (1923: 61), they were, except for the factor of linguistic conservatism, practically indistinguishable from Tai Lü, and it is probable that they represent a case of Wa "becoming Tai." ● The hill tribes in Yunnan and Laos are incorporated within the traditional Lü sociopolitical organization through the institution of *lam*. The *po lam*, "father" or "patron," is a member of a chiefly family or some other local notable who receives as appanage the dependency of a number of hill villages. He serves as intermediary between the latter and Lü officialdom, receiving in return a portion of the taxes and tribute passing through his hands. In Laos, Akha villages are virtually under Lü control, each Lü personage being *po lam* to several Akha villages. Important Lü villages, such as Muong Sing, Muong Nang, and Bun Tay, organize markets every five days, and by this means maintain contact with the hill tribes. [Chiang 1950: 103; Rispaud 1937: 119; Lafont 1962b.]

SETTLEMENT PATTERN AND HOUSING. **Settlement pattern.** Chen (1949: 39) gives an average for the Sip Song Panna of 30 houses per village, based on a survey of 44 villages. This is in accord with a figure for Laos of 20 houses per village (Lafont 1962b). Lafont adds that villages may be as large as 80 houses. Chiang (1950: 164) says, however, that in Yunnan Lü villages range in size from fewer than 10 to over 300 houses. Moerman (1962) reports a population of about 600 in a Lue village in Chiengrai, northern Thailand, and Carey (1899: 382) says that Lü villages in Yunnan average 500 inhabitants. The more important centers, such as Chiengrung, have historically been walled towns, designed and located for defensive purposes. **Housing.** The house is normally built on piles about seven or eight feet above the ground. A ladder leads up to a single room, with a gable roof coming down on both sides directly onto the flooring. The room is frequently divided by a partition into living and sleeping quarters. A fire basin is placed in the center and a covered veranda constructed at one end. Cattle are tied to the posts underneath the house at night. In Yunnan the *chao* (rulers) and members of their immediate families live in houses which tend to be larger and made of planks rather than bamboo, with tiled rather than thatched roofs. [Chiang 1950: 165 ff.; Lafont 1962b.] Lue emigrants in Chiengrai province in northern Thailand lived until quite recently in multifamily longhouses, possibly a response to a pioneering situation (Moerman 1963).

ECONOMY. Primarily wet-rice farmers. Domestic animals are economically important, and contribute a major portion of the diet, along with rice, beans, and vegetables. Fish are present in rivers and canals and are eaten whenever available. Hunting is of less importance. Insects, maggots, grubs, greens, and wild fruits are gathered, and contribute a minor but highly regarded portion of the diet. **Agriculture.** Cultivable valley plains in the Sip Song Panna are estimated by Wissmann (1943: 22) at about 30,000 acres, only one-half of which are in use. According to Chen (1949: 45), 26 per cent of the cultivable land in Ch'eli district has never been cultivated. Land, therefore, is apparently not a problem. Glutinous rice, grown in irrigated fields, is the main crop. Some dry rice is grown on valley sides and slopes; about one-half of the villages surveyed by Chen (1949: 28) sup-

plemented their irrigated rice in this manner. Double cropping, although feasible, is generally not practiced. Field rotation and fallowing take the place of fertilizer. Field implements, of iron, resemble those of the Chinese. Fields are irrigated for rice by diverting the rivers into side canals and, where necessary, lifting the water to the level of the fields by means of basket water wheels. Buffalo and sometimes cattle are used to draw the plow. Paddy is cut and dried in the field, threshed with a stick on a flat piece of ground, and winnowed by tossing in the air. Rice is plentiful and may on occasion be fed to domestic animals. Rice liquor is popular and is consumed in quantity on festive occasions. ● Other field crops include beans, peppers, maize, vegetables, sugar cane, and tobacco. Fruits are grown near the houses in the villages. Cotton is grown in small amounts by most families and sold to Chinese traders. P'u-erh tea is an economically important and widely-known product of the area, and is grown both by the Lü and by the hill tribes. Haw merchant caravans, and also horse caravans from as far away as Tibet, come annually to collect this tea. Opium is not grown by the Lü, nor are they widely addicted to its use. They do, however, traffic to some extent in opium, acting as middlemen between Chinese merchants and the hill people who grow it. Betel chewing is popular and for this the nut of the areca palm is important. Camphor, shellac, and bamboo are other important forest products. [Chiang 1950: 137-45.] **Fishing and hunting.** The products of rivers and canals—including fish, turtles, eels, snails, mussels, and shrimp—are eagerly sought, and contribute greatly to the diet. Elaborate organization of communal fishing enterprises is reported for the Lue of northern Thailand. [Chiang 1950: 168; Moerman 1963.] **Domestic animals.** Cattle, buffalo, horses, chickens, pigs, ducks, dogs, and cats. Pork is the most popular meat, followed by beef, chicken, and duck. Oxen are used for transport. Elephants were formerly associated with a *chao fa's* court paraphernalia, and were important in warfare. [Chiang 1950: 84.] **Industrial arts.** Economic pursuits are not highly specialized in Lü society. The people are not known as traders or merchants, and there is relatively little craft specialization. Home handicrafts for family consumption include work in bamboo, weaving, embroidery, and pottery making. Chiang (1950: 149) says that iron working is limited to crude farm implements; Seidenfaden (1958: 26), however, speaks of the "famous Lü swords with excellent blades." Jewelry, much of it showing Indian influence, is fabricated locally by silversmiths. Bamboo is used extensively in the construction of houses, utensils, furniture, roads, and bridges. Chiang mentions that paper is made by native methods from the pulp of a wild plant, *Broussonetia papyrifera*. **Trade.** Markets are held weekly in the larger towns and are usually rotated among four or five villages. The Yunnan Tai do not, however, trade on as large a scale as the Shan Tai in Burma. Women are active traders in the village markets, exchanging food products and bamboo, salt, fuel, herbs, fruits, and opium. Itinerant Chinese traders deal in cloth, cosmetics, and medicines. [Chiang 1950: 150-51.] **Division of labor.** Persons without land hire themselves out as agricultural workers under a variety of arrangements. Some may be hired to serve in place of a family member when a labor levy is imposed by the *chao muong* (Chiang 1950: 144). Women help in the fields, but their status in Lü society is relatively high. A married woman is economically independent of her husband, and is free to make her own living if she wants to. Men help with the children at home, and a man may be found at home baby-sitting while his wife is off trading at a nearby village market. **Land tenure.** According to Chiang (1950: 129 ff.), land is considered to belong ultimately to the state, with its year-to-year management in the hands of village chiefs and above them, the *muong* chiefs. The Lü peasant farmer therefore does not own the land he tills in the sense of being able to sell or lease it. Commoner families do, however, have usufruct rights which are handed down from generation to generation and which cannot be arbitrarily terminated. Traditional usage defines firmly the respective rights of the various parties. The *chao* receive taxes and produce from the villagers within their districts, tribute which is in part based on the size of land holdings. Within the Sip Song Panna, according to Chiang, this relationship is not as marked as it is among the Tai of the Chinese Shan States, where the people have fewer traditional rights with respect to land, and where taxes and other obligations to the *muong* chiefs are based directly on the land factor. • Chen (1949: 29-31) describes four different categories of land ownership among the Yunnan Lü: (1) village-owned land subject to periodic redistribution; (2) official-owned land worked by whole villages or individual peasant families, on which labor, produce, and taxes are due the owner, who is usually a member of one of the ruling families; (3) unclaimed lands and newly-opened lands to which peasants have usufruct rights approaching a permanent leasehold; and (4) temple-owned lands. Chen found that in the Ch'eli area 60 per cent of all cultivated land was in the official-owned category.

KIN GROUPS. The nobility among the Lü are characterized by patrilineal surname groups (common descent groups) similar to those found among the Chinese, and presumably the result of Chinese influence (Chiang 1950: 208-20). Only among the more sinicized ruling families, however, is a common surname regarded as evidence of actual kinship and marriage prohibited between persons of the same surname. Ruling families maintain genealogies, but only for individuals in the direct line of succession to the position of *chao* (ruler). There is no evidence of an ancestor cult at any level of Lü society; the Lü (except for the sinicized nobility) place little emphasis on remembering their ancestors, and pay little attention to kinship ties beyond those of the immediate family and kindred. • At the commoner level, the only kin group recognized, aside from the immediate household group, is what appears to be the bilateral kindred. As phrased by Chiang (1950: 222), "their idea of relatives includes the father's family, the mother's family, and the wife's family." These are the kinsmen who come together at crisis periods in the life cycle, such as marriage and death. • Moerman found no evidence of unilinear descent among the Lue of northern Thailand. Property inheritance and kin terminology are bilateral, marriage is permitted—and is not infrequent—between first cousins, and there are no behavioral or terminological distinctions between parallel and cross cousins (Moerman 1963). **Kin terminology.** Lü kinship terms given by Chiang (1950: 222-23) are characterized by lineal terminology for the first ascending generation and Hawaiian terminology for cousins. Age distinctions are important, and appear in both sibling and parents' sibling terms. Terms for consanguineal relatives are extended to include members of Ego's wife's family.

MARRIAGE AND FAMILY. According to Chiang (1950: 179), marriage among the Yunnan Lü is strictly within hereditary class lines, i.e. the members of chiefly families marry only among themselves, and commoners marry only commoners. These Lü do not intermarry with the various hill peoples within their domain, with the possible exception of the Buddhist Wa. They have for some time, however, intermarried with Han Chinese. Moerman (1962) reports Lue endogamy in Thailand with respect to their Tai-speaking neighbors, the Yuan. **Mode.** Within chiefly families marriage customs are heavily sinicized. Marriage is by parental arrangement and includes a go-between and a sizable bride price. A woman's prestige is judged by the size of the latter. According to Chiang (1950: 179), a member of the hereditary nobility must marry outside his *muong*, since noble families within a *muong* usually belong to the same patrilineal surname group. Noble marriages usually occur within the Sip Song Panna area, although some chiefly families have relations through marriage with those in neighboring Tai states in Kengtung and Chiengmai. • Among commoners, marriage is more in accord with traditional Tai custom (Chiang 1950: 182 ff.). The preliminaries are initiated by the young people themselves, and relative freedom is allowed during courtship. Religious festivals and evening gatherings at the village rice mill afford traditional opportunities for courting and for young couples to slip off by themselves with the tacit approval of their elders. Sisawat (1952: 205) reports the existence of courting platforms. Musical ability plays a prominent role in courtship; mastery of the reed organ and cleverness in singing and extemporaneous composition are greatly admired. When a couple reach the point of marriage, the boy's family arranges for a go-between who negotiates the bride price. A marriage ceremony takes place in the bride's house, and may be solemnized by a monk. If the families cannot agree on the amount of the bride price, they may resort by mutual agreement to a mock kidnap wedding and later renegotiation of the bride price, thus saving face all around; or the couple may elope to another *muong*, living there long enough to accumulate the required bride price. **Form.** Polygyny is a common practice among chieftains. In the past the royal Chiengrung household included numerous wives and concubines (Chiang 1950: 180). Lafont (1962b) reports polygyny among well-to-do families in Laos. Marriage among Lü commoners is normally monogamous. **Extension of incest taboos.** Long ago the Chinese bestowed honorific titles and surnames on the *muong* chiefs in the Sip Song Panna area. Today these families are organized as patrilineal surname groups along Chinese lines, although the surname does not appear to carry quite the degree of relatedness that it does among the Chinese, nor does the principle of surname group exogamy appear to be observed as strictly. Among the Lü of Muong Sing (Laos), cross-cousin marriage is recognized but not preferred (Lafont 1962b). **Residence.** In conformity with the patrilineal orientation of the Lü nobility, residence after marriage within this group is strictly patrilocal (Chiang 1950: 181). Among commoners, residence is more variable, but there is an apparent pattern whereby the couple may live alternately with (or near) the parents of both the bride and groom for a time, before establishing an independent household. A family lacking a son may adopt a son-in-law, who then resides matrilocally and inherits his adopted parents' property on their death. [Chiang 1950: 188; Lafont 1962b; Sisawat 1952: 194 ff.] **Domestic unit.** Patrilineal extended (or large polygynous) families characterize the Lü nobility. Commoner households in Yunnan are of the independent nuclear type, averaging four members, according to Chinese *hsien* census figures. [Chiang 1950: 181, 188.] **Inheritance.** It is customary for a couple to make provision for the division of their property before their death. The eldest son inherits the family homestead, and the rest of the property is equally divided among all the sons. [Chiang 1950: 225-26.] Among the Lue of northern Thailand, Moerman (1963) found all children inheriting equally regardless of sex or seniority, with the exception that the house and its compound goes to the oldest married child still residing with the parents at the time of their death. In practice this is often a younger child, thus giving the appearance of ultimogeniture. **Divorce.** Divorce is relatively easy, although apparently not common, with laziness and unchastity the two most frequent causes. A woman simply returns to her parental home and stays there;

a man wishing to terminate a marriage hands his wife a piece of wood with symbolic marks cut on it. Women are relatively independent economically and thus usually do not object to a divorce, nor is there any prejudice against a divorced woman. Children usually go with the mother. [Chiang 1950: 186-88.]

SOCIOPOLITICAL ORGANIZATION. **The Sip Song Panna.** The exact nature of the indigenous political structure within the Sip Song Panna area is largely a matter of conjecture; Tai historical records are fragmentary and the long period of Chinese penetration has blurred the original picture. Furthermore the documentary evidence that is available, being largely Chinese, is likely to result in a somewhat skewed understanding of native political concepts and relationships. It is probable that the kingdom of Alopi—which according to Lü histories was founded by Patseng in 1180 A.D.—was made up of a number of chiefdoms (semifeudal fiefs or principalities) loosely controlled by a paramount chief or "king," himself possibly a vassal of the Han Chinese. Political control may have been concentrated within a single family or related families—possibly descendants of Patseng—whose members occupied the positions of paramount chief and chiefs of the various fiefdoms within the kingdom. Political control may have been solidified and sanctioned by a cult of the spirit of the soil (with an accompanying myth), as among the Black Tai, where only members of a ruling family (or families) are empowered to conduct annual sacrifices for the welfare of the *muong* and its inhabitants. Among the Lü in Laos, at the present time, the *chao fa* of Muong Sing annually sacrifices to the *phi muong* on behalf of the people (Lafont 1962b). ● The Lü territory in southern Yunnan is known today by the Tai term Sip Song Panna or (in older Western language sources) as the kingdom or state of Kenghung (Chiengrung, Xieng Hong). The name Sip Song Panna is variously translated "Twelve Thousand Rice Fields" or "Twelve Farming Areas." According to Rispaud (1937: 78), the literal meaning is more correctly "Twelve Principalities," or "Twelve Fiefdoms." According to Garnier (1873: 407), the term refers to the number of registered inhabitants in each of a number of territorial units. Scott and Hardiman (1900: 329) say that, as in the Southern Shan States, the term probably refers to the number of baskets of rice (a thousand) paid to the overlord of each of 12 (or more) territorial units. Petty political domains are mentioned historically throughout the area of the southwestern Tai peoples; this propensity for establishing semifeudal principalities plays a considerable role in the history of such modern states as Thailand, Assam, Laos, and Burma. The usual Tai term for such entities is *muong* (*mong, mang, meng*) and for the "prince" or chief of same, *chao fa* (*saohpa*). Much of the history of this area is concerned with the combinations of *muong* domains into petty kingdoms and their subsequent dissolution and recombination under the vicissitudes of inter-*muong* warfare, political intrigue, and attack from neighboring states. The Sip Song Panna represents still another example of this more generalized Tai pattern. For the past 150 years, at least, it has been traditionally composed of 12 *pannas* (*muongs*), although one, Muong Sing, has been situated in northern Laos since the period of French intervention. It is probable that the actual number has varied as larger *muong* domains have segmented into lesser ones. Chiang (1950: 68) reports that at a Chinese-sponsored council of all *chao muong* in 1780 some 20 *muong* areas were assigned to one or another of 12 *pannas*. In 1950 Chiang reported "over 30" *muong* areas in the Sip Song Panna, each ruled by a *t'u-ssu*. The question of the number of *muong* areas is difficult to deal with precisely because the Tai, as pointed out by Leach for Burma (1954: 122), are not themselves precise in their use of the term, using it at times to mean a village or town, and at other times to mean a larger political domain. According to Rispaud (1937: 105), the number "twelve" in the designation Sip Song Panna should not be taken too literally, representing as it does a Tai convention of preceding the name of a territory with a number, e.g. the Hok Chao or Six Kingdoms of Nanchao and the Sip Song Chao Tai or Twelve Tai Principalities in Tonkin. A Lü *muong* may be as much as 200 square miles or more in extent; one, considered "quite large" by Dodd, was some 20 miles in length, and contained 70 Lü villages and about 30 villages belonging to various hill tribes. **Political organization.** The political structure of the Sip Song Panna, as observed by Chiang in the 1940s, was not unlike that of a nineteenth-century Burmese Shan State (Chiang 1950: 89-126). Political power is concentrated in the person of the *chao fa* of Chiengrung (Chinese title Hsuan-wei-shih). Although exercising a good deal of authority, the *chao fa* is responsible to the local Chinese magistrate, particularly in matters of taxation and military levies. Succession to the position is strictly patrilineal and by primogeniture. In the absence of a son, a brother or brother's son may succeed. [In 1942 Tao (Chao) Shih-hsun succeeded his uncle, Tao Tung-liang, who died without a male heir.] If the royal heir is under age a regent may be appointed, usually a brother of the deceased *chao fa*. Under such circumstances the "Queen Mother," if she is still alive, may exercise considerable authority, even over the regent. ● The court at Chiengrung consists of some 50 titled and graded officials, with responsibility for such things as the royal food supply, the royal horses, and particular kinds of economic pursuits, e.g. markets and trade fairs. According to Chao (1953: 16), two of these high officials are specifically charged with responsibility for irrigation works throughout the kingdom. Chen (1949: 41-42) says, however, that groups of villages characteristically control their water supply through elected officials whose position is confirmed at the *muong* level. A position equal to that of the *chao fa* may be held by one of his brothers, in a sort of "second government," although the status is rather vaguely defined. The *chao fa* is assisted by a premier and a council of high court officials and *muong* representatives. The council, which meets irregularly, serves to some extent to check the absolute power of the *chao fa*. According to Chen (1949: 19), the council is mainly concerned with the appointment of lesser *muong* officials. ● The higher court positions are hereditary (Chao 1953: 15), and together with the chieftaincies of the larger *muongs* are occupied by members of the nobility—those related to the family line of the *chao fa*. This aspect of Lü culture, including the granting of lands as virtual fiefdoms, is well documented by Chen (1949: 16 ff.). Land-owning officials "live off the people" by exercising traditional rights to levies of labor, economic goods, and taxes. ● Chen (1949: 16 ff.) mentions five grades of *chao muong*, 24 of whom maintained some degree of political liaison with the court at Chiengrung. Although the *chao muong* are theoretically under the control of the *chao fa,* in practice they have considerable freedom in the administration and exploitation of their own domains. The *chao muong's* village or town tends to be the political capital of his *muong*, and duplicates on a smaller scale the court and its bureaucracy as found in Chiengrung. At the bottom of this administrative hierarchy are various grades of village headmen. ● Some at least of this administrative elaboration is probably the result of Chinese acculturative influence. The administrative structure of the Sip Song Panna must have been influenced by the *t'u-ssu* system, whereby local chieftains were granted hereditary titles as rulers of their territories, which in effect became feudatories of the imperial court. On the other hand, the Lü system bears many similarities to indigenous Tai administrative bureaucracies found farther west and south in non-Chinese areas. **Social stratification.** Lü society is divided into two hereditary classes, nobility and commoners. In Yunnan the nobility, who make up about a tenth of the population, are the landowners, receiving rent from commoner-peasants who work the lands within their domains, but exempting themselves from taxes and rentals based on landownership. The nobility also furnish the higher grades of officials who staff the administrative bureaucracy. Whether there is, or was, a class of slaves (either debt slaves or captives in warfare) is not clear. Chen in 1940 found no trace of slavery (1949: 34). The ruling families are relatively highly sinicized, and this, plus their higher standard of living and class endogamy, tends to set them apart from commoners. The higher nobility speak Chinese, and the *muong* courts usually maintain a Han teacher. Travel to visit relatives in Burma and northern Thailand is not infrequent, and a few have traveled and studied in China. Although comparatively wealthy, the nobility in the Sip Song Panna do not live as ostentatiously as do their counterparts in neighboring Kengtung state or the Chinese Shan States. ● A variety of traditional economic obligations are placed on commoners vis-à-vis nobility. These include an annual monetary tax collected from every household for support of the *chao fa* and other high officials and their families; an annual grain rent determined in part by the amount of land tilled; labor service, which includes furnishing servants for noble households; supplies, such as food, charcoal, and opium; and special levies on occasions such as births, festivals, or the marriage of a noblewoman (Chiang 1950: 133 ff.). Differences in social status and rank are expressed in a number of ways. Because yellow is the traditional color of the nobility, commoners are prohibited from wearing it on many occasions. In greeting a superior, a commoner must kneel and knock his forehead on the ground. In approaching a *chao*, he moves forward on his knees, saluting every three steps, and repeats this procedure when departing from an audience. Status is indicated also by names (Chiang 1950: 215-16). Acculturated nobility have Chinese surnames, which is not true of the less sinicized Lü. Given names are, however, a status indicator in all cases. Generally speaking, an individual has at least five given names, which change at various stages of life: his pet name, monk name, secular name, parent name, and official name. The parent name is given after the birth of a child and follows the rules of teknonymy. The first word in a name indicates class membership, e.g. the first word in the pet name of a male commoner must be Yai. The second word indicates order of birth. Thus the first two words in the name of an eldest son of a commoner must be Yai-wei. Within the nobility finer distinctions in social rank are indicated by changes in a man's official name as he moves upward in the bureaucratic hierarchy. Children of the nobility are ranked according to the rank of their parents, e.g. children within the direct line of descent of a *chao muong* rank above their cousins. **Warfare.** Dodd (1923: 66) mentions the "petty [inter-*muong*] wars for which the Sip Song Panna is famed," but the literature contains little information on this. It is probable that warfare, once an important aspect of Lü culture, has declined in importance during the past 50 years.

RELIGION. **Major religions.** The Lü are Theravada Buddhists, with many similarities in text and ritual language to those of the neighboring Buddhist states of Siam and Laos. Old men among the emigrants to northern Thailand tell legends, however, of the days before Buddhism came to the Sip Song Panna (Moerman 1963). Christian missionaries have been at work in the area since about the turn of the century, but have made little headway. Larger villages have at least one Buddhist temple; in Yunnan these are imposing structures with red tiled roofs. Boys are expected to enter a monastery for at least a brief period, and the Lü are relatively strict about this and other Buddhist observances. There are various grades of monkhood, with the highest that of abbot of a village temple. There is no over-all organization of the monkhood within a *muong* or within the Sip Song Panna as a whole. The Buddhist New Year in April and the period of Lent, during the rainy season, are both widely observed. [Chiang 1950: 227-50.] **Indigenous religion.** Along with Buddhist beliefs and practices the Lü believe in a variety of spirits, some of which appear to be analogous to the *phi* of Thailand and Laos. Many are held to be malevolent, and women in particular may be possessed by evil spirits, or may gain control over them in order to harm other persons. **Supernaturals.** The Lü of Laos believe in good and bad *phi*, multiple souls, major spirits or genii, and a house spirit invoked by the head of the family; they do not, however, have a developed ancestor cult. Each village possesses a *lak ban*, a post stuck in the earth symbolizing the god of the local soil. *Muong* capitals have a *lak muong*, symbolizing the god of the feudal soil, *phi muong*. The cult of the *phi muong* is celebrated at Muong Sing annually by the *chao muong* assisted by a priest. [Lafont 1962b; Izikowitz 1962: 76-78.] **Practitioners.** Belief in malevolent spirits and sorcery enters heavily into Lü concepts of sickness and disease, according to Chinese sources. Chiang (1950: 190) says that according to Tai belief, malaria is caused by a gas discharged from the bodies of poisonous or loathsome creatures such as snakes, toads, centipedes, and scorpions, who become evil spirits when hidden underground for a time. This belief appears to be related to what Chiang (1950: 255 ff.) reports as *fang-ku*, or insect poisoning, among the Lü. Women in particular are adept at this practice, whereby a variety of poisonous insects are buried in a jar and left to feed on one another until only one is left—this is the *ku*, the spirit or essence of all the poisons of all the creatures in the jar. The sorcerer swears to live and die by the *ku*, which can be released to harm others. If the *ku* dies, the sorcerer will also sicken and die. Similar beliefs and practices relating to *ku* poisoning are found among Miao groups in Kweichow and Szechwan. It is evidently an old and widespread belief among both Miao and Tai peoples in southern and southwestern China (Feng and Shryock 1935; Wiens 1954: 49 ff. in trait lists taken from Eberhard). Women are thought to cause illness and to work magic in still other ways: by incantations they can cause an object to shrink and enter the most solid of objects, or cause poison to be introduced into food. A woman is said to use these methods, or the threat of them, to keep a man near her (Chiang 1950: 253-54). Belief in the ability of some individuals to transform themselves into animals is also reported by Chiang, as well as a belief in spirit possession, whereby the soul of the person possessed is commanded to enter into the body of another. The symptoms of this and other kinds of magical afflictions are stomach cramps, dizziness, fainting, speech abnormalities, and bizarre behavior. • Chiang (1950: 259-60) makes little mention of the role of medicine men or shamans in exorcising evil spirits or counteracting the magic of sorcery. In such cases, he says, the Lü have recourse to Buddhist monks, who use incantations, massage, charms, and talismans as counteractive measures. Lafont (1962b) mentions priests or sorcerers (*mwod phi*), and diviner-healers (*mwod mod*), for the Lü of Laos. **Tattooing.** Tattooing is mentioned in early Chinese records as a characteristic Tai trait, and it is still practiced by the Lü. Performed on males only, the designs extend generally from knee to navel. Tattooing is done between the ages of 11 and 20, and is said by the Lü to constitute a sign of manhood without which no man could successfully court a Lü girl. [Chiang 1950: 176.] **Teeth blackening.** Today the women of the Chinese Shan States area in Yunnan blacken the teeth with a kind of vegetable juice as a sign of marriageability. According to Chinese records, this custom was formerly present among all the Tai people of southern Yunnan. [Chiang 1950: 176.] **Soul, death, and afterlife.** Among the Lü of Laos the soul remains with the corpse after death. If it is not given sufficient offerings, it torments living members of the deceased's family (Lafont 1962b). According to Moerman (1963), the Lue of northern Thailand inter only those who die "bad deaths;" others are cremated. Chiang, on the other hand, says that among the Yunnan Lü, commoners and nobility alike are interred in rough wooden coffins. Buddhist monks and honored old men are cremated. The Lü pay relatively little attention to ancestors or to an ancestor cult. Aside from the most sinicized of the nobility, they do not keep genealogies, nor do they tend the grave after burial. There are no formally kept cemeteries. The corpse is laid out in a coffin in the home, but with little ritual other than some chanting on the part of monks on the day of burial. The Yunnan Lü reportedly at one time conducted a family sacrifice ceremony at home while the corpse lay in state, apparently an occasion for eating, drinking, and dancing, i.e. "entertaining the corpse." [Chiang 1950: 192 ff.]

BIBLIOGRAPHY. Abadie 1924; Carey 1899; Chao 1953; Chen 1949; Chiang 1950; Clarke 1911; Dodd 1923; Feng and Shryock 1935; Garnier 1873; Halpern 1961b; Izikowitz 1962; Lafont 1962a, 1962b; Leach 1954; Moerman 1962, 1963; NNCDT 1959; Rispaud 1937; Scott and Hardiman 1900; Seidenfaden 1958; Sisawat 1952; Wiens 1954; Wissmann 1943.

KHÜN

Synonyms. *Hkün, Kün*

ORIENTATION. **Identification and location.** The term Khün (Hkün, Kün) refers to the Tai-speaking population in and around the old walled town of Kengtung (Chiengtung) in the Burmese Shan State of the same name. Formerly the Khün were distinguished from neighboring Tai populations by slight differences in dialect and by peculiarities of women's dress. The Khün are limited largely to the main Kengtung valley in the center of the State, whereas a major portion of the population as a whole consists of closely-related Tai Lü from across the border in southern Yunnan. Wa, Lahu, and Akha swidden agriculturists occupy the hills, particularly in the east. **Linguistic affiliation.** Tai speakers, closely related to the Lü. **History and cultural relations.** The history of Kengtung is associated with that of other thirteenth-century Tai principalities along the middle Mekong. Mangray, the traditional founder of Chiengmai, is also regarded as the legendary founder of Kengtung. Seidenfaden (1958: 49) thinks that the Kengtung valley area was settled by Tai emigrants from Nanchao, who imposed their rule on a Mon-Khmer population called Khüns. Until recently Wa tribesmen played a traditional role in major state ceremonies. • Prior to British annexation, the Burmese claimed suzerainty over Kengtung and beyond to the Lü country, and the British attempted to keep Kengtung within the political sphere of the Burmese Shan States. Culturally, historically, and by virtue of prevailing trade relationships, however, Kengtung has been oriented to China and Thailand rather than to Burma. In the 1920s Chinese caravans entered Kengtung town almost daily during the dry season. The Khün dialect and religious script are on the whole similar to those of the Yuan, Lü, and Lao.

ECONOMY. The Khün are predominantly wet-rice growers and cattle breeders. They are more active in trade than their relatives the Burmese Shans.

SOCIOPOLITICAL ORGANIZATION. As observed by Western missionaries and administrators in the late nineteenth century, the state of Kengtung, with a total population of around 300,000, was ruled by a Tai prince or *chao fa* (*saohpa*), with his court, *haw*, at Kengtung town. The *chao fa* and members of his own and related families constituted the ruling elite. The royal court, maintained with pomp and ceremony reminiscent of the Burmese court, included a council of ministers, *hpaya*. The countryside was divided into districts, *muong*, ruled by *chao muong*, who annually took an oath of allegiance to the *chao fa*. The Kengtung ruling families have traditionally been active in the opium trade, adding considerably to their income thereby.

RELIGION. The Khün are Theravada Buddhists, their ceremonies and temples showing both Burmese and Chinese influence. There is a pronounced belief in local spirits. Ceremonies may be private or public, and are reported to include the official expulsion of evil spirits from Kengtung town every three years. [Scott and Hardiman 1900: 205-07; Enriquez 1918; Dodd 1923: 200-03; Seidenfaden 1958: 48, 49, 53-54; Coedès 1944: 252.]

BIBLIOGRAPHY. Coedès 1944; Dodd 1923; Enriquez 1918; Scott and Hardiman 1900; Seidenfaden 1958.

YUAN

Synonyms. *Lanatai, Lao, Youanne, Youon, Yün*

ORIENTATION. **Identification.** Indigenous Tai speakers of northern Siam, particularly the Chiengmai area, are known locally as Tai Yuan (Yün or Yün Tai). They are called Lanatai (Tai Lan Na) by the Siamese, and Lao by most missionary writers. The term Yuan or Yün, in the sense of a complex of traits associated with northern Pali language Buddhism—script, polite terms, temple architecture—can refer to Lao, Yuan, Khün, Lü, or Nüa, all of whom share this trait complex—or to all together as part of a "cult area" (Dodd 1923: 76). **Linguistic affiliation.** Tai, related to Lü and Khün. **Location and demography.** The Tai Yuan area comprises the former vassal states of Chiengmai, Lamphun, Lampang, Nan, and Phrae, with a population of somewhat more than 2,000,000 (Credner 1935a: 176). This is the area of the old Tai state of Lan Na, founded in 1296 A.D. Yuan are also found across the border in Laos, in the province of Haut Mekong. The Yuan of the Haut Mekong, mentioned by Izikowitz (1951: 23-24) and by Lafont (1962a: 377), number between 3,000 and 5,000, and are shown on French maps as Youon or Youanne. The Yuan dialect of Tai serves as a lingua franca in southern Haut Mekong, according to Izikowitz. There are also numerous Yuan in the province of Sayaboury. **History and cultural relations.** Today the Yuan are undergoing assimilation to a national culture pattern radiating outward from Bangkok. Historically and culturally, however, there is justification for considering them apart from the central Siamese. Yuan political history is associated with the old Tai principalities of the middle Mekong, and Yuan written (religious) characters are similar to those of the Lao of Laos, thus linking these Tai of northern Siam with their relatives on the Mekong rather than the Chao Phraya. Traditionally, the Yuan (or Lao) of northern Siam have been distinguished from the Lao of northeastern Siam by the fact that the former (Lao Phung Dam) tattooed on the stomach, whereas the latter (Lao Phung Khao) did not. In addition, Brown (1962) has demonstrated dialect differences between the two

areas. [Seidenfaden 1958: 109-13; Dodd 1923: 234 ff.; Sharp et al. 1956: 70; Coedès 1944: 252.]

SOCIOPOLITICAL ORGANIZATION. The writings of travelers and missionaries in northern Siam during the middle and late nineteenth century give a fair picture of the sociopolitical organization of the state of Chiengmai, as it was just before and during the early days of Siamese domination under King Mongkut. The picture is generally similar to that drawn by early visitors to the Burmese Shan States and to Luang Prabang prior to the French protectorate. McGilvary (1912), who first went to Chiengmai in 1850, makes it clear that the Chiengmai prince, although in theory a vassal of the King of Siam, in actuality ruled as an absolute monarch. Political power centered in the court at Chiengmai, where annually the landed nobility came to offer allegiance to their prince. At death, the body of the prince was preserved for a year and then cremated at a week-long ceremony attended by the great *chao* of the land together with princes invited from neighboring states. As in the Shan States and Laos, there was the institution of the *maha oupahat,* or second king. Female members of the nobility were on occasion powerful political figures behind the scene, and court life was marked by elaborate ceremony and colorful regalia. ● The picture drawn by McGilvary, and somewhat later by Colquhoun (1885) and Freeman (1910), is one wherein the personal rights and property rights of farmers and artisans were circumscribed by demands on the part of the nobility. Corvée labor and military conscription were imposed (often arbitrarily) from above. Taxes and special requisitions were levied on field produce and the work of artisans, as in the case of the village of ironworkers described by Colquhoun (1885: 51), which paid an annual tax to the Chiengmai court in the form of finished iron products—elephant chains, cooking pots, and the like. Slavery, in various forms, existed well into the late nineteenth century (Freeman 1910: 98-100). Warfare, and population raids to resettle areas decimated by warfare, resulted in frequent dislocation of individuals or whole villages. Colquhoun, who visited Zimmé (Chiengmai) in 1884, estimated that despite efforts at resettlement, only one-twelfth of the available land in the Ping river plain was actually under cultivation (1885: 86). ● The extraordinary amount of contact and movement of peoples in northern Siam and adjacent regions about the turn of the century is well documented by Freeman (1910: 90-94). Much of this was the result of extensive trading patterns. The Chinese Haws ran annual caravans from Yunnan down to Chiengmai, and from there to Moulmein and back by the same route. The Yuan traded extensively in and around Chiengmai state, and also ran caravans (including cattle) to Burma. There was in addition much trade up and down the river to Bangkok. As phrased by Freeman: "All through the season when the roads are good and farm work light, multitudes of men yield to the 'wanderlust' that is a marked feature of Laos life, and seek profit as well as pleasure in a trading expedition." ● The Tai Yuan of a somewhat later period are portrayed by LeMay (1926), who was able to cite numerous differences in custom between these northerners and the Siamese to the south. A still later stage in the assimilation of the Yuan to the national culture of Thailand is described by Kingshill (1960).

BIBLIOGRAPHY. Brown 1962; Coedès 1944; Colquhoun 1885; Credner 1935a; Dodd 1923; Freeman 1910; Izikowitz 1951; Kingshill 1960; Lafont 1962a; LeMay 1926; McGilvary 1912; Seidenfaden 1958; Sharp et al. 1956.

LAOTIAN TAI

Synonym. *Phou Lao*

ORIENTATION. **Identification.** The Siamese at times refer to the Tai-speaking, glutinous-rice eaters living in the plains and lowland river valleys to the north and northeast of central Thailand as Lao. The term Laotian Tai is here used to distinguish those Lao living within the political boundaries of Laos, but also includes recent refugees into northeastern Thailand. **Location.** The Laotian Tai live mainly along the Mekong river valley, as well as the lower valleys of its major tributaries, from Luang Prabang south to Khone in Laos. **Geography.** Laos is largely mountainous and forest covered. The Annam Cordillera, running the length of the country, is buttressed on the west by a series of plateaus from which the land falls off rather sharply toward the alluvial plain of the Mekong. Precipitation, latitude, and soil conditions make the country a land of tropical forests. Relative humidity is high throughout most of the year. A wet rainy season lasts from May to October, and a relatively dry cool season from November to April. Fauna include deer, elephants, tigers, bears, and wild pigs. Fish are plentiful. [Canada Department of Mines 1953; Seidenfaden 1958: 82-83; LeBar and Suddard 1960: 25-35.] **Linguistic affiliation.** Lao is a Tai language, closely related to Siamese and Shan, with borrowings from Sanskrit, Pali, Cambodian, and French. **Demography.** Of the total population of Laos, approximately two million, about one-half are Laotian Tai, who constitute a majority in Vientiane, Cammon, Champassak, and Savannakhet provinces. The other provinces have notably fewer Laotian Tai: Luang Prabang has only about 35 per cent; Sam Neua and the other provinces bordering on Vietnam, practically none. [Halpern 1961b.] **History.** The early history of the Tai along the middle Mekong is obscure. Tai speakers were probably infiltrating the area prior to the fall of Nanchao in the thirteenth

century A.D. By the end of the century they had founded a number of small political enclaves, *muong*, similar in organization and function to medieval European principalities. Some of these *muong* were located in areas now occupied by Luang Prabang, Vientiane, Xieng Khouang, Savannakhet, and Champassak. Characteristically they warred among themselves, combining and recombining into semifeudal kingdoms or confederations as one or another prince gained ascendancy. At various times they were forced to acknowledge suzerainty of their powerful neighbors, Sukhothai and Cambodia. ● Fa Ngoun, the heir to Muong Swa (Luang Prabang), in 1340-50 succeeded by conquest in welding the middle Mekong principalities into a strong state, Lan Xang, which lasted into the early eighteenth century, extending its power north to Yunnan and west to Chiengmai in what is now northern Thailand. The decline of Lan Xang in the eighteenth century was followed by a confused period during which the Laotian Tai were conquered by Siam and then by Annam. The Lao states along the Mekong were controlled by resident Siamese commissioners when the French entered the area in the late nineteenth century and established a protectorate. An artificial boundary between the Lao on the right and left banks of the Mekong was created by the French, who dealt with the royal family of Luang Prabang as the heirs to the old kingdom of Lan Xang. When independence within the French Union was granted in 1949, the king of Luang Prabang became head of the Lao state. Formal political independence followed the end of the Indochina war and the Geneva agreements of 1954. [Le Boulanger 1931: 30-57; Coedès 1944: 287-90; LeBar and Suddard 1960: 6-24.] **Cultural relations.** The Laotian Tai are closely related to, if not identical with, the Lao of northeastern Thailand. Relations between those on the left and right banks of the Mekong are maintained by trade and migration, often seasonal in nature. Migration has been mostly across the Mekong out of Laos, partly as a consequence of former Siamese conquests and population raids but also as part of the historic movement of Tai peoples southward. The Lao of northeastern Thailand are subject to cultural influences radiating from Bangkok. They differ from the Siamese with respect to such traits as dialect, music, preference for glutinous rice, and a general cultural conservatism (Halpern 1961h: 185). The Siamese tend to regard all Lao as rustics, and in return, the Laotian Tai admire the Siamese but do not altogether trust them. Under the French, Laos was oriented away from Bangkok in the direction of Saigon; with independence this trend has been reversed. ● The Laotian Tai sharply distinguish themselves from the upland Tai (Black Tai, Red Tai, Phuthai, Tai Neua, Tai Phuan) of northern Laos (Halpern 1961c: 7). Trade relations with Meo and Khmu groups in northern Laos are frequent at the rural village level, and the Lao and Khmu sometimes participate jointly in buffalo sacrifices (Halpern 1961f: 86). The feeling of the Laotian Tai for the Vietnamese, mainly one of distrust and hostility, goes back at least as far as French colonial days, when Vietnamese were brought in as civil servants in preference to native Lao.

SETTLEMENT PATTERN AND HOUSING. **Settlement pattern.** Villages are characteristically located near water, among groves of coconut palms and bamboo, and surrounded by rice fields. Homesteads are spaced irregularly, each with its own vegetable garden and fruit trees. The Buddhist temple compound, *wat*, is the most prominent structure in the village. Although the villages appear permanent when compared to those of shifting agriculturists, they may be moved from time to time, and in fact the extent of this movement may be greater than is normally thought (Halpern 1961c: 7). Villages range in size from 50 to 1,000 inhabitants, the average in Vientiane province being 350 (Kaufman 1961: 1). **Housing.** Houses are similar to those of other Tai groups in Burma and Thailand. Constructed largely of bamboo, they are raised on piles, with a veranda in front and a division within into living and sleeping quarters. The space underneath is used for storing tools and for securing livestock at night. A raised granary stands a short distance from the house.

ECONOMY. Domestic economy is based chiefly upon agriculture. Fishing and animal husbandry are important supplementary activities. Also of economic importance are a variety of cottage industries and small-scale trading with the surrounding hill tribes. Hunting and gathering contribute relatively little to the food supply. [Halpern 1961f.] **Agriculture.** The chief crop is glutinous rice. Irrigated paddy fields, *na*, predominate, but are supplemented in northern Laos in particular by dry-rice fields, *hai*. An estimated 20 per cent of the farmers in Vientiane province, for example, supplement their wet-rice crops with dry. Fields are prepared for planting by plowing with a buffalo-drawn plow. Rice seedlings are grown in special beds and then transplanted. The mature rice is threshed by beating, stored in mat bins or in small storerooms raised on piles, and then milled with a wooden mortar and pestle device. Single cropping is the rule, and little use is made of compost or fertilizer (Kaufman 1961: 3-8). Other crops include maize, beans, tobacco, cotton, and sugar cane. Vegetables (chili peppers, cucumbers, cabbages, eggplant, melons, onions, tomatoes) are grown in household gardens. Fruits include bananas, mangoes, pineapples, oranges, and papaya. Mulberry trees are important in connection with silkworm culture. [Seidenfaden 1958: 89-97.] **Fishing.** Although the Laotian Tai are fond of fishing, they fish mainly in response to family needs. Nets and traps are used, and an entire family may participate. Fish and fish products are important in the diet, with consumption averaging twice a week (Halpern 1958: 39). **Gathering.** Cicadas, crickets, larvae, frogs, shrimp, crabs, and snails constitute a minor but highly prized part of the diet. **Domestic animals.** Cattle are raised mainly as a source of prestige and for religious sacrifice. Other domesticated animals include buffalo, oxen, chickens, ducks, and pigs. Pork is an important part of the diet. Elephants are associated with royalty, and are also used in parts of Laos for work in the forests. **Food and stimulants.** Betel chewing is popular, as is the consumption of tobacco. Opium addiction is rare. Water is the main beverage although considerable quantities of distilled rice spirits are consumed on festive occasions. **Industrial arts.** Include brass founding and casting using the lost-wax process, silversmithing, blacksmithing (sometimes hereditary within families), charcoal making, pottery making, basketwork, and weaving. Embroidery is highly developed among the women. Most of this work is for home or village consumption and is carried out on a part-time basis. Village-wide specialization is limited mainly to the area in and around Luang Prabang, where such specialties as pottery making, silversmithing, and weaving seem to be holdovers from the days when such villages served the Luang Prabang royal house. [de Reinach 1901: 453-68; Halpern 1961f.] **Trade.** Between the Laotian Tai of the valleys and the various hill peoples (particularly the Meo and Khmu) trade is extensive, occurring both at village markets and also through the institution of *lam*, whereby the interests of a group of hill peoples vis-à-vis the outside world are represented by a Laotian Tai patron or protector (Rispaud 1937: 119; Halpern 1961a: 9-10). There is, however, little specialization and trade among Lao villages. Formerly, caravans from Yunnan traded throughout northern Laos, bringing in Chinese, Indian, and Tibetan products in exchange for opium (Halpern 1961f: 27). Today considerable amounts of opium—very little of which is grown by the Laotian Tai themselves—are smuggled out of the country. **Division of labor.** Women spin, weave, care for livestock, pound rice, cook, and engage in trade in market bazaars. Men, in addition to performing the heavy work in the fields, pursue blacksmithing, silversmithing, and carpentry. Both sexes may engage in fishing, trading, pottery making, and the transplanting and harvesting of rice. In general, strict sexual division of labor is absent. **Land tenure.** It is probable that in former times the land in a *muong* was considered to be ultimately the property of the *chao muong*, a hereditary position occupied by a member of the nobility. Ceremonies held until recently at Vientiane, Luang Prabang, Muong Sing, and other old *muong* capitals indicate the former existence of a cult of the spirit of the soil. Such activities as the participation of the *chao muong* in sacrifices made at the *lak muong* (a post set up in the *muong* capital) to the *phi muong* are indicative of a cult analogous to that among the Black Tai, in which noble families, by virtue of their exclusive right to communicate with the *phi muong*, obtained a supernatural sanction to the title of lands within their *muong* domains (Sinavong 1957: 2; Lévy 1959: 162-70). Under this system, commoners tilled the land as usufructuaries, contributing labor and taxes in return for protection. The rights and duties of both parties were firmly established by custom. Should a farmer emigrate, his lands reverted to the village and were ultimately redistributed. [Halpern 1961f: 43; de Reinach 1901: 500.] Today the land tenure system in Laos is not as clear-cut. Although in theory land may belong to the state, in practice most farmers appear to own their land outright, including the right of alienation (Kaufman 1961: 23). However, throughout most of Laos it is still necessary to get the approval of the traditional leader of the district before making any land transfers (Halpern 1961f: 41); and in the area of Luang Prabang town, at least, a good portion of the irrigated land belongs to the royal family or members of the nobility (Halpern 1961f: 43). The extent of the fragmentation of land holdings in modern Laos is indicated in the results of a survey by the Ministry of Agriculture of wet-rice agricultural villages; the figures given below are averages for the wet-rice fields in the 30 villages surveyed (Halpern 1961d: Table 6):

Number of proprietors per village	55.00
Extent of area cultivated per village (in hectares)	81.00
Number of parcels per proprietor	30.60
Average parcel size (in square meters)	480.00
Average holding per proprietor (in hectares)	1.47

This fragmentation seems to be in part a result of the system of inheritance, whereby land may be divided equally among children.

KIN GROUPS. **Descent.** Society at the commoner level is bilaterally structured. Kinship ties are felt to be equally strong on both the mother's and father's side. Today surnames are by law patrilineally inherited, but this is a recent innovation and not yet fully accepted in the villages. Traditionally, people are known by their given names, e.g. pet names and monk names. Studies made in the villages have found no formally constituted kin groups larger than the family (household) unit. There are indications, however, that something like a loosely constituted bilateral kindred does function at life crisis situations (Kaufman 1961: 19). **Kin terminology.** Villagers pay relatively little attention to genealogies, and are rarely able to trace their ancestry for more than three generations. The kinship system is similar to that among neighboring Tai groups, e.g. the Siamese, and is in general suggestive of a bilateral kindred grouping. Benedict (1943) gives the following terms:

Mo	*me*
Fa	*p'o*
FaElSi, MoElSi	*pa*
FaElBr, MoElBr	*lung*
FaYoSi	*a*
FaYoBr	*au*
MoYoBr, MoYoSi	*na* plus sex modifier
ElBr, ElSi	*p'i* plus sex modifier
YoBr, YoSi	*nong* plus sex modifier
Cousins	Sibling terms. Age-graded according to relative ages of kin through whom relationship is traced. [Ayabe (1961: 23-26) adds the prefix *luk* (child), e.g. FaBrDa, *luk nong.*]

MARRIAGE AND FAMILY. **Mode.** Marriages are normally the outcome of a period of courtship, *linsaw.* Opportunities for courtship are frequent, and considerable freedom is allowed. Girls set up booths at temple festivals, where young men compete for their attention. Girls are also serenaded at home in the evening as they sit spinning or sewing on the veranda. Poetic conversation and skill in playing the multi-reed organ, *khene*, figure prominently on these occasions. When a young couple have made their choice, the boy notifies his parents, who then arrange for a go-between (Kaufman 1961: 47-48). A bride price is normally paid in silver. A legal code formerly specified the amount, graded according to the rank of the girl's parents (Halpern 1961h: 130). Elopement may occur if the bride price cannot be met by the boy's family. **Form.** Marriages are predominantly monogamous; polygyny is possible, but in practice limited to the wealthy. In the past, polygynous marriages were strongly associated with royalty (de Reinach 1901: 193-94). **Extension of incest taboos.** A high percentage of marriages are of the romantic love type and occur within the same village. Village endogamy is estimated at about 80 per cent by both Kaufman (1961: 50) and Ayabe (1961: 96). Bilateral cousin marriage is allowed, particularly in the case of second cousins, according to Kaufman (1961: 50-51). Ayabe reports a tendency among commoners to avoid cousin marriage, but adds that among descendants of former chiefs and nobles bilateral cross-cousin marriage is allowed, provided the spouse's parent is younger than Ego's parent (1961: 17-18). **Residence.** Residence after marriage is ideally matrilocal for a time (about two years), and then neolocal. A daughter normally inherits the family homestead, in which case she may, if married, reside matrilocally and never progress to neolocality. [Kaufman 1961: 21; Ayabe 1961: 19-20.] **Domestic unit.** The nuclear family normally constitutes the household unit, which averages slightly over five persons; stem families (most often a married daughter living matrilocally) constitute a minority of cases (Ayabe 1961: 13). **Inheritance.** The family homestead and the land it stands on is inherited matrilineally—often by the youngest daughter, since she is normally the last to marry. Paddy lands are in theory divided by mutual consultation among all the surviving children; in practice, however, sons seem to be favored in the inheritance of agricultural lands. [Halpern 1961h: 37; Ayabe 1961: 20-21; Kaufman 1961: 21.] **Divorce.** Divorce is possible for either partner, and no particular stigma is attached. Female children go with the mother; older male children with the father.

SOCIOPOLITICAL ORGANIZATION. **Old Lan Xang.** The sociopolitical structure of old Lan Xang has been described by Le Boulanger (1931: 53-57), who based his remarks on French translations of chronicles pertaining to the reign of King Sam Sene Thai (1373-1416 A.D.). Inhabitants of the kingdom were registered [probably for purposes of taxation and military duty]. Of those who spoke Tai and practiced Buddhism, some were nobles and some commoners. The nobles were given certain privileges [probably including title to small fiefdoms and the right to withhold a portion of the taxes and other benefits derived therefrom]. Commoners were generally traders [and probably military conscripts] rather than farmers, the work in the fields being left to dependents of an inferior race [possibly Mon-Khmer tribesmen] or to slaves. [There may be indicated here a situation of a relatively small number of Tai speakers imposed on a base of non-Tai, the former engaging primarily in trade, warfare, and administration.] An army of five corps, plus coolies responsible for provisioning, was divided into security, defense, and reserve forces. Warriors fought on horseback or on elephants, using lances and swords. Under this system the king, seated at Muong Swa (Luang Prabang), was an absolute monarch. The *maha oupahat* (second king) was in actuality the military leader—the leader of the advance guard. Halpern (1961h: 121-22) adds that high military leaders were given territories, and were responsible for their defense. **The Luang Prabang state in the late eighteenth century.** Further evidence of indigenous sociopolitical structure is contained in descriptions of Luang Prabang at the time the French first established their protectorate (cf. de Reinach 1901: 490-97). The royal court at Luang Prabang consisted of the king, *somdet pra-chao;* the second king, *chao maha oupahat;* four minister princes of noble blood entitled to the hereditary title of *chao;* three high officials with the title *phaya,* who were responsible for justice, public service, and transport; a five-man council, *senam,* selected from the officials listed above; judges; lesser officials in charge of tax collection and labor corvée; certain minor functionaries such as the keeper of the royal elephants; and various artists, craftsmen, mu-

sicians, and so on. ● The state was divided into provinces, *muong,* in the charge of *chao muong,* with seats of government and courts similar to those at the capital, but without the institution of the council. *Muong* were administratively divided into cantons, governed by officials with the title of *tasseng.* At the bottom of the structure were the villages, each with a headman, *pho ban* or *nai ban,* assisted by a council of village notables. The higher court officials and the *chao muong* were princes of the royal blood or members of families related to the royal line. The various officials in this hierarchy "lived off the people" by retaining some of the taxes and tribute which were funneled upward through the hierarchy. Most vestiges of the once-powerful military force had disappeared by the time of French intervention; otherwise the administrative system was maintained largely intact under the French protectorate. **Modern political organization.** Today the provincial governors, *chao khoueng,* are part of a governmental bureaucracy with its center in the administrative capital, Vientiane. Until recently, the power of these governors was virtually absolute (Kaufman 1961: 23). Provinces are still divided into districts, *muong,* and these in turn into cantons, each composed of a number of villages. The *chao muong,* in charge of anywhere from 80 to over 300 villages, is a key person within the civil service. Working through the canton leaders, *tasseng,* he is responsible for taxes, military conscriptions, and corvée labor, and he also has some judicial functions. Government and politics are dominated by an elite group, whose members tend to intermarry. There are, however, numerous instances in recent years of individuals rising from humble beginnings into an elite family through marriage. Since the coming of the French, this practice, together with education, has provided the main avenue to upward mobility in Laos. The concept of nobility, except within the royal lineages, has probably never been too strictly defined among the Laotian Tai. [Halpern 1958: 124; Kaufman 1961: 23-28.] **Social stratification.** Social relationships at the village level are remarkably loose in structure. Individual status differences due to leadership ability or marked religious piety are present, but inherited class distinctions and closed group affiliations are absent. In this respect, the society is strongly individualistic, a trait sometimes associated with Buddhism's emphasis on the individual's responsibility for his own spiritual welfare. Society as a whole, however, is sharply stratified between peasant farmers and members of the intellectual elite, reflecting the former dichotomy between nobility and commoners. The elite group in Laos is made up primarily of descendants of some twenty or more noble families—the princely rulers of the old principalities which made up the kingdom of Lan Xang. The bases of the old order—the concentration of land ownership in the hands of the nobility and the organization and mobilization of the population for warfare—have largely disappeared, although vestiges remain. ● Lao society still retains numerous evidences of traditional status distinctions. Members of the elite bear titles such as *tiao* (*chao*), *maha*, and so on. The legal statutes of the 1950s retained provisions for the assessment of fines and penalties graded according to the traditional hereditary rank of the plaintiff (Halpern 1961h: 63). Special terms are still used in addressing superiors, including an honorific language reserved for the king alone. Formerly, commoners prostrated themselves when approaching the king or a prince of the royal blood. The position of women in society is an interesting one. Although nominally low in the formal social hierarchy, women have a considerable voice in family economy, and they have on occasion entered national politics.

RELIGION. Religious behavior is a synthesis of Theravada Buddhism with remnant Brahmanistic beliefs and rituals and a strong underpinning of indigenous animism. It is often said that the Laotian Tai love their Buddhism and practice it as a preparation for the next life; but that in dealing with day-to-day problems and hardships they are likely to turn to the world of the spirits, *phi*. **Major religions.** Buddhism is the state religion, and the king and members of the royal family participate extensively in Buddhist ceremonies. A Buddhist hierarchy parallels that of the secular government. Every village has at least one temple with its complement of monks and novices. The temple compound, *wat*, is the center of both secular and religious life. The *wat*, consisting of a public hall, a convocation hall (reserved for ordinations and other sacred occasions), and separate living quarters for monks, is kept up by the voluntary labor and material contributions of the villagers. *Wat* schools were formerly the sole means of formal education. The custom of ordination remains popular, and novices, boys ranging in age from nine to nineteen, are numerous. The ordination ceremony, whereby a young man, sponsored by his family, enters the monkhood for a period of about two years, is a high point in the life cycle. The ordination ceremony and the novitiate confer religious merit on both the youth and his family. Merit making is an important motivating factor in Laotian Tai behavior, and much time and money are spent in this fashion. The Buddhist clergy is not a closed corporation. Males over twenty can enter and leave the monkhood at will, and a villager, particularly as he grows older, may go into retreat for a period of months or years. ● Religious festivals, *boun*, are most frequent during the fourth and fifth lunar months (April and May). Ordinarily, a village selects which *bouns* it will sponsor in consultation with its neighbors, so that no two villages in the same area will sponsor the same ones. Villagers are thus afforded frequent festive holidays

and opportunities to visit. A *boun* may last anywhere from one to five days and include sermons by the monks and frequent visits to the temple. Evening entertainment includes dancing and gambling, while stalls serve food and drink. Eligible daughters of the leading men of the village may act as dancing partners on these occasions, the men paying for dances and the proceeds going to the local *wat*. In late March or early April, the Festival of the New Year, Songkran, is widely observed. This is an occasion for much merit making, including sprinkling of Buddha images and mutual dousing of participants. In former times royal processions took place in the capital, ending with the drinking of an oath of allegiance to the king by the assembled princes of the realm. Vixakha Bouxa, commemorating the birth, enlightenment, and death of the Buddha, is held in May. In urban centers it is a major holiday and the occasion for firing rockets made by monks. The rockets are said to break the clouds, thereby bringing the life-giving rains of the summer monsoon. [Kaufman 1961: 55-71; de Reinach 1901: 146-74; Seidenfaden 1958: 89-97.] **Indigenous religion.** Interwoven with Buddhism are beliefs in various Brahmanic deities and local spirits. In general these beliefs and practices predate the introduction of Buddhism. **Supernaturals.** The *phi*, spirits, are ever-present, in trees, rivers, gardens, villages, houses, crops, and ancestors. They must be placated or propitiated by offerings of food; and small *phi* shrines are conveniently located along village lanes, beside hedges, and under the eaves of houses. A considerable portion of a farm family's capital is expended in the form of animal sacrifices to the *phi*. The Laotian Tai also believe in the 32 *kwan* (bodily spirits or souls), 20 of which are inherited from the father, and 12 from the mother. Much of the religious behavior involving belief in *phi* is performed by an individual alone or by a household head on behalf of his family. In practically every village there is in addition one older person, usually a male, with special knowledge of spirits and how to deal with them. Combining this knowledge with astrology and other occult lore, he may be called upon to choose an auspicious day for a wedding, locate lost property, conduct household rites, or perform the yearly ritual of feeding the village spirits. This is a part-time specialty, for there is no formal organization or training of such individuals. Propitiation of *phi* is associated with the all-important activity of growing and harvesting rice. Ceremonies at the time of spring plowing formerly required the participation of royalty; such was the case for example at Luang Prabang, Xieng Khouang, Champassak, and Muong Sing. There was felt to be a special degree of kinship between these royal lines and the protecting spirits of the *muong* land, akin to the cult of the *phi muong*, or guardian spirit of the *muong* land, and its association with noble lineages among the Black Tai.

Like the Black Tai, the Laotian Tai have the concept of a *chao phi*, or guardian spirit of the village and its lands. [Halpern 1958: 17-19; Kaufman 1961: 71-78; Sinavong 1957: 2; Ayabe 1961: 39; Lévy 1959: 162-70.] **Practitioners.** Illness and disease are most frequently attributed to evil spirits or to soul loss. Several kinds of practitioners specialize in the treatment of illnesses, although different skills may in some cases be combined in the person of a single practitioner. The type of illness, and thus the kind of practitioner required, is customarily decided by means of egg divination. Monks may be called in to treat illness by sprinkling the patient with holy water, at the same time reciting Pali scripture. Herb doctors work with an extensive pharmacopoeia as well as with the concept of the basic elements of air, fire, and water; the idea of 32 souls, all of which must be present for complete health; and the concept of nine body openings, including the palms of the hands, through which evil spirits may enter or leave the body. A female exorcist may be called in if it is determined that certain kinds of spirits are causing the trouble. The exorcist works with a variety of paraphernalia, including food offerings to the spirit afflicting the patient as well as to the guardian spirit of the practitioner herself. She attempts to drive out the offending spirit by dancing about the patient with swords and lighted candles. ● Shamanistic skills may be required if it is determined that illness is caused by the intrusion of a foreign object into the body. This in turn seems to be related to the belief in *phi pop*, persons possessed by evil spirits and capable of casting spells, or of causing death by incantations, evil eye, or the introduction of a harmful object into the body of a victim. A *phi pop* can reduce a buffalo hide to minute size and cause his victim to swallow it; the hide then swells in the stomach, causing suffering, madness, or death. Apparently *phi pop* may acquire their skill (or their affliction) from a parent or relative. They are much feared by villagers, and there are instances of suspected *phi pop*, frequently women, being ostracized from their own villages or put to death by an enraged populace. It also seems to be the case that the victim of a *phi pop* may himself become a *phi pop*, by a kind of transference mechanism. A *phi pop* may on occasion be induced to counteract his own magic and cure a victim. In other cases an equally powerful practitioner must be called in to rid the patient of the cause of his suffering, usually by locating the foreign object and magically removing it by blowing or pretending to bite the afflicted area, or by inducing the patient to regurgitate. [Halpern 1961g: 10-20; Souvannavong 1959: 301-06; de Reinach 1901: 151-52.] **Birth.** A woman is normally attended by a midwife when giving birth, which is accomplished in a kneeling position. The Laotian Tai observe the custom of "mother roasting," termed *jukam*

(living in penitence). During the period—twenty days for a first child, less thereafter—the mother does not leave the house but remains beside a constantly replenished fire. [Kaufman 1961: 42-43.] **Tattooing.** Before the age of marriage, boys used to be tattooed from knee to thigh. This custom is dying out and is no longer practiced in Vientiane province. Tattoos served as a symbol of virility, and also functioned as charms against illness, battle wounds, snake bite, and the like. The Laotian Tai are said to have blackened their teeth with a kind of gum made from tanbark and other substances. [de Reinach 1901: 185.] **Death.** At death, the corpse is prepared by members of the immediate family, and a service is chanted by Buddhist monks. Cremation is the ideal, but poorer people are often buried in a coffin. In cases where cremation is postponed for any length of time (a year or more in the case of royalty; somewhat less for the Buddhist clergy, the wealthy, and members of the nobility), the body is desiccated and perfumed with aromatic plants. The corpse is borne to the grave or funeral pyre by close relatives, often male first cousins of the deceased. In case of burial a simple marker is used and the grave soon forgotten. There are no cemeteries. In case of unusual deaths (women who have died in childbirth, persons struck by lightning, or those who have died from cholera) the body is hurriedly buried in an unmarked grave far from the village. [Kaufman 1961: 53-55; de Reinach 1901: 200-02.]

BIBLIOGRAPHY. Ayabe 1961; Benedict 1943; Canada Department of Mines 1953; Coedès 1944; Halpern 1958, 1961a, 1961b, 1961c, 1961d, 1961f, 1961g, 1961h; Kaufman 1961; LeBar and Suddard 1960; Le Boulanger 1931; Lévy 1959; de Reinach 1901; Rispaud 1937; Seidenfaden 1958; Sinavong 1957; Souvannavong 1959.

CENTRAL UPLAND GROUPS

BLACK TAI

Synonyms. *Tai Dam, Tay Den, Thai Noir*

ORIENTATION. **Identification.** The Black Tai, Tai Dam (Tai designation), Tay Den (Vietnamese), or Thai Noir (French) are so called for the characteristic black of the women's costume. The Black Tai of Nghia Lo and Son La in the heart of the Sip Song Chau Tai (Twelve Tai Chau) between the Red and Black rivers in northern Vietnam differentiate themselves according to the *muong* (or *chau*, a political-territorial unit) in which they live. For example, those from Muong Lo refer to themselves as Tai Lo. [Lafont 1955: 806.] **Location.** Usually found in the upland valleys of northern Vietnam and Laos. The greatest concentration is in northern Indochina in the area between the Red and Black rivers. There also are Black Tai groupings in the areas of Pa Kha, Hoang Su Phi, and in the Song Chay valley and on the right bank of the Red river in northern Vietnam. Since World War II, large numbers of Black Tai have migrated into northern Laos. At the present time there are large groupings (an estimated 3,500) in the Laotian province of Hua Phan. In Haut Mekong province there are around 4,000 Black Tai, and in the province of Luang Prabang they are scattered throughout the Nam Bac valley and the Nam Pat valley. There are scattered villages in the vicinity of Sop Khao and Xieng Khouang town in Xieng Khouang province, and in Vientiane province there are some 1,000 Nghia Lo and Son La Black Tai refugees 35 kilometers distant from Vientiane on the Luang Prabang road. [Hickey 1958: 130; Lafont 1962b.] **Linguistic affiliation.** Tai-speaking. **Demography.** A recent North Vietnamese source reports the population of the Black Tai and White Tai (both of which they refer to as Tay) to be 344,628, without giving the figure for each group. [NNCDT 1959: 242.]

SETTLEMENT PATTERN AND HOUSING. **Settlement pattern.** Settlements vary in size from 20 to 50 houses, depending on the availability of arable land. Villages are located near wooded areas and water courses. Within the village, there is no defined orientation for the houses. There is sufficient space around each house for a kitchen garden and an open area for drying paddy, herbs, and animal hides. Paddy fields are located near the village, and swidden agriculture may be carried on in the nearby hills, necessitating temporary shelters where the young men remain during the planting season. [Hickey 1958: 130-33.] **Housing.** Houses are constructed on piling. Logs, sticks, and bamboo are used in the frame, and the high hip roofs are thatched. A platform extending from the front of the house is used for weaving and dyeing, and also serves as a veranda where the family and guests gather. The area under the house is divided into several parts, the largest of which is the stable. Other sections are used for storing, husking, and grinding rice and maize as well as for storing tools and farm implements. The houses of the Black Tai nobility are distinguished by "Tai crosses" on the two extremities of the roof top. • The interior of the house is divided into several compartments. Meals are prepared on a common hearth in the main room, regardless of household composition. The head of the house usually has a separate sleeping room, as do the unmarried females. Mats on the floor and camp beds are used for sleeping. Boxes containing personal belongings, tools, traps, and weapons are piled along the walls or hung from the rafters of the main room. The bulk of the cereal crops is stored in a granary near the house. [Lunet de Lajonquière 1906: 175; Lafont 1962b; Hickey 1958: 133-34.]

ECONOMY. **Agriculture.** Predominantly wet-rice cultivators. Since they live in mountain valleys where there is often insufficient bottom land for paddy cultivation, some Black Tai also cultivate upland rice on the slopes by the swidden method. Fields so cultivated are abandoned after three years to lie fallow for eight to ten years before they are recultivated. [Diguet 1908: 57; Hickey 1958: 135.] In the vicinity of Nam Tha in northern Laos, seasonal rainfall and flooding are the major sources of irrigation. A system of shallow channels is dug through the fields to distribute the water. Tools include plows with iron cutting blades, spades, hoes, and a variety of cutting instruments. Threshing is done by beating the stalks against the edge of a basket. Buffalo are used as draft animals. [Hickey 1958: 135-38.] **Fishing and hunting.** The Black Tai are avid hunters and fishermen, and both activities provide necessary supplementary food. Crossbows are the common hunting weapons, and some Black Tai make firearms resembling ancient European muskets with iron purchased from Chinese merchants. Powder is made from sulphur and saltpeter, also purchased from the Chinese. A wide variety of nets and traps are employed for fishing. [Hickey 1958: 136.] **Domestic animals.** Buffalo and small Mongolian horses are bred for draft animals. Buffalo are used in the fields, and occasionally as sacrificial animals. Horses are widely used for transporting goods. The Black Tai also raise pigs, goats, chickens, and dogs. [Hickey 1958: 136.] **Industrial arts.** Each family produces its own tools, weapons, baskets, and most of its cloth, although the Black Tai have been purchasing cloth from Chinese and Vietnamese merchants in increasing amounts. Village specialists include carpenters and wood carvers. [Hickey 1958: 138.] **Trade.** Commerce is not highly developed. Markets are held periodically in larger villages and in towns such as Son La. In addition, Chinese and Vietnamese merchants travel throughout the Black Tai areas selling manufactured goods and purchasing opium produced by the villagers. [Hickey 1958: 137.] **Land tenure.** In areas such as the Sip Song Chau Tai, where the traditional *muong* domains of the Black Tai formed a collection of principalities ruled by noble families, the ruling elite held title to all the land. French reforms deprived this group of their hereditary right to land in the *muong*, and individual families received title to the land they were cultivating. In areas where the Black Tai are scattered, individual family ownership of land has been traditional. [Lunet de Lajonquière 1906: 178-80.] Families practicing swidden agriculture had use of the land, and implicitly the right to continue cultivation after the fallow period (Hickey 1958: 137).

KIN GROUPS. **Descent.** From the viewpoint of structure manifest in terminology, the Black Tai kinship system appears bilateral. Descent, however, is patrilineal, inheritance is in the male line, and males have a dominant role in the family. Terminologically, there is no bifurcation of kin in the third and second ascending generation. In the first ascending generation there are common terms for parents' older brothers and parents' older sisters, but other kin of this generation are distinguished according to lineal affiliation. All kin in Ego's generation are age-graded relative to Ego. [Hickey 1958: 157-58.] **Kin groups.** Lafont (1955) described great families among the Black Tai—*"les familles patronymiques"*—which appear to have some sib, possibly patrisib, functions. In the heart of the Black Tai country, around the northern Vietnamese towns of Nghia Lo and Son La, there are eleven family names: Cam, Lo, Vi, Lu, Leo, Luong, Ka, Tong, Kwang, Ma, and Nguyen. These families are divided along class lines. The Lo and Cam comprise the sociopolitical elite of Black Tai society. Because the Ka and Luong families provide priests of a particular type, they are considered sacerdotal families, and the remaining families form the commoner class. • According to Lafont, there is some indication that in the past these families were exogamous, although, with explicit exceptions, it is possible to marry someone with the same surname if the relationship is not within one degree. Members of the Lo and Cam families are forbidden to marry into the families of the Nguyen (a common Vietnamese surname) or the Ma, both of which are considered mixed-blood Tai, nor may they marry Vietnamese, Chinese, or anyone else who is not "pure Black Tai." Any members of the Ka and Luong families who are (or intend to become) priests cannot marry members of the Ma or Nguyen families. [Lafont 1955: 801.] Neither the Lo nor the Cam families are permitted to marry the Tai Fieng, a group of eight families in the Nghia Lo–Son La area. Although the Tai Fieng are not known as a mixed-blood group, they are considered by the Black Tai to be inferior people. [Lafont 1955: 803.] **Role of women.** The woman keeps her maiden name after marriage, and after her parents die she keeps her own ancestral altar in their honor. She also maintains considerable contact with her kin after marriage. [Lafont 1955: 806.] **Taboos.** Some of the Black Tai families have food taboos which, if violated, are supposed to cause the guilty party to lose his teeth. The Lo and Cam families are forbidden to eat *kam tanh* (a local vegetable), shoots of the *sen kam* and *lay lo* (varieties of bamboo), and the pulp of the *lang kam* tree. The Lo also are forbidden the flesh of the *noc tang,* a bird with green plumage, and the flesh of a black-plumed bird called *noc chan lo.* The Tong have no food taboos, but they cannot use wood of the *may tong* tree in their house construction. The

only families without specific taboos are the Ma and Nguyen. [Lafont 1955: 801-03.]

MARRIAGE AND FAMILY. **Mode.** Marriages are arranged by the parents. Custom requires that the boy spend a service period working for his fiancée's parents. Sons of nobles (Lo and Cam) are expected to do from eight to ten years of service, while a briefer period is required of commoners. After the service period, the marriage takes place, and the girl's parents must present the groom with a dowry. The only exception to the service rule is when the fiancée's family does not have enough males to assist with cultivation, in which case the marriage may take place immediately after preliminary arrangements have been completed, and the groom goes to live with his wife's family. **Residence.** Normally residence after marriage is patrilocal for the eldest son and neolocal for other sons, although they are expected to remain in the vicinity of the paternal house. [Hickey 1958: 157-58.] **Inheritance.** Among the Black Tai of northern Vietnam, primogeniture determines the inheritance of the paternal house and the greatest share of family land. In northern Laos, however, the pattern is for all sons to share the inheritance equally. [Hickey 1958: 158.]

SOCIOPOLITICAL ORGANIZATION. In the traditional political system, the *muong* functioned as a principality in which the *tao* or Black Tai nobility (comprised of the Lo and Cam families) ruled. The *chau muong,* chief of the *muong,* held title to the land—a hereditary title passed from father to eldest son—and his role as *chau muong* was also hereditary. The French altered the land tenure system, granting title to individual cultivators, but they were unable to change the hereditary prerogative of the Lo and Cam to the role of *chau muong.* The right to this role appears to be reinforced by a legend which establishes a special relationship between the Lo and Cam and the supreme spirit of the soil. Since the *chau muong* must have power to invoke the presence of the spirit of the soil at important *muong* rituals, the *chau muong* must be of the Lo or Cam, and French efforts to make this position appointive were without success. The Luong and Ka families have the exclusive right to the role of *mo,* the official priests who participate in the rituals honoring the spirit of the soil. The remaining families provide soldiers, artisans, and farmers. [Lafont 1955: 780; Diguet 1908: 90; Maspéro 1929-30: 237-40.]

RELIGION. **Supernaturals.** There is belief in a wide range of spirits known collectively as *pi* (sometimes spelled *phi*), also known among the Black Tai in parts of northern Vietnam as *fi.* A variety of *pi* known as *ten* are the spirits of the soil, arranged in a ranked hierarchy. *Ten luong* is the supreme spirit of the soil, the source of soil fertility and abundant harvests, while *pi muong* is the spirit of the soil of the *muong*. At the village level there is the *pi ban*. *Long ton,* an important annual ritual honoring the spirits of the soil, precedes planting, following which the *chau muong* is the first to begin cultivation. Several rituals are observed by individual farmers—one for the ancestors when the buds appear, and a pig or chicken sacrifice for the new rice. The spirit of the soil is again honored at harvest. Following the harvest, each farmer offers a simple sacrifice to invite the rice spirit (*kwan kuu*) to sleep in the granary. [Lafont 1955: 801-06; Maspéro 1929-30: 238; Hickey 1958: 145.] A person's 32 souls are fashioned by three spirits, two of which—*po chang lo* and *po chang ty*—are male, while *me ban,* the third spirit, is female. Again, the Lo and Cam families are unique in having six of their 32 souls created by the *ten luong,* the supreme spirit of the soil. [Lafont 1955: 806.] The cult of the ancestors is also practiced. Ancestral altars, consisting of a table and candles, are found in Black Tai houses in northern Vietnam, and in northern Laos there are similar ancestral altars attached high on the rear wall of the house. Periodic rituals are held, with the eldest male officiating. [Hickey 1958: 148; Lafont 1962b.] **Practitioners.** The type of Black Tai priest known as *mo* comes from the Luong and Ka families. This role is passed from father to son, and the initiate must undergo training in prayers, ritual forms, healing techniques, and other kinds of sorcery. After a period as an apprentice, the postulant moves up to a higher level, eventually attaining the title of *mwo lam.* Only the *mwo lam* can perform an official role in rituals honoring the spirits of the soil. In addition to the trained *mo,* in the Sip Song Chau Tai area of Vietnam there are individual priests called *mot* (males) and *nang thiem* (females) who are considered naturally gifted with the ability to contact the spirits; they usually practice sorcery for individual clients. [Hickey 1958: 145; Lafont 1955: 801-06.] In northern Laos, sorcerers called *mo mot* are hereditary within the Luong family. They officiate at village rituals honoring the spirit of the soil, the guardian *pi* of the village, and a variety of other *pi.* A buffalo and pig are offered for the guardian *pi* of the village, a duck is sacrificed for the water *pi,* and a dog is considered the appropriate offering for the forest *pi.* Chickens are offered for the *pi* of heaven and also for the *pi* that guard the entrance to the village. At all rituals, a small tray of offerings is intended for the errant *pi.* [Hickey 1958: 148.] According to Diguet (1908: 90), *ong chang* is a generic designation for Black Tai priests. *Ong mo* are those of the lowest category while the highest category bears the title *ong nghe.* The individual, untrained sorcerers are *mot* (male) and *mot nhing* (female). The *mot nhing* are renowned for their ability to cure a variety of illnesses by means of a special ritual

wherein the evil spirits causing the ailment are invited to enter the body of a caged chicken which subsequently is killed. **Illness and medicine.** Among the Black Tai in Laos, an illness due to natural causes is treated by a healer (*mwod*), who examines the patient, and then prepares a medicine composed of organic elements. Usually these healers have learned the trade from their fathers. Illnesses caused by spirits are treated by sorcerers (*mwod mod*), who use only magical techniques. [Lafont 1959: 819-40.] **Soul, death, and afterlife.** The Black Tai believe that each human has 32 souls which leave the body after death. Some go "beyond the sky," while others remain on the altar of the ancestors. Black Tai social stratification extends to their concept of the afterlife. Commoners and those who die before the age of five enter Lam Loi, a village of the next world where existence is much the same as it is in life. "Great chiefs" of the Lo and Cam families remain in the celestial village of Tup Hoang No Fa, where existence is idyllic. Lesser aristocracy go to the village of Gien Pan Noi, where existence is also idyllic, but eventually their souls return to earth. Other members of the Lo and Cam go to the village of Gien Pan Luong, a place much like Gien Pan Noi. Normally the souls of a woman go to the family house of her husband. Souls of Lo and Cam wives go to Gien Pan Luong, but if a Lo or Cam woman should marry a commoner her souls would go to the village of Lam Loi and, like other souls in that village, eventually return to earth and oblivion. [Lafont 1955: 804-07.] After death, animal sacrifices are made to provide offerings to the spirit of the deceased, and also to provide food for the kin and friends who gather for the funeral. The corpse is placed on a stand in the house while kin and friends gather. The Black Tai cremate their dead. The ashes are collected and placed in an earthen jar which is then buried. [Hickey 1958: 158.]

BIBLIOGRAPHY. Diguet 1908; Hickey 1958; Lafont 1955, 1959, 1962b; Lunet de Lajonquière 1906; Maspéro 1929-30; NNCDT 1959.

WHITE TAI

Synonyms. *Tai Khao, Thai Trang*

ORIENTATION. **Identification.** Lafont (1962b) notes that Diguet and Maspéro do not consider the White Tai an ethnic group separate from the Black Tai. Lafont believes that they are separate, and feels furthermore that Maspéro failed to realize that the Vietnamese use the term Tho to indicate all Tai groups east of the Red river, and that he therefore concluded that the White Tai and Tho should properly be considered one group. A recent North Vietnamese source refers to the White Tai by the Vietnamese designation Thai Trang (NNCDT 1959: 242). **Location.** There are major groupings along both banks of the Red river from the delta to the frontier of Yunnan, and along the Black river and its tributaries. There also are White Tai in the vicinity of Lai Chau, in the Na Ho area along the Phong Tho river, and in the areas of Muong Mo, Chieng Nua, Chieng Chan, Ban Pa Tan, and Muong So. [Roux and Tran 1954: 364-65.] **Linguistic affiliation.** Tai speakers. According to Silvestre (1918: 10), they have traditionally had their own script. The prevalent lingua franca in the Red river area is Vietnamese, while Chinese *kwan hoa* is used in the Black river area (Roux and Tran 1954: 364-65). *Kwan hoa,* also spelled *quan hoa* and *kouan-hoa,* simply means "Mandarin" in Chinese. More than likely it is a variation of southwestern Mandarin, a dialect of Sino-Tibetan spoken in a wide area including Yunnan and northern Kwangsi (cf. Hu et al. 1960: 97). **Demography.** Roux and Tran (1954: 365) report 18,000 White Tai in northern Vietnam. NNCDT (1959: 242) gives 344,628 as the combined total for White Tai and Black Tai. **History and cultural relations.** According to the family history of the Dieu or Deo of the Lai Chau area, one of their ancestors was of Cantonese origin—the chief of a group of Chinese raiders who settled in the area (Diguet 1908: 92).

SETTLEMENT PATTERN AND HOUSING. **Settlement pattern.** Settlements are very similar to those of the Black Tai. They are reported to be larger than those of the Tho, with 50 or more houses not unusual. [Abadie 1924: 69.] **Housing.** Houses resemble those of the Black Tai, and are constructed on piling. A platform extending from the front of the house is used as a work area, particularly for weaving and dyeing cloth, and also as a gathering place for family and friends. The interior is one large, undivided room unless there is more than one nuclear family residing in the house, in which case it is divided by bamboo partitions. [Abadie 1924: 69; Silvestre 1918: 10-13.]

ECONOMY. According to Abadie (1924: 64-65), White Tai agriculture is similar to that of the Tho. Wet rice is the staple, and with the exception of buckwheat (grown by the Tho and not by the White Tai), the crops cultivated are the same. Agricultural techniques also are similar. The White Tai cultivate betel and areca as well as poppies to produce opium for their own use. They also practice some swidden agriculture. In some areas they purchase vegetables from the neighboring Man (Yao) and Meo. **Agriculture and division of labor.** Agricultural activities are family-oriented. A household composed of a nuclear family may require the assistance of a related household, but most are extended families in which all members aid in the common agricultural activities. Men prepare

the fields, and women do the transplanting. Both men and women work at cutting and threshing at harvest time, and both sexes carry paddy to the granary. [Silvestre 1918: 19.] **Fishing and hunting.** Fish for food are taken with nets, traps, trained cormorants, and a poison produced from lime. Hunting is enjoyed as a sport. [Abadie 1924: 64-65; Diguet 1908: 69-70; Silvestre 1918: 23-28.] **Domestic animals.** The White Tai of Phong Tho raise horses, buffalo, cattle, chickens, ducks, pigeons, pigs, dogs, and cats (Silvestre 1918: 19-20). **Industrial arts.** Home industries include weaving, dyeing, alcohol production, and some sugar production from cane. Some families also process opium from their own crops of poppies. Village specialists are carpenters and joiners. [Abadie 1924: 70; Diguet 1908: 69-70; Silvestre 1918: 21-23.] **Trade.** Markets are held in the larger towns, but commerce is not highly developed (Roux and Tran 1954: 370). **Land tenure.** According to Abadie (1924: 71), the traditional land tenure system resembled that of the Black Tai—the *chau muong* held title to the land, which was periodically redistributed among the peasants for their use. Due to French influence this system has been changing, with an increase in private ownership. In the Red river area, repartitioning of land has died out, and some former local officials who were given use of land while they were in office have assumed permanent title to it. The practice continues of allotting abandoned or unused land to needy families in the villages. [Diguet 1908: 69-70; Roux and Tran 1954: 370.] In some areas, however, the tradition of redistributing land in the *muong* every three years is still observed. According to Silvestre (1918: 18), land is divided each year among the White Tai of Phong Tho in northern Vietnam. The White Tai of Muong So have two types of land: public land, title to which is held by the *chau muong* (redivided every three years according to the relative size of the family); and private land, to which families hold titles granted by the *chau muong* (Hickey 1956-58).

KIN GROUPS. **Descent.** Similar to Black Tai, i.e. patrilineal at least within the elite family lines. **Kin groups.** According to Maspéro (1929-30: 239), the same "great families" found among the Black Tai are also found among the White Tai. He describes them as exogamous clans organized along class lines. The Lo and Cam comprise the political elite, while the Vi, Kuan, Ka, Lu, and Non are commoner clans. Lafont (1953) is not in agreement with this statement. He contends that there is no family named Cam among the White Tai, and that in the Lai Chau area the White Tai *"familles patronymiques"* are the Deo (ruling family), Kwang, Mao, and Lo (sometimes called Lu). The White Tai of the Nghe An area are described as having phratries, with all clans grouped either in the Hun or Kwan phratry. Those in the Hun phratry are reported to have a special place of honor at White Tai rituals (Maspéro 1929-30: 240).

MARRIAGE AND FAMILY.

Mode. According to Maspéro (1929-30: 239), a boy may select a mate without his father's approval. Hickey (1956-58) found that in the Muong So area the boy's parents make the first overtures. Intermediaries called *mar po* or *ma su* negotiate the marriage agreement. The service period among the White Tai varies. Silvestre (1918: 30) reports a period of from seven to ten years; for the Muong So area Hickey (1956-58) found a three-year period. **Form.** Many wealthy White Tai have more than one wife. In 1913 the *ly truong* of Phong Tho had five wives (Abadie 1924: 71; Silvestre 1918: 32-33). **Inheritance.** The first-born son inherits the responsibilities and prerogatives of the father, and at his death receives the largest share of property, including the paternal house. All children, however, inherit some property from the father. In the absence of male offspring, it is necessary to either adopt or purchase a male child to carry on the family name and the cult of the ancestors. [Abadie 1924: 71; Silvestre 1918: 32-39.] **Divorce.** In the event of adultery by a wife, a husband may reject her. He meets with both his and her parents and the village leaders to announce the divorce in public (Silvestre 1918: 39).

SOCIOPOLITICAL ORGANIZATION.

The Deo family has remained the ruling family among the White Tai. The Vietnamese were reluctant to change the traditional political system, requiring only the acceptance of Vietnamese political nomenclature. The hereditary right of the Deo family to political leadership was respected. The French brought about some changes by appointing leaders from families other than the Deo. [Lunet de Lajonquière 1906: 179; Abadie 1924: 71.] According to Maspéro (1929-30: 239), the elite of the White Tai have personal relationships with the spirits of the soil. Each *chau muong* (chief of a *muong*) has a personal spirit of the soil which functions as the guardian spirit of the *muong*, symbolized by a wooden post called a *lak sua* or *lak xuon*. It is taboo to disturb the soil in which this post is placed, and each newly appointed *chau muong* tears up the post of his predecessor, replacing it with his own, according to Maspéro. Among the White Tai of Phu Qui in northern Vietnam, the post has lost its original significance, and has been replaced by a sacred tree to which sacrificial animals are tied during rituals honoring the spirit of the soil of the *muong*. Lafont disagrees with Maspéro's version of the *lak sua*. He maintains that traditionally, in the period when the White Tai had independent principalities, the founder of a dynasty within a *muong* domain installed a *lak muong*, symbolizing the spirit

of the soil of the principality, and that his successors respected the symbol. Only when there was a change in the ruling dynasty did the new rulers replace the old *lak muong* with a new one. In the modern period, however, with the *muong* no longer independent, and with no ruling dynastic families, the significance of the *lak muong* has changed. The *chau muong*, named by the administration for an indefinite period, installs a *lak muong* which does not symbolize his relationship with the *pi muong*—the spirit of the soil of the *muong*—but rather his delegated authority. When the *chau muong* is deposed, for whatever reason, his successor removes his *lak muong*, replacing it with a new one. According to Lafont, this symbolizes the destruction of the former political order and the acquisition of the territory in the name of the new authority. [Lafont 1953.] In Muong So (northern Vietnam), the *truong muong* is the chief of the *muong*, assisted by the *tao muong* and *tao tang*. The *tao ban* is the village headman (Hickey 1956-58). Among the White Tai of Phong Tho in northern Vietnam, there are 16 notables, ranking from *truong muong* to *quang di*. Each has well-defined responsibilities, and, according to Silvestre (1918: 17-18), members of the Deo family hold most of the more powerful positions.

RELIGION.

Religious beliefs and practices resemble closely those of the Black Tai. The *pi muong*, the spirit of the soil of the *muong*, is probably the most important spirit of the pantheon. [Silvestre 1918: 40-56.] **Practitioners.** The *mwo muong*, or sorcerers, play an important part in White Tai rituals. Their role is hereditary, and usually there is one for each group of villages. [Lafont 1953.] **Ceremonies.** *Lon ton*, the ritual to open the planting season, has the same significance and the same general form as the *long ton* of the Black Tai. Among the White Tai of Muong So, in the Red river area near the Chinese frontier, *pu ko di nen ban* and *pu ko lan het muong* (two types of spirits of the soil) are honored in the *lon ton* ritual. The *chau muong* (always a member of the Deo family) and the sorcerer officiate at this ritual, which takes place on a river bank. A buffalo is sacrificed, after which buffalo blood and river water are mixed and spread on the fields as an offering to the spirits of the soil. In the course of the ritual, the name of the *chau muong* must be invoked; as a member of the Deo family, his special relationship with the spirits of the soil is reiterated. A less elaborate ritual sacrifice is made after the harvest. *Kin pang* is the ritual gathering of medicinal plants and flowers by female healers dressed in special costumes with elaborate headdresses. The flowers are subsequently offered to the spirits. [Hickey 1956-58.] The Feast of Alcohol, held in September and lasting three days, is accompanied by much feasting and dancing. During the period, no one may enter or leave the village. The lunar new year is reported to be celebrated as it is among the Tho. [Abadie 1924: 72.] According to Abadie (1924: 72), the White Tai of the Red river area practice the cult of the ancestors with greater rigor than do the other White Tai. Only ancestors of the first and second ascending generations are honored in a cult, and when a girl marries, she brings a small altar to her husband's house to maintain her own ancestral cult (Silvestre 1918: 35). **Soul, death, and afterlife.** The White Tai bury their dead and maintain their tombs carefully. Funerals of the well-to-do are elaborate, with a large catafalque of carved wood. In the Muong So area, the daughters of the deceased prostrate themselves before the catafalque as it is passed over them (Hickey 1956-58). Abadie (1924: 70, 72) and Silvestre (1918: 37-39) report that graves or tombs are abandoned after the funeral.

BIBLIOGRAPHY. Abadie 1924; Diguet 1908; Hickey 1956-58; Hu et al. 1960; Lafont 1953, 1962b; Lunet de Lajonquière 1906; Maspéro 1929-30; NNCDT 1959; Roux and Tran 1954; Silvestre 1918.

RED TAI

Synonym. *Tai Deng*

ORIENTATION. **Identification.** Strictly speaking, the Red Tai or Tai Deng are the Tai-speaking inhabitants of the Muong Deng area in Thanh Hoa province of northern Vietnam. By extension, however, the term is used for other groups with similar language and customs in the same general area; thus the Tai of Lang Chanh, Quan Hoa, Ngoc Lac, and Nhan Song are all called Red Tai. The Red Tai are closely related to the Black Tai just to the north. The Tay (Tai) Jo, a distinguishable group of Tai speakers in Thanh Hoa province, have considerable contact with the Red Tai. [Robert 1941: 1-8.] **Location.** The main areas of concentration are in the highlands inland from Thanh Hoa town, near the Laos border. They are most numerous in the middle Nam Ma valley, along its right bank tributaries, and along the left bank tributaries of the Nam Xam. [Robert 1941: 1-8.] **Geography.** The Red Tai inhabit an upland region, less fertile and less easy to work agriculturally than the country of the Muong farther east in Thanh Hoa province. **Linguistic affiliation.** Tai speakers, their dialect resembling that of the Black Tai and the Tai of the Sam Neua area of Laos (the Tai Neua). **Demography.** Lafont (1962a: 386) reports some 15,000 Red Tai in Laos. **History and cultural relations.** The area has been inhabited by Tai speakers for a long time, and the migration and assimilation that has characterized the history of the region is still in progress. How long the Red Tai have been in their present location is difficult to say, but some of the old men say that they invaded from the west some 250 years ago. [Robequain 1929: 110.]

SETTLEMENT PATTERN AND HOUSING. **Settlement pattern.** The significant residential group is a hamlet of from two to ten houses placed in no particular pattern on flat or slightly sloping ground near the bottom of a cultivated valley. There are no communal houses and no distinctive structures. **Housing.** Houses are rectangular, thatched-roof, gable-end structures raised on piles. An altar to the ancestors is located just inside the main door. [Robert 1941: 10-15.]

ECONOMY. **Agriculture.** The staple is glutinous rice, cultivated wherever possible in permanent irrigated rice fields. Additional crops include maize, cotton, manioc, sweet potatoes, bananas, and taro. **Fishing and hunting.** Eleven kinds of fish are known and eaten. These are caught in the rivers and in the rice fields. Hunting also appears to be important as a source of food. Porcupines, squirrels, turtles, monkeys, rats, snails, and toads are eaten. **Gathering.** Sweet chestnuts, palm shoots, bamboo pods and shoots, wild banana roots, and latania palm fruit are all gathered and eaten. **Domestic animals.** Include buffalo, horses, some goats, chickens, and bees. **Food.** The ordinary diet consists mainly of rice with salt and vegetables; meat is consumed only at festivals or sacrifices or after a successful hunt. Only the well-to-do regularly have meat and spices along with their rice and vegetables. **Industrial arts.** The Red Tai engage in weaving and basketwork, but there is little or no work in ceramics or metal. **Trade.** Some trade is carried on with the Vietnamese, mainly in tung wood, areca, bamboo, and other jungle products in return for salt, cloth, and metal tools. **Division of labor.**

Men and boys	Women and girls
Do woodworking and carpentry	Harvest rice
Manage buffalo	Transplant rice
Cut wood	Raise cotton
Look after carts	Spin and weave
Sow rice	Carry water
Make baskets	Cook
Make nets	Gather firewood
Watch animals at pasture (small boys)	Gather edible roots and leaves
Look after bees	Fish with basket net
Fish with cast net	Dye cloth
Hunt	

Land tenure. There are three types of cultivable land: land privately owned by families, fief land, and common land. [Robert 1941: 17-20.]

KIN GROUPS. **Descent.** Patrilineal (Robert 1941: 39). **Kin groups.** According to Robert (1941: 39), the Red Tai are divided into patrilineal, exogamous *chao*. Currently there are nine such kin groups in the Lang Chanh area: Lo Kham, Kha Khun, Lu Ong, Vi, Loc, Pui, Khoang, Ngan, and Lu. There is some association of these groups with animals such as the snake and tiger. **Kin terminology.** Robert (1941: 129) gives the following Red Tai kin terms:

Fa	*po*
Mo	*me*
FaElSi	*pa oc*
FaYoSi	*kua*
FaElBr	*ung*
FaYoBr	*ao*
MoElSi	*pa*
MoYoSi	*na nhing*
MoElBr	*ung*
MoYoBr	*na chai*
PaElSibSo	*pi ai ho*
PaElSibDa	*pi u'o'i ho*
PaYoSibSo	*nang chai ho*
PaYoSibDa	*nang xao ho*

MARRIAGE AND FAMILY. **Mode.** A first-rank marriage is a long and involved process, carried out in its entirety only by the rich. Among noble families, the spouse is chosen by the head of the family. Among commoners, there is usually free personal choice, followed by the consent of the families. In a proper first-rank marriage, the proceedings are initiated by the young man, who uses the services of a go-between. The arrangements take several months, and involve a series of presentations from the young man's family to that of the girl. After the third presentation, the two are formally engaged and the families are said to be in alliance. Some time after this, and following two further presentations by the man, a small wedding ceremony is held. The total amount given by the man's family is considerable, running to several buffalo and bars of silver, as well as many smaller items. Only the final presentation at the time of the wedding is formally called a bride price. ● Alternative modes of marriage include abduction (with the consent of the girl and ultimately of her parents) and marriage by the adoption of the son-in-law. A man with no sons may acquire a son-in-law by offering his daughter in marriage, in which case the groom resides matrilocally with his parents-in-law. **Form.** Polygyny is allowed. Among the nobility a man may have up to four wives acquired through first-rank marriage. **Extension of incest taboos.** Marriage is exogamous with respect to the *chao*. Marriage between a noble woman and a commoner man is forbidden. There is no evidence of prescribed or preferred cross-cousin marriage. **Residence.** Except in the case of an adopted son-in-law, the newly-married couple live with the man's parents if the man is the first male of his generation to be married. If not, they live in a separate house near that of the man's parents. **Domestic unit.** A typical household group contains two grandparents, a married son with his wife and children, and some of this son's unmarried siblings. **Divorce.** Divorce is difficult in cases of a first-rank marriage, but in other cases it is a relatively easy matter. Concubinage occurs, and always requires a large presentation to the girl's family. [Robert 1941: 43-59.]

SOCIOPOLITICAL ORGANIZATION. The Red Tai country is divided into *muong* districts. At the head of each *muong* is the "lord," the *tao* (*chao*) *muong*. Under him are five junior nobles. These positions are hereditary in the male line. The over-all political organization is feudal. A *tao* hereditary nobility, centered on the *tao muong*, holds land and rights to corvée and taxes from commoners. The authority and responsibility of the *tao muong* are fixed by tradition. He gives frequent buffalo feasts, shared by all commoners who have worked on his houses and land. If the *tao muong's* sons or daughters have illicit sexual intercourse with commoners, the commoners are paid reparation. On the death of a *tao muong*, nobles must mourn for one year, commoners for three months. During the mourning period marriage and house construction are theoretically forbidden. ● Under the *tao muong* come the *tao pong*, who have direct suzerainty over two or three hamlets. The hamlet chief is the *quan ban*, assisted by the *cha ban*, both of whom are heads of families, usually old men. They are chosen by election in the hamlet. Their duties are to use their influence in disputes and to keep the *tao muong* informed of the state of affairs in their hamlets. ● Living among the Tay Jo, who are in close contact with the Red Tai, are members of the Cam family, the sociopolitical elite of the Black Tai. The Cam cremate deceased males, a practice unknown among other Tay Jo. [Robert 1941: 10ff.] **Warfare.** The Red Tai took their present territory by force of arms, but warfare has not been possible since the French penetrated the area. [Robert 1941: 90ff.]

RELIGION. **Supernaturals.** Red Tai religion is tied to an elaborate cosmology in which heaven is a magnified and more wonderful replica of the earth. This heaven is divided into districts, some of which are reserved for lepers and sufferers from scrofulous diseases. Another district is near heaven, but not of it: here there is no work, and an abundant supply of rice is brought in on the wind. Each *chao* [patrilineal surname group] on earth has its corresponding village in heaven. A capital city is reserved for the gods, *then*, who are arranged in a hierarchical order according to their authority: a supreme god, *po then kham* (lit., golden father god), who presides over the capital city and over all the other gods; a creator of men, animals, and all things; an intermediary god between the higher gods and the lower spirits; and a distributor of the winds. Below this hierarchy of gods are innumerable spirits: nature spirits, spirits of the river, ancestor spirits, and the souls of dead sorcerers who have become sorcerers' familiars. It is these lower spirits, who can affect the lives of men, who must be propitiated. **Practitioners.** Include female diviners, *me juong,* and stick diviners, *mo mo.* A male *kun du xay* divines the causes of sickness by scrutinizing eggs. The *mo xo* propitiates the spirits with prayers and offerings. The sorcerer, *me mot,* is supposed to be born with a placenta around his neck. He studies under a practicing sorcerer for two years and may become a powerful figure within the community. There are also *mo mun,* or curers. **Ceremonies.** Major ceremonies are held every year to thank the gods for abundance. Other ritual occasions center around asking for rain, starting to build a house, planting rice, or embarking on a fishing expedition. The spirits are also invoked ritually in curing, divining, augury, black magic, and in the creation of love potions. **Soul, death, and afterlife.** The Red Tai doctrine concerning the afterlife rests on a division between the souls of the head and the souls of the body. Each individual has many souls. Those from his body go to the cemetery at his death, and stay there. Those from his head go to heaven. Three days after death these spirits become ancestors and are honored at the ancestor altar in each house. [Robert 1941: 61-77.]

BIBLIOGRAPHY. Lafont 1962a; Robequain 1929; Robert 1941.

NEUA

Synonyms. *Nua, Nüa*

ORIENTATION. **Identification and location.** Neua is a lowlander term distinguishing the original Tai-speaking population of the Hua Phan (Sam Neua) area of northeastern Laos. It may also be used for those Sam Neua upland Tai who have emigrated to other parts of Laos, e.g. those in the vicinity of Vientiane and Luang Prabang (Iwata 1961a). According to Lafont (1962a: 390), Tai Neua are found in the uplands of Tonkin and also in Laos in the Hua Phan, Xieng Khouang, Haut Mekong, and Phong Saly areas. **Linguistic affiliation.** Tai. Dialect apparently influenced by Vietnamese. **Demography.** Lafont (1962a: 390) records 25,000 Neua in the Hua Phan, 10,000 in Xieng Khouang, and 3,500 in Haut Mekong. **History and cultural relations.** The Neua of Hua Phan are Buddhists, growing both wet and dry rice. This is the area of an old Tai confederacy of *muong,* the Hua

Phan Thang Hok or "Six Muong of One Thousand Registry Each." In the early twentieth century, these *muong,* each administered by a hereditary prince assisted by a council of ministers, were tributary to Luang Prabang. Peasant farmers had usufruct rights to land in return for labor and taxes paid to the various *chao muong.* [Seidenfaden 1958: 89-90; Bourlet 1906: 521-28.]

BIBLIOGRAPHY. Bourlet 1906; Iwata 1961a; Lafont 1962a; Seidenfaden 1958.

PHUAN

ORIENTATION. **Identification and location.** Phuan is a lowlander term distinguishing the Tai-speaking population of the former principality of Xieng Khouang in northern Laos (Seidenfaden 1958: 89-90). The term may also be used locally to distinguish those upland Tai from Muong Phuan in Xieng Khouang province who have migrated in the last few centuries westward to the vicinity of Vientiane and Luang Prabang. In some cases these emigrants still maintain kinship ties with their places of origin. [Iwata 1961a.] **Linguistic affiliation.** Tai.

BIBLIOGRAPHY. Iwata 1961a; Seidenfaden 1958.

PHUTHAI

Synonym. *Puthai*

ORIENTATION. **Identification and location.** Phuthai, from Phu, meaning "people," is a lowlander term for various Tai-speaking populations in northeastern Laos. More specifically, the term is used by some writers (cf. Seidenfaden 1958) as a generic term for upland Tai who have migrated out of the area of the Hua Phan in northeastern Laos and the Sip Song Chau Tai in northwestern Tonkin and are today found in pockets throughout northern Laos, and for communities of Tai speakers, also upland Tai emigrants, in extreme northeastern Thailand who are only recently removed from Laos—people who were, or who still maintain ties with, the upland Tai; e.g. the White Tai and Black Tai. Those in the Udon–Roi Et area are sometimes called Lao Khao (Kao), a reference to the White Tai element. The Phuthai in Thailand, estimated at 70,000 to 100,000, usually go through an intermediate stage of living among the Laotian Tai in the lowlands of Laos before migrating on beyond the Mekong. [Seidenfaden 1958: 109-13.] Iwata (1961a: 8) adds that the Laotian Tai sometimes use the term Phuthai to include Black Tai and Red Tai. **Linguistic affiliation.** Tai.

BIBLIOGRAPHY. Iwata 1961a; Seidenfaden 1958.

EASTERN GROUPS

CHUNG-CHIA

Synonyms. *Dioi, I-chia, I-jen, Jui, Pu-yi, Yoi*

ORIENTATION. **Identification.** The term Chung-chia is used by the Chinese to refer to Tai speakers centering in Kweichow province. They are also known by the terms Jui, Yoi, I-chia, I-jen, and Pu-yi. Dioi, often encountered in the Western language literature, is a corruption of Jui or Yoi. The term Pu-yi is the official designation used by the Chinese People's Republic. Jui, 'Jui, and 'Joi are regional dialectal variations of terms used by the people themselves to refer to their own language (and presumably to themselves as speakers of the language). As Dodd (1923: 95) points out, Tai speakers in eastern Yunnan, Kwangsi, Kweichow, and Kwangtung do not refer to themselves as Tai, as do the Lü, Shans, Siamese, and Lao. [Li 1943; 1957; 1959.] The Trung-cha of northern Tonkin, along the border with China, are presumably related to or derived from the Chung-chia of Kwei-chow: according to Diguet (1908: 100), the Trung-cha originated in Kweichow, migrating through Kwangsi into northern Tonkin in the tenth century. **Location.** Mainly in western and southwestern Kwei-chow, reaching into central Kweichow around Kwei-yang city. A few thousand spill over into Yunnan. **Linguistic affiliation.** Classed with northern Tai dialects by Li. There are some minor dialect differences. They have had no written language of their own, using Chinese where necessary. **Demography.** Population estimates vary: Bruk (1960: 25) gives 1,250,000; Wiens (1954: 278-79), using 1952 data, gives 1,600,000; deBeauclair (1956: 264-65) gives 2,000,000. Wu and Ch'en (1942: 4) estimate that 40 per cent of the total Kweichow population is non-Han. The most numerous of these non-Han peoples are the Chung-chia, followed closely by Miao speakers. **Cultural relations.** Heavily sinicized. Majority can speak Chinese. In dress and physical appearance they can scarcely be distinguished from Chinese peasants, although in some places the women still wear distinctive dress. Many Chung-chia live in towns, where they engage in trade and are reckoned as Chinese. They are recognized as a nationality group by the Chinese Communists, who have created a Pu-yi Autonomous Chou in southern Kweichow province. Almost everywhere in Kweichow the Chung-chia are in close contact with Miao speakers. They tend to look down on the Miao, regarding themselves as more closely related to the Chinese than are the Miao. In the area of Kweiyang and other large towns the Chung-chia may be in active economic competition with the Miao.

SETTLEMENT PATTERN AND HOUSING. **Settlement pattern.** Villages are characteristically located away from the main roads, and are enclosed by stone walls or bamboo stockades. The maximum size of villages in rural areas is about 100 families, or 500 people (Betts 1899: 87). In more urban areas, as around Kweiyang, villages may contain as many as 200 families (Clarke 1911: 95). Bronze drums are found in many Chung-chia villages. They are beaten on festive occasions and are the property of the village as a whole (deBeauclair 1960: 152). **Housing.** House type varies. Houses of stone and mortar built directly on the ground seem to predominate. However, houses on piles and houses built on a slope with the projecting portion supported on piles are reported (Seidenfaden 1958: 57). Lin (1940: 292), citing an 1899 source, also records houses on piles among the Chung-chia. Such dwellings were divided within, and the space beneath the house used as a cattle pen.

ECONOMY. Settled agriculturists, the staple crop being rice grown in irrigated fields. Fields are plowed with the help of buffalo. Other domestic animals are oxen, ponies, pigs, and poultry. Bananas, melons, gourds, and other fruits and vegetables are grown in gardens. Agricultural methods, tools, and techniques are similar to those of the Han Chinese. The Chung-chia understand both *ikat* and *plangi* techniques of resist dyeing (deBeauclair 1960: 148).

KIN GROUPS. The Chung-chia have apparently taken over the Chinese system of patrilineal descent (surname) groups. Betts (1899: 89) mentions villages of up to 100 families all of the same surname. **Kin terminology.** The essentially bilateral kinship system characteristic of other Tai-speaking groups is reported also for the Chung-chia by Benedict (1943: 169-72), using data of about the turn of the century:

Fa	*po*
Mo	*me*
FaElBr, MoElBr	*po long*
FaElSi, MoElSi	*me pa*
FaYoBr	*po au*
MoYoSi	*me na*
MoYoBr	*po na*
ElBr, ElSi	*pi* (plus suffixed sex modifier)
YoBr, YoSi	*nuang* (plus suffixed sex modifier)
Cousins	Sibling terms, based on relative age of kin through whom relationship is traced, e.g. parents' older brother's child is *pi*

MARRIAGE AND FAMILY. Marriage is preceded by a period of courtship, and young people are given some freedom in the selection of marriage partners. At markets and festival occasions young people may engage in group antiphonal singing. Love songs, of an interrogative and responsive pattern, are popular.

Once a couple have decided on marriage, the boy informs his parents, who then engage a go-between to negotiate the bride price (paid in silver). Lin (1940: 292), citing data from about 1840, records the payment of bride price in cattle. As among the Miao in the same area, a bride returns to her parents' house after marriage and remains there until her first child is born, after which she goes to live permanently with her husband. Around Kweiyang and Anshun cities the Chung-chia are more like the Chinese with respect to courtship and marriage. [Betts 1899: 88 ff.; Wu and Ch'en 1942: 195-99.]

SOCIOPOLITICAL ORGANIZATION. Seidenfaden (1958: 59) says that until about the turn of the century, the Chung-chia were still governed by their own feudal chiefs. If they ever formed small semifeudal principalities on the order of those among the Mekong river Tai, the long period of domination and acculturation under the Han Chinese has by now removed all evidence of their existence. ● The Chung-chia have for some time been incorporated into the Chinese administrative system, with villages and districts governed like those of rural Chinese. Near *hsien* cities, village headmen are directly responsible to local Chinese magistrates. In areas farther removed, there are intermediate Chung-chia *t'u-ssu* officials between groups of villages and the nearest Chinese magistrate (Betts 1899: 87; Clarke 1911: 109). These hereditary *t'u-ssu* positions, created in Ming dynasty times, may have been founded on the basis of a native Tai aristocracy or nobility similar to that found farther west today. Under the Chinese Communists, former administrative arrangements have been altered with the creation of an autonomous nationality area in southern Kweichow.

RELIGION. The Theravada Buddhism of the Mekong river Tai is not found among the Chung-chia. Their religion is best described as a mixture of Taoism and animism (Seidenfaden 1958: 57 ff.). The paraphernalia and techniques of native priests resemble those of Taoist priests among the Chinese (Clarke 1911: 98). Animistic beliefs and practices, including the propitiation of ancestral spirits, appear to predominate. Ancestral altars are maintained in the home; food offerings are left at the foot of certain trees and in small shrines outside the village (Betts 1899: 95). **Soul, death, and afterlife.** Death is followed by a period of mourning during which the corpse, fully clothed, lies in a wooden coffin. The day of burial is chosen by the native priest. The latter conducts an "opening-the-way" ceremony for the soul of the deceased, chanting from a liturgical book in corrupt Chinese. A buffalo, tethered to a stake outside the village gates, is slaughtered by repeated stabs of a knife after all have paraded around the animal. To the accompaniment of trumpets and drums, the priest leads a procession to the grave, which has been selected by geomancy. Paper money and incense are burned. Three years after burial the body is disinterred and the bones placed in an earthen jar for reburial. [Ch'en 1942.]

BIBLIOGRAPHY. DeBeauclair 1956, 1960; Benedict 1943; Betts 1899; Bruk 1960; Ch'en 1942; Clarke 1911; Diguet 1908; Dodd 1923; Li 1943, 1957, 1959; Lin 1940; Seidenfaden 1958; Wiens 1954; Wu and Ch'en 1942.

CHUANG

Synonyms. *Tho, T'u, T'u-jen*

ORIENTATION. **Identification and location.** The term Chuang generally refers to a heavily sinicized Tai-speaking population centering in Kwangsi province. [Bruk (1960: 26) specifically names the Molao and Maonam, two small Tai-speaking populations located in the Chuang area, northwest of the city of Liuchow in northern Kwangsi.] These people are for the most part plains dwellers practicing wet-rice agriculture side by side with the Chinese, or, where sufficient bottom land is not available, growing rice and other crops on terraced hillsides. Speaking Chinese as well as Tai, their way of life is in many respects indistinguishable from that of the Han Chinese peasantry. ● Used in the above sense, the term Chuang is on a level with Pai-i, a Chinese term for similarly circumstanced Tai speakers farther west in Yunnan. T'u or T'u-jen, meaning "soil" or "people of the soil," is sometimes used in a generic sense for the Chuang Tai of Kwangsi (Wiens 1954: 35). The term is presumably cognate with Tho, the literary Vietnamese term for "soil," used in a somewhat similar sense for the Tai of northern Tonkin. The T'u or Tai (Chuang) of Kwangsi are sometimes, by extension, called Tho (Seidenfaden 1958: 64-65). Tho, T'u, and Chuang are very likely local generic terms referring to an originally undifferentiated Tai population within the area of Kwangsi–Kwangtung–Tonkin. Lacking the literate Buddhist traditions of the Tai farther west and south, and apparently lacking also the patterns of politico-military organization and social stratification characteristic of these other Tai peoples, they have more easily and much earlier succumbed to Chinese and Vietnamese acculturative forces. **Linguistic affiliation.** The Chuang speak what Li (1959) has called Northern Tai dialects. **Demography.** Bruk (1960: 25) reports slightly over 7,000,000. **History and cultural relations.** The Chinese literature on the Chuang Tai of Lingnan (Kwangsi–Kwangtung) appears to consist largely of documentary studies of an historical nature (e.g. Hsü 1939). However, scattered references to such traits as wet-rice agriculture, cotton cloth manufacture, tattooing, betel chewing, pile dwellings, and polygyny point to Tai affiliations. De-Beauclair (1960: 137) observed Chuang villages in southern Kweichow in 1947. She reports the following: villages located in river valleys; reliance on wet (glutinous) rice agriculture with the use of the buffalo; houses on piles with wide verandas and interiors divided into two or three rooms; and the use of batik technique. She adds that the literature records spring festivals with sexual freedom and the use of *ku* (insect) poison.

BIBLIOGRAPHY. DeBeauclair 1960; Bruk 1960; Hsü 1939; Li 1959; Seidenfaden 1958; Wiens 1954.

TUNG-CHIA

Synonyms. *Kam, Nin Kam, Tung, Tung-jen*

ORIENTATION. **Identification.** The Chinese term is Tung-chia or Tung-jen. They call themselves Nin Kam (deBeauclair 1960: 172), and are sometimes known locally as Kam (Li 1943). **Location.** Mostly in southeastern Kweichow but also in neighboring parts of Hunan and Kwangsi. This limited territory is, according to Bruk (1960: 26), occupied by the Tung as an unbroken mass. **Linguistic affiliation.** Classed by Li as belonging to a Kam–Sui dialect group, consisting of Kam, Sui (Shui), Mak, and T'en—all located in the area of southeastern Kweichow and northern Kwangsi. Although related to modern Tai dialects such as Dioi (Chung-chia), Tho, and Siamese, the Kam–Sui dialects represent an early separation from the main stream of Tai linguistic development. [Li 1943.] **Demography.** Population estimates range from 200,000 (deBeauclair 1960: 137) to 700,000 (Bruk 1960: 25). **Cultural relations.** The Tung have been for a long time in direct contact with Han Chinese, particularly in the larger towns. Their contacts with other groups are mainly with the He and Sheng Miao of southeastern Kweichow and the Chuang (Tai) of northern Kwangsi. Wu and Ch'en (1942: 190) state that although the Tung are basically Tai, many of their customs are borrowed from the He Miao.

SETTLEMENT PATTERN AND HOUSING. The house is characteristically raised on posts or piles above the ground (deBeauclair 1960: 137). Villages are located near water if possible. A unique structure is the so-called drum tower. These towers, of wood with tiled roofs, may reach 100 feet in height. The ground floor space serves as a combination village meeting hall and men's house. A wooden drum, suspended from the roof, is beaten in times of emergency and as a preliminary to village meetings. During the period between planting and harvesting, when farmwork is light, villagers gather at the drum tower, often

inviting young people from neighboring villages. On these occasions the two sexes may sing antiphonally throughout the night. The towers are said to be old in Tung culture, but there is relatively little mention of them in the historical literature. [Wu and Ch'en 1942: 190 ff.; deBeauclair 1960: 173-77.]

ECONOMY. Mainly valley dwellers, cultivating irrigated glutinous rice and also cotton. The Tung are excellent hunters of birds, using both snare and liming techniques. They are also expert fish breeders, and construct special ponds for the purpose. The women weave cotton cloth, and older sources mention silkworm culture and the spinning and weaving of silk. The Tung have the reed organ, *lu-sheng,* and a variety of string instruments. [Cf. deBeauclair 1960: 137, 144, 149, 172.]

KIN GROUPS. According to deBeauclair (1960: 184), the Tung have patrilineal surname groups which they have adopted from the Chinese.

MARRIAGE AND FAMILY. Among the linguistically related Sui (Shui), also resident in southeastern Kweichow, marriages are contracted entirely by parents. Unmarried girls are watched closely by elder male relatives, and young people are denied the freedom in the choice of a partner that is found among some other Tai-speaking groups in the same area. A young girl spends much time in sewing and embroidery to make the fine trousseau that will help establish her family's social status at her marriage. Marriages are negotiated by a go-between, and the marriage ceremony itself is marked by an exchange of gifts between the two families; the groom's family contributes a sum of money proportional to the dowry (quilts, clothing, and cattle) presented by the bride's family. Following a brief period of alternating residence, the girl goes to live permanently with her husband. [Wu and Ch'en 1942: 77 ff.]

SOCIOPOLITICAL ORGANIZATION. The Tung, like neighboring non-Han minorities, have been incorporated into the Chinese administrative system. The Communists have created a Tung and Miao Autonomous Chou in southeastern Kweichow.

RELIGION. Periodic water buffalo fights are a highly characteristic feature of Tung culture. These fights appear to have some religious significance in the sense of assuring good crops, but in many respects they seem to be a spectator sport, purely for amusement. Although fights between male buffalo are held also by the Miao in Kweichow, this spectacle has reached its most elaborate form among the Tung, who expend much care in breeding good fighting animals. Neighboring villages compete in these affairs, which are held every spring. A buffalo fight is also the occasion for a bazaar, and may be attended by several thousand people. Defeated animals are slaughtered and eaten at a large feast. Fights appear to be sponsored by villages rather than individual families—the latter being the case among some of the Kweichow Miao. [Cf. deBeauclair 1960: 178-79; Dodd 1923: 28-29.] The linguistically-related Sui (Shui) of southeastern Kweichow believe in a variety of supernaturals, many of them Chinese in origin. Family sacrifices, some of which are fixed annual occasions, are carried out in the home or at special shrines. Persons who are ill or families in distress or faced with disaster consult female shamans who have the power to summon a variety of spirits and to foretell and divine present and past events. They are thought to be possessed by a spirit or spirits, as indicated by signs of mental derangement and the ability to sing spirit songs. [Wu and Ch'en 1942: 77 ff.]

BIBLIOGRAPHY. DeBeauclair 1960; Bruk 1960; Dodd 1923; Li 1943; Wu and Ch'en 1942.

THO

Synonym. *Tay*

ORIENTATION. **Identification.** The literary Vietnamese term for "soil," *tho,* is sometimes used to designate one who lives in the remote country, and the term Tho is therefore also used to designate a relatively large Tai-speaking population in rural northern Vietnam. Lafont (1961), however, considers the designation Tho a Vietnamese term for the Tai groups east of the Red river, and contends that it includes some White Tai and Black Tai. Claiming that Tho is a pejorative term, a recent North Vietnamese source refers to them as Tay (NNCDT 1959: 37). **Location.** To the north and northeast of the Red river delta, with the densest groupings in the Clear river area and in the vicinity of Cao Bang. There are Tho settlements throughout the vicinity of Lang Son, and along the frontier of the Chinese province of Kwangsi. [Hickey 1958: 93.] **Geography.** Gourou (1936a: 25) refers to the area above the Red river delta as the "middle region," physiographically a karst area of near-level plains broken by precipitous limestone hills. It is relatively accessible to the Red river delta. **Linguistic affiliation.** The Tho are Tai speakers. Those in the eastern provinces of Lang Son, Cao Bang, Thai Nguyen, and Bac Kan have a script based on the Vietnamese *chu nom,* very closely related to Chinese calligraphy. [Nguyen 1940: i-iii.] **Demography.** One source (Morechand 1952: 354-61) reports the total Tai population of northern Vietnam to be 830,000, some 400,000 of whom are estimated to be Tho. A North Vietnamese source reports that the Tho (or Tay, as they call them) number 437,019.

[NNCDT 1959: 242.] **History and cultural relations.** The Tho are considered the most Vietnamized of the Tai groups in northern Vietnam. Within Tho society there is a sociopolitical elite known as the Tho-ti, descendants of Vietnamese mandarins sent into the Tho area in the seventeenth century to establish outposts of the central Vietnamese administration. [Hickey 1958: 32-33.]

SETTLEMENT PATTERN AND HOUSING. **Settlement pattern.** Some settlements are loose-knit agglomerations, either surrounded by rice fields or strung along river banks. Others are more compact and enclosed by a mud wall or hedge growth. These latter are frequently found near the Chinese frontier, where raids by river pirates, bandits, and marauding armies require protection. Settlements vary in size, depending on the amount of arable land available. Walled market towns average 50 or more farmsteads. The position of buildings is in many cases determined by geomancy. Every village has a special place for the house of the headman. The Tho farmstead includes a kitchen garden and usually a small fruit grove. [Hickey 1958: 96.] **Housing.** The traditional Tho house is constructed on piling, with notable exceptions in settlements located near the Vietnamese urban centers of Cao Bang or Lang Son. In pile dwellings, the area under the house is used as a stable and storage area. Each house also has a veranda which serves both as a gathering place for family and friends and a work area where cloth is dyed and woven, and tools, traps, and weapons are repaired. With the exception of those of the well-to-do, who favor walls of wood planks, Tho houses have walls of split bamboo which are attached to the log frame supporting the thatched roofs. The interior of the house is divided into several rooms by split-bamboo partitions. A large room at the entrance is a gathering place for the family and a reception room for visitors as well as being a common sleeping room for unmarried males. There are separate sleeping quarters for the head of the family and his wife and their eldest son and his wife. Unmarried females share a room, and the kitchen is located in one of the small rear rooms of the house. The floors are covered with woven mats. Personal and family property is stored in whatever space is available. Maize and seeds are stored in the upper parts of the house to keep them dry. Paddy is stored in a separate granary, a small structure built on piling and located near the house. [Hickey 1958: 96.]

ECONOMY. The economy is based on rice agriculture. Varieties of glutinous and nonglutinous rice are cultivated in paddy fields, some of which are terraced, and upland rice is cultivated by the swidden method. Hunting and fishing are done more for sport than to supplement the food supply. Cottage industry is important. The Tho also engage in market commerce—markets rotate from village to village within a geographical area according to a patterned cycle. **Agriculture.** In the area immediately north of the delta of the Red river, there is sufficient bottom land close to sources of water to maintain fairly extensive paddy fields. When possible, sloping land on the hills and lower areas of the karst formations are graded into wide terraces. At higher elevations, where slopes are steeper, the Tho resort to shifting agriculture. In general, the cultivation cycle is as follows: during the fourth lunar month, after the first rains, the seed beds are plowed, fertilized with animal manure, and seeded; the seed beds are tended during the fifth lunar month, and when the rains have moistened the fields sufficiently they are plowed and the seedlings transplanted; transplanting continues during the sixth lunar month, and the fields are weeded and irrigated if necessary; the first buds appear during the seventh month, and during this and the succeeding month, weeding and irrigation continue; harvesting begins during the ninth lunar month. Bottom-land paddy fields are irrigated by rainfall and water from nearby streams and rivers carried to the fields by small channels. For lifting water to a higher level, the Tho employ a large water wheel with bamboo containers on the outer rim. In areas where the water supply is sufficient, there usually is a second rice crop. The Tho plow is somewhat larger than that of the Vietnamese. Hoes, harrows, square and round spades, rakes, sickles, winnowing machines, and various types of cutting instruments, including a special knife for cutting glutinous rice, are used, as well as sieves, scrapers, flails for husking paddy, mortars, and pestles operated both by water power and by hand. [Abadie 1924: 41; Diguet 1908: 57; Hickey 1958: 100-01.] Maize and buckwheat are cultivated by the shifting method in fields located near the paddy fields and along the river banks. Watercress is planted along the edge of the paddy fields. Sugar cane, mulberry trees, manioc, and betel are cultivated in small plots. Kitchen gardens contain sweet potatoes, tomatoes, string beans, eggplant, lettuce, and a variety of other green vegetables, as well as peppers and ginger. Industrial crops include tobacco, cotton, indigo, and in some areas poppies for the production of opium. The French introduced anise, turpentine trees, and colza. [Abadie 1924: 41-42.] **Fishing and hunting.** Fishing is considered a leisure-time activity. Hunts are organized to track wild beasts causing damage to fields and gardens. Some small game and wild fowl are hunted to provide variations in the diet. The Tho make their own weapons—crossbows for the most part, although some make firearms. [Hickey 1958: 103.] **Domestic animals.** Cattle and buffalo serve as draft animals, and are occasionally used for sacrifices. The Tho are celebrated horse breeders. They sell horses to neighboring groups, as well as

using them for transport. They also raise pigs, chickens, ducks, and goats for food. Sheep reportedly are raised in a few areas. [Abadie 1924: 40.] **Industrial arts.** Cottage industry includes weaving and dyeing (by the women), basketry (by the men), and the husking and grinding of paddy, maize, and buckwheat. Sugar production as well as extraction of colza oil and turpentine are carried out by some families, and many families produce rice and maize alcohol. Poppies are cultivated for opium production, and salt is mined in some areas. A number of villages specialize in pottery, and the rough paper used in cult rituals is prepared in a few villages. In most settlements there is at least one iron worker, carpenter, and joiner. [Abadie 1924: 40-45; Hickey 1958: 103-04; Diguet 1908: 60.] **Trade.** Aniseed, turpentine, and colza oil are sold to visiting Chinese and Vietnamese merchants. Vietnamese horse dealers also visit the Tho areas to purchase horses from individual farmers. Salt from the marine salt areas of the Red river delta is sold, and the Tho purchase paper from Vietnamese merchants. Much of the trade occurs in the markets held in different villages in a fixed cycle. Vietnamese and Chinese merchants sell manufactured goods to the Tho farmers, who usually pay in kind. Well-to-do Tho usually retain the services of Vietnamese carpenters and joiners for house construction. [Hickey 1958: 104-05.] **Land tenure.** Swidden fields are considered a family usufruct; other fields are family property. Vietnamese civil codes require each village to have communal land, but most Tho villages have failed to conform to this requirement. The only exceptions are some villages near urban centers where the Vietnamese constitute the majority population. [Hickey 1958: 99.]

KIN GROUPS. **Descent.** Descent is patrilineal. Terminologically, with the exception of a common term for parents' older sisters, there is a complete bifurcation of kin according to male or female line. Age-grading is carried out on both sides of the family and with both sexes. **Kin groups.** The *tinh* is the name-sib, an exogamous group that includes all those with the same family name. Exogamy appears to be the only function of the *tinh*. The *choc* is the patrilineal common descent group which includes kin related to a common male ancestor in the fourth ascending generation. The eldest male of the eldest line is the *truong toc* (a Vietnamese term), or head of the *choc*. The *truong toc* is responsible for performing cult rituals honoring the common ancestor, and is charged with the upkeep of the tomb of the common ancestor. He also keeps the genealogy book of the *choc*, and holds title to *choc* land. The *choc*, rather than the *tinh*, functions as the important corporate group; it is a social institution in which the members participate in common activities such as the rituals and feasting associated with the cult of the ancestors. [Hickey 1958: 122.] **Kin terminology.** Hickey (1958) records the following kin terms:

Fa	*po thau, po ooc*
Mo	*me thau, me ooc*
FaElBr	*po bac, po gie*
MoElBr	*po khu bac, po lung*
MoElSi	*me pa*
FaElSi	*me co*
FaYoBr	*po ao, po chu*
MoYoBr	*po khu*
FaYoSi	*me a*
MoYoSi	*me na*
ElBr	*pi chai, pi bao*
ElSi	*pi nhing, pi sao*
YoBr	*nong chai, nong ao*
YoSi	*nong nhing, nong sao*
Older male cousin	*pi chai*
Older female cousin	*pi nhing*
Younger male cousin	*nong chai*
Younger female cousin	*nong nhing*

MARRIAGE AND FAMILY. Mode. Either the father selects mates for his sons or they make their own choices with paternal approval. Well-to-do families consult genealogy books to ascertain that the couple are not related. Once arrangements are made, the marriage follows closely. The high-ranking Tho-ti have marriage restrictions not applicable to other Tho. Whereas Tho-ti men are free to marry non-Tho-ti women, who then assume Tho-ti status, Tho-ti women cannot marry outside their own group within the *chau* (district). If they marry non-Tho-ti men from another *chau*, their children do not have the rank of Tho-ti. A bride price is paid on the day of the marriage. If the groom is too poor to pay one, he may do service for his future parents-in-law for a specified period. The Tho marriage ritual is similar to that of the Vietnamese. The groom and his party go to the bride's house, where the bridal couple kowtow before her ancestral altars. After a meal, they return to the groom's house to kowtow before his ancestral altars. They also kowtow before the assembled kin, and there is a feast. **Form.** Polygyny is common among the well-to-do. **Residence.** Patrilocal for the eldest son, who will inherit the bulk of family property and the role of family head. Residence for other sons is neolocal, although they are expected to establish their households near the paternal house. **Inheritance.** On the death of the father, the sons divide the inheritance, the eldest son receiving the largest share. Daughters may inherit some movable goods or animals, but never land. Married sons already established in their own households usually receive the use of some family land until the death of the father, when they receive title. Land passed to the eldest son is "family land," and while

it is alienable, it is rarely sold. To sell it would be considered an affront to the ancestors. If there are no sons, it is common practice for the father to select a husband for one of the daughters with the specific understanding that he adopt the name and ancestors of his wife's family. As a male member of the family, he is qualified to succeed the father as head of the family. If a couple is childless in their later years, they usually adopt one of the husband's nephews as a son. The last resort is to adopt an unrelated male child. **Divorce.** Rare among the Tho, but should it occur, the woman returns to her paternal house. [Hickey 1958: 123-26; Lunet de Lajonquière 1906: 155-56.]

SOCIOPOLITICAL ORGANIZATION. In the fifteenth and sixteenth centuries, when the Vietnamese emperors of the Le dynasty were extending political control over northern Vietnam, they sent mandarins into the Tho area with absolute authority to administer the local groups. These took Tho wives, and, unlike other mandarins in the Vietnamese system, they passed on their official prerogatives to their sons. As a result, a Tho-Vietnamese sociopolitical elite known as the Tho-ti emerged. In addition to their inherited political prerogatives and their position as the social elite, the Tho-ti have retained the exclusive right of officiating at the rituals honoring the spirit of the soil (just as Lo and Cam families have done among the Black Tai). The French, pursuing a policy of weakening the power of traditional leaders among the ethnic groups of northern Indochina, made all Tho political offices appointive. As a result, non-Tho-ti have assumed more political authority, although the Tho-ti have retained their place as the social elite. [Hickey 1958: 106-07.] ● The *ban*, usually only six or seven households, is classified administratively as a hamlet, and is the smallest unit in the Tho political system. Political authority is vested in a council of male heads of families, which elects the *po ban*, or headman. The *xa* is composed of several *ban*, and is classified administratively as a village or commune. The *cai thon* is the council of all the *po ban* in the *xa*, which elects the *ly truong* or *xa truong*, the headman of the commune. The headman and the council are responsible for communal affairs, and the former is the keeper of the communal seal with which all public documents are stamped. The council meets periodically at the house of the headman to discuss communal problems and to resolve any difficulties or disputes brought to their attention by residents of the *xa*. The *tong*, or canton, represents the level above the *xa* in the French administrative system. The *chang tong* is the administrative head of this unit, appointed by the central government. His assistants are the *pho tong* and the *tong doan*. Several *tong* form a *chau*, supervised by an appointed *quan chau* or *tri chau*. The *tinh,* or province, is the highest Tho administrative unit. The *tuan phu* or *tong doc* is the province chief. In most provinces the *tuan phu* is Vietnamese, although the majority of his subordinates are Tho. [Hickey 1958: 107-09.]

RELIGION. **Major religions.** Organized Mahayana Buddhism is found only among the Tho-ti. They construct pagodas, maintain and use them, and bring in Vietnamese monks to officiate at the periodic rituals (Hickey 1958: 114). Other Tho have ill-defined beliefs in Buddhist deities such as Quang Am (Kwan Yin) and Muc Lien, and they refer to Buddha as Put (Diguet 1908: 39; Abadie 1924: 54). There are numerous Confucianist shrines in the Tho area, and each spring and fall notables officiate at rituals honoring Confucius. Tho sorcerers use some Taoist incantations in their rituals. [Diguet 1908: 39.] **Supernaturals.** *Pi* is a generic term for a wide variety of spirits, including the errant spirits of humans and animals that wander in search of cult offerings. *Pi mit* are spirits of people who have died violently; *pi mang* are spirits of those who have taken false oaths before death; and *pi xan* are spirits of men who have died in battle. The spirits of chickens, *pi cay,* are particularly malevolent. *Pi* associated with nature are objects of cult rituals aimed at bringing about favorable weather and soil fertility. The most powerful *pi* in the Tho pantheon are the *tho cong* or *tho than,* the spirits of the soil. Each village maintains a shrine to the spirit of the soil as a guardian spirit. [Hickey 1958: 111; Lunet de Lajonquière 1906: 129-33.] **Practitioners.** Male and female sorcerers, *mo ten,* are considered predestined for their roles, and therefore receive no formal training. The *mo ten* lay claim to spirits with whom they have special relationships and from whom they derive their occult powers. Other Tho sorcerers receive formal training for their hereditary roles, and are ranked according to their occult powers. The lowest rank is *p'u put. P'u giang* (males) and *me put* (females) rank slightly higher than the *p'u put.* The highest rank is *p'u tao,* within which group there are specializations, e.g. some are skilled at geomancy while others are active in arranging marriages. Most *p'u tao* have roles in public rituals, particularly those honoring the spirit of the soil. [Hickey 1958: 111-12.] **Ceremonies.** The Tho cult of the ancestors closely resembles its Vietnamese counterpart in form and content. Ancestral altars are located in the paternal house, and as each son establishes his own household, he is expected to maintain his own altar. Tho altars tend to be simpler than those of the Vietnamese. They generally consist of tablets containing the names of ancestors up to the fourth ascending generation, incense burners, offering dishes, and candles. Rituals honoring the ancestors are held during *king nen* or *kin chieng,* the Tho lunar new year. On the first day of the new year, rituals and feasting take place at the house of the head of the family. The sorcerer is invited to select subsequent days during the first month of the new year for large rituals in which the family gathers to kowtow before the ancestral altar and make offerings of food. Rituals also are held on the anniversaries of the ancestors' deaths. [Hickey 1958: 126-27; Lunet de Lajonquière 1906: 133-34.] The **Tho** have adopted the Vietnamese cult of *ong tao,* the spirit of the hearth, and they observe the rituals of this spirit during the new year period (Lunet de Lajonquière 1906: 107). **Soul, death, and afterlife.** A male principle is associated with the sun and sky, and a female principle with the moon. A person is thought to have multiple souls: those called *hon* emanate from the male principle and may number up to three; *via* emanate from the female principle and number seven for males, nine for females. After death, the *hon* are purified in the fires of hell while the *via* return to earth. Offerings can be made to alleviate the sufferings of the *hon.* [Abadie 1924: 54; Lunet de Lajonquière 1906: 126-27.] The Tho bury their dead, and maintain a cult of the tomb afterward. Their funeral rituals resemble those of the Vietnamese. The eldest son and the *p'u tao* prepare the corpse and officiate at the ritual. The Tho-ti have more elaborate rituals than other Tho, and retain the services of a geomancer to select the site of the family graves. On the third day after burial, a ritual is held, and the family visits the grave. There are other rituals on the forty-ninth and the hundredth day, and, like the Vietnamese, the Tho observe each death anniversary ritually. Unlike the Vietnamese, however, they do not exhume the bones after a given period. [Hickey 1958: 127-28; Lunet de Lajonquière 1906: 163-65.]

BIBLIOGRAPHY. Abadie 1924; Diguet 1908; Gourou 1936a; Hickey 1958; Lafont 1961; Lunet de Lajonquière 1906; Morechand 1952; Nguyen 1940; NNCDT 1959.

TRUNG-CHA

Synonyms. *Chong Kia, Chung-tra, Heu Y*

ORIENTATION. **Identification.** Trung-cha is the Vietnamese designation for this relatively small Tai-speaking group located in the China–Vietnam border area. The Chinese refer to them as Chong Kia or Heu Y (Diguet 1908: 100; Lunet de Lajonquière 1906: 203). According to Diguet, the Trung-cha originated in Kweichow province in China, and migrated through Kwangsi into Tonkin in the tenth century. A North

Vietnamese source (NNCDT 1959: 243) refers to this group as the Chung-tra. **Demography.** There are reportedly 180 Trung-cha in northern Vietnam (NNCDT 1959: 243).

SETTLEMENT PATTERN AND HOUSING. **Settlement pattern.** In 1906 a Trung-cha settlement in the Quan Ba sector was reported to have consisted of several dispersed farmsteads; while settlements in the Dong Van area were closely-knit clusters of eight to twelve houses. There also were some mixed settlements, containing families of Trung-cha, Nung, Nhang, and Tho. [Lunet de Lajonquière 1906: 204.]

ECONOMY. The Trung-cha cultivate paddy rice, maize, and buckwheat. Their agricultural techniques are said to resemble those of the Nung and Tho. Economic specialization includes forging, carpentry, stone cutting, jewelry production, ceramics, and weaving. [Diguet 1908: 100; Lunet de Lajonquière 1906: 205.]

MARRIAGE AND FAMILY. **Mode.** The young man has the prerogative of selecting his own mate. He initiates the courtship through the services of a female intermediary, who presents the girl with symbolic gifts of rice alcohol and a cock, and **arranges** the bride price—usually in cash. On the day of the wedding, the groom sends additional gifts of food and alcohol. As part of the marriage ritual, which takes place at the groom's house, the sorcerer, *p'u tao*, exorcises any evil spirits that may be present. The bride returns to her parents' house, which the groom is free to visit, and remains there until she becomes pregnant. **Form.** Polygyny is permitted only when the wife fails to have children. The levirate is common, but not obligatory. [Lunet de Lajonquière 1906: 206-07.]

RELIGION. The Trung-cha are reported to have a cult of the ancestors. They believe that there are 36 vital spirits in each human body, and that after death they disperse—some to the altar of the ancestors, some to the grave. Any which become evil spirits are known as *vang*, and can be reincarnated into another person (but not into a kinsman of the deceased). Some sorcerers are capable of communicating with the *vang*. Offerings are made to keep the vital spirits that remain on the ancestral altar contented. Rituals honoring the ancestors are held on the first day of the new lunar year, on the third day of the third month, the sixth day of the sixth month, and on the fourteenth day of the seventh month. The head of the family, wearing a long blue robe, officiates at the family rituals. [Lunet de Lajonquière 1906: 205-06.]

BIBLIOGRAPHY. Diguet 1908; Lunet de Lajonquière 1906; NNCDT 1959.

NUNG

ORIENTATION. **Identification.** Seidenfaden (1958: 65-66) and Lin (1940: 296) describe the Nung as an identifiable Tai group in China. Bruk (1960: 26) writes that although the Nung have been considered a separate ethnic group, they now should be viewed as a subdivision of the Chuang. Some of the subgroups of the Nung in Vietnam are named for their places of origin in China, e.g. the Nung Inh, Nung Loi, Nung An, and Nung Chan (Gourdon 1931: 82). A recent North Vietnamese source reports similar subgroupings of Nung, such as the Nung Phan Sinh, Nung Chao, Nung Tung (also known as the Nung Xuong), Nung Loi, Nung Qui-rin, Nung An, and Nung Inh (NNCDT 1959: 243). Le (1955: 47) raises the question of whether the Nung really should be classified with other Tai groups, since they have been so strongly influenced by the Vietnamese and Chinese. Lunet de Lajonquière (1906: 197), in noting that the Nung employ Chinese calligraphy, considers them a mixed Chinese-Tai group. **Location.** The Vietnam Nung are located at relatively high elevations along the upland area of the Chinese border, with the densest concentrations in the vicinity of Cao Bang. In some areas of northern Vietnam the Nung are reported to have occupied land abandoned by the Tho, who fled Chinese bandits during the nineteenth century. [Abadie 1924: 77; Gourdon 1931: 82.] **Linguistic affiliation.** Tai speakers, classified by Li as using a Central Tai dialect (1959). **Demography.** Early estimates placed the Nung population in Vietnam at around 80,000 (Abadie 1924: 77; Gourdon 1931: 82). Le (1955: 47) estimated that there were around 90,000 in northern Vietnam, and the NNCDT (1959: 243) places the Nung population at 270,810. Seidenfaden (1958: 65-66) contends that around 40 years ago, the Nung in China numbered some 200,000, and that there were also about 100,000 in the upland valleys of northern Vietnam.

SETTLEMENT PATTERN AND HOUSING. **Settlement pattern.** Nung villages usually have from 20 to 30 houses. The farmsteads are clustered in the upland valleys close to their fields. [Abadie 1924: 77.] **Housing.** House types vary from region to region. In the Hsi Chiang basin and the Clear river area, they are constructed on piling in the traditional Tai manner, with the stable under the house. An extended platform at the entrance to the house is used for weaving and as a gathering place for friends and family. The Nung of the Song Chay and Red river areas, however, build their houses on the ground, and the well-to-do prefer masonry and tile houses of Chinese architecture. In spite of these variations, the interiors of Nung houses tend to be very similar. If the house is occupied by an extended family, the interior is partitioned into several rooms. There is one large room where the inhabitants gather, and where guests are received. The Nung have simple furnishings, and they prefer sleeping on floor mats. [Abadie 1924: 77-82.]

ECONOMY. **Agriculture.** Maize is the staple crop. When the rains begin in January, dried stalks and weeds are cleared from the fields and the first plowing takes place. Buffalo dung is spread on the fields before the second plowing. Women plant the maize. By mid-April the first ears appear, and in mid-May the harvest usually begins. Maize is stored in the upper parts of the house, where it dries from the heat of the kitchen fires. Buckwheat is cultivated by a similar method. Three months after planting the harvest takes place. Most Nung have an annual double crop of buckwheat. [Diguet 1908: 74-75.] Secondary crops include cotton, millet, tobacco, beans, and sweet potatoes. Poppies are grown for opium production. A variety of green leafy vegetables as well as tuberous plants are cultivated in kitchen gardens. Pumpkins are grown primarily as food for pigs. [Diguet 1908: 75; Abadie 1924: 82; Lunet de Lajonquière 1906: 193.] ● Since the Nung are located at relatively high altitudes, the problem of irrigation limits paddy cultivation. Gourdon (1931: 82) reports some terracing. According to Abadie (1924: 82), when the Nung obtain a plot of bottom land they shift from maize to paddy cultivation. Gourdon (1931: 82) considers Nung and Tho agricultural techniques to be very similar. **Industrial arts.** Home industries include the production of cloth, maize and rice alcohol, and fuel oil from the colza plant. The Nung also engage in smithing and carpentry. **Trade.** Along the frontier of Yunnan, some Nung operate inns for the many caravans that pass through. In the areas of Bo Gai and Bao Luc, they lumber a hardwood which Chinese and Vietnamese coffin manufacturers value highly. They also trade opium, alcohol, surplus paddy, and maize in return for oil, matches, tobacco, and small manufactured items with the Chinese and Vietnamese merchants who visit their areas. [Abadie 1924: 83; Lunet de Lajonquière 1906: 193; Diguet 1908: 75.]

KIN GROUPS. **Descent.** The kinship system of the Nung is similar to that of the Tho. Children take their father's family name. The father has title to all family property. The eldest son inherits the prerogatives and responsibilities of head of the family —the duty to perform the prescribed rituals of the cult of the ancestors, title to most of the family property, and authority over the members of the family. Married sons receive the use of some family land, and upon the death of the father they receive title to it. [Abadie 1924: 84; Diguet 1908: 73.] **Kin groups.** Lunet de Lajonquière (1906: 185-86) describes the Nung as divided into "clans" named for their place of origin in southern China. For example,

the Nung Inh originated in the area of Long Inh, west of Tai Ping Fu in Kwangsi province. Other such "clans" are the Nung An, Nung Loi, Nung Phan Sinh, Nung Chao, Nung Si Kiet, Nung An Sich, Nung Quay Son, and Nung Giang.

MARRIAGE AND FAMILY. **Mode.** Persons with the same family name are forbidden to marry. Marriage with other ethnic groups is not uncommon, although there is some disagreement concerning marriages between the Nung and Tho—whereas Diguet (1908: 195) contends that while the Nung and Tho often live in proximity, they seldom intermarry, Abadie (1924: 85) reports that the Nung often take Tho women as second or third wives. In the Song Chay area, a boy selects his own wife, subject to his father's approval. Should the father make the choice, the boy has the right to refuse it. The couple kneel before the groom's ancestral altar while an aged male member of the groom's family requests the ancestors' approval of the union. After the ritual, the bride returns to her paternal house where the groom is free to visit her. Cohabitation is not allowed until pregnancy occurs, and if this does not occur within three years, the marriage is nullified. **Form.** Polygyny is practiced among the well-to-do, and all children are considered equal. **Residence.** The eldest son resides patrilocally after marriage, while the other sons settle nearby. **Inheritance.** The eldest son inherits the bulk of family property (Abadie 1924: 84-85).

SOCIOPOLITICAL ORGANIZATION. In addition to having their own village chiefs, the Nung in some areas are reported to be gaining control of higher political positions; the *ly truong* of Muong Khuong in the Lao Kay area was reported by Abadie (1924: 84) to be a Nung, as were other commune officials in the vicinity. Abadie attributes the growing Tung political ascendancy to their continual acquisition of land, much of which is purchased from neighboring Tho.

RELIGION. The Nung have the pantheon of *pi* found among the Black Tai and Tho. They also hold an ill-defined amalgam of Buddhist, Confucianist, and Taoist beliefs which vary from one subgroup to another. The rituals associated with both the cult of the ancestors and the spirit of the hearth are performed at the same altar. The domestic altar of the Nung Inh has two shelves, one of which contains the ancestors' tablets, and the other the accouterments for the cult of the spirit of the hearth. Major annual rituals include the fixing of tombs in the third lunar month; the ritual of the fifteenth day of the fourth lunar month; and the feast of the new rice in the tenth lunar month. [Abadie 1924: 86; Diguet 1908: 75.] **Soul, death, and afterlife.** Funeral rituals are described as being very similar to those of the Tho. The Nung maintain their family graves, and visit them each year on the third day of the third lunar month. The importance of the grave is illustrated by the practice of moving it if misfortune should strike a family. [Abadie 1924: 86.]

BIBLIOGRAPHY. Abadie 1924; Bruk 1960; Diguet 1908; Gourdon 1931; Le 1955; Li 1959; Lin 1940; Lunet de Lajonquière 1906; NNCDT 1959; Seidenfaden 1958.

NHANG

Synonyms. *Giai, Giay, Nung, Nyang, Yang*

ORIENTATION. **Identification.** Neighboring groups refer to the Nhang variously as Nung, Giai, or Giay, and the Lao refer to them as Yang. They appear on French maps as Nyang. **Location.** In northern Vietnam, along the China border. Especially numerous along the Clear river (in Yunnan as well as Vietnam), the Song Chay, and the right bank of the Red river. **Linguistic affiliation.** The Nhang are reported to speak a dialect of Tai very similar to that spoken by the Nung. They employ a Chinese calligraphy. [Abadie 1924: 88; Lunet de Lajonquière 1906: 202.] **Demography.** Lunet de Lajonquière (1906: 200) reported 7,000 Nhang. NNCDT (1959: 243) places the Nhang population at 14,387.

SETTLEMENT PATTERN AND HOUSING. **Settlement pattern.** Most settlements have from 10 to 12 farmsteads. Occasionally settlements of 20 or 30 are found. Settlements are described as being isolated along the China–Vietnam border, where the Nhang are reported to have occupied land abandoned because of bandit raids. [Abadie 1924: 88; Diguet 1908: 99.] **Housing.** Houses are commonly constructed on the ground. Bamboo logs are used for the frame, and split bamboo for the walls, while the roof is of thatching. Occasionally mud is plastered on the exterior of the walls. The house interior is divided into several rooms—the main room contains the altar of the ancestors, and serves as a gathering place for the family and a place to receive guests. The stable is a small outbuilding. The Nhang usually construct a bamboo fence around the house and outbuildings. [Abadie 1924: 89; Diguet 1908: 99; Lunet de Lajonquière 1906: 199-200.]

ECONOMY. The Nhang are reported to cultivate the same crops by the same techniques as the Black Tai. Because they are located at higher elevations, however, the Nhang must resort to terracing. In addition to rice, they cultivate maize, indigo, sugar cane, and cotton. The only outstanding characteristic of Nhang industry is an elaborate cotton gin not found among other Tai groups. [Abadie 1924: 89-90; Diguet 1908: 98.]

KIN GROUPS. Lafont (1961) reports that the Nhang are patrilineal, and have exogamous kin groupings. He also reports that they prefer to have married sons live near the paternal house. Unlike other Tai groups in northern Vietnam, cohabitation takes place immediately after marriage. Polygyny is common, and second or third (but not first) wives may be taken from neighboring groups. The Nhang also have the levirate. [Diguet 1908: 102; Abadie 1924: 90.] **Kin terminology.** Durand (1952: 216-17) gives the following kin terms for the Nhang of northern Vietnam:

Fa	*pyo*
Mo	*me*
FaBr	*lung ao*
FaSi	*pa (yeo, sin)*
MoBr	*pa (na, lung)*
MoSi	*pa*
ElBr	*ko lao*
YoBr	*nuon sai*
ElSi	*tche lao*
YoSi	*nung kwo (nung buk)*
FaBrSoDa	*syu*
FaSiSoDa	*syu*
MoBrSoDa	*sin*
MoSiSoDa	*sin*

SOCIOPOLITICAL ORGANIZATION. Since they are relatively dispersed, the Nhang usually live under the political dominance of a more populous neighboring group, although they do have their own *siao phay*, or village headman. Even in such areas as Tai Nien and Ban Tai, where the Nhang are numerous, higher administrative positions are held by the Tho. [Abadie 1924: 90.]

RELIGION. On the third day of the third month, rituals are performed honoring the ancestors. Guardian spirits in each Nhang village are honored in annual rituals during which the village is taboo to outsiders. [Diguet 1908: 99; Lunet de Lajonquière 1906: 200; Abadie 1924: 90-91.]

BIBLIOGRAPHY. Abadie 1924; Diguet 1908; Durand 1952; Lafont 1961; Lunet de Lajonquière 1906; NNCDT 1959.

T'OU LAO

Synonym. *Thu Lao*

ORIENTATION. **Identification and location.** The Chinese use the generic term T'ou Lao, meaning "native" or "people of the soil," for a large number of Tai-speaking groups. In northern Tonkin, T'ou Lao is used for a specific group of some dozen hamlets, numbering around 200 persons, in the Song Chay area of the Chinese frontier. [Abadie 1924: 96;

Lunet de Lajonquière 1906: 197-98.] **Linguistic affiliation.** Tai. **Demography.** A recent North Vietnamese source estimates the Thu Lao (Vietnamese transcription) at 528 (NNCDT 1959: 243).

SETTLEMENT PATTERN AND HOUSING. **Housing.** Houses are constructed on the ground, sometimes with wattled walls. The interior is divided into two rooms—a main room where the altar of the ancestors is located, and a room that serves as the kitchen and women's quarters. [Abadie 1924: 97.]

ECONOMY. Methods of agriculture and home industries are similar to those of nearby Meo groups (Abadie 1924: 97).

BIBLIOGRAPHY. Abadie 1924; Lunet de Lajonquière 1906; NNCDT 1959.

PA-Y

Synonym. *Pa-di*

ORIENTATION. **Identification.** The Pa-y are described as relatively recent arrivals from China into northern Vietnam. Their largest groupings are in the mountainous region of Pa Kha and in the vicinity of Muong Khuong, near the Chinese border just east of the Red river. They are divided into two groups—the Peu Pa-y (White Pa-y) and the Hoang Pa-y (Yellow Pa-y). [Abadie 1924: 92.] **Linguistic affiliation.** Tai speakers, related to the Tai (Pai-i) of Yunnan. **Demography.** Abadie (1924: 92) reports that there are "several hundred" Pa-y. A North Vietnamese source estimates that the number of Pa-di (Vietnamese transcription) is 533 (NNCDT 1959: 243).

ECONOMY. The Pa-y cultivate maize and mountain rice. Few cultivate paddy rice. [Abadie 1924: 92.]

MARRIAGE AND FAMILY. Marriages between the Nung and Pa-y are common. Newly-married couples cohabit from the day of the marriage. [Abadie 1924: 92.]

RELIGION. The Pa-y practice the cult of the ancestors. They also believe in spirits, *pi*. [Abadie 1924: 92.]

BIBLIOGRAPHY. Abadie 1924; NNCDT 1959.

KADAI

THE INCLUSION IN THE PRESENT VOLUME of cultural summaries on four so-called Kadai groups rests primarily on linguistic evidence presented by Benedict. As might be expected, speakers of these languages, with the possible exception of the Li of Hainan, are highly marginal with respect to stronger and more dominant peoples with whom they have come in contact. Ethnographic data, particularly for the Kelao, Laqua, and Lati, are meager, and distinctive cultural features difficult to delineate. Stübel, working with elements of language and material culture among the Li tribes of Hainan, reports similarities with Malayo-Polynesian-speaking aboriginal tribes on Formosa as well as Tai-speaking groups on the mainland. ● Benedict's original hypothesis, in which he groups Tai, Kadai, and Indonesian as a single linguistic complex, with Kadai as the "transitional" member, has been accepted by Greenberg but is regarded with some reserve by both Sebeok and Li Fang-kuei. Chang (1959), working from recent archaeological evidence, posits a common south China neolithic substratum with some local variation due to peculiar environmental and historical influences. He further concludes that these neolithic cultures belonged to an "undifferentiated Sino-Tibetan/Malayo-Polynesian Complex" out of which differentiated a southwestern branch (Tai, Miao, Lolo, etc.) and a southeastern branch (Indonesians, Chams, etc.). These suggestions, derived independently of linguistic analysis, are of interest in light of Benedict's hypothesis concerning the probable relationship of Tai and Indonesian.

LI

Synonyms. *B'lai, B'li, Dai, Dli, Hiai, K'lai, Lai, Le, Loi, S'lai*

ORIENTATION. **Identification and location.** The Li tribes of Hainan are concentrated in the mountainous southern portion of the island, an area also inhabited by scattered populations of so-called Miao (probably Yao). The area has been designated the Hainan Li and Miao Autonomous Chou by the Chinese People's Republic. They are known to the Chinese by the generic term Li (Loi, Lai), to which is usually added a term referring to some characteristic of dress, dialect, habitat, or degree of acculturation, e.g. Sansheng Li, Pen-ti Li, Seng-t'i Li. Their names for themselves differ according to dialect, e.g. Dli, B'li, Le, Lai, Loi, Dai, B'lai, K'lai. Five major tribes are distinguished by Stübel and Odaka on the basis of field work: (1) The Ha Li comprise the largest group, located in the southern part of the area, primarily in Tungfang, Lotung, and Yai districts. The majority of Ha Li have been deeply influenced by Chinese culture. (2) The Ki Li, numbering some 80,000, live in the heart of the Li area in the Wu-chih mountains of Paoting, Lotung, and Ch'iungchung districts. They are among the least acculturated of the Li groups. (3) The Pen-ti Li are located on the northern periphery of the area, primarily in Paisha district. (4) The Me-fu (Moi-fau) Li, who are heavily sinicized, live primarily in Tungfang district on the western periphery of the mountains. (5) The Lai, sometimes considered a subgroup of the Ha. Stübel considers the Pen-ti an indigenous group, the others having arrived on the island in successive migrations. These groups differ somewhat in physical appearance, dialect, dress, and house type, the most noticeable difference among them being their degree of acculturation to the surrounding Chinese. [Stübel 1937: 20-21; Odaka 1950: 13; Benedict 1942: 580; Bruk 1960: 27.] **Geography.** Although Hainan has a tropical climate, much of the land has been extensively deforested by swidden cultivation, so that many Li settlements are located in badly eroded hilly country (Stübel 1937: 279-81; Wiens 1954: 277). **Linguistic affiliation.** There are many dialects which, according to Benedict, can be classified into Northern Li and Southern Li. The Li dialects are included, with Lati, Laqua, and Kelao, in Benedict's Kadai stock, related to Tai and Malayo–Polynesian (Benedict 1942). The Tai element in Li was, according to Benedict, noted more than a half century ago; Greenberg (1953: 282) feels that the Li-Tai relationship is particularly close. There is no indigenous system of writing, and only a few Li are literate in Chinese. Many, however, particularly among the Ha and Me-fu groups, speak Chinese (Odaka 1950: 13-14; Stübel 1937: 283). **Demography.** Wiens (1954: 277), citing 1952 Chinese Communist figures, gives an estimated total of 220,000 Li. Bruk (1960: 25), using 1953 CPR census figures, gives a total of 358,000 Li in Kwangtung (mainly Hainan) province. **History and cultural relations.** Wang Hsing-jui, after studying the Li at firsthand and reviewing the historical literature, concludes that they have been on Hainan since prehistoric times, their contact with Han Chinese extending over a 2,000 year period dating from the establishment of provinces on the island by the Emperor Wu in 110 B.C. Wang further concludes that lack of consistent, constructive policies led to economic exploitation and consequent Li uprisings, in which the Li gained a reputation among the Han for ferocity and cannibalism. The so-called Miao (Yao) on the island are thought to be descendants of troops brought from the mainland in the sixteenth century to put down Li uprisings. The Chinese have occupied the northern flatlands and coastal areas, and the Li (and later the Miao) have been forced back into the interior mountainous regions. The long period of contact has meant that practically all Li are to some degree sinicized, particularly those near the coast. Here the Li live much as Chinese, and some are themselves landlords, owning land in the interior occupied by Li and Miao tenants. ● The Li and the Miao on Hainan have been in contact for several centuries, resulting in cultural borrowing and cultural similarities between the two. The Miao have often been exploited by neighboring Li, with the result that attempts at land reform and education on the part of Nationalist and Communist governments in recent years have been generally well received by Miao. The more diffuse and complex economic situation of the Li has resulted in mixed and often conflicting reactions to these overtures. The Li landlords, in particular, have resisted attempts at land reform. ● The prolonged period of cultural blending on Hainan renders any reconstruction of aboriginal Li culture highly uncertain. Working with elements of language and material culture, Stübel sees similarities with peoples of Austronesian or Malayo–Polynesian stock (in particular the aboriginal tribes of Formosa), as well as with Tai-speaking peoples on the Asiatic mainland. [Wang 1948: 112-22; Stübel 1937: 1-3, 290-97; Odaka 1950: 12-14.]

SETTLEMENT PATTERN AND HOUSING. **Settlement pattern.** The Li settle in river valleys and grow wet rice wherever they are able to do so, e.g. along the upper river valleys of Tungfang and Lotung districts. Many villages in the more mountainous interior, however, do not have ready access to areas suitable for paddy rice. The settlements are usually located off main paths and roads and concealed by trees or bamboo groves. In some areas the village is fenced in by a dense hedge or dirt wall as a protection against raiders. Houses in larger villages may be laid out in rows, with the granaries located on the village periphery. A local shrine is ordinarily found near the village entrance. Villages range in size from 20 to some 1,000 persons, the smaller settlements in general being in the more remote mountainous areas. [Stübel 1937: 282-83 passim; Odaka 1950: 17.] **Housing.** Pen-ti Li houses are built on piles, preferably against a slope, with a space below for domestic animals. Walls and flooring are of bamboo and plank respectively, and a large straw roof reaches almost to the ground. The single large room is divided by a woven bamboo partition into living-cooking and sleeping quarters. The Ki Li house is raised slightly above the ground, its split bamboo floor resting on stone supports. The large barrel-shaped straw roof reaches the ground, making side walls unnecessary.

Entrances are cut through bamboo walls, front and back. The more sinicized Me-fu and Ha build their rectangular houses directly on the ground. The floor is of tamped earth, the low side and end walls of logs smeared with mud, and the gable roof thatched with straw. The interior is partitioned to provide sleeping quarters in one corner. Some of the wealthy Li on the lowlands have adopted Chinese-style houses of brick with tile roofs. [Stübel 1937: 278 passim; Odaka 1950: 18-20.]

ECONOMY. Agriculture is the main source of livelihood. Although paddy rice is the preferred crop, grown wherever the water supply and topography are suitable, most Li groups cultivate both wet and dry rice. The food supply is supplemented by animal husbandry, fishing, and gathering. Hunting is a popular pastime, but its economic importance is minor. Water buffalo and cattle are of considerable economic importance, both as a symbol of wealth and as sacrificial animals, and large herds are maintained in some areas, as among the Pen-ti. Industrial arts, such as weaving, are well developed, although the Li depend on the Chinese for iron implements. **Agriculture.** In addition to rice, food crops include millet, maize, sweet potatoes, sesame, taro, beans, and sugar cane. Papaya, coconut, and sago palms are cultivated, as are cotton, tobacco, and indigo. Peppers, garlic, pumpkins, and bananas are raised in kitchen gardens. Methods of paddy cultivation are similar to those of the Chinese except that buffalo dung is the only fertilizer used, and sometimes the fields are prepared for tilling by driving buffalo and cattle over them repeatedly. Upland swiddens planted to dry rice are prepared by the slash-and-burn method. [Odaka 1950: 37; Stübel 1937: 279-81 passim.] **Fishing and hunting.** Fishing is of little economic importance among many Li groups. Those near rivers or streams utilize hooks, bamboo traps, hand nets, bows and arrows, and poison. An entire village may participate in damming a stream and poisoning the water to take the fish. Game is plentiful, and the Li enjoy hunting as a pastime, utilizing old muzzle loaders obtained from the Chinese, bows and arrows, and traps. Wild boar, deer, birds, monkeys, rats, and rabbits are among the animals taken. Antlers and hides are sold to the Chinese; the meat may be consumed in feasts or sold to the Chinese. [Odaka 1950: 41-46; Stübel 1937: 281-82 passim.] **Gathering.** Frogs, beetles, insects, and edible plants are gathered as dietary supplements. Gathering is not, however, of major economic importance even among the most isolated Li (Stübel 1937: 281-82). **Domestic animals.** Most Li villages contain some or all of the following: water buffalo, cattle (light brown with one hump), horses, pigs, goats, chickens, ducks, geese, dogs, and cats. Honey bees are kept by some groups. Buffalo and cattle serve as work animals. In addition, the buffalo

is a symbol of wealth, its relative worth being determined by sex and length of horns. Buffalo are used in ceremonies, as sacrifices, and for payment of fines and bride price. Wealthy individuals among the Pen-ti are reported by Stübel to have quite large herds of buffalo—up to 100 animals in some cases. [Stübel 1937: 49, 281; Odaka 1950: 39-40.] **Food and stimulants.** Among the Me-fu and Pen-ti Li, the main dish is a thick rice gruel flavored with salt (Odaka 1950: 25; Stübel 1937: 52). Side dishes include boiled rape, various kinds of beans, and pumpkin. Small animals, such as rats, which are caught in the fields or around the house, are eaten boiled and apparently supply some degree of protein. Game and domestic animals are consumed only on special occasions. Tobacco, smoked in pipes, is popular, as is betel. The Li reportedly consume a great deal of rice wine and sweet potato whisky, and they make both distilled and fermented varieties of each. [Odaka 1950: 24-28.] **Industrial arts.** Li men weave baskets, mats, fish traps, and rain gear out of bamboo, rattan, and pandanus. They also make cowhide wallets and the wooden parts of farm tools and oxcarts, the iron parts being imported from the Chinese. Li women spin thread, weave it into cloth on a simple belt loom, and dye the cloth with dark blue and brown vegetable dyes. Hemp is woven for nets, and kapok for blankets. The Ha make most of the Li pottery, which is shaped by coiling, dried in the sun, and hardened by fire. Many women still tattoo the face and body. According to Odaka, the designs vary among the different tribal groups. [Odaka 1950: 20-30, 46-50; Stübel 1937: 282 passim.] **Trade.** Trade, usually in the form of barter, is in Chinese hands. The Li frequent Chinese market places, and in each large Li village there is at least one Chinese shopkeeper. Much trade is also conducted by Chinese peddlers. From the Chinese the Li obtain plowshares, sickles, iron parts of farm implements, muzzle loaders, gunpowder, bullets or lead, fishing gear, tools, needles, fabrics, salt, sugar, candles, dishes, and thread. Li export items include unhulled rice, sweet potatoes, beans, cattle, pigs, chickens, deer antlers and skins, monkeys, lumber, honey, and medicinal herbs. The difficulty of transportation in the Li territory has always limited trade between the Li and the plains-dwelling Chinese. [Odaka 1950: 10, 74-79; Stübel 1937: 282 passim.] **Division of labor.** Strict division of labor is lacking. In general, men burn and clear the fields, till, care for cattle, chop wood, hunt, fish, peddle surplus products, weave baskets and fish traps, and engage in politics and war. Women transplant, reap, thresh and mill rice, carry water, gather fruit and bamboo shoots in the mountains, cook, spin, weave, dye, take care of children, keep pigs and chickens, and garden. The women also make the pottery in groups where it is manufactured. Boys care for water buffalo and gather firewood; girls fetch water for the household and help their mothers (Odaka 1950: 25, 50-53; Stübel 1937: 285). **Land tenure.** Ownership of land varies greatly. In some cases the Li are tenants on land owned by Li or Chinese landlords; others may themselves be landlords, or independent farmers. In the sinicized Me-fu and Ha areas, the Chinese have utilized the *kom* as the basic territorial division in governing the Li, with each *kom* consisting of a number of villages—not necessarily of the same tribe. Hills and forests are owned in common by the inhabitants of a *kom*, and unused *kom* land can be reclaimed at will. Dry-land farms are owned by the individual who cleared them; wet-rice fields are considered the property of the village, although individual family holdings are well defined. Hunting grounds and streams are considered *kom* property, and are not claimed by any one village. [Odaka 1950: 63-69.]

KIN GROUPS. In many areas family names, similar to those among the Chinese, are inherited patrilineally, but people of the same surname are not necessarily prohibited from marrying. [Stübel 1937: 286; Odaka 1950: 16.]

MARRIAGE AND FAMILY. Most Li tribes permit premarital intercourse. In the least acculturated villages houses are set aside for courtship, or an individual family may build a hut where an unmarried daughter can entertain visitors. In villages where Chinese influence is strong, there is less freedom. **Mode.** Li uninfluenced by Chinese culture have free choice of marriage partners. Bride price and marriage are officially arranged by a go-between sent by the boy's parents. Bride price is comparatively light and is paid in buffalo, pigs, wine, and money. Among Li influenced by Chinese culture, parents have stricter control over the choice of marriage partners, and the bride price is heavier. [Stübel 1937: 285-87.] **Form.** Marriage is generally monogamous, although a wealthy man may take two wives, both of whom have equal rights (Stübel 1937: 285-87). **Extension of incest taboos.** Rules of marriage vary considerably, but village exogamy is usual. Unlike the Chinese, the Li do not forbid the marriage of persons with the same surname. The levirate is found among some groups. [Stübel 1937: 285-87.] **Residence.** In the least acculturated villages a young bride may return to her parental home, where any of the village youths may have access to her. Not until her first child is born does she return to her husband's home. From then on infidelity is strictly punished. This duolocality is dying out in the more acculturated regions, where the bride joins her husband directly or merely pays a token visit to her parental home, and residence is patrilocal. [Stübel 1937: 285-87.] **Domestic unit.** The patrilocal stem family appears to be common among at least some Li tribes. One married son, usually but

not necessarily the eldest, remains permanently in the parental home. [Odaka 1950: 65a, 70, 71.] **Inheritance.** All sons inherit equally from their parents, although the eldest usually gets the house and a slightly larger share of the land and animals (Stübel 1937: 285-87). **Divorce.** Divorce is easy and common among unacculturated groups; difficult where Chinese influence is strong. Either party can initiate divorce. If the woman leaves the man, the bride price is generally returned (Stübel 1937: 285-87).

SOCIOPOLITICAL ORGANIZATION. **Political organization.** Prior to their final subjugation, the Li seem to have had a strong tribal organization capable of resisting Chinese military forces. The last great campaign against the Li occurred in 1887, after which the Chinese introduced indirect rule. Influential Li, appointed chiefs of administrative districts composed of a number of *kom*, served under Chinese officials of the Li Pacification Bureau. The establishment of *hsien* districts in the Li area in 1935 did little to change this arrangement. The village remained the smallest political unit, governed by a village headman and a council of elders. The headman was responsible for witnessing contracts, judging minor thefts, and settling quarrels, although serious cases, e.g. the theft of a buffalo, were judged by a court made up of headmen and elders from several communities. A headman was usually succeeded by his son. In 1952 the Communist government inaugurated the Hainan Li and Miao Autonomous Chou, a single administrative entity under the direct control of the provincial government. The introduction of agricultural cooperatives and communes has altered the old political structure. [Stübel 1937: 287-90; Odaka 1950: 55-56; Wang 1948: 1-2.] **Social stratification.** The population is divided into landlords who rent out land, independent farmers who till their own land, and tenant farmers who rent all or part of the land they till. Wealth is based on ownership of land and buffalo. Within the average Li village, however, there is little evidence of class or status distinctions based on wealth. [Stübel 1937: 281; Odaka 1950: 69-71.] **Warfare.** Chinese historical records portray the Li as tenacious warriors adept at mountain warfare. The Li have not only warred against the Chinese but also have carried on local (usually intratribal) feuds over buffalo theft and land rental. Some tribes have the reputation of being quite warlike. Although firearms are used, battles are usually brief. Peace negotiations often follow the first attack. Treaties are made by the headmen and elders, with buffalo used as payment. [Stübel 1937: 287-90; Odaka 1950: 12.]

RELIGION. **Major religions.** The Li do not appear to have been deeply influenced by any of the major religions, although they have borrowed aspects of ancestor worship and magico-religious practices from the Chinese. **Indigenous religion.** The Li worship local deities called *tau-ti*, earth gods which Odaka (1950: 88) says are of Chinese origin. Near the entrance to each village is a shrine, where offerings of rice and wine are made to the local *tau-ti* (Stübel 1937: 284-85). **Supernaturals.** Supernaturals include local deities and also ancestral and other spirits. These spirits are able to cause sickness, which can be diagnosed by divination and treated by sacrifice (Stübel 1937: 284-85; Odaka 1950: 82-89). **Practitioners.** Chiefly diviners and exorcists. The diviners, by means of chicken legs, diagnose illness and try to influence the course of hunting, war, and trading expeditions. Practitioners are usually part-time specialists, generally elderly men or widows. Young people with a tendency toward induced hysteria may become apprenticed to a diviner. Exorcists perform demon-chasing rites after the diviner has identified the offending spirit. [Stübel 1937: 284-85; Odaka 1950: 81-88.] **Ceremonies.** Include ritual offerings of wine and rice to local deities, various methods of divination with chicken leg bones, and exorcistic rites. [Stübel 1937: 284-85; Odaka 1950: 82-89.] **Illness and medicine.** Ancestral and other spirits and demons can cause sickness, which is diagnosed by divination and treated by the sacrifice of chickens, pigs, dogs, and buffalo under the supervision of an exorcist. [Stübel 1937: 284-85; Odaka 1950: 82-89.] **Soul, death, and afterlife.** Elaborate funeral feasts include the sacrifice of a water buffalo. In some regions the house of the deceased is burned. The corpse is usually buried in a wooden coffin. Silver coins are placed in the deceased's hand or mouth as an offering. Special offerings are made to pacify the soul of a person who has died a violent death so that the spirit will not remain in the vicinity and cause trouble for the living. [Stübel 1937: 287.]

BIBLIOGRAPHY. Benedict 1942; Bruk 1960; Greenberg 1953; Odaka 1950; Stübel 1937; Wang 1948; Wiens 1954.

KELAO

Synonyms. *Ch'i-lao, I-lao, Kei-lao, Kha Lao, Khi, Lao, Thi, Thü, Xan Lao*

ORIENTATION. **Identification.** The Kelao (Keh-lao, Kei-lao) call themselves Thü or Thi (Benedict 1942: 579; Embree and Thomas 1950: 105). In Indochina they are called Kha Lao or Xan Lao by the Tai-speaking Tho, and Khi by the Meo (Embree and Thomas 1950: 105). In China they are referred to as Kelao, Ch'i-lao, I-lao, or Lao (Bruk 1960: 33; deBeauclair 1946; Clarke 1911: 13ff.; Lin 1940; **Ling and Ruey 1947: 51ff.**). The Chinese further distinguish subgroups according to characteristics of dress, habitat, and economy. Mickey (1947: 7) records ten such Kelao subgroups in Kweichow, e.g. Ch'ing (Blue), Hung (Red), Ch'ien-t'ou (Head-shaving), Ta-ya (Tooth-knocking), Ta-t'ieh (Iron-working). Lin (1940) lists these same groups, and adds, among others, the Mu-lao. **Location.** Found at present chiefly in north-western Kweichow province. There are scattered small populations in Hunan, Yunnan, Kwangsi, and extreme northern Vietnam along the border with China. Evidently once more numerous and wide-spread than at present. [Benedict 1942; deBeauclair 1946.] **Linguistic affiliation.** Grouped with Laqua, Lati, and Li as Kadai, a language group related to Tai. The Tai-Kadai family in turn shows relationships to Malayo-Polynesian. [Benedict 1942.] DeBeauclair (1946: 29-40) found dialect differences among the various named subgroups of Kelao in Kweichow. **Demography.** Bruk (1960: 33) records 21,000 Kelao in Kweichow province. **History and cultural relations.** According to Clarke (1911: 13ff.), the few surviving Kelao speakers in Kweichow claim to be the real aborigines of the region. DeBeauclair, who surveyed these same Kelao in the Anshun area in the early 1940s, feels that they are representatives of the ancient Lao of Chinese historical records. The Lao, under various names, appear in late Chou in what is now Szechwan, and by 116 B.C. were located in Kweichow, Hunan, and Kwangsi. By Sung dynasty times they were under strong acculturative pressure from the Han Chinese. Distinctive Lao culture traits, as culled from the records, include pile dwellings, slavery, tooth breaking, bronze drums, drinking through the nose by means of bamboo or metal tubes, burial high among rocks or in caves, second burial, and absence of the crossbow. Traits such as these, according to deBeauclair (1946: 1-29), would link the Kelao with widely-dispersed groups in Assam, Indochina, and Indonesia, including Karens, Dyak, Toradja, and various mountain Mon-Khmer populations in South Vietnam and Cambodia. Today the Kelao are everywhere a distinctly marginal people, rapidly being absorbed into larger populations of Chinese and Tai speakers. In Kweichow, where they have been pushed into the inaccessible and less desirable hill areas, they have adopted Chinese surnames and live the life of Kweichow farmers, as tenants on land owned by the Chinese (deBeauclair 1946: 29-40).

BIBLIOGRAPHY. DeBeauclair 1946; Benedict 1942; Bruk 1960; Clarke 1911; Embree and Thomas 1950; Lin 1940; Ling and Ruey 1947; Mickey 1947.

LAQUA

Synonyms. *Ca Beo, Ha Beo, Ka Beo, Man Laqua, Pu Peo*

ORIENTATION. **Identification and location.** Laqua, or Man Laqua, is the Vietnamese term for this small hill-dwelling population in the upper Clear river area along the Vietnam–Yunnan border, near the town of Ha Giang. They call themselves Ka Beo (Ca Beo, Ha Beo) and are called Pu Peo by the neighboring Meo. [Embree and Thomas 1950: 105; Bonifacy 1908: 532.] **Linguistic affiliation.** Benedict includes Laqua, Lati, Kelao, and the dialects of the Li on Hainan in a Kadai group, related to Tai. The Tai-Kadai family in turn shows certain relationships to Malayo-Polynesian. [Benedict 1942.] **Demography.** Less than 200 (Embree and Thomas 1950: 105). **History and cultural relations.** The Laqua and Lati regard themselves as indigenous to the area and are in general marginal to the other groups such as Meo and Lolo. The economy and culture of the Laqua appear to be patterned on that of the neighboring Meo, to whom they are politically subordinate. [Bonifacy 1908.]

BIBLIOGRAPHY. Benedict 1942; Bonifacy 1908; Embree and Thomas 1950.

LATI

Synonyms. *A-khu, Ak'ou, Fou-la, Lachi, P'ou-la*

ORIENTATION. **Identification and location.** Lati or Lachi is a Tho (Tai) word used by Vietnamese and French to refer to this small population of hill dwellers in the upper Clear river area along the Vietnam–Yunnan border, near the town of Ha Giang. The Tho call them Fou-la (P'ou-la), whereas the Lati refer to themselves as A-khu (Ak'ou). [Embree and Thomas 1950: 105; Bonifacy 1906: 271.] **Linguistic affiliation.** Benedict (1942) groups Lati, Laqua, Kelao, and the Hainanese Li dialects as Kadai. He sees an essential relationship of this Kadai group with Tai, and furthermore posits a relationship of the Tai-Kadai family to Malayo-Polynesian. **Demography.** A total of 450, in 78 families, according to Bonifacy (1906: 271), with more across the border in China. **History and cultural relations.** The Lati consider themselves autochthonous. They rank below the neighboring Meo and Lolo, and are administratively responsible to Tho chieftains (Benedict 1942: 579; Bonifacy 1906: 272). The Tho appear to be rapidly assimilating the few remaining Lati in northern Vietnam.

BIBLIOGRAPHY. Benedict 1942; Bonifacy 1906; Embree and Thomas 1950.

PART IV. MALAYO-POLYNESIAN

CHAM

CHAM SPEAKERS ARE SCATTERED throughout southern Vietnam and parts of Cambodia. The majority are found in the south-central coastal plain in Vietnam, and there are groupings in the area of the Tonle Sap in Cambodia as well as in the Chau Doc area along the southern Vietnam-Cambodia border. The language is generally classified as Malayo-Polynesian (Austronesian), and shows definite links with Atjeh on the northern tip of Sumatra (Capell 1962: 393). First influenced by Hinduism and later by Islam, the Chams have retained some beliefs and practices of both traditions. Those in Cambodia are more orthodox in the practice of Islam. The South Vietnam Jarai, Rhadé, and Raglai are in varying degrees Chamized hill peoples—speakers of Malayo-Polynesian showing cultural and linguistic influences of the once-powerful kingdom of Champa (cf. Embree and Dodson 1950: viii). The authors of the present volume follow Bruk (1959b) in classifying these people as upland (or mountain) groups, related linguistically to lowland speakers of Cham in the same area.

LOWLAND GROUPS

VIETNAM CHAMS

Synonym. *Nguoi Cham-pa*

ORIENTATION. **Identification.** The Chams remaining in Vietnam are descendants of the ancient kingdom of Champa. They are sometimes referred to by the Vietnamese as Nguoi Cham-pa. A recent North Vietnamese source mentions a subgroup of mixed Vietnamese-Chams known as the Kinh Cuu (NNCDT 1959: 248). **Location.** Mainly along the south-central coastal plain of Vietnam. There are also small groups along the southern Vietnam–Cambodia border. **Geography.** The Cham area of the south-central coast of Vietnam is a desiccated plain with little rainfall. Villages are built on ancient dunes which will not support growth—trees, gardens, or even hedge growths. [Nguyen 1944: 219-23.] **Linguistic affiliation.** The Chams speak a language of the Malayo-Polynesian stock. They have had considerable contact with neighboring groups, some of which speak languages of the same stock. Contact with non-Malayo-Polynesian speakers has affected the language (Maspéro 1928: 6-8; Benedict 1942: 599). The traditional script, of Indian origin, has been preserved to some extent. The Chams also have a romanized script devised by the French, and many know the written Viet-namese *quoc ngu* or romanized Vietnamese (Nguyen 1944: 220-23). **Demography.** The Cham population appears to be increasing slowly, although vital statistics from the Phan Rang and Phan Ri areas where they are concentrated are poor. The Cham population of Phan Ri is estimated at 3,674, and that of Phan Rang at 8,899 (Nguyen 1944: 213-23). In 1951, Olivier and Chagnoux (1951: 272) reported some 100,000 Chams in Vietnam and Cambodia. The NNCDT estimates the Cham population to be 45,000 for all of South Vietnam (1959: 248). **History and cultural relations.** According to Maspéro (1928: 8-12), when the Chams first appeared in history toward the end of the second century A.D., a strong Hindu influence was already evident. They venerated the three gods of the Indian Trimurti—Brahma, Vishnu, and Siva (and the Sakti, or spouses of the latter two). They also practiced some Buddhism, and at times combined veneration of the gods of the Trimurti with that of the Master of the Law. Siva, represented by a stone *linga,* was the most important deity. Brahma was represented in temple decorations, but there was no sanctuary dedicated to him. ● Islam was introduced into Champa at an early, somewhat indeterminate date. Maspéro quotes Huber as stating that some Chams may have been converted to Islam as early as the Sung dynasty in China. Two Kufic inscriptions were found in what was southern Champa date around 1030 A.D., and there is some indication of a Muslim community in Champa in the tenth century.

Religion played an important part in the kingdom of Champa. The Cham emperors expended considerable wealth on the temples. Each had its own domain, the income from which went to the upkeep of the temple. The temple complex included a sizable population of priests, servants, slaves, dancers, and musicians, and a gynaeceum in which the women had their own servants. Art was highly developed (cf. Parmentier 1918). A series of dynasties led to a florescence of Cham culture and an expansion of the kingdom of Champa between the sixth and thirteenth centuries. There was also a series of wars with the Khmer and Vietnamese during this period. Maspéro (1928: 193-219) considers the eleventh dynasty (the end of the twelfth century) as the beginning of Cham decline. They had made a series of territorial concessions to the southward-expanding Vietnamese, and were finally defeated in 1471 by the Vietnamese emperor Le Thanh Ton. The elite fled to Cambodia, followed by most of the population, leaving remnants of the peasantry in the coastal area of central Vietnam (Maspéro 1928: 43-242; Leuba 1923: 20-36). ● Since the time of the Cham-Vietnamese wars, there has been considerable contact between the two groups. Mixed marriages are common, and Vietnamese influence is very strong. At An Phuoc the official language is Vietnamese, but as late as 1944 Nguyen noted that at Phan Ri the official language was still Cham. The Chams have adopted many Vietnamese customs—house style, clothes, lunar calendar, and the twelve-animal cycle of years. [Nguyen 1944: 221; Leuba 1923: 87.]

SETTLEMENT PATTERN AND HOUSING. Settlement pattern.

Villages appear rather desolate, since they usually are located on dunes and other arid areas, without trees or hedge growths (Nguyen 1944: 219-23). According to Leuba (1923: 65), however, in some villages edible gourds grow on the palisades, and some have enclosures of pineapple plants. **Housing.** The traditional house was constructed on piling, and resembled some of the house types of the highland groups in southern Vietnam. Acculturation and contact with the Vietnamese have led the Chams to adopt a Vietnamese type of house—thatched, and constructed on the ground, with one main room. Some houses are of masonry. [Nguyen 1944: 220-21.]

ECONOMY. Agriculture.

The area occupied by the bulk of the population is not amenable to extensive paddy cultivation. Maspéro (1928: 3-4), citing early Chinese sources, describes Cham agriculture as historically dominated by market gardening rather than paddy agriculture. Crops included sugar cane, maize, a variety of fruit trees—the most important of which were coconut and banana trees—green beans, peas, eggplant, cucumbers, millet, sesame, peppers, and areca and betel leaves (both of which were used in the production of an alcoholic drink). Hemp, reeds, and latania palms were used in weaving and thatching. ● Aymonier (1891: 26-28) describes the Chams of Binh Thuan as cultivating paddy, using a plow and buffalo. They also cultivate some maize, peas, manioc, sesame, and ground nuts. Tobacco, castor beans, and cotton are also cultivated. He notes that they do not, however, cultivate areca or betel leaves. ● Wet-rice fields are irrigated by canals, into which river water is diverted by means of dams. Owners of fields watered by a particular canal system are obliged to see that the irrigation system is repaired annually. As the rice ripens, watchers station themselves in shelters built on piles in the paddy fields and frighten marauding animals and birds by beating drums, blowing on conch shells, or shouting (Leuba 1923: 116). Upland rice is cultivated in swiddens, as are maize, castor-oil plants, manioc, peanuts, tobacco, some fodder crops, and some leguminous plants (Leuba 1923: 118). **Domestic animals.** The Chams breed buffalo, chickens, ducks, and many goats. Due to their Brahman origins, however, they do not raise cattle, and pigs are rare, even among the non-Muslim Chams. [Aymonier 1891: 27; Eickstedt 1940: 73.] **Industrial arts.** According to Aymonier (1891: 27-28), there are few crafts. The women weave cloth, but not as well as the Khmer. Since the Chams lack specialists for house construction, they hire Vietnamese for this purpose. **Division of labor.** Women do housework, cook, care for the children, weave, cultivate kitchen gardens, winnow husk paddy, pound grain, and fetch water (Leuba 1923: 96).

KIN GROUPS. Descent.

Descent is matrilineal (Aymonier 1891: 29-32). **Kin groups.** According to Maspéro (1928: 17-19), the Chams had a clan system predating Hindu influence. Clan names marked these kin groupings, and each clan also had a totem to distinguish it further. Two such clans mentioned in legends are the coconut tree clan and the *kramukavansa*, or areca nut tree clan. These two are reported to have struggled for supremacy. The areca nut tree clan ruled the state of Panduranga in what is now central Vietnam, and the coconut tree clan dominated the area farther north. There is strong evidence that the clans were matrilineal. In the annals, King Harivarman III is stated to have belonged to the clan of his mother, the areca nut tree clan. Although the Cham kinship system retained its matrilineal character, Maspéro (1928: 19-20) states that succession in the royal line was patrilineal in keeping with Hindu practice.

MARRIAGE AND FAMILY. Mode.

According to Aymonier (1891: 29-33), parents permit their daughters great freedom of choice in marriage. The girl's parents make the overtures in asking the boy in marriage. Among the non-Muslim Chams there is no ritual. When marriage is agreed upon, the boy goes to live in the compound of the girl's family. A feast is held, and the boy presents the girl with gold or silver as a symbol of the marriage. Among the well-to-do, this gift may be larger—much silver, or several buffalo. ● Leuba (1923: 186-90) notes that the Kaphir (Brahman) marriage takes place without religious or civil ritual. There is a simple feast given by the two families as recognition of the marriage. Muslim marriages, however, do entail a ritual. *Imams* act as witnesses, and the parents have a role in the ritual. The girl's parents ask the groom if he accepts their daughter in marriage, and he is expected to respond positively. A large feast follows (Aymonier 1891: 50-100). Among the Chams of Parik and Karang, according to Aymonier, the marriage is somewhat different, probably due to Vietnamese influence. The boy may ask the girl in marriage, and on the evening of the marriage an intermediary, carrying candles, escorts the boy to the girl's house. **Form.** Aymonier (1891: 31) reports that the Chams of Binh Thuan are too poor to practice polygyny, although it is allowed. For those few who can afford it, the consent of the first wife is necessary. **Residence.** Matrilocal. The boy goes to live in the compound of the girl's family. [Aymonier 1891: 29-32.] **Inheritance.** Females inherit the family property (Aymonier 1891: 29-32). **Divorce.** Divorce is generally demanded by the woman, who gets the house as well as two-thirds of the common property (Aymonier 1891: 30-31).

SOCIOPOLITICAL ORGANIZATION. During the imperial phase of Cham history, society was divided into four castes—Brahmans, Ksatriyas, Vaisyas, and Sudras. The division, however, was not completely rigid. A woman of nobility could marry a man of low caste if he had the same family name. [Maspéro 1928: 17-19.] Following their conquest by the Vietnamese, the Chams lost all semblance of their traditional sociopolitical organization. Villages were organized along the lines of the traditional Vietnamese village. Each was composed of several hamlets, administered by a group of notables who were elected by the residents. The number of notables varied from five to fifteen, and they were charged with the complete administration of the village. The *ly truong*, or headman, was in charge of all village affairs. Each village had some communal land. Several villages were organized into a canton, with the *huyen* as the largest local administrative unit. [Leuba 1923: 196-99.]

RELIGION. **Brahmanism.** According to Aymonier (1891: 35-38), Cham religion incorporates a degenerate type of Brahmanism. The *po-yang* are the gods, and they are numerous. The three principal deities are Po Nagar, Po Rome, and Po Klong Garai—the last two Cham royalty who have achieved divine status. There are a number of important feminine deities, among them Po Nagar, "Goddess Mother of the Kingdom," a Cham version of the ancient Bhagavati, the Cakti of Civa. Another is Patao Kumei, "Queen of

Women," associated with the paddy fields and fertility; she is alleged to have taught the Chams the art of irrigation. The Brahman Chams have retained some of the ancient beliefs in spirits, and they also have adopted some of the Muslim deities. They venerate Ovloh (Allah), whom they believe to have been an ancient Cham ruler. **Islam.** In 1891 Aymonier pointed out that relations were excellent between the non-Muslim priests and Muslim priests. The Muslims, he noted, were isolated from the Islamic world, and consequently had no spirit of proselytizing. Their religious practices were adulterated: prescribed ablutions were not observed, and the five *vaktou*, daily adorations, were observed only on Fridays and during Ramadan. The study of the Koran in Arabic had faded, and while they observed the taboo against eating pork, the Cham Muslims did drink alcoholic beverages. [Aymonier 1891: 79-80.] Ner (1941: 154-55), writing at a later date, felt that the Muslims were more on the margin of Islam than a part of it. They have retained some pre-Muslim beliefs, and have also adopted some beliefs and practices of neighboring groups. Ner found that they do not observe the daily prayers, nor do they observe the taboos against alcohol or pork. They have, however, preserved a recognition of Muslim deities. Even the non-Muslims have some veneration for Allah. The Muslim Chams also believe in Mahamet (Mohammed), and in the incarnation of Po Rathulak (Rasul Allah, one of the names of the prophet). Other deities include Djiburaellak (Gabriel) who was created by Mahamet, and Po Haova (Eve) and Po Adam, both created by Ovloh. [Aymonier 1891: 40-47.] **Practitioners.** According to Aymonier (1891: 42-46), one of the last Brahmanic remnants among the Chams are the *basheh*, priests who are found in many of the non-Muslim villages of the Binh Thuan area of central Vietnam. The *basheh* are not specialists. They cultivate their fields, or engage in other forms of economic activity. Their male children usually learn the métier from their fathers, and undergo a series of initiations. A *basheh* must be married, and in most instances he reaches the age of 25 or 30 before his final initiation. The *basheh* plays an important role in non-Muslim rituals, particularly cremations. He is subject to caste-associated food taboos, which include beef, pork, the meat of the antelope or wild goat, frogs, and *hakan*, the common fish of the area. *Tchamenei* are priests of an order somewhat lower than the *basheh*, functioning primarily as guardians of the cult accouterment—platters, cups, bowls, and silver spittoons. The *tchamenei* observe the same abstinences as the *basheh*. *Kathar* or *kadhar* are singers and musicians who play a role in many rituals. *Padjao* are priestesses at the *tchamenei-kathar* level, and *kaing-yang* are priestesses of a somewhat lower order. The lowest order of priest is the *ong-banoek*, who performs rituals associated with irrigation canals and waterways. The *ong-banoek* may not eat the *hakan* fish, and must abstain from sexual relations during the time of ritual performances. Among the Muslim Chams the *radja* are priestesses who perform special rituals. They are allowed to marry, but they must avoid eating pork and sand lizard. The *medouon* or *padouon,* found among the Muslim Chams, are singers and musicians who, together with the *radja,* perform certain domestic rituals to the accompaniment of drums and stringed instruments. [Aymonier 1891: 42-50; Durand 1907: 318-19.] **Ceremonies.** A single mosque serves several villages. These are ramshackle structures of thatch. On Friday, the faithful gather to venerate Ovloh (Allah) and Po Dibata Thuor (Lord of Heaven), an ill-defined deity often confused with Allah. At these rituals, the *ong-grou,* two *imams,* two *katip,* and a *medine,* as well as all eight priests, must be present, along with a number of the faithful. Women bring food, which is consumed at a feast which follows the prayers. Tubah is a ritual of spiritual cleansing for the faithful, particularly the elderly. This is essentially a family fete, with a special shelter, food, and the necessary accouterment provided by each family. The *ong-grou, imams,* and *katip* are invited to officiate. Circumcision takes place around the age of 15. For girls of the same age, the Muslim Chams have a ritual called Karoeh (closure, closing), and until this ritual has been performed, a girl is sexually inaccessible. [Aymonier 1891: 79-87.] **Cult of the ancestors.** According to Aymonier (1891: 57-66), the non-Muslim Chams practice a cult of the ancestors. After cremation, some of the bones are collected and kept in a box in the house. There are prescribed rituals on the third, tenth, and one hundredth days after the cremation. On the first anniversary the bones are buried with those of other deceased kin in a family plot known as *kout.* According to Mus (1933: 379), the burial ground is located in the paddy fields, in a specific place where sacred rice is grown, and on it stand a number of more or less worked stones called *kut—* five stones for men, two for women. Ancestors are honored at the Kate and Tchabaur fetes, and also at the Radja celebration. Periodical rituals are also held at the graves, and if the family is well-to-do, a *basheh, kadhar,* or *padjao* may officiate. The ancestors counsel their descendants through the mouth of a *padjao.* [Aymonier 1891: 57-66.] **Soul, death, and afterlife.** Muslim Chams bury their dead without great ceremony. The corpse is kept in the house for several days, during which prayers are recited and visitors pay their respects. Among wealthy Brahman Chams, the corpse is exposed as long as 17 days, and a special shelter may be constructed for the bier, with the head orientated in the direction of the rising sun. A number of amulets are prepared by the priest, and the corpse is garbed in special vestments. There are rituals and prayers, and a cortege carries the corpse to the pyre for cremation. [Leuba 1923: 188-96.]

BIBLIOGRAPHY. Aymonier 1891; Benedict 1942; Durand 1907; Eickstedt 1940; Leuba 1923; Maspéro 1928; Mus 1933; Ner 1941; Nguyen 1944; NNCDT 1959; Olivier and Chagnoux 1951; Parmentier 1918.

CAMBODIA CHAMS

ORIENTATION. **Identification and location.** The Chams located in Cambodia, mostly around the Tonle Sap, are the descendants of refugees from central Vietnam, who fled following the collapse of Champa in the fifteenth century. Aymonier (1891: 95-111) noted that they had retained their cultural identity, and more recently Olivier and Chagnoux (1951: 271-318), in a comparative anthropometric study including a sample of 92 Chams in Cambodia, concluded that they have retained identifiable group physical characteristics. **Linguistic affiliation.** Malayo-Polynesian.

SETTLEMENT PATTERN AND HOUSING. Cham settlements tend to be similar to Khmer settlements —usually oriented along water courses. [Aymonier 1891: 95-97.]

ECONOMY. The Cambodia Chams engage in fishing, and cultivate some industrial crops such as cotton, indigo, and sesame. They also produce jewelry and sculpture, and engage in boat construction. Cham women weave silk and make mats. The Chams are also considered particularly adept at raising buffalo. [Aymonier 1891: 95-98.]

RELIGION. **Major religions.** The Chams of Cambodia are Muslim, and, according to Aymonier (1891: 95-111), more orthodox than those of central Vietnam. They venerate Allah both in mosques and in private shrines, and observe the daily adorations facing Mecca. There is a well-structured religious hierarchy. The head is the *muphti (mufti).* Below him are three dignitaries—*tun kalik, radjak kalik,* and *tuon pake.* The next level is that of the *hakem* or *me vat,* chiefs who are in charge of the *imams* in each mosque. *Katip* are those who engage in and lead prayers. *Bilal* are keepers of religious discipline. **Ceremonies.** The major rituals are Boulan Oek (Ramadan); Boulan Oek Hadjih (the month of the pilgrims), also called Boulan Ovloh (the month of Allah); Melut or Molot, a type of initiation ritual for children; and Soura, honoring the distress of Mohammed. Tamat is a ritual honoring young men who have become Monomat Koroan, masters of the Koran. Tapat is similar to Tubah of the Vietnam Muslim Chams, a ritual in which the elderly are absolved spiritually. There also are rituals associated with planting and with the new year, fixed by the Cambodian court. **Practitioners.** *Imams* are found in all Muslim villages, and are exempt from corvées. In each village the *imams* are associated with a mosque in which the leader, the *ong-grou,* officiates at all rituals. Below him are the *katip* or *medine* (also known as the *medouon* or *padouon*). [Aymonier 1891: 77-95.]

BIBLIOGRAPHY. Aymonier 1891; Olivier and Chagnoux 1951.

UPLAND GROUPS

BIH

Synonym. *Pih*

ORIENTATION. **Identification.** Thomas (1962: 6) believes the Bih may originally have been a Rhadé group, but that they have diverged due to long contact with the Mnong. Maitre (1912: 400) reported that the "Pih" (undoubtedly referring to the Bih) spoke a corrupt Rhadé dialect. **Location.** South of the Rhadé in the vicinity of lower Krong Kno in southern Vietnam (Maitre 1912: 400; Dam Bo 1950: 961; *Carte ethnolinguistique de l'Indochine* 1949). **Linguistic affiliation.** Varied opinions exist as to the linguistic placement of the Bih. Dam Bo (1950: 1000) describes them as a group that speaks a Cham dialect. Pinnow (1959: 3) classified Bih as a Mon-Khmer language, whereas Thomas (1962: 6) notes that Bih is mutually intelligible with Rhadé and should be classified as a Malayo-Polynesian language. **Demography.** The NNCDT (1959: 248) reports a combined total of 40,000 for the Bih, Churu, Raglai, and Noang.

ECONOMY. **Agriculture.** According to Maitre (1912: 400), the Bih have converted extensive marshes in their territory into paddy fields. **Industrial arts.** In certain villages near beds of fine pottery clay, the women engage in small-scale pottery industry, producing a variety of pots for domestic use. Sabatier, while *résident* in Ban Me Thuot, established a small brick kiln in the Bih area. [Botreau-Roussel and Jouin 1943: 387-89.]

BIBLIOGRAPHY. Botreau-Roussel and Jouin 1943; *Carte ethnolinguistique de l'Indochine* 1949; Dam Bo 1950; Maitre 1912; NNCDT 1959; Pinnow 1959; Thomas 1962.

CHURU

Synonyms. *Chru, Curu*

ORIENTATION. **Identification.** Churu is sometimes spelled Chru (Thomas 1961) or Curu (Queguiner 1943: 395). **Location.** In the vicinity of the valley of Dran, between Dalat and Phan Rang, in South Vietnam (Maitre 1912: 12). **Linguistic affiliation.** The Churu speak a language of the Malayo-Polynesian stock (Thomas 1961). **Demography.** A North Vietnamese source groups the Churu with the Raglai and the Noang, and reports their total population at 40,000 (NNCDT 1959: 248). A South Vietnamese government source (NCTXH 1960) reports 6,808 Churu. Phillips (1961: 12) reports 10,000.

ECONOMY. **Agriculture.** According to Gourou, the agriculture of the Churu is relatively advanced for a highland group. They have been in contact with the Chams, and have learned paddy cultivation, among other things, from them. They use the buffalo and plow. The Churu rent their slope areas, which they do not cultivate, to the Kil, who practice shifting agriculture. [Gourou 1945: 454.]

BIBLIOGRAPHY. Gourou 1945; Maitre 1912; NCTXH 1960; NNCDT 1959; Phillips 1961; Queguiner 1943; Thomas 1961.

HROY

Synonyms. *Bahnar Chams, Cam*

ORIENTATION. **Identification.** Guilleminet (1952: 7) considers the Hroy (whom he refers to as Cam) as a subgroup of the Bahnar. Smith (1959) maps the Hroy as a separate group called Bahnar Chams, and Phillips (1962) considers them a separate Malayo-Polynesian-speaking group. **Location.** East of Cheo Reo in South Vietnam. **Linguistic affiliation.** Thomas (1961) places Hroy with the Malayo-Polynesian languages. Phillips (1961: 12) notes that Hroy is very similar to Cham. **Demography.** Phillips (1961: 12) reports 10,000 Hroy. The NCTXH (1960) reports 6,176.

SETTLEMENT PATTERN AND HOUSING. According to Phillips (1961: 12), Hroy houses, which are on piles, resemble those of the Jarai.

BIBLIOGRAPHY. Guilleminet 1952; NCTXH 1960; Phillips 1961, 1962; Smith 1959; Thomas 1961.

JARAI

Synonym. *Djarai*

ORIENTATION. **Identification.** The name Jarai often is spelled Djarai by French investigators. The NNCDT (1959: 248) reports several Jarai subgroupings—the Hdrung, Hbau, A-rap, and To-buan. Lafont (1963: 11) lists the Arap, Habau, Hodrung, Sesan, Chu Ty, and Plei Kly. Maitre (1912: 398) reports the He Drong or He Grong, Habau, and Arap. **Location.** The Darlac plateau of the south central Vietnamese highlands. The major town is Pleiku. Jarai territory extends into Cambodia on the west and is contiguous with the Rhadé area to the south. **Linguistic affiliation.** The Jarai speak a language of the Malayo-Polynesian linguistic stock (Thomas 1961). **Demography.** The NNCDT (1959: 246) reports 160,000 Jarai, and the NCTXH (1960) 137,549; Lafont (1963: 11) estimates 150,000; Phillips (1961: 13) claims there are 200,000.

SETTLEMENT PATTERN AND HOUSING. **Settlement pattern.** Jarai villages, closely resembling those of the Rhadé, have longhouses oriented north–south, and are located on high ground near a good water supply. Most have between 20 and 60 longhouses, although there are a few small villages of 3 or 4 longhouses, usually occupied by members of the same sib. Kitchen gardens are near the houses, and granaries are clustered on the edge of the village. Some villages are enclosed by hedge growths. [Hickey 1956-58; Lafont 1963: 156-57.] **Housing.** Houses resemble those of the Rhadé. They are constructed on piling, with an extended platform at the end where the entrance is located. The interior is divided into compartments, most of which are occupied by matrilineally-linked nuclear families. There is a common room for family gatherings and receiving guests. [Hickey 1956-58; Lafont 1963: 156.]

ECONOMY. Little information is available on the economic activities of the Jarai. They appear to practice swidden upland rice agriculture, and to cultivate the same secondary crops as the Rhadé. Hunting and fishing also appear to have the same role that they do in Rhadé society.

KIN GROUPS. Both Jarai and Rhadé have matrilineal descent and exogamous matrisibs. In some areas, such as Cheo Reo, sibs seem to be better defined than in others. Lafont (1963: 148-51) lists seven Jarai clans [matrisibs]: the Romah, Rochom, Siu, Rohlan, Kopa, Roo, and Ksor. Matrisibs often have taboos relating to certain animals with whom they have alliances. The Rochom have an alliance with domestic and wild buffalo, the Ksor with reptiles, and the Siu with the iguana, the kite bird, and the toucan. The taboo includes restrictions against consuming the flesh of the animal or having the animal in the house. [Lafont 1963: 153-56.]

MARRIAGE AND FAMILY. **Mode.** As among the Rhadé, the female asks the hand of the male in marriage. Her family initiates the engagement procedures by obtaining the services of an intermediary, who offers a bracelet to the man's family. Marriage usually follows soon after (a week in most instances). The marriage ritual takes place at the bride's house, where there is a symbolic exchange of a bracelet and pieces of chicken. After the dowry is agreed upon, the groom visits the village water source to expose himself to the spirits there. A feast ends the marriage celebration. [Lafont 1963: 160-69; Hickey 1956-58.] **Form.** Polygyny is practiced among the Jarai (Lafont 1963: 170-72). **Residence.** According to Lafont (1963: 150), a newly-married couple reside matrilocally until the birth of the first child, and then, with the agreement of the wife's family, are free to establish their own household. **Domestic unit.** The Jarai household is made up of a number of matrilineally-linked nuclear families (Hickey 1956-58; Lafont 1963: 151-53). **Inheritance.** Those goods of the deceased not sacrificed at his tomb are divided by the "person who continues the house," i.e. by the one who becomes head of the house, by calling together the heirs and agreeing on a division of the property (Lafont 1963: 199-203). **Secondary marriage.** When a woman dies, her unmarried sister must marry the widower. If there are no unmarried sisters, the widower returns to his maternal longhouse while his children remain at their mother's longhouse (Hickey 1956-58).

SOCIOPOLITICAL ORGANIZATION. Although the sorcerer known as the Sadet of Fire was also a powerful political leader in the past, there exists no traditional tribal sociopolitical system among the Jarai, nor do the subgroupings function as political units. The adult village population selects a headman from among the household heads, and the elderly males form a council which functions as an advisory body to the village headman and a tribunal for resolving disputes. Since wealth is a manifestation of the spirits' approval, well-to-do villagers have considerable influence in village affairs. Bachelors and spinsters have very low status. [Lafont 1963: 156-59; Guilleminet 1952: 224; Hickey 1956-58.]

RELIGION. **Supernaturals.** The Jarai, like the Rhadé, have an extensive pantheon of *yang*, or spirits. **Practitioners.** The Sadet of Fire, the Sadet of Water, and the Sadet of the Wind are the three most powerful sorcerers in the Jarai area. According to Jarai tradition, as keeper of the sacred saber (alleged to be the Prah Khan saber of the ancient Khmer), the Sadet of Fire derives his unusual power from the host of spirits associated with the saber (the spirits are believed to live in the Sadet), giving him great strength in battle as well as power to dispel epidemics (Bourotte 1955: 31-33). Jouin (1951a: 73-83) contends that the last real Sadet of Fire was a Jarai named Y-Thih, who lived in the nineteenth century, and even though his successors are often referred to as *ae m'dao*, masters of the saber (also a designation for the Sadet of Fire), they should be called *ae buom*, guardians of the house of the saber, as they are not proper Sadets. • All investigators agree that when the Sadet of Fire grows old, Jarai tradition demands that his kinsmen slay him. There are two reported versions of the means by which the successor is chosen. One is that prior to death the Sadet throws his copper bracelet into the pool at Plei Mtao (the village where the saber is kept and where the Sadet resides), and that the male who emerges from the pool with the bracelet on his arm is the new Sadet (Ezzaoui 1940: 169-74). Another version is that after the death of the Sadet (Bok Redau), the young warriors gather in the communal house to sleep. While they sleep, one of the elders demands: "Who will be Bok Redau?" When one of them responds, "It is I," a bracelet is placed on his arm as a symbol of his new role (Bourotte 1955: 33). **Soul, death, and afterlife.** Jouin (1949: 21-131) describes the elaborate rituals associated with death, the establishment of the tomb, and in some cases, the subsequent abandonment of the tomb, that are practiced by the Jarai located in Darlac province (numbering some 3,249, and referred to by Jouin as the Rhadé Djaray). The rituals vary, depending on the type of death; the Jarai differentiate natural death, death far from the village, accidental death, miscarried fetus or stillborn, death by contagious disease, death by poisoning, and death by condemnation.

BIBLIOGRAPHY. Bourotte 1955; Ezzaoui 1940; Guilleminet 1952; Hickey 1956-58; Jouin 1949, 1951a; Lafont 1963; Maitre 1912; NCTXH 1960; NNCDT 1959; Phillips 1961; Thomas 1961.

KRUNG

ORIENTATION. **Identification.** Krung is the only name reported for this group. **Location.** Along the upper Ya Liau, Ya Hiau, and Kra Bou rivers north of Ban Me Thuot. Some extend into the area of Cheo Reo. [Maitre 1912: 399; Maurice and Proux 1954: 149.] **Linguistic affiliation.** The Krung speak a language of the Malayo-Polynesian stock. [Thomas 1961.] **Demography.** The NCTXH (1960) reports 5,677 Krung.

BIBLIOGRAPHY. Maitre 1912; Maurice and Proux 1954; NCTXH 1960; Thomas 1961.

NOANG

Synonym. *La-Dang*

ORIENTATION. **Identification and linguistic affiliation.** The Noang, also called La-Dang, are Malayo-Polynesian speakers (NNCDT 1959: 248; Dam Bo 1950: 1000). **Location.** Southeast of Dalat in South Vietnam (Dam Bo 1950: 961). **Demography.** According to the NNCDT (1959: 248), the Bih, Churu, Raglai, and Noang together number 40,000.

KIN GROUPS. According to Dam Bo (1950: 1086), the Noang are matrilineal. Residence after marriage is matrilocal.

RELIGION. There are male and female sorcerers, *bojou* (Dam Bo 1950: 1125).

BIBLIOGRAPHY. Dam Bo 1950; NNCDT 1959.

RAGLAI

Synonym. *Orang Glai*

ORIENTATION. **Identification.** Maitre (1912: 400) reports that the Raglai are also known as the Orang Glai, or "Men of the Forest." A distinction is usually made between southern and northern Raglai, since these groups are separated by populations of Cham speakers. Dam Bo (1950: 1094) considers the southern Raglai closely related to the Noang and heavily influenced by the Chams. **Location.** The northern Raglai occupy a mountainous area inland from the coastal city of Nhatrang in South Vietnam. The southern Raglai are inland from Phan Rang city, south of Dalat. [*Carte ethnolinguistique de l'Indochine* 1949; Maitre 1912: 400.] **Linguistic affiliation.** Phillips (1961: 12) places Raglai in the Malayo-Polynesian stock, and distinguishes southern from northern Raglai. **Demography.** Phillips (1961: 12) reports a total of 40,000, divided equally between northern and southern Raglai. The NCTXH (1960) reports a population of 31,125.

KIN GROUPS. According to Dam Bo (1950: 1086), the Raglai are matrilineal. Females have title to family property, and jural authority rests with the mother's brother. Residence after marriage is matrilocal.

RELIGION. There are several grades of male sorcerers. The Raglai village of Choah is considered a religious sanctuary to which sorcerers make annual pilgrimages. [Dam Bo 1950: 1125.]

BIBLIOGRAPHY. *Carte ethnolinguistique de l'Indochine* 1949; Dam Bo 1950; Maitre 1912; NCTXH 1960; Phillips 1961.

RAI

ORIENTATION. **Identification.** The Rai are identified by Thomas (1963) as a small Malayo-Polynesian-speaking group. They are located inland from Phan Thiet in the vicinity of the Chrau and Nop groups in the area northeast of Saigon in South Vietnam.

BIBLIOGRAPHY. Thomas 1963.

RHADÉ

Synonyms. *Raday, E-De*

ORIENTATION. **Identification.** Rhadé is the spelling most commonly used for this group, but some American investigators (Smith 1959; Phillips 1962) spell it Raday and the Vietnamese (NNCDT 1959: 248) spell it E-De. Jouin (1949: 132-93) reports these subgroups: Rhadé Kpa (known as the "true Rhadé"), Rhadé M'dur, Rhadé A'dham, K'tul, Epan, Blo, K'ah, K'drao, and H'wing. Jouin classifies the Bih as a Rhadé subgroup. **Location.** The Darlac plateau in the highlands of southern Vietnam in a large area extending westward into Cambodia (Maurice and Proux 1954: 129-31). **Linguistic affiliation.** Malayo-Polynesian (Thomas 1961). **Demography.** On the basis of a 1944-45 survey, Jouin (1950a: 280) reported the Rhadé population at 58,473; Maurice and Proux (1954: 129) reported 80,000. More recently the NNCDT (1959: 248) and the NCTXH (1960) have both published a figure of 120,000, which agrees with the figure given by a missionary source (Phillips 1961: 13).

SETTLEMENT PATTERN AND HOUSING. Settlement pattern.

Rhadé villages, preferably on high ground and always near a water source, usually have from ten to twenty longhouses strung along wide paths which run through the village. Ample space is left between houses to guard against fire and to allow for sizable kitchen gardens. Pigsties, enclosed by bamboo fences, are located to the rear of the houses, as are the granaries, which, like the houses, are constructed on piling. A feature in every village is the large clump of bamboo specially tended as a sacred grove. There is no separate building for the village council, whose meetings are generally held in the front section of the village headman's house. As the swiddens are often located a considerable distance from the village, temporary shelters are constructed during the planting season for the young men who guard the fields. [Hickey 1956-58; Maurice 1942: 87-90.] **Housing.** Longhouses constructed on piling, which vary in length according to the number of residents. The framework is of thick logs cut to fit together, set in place by elephants, and secured by thick rattan cord. The walls and floors are of poles, often bamboo, and the roof is thickly thatched with local long grass. At the front of the house is a large platform which serves as a veranda and work area, reached by steps cut in a log resting on the outer edge. The front entrance is for general use; a small rear entrance is used exclusively by the family. The orientation of the houses varies. It depends on the character of the terrain in the southern part of the Rhadé area—between the Donnai and Srepok rivers—and it is almost invariably north–south in the northern part. ● The interior of Rhadé houses—everywhere the same—is dominated by a large multipurpose room at the front which serves as the reception room for visitors, the place for feasts and some sacrifices, a gathering place for the members of the family, a general work area, and a place to store jars, gongs, weapons, and tools. The remainder of the interior is divided into small compartments which open on a common corridor running the length of

the divided part of the house. Each nuclear family has its own compartment. In addition, there is a special compartment for older members of the family and one set aside as a gathering place for female members and their guests. The compartments are large enough to contain beds, personal effects, and an open hearth. There also are open hearths in the corridor, which are used for preparing meals. [Hickey 1956-58; Maurice 1942: 90-119; Monfleur 1931: 34-35.]

ECONOMY. **Agriculture.** The cultivation of upland rice in swiddens is estimated by one source (Maurice and Proux 1954: 150) to constitute 80 per cent of Rhadé subsistence. The site of a new swidden is chosen with regard to a number of omens and taboos —e.g. to hear the cry of a wild goat is a good omen, and it is forbidden to cut a swidden around a grave that has not yet been abandoned. After the selection is made, the site is marked and a talisman, such as two goat's feet, may be buried in the soil to assure favorable work. The cutting of brush and small growth begins in September during the interim period in the rains known as the "little dry season," and continues into December. In February and March the trees are cut, and by late March or early April the fires are set, with the dried brush serving as kindling. In March a ritual planting of a field specially set aside precedes the general planting, with the entire village participating. The men move along in rows, making holes with digging sticks, followed by the women carrying the seeds in a bamboo container. [Maurice and Proux 1954: 149-61; Hickey 1956-58.] **Paddy cultivation.** Where there are streams or accessible bottom land, the Rhadé arrange paddy fields. Those designated "summer paddy fields" are sown in lowland rice in December and harvested in May or June. The excess of water in the fall prevents a second planting. The "rain paddy fields," those inundated by the rains, are planted in July and August and harvested in December or January. As with swidden agriculture, there are numerous rituals. The Rhadé apparently have no plows, and use hoes to prepare the moistened fields and buffalo to flatten the soil. Seeds are germinated before planting by four days of soaking. Women level the mud of the inundated field with their feet while the men scatter the seeds, which then sink into the mud. Low dikes hold water in the fields and small channels are arranged for water control. Some Rhadé transplant. [Maurice and Proux 1954: 191-94.] **Secondary crops.** Maize is important and is planted in a small part of the swidden—never in a full field—in April when the upland rice is being planted (Maurice and Proux 1954: 160-61). **Division of labor.** Heavy agricultural labor, such as preparing the swiddens and paddy fields for planting, is performed by the men. Those residing in the same longhouse constitute a common work force, and the longhouses within a village aid one another with the heavier agricultural tasks. Males are also responsible for paddy field irrigation and for guarding the swiddens during the growing season. Females are responsible for some of the lighter agricultural tasks such as broadcast sowing of rice or planting seeds in the swiddens in holes made ready by the men. Both sexes cooperate in clearing and weeding fields and in cutting and threshing crops such as rice. [Maurice and Proux 1954: 158-93.] **Land tenure.** Subsibs have set territories, and the Rhadé concept of ownership extends to trees, grass, and other growth on the land as well as to any lakes or streams. Title to the subsib's territory rests with the eldest female of the senior line, who is called the *po-lan* (*po,* proprietor; *lan,* land). Since under Rhadé law the land is inalienable, anyone desiring to cultivate a swidden within the territorial limits of a subsib must obtain the permission of the *po-lan*. Other responsibilities of the *po-lan* as guardian of subsib territory include periodic prescribed sacrifices and annual visits to the boundaries of the territory. In addition, she prescribes expiatory ritual sacrifices for violations of the territory—incest committed in the territory, cutting wood without permission, etc.—which may anger the souls of the ancestors and cause misfortune. [Sabatier 1940: 279-86; Maurice and Proux 1954: 204-16; Hickey 1956-58.]

KIN GROUPS. **Descent.** Matrilineal. Children belong to their mother's sib, and family property is in the hands of females. **Kin groups.** The matrilineal longhouse group is the corporate kin group of most importance. It is the mutual aid group which, in addition to sharing and maintaining the longhouse, often shares food, and always participates in cultivation of the common longhouse swiddens. Gongs, jars, cattle, and paddy, as well as the house, are lineage property, the title to which is held by the senior female of the lineage. Matrilineages are grouped into exogamous matrilineal sibs (Murdock's matrisibs), and these in turn into two phratries which also regulate marriage. [Hickey 1956-58; Condominas 1955a: 561-65; Sabatier 1940: 55.] The head of the lineage longhouse is a male. When he dies he is replaced either by his son-in-law or the husband of one of his wife's sisters. If the successor should be a minor, the eldest male in the house can temporarily assume the role of household head. In the absence of a son-in-law or brother-in-law, a nephew may succeed. A man residing matrilocally is expected to avoid any contact with his mother-in-law that might be interpreted as intimate. He must avoid her compartment and must treat her with distant respect. Above all, he must avoid joking with her. [Hickey 1956-58.] **Kin terminology.** The following kin terms were recorded by Hickey (1956-58):

Fa	*ama*
Mo	*ami*
FaElBr	*aprong ekei*
FaYoBr	*mneh ama neh*
FaElSi, MoElSi	*aprong m'nie*
FaYoSi, MoYoSi	*neh ami neh*
MoElBr	*awa*
MoYoBr	*amiet ekei*
ElBr	*ayong*
ElSi	*amai*
YoSb (f.)	*adei (mnie)*
YoSb (m.)	*adei (ekei)*

MARRIAGE AND FAMILY. **Mode.** Among the Rhadé the girl's family requests the boy in marriage and, when marriage has been agreed upon, the two young people exchange gifts. Her family is expected to pay a dowry, the size of which varies according to the family's wealth. [Sabatier 1940: 129-30.] **Extension of incest taboos.** Rhadé matrisibs are strictly exogamous with respect both to intercourse and marriage, and a couple guilty of sib incest must sacrifice a white buffalo. Marriage restrictions also apply at the phratry level: members of the Nie Kdam phratry can marry any member of the Eban phratry, but are forbidden to marry within their own phratry and with members of the Buon To matrisib. Restrictions within the Eban phratry exist only between certain sibs. Violations of these prohibitions, while not regarded as seriously as sib incest, require that the guilty parties sacrifice a pig to the spirits of their ancestors. [Hickey 1956-58; Sabatier 1940: 203-06.] **Residence.** Matrilocal. The new couple are usually given one of the compartments in the longhouse. **Domestic unit.** The longhouse, inhabited by the women of a matrilineage and their in-marrying spouses. **Inheritance.** Lineage property, including land, is in the hands of females, and females inherit from their mothers. **Divorce.** With the belief that marriage, once contracted, should be indissoluble, the Rhadé have strong sanctions against separation. If a couple does separate, the husband goes back to his own lineage longhouse and both the gifts exchanged at marriage and the dowry must be returned (Sabatier 1940: 170). **Secondary marriage.** If a husband dies, one of his younger brothers is expected to take the widow as his wife. If the eligible brothers are already married, one of them may take the widow as a second wife although this is not obligatory. It is taboo for a man to marry the widow of his younger brother. The rules of the sororate are similar to those of the levirate. In either case, if the family of the deceased is unable to furnish a replacement, a prescribed fine must be paid. [Hickey 1956-58; Condominas 1955a: 555-68; Sabatier 1940: 130-31.] According to Rhadé custom, an elderly woman who takes a young man as replacement for her deceased husband must provide him with a concubine so that he may have children. By the same token, if the replacement is too young, the wife is free to take a lover (Sabatier 1940: 135-45).

SOCIOPOLITICAL ORGANIZATION. Rhadé society is village-oriented and, according to Condominas (1955a: 561), villages were more or less autonomous prior to the arrival of the French. Each village was ruled by an oligarchy of leading families. Occasionally a village would become dominant in a local area, forcing other villages to recognize its leadership, although none ever attained a politically significant area or following. Condominas notes that the epic poem of the Rhadé, *The Song of Dam Son*, underlines several characteristic patterns of Rhadé life, e.g. the intermarriage among the families of chiefs, the first stirrings of a class sentiment, and the acceptance of slavery (1955a: 561-65). ● Under the French, districts and provinces were organized in the Rhadé area and new village chiefs named by the provincial administration. While the *résident* and higher provincial officials invariably were French, many of the lower-echelon provincial positions and almost all of those at the district level gradually came to be held by trained Rhadé. Rhadé law demands absolute obedience to the village chief and specifies fines for flouting his authority. [Sabatier 1940: 53-56.] **Village taboo.** In order to maintain the well-being of the village during periods when diseases tend to strike, the village chief may declare the village taboo to outsiders. Taboo signs are placed along the paths, and any violation may be punished. [Sabatier 1940: 115.]

RELIGION. **Supernaturals.** The pantheon of Rhadé spirits is ranked, the highest spirit being Ae Die, the lord of heaven, whose name is invoked repeatedly during the many rituals associated with agriculture. His sister, Dung Dai, is the spirit who protects the paddy, and her husband, Ae Du, the assistant of Ae Die, is associated with the sharing of paddy. Spirits usually represented in human form are Mtao Kla and his wife, H'Bea Klu, both lower than Ae Du in rank and both associated with cereals and other edible plants. At the lowest echelon of spirits are Ae Mghan, protector of paddy and millet, Yang Lie, an evil spirit associated with thunder, and his assistant Mjoa. Ae Yut is the rain spirit, and among the celestial spirits are Yang Hroe, the sun spirit, and Yang Mlan, the moon spirit. In addition, there are a large number of errant spirits, known generically as *ksok*, who are capable of great evil and are thought to inhabit caverns and the dark recesses of forests and mountains. Spirits of the dead are also revered. [Maurice and Proux 1954: 129-258.] **Rituals.** The Rhadé have a wide variety of prescribed rituals ranging from agricultural through household to the personally expiatory. **Agricultural rituals.** Swidden, paddy, and garden cultivation all have special rituals honoring the spirits and, in the case of swidden and paddy cultivation, the "soul of the rice." When a new swidden has been cleared and burned, there is a ritual to the spirit of the swidden. In February,

prior to clearing the fields, each household performs a rite for the wind to ensure sufficient rain for an ample crop. Another rite marks the clearing of each household's fields. Around the end of March an elaborate village planting ritual takes place at a special field to honor the highest spirit, the lord of heaven, and to keep the evil spirits away from the swiddens. Predatory animals that damage the crop are symbolically destroyed at this time. On the morning of the actual planting a purification rite honors the spirit of the land. As the buds appear, usually in June or July, a ritual is held in each swidden to bring back the "soul of the rice" and to attract the spirits of good harvest. ● Several rituals precede planting in paddy cultivation. Any ominous signs call for a ritual to propitiate the evil spirits, and several days prior to sowing there is a brief ritual blessing the grains. Ritual prayers precede the harvest and a ritual of the new rice follows, at which time the spirits associated with agriculture are invited to partake of the first rice. There is also a village harvest ritual. Ritual offerings are made to invite the "souls of the paddy" to enter the granary. [Maurice and Proux 1954: 150-202.] **The cult of the land.** The *po-lan*, the female guardian of subsib land, is the officiant at rituals associated with this cult. The *po-lan* makes an annual sacrifice after the harvest, and every seven years on her visit to all parts of the subsib territory she makes a prescribed ritual offering to the high spirits of the Rhadé pantheon. If violation of an incest taboo occurs in a subsib territory, the *po-lan* must see to it that the proper expiatory sacrifice is performed by the guilty parties. In the case of drought, the *po-lan* officiates at a rain-making ritual. [Maurice and Proux 1954: 204-16; Sabatier 1940: 203-05.] **House-building rituals.** Taboos and prescribed divinations surround the choice of a site for the longhouse, and a propitiatory ritual precedes construction. Selection of construction materials also involves regard for taboos and magical omens. If an elephant is used in transporting logs to the construction site, a ritual is held to protect the animal from accidents. The ritual sacrifice of a chicken also precedes the placement of the large columns which constitute the main support of the house. Use of "male" and "female" varieties of bamboo are well defined in Rhadé house construction. An offering to the spirits is made when the house is three-quarters completed, and a chicken or pig is sacrificed to the spirits of the hearth and the land when the hearth is installed. A three-day celebration highlighted by a pig or buffalo sacrifice for the mistress of the house marks the end of construction. [Maurice 1942: 87-106.] **Animal rituals.** Associated with the cycle of agricultural rituals are special rituals for invoking the spirits to protect the draft animals, with offerings of particular foods for particular animals, e.g. only pork and eggs can be offered in behalf of elephants. [Maurice and Proux 1954: 144.] **Rice mystique.** Maurice and Proux (1954: 216-17) see an association in Rhadé rituals between the role of women and the fertility of rice plants. There also are ritual bonds between rice and other plants, notably millet, maize, tobacco, cotton, gourds, indigo, and eggplant, as well as such domestic animals as pigs, buffalo, and chickens. Most predatory animals, on the other hand, are enemies of the rice spirit—although toads have a special place in rice-agriculture rituals. The rice *mystique* is also found in other rituals: a good example is the prayer to rice in funeral rites. [Maurice and Proux 1954: 216-21.] **Stick consultation.** A special spirit, Yan Gie, associated with sticks of bamboo, may give protection or bring health or good fortune to a family. Any male may contact the spirit through the agency of a special intermediary who employs a bamboo stick as his object of consultation. Males between 18 and 22 manifest this power. Usually there are several such agents in each village. [Kerrest 1941: 216-23.] **Preventive rituals.** Jouin (1951b: 85-88) describes a ritual among the Rhadé K'drao, a subgroup located in five villages of M'drack district, wherein the first offering to guardian spirits is made while the sacrificial buffalo still lives and the jar alcohol remains

untouched. After the sacrifice has been made and leaves have been placed in the jar, a second appeal is made to benevolent spirits, including spirits of the dead, for good fortune and happiness. A third appeal is followed by great feasting and drinking. **Origin myth.** According to Jouin (1950a: 357-79), the Rhadé legends account for world history in five epics. In the first epic, the earth was consumed by fire; in the second, the earth cooled, but neither plant nor animal life yet existed; in the third, life appeared and there was a great flood, killing all humans but one couple who in the fourth epic multiplied into different groups that migrated in search of food; during the fifth epic, the Rhadé emerged from a hole in the ground, and subsequently left their natal islands on rafts, finally landing on the coast of what is now Vietnam.

BIBLIOGRAPHY. Condominas 1955a; Hickey 1956-58; Jouin 1949, 1950a, 1951b; Kerrest 1941; Maurice 1942; Maurice and Proux 1954; Monfleur 1931; NCTXH 1960; NNCDT 1959; Phillips 1961, 1962; Sabatier 1940; Smith 1959; Thomas 1961.

MALAY

THE VARIOUS DIALECTS OF MALAY, spoken in Malaya north to the Mergui archipelago and throughout much of Indonesia, are included within the Indonesian family of Malayo-Polynesian (Austronesian) languages (Capell 1962). Malay speakers engaged in trade and religious propagation have expanded over a wide area, coming into contact with a great variety of local populations. The result has been an intricate complex of Malay, Malay-like, and Malay-influenced languages and dialects. Thus the speech of the Moken or Sea Gypsies—the boat people of the Mergui coast and the coastal waters of western Malaya—is basically Malay but with vocabulary additions and peculiarities of pronunciation foreign to the standard Malay of the Peninsula. Likewise the Jakun, Aboriginal Malays of Johore, speak a basically Malay tongue but with an "archaic" accent, possibly due to Senoi influence.

MALAYS[1]

Synonym. *Orang Melayu*

ORIENTATION. **Identification.** The term Malay is the English version of the Malay word *melayu*. The Malays speak of themselves as Orang Melayu, or Malay people. Malay is not to be confused with

Malayan, which refers to all citizens of the Federation of Malaya, including members of other ethnic groups. **Location.** The Federation of Malaya, comprising the states of Perlis, Kedah, Perak, Selangor, Negri Sembilan, Johore, Kelantan, Trengganu, and Pahang, and the former settlements of Penang and Malacca, covers an area of approximately 51,000 square miles in the southern portion of the Malay Peninsula, from approximately 1° to 7° N. **Geography.** In the north, the Peninsula is divided by a series of low, jungle-clad mountain ranges, reaching a maximum altitude of over 6,000 feet in the north–central area. Lower hills, still steep and jungle-covered, dominate the center of the southern half of the country. Since the main mountain chain runs ap-

[1] This account of Straits Malay culture was contributed by R. E. Downs, who spent from July 1957 to December 1958 in Singapore and Malaya, most of the time in Kelantan studying an inland village in the district of Pasir Puteh. Some of the results of this research have appeared in Downs (1960). The author's corrections of final editorial changes and additions were received too late to be incorporated in the present edition.

proximately parallel to and about 50 miles inland from the west coast from Thailand to Malacca, the west coast has relatively short rivers with steep gradients, whereas those of the east coast are longer and descend more gradually. Most rivers have a trellislike drainage pattern, with transverse streams or gullies cutting the hill slopes. [IBRD 1955: 1.] Alluvial deposits along the river valleys and coasts up to 40 miles inland support the chief areas of settlement. Rice cultivation is concentrated on the relatively fertile deposits of the valleys and deltas of the larger rivers, particularly in Kedah, Province Wellesley, Perak, and Kelantan. Some rice is also grown in small areas between sandy ridges along the coasts of Kelantan and Trengganu. Mangrove swamps, from 50 yards to 12 miles wide, are typical of the west coast, whereas a 60 foot-wide fringe of *Casuarina* trees extends along most of the beaches of the east coast. [Dobby 1960: 91, 100, 106ff.] Nearly four-fifths of the country is covered by tropical rain forest closely resembling that of Borneo and Sumatra. This forest is a source of a great variety of woods and other products such as canes, bamboo, damar, and (formerly) gutta-percha. The enormously rich fauna is homogeneous with that found in Sumatra, Borneo, Java, and Tenasserim. [Foxworthy 1923: 42ff.; Robinson 1923: 47; Dobby 1960: chaps. 4, 6.] The climate is equatorial, with high and relatively uniform temperatures throughout the year, abundant rainfall, and high humidity. The west coast receives most of its rain during two intermonsoon seasons from March to the middle of May and from mid-September to the end of October, but the east coast gets most of its rain during the northeast monsoon, from November to February. [IBRD 1955: 1ff.] Tin has been Malaya's greatest mineral resource, although gold (for which the country was once noted) and some other minerals, of which iron ore is by far the most important, are also produced. [IBRD 1955: 71.] **Linguistic affiliation.** Malays are found in the southern provinces of Thailand, on Singapore Island, in the Riau Lingga archipelago, along the east coast of Sumatra, and along the coasts of many of the islands of Indonesia. They are closely related linguistically and culturally to most of the other Malayo-Polynesian speakers of Indonesia. The people of the state of Negri Sembilan on the west coast of the Peninsula came from Minangkabau on the west coast of Sumatra. The culture of the Malays in Thailand, at least in the southernmost province of Patani, where they constitute 75–80 per cent of the population, appears to be essentially the same as that of the Malays in the northern states of the Federation, except for their political institutions, which are dominated by the Siamese (cf. Fraser 1960; Graham 1924: *1*, Pt. II; Annandale and Robinson 1903). **Demography.** According to the 1947 census of Malaya, the Malays totaled 2,118,834, and constituted 43 per cent of the population. Some 309,000 "other Malaysians" (closely related immigrants from Southeast

Asia—primarily Indonesia), 1,884,534 Chinese, and 530,868 Indians made up most of the rest. The northern states of Perlis, Kedah, Kelantan, and Trengganu have the largest percentages of Malays, most of whom live in rural areas. [Tufo 1949; see also Smith 1952 for modern trends.] **History.** The earliest ancestors of the Malays seem to have entered the area from mainland Southeast Asia during the period between 2500 and 1500 B.C. (Heine-Geldern 1945: 138ff.; Tweedie 1953: 63). Historical records reveal the existence at about the second century A.D. of several small "Hinduized" kingdoms on the Isthmus of Kra, in the northern and eastern parts of the Malay Peninsula, and later in southern Kedah, Perak, Kelantan, Trengganu, and Pahang (Coedès 1948: 71, 88). These kingdoms seem from the beginning to have been dominated by a succession of empires based on mainland Southeast Asia or Indonesia: Funan, on the lower valley of the Mekong; Srivijaya and Djambi on Sumatra; Sukhothai and Ayuthia in Siam; and Madjapahit on Java. [Coedès 1948; see also Wheatley 1962.] The fifteenth century saw the increasing development of the southern states and the rise of Malacca, which was founded in 1403 and gradually came to dominate the Peninsula at the expense of the Siamese. By the time Malacca fell to the Portuguese in 1511, it had become the greatest port in Southeast Asia. Its control extended as far north as Kedah on the west coast and Patani on the east, and included as well the Riau Lingga archipelago and the kingdoms of Rokan, Siak, Kampar, and Indragiri on the east coast of Sumatra. By the middle of the fifteenth century Malacca had been converted to Islam, and it was influential in converting the rest of the Peninsula during that century, although the first record of the presence of Islam in Malaya dates from 1326 or 1386 at Kuala Berang in Trengganu. [Hall 1955: chap. 10; Moorehead 1957: 137; Wheatley 1962: 309.] With the fall of Malacca, the Siamese reasserted their control over the northern part of the Peninsula. Although Sultan Mahmud of Malacca moved to the Riau Islands and founded the Riau Johore sultanate, the southern part of the Peninsula was dominated by the Portuguese and to an even greater extent by the Achinese from Sumatra. The Dutch succeeded the Portuguese in Malacca in 1641, but the major influence in the area during the eighteenth century was exerted by the Buginese from Celebes. [Tregonning 1961: 15; Hall 1955: chap. 17.] In 1786 Francis Light acquired Penang from Kedah for the East India Company, and in 1800 took Province Wellesley as well. In 1819 the British acquired Singapore, and in 1824 took final possession of Malacca from the Dutch. In 1896 a Federation was formed, comprising Perak, Selangor, Negri Sembilan, and Pahang, and in 1909 Britain acquired by treaty from Siam the four northern states of Perlis, Kedah, Kelantan, and Trengganu, which together with Johore in 1914 formed the Unfederated States of Malaya. [Hall 1955: 421-52, chap.

29; Swettenham 1929; Parkinson 1960; Cowan 1961.] In 1946 Great Britain proposed a Malayan Union with a strong centralized government, but the plan was opposed by the rulers of the several states. A federal form of government was finally agreed to in February 1957, on the basis of a report by a Constitutional Commission, and independence was granted to the Federation of Malaya on August 31, 1957 (Federation of Malaya 1958a: 505-07; King 1957). **Cultural relations.** Throughout their history the Malays have been in more or less intensive contact with other peoples and cultures. They share much of their cultural tradition and history with Indonesia, for which their language has provided a lingua franca. The cultural legacy of Java is still evident in the *wayang* (shadow play) of Kelantan; Negri Sembilan still maintains the matrilineal social organization of Minangkabau, its country of origin; and immigrants from Indonesia constitute about 13 per cent of the present Malaysian population of the Federation. The northern Malay states of Perlis, Kedah, Kelantan, and Trengganu were at one time subject to Thailand, and Siamese influence is still evident in the first three. There are, moreover, quite a number of Siamese villages within the borders of Kelantan, Kedah, and Perlis (Tufo 1949: 81). ● The greatest cultural influence on the Malays, as on the peoples of Southeast Asia generally, has been that of Hindu India, which has made itself felt in language, religion, and social structure. In modern times large numbers of Indians, primarily Tamil-speaking, have come as manual laborers, mostly to work on European-owned rubber estates. Others are found in professional, clerical, and trading occupations. They have not been absorbed into Malay society as have the "other Malaysians," but form a more or less distinct community of their own. ● China has long played an important political role in Southeast Asia, but its cultural influence in Malaya has been far less than that of India. Chinese contact with the Peninsula dates back to the fifteenth century, but it was mostly restricted to Malacca, where mixture with the Malays produced the Baba. After the arrival of the British, especially during the nineteenth century, Chinese came in great numbers from southern and southeastern China to work first in the tin mines and later on rubber estates. They now constitute about 38 per cent of the population and are found primarily in mining and trading occupations, living mainly in urban areas. Because of the religious barrier, there has been little intermarriage with the Malays. ● The adoption of Islam has had profound effects on the Malays. It has not only brought them new religious concepts but has also increased their contact with other parts of the world, strengthened their feelings of solidarity with the rest of the (Islamic) Malaysian world, and provided many of their basic social and economic codes. [Coedès 1948; Hall 1955; Winstedt 1950.] Relations of the Malays with the pagan tribal peoples of the

Peninsula have been sporadic, and have produced little understanding or good will on either side. Until the nineteenth century the Malays raided such groups as the Senoi for slaves and women; their term for these people, "Sakai," is a pejorative term disliked and resented by the Senoi. Senoi living near Malay communities may adopt wet-rice agriculture, but they rarely adopt Islam. There are relatively few cases of Senoi "becoming Malay" in this sense.

SETTLEMENT PATTERN AND HOUSING. **Settlement pattern.** The typical Malay settlement is the rural village (*kampong*), which may contain anywhere from 50 to 1,000 people. Except on the east coast, the towns tend to be inhabited more by Chinese, Indians, and other ethnic groups than by Malays. Malay villages are located primarily along rivers and roads or along the coasts. Towns are found at strategic communication points—ferry, road, or river junctions and river mouths—and serve as distribution centers. The form of the village varies with the terrain: it may stretch in parallel ribbons halfway up the slopes of a valley (as in Negri Sembilan), or along a raised river bank, or it may be built on raised ground in the midst of rice fields. Although the villages are not tightly nucleated and the houses not arranged in regular patterns, they usually form a continuous area containing kitchen gardens and coconut, fruit, and sometimes rubber trees. Rice fields and more extensive orchards and rubber stands surround this area. [Dobby 1942; Winstedt 1925b: 1-8.] Some villages contain a mosque (one to each religious district), and most have one or more smaller religious buildings for instruction and prayer. A village may also have a government primary school. All but the smallest have a certain number of sundry and coffee shops. Shops are built directly on the ground in Chinese fashion. **Housing.** Dwellings and the rice barns which commonly accompany them are raised on piles about four to eight feet from the ground. The simpler houses have split bamboo or nibong palm flooring, walls made of woven bamboo, palm, or reed, or occasionally of bark sheets, and gable roofs of thatch made from any of various palm fronds or grasses. More elaborate houses are made of wooden planks, and have tile roofs. The standard house form includes a veranda, a front room for receiving guests, one or more sleeping rooms or areas, and a kitchen area (which may be in an attached building) primarily for the women. The space under the house is used for storage. [Winstedt 1925b: 9-30.]

ECONOMY. The great majority of the Malays are dependent on agriculture, although a small percentage along the coasts are primarily engaged in fishing (cf. Firth 1946). Fish are also caught in ditches, swamps, streams, and rice fields. Hunting and gathering of wild products are carried on by Malays living near the jungle. Cottage industries are also of some economic importance in certain parts of the country. Rice is the principal crop and staple food, but rubber is the chief commercial product. Coconut and areca nut palms, betel vines, and tobacco are found in all villages, with commercial production of copra concentrated chiefly along the coasts. Other food crops of lesser importance include sago, tapioca, a great variety of vegetables (including cucumbers, peas, beans, chilies, and *keladi*), and fruits (such as durian, mangosteens, rambutan, papaya, bananas, pineapples, and limes). [Grist 1936.] **Agriculture.** Most rice is grown in flooded fields. Usually the necessary water is provided by rainfall, but in a few areas adequate water supplies and a sufficiently dense population have made the installation of permanent irrigation facilities worthwhile. Until the practice was forbidden by the British for reasons of soil conservation, water was obtained in many areas by damming the rivers during the flood season and digging ditches to the nearby fields. The traditional use of organic fertilizer is now being supplemented by artificial fertilizers. Except in a few favored localities with year-round irrigation facilities, only a single rice crop is produced annually. In some places catch crops of vegetables, which require relatively little water, may be grown on some of the rice fields in the off season, but generally the ground is grazed over by livestock between crops. Rice seedlings are raised in nurseries (usually dry) and then transplanted. The chief agricultural implements are the plow (wooden with metal blade), harrow (with wooden or metal teeth), hoe, and harvesting knife, which in some places has been superseded by the sickle. When the grain is harvested with the knife, it is stored on the stalk in granaries and threshed as needed; when it is cut with the sickle, it is threshed in the field and stored in wooden bins or woven baskets. Oxen or water buffalo are used for plowing. Terracing is rare. Dry rice is also grown, not only as a first crop after clearing a piece of jungle, but also on permanent fields not suitable for flooding, particularly in Kelantan and Trengganu. The seed is dibbled into the plowed and harrowed ground and is not transplanted. ● Rubber trees are cultivated mostly in small lots varying from a fraction of an acre to a few acres in size. The Malay smallholder normally taps the latex, coagulates it with acid and water, and rolls it out into corrugated sheets which are sundried and sold to a rubber dealer, who in turn sells them to a factory for further processing. Any coconuts which are not consumed or sold whole to dealers are made into copra. The nuts are split open and their flesh smoke-dried on a rack over a fire of coconut husks and shells, which may be enclosed to form a kiln. Occasionally oil is still made from copra in the home, a practice which used to be general. [Grist 1936; IBRD 1955: Pt. V, Report 1; Federation of Malaya 1956; Bauer 1948; Shaw 1926; Hill 1951.]

Domestic animals. Water buffalo and cattle (of the Siamese humped variety) are kept as draft animals and may occasionally be eaten. Sheep and goats are also raised on a much smaller scale for food. Fowl are found in all villages, and ducks (including the Muscovy duck) are common. **Food and stimulants.** The diet, which is highly spiced, consists mainly of rice, vegetables, coconuts, and fruit, supplemented with fish, beef, chicken, and eggs. Sago and tapioca are also eaten. Beverages include water, tea, coffee, and commercial soft drinks. The chewing of betel and areca nuts with lime and the smoking of tobacco are widespread, although the former is declining. **Industrial arts.** Cottage industries include basketry, mat making, weaving, pottery, and metal work in brass, copper, silver, and gold. Trengganu produces an alloy of tin, copper, and antimony. A declining number of village blacksmiths produce knives, plowshares, and other tools. Boat building ranges from dugouts to ocean-going fishing and cargo boats. [Winstedt 1925a; 1929; 1950: 161-75; IBRD 1955: 301-16; Warington Smyth 1902; Gibson-Hill 1949.] **Trade.** In the past, the many small Malay kingdoms located at river mouths and along river courses were supported to a large extent by duties levied on products passing through them, and the Malays themselves engaged extensively in trading. In recent times, however, most trade has been in the hands of Chinese, Indians, and Europeans. Malays still predominate in fishing and in the sale of fish, and on the east coast they handle much of the petty trading throughout the countryside and at the markets found in most towns. Recent improvements in transportation have led to the abandonment of village markets in favor of those in the towns. There are shops in all but the smallest villages, and village produce is also sold and bartered informally within and between neighboring villages. Traveling vendors (usually Indians) sell fish and sundries. The sale of the principal cash crops, such as rubber, coconuts, and areca nuts, is handled through local dealers, who are mostly Chinese. **Division of labor.** The social distinction and separation of the sexes is well marked, but the division of labor is not strict. Normally women spin and weave, keep house, cook, polish rice, tend vegetable gardens, transplant rice seedlings, and shop and sell at the markets; whereas men work metal, do carpentry (including house and boat building), fish at sea, and do the heavy work in the fields, such as clearing ground, plowing, and hoeing. Both sexes work together harvesting and threshing rice, and both tap latex and roll it out into sheets, although women generally coagulate it. Men and boys tend cattle and water buffalo. **Land tenure.** Traditionally individuals have held usufructuary and occupational rights to land, although in theory all land has always belonged ultimately to the rulers of the several states. Individual rights could be handed down from generation to generation, provided the land remained in use and produce taxes were paid on it to the rulers via their chiefs. These holdings were never secure, however, and the individuals were further liable to forced labor and exactions on their personal property. The British introduced the Torrens system of registration, under which individual landholders were given permanent, registered title to their land with full rights of alienation and inheritance, subject to the payment of a land tax. [IBRD 1955: 223-33; Maxwell 1884; Wilson 1958: 7-11.] The Malays and "other Malaysians" have been protected in their possession of cultivable land by a series of tenure and reservation enactments passed between 1909 and 1941 (in all the states but Penang and Province Wellesley), which prohibit other people from acquiring land in reserved areas and Malays from leasing or charging such land to other people (IBRD 1955: 227ff.). Various other types of land tenure agreements also exist, including fixed rent, crop sharing, lease, loan, and mortgage. Although the popularity of these types of tenure varies from region to region and state to state, generally speaking share cropping is practiced on the east coast and rental of land is the most common arrangement on the west coast (Wilson 1958: chap. 2).

KIN GROUPS. **Descent.** In Negri Sembilan descent is matrilineal and the people are divided into a series of descent groups (*perut, suku*) and territorial units (*negeri* or *luha'*) with a kinship basis. Elsewhere descent is reckoned bilaterally, except that no corporate kin groups exist, and that succession to offices (primarily limited to the upper classes) has tended to be patrilineal. One writer has reported a tendency to agnatic grouping about a politically dominant family in a village in Johore (Burridge 1956). Personal kindreds (reckoned laterally as far as third cousins) are known, and apparently villages used to be composed primarily of consanguineous relatives (Gullick 1958: 32ff.). Even today it is the general rule (at least on the east coast) that affinal or consanguineal ties with another village inhabitant are required for residence, which means that the great majority of the people in a village are related to each other. **Kin terminology.** Basic kin terms of reference are as follows (cf. Djamour 1959: 26ff.):

Fa	*bapa (pak)*
Mo	*(ě) mak*
So, Da	*anak*
ElBr	*abang**
ElSi	*kakak**
YoBr, YoSi	*adik*
FaBr, MoBr	*bapa (pak) saudara*
FaSi, MoSi	*(ě) mak saudara*
FaFa, MoFa	*datok*
FaMo, MoMo	*nenek* (or *datok*)
Grandchild	*chuchu*

| Great-grandparent | *moyang* |
| First (second, third) cousin | *sa-pupu (dua pupu, tiga pupu)* Older cousin: *abang** or *kakak** *sa-pupu*, etc. Younger cousin: *adik sa-pupu*, etc. |

*In Kelantan *kakak* is used for both sexes.

MARRIAGE AND FAMILY. In former times, despite the fact that girls were more or less secluded, amorous adventures were one of the chief sports of young men (particularly of the upper classes). At the present time, premarital sexual relations are disapproved of, but greatly feared, and early marriage is encouraged to ensure the virginity of the bride. **Mode.** Marriage proposals are handled by go-betweens or by the parents of a prospective couple. Although marriages used to be arranged by the parents without regard to the wishes of the principals (Swettenham 1929: 153), nowadays more account is taken of their wishes. Small presents are offered by the parents of the groom to those of the bride when an engagement is settled, and a sum of money is paid by the groom to the bride as the principal marriage payment. This payment is the Moslem *mahr*, but is also known as *mas kahwin*, or "marriage gold," which term was formerly applied to a payment made to the bride's family (Winstedt 1950: 47; Annandale and Robinson 1903: Pt. II, 74). Presents are also given to the couple by both families and by other guests at the wedding. Afterwards, when they are first visited by the couple, both families offer presents again. Most of the wedding presents contributed by the guests are kept by the bride's father. ● The marriage ceremony itself consists of two main parts. The first, called *nikah*, is required by Moslem law, and consists of the legalizing by a *kathi* or *imam*, in the presence of witnesses, of a contract agreed upon by the husband and wife (in person or through proper representatives), and the payment, or promise to pay, of the *mas kahwin*. The second part, which follows the *nikah* in the case of first marriages, is a traditional ceremony called *bersanding*, reflecting considerable Hindu influence. Guests are invited to the house of the bride's parents for feasting and the presentation of gifts (Winstedt 1950: 45ff.; 1951: 115-23; Djamour 1959: 73-79; Wilkinson 1920: 19-37). In Negri Sembilan the *suku* or *perut* of the two parties are directly involved in the traditional ceremonies and exchange of presents (de Josselin de Jong 1951: 127). **Form.** Polygyny to a maximum of four wives is permitted by Moslem law, but it is rare and found most frequently among the wealthy and the nobility. **Extension of incest taboos.** All cousins are permissible marriage partners, although there is some prejudice against marrying first cousins (Winstedt 1950: 190) and in some places against the marriage of two brothers' children (Djamour 1959: 69). In Kelantan, even though there is a stated preference for marriage with cousins, particularly second cousins, few such marriages actually occur. Marriages within the village are frequent but by no means the rule. Normally they are contracted by members of the same class, although it is not unusual for members of the nobility to marry lower class women, particularly as secondary wives. Formerly marriage within the kindred is supposed to have been more frequent and is still said to be common in Singapore (Djamour 1959: 68). In Negri Sembilan marriage between parallel cousins is forbidden. The *suku* is theoretically exogamous and the *perut* is so in fact as well as in theory. Some *biduanda suku* practice endogamy (de Josselin de Jong 1951: 126ff.). **Residence.** Residence is generally neolocal or ambilocal following an initial stay for a varying period with the bride's parents, although there are reports that matrilocality was once the rule in certain west coast areas (Gullick 1958: 33) and is frequent even now in some others, e.g. Singapore (Djamour 1959: 80ff.). In Negri Sembilan, residence is normally matrilocal, but after the birth of the first child it is neolocal on the same property. **Domestic unit.** The typical domestic unit is the nuclear family, although the stem family also occurs not infrequently. Occasionally a group of brothers or sisters and their spouses live in adjacent or connected houses. In Negri Sembilan the nuclear family is also the norm after the birth of the first child, although it is far less independent than among the bilateral Malays. ● The theory and outward appearance of male superiority are maintained in all matters, but women have considerable freedom in their everyday activities, and generally play a by no means submissive role in the family. They may own more property than their husbands and they frequently manage the household finances (cf. Firth 1943: chap. 2). **Inheritance.** Inheritance is based on Moslem law, which provides in detail for the division of property among the close relatives. Deviations ˮfrom these rules are allowed when agreed upon by the heirs, however. Generally sons and daughters share equally, instead of the sons receiving double shares as stipulated by law, and widows receive from one-third to one-half of their deceased husbands' property instead of their legal share of one-eighth (cf. Winstedt 1950: 114; Taylor 1937: 8, 10). There are earlier, but conflicting, reports that sons and daughters used to inherit different kinds of property (Maxwell 1884: 127; Rigby 1929: 34). **Divorce.** Divorce is easily obtained by men under Moslem law and is frequent among all the Malays of the Peninsula. Although the legal grounds for women to obtain divorce are few, wives are usually able to persuade their husbands to divorce them. Young children normally accompany their mother in cases of divorce.

SOCIOPOLITICAL ORGANIZATION. Political organization: traditional. The chief places of settlement of the Malays have been at river mouths or along river courses toward the interior, where they have lived primarily as wet-rice agriculturists, fishermen, and seafarers. In pre-British days they were politically organized into a number of independent feudal states. The population was composed of a ruling and a subject class, with the former divided into a royal patrilineage and a lesser nobility of various ranks and titles. There was also a relatively small class of debt bondsmen drawn from the subject class and slaves of foreign origin (mostly Africans, Bataks from Sumatra, and Malayan aborigines). The division between the two main classes was strict, and it was extremely difficult for a commoner to attain noble rank. Male nobility were permitted to marry beneath them, but women were not. ● The head of state bore the title of *yang di-pertuan* "he who is made lord," and, in most cases, that of Sultan as well. He was a member of the royal lineage, and was invested with supernatural power and dignity, which gave him theoretically absolute authority in civil, military, and religious affairs. He had a collection of sacred regalia, and maintained one or more royal residences, which often housed a harem and a large group of secretaries, armed retainers, domestic servants, boatmen, watchmen, destitute people, and fugitives. He ruled his country through a hierarchy of advisers and officials, both members of the royal lineage and chiefs of the districts into which each state was divided. The chiefs were in theory appointed by the Sultan, but their positions tended to be hereditary in the male line, and they held their offices primarily through their own strength. The power of the ruler was restricted by the power of these officials and of the district chiefs, and his position (succession to which was not automatic, though usually confined to the royal lineage) was frequently the object of struggle among the members of the royal lineage and the local chiefs whose support was necessary to them. These struggles often brought intervention from other states. [Gullick 1958.] ● The great majority of the Malay population has always lived in villages. In pre-British times the official head of a village was a local man of the subject class, appointed by the ruler of the state via the district chief. As their representative he had considerable authority, although he could not carry out his duties without the consent of his fellow village elders (Gullick 1958: 34ff.). During British and post-British times, however, the authority of the village head has been reduced or eliminated, and leadership has become more informal. In Kelantan there is normally both a village head appointed by the government and an unofficial head chosen by his fellow villagers, not on the basis of heredity, but rather for his personal qualities and capacities. His functions include not only maintaining order within the village, counseling its inhabitants, and directing its activities but also representing it in relations with other villages. His authority is limited, however, and depends on the continued support of the village. He shares the leadership of the village with a small number of men prominent for reasons of wealth, knowledge, character, intelligence, age, or family, whose unanimous approval is usually necessary for carrying out any activities concerning the village as a whole. **Contemporary government.** The present constitution of the Federation of Malaya, under which the Malays enjoy a protected status vis-à-vis the other ethnic groups, provides for a Paramount Ruler, the *yang di-pertuan agong*, chosen by the rulers of the several states from among themselves; a cabinet headed by a Prime Minister and responsible to the Parliament; and a Parliament consisting of a 38-member Senate (22 elected and 16 appointed) and a House of Representatives of 104 elected members. The state governments are modeled on the federal one. For administrative purposes the states are divided into districts, headed by district officers, and subdistricts, headed by *penghulu* (west coast) or *penggawa* (east coast), all of whom are appointed officials. On the east coast there are government-appointed village heads (*penghulu*) as well. Each state has its own police force, but statute law, introduced by the British and based largely on English and British Indian sources, is administered by federal officers in the courts (except for minor cases heard by the subdistrict heads). In addition to the state governments, some areas have various types of local governments —municipal committees and rural boards in Penang and Malacca, town boards and councils, and local councils elsewhere. More and more, the membership in these bodies is becoming elective. [Jones 1953: 97ff.; Ginsburg and Roberts 1958: 226ff.] A religious administration parallels the civil administration in each state. The districts are divided into a number of parishes (*mukim*), each with a mosque, under the charge of an *imam*, who not only leads prayers in the mosque but also records marriages and divorces and collects religious taxes. There is a *kathi's* court in each district and a *mufti* as chief religious judge in the state capitol. In Kelantan a religious council (*majlis ugama*) plays an important role, including the collection and distribution of religious taxes. [Federation of Malaya 1958a: 509ff.; 1958b; Jones 1953.] **Social stratification.** Class distinctions are still strongly marked in Malay society, although the nobility no longer have as much authority over the commoners as they once enjoyed. Government officials are still largely recruited from the upper classes, and in spite of postwar educational, economic, and political developments, there is a considerable gulf separating the ordinary villager in most areas from the government and its representatives and from townspeople in general. The sociopolitical structure of Negri Sembilan is atypical. With the exception of the royal house, which is patrilineal, all the people

are organized into a series of matrilineal kin groups and territorial units: *perut* (matrilineages of varying sizes), headed by an *ibu-bapa* or *buapa'*, twelve *suku* (matrisibs) each made up of related *perut* and headed by a *lembaga,* and an historically varying number of territorial units called *negeri* or *luha',* now totaling 13 including that of the ruler (*yang di-pertuan*), each headed by an *undang.* Four of the latter choose the ruler, whose authority is largely symbolic and religious. [De Josselin de Jong 1951: chaps. 8, 9; Swift 1956: 2ff.]

RELIGION. **Major religions.** All Malays are adherents of the Shafiite school of Islam, to which they were converted for the most part during the fifteenth century. They follow more or less faithfully the regular Muslim forms of worship, observe Muslim holidays and ceremonies connected with birth, circumcision, marriage, and death, and follow, with modifications, the Muslim law with respect to marriage, divorce, and the inheritance of property. [Zainal Abidin 1949.] Many Malay religious beliefs and practices, although intermingled with Islamic ones, are Hindu, pan-Malaysian, or indigenous in origin. The principal marriage ceremony (*bersanding*), the enthronement of the Sultan, and other state ceremonies are largely based on Hindu ritual. Birth customs, including the "roasting" of the mother for 40 days, are mostly indigenous, and circumcision for boys and clitoridectomy for girls, although they are in accord with Muslim custom, are also native to the area. [Wilkinson 1920; Winstedt 1950: chap. 3.] **Supernaturals.** The Malays believe in a host of spirits (*hantu*) of the earth, forest, trees, hills, water, animals, the sea, and the dead, which are capable of causing anything from annoyance to serious illness and death, and which, although they are sometimes accorded the Arabic title of *jinn* (genie), are of Hindu and native origin. **Practitioners.** A variety of medicine men or shamans (occasionally women) called *pawang, bomah,* or *peteri,* specialize according to the way in which they come into contact with the spirits, or the particular spirits they contact, or the diseases they treat. One type (*belian*) is thought capable of turning into a particular animal (the tiger), but most are supposedly possessed by the spirits. At a séance in Kelantan, which is attended by the patient, his family, friends, and neighbors, the *peteri* is always accompanied by a *mindok,* who plays a kind of violin and acts as his chief assistant and interlocutor, and by a varying number of other instrumentalists playing drums, tambourines, or little gongs. It is characteristic of the *peteri* that he enters into his trance to the accompaniment of violent shaking and twirling of the head and torso. Medicine men also treat disease with medicines derived from natural sources, lead the planting and harvesting rituals by propitiating spirits of the soil and forest and the "soul" of the rice, and direct the offerings made by fishing villages to the spirits of the sea. [Winstedt 1951; Skeat 1900; Gimlette 1923.] **Soul, death, and afterlife.** Funeral rites follow in general Moslem law, with an *imam* in attendance at the time of death. Burial follows within 24 hours after death. The corpse is washed, perfumed, shrouded, and borne in procession to a cemetery. The body is placed in a grave, protected by a three-sided coffin of wood. Relatives hold postfuneral feasts periodically up to the hundredth day after death. Grave sites are distinguished by wood or stone markers. There is some evidence of former tree burial and also (probably due to Hindu influence) of cremation. [Wilkinson 1920: 53-56; Winstedt 1950: 24.]

BIBLIOGRAPHY. Annandale and Robinson 1903; Bauer 1948; Burridge 1956; Coedès 1948; Cowan 1961; Djamour 1959; Dobby 1942, 1960; Downs 1960; Federation of Malaya 1956, 1958a, 1958b; Firth 1946; Firth 1943; Foxworthy 1923; Fraser 1960; Gibson-Hill 1949; Gimlette 1923; Ginsburg and Roberts 1958; Graham 1924; Grist 1936; Gullick 1958; Hall 1955; Hill 1951; Heine-Geldern 1945; IBRD 1955; Jones 1953; de Josselin de Jong 1951; King 1957; Maxwell 1884; Moorehead 1957; Parkinson 1960; Rigby 1929; Robinson 1923; Shaw 1926; Skeat 1900; Smith 1952; Swettenham 1929; Swift 1956; Taylor 1937; Tregonning 1961; Tufo 1949; Tweedie 1953; Warington Smyth 1902; Wheatley 1962; Wilkinson 1920; Wilson 1958; Winstedt 1925a, 1925b, 1929, 1950, 1951; Zainal Abidin 1949.

JAKUN

Synonyms. *Aboriginal Malay, Benua, Binua, Darat, Proto-Malay, Sakai*

ORIENTATION. **Identification.** As early as Portuguese times notice was taken of numerous small, predominantly non-Muslim, populations in the southern portion of the Malay Peninsula. Malays, Portuguese, and later European travelers and ethnologists have given to these groups names which often reflect local dialect differences, e.g. Beduanda (Biduanda), Belanda (Belana, Blanda, Landa), Berembun (Birmun), Besisi (Cellate, Mah Meri, Sisi), Kenaboi, Mantra (Mentera, Mentira, Mintra), Temuan, and Udai. [Skeat and Blagden 1906: *1*, 19-24, 32-34, 75-78, 81-82; Evans 1923: 263; Wilkinson 1926: 25-32.] Evidencing in most instances a cultural similarity to the groups with whom they are in most frequent contact, i.e. the Senoi to the north and the coastal Malays to the south, they nevertheless show some distinctive traits with respect to language, political organization (a community-level hierarchy of ranks or titles with quasi-political functions), and religion (elaboration of graves and grave goods). [Williams-Hunt 1952: 20; Wilkinson 1926: 32; Evans 1923: 266-67.] It has been largely

on the basis of linguistic peculiarities and problems that they have been grouped within a single category, in the classic trilogy of Semang (Negrito), Senoi (Sakai), and Jakun. [Cf. Skeat and Blagden 1906.] The name Jakun appears to be derived from Senoi *jah-kudn,* meaning "man" or "male person" (Wilkinson 1926: 30). Although at least one group calls itself by this term, most of the populations generally designated as Jakun do not recognize the term. The Malays call them Sakai, a generic and pejorative term for all pagan groups in the peninsula, or Orang Darat (Land Jakun), as opposed to Orang Laut (Sea Jakun). Early travelers and ethnologists frequently referred to these people as Benua or Orang Benua (Binua). More recently they have been called Aboriginal Malays or Proto-Malays (cf. Williams-Hunt 1952), terms which in the light of the probable origin of at least some of these groups are not altogether satisfactory. The terminological indecision reflects the paucity of reliable ethnographic and linguistic data, and until such data are at hand the ethnological position of the Jakun groups in Malaya will remain unclear. **Location.** Primarily the states of Selangor, Malacca, Negri Sembilan, Johore, and adjacent areas of southern Pahang. Most often on the upper reaches of rivers, e.g. the Selangor, Langat, Muar, Johore, Endau, and Pahang, including the southern extension of the main range and much of interior Johore. In areas not pre-empted by coastal Malays, groups of Jakun are also found around the mouths of rivers and along lower river courses, as along the eastern coast of Johore. Extensive physical and cultural assimilation renders the line of demarcation between Jakun and other groups—Semang, Senoi, and Malay—extremely indistinct. [Hervey 1881: 101; Wilkinson 1926: 29-31, 34; Evans 1923: 263; Noone 1936: 2.] **Geography.** Much of the country inhabited by Jakun groups is covered by thick jungle growth. Climate is tropical and the lower areas tend to be wet and foggy much of the year. **Linguistic affiliation.** Present usage defines at least the following named groups, based largely on dialect differences and degree of acculturation to surrounding peoples: Belandas (Belanas, Biduanda), in the foothills of the main range in interior Selangor–Negri Sembilan, east of Kuala Lumpur and Seremban; Temuan (Mentera, Mentira), in the southern extension of the main range in the Selangor–Negri Sembilan–western Pahang border area; Semelai, east of the Temuan in southern Pahang–northern Johore; Temoq, in southern Pahang; Jakun (or "Jakun Proper"), scattered over much of Johore; and Kanaq, in southeastern Johore (Williams-Hunt 1952; Dentan 1963). The Jakun dialects of Johore are generally regarded as Malayo-Polynesian. Farther north, in the Negri Sembilan–Selangor–Pahang belt, the Temuan, Belanda, Semelai, and Temoq groups appear to be basically Senoi (Mon-Khmer), with a good many Malay accretions (Wilkinson 1926: 29-30). The Mah Meri (Besisi) of the Selangor coastal area live much as Malays and are sometimes regarded as Aboriginal Malays (cf. Williams-Hunt 1952); on linguistic grounds, however, they can be classed as Senoi (Dentan 1963). The hybrid nature of these groups, whom Wilkinson (1926: 35) called "mongrel communities," makes classification extremely difficult. **Demography.** Williams-Hunt (1952: 11-13) cites 1947 census figures for Aboriginal Malays totaling 7,489. His own estimates, regarded as conservative, total slightly over 14,000, distributed as follows: Selangor, 2,590, primarily in Ulu Selangor, Ulu Langat, and Kuala Langat districts; Negri Sembilan, 1,400, primarily in Kuala Pilah and Jelebu districts; Malacca, 170, in Alor Gajah and Jasin districts; Pahang, 7,495, primarily in Raub, Temerloh, and Pekan districts; and Johore, 2,370, primarily in Kluang, Pontian, and Batu Pahat districts. **History and cultural relations.** Variously regarded as aboriginal Proto-Malays forced inland by later incursions of coastal Deutero-Malays from Sumatra, as non-Malays who intermarried with Proto-Malays fleeing conversion to Islam, etc. There is some support for the theory that they are in large part Senoi who are in the process of adopting permanent agriculture and the Malay language, i.e. of "becoming Malay" (cf. Wilkinson 1926: 31-32; Dentan 1963). The so-called "archaic Malay" spoken by Jakun in Johore may emerge as Malay with a Senoi accent. This point of view is supported by the apparent fact that groups of lowland Senoi in Pahang (Jah Hut, lowland Semai) are today culturally more akin to Aboriginal Malays than they are to highland Senoi (Temiar and highland Semai). Although adults among some "Senoi" groups in southern Perak speak a Semai dialect, they deny that they are Semai and intermarry more often with Temuan than with Semai; Malay loan words are much in evidence, and the children speak Malay rather than Semai. Dependence on Chinese among such groups is also common. [Dentan 1963.] Whatever their ultimate origin, the Jakun groups have for centuries been economically exploited by Mohammedan Malays and are gradually being absorbed into the coastal Malay population.

ECONOMY. Practically all groups engage in some form of agriculture, supplemented by hunting, fishing, and gathering. The economy in some areas is heavily dependent on the gathering of jungle produce for trade to Malays, and economic dependence on Malays is common. **Agriculture.** Agricultural patterns range from swidden farming accompanied by periodic shifting of settlements through combinations of settled plantation farming with upland swiddens to wet-rice farming in permanent settlements (Williams-Hunt 1952: 44). Crops include rice, maize, tapioca, sweet potatoes, chilies, beans, cucumbers, bananas, and tobacco. **Fishing and hunting.** Fishing techniques include the use of hook and line, traps, nets, weirs, poisons, and spears. Hunting is done with blowguns, fall and spring traps, game fences, and (more recently) firearms. Wild hogs, deer, mouse deer, monkeys, snakes, frogs, wild pigeons, partridge, and pheasant are taken. [Skeat and Blagden 1906: 1, 93, 214-24.] **Trade.** Barter trade with Malays has been carried on for centuries. Among the Johore Jakun small bands of a few families each roam the forest collecting jungle produce such as rattan, eaglewood, camphor, resin, and fruits, which they trade for rice, tobacco, salt, clothing, and knives. In such cases virtual dependence on Malay traders, frequently accompanied by exploitation and indebtedness, is common. [Hervey 1881: 98, 120-22; Skeat and Blagden 1906: 1, 95, 230-39; Wilkinson 1926: 28; Dentan 1963.]

SOCIOPOLITICAL ORGANIZATION. Skeat and Blagden (1906: 1, 510-17) reported ranked and titled statuses with quasi-political functions for most Jakun groups. A *batin,* headman or chief, acted as arbiter of all disputes and in addition served as priest and magician on occasion. The *batin* had absolute authority within his own jurisdiction and was assisted in his duties by a variety of officials corresponding to executive officer, war chief, legal expert, herald, and the like. According to Williams-Hunt (1952: 20), there may be a *batin* in each community as well as an over-all *batin* for an entire group.

BIBLIOGRAPHY. Dentan 1963; Evans 1923; Hervey 1881; Noone 1936; Skeat and Blagden 1906; Wilkinson 1926; Williams-Hunt 1952.

MOKEN

Synonyms. *Mawken, Selon, Selong, Selung*

ORIENTATION. **Identification and location.** Semi-nomadic boat people were located as late as the 1930s in relatively large numbers along the coast and among the islands of the Mergui archipelago in extreme southern Burma, particularly Elphinstone and Ross islands, together with St. Luke's, St. Matthew's, and Loughborough islands. These people call themselves Moken or Mawken, and are known to the Burmese as Selung, Selong, or Selon (White 1922: 55-56; Bernatzik 1938: 30). Related groups, living a seminomadic life in boats or settled near river mouths or on marshy coastal areas, occur southward along the west coast of Malaya and throughout much of Indonesia. In the Phuket Island area south of Mergui they are called Chaonam by the Siamese (Seidenfaden 1958: 123-24), while on the Johore coast and Singapore Island they are known as Orang Laut or Rayat Laut by the Malays (Skeat and Blagden 1906: 1, 87-88). In Indonesia, along the coasts of Borneo, Celebes, Halmahera, Flores, and Sumbawa, they are known collectively as Badjo. In the Riau Lingga archipelago they are known as Barok, in the Banka-Billiton area as Sekah, Rayat, or Juru, and along the east coast of Sumatra as Rayat or Kuala (Kennedy 1935: 308-20). ● Finer terminological distinctions occur locally, reflecting places of origin, dialect differences, or incidents of past history. For Mergui, White (1922: 157) lists four named dialect areas: Dung, Ja-it, Lbi, and Lawta. In Malaya, the Seletar (Sletar), Kuala, and Desin Dolaq live along the Pontian coast of western Johore State, and the Selat live on Pulau Brani in Singapore harbor (Williams-Hunt 1952: 51). Groups of Orang Laut formerly reported in the Singapore–Johore area include the Biduanda Kallang, Sabimba, Muka Kuning, and Akik; the Kallang and Sabimba have since become land dwellers. On the Southeast Asia mainland only the Moken of Mergui appear to have retained their indigenous culture and even here it was fast disappearing in the years prior to World War II. In Malaya many Laut have settled down in coastal fishing villages and accepted Islam. **Linguistic affiliation.** All of the so-called Sea Gypsies, including Moken, Orang Laut, and Badjo, speak Malayo-Polynesian dialects related to Malay. Peculiar pronunciation and the use of strange words, however, may make it difficult for them to be understood by a Malay speaker. There are numerous dialects, e.g. four within the Mergui area. The American Baptist Mission devised a script for Moken, and a primer was published in 1846. [White 1922: 132, 155-57; Kennedy 1935: 308-20.] **Demography.** White (1922: 189) estimated close to 5,000 Moken in the Mergui archipelago in the 1920s. The number of known Laut in the Johore–Singapore area in the nineteenth century was in the vicinity of 1,000, probably a low figure (Skeat and Blagden 1906: *1*, 88, 239-40). Those presently on the Pontian coast of Johore, including Seletar, Kuala, and Desin Dolaq, are estimated to number close to 1,200 (Dentan 1963). **History and cultural relations.** The Moken and their relatives to the south are generally regarded as originally Proto-Malay stock, having reached their present distribution from a homeland in the Malacca Straits area, and thus being related to the Jakun (Orang Darat or Land Jakun) of southern Malaya. Moken tradition speaks of original settlements on the mainland, from which they were driven by constant exploitation and harassment from the Malays. In desperation they took to life in boats as a means of escape. ● As observed by White, the maritime Moken avoid contact with other groups. In some cases, they allow their women to marry Chinese or Malay traders, thus setting up a relationship whereby the members of the woman's boat group collect sea and forest products in return for the trader's protection. Even in White's time, the Moken were settling on the coast and adopting Burmese dress and language. To the south, in Malaya, some Laut still cling to their boats, selling crabs and other sea produce to Chinese middlemen. Most live in coastal villages or near rivers and swamps, where they are fishermen or gatherers of mangrove wood, and usually in debt to Chinese and Malays (Williams-Hunt 1952: 51; Dentan 1963). They are gradually undergoing assimilation and acculturation to the dominant group, in the one case Burmese, in the other, Malays. [White 1922: 57-59, 66-71, 304-11; Bernatzik 1938: 45; Kennedy 1935: 308-20.]

SETTLEMENT PATTERN AND HOUSING. **Settlement pattern.** The maritime Moken travel in fleets of boats numbering from 10 to 40. These boat groups, or nomadic bands, are the equivalent of the community, the normal face-to-face group within Moken society. Although they may occasionally go ashore for longer or shorter periods, the time of the northeast monsoon is normally spent afloat. [White 1922: 84, 172.] **Housing.** The maritime Moken's house is his boat, a dugout some 20 to 25 feet long, decked over and fitted with a mast for sails and an earthen fireplace. At one end is a crude hut consisting of two hooped supports covered with palm leaves. This shelter can be removed and set up ashore when camping. Some groups maintain one-room pile dwellings ashore as a base of operations. [White 1922: 38-48, 106.]

ECONOMY. Maritime Moken rely overwhelmingly on fishing and collecting for food, although they may raise a few vegetables and fruits on islands which they visit regularly. Most Moken, however, as well as the Laut along the Malaya coast, engage in trade for rice, salt, clothing, and other necessities. **Fishing and hunting.** The Moken fish mainly with spears, and the catch is correspondingly small (White 1922: 85, 110-11). The Laut of Malaya make some use of nets. Trained dogs are used by some groups to hunt wild pigs, deer, and crabs on the larger islands. **Gathering.** The single most important activity is probably gathering of sea and forest products, both as a direct source of food and as a means of obtaining additional food and necessities through trade. Sources of food include limpets, crabs, shellfish, oysters, snails, and beach worms. White comments on the extraordinary elaboration of terms by which the Moken recognize the varieties of shellfish and edible miscellany which they collect at low tide. Diving for pearl oysters and sea snails and raking the sand for sea slugs provide products for trade, and from the land the Moken collect edible birds' nests, tanbark, and cordwood. For their own use they collect such items as wild fruits, berries, roots, and honey. [White 1922: 107-12; Bernatzik 1938: 24, 30-31.] **Domestic animals.** Chickens, dogs, and cats are reported by White for the Mergui Moken (White 1922: 172, 186-87). **Food and stimulants.** The staples are fish, together with rice, which is obtained by barter. These staples are supplemented by game, wild fruits, berries, roots, vegetables, mudfish, and shellfish. Bananas and pawpaws are sliced and sun dried on the roofs of the boats.

The Moken chew betel, a practice said to have been learned from the Burmese. Tobacco and opium are obtained from Malay and Chinese traders. [White 1922: 36, 52, 85-86.] **Industrial arts.** The Moken make most of their own equipment, being especially skilled in boat building and mat making. Cordage, lanyards, and cables are made from grass, lianas, and bast fiber. Women make clay pots and containers. Iron and metal implements are obtained by barter. [White 1922: 177, 241, 249, 266-86.] **Trade.** The economy relies heavily on barter for such items as rice, salted fish, opium, knives, iron skillets, and cloth in return for amber, pearls, mother-of-pearl, snails, sea cucumbers, birds' nests, tanbark, and cordwood. Chinese and Malay traders, equipped with their own boats, visit the islands frequented by Moken. The latter are reportedly exploited by these traders, who have introduced opium smoking as a means of controlling and coercing them. [White 1922: 45, 86, 106, 110-11, 250-52, 255-56; Bernatzik 1938: 24.]

KIN GROUPS. **Kin terminology.** Kin terms, as reported by White (1922: 211-14), are as follows:

Fa	*apong*
Mo	*enong*
So	*anak kanai*
Da	*anak binai*
FaElBr, MoElBr	*tawba kanai*
FaYoBr, MoYoBr	*nyi kanai*
FaElSi, MoElSi	*tawba binai*
FaYoSi, MoYoSi	*wa binai*
ElBr	*aka kanai*
YoBr	*uui kanai*
ElSi	*aka binai*
YoSi	*uui binai*
GrSo	*chocho kanai*
GrDa	*chocho binai*

According to White (1922: 209-10), the Moken have no term for cousin; even first cousins are considered outside the "inner circle" of family, and a cousin is referred to as *ja*, the word for friend.

MARRIAGE AND FAMILY. **Mode.** Marriage usually takes place within the same band or boat group. If a man is from another group he may make a prolonged visit to the girl's group, living and working with it. When a couple decide on marriage, "joiners" are sent by the young man to the boat of the girl's parents. If the answer is favorable he comes in person and takes his bride away. [White 1922: 203-04.] **Form.** White found no cases of plural marriage or concubinage among the Moken (White 1922: 199). **Residence.** A young couple lives with the groom's parents in their boat until he strikes out for himself by building his own boat, often following the birth of the first child (White 1922: 203-04). **Domestic unit.** Those persons normally residing on a single boat constitute the domestic unit. This averages seven persons, with a range of from four to ten (White 1922: 183).

SOCIOPOLITICAL ORGANIZATION. The nomadic boat groups or bands acknowledge no chiefs, according to White (1922: 84). In the Malacca Straits area the oldest man or best navigator within a boat group functions as leader; in this same area the settled Laut are reported formerly to have had a hierarchy of titled chiefs and officials similar to the Jakun (Skeat and Blagden 1906: *1*, 520).

RELIGION. In the Malay area many Orang Laut now settled along the west coast have accepted Islam, and in the north the Moken were visited by Christian missionaries as early as the 1830s and '40s. The indigenous religion of the Moken of the Mergui archipelago is, according to Bernatzik (1938: 36), a form of shamanism. **Supernaturals.** White (1922: 119) reports incipient belief in a kind of supreme being, Thida, apparently a borrowing from the Siamese. Otherwise the Moken believe in a variety of spirits, good and bad, controlling such misfortunes as death, sickness, storms, lightning, thunder, and food shortages. To propitiate these spirits, they place carved and painted wooden posts just above the high water mark on the islands which they frequent and on which they maintain their small fruit and vegetable plantations. [White 1922: 95-96, 143-45, 288; Bernatzik 1938: 33.] **Practitioners.** The shaman, *micha blen*, functions mainly in healing ceremonies, during which he enters a state of possession manifested by bodily trembling and quivering. The *micha bap* are sorcerers, or witch doctors, who can cause sickness and death by constructing a wax image of the victim or by obtaining the sand from his footprints. [White 1922: 76-82; Bernatzik 1938: 31-32.] **Ceremonies.** Sacrifices, summoning the aid and protection of beneficent spirits, are conducted by the *micha blen* on behalf of the group. Offerings of roots, shells, rice, stewed chickens, opium, and blood are placed in square sacrificial bowls, and a candle is lighted; at this juncture the shaman is possessed—staring, jerking, and finally collapsing in exhaustion, following which he enters into communication with the spirits. [White 1922: 220-21; Bernatzik 1938: 36.] **Illness and medicine.** According to Moken belief, most illnesses are caused by evil spirits. The souls of deceased persons may become agents of evil. It is also possible for malevolent spirits to enter the body through wounds. It is customary to change one's name following a severe illness in order to mislead the spirits and discourage their return. The shaman, *micha blen*, after going into a trance and summoning supernatural aid, sucks the evil influences from the patient's body and expectorates them into the wind. [White 1922: 217-21, 236-37; Bernatzik 1938: 38.] **Soul, death, and after-life.** According to White, the older and preferred method of disposing of the corpse is by exposure on a low platform built on a deserted island. Alternatively, the body of a man may be left above ground in a kind of coffin made by splitting his canoe in half, one piece serving as a resting place for the corpse, the other as a lid. The Moken are also known to bury their dead in graves dug in the sand, although they reportedly believe that the soul of a person buried in the earth cannot survive in the afterworld. [White 1922: 229-30, 239; Bernatzik 1938: 38.]

BIBLIOGRAPHY. Bernatzik 1938; Dentan 1963; Kennedy 1935; Seidenfaden 1958; Skeat and Blagden 1906; White 1922; Williams-Hunt 1952.

BIBLIOGRAPHY

ABBREVIATIONS

AA	*American Anthropologist*, Menasha, Wisconsin.
BEFEO	*Bulletin de l'Ecole Française d'Extrême-Orient*, Hanoi, Saigon, Paris.
BSEI	*Bulletin de la Société des Etudes Indochinoises*, Saigon.
HJAS	*Harvard Journal of Asiatic Studies*, Cambridge.
IIEH	*Institut Indochinois pour l'Etude de l'Homme, Bulletins et Travaux*, Hanoi.
JAOS	*Journal of the American Oriental Society*, New Haven.
JBRS	*Journal of the Burma Research Society*, Rangoon.
JRASB	*Journal of the Royal Asiatic Society of Bengal*, Calcutta.
JRASMB	*Journal of the Royal Asiatic Society, Malayan Branch*, Singapore.
JRASNCB	*Journal of the Royal Asiatic Society, North China Branch*, Shanghai.
JRASSB	*Journal of the Royal Asiatic Society, Straits Branch*, Singapore.
JSS	*Journal of the Siam Society*, Bangkok.
JWCS	*Journal of the West China Border Research Society*, Chengtu.
PMAAE	*Papers of the Peabody Museum of American Archaeology and Ethnology, Harvard University*, Cambridge.

Asterisked titles indicate HRAF translations, available at member institutions or on file in New Haven.

Abadie, Maurice
*1924 *Les races du Haut-Tonkin de Phong-Tho à Lang Son*, Paris, Société d'Editions Géographiques, Maritimes et Coloniales.

Aitchison, C. U., comp.
1931 *A Collection of Treaties, Engagements and Sanads Relating to India and Neighbouring Countries, vol. XII, Containing the Treaties, etc., Relating to Jammu and Kashmir, Sikkim, Assam and Burma*, Calcutta, Government of India Central Publication Branch.

Andrews, James M.
1943 "Evolutionary Trends in Body Build," *PMAAE*, 20, 102-21.

Annandale, Nelson and H. C. Robinson
1903 *Fasciculi Malayenses: Anthropological and Zoological Results of an Expedition to Perak and the Siamese Malay States, 1901-1902, Pts. I, II*, "Anthropology," London, University Press of Liverpool, Longmans, Green.

Ao, P. Shilu
1953 "The Nagas," *Vanyajati*, 1, 54-57, 69-71.

Arutiunov, S. A. and A. I. Mukhlinov
1961 "Materialy po Etno-Lingvisticheskoi Klassifikatsii Narodov V'etnama [Materials for the Ethnolinguistic Classification of the Peoples of Vietnam]," *Sovetskaia Etnografiia*, 1, 72-82.

Associates for International Research
1956 *Peoples of Burma*, Cambridge, Mass.

Ayabe, Tsuneo
1961 *The Village of Ban Pha Khao, Vientiane Province, Laos Project Paper No. 14*, ed. Joel M. Halpern, Los Angeles, University of California (mimeographed).

Aymonier, Etienne
1891 *Les Tchames et leurs religions*, Paris, Leroux.
1900 *Le Cambodge*, 3 vols. Paris, Leroux.

Bacot, Jacques
1913 *Les Mo-so*, Leiden, E. J. Brill.

Baradat, R.
1941 "Les Samrê ou Péar, population primitive de l'ouest du Cambodge," *BEFEO*, 41, 1-150.

Bare, Garland
1961 "The T'in and Kha Phai," Pua, Nan province, Thailand (mimeographed). (A background study for a conference of American Bible Society personnel and American Church of Christ missionaries.)

Bareh, Hamlet
1962 *A Short History of Khasi Literature*, Shillong.

Barney, George L.
1961 *The Meo of Xieng Khouang Province*, Laos Project Paper No. 13, ed. Joel M. Halpern, Los Angeles, University of California (mimeographed).

Bauer, P. T.
1948 *Report on a Visit to the Rubber-growing Smallholdings of Malaya, July-September, 1946*, Great Britain, Colonial Office, Colonial Research Publication No. 1, London, H. M. Stationery Office.

Beauclair, Inez de
1946 "The Keh Lao of Kweichow and their History According to Chinese Records," *Studia Serica*, 5, 1-44.
1956 "Ethnic Groups," in *A General Handbook of China*, ed. Hellmut Wilhelm, HRAF Subcontractor's Monograph No. 55, New Haven (mimeographed).
1960 "A Miao Tribe of Southeast Kweichow and its Cultural Configuration," *Bulletin of the Institute of Ethnology, Academia Sinica*, 10, 127-99.
1961 "'Miao' on Hainan Island," *Current Anthropology*, 2, 394.

Becker, C.
1909 "Die Nongkrem-Puja in den Khasi-Bergen (Assam)," *Anthropos*, 4, 892-902.
1924 "Familienbesitz und Mutterrecht," *Zeitschrift für Buddhismus und verwandte Gebiete*, 6, 127-38, 300-10.

Benedict, Paul K.
1941 "Kinship in Southeastern Asia," unpublished Ph.D. dissertation, Harvard University.
1942 "Thai, Kadai, and Indonesian: A New Alignment in Southeastern Asia," *AA*, 44, 576-601.
1943 "Studies in Thai Kinship Terminology," *JAOS*, 63, 168-75.
1945 "Chinese and Thai Kin Numeratives," *JAOS*, 65, 33-37.

Benedict, Ruth
1952 *Thai Culture and Behavior*, Data Paper No. 4, Ithaca, Cornell University, Southeast Asia Program.

Bernatzik, Hugo Adolf
°1938 *Die Geister der gelben Blätter,* Munich, F. Bruck-
mann.
°1947 *Akha und Meau: Probleme der angewandten Völkerkunde in Hinterindien,* 2 vols. Innsbruck, Wag-
nerische Universitäts Buchdrückerei.

Bertren, Muraire de
1944 "Le Nam-Giao," *Ethnographie, 42,* 54-61.

Berval, René de, ed.
1955 "Présence du Cambodge," *France-Asie,* Special No.
12.

Betts, G. E.
1899 "Social Life of the Miao Tsi," *JRASNCB, 33,* 84-104.

Bezacier, Louis
1942 "Note sur quelques tatouages des Moi 'Ka-tu',"
IIEH, 5, 117-25.

Bhuyan, S. K.
1949 *Anglo-Assamese Relations 1771-1826,* Gauhati, Government of Assam, Department of Historical and
Antiquarian Studies.

Bitaro, P.
1952 "Rites agraires des Kha Braou," *BSEI, 27,* 9-17.

Blanchard, Wendell et al.
1958 *Thailand: Its People, Its Society, Its Culture,* New
Haven, HRAF Press.

Bonifacy, Auguste
1906 "Etude sur les coutumes et la langue des La-ti,"
BEFEO, 6, 271-78.
1908 "Etude sur les coutumes et la langue des Lolo et
des La-qua du Haut-Tonkin," *BEFEO, 8,* 531-58.
1919 *Cours d'ethnographie indochinoise,* Saigon-Haiphong,
Imprimerie d'Extrême-Orient.

Botreau-Roussel and Bernard Jouin
1943 "Les potières Bih de Buon Tur H'ma," *IIEH, 6,*
387-91.

Boulbet, Jean
1957 "Quelques aspects du coutumier (N'dri) des Cau
Maa," *BSEI, 32,* 108-78.
1960a "Description de la végétation en pays Ma," *BSEI,
35,* 544-74.
1960b "Bo'rde au rendez-vous des génies," *BSEI, 35,* 627-
50.

Bourlet, A.
1906 "Socialisme dans les Hu'a Pha'n (Laos, Indo-Chine),"
Anthropos, 1, 521-28.

Bourotte, Bernard
1943 "Mariages et funérailles chez les Meo," *IIEH, 6,*
33-57.
1955 "Essai d'histoire des populations montagnards du
Sud-Indochinois jusqu'à 1945," *BSEI, 30,* 1-133.

Brandt, J. H.
1961 "The Negrito of Peninsular Thailand," *JSS, 49,*
123-60.

Brant, Charles S.
1956 "The Shans," in *Burma,* ed. Frank N. Trager, HRAF
Subcontractor's Monograph No. 37, New Haven
(mimeographed).

Briggs, Lawrence P.
1951 "The Ancient Khmer Empire," *Transactions of the
American Philosophical Society,* vol. *41,* Pt. I.

Brohm, John
1956 "Religion," in *Burma,* ed. Frank N. Trager, HRAF
Subcontractor's Monograph No. 37, New Haven
(mimeographed).
1963 "Buddhism and Animism in a Burmese Village,"
Journal of Asian Studies, 22, 155-67.

Brohm, John, Charles Brant, and M. Lois Jackim
1956 "Social Structure and Social Values," in *Burma,* ed.
Frank N. Trager, HRAF Subcontractor's Monograph
No. 37, New Haven (mimeographed).

Brown, James Marvin
1962 "From Ancient Thai to Modern Dialects: A Theory,"
unpublished Ph.D. dissertation, Cornell University.

Bruk, Solomon Il'ich
1959a *Karta Narodov Kitaia, MNR i Korei* [Map of the
Peoples of China, Mongolian People's Republic and
Korea], Moskva, Glavnoe Upravlenie Geodezii i
Kartografii MVD SSSR, Institut Etnografii imeni
N. N. Miklukho-Maklaia Akademii Nauk SSSR.
1959b *Karta Narodov Indokitaia* [Map of the Peoples of
Indochina], Moskva, Glavnoe Upravlenie Geodezii
i Kartografii MVD SSSR, Institut Etnografii imeni
N. N. Miklukho-Maklaia Akademii Nauk SSSR.
1960 *Peoples of China, Mongolian People's Republic, and
Korea [Naseleniye Kitaya, MNR i Korei],* Moscow,
Academy of Sciences USSR, Institute of Ethnog-
raphy imeni N. N. Miklukho-Maklay, 1959 (trans-
lation by United States Joint Publications Research
Service, No. 3710, Washington, D.C.).

Buck, John Lossing
1937 *Land Utilization in China,* Shanghai, Commercial
Press.

Burling, Robbins
1963 *Rengsanggri: Family and Kinship in a Garo Village,*
Philadelphia, University of Pennsylvania Press.

Burma (Union). Karen Special Enquiry Commission
1951 *Report,* Rangoon, Superintendent of Government
Printing and Stationery.

Burridge, Kenelm
1956 "The Composition of a Village in Johore," *JRASMB,
29,* Pt. III, 60-77.

Buttinger, Joseph
1958 *The Smaller Dragon: A Political History of Vietnam,*
New York, Praeger.

C., W.
1832 "Smelting of Iron in the Kasya Hills," *JRASB, 1,*
150-51.

Cadière, Léopold Michel
1940 "Note sur les Moi du Quang-Tri," *IIEH, 3,* 101-07.
1955 *Croyances et pratiques religieuses des Vietnamiens,*
vol. 2, Saigon, Imprimerie d'Extrême-Orient.
1957 *Croyances et pratiques religieuses des Vietnamiens,*
vol. 3, Paris, Imprimerie d'Extrême-Orient.
1958 *Croyances et pratiques religieuses des Vietnamiens,*
vol. 1, Saigon, Imprimerie d'Extrême-Orient.

Cady, John F.
1956 "The Karens," in *Burma,* ed. Frank N. Trager,
HRAF Subcontractor's Monograph No. 37, New
Haven (mimeographed).
1958 *A History of Modern Burma,* Ithaca, Cornell University Press.

Cameron, A. A.
1912 "A Note on the Palaungs of the Kodaung Hill
Tracts of Momeik State," Appendix A in *Census
of India, 1911, 9,* Pt. I, i-xlii.

Canada. Department of Mines and Technical Surveys
1953 *Indochina: A Geographical Appreciation,* Foreign
Geography Information Series No. 6, Ottawa.

Cantlie, Keith
1934 *Notes on Khasi Law,* Aberdeen, Munro.

Capell, Arthur
1962 "Oceanic Linguistics Today," *Current Anthropology,
3,* 371-96.

Carey, Fred W.
1899 "A Trip to the Chinese Shan States," *Geographical
Journal, 14,* 378-94.

Carey, Iskandar Yusof
1961 *Tengleq Kui Serok: A Study of the Temiar Language with an Ethnographical Summary,* Kuala
Lumpur, Dewan Bahasa dan Pustaka.

Carpenter, C. H.
1875 *The Anglo-Karen Hand-book and Reader*, Rangoon, American Baptist Mission Press, C. Bennett.

Carrapiett, W. J. S.
1929 *The Kachin Tribes of Burma: For the Information of Officers of the Burma Frontier*, Rangoon, Superintendent of Government Printing and Stationery.

Carte ethnolinguistique de l'Indochine
1949 (Dressée sous la direction de l'Ecole Française d'Extrême-Orient), Hanoi, Service Géographique de l'Indochine.

Carthew, M.
1952 "The History of the Thai in Yunnan," *JSS, 40*, Pt. I, 1-38.

Chang, Kwang-chih
1959 "A Working Hypothesis for the Early Cultural History of South China," *Bulletin of the Institute of Ethnology, Academia Sinica, 7*, 75-103.

Chao, Shun-hsiao
*1953 *Pai-i Pien Min Yen-chiu* [A Study of the Pai-i Border People], Hongkong, Freedom Press.

Chassigneux, E.
1929-30 "Géographie physique," in *Un empire colonial français: L'Indochine*, ed. G. Maspéro, 2 vols. Paris, G. Van Oest.

Chatterji, Suniti Kumar
1953 *The Indian Synthesis, and Racial and Cultural Intermixture in India*, presidential address, All-India Oriental Conference, 17th Session, Ahmedabad (Gujarat), Bombay State, October 30 and 31 and November 1, 1953, Ahmedabad and Poona.

Chattopadhyay, K. P.
1941 *Khasi Kinship and Social Organisation*, University of Calcutta Anthropological Papers, n.s. No. 6, pp. 1-39.

Chau Thanh Kien
1940 *Essai d'une réforme sur le crédit agricole mutuel en Cochinchine*, Bordeaux, Bière.

Chen, Han-seng
1949 *Frontier Land Systems in Southernmost China*, New York, Institute of Pacific Relations.

Ch'en, Kuo-chün
*1942 "Kuei-chou An-shun Miao-I te Tsung-chiao Hsin-yang [Religious Beliefs of the Miao and I in Anshun, Kweichow]," *Frontier Affairs, 1*, 88-92.

Ch'en, Tsung-hsiang
1947 "The Dual System and the Clans of the Li-su and Shui-t'ien Tribes," *Monumenta Serica, 12*, 252-59.

Chiang, Ying-liang
*1948a "K'un-ming Ching Nei te I-min [The Yi People in the Kunming Region]," *Hsi-nan Pien-chiang Min-tsu Lun-ts'ung* [On the Peoples of the Southwest Frontier Regions], chap. 1, Canton, Chu-hai University.

*1948b "Kuang-tung Yao-jen chih Tsung-chiao Hsin-yang [Religious Beliefs of the Yao of Kwang-tung]," *Hsi-nan Pien-chiang Min-tsu Lun-ts'ung* [On the Peoples of the Southwest Frontier Regions], chap. 6, Canton, Chu-hai University.

*1950 *Pai-i te Sheng-huo Wen-hua* [The Life and Culture of the Pai-i], Shanghai, Chunghua Book Co.

Claeys, Jean Y.
1939 *A propos d'un sacrifice rituel chez les Katu "Chasseurs de Sang" à Ben-Giang (Quang-nam)*, Hanoi, Imprimerie d'Extrême-Orient.

1942 "L'Annamite et la mer: Les radeaux de pêche de Luong-Nhiem (Thanh-hoa) en bambous flottants," *IIEH, 5*, Pt. I, 17-28.

Clarke, Samuel R.
1911 *Among the Tribes of Southwest China*, London, China Inland Mission.

Coedès, Georges
*1944 *Histoire ancienne des états hindouisés d'Extrême-Orient*, Hanoi, Imprimerie d'Extrême-Orient.

1948 *Les états hindouisés d'Indochine et d'Indonésie*, Paris, Boccard.

Collis, Maurice S.
1938 *Lords of the Sunset: A Tour of the Shan States*, London, Faber and Faber.

Colquhoun, Archibald R.
1885 *Amongst the Shans*, London, Field.

Condominas, Georges
1955a Introduction to "Chant épique de Kdam Yi," by F.-P. Antoine, *BEFEO, 47*, 549-615.

1955b "Notes sur le Tam Bo Mae Baap Kuon (Echange de sacrifices entre un enfant et ses père et mère) Mnong Rlam," *International Archives of Ethnography, 47*, Pt. II, 127-59.

1957 *Nous avons mangé la forêt*, Paris, Mercure de France.

1960 "The Mnong Gar of Central Vietnam," in *Social Structure in Southeast Asia*, ed. G. P. Murdock, New York, Viking Fund Publications in Anthropology No. 29.

Condominas, Louis
1951 "Notes sur les Mois du haut Song Tranh," *BSEI, 26*, 13-38.

Cook, T.
1936 "The Independent Lolo of South-west Szechwan," *JWCS, 8*, 70-81.

Cordier, Henri
1908 "Les Mosos," *T'oung Pao*, Ser. 2, 9, 663-82.

Cornell Thailand Project
1948-57 Field notes written by various persons between 1948 and 1957 in Bang Chan, Thailand. Ithaca, Cornell University.

Costa, G.
1936 "Ka Riti jong Ka Ri Laiphew Syiem [Customs of the Land of Thirty Chiefs]," *Ka Jingroi ka Ri Khasi*, vol. 1, Shillong, St. Anthony's College.

1937 "Ka Riti jong Ka Ri Laiphew Syiem [Customs of the Land of Thirty Chiefs]," *Ka Jingroi ka Ri Khasi*, vol. 2, Shillong, St. Anthony's College.

1958 "The Origin of the People," *Ka Syngkhong Jingtip*, vols. 1 and 2, Shillong.

1960 "The Origin of the People," *Ka Syngkhong Jingtip*, vol. 3, Shillong.

Coughlin, Richard J.
1960 *Double Identity: The Chinese in Modern Thailand*, Hongkong, Hongkong University Press.

Coulet, Georges
*1926 *Les sociétés secrètes en terre d'Annam*, Saigon, Imprimerie Commerciale C. Ardin.

Cowan, Charles Donald
1961 *Nineteenth-Century Malaya: The Origins of British Political Control*, London, Oxford University Press.

Credner, Wilhelm
*1935a *Siam: Das Land der Tai*, Stuttgart, J. Engelhorns Nachfolger.

1935b *Cultural and Geographical Observations Made in the Tali (Yünnan) Region with Special Regard to the Nan-chao Problem*, translated from the German by E. Seidenfaden, Bangkok, Siam Society.

Cresson and R. Jeannin
1944 "La toile Meo," *IIEH, 6*, 435-47.

Cuisinier, Jeanne
1948 *Les Muong: Géographie humaine et sociologie*, Paris, Institut d'Ethnologie.

Cushing, Josiah N.
1914 *A Shan and English Dictionary*, 2d ed. Rangoon, American Baptist Mission Press.

Dam Bo (Jacques Dournes)
  1950 "Les populations montagnards du Sud-Indochine," *France-Asie*, Special No. 5, pp. 931-1208.
Dang The Binh
  1950 "The Vietnamese," in *Ethnic Groups of Northern Southeast Asia*, John F. Embree and William L. Thomas, Jr., New Haven, Yale University, Southeast Asia Studies (mimeographed).
Dao Duy Anh
  *1938 *Viet-Nam Van-Hoa Su-Cuong* [Outline History of Vietnamese Culture], Hue, Quan-Hai Tung-Thu.
Darrah, H. Z.
  1896 "Iron Smelting in the Khasi Hills," in *Three Manufactures of Assam*, Shillong, Assam Secretariat Printing Office.
Das, T. C.
  1954 "Land Tenure among the Tribal Population of Assam," *Vanyajati*, 2, 12-17.
Davies, H. R.
  1909 *Yünnan: The Link between India and the Yangtze*, Cambridge, Cambridge University Press.
Delvert, Jean
  1958 "La vie rurale au Cambodge," *France-Asie*, 15, 95-104.
  1961 *Le paysan cambodgien*, Le Monde d'Outre-Mer, Paris, Mouton.
Dentan, Robert
  1962 Unpublished map of hill tribes of Malaya.
  1963 Personal communication.
Devereux, G.
  1937 "Functioning Units in Ha(rh)ndea(ng) Society," *Primitive Man*, 10, 1-8.
  1961 Lecture notes. (Lectures delivered at Columbia University, recorded by May Ebihara, and subsequently corrected in manuscript by the author.)
DeYoung, John E.
  1955 *Village Life in Modern Thailand*, Berkeley, University of California Press.
Diguet, Edouard
  *1908 *Les montagnards du Tonkin*, Paris, Challamel.
Djamour, Judith
  1959 *Malay Kinship and Marriage in Singapore*, Monographs on Social Anthropology No. 21, London, London School of Economics.
Dobby, E. H. G.
  1942 "Settlement Patterns in Malaya," *Geographical Review*, 32, 211-32.
  1955 "Padi Landscapes of Malaya," *Malayan Journal of Tropical Geography*, 6, 1-94.
  1960 *Southeast Asia*, 7th rev. ed. London, University of London Press.
Dodd, William C.
  1923 *The Tai Race*, Cedar Rapids, Torch Press.
Downer, G. B.
  1961 "Phonology of the Word in Highland Yao," *Bulletin of the School of Oriental and African Studies, University of London*, 24, 531-41.
Downs, R. E.
  1960 "A Rural Community in Kelantan," in *Studies on Asia 1960*, 1, ed. Robert Sakai, Lincoln, University of Nebraska Press.
Dumont, R.
  *1935 *La culture du Riz dans le delta du Tonkin*, Paris, Société d'Editions Géographiques, Maritimes et Coloniales.
Dumoutier, G.
  1891 *Les symboles: Les emblèmes et les accessoires du culte chez les Annamites*, Paris, Leroux.
Du Perron, P. C.
  1954 "Etude d'un peuplement Man Xanh-Y," *BSEI*, 29, 23-42.

Durand, E. M.
  1907 "Notes sur les Chams," *BEFEO*, 7, 313-55.
Durand, Maurice
  1952 "Notes sur les pays tai de Phong-tho," *BSEI*, n. s. 27, 193-231.
  1959 *Technique et panthéon des médiums vietnamiens (Dông)*, Ecole Française d'Extrême-Orient, Publications, vol. 45, Paris.
Dussault, C.
  1924 "Les populations du Tonkin Occidental et du Haut-Laos," *Cahiers de la Société de Géographie de Hanoi*, vol. 5.

Eberhard, Wolfram
  1942 *Kultur und Siedlung der Randvölkers Chinas*, Leiden, Brill.
Ehrenfels, U. R.
  1950 "The Double Sex Character of the Khasi Great Deity," *Journal of the Madras University, Section A, Humanities*, 22, 26-39.
  1953 "Khasi Kinship Terms in Four Dialects," *Anthropos*, 48, 396-412.
  1955 "Three Matrilineal Groups of Assam: A Study in Similarities and Differences," *AA*, 57, 306-21.
Eickstedt, Egon von
  *1940 "Forschungen in Süd-und Ostasien. IV. Die Annamiten und der Untergang von Tchampa. V. Untersuchungen bei der indochinesischen Urbevölkerung des Moi," *Zeitschrift für Rassenkunde*, 11, 21-79, 115-53.
  1944 *Rassendynamik von Ostasien; China und Japan: Tai und Kmer von der Urzeit bis heute*, Berlin, Gruyter.
Elwin, Verrier
  1961 *Nagaland*, Shillong, Research Department, Adviser's Secretariat.
Embree, John F. and Lillian O. Dotson
  1950 *Bibliography of the Peoples and Cultures of Mainland Southeast Asia*, New Haven, Yale University, Southeast Asia Studies.
Embree, John F. and William L. Thomas, Jr.
  1950 *Ethnic Groups of Northern Southeast Asia*, New Haven, Yale University, Southeast Asia Studies (mimeographed).
Enriquez, Colin M.
  1918 *A Burmese Loneliness*, Calcutta, Thacker Spink.
  1923 *A Burmese Arcady*, London, Seeley, Service.
Evans, Ivor H. N.
  1923 *Studies in Religion, Folk-Lore, and Custom in British North Borneo and the Malay Peninsula*, Cambridge, Cambridge University Press.
  1937 *The Negritos of Malaya*, Cambridge, Cambridge University Press.
Ezzaoui, J.
  1940 "Une version de la légende des deux Sadets," *IIEH*, 3, 169-74.

Fall, Bernard B.
  1960 *Le Viet-Minh*, Paris, Armand Colin.
Fea, Leonardo
  1896 *Quattro anni fra i Birmani e le tribù limitrofe* [Four Years among the Burmese and the Border Tribes], Milano, Ulrico Hoepli.
Federation of Malaya
  1956 *Final Report of the Rice Committee*, Kuala Lumpur, The Government Printer.
  1958a *Annual Report, 1957*, Kuala Lumpur, The Government Printer.
  1958b *Malayan Constitutional Documents*, Kuala Lumpur, The Government Printer.

Feng, Han-yi and J. K. Shryock
1935 "The Black Magic in China Known as Ku," *JAOS*, *55*, 1-30.
1938 "The Historical Origins of the Lolo," *HJAS*, *3*, 103-27.
Ferrars, Max and Bertha Ferrars
1901 *Burma*, 2d ed. London, Sampson Low, Marston.
Firth, Raymond
1946 *Malay Fishermen: Their Peasant Economy*, London, Kegan Paul.
Firth, Rosemary
1943 *Housekeeping among Malay Peasants*, Monographs on Social Anthropology No. 7, London, London School of Economics.
Fitzgerald, C. P.
1941 *The Tower of Five Glories*, London, Cresset Press.
Fortune, Reo, ed.
1939 "Yao Society: A Study of a Group of Primitives in China," *Lingnan Science Journal*, *18*, 341-455.
Foxworthy, F. W.
1923 "Flora and Forests," in *Malaya: The Straits Settlements and the Federated and Unfederated Malay States*, ed. R. O. Winstedt, London, Constable.
Fraisse, A.
1950a "Les tribus So de la province de Cammon," *BSEI*, *25*, 171-86.
1950b "Les tribus Sek et Kha de la province de Cammon," *BSEI*, *25*, 333-48.
1951 "Les villages du plateau des Bolovens," *BSEI*, *26*, 52-72.
Fraser, Thomas M., Jr.
1960 *Rusembilan: A Malay Fishing Village in Southern Thailand*, Ithaca, Cornell University Press.
Freeman, John H.
1910 *An Oriental Land of the Free*, Philadelphia, Westminster Press.
Fromaget, J.
1937 "Etudes géologiques sur le nord-ouest du Tonkin et le nord du Haut-Laos," *Bulletin de la Société Géologique Indochinoise*, vol. 23.
Fürer-Haimendorf, Christoph von
1946 *The Naked Nagas*, Calcutta, Thacker Spink.
Furnivall, John S.
1948 *Colonial Policy and Practice: A Comparative Study of Burma and Netherlands India*, Cambridge, Cambridge University Press.

Gait, Edward
1926 *A History of Assam*, 2d rev. ed. Calcutta and Simla, Thacker Spink.
Garnier, Francis
1873 *Voyage d'exploration en Indochine*, Paris, Hachette.
Gatphoh, U. Primrose
1947 *Ki Khanatang bad U Sier Lapalang* [Tales, Including the Deer Lapalang], 2d rev. ed. Shillong.
Gerber, T.
1951 "Coutumier Stieng," *BEFEO*, *45*, 228-69.
Gibson-Hill, C. A.
1949 "Cargo Boats of the East Coast of Malaya," *JRASMB*, *22*, Pt. III, 106-25.
Gilhodes, Charles
1922 *The Kachins: Religion and Customs*, Calcutta, Catholic Orphan Press.
Gimlette, J. D.
1923 *Malay Poisons and Charm Cures*, 2d ed. London, Churchill.
Ginsburg, Norton and Chester F. Roberts, Jr.
1958 *Malaya*, Seattle, University of Washington Press.
Gittinger, J. P.
1959 "Communist Land Policy in North Viet Nam," *Far Eastern Survey*, *28*, 113-26.

Gjessing, Gutorm
1956 "Chinese Anthropology and New China's Policy toward Her Minorities," *Acta Sociologica*, *2*, 45-66.
Gobron, G.
*1949 *Histoire du Caodaïsme*, Paris, Dervy.
Gogoi, Padmeswar
1956 "The Political Expansion of the Mao Shans," *JSS*, *44*, Pt. II, 125-37.
Goldsen, Rose K. and Max Ralis
1957 *Factors Related to Acceptance of Innovations in Bang Chan, Thailand: Analysis of a Survey Conducted by the Cornell Cross-Cultural Methodology Project, May 1955*, Data Paper No. 25, Ithaca, Cornell University, Southeast Asia Program.
Goudal, J.
1938 *Labour Conditions in Indo-China*, International Labour Office Studies and Reports, Ser. B, No. 26, Geneva.
Goullart, Peter
1957 *Forgotten Kingdom*, London, John Murray.
Gourdon, Henri
1931 *L'Indochine*, Paris, Larousse.
Gourou, Pierre
*1936a *Les paysans du delta tonkinois: Etude de géographie humaine*, Paris, Editions d'art et d'histoire.
*1936b *Esquisse d'une étude de l'habitation annamite dans l'Annam septentrional et central du Thanh Hoá au Binh Dinh*, Paris, Editions d'art et d'histoire.
1945 *Land Utilization in French Indochina*, 3 vols. New York, Institute of Pacific Relations.
Graham, David C.
1937a "The Customs of the Ch'uan Miao," *JWCS*, *9*, 13-70.
1937b "The Ceremonies of the Ch'uan Miao," *JWCS*, *9*, 71-119.
Graham, W. A.
1924 *Siam*, 3d ed. 2 vols. London, De La More Press.
Granet, Marcel
1932 *Festivals and Songs of Ancient China*, New York, Dutton.
Greenberg, Joseph
1953 "Historical Linguistics and Unwritten Languages," in *Anthropology Today*, ed. A. L. Kroeber, Chicago, University of Chicago Press.
Grierson, G. A.
1903-28 *Linguistic Survey of India*, 11 vols. Calcutta, Office of the Superintendent of Government Printing.
Grist, Donald H.
1936 *An Outline of Malayan Agriculture*, Kuala Lumpur, Department of Agriculture, Straits Settlements and Federated Malay States.
Grossin, P.
1926 "Les coutumes des Meos de la région de Long-He," *Extrême-Asie*, vol. 1.
Guillemet, E. and K. O'Kelly
1916 "En colonne dans le Haut-Laos," *Revue Indochinoise*, *11-12*, 383-84.
Guilleminet, Paul P.
1941 "Recherches sur les croyances des tribus du Haut-Pays d'Annam, les Bahnar du Kontum et leurs voisins, les magiciens," *IIEH*, *4*, 9-33.
1943a "Note sur les amas d'objets à sens religieux dans le Haut-Pays Moi," *IIEH*, *6*, 261-64.
1943b "Note sur le culte du chien et des animaux chez les Moi du Kontum," *IIEH*, *6*, 369-71.
1949 "La tribu Bahnar du Kontum," *Actes du XXIe Congrès des Orientalistes*, Paris, Imprimerie Nationale, Société Asiatique de Paris, pp. 383-84.
1951-52 "La tribu Bahnar du Kontum," *BEFEO*, *45*, 393-561.
1952 *Coutumier de la tribu Bahnar des Sedang et des Jarai (de la province de Kontum)*, Ecole Française

d'Extrême-Orient, Publications, vol. 32, Paris, Boccard.
1960 "Langages spéciaux utilisés dans la tribu Bahnar
de Kontum," *BEFEO*, 50, 117-43.

Gullick, J. M.
1958 *Indigenous Political Systems of Western Malaya*,
Monographs on Social Anthropology No. 17, London, London School of Economics.

Gurdon, P. R. T.
1907 *The Khasis*, London, David Nutt.

Hall, D. G. E.
1955 *A History of South-East Asia*, London, Macmillan.

Halliday, Robert
1917 *The Talaings*, Rangoon, Superintendent of Government Printing and Stationery.

Halpern, Joel M.
1957 "Trade Patterns in Northern Laos," paper read at
the Ninth Pacific Science Congress, Bangkok (dupli-
cated).
1958 *Aspects of Village Life and Culture Change in
Laos*, Special Report Prepared for the Council on
Economic and Cultural Affairs, New York.
1960 "Laos and Her Tribal Problems," *Michigan Alum-
nus Quarterly Review*, 67, 59-67.
1961a *Capital, Savings and Credit among Lao and Serb
Peasants: A Contrast in Cultural Values*, Laos Project Paper No. 2, Los Angeles, University of California (mimeographed).
1961b *Population Statistics and Associated Data*, Laos
Project Paper No. 3, Los Angeles, University of
California (mimeographed).
1961c *Geographic, Demographic and Ethnic Background
on Laos*, Laos Project Paper No. 4, Los Angeles,
University of California (mimeographed).
1961d *Laotian Agricultural Statistics*, Laos Project Paper
No. 9, Los Angeles, University of California (mimeographed).
1961e *Laos Profiles*, Laos Project Paper No. 18, Los Angeles, University of California (mimeographed).
1961f *The Rural and Urban Economies*, Laos Project Paper No. 19, Los Angeles, University of California
(mimeographed).
1961g *Laotian Health Problems*, Laos Project Paper No.
20, Los Angeles, University of California (mimeographed).
1961h *Government, Politics, and Social Structure of Laos:
A Study of Tradition and Innovation*, Laos Project
Paper No. 21, Los Angeles, University of California
(mimeographed).

Hanks, Jane R.
1960 "Ontology of Rice," in *Culture in History: Essays
in Honor of Paul Radin*, ed. Stanley Diamond, New
York, Columbia University Press.

Hanks, L. M., Jr.
1959 "Indifference to Modern Education in a Thai Farming Community," *Human Organization*, 17, 9-14.
1962 "Merit and Power in the Thai Social Order," *AA*,
64, 1247-61.

Hanks, L. M., Jr. and Jane R. Hanks
1963 "Thai Equality of the Sexes," in *Women in the
New Asia*, ed. Barbara E. Ward, Paris, UNESCO.

Hanks, L. M., Jr. and Herbert P. Phillips
1961 "A Young Thai from the Countryside," in *Studying
Personality Cross-Culturally*, ed. Bert Kaplan, Evans-
ton, Row, Peterson.

Hanson, Ola
1913 *The Kachins: Their Customs and Traditions*, Rangoon, American Baptist Mission Press.
1954 *A Dictionary of the Kachin Language*, Rangoon,
Baptist Board of Publications.

Harvey, Godfrey E.
1925 *History of Burma*, London, Longmans, Green.
1957 "The Wa People of the China-Burma Border," *St.
Antony's Papers*, Oxford University, St. Antony's
College, No. 2, London, Chatto and Windus.

Haudricourt, André G.
1953 "La place du vietnamien dans les langues austro-
asiatiques," *Bulletin de la Société Linguistique de
Paris*, 49, 122-28.
1962 "Comment," *Current Anthropology*, 3, 410.

Heine-Geldern, Robert von
1945 "Prehistoric Research in the Netherlands Indies,"
in *Science and Scientists in the Netherlands Indies*,
New York, Board for the Netherlands Indies, Suri-
nam, and Curaçao.

Hendry, J. B.
1959 *Report on the Study of a Vietnamese Rural Community: Economic Activities*, Saigon, Michigan State
University Viet Nam Advisory Group (mimeographed).

Henry, Augustine
1903 "The Lolos and Other Tribes of Western China,"
Journal of the Royal Anthropological Institute, 33,
96-107.

Henry, Y.
1932 *Economie agricole de l'Indochine française*, Hanoi,
Gouvernement Général de l'Indochine.

Hervey, D. F. A.
1881 "The Endau and its Tributaries," *JRASSB*, 8, 93-124.

Hickey, Gerald C.
1956-58 Field notes on southern Vietnamese highland
groups.
1957 Katu field notes.
1958 "Social Systems of Northern Viet Nam: A Study
of Systems in Contact," unpublished Ph.D. dissertation, University of Chicago.
1960 *Report on the Study of a Vietnamese Rural Community: Sociology*, Saigon, Michigan State University Viet Nam Advisory Group (mimeographed).
1964 *Village in Vietnam*, New Haven, Yale University
Press.

Hill, A. H.
1951 "Kelantan Padi Planting," *JRASMB*, 24, Pt. I, 56-76.

Hodson, Thomas C.
1908 *The Meitheis*, with an introduction by Sir Charles
Lyall, London, David Nutt.

Hoffet, J.
1933 "Les Moïs de la chaîne annamitique," *Terre, air,
mer: La géographie*, 59, 1-43.

Hooker, Joseph Dalton
1891 *Himalayan Journals; or, Notes of a Naturalist in
Bengal, the Sikkim and Nepal Himalayas, the
Khasia Mountains, etc.*, London, New York, and
Melbourne, Ward, Lock, Bowden.

Hsu, Francis L. K.
1943 "Magic and Science in Western Yunnan," in *Social Change in Southwest China*, ed. F. L. K. Hsu,
New York, Institute of Pacific Relations.

Hsü, Sung-shih
*1939 "Ling-nan te Chuang-tsu [The Chuang Tribe of
Lingnan]," *Yüeh Chiang Liu-yü Jen-min Shih* [His-
tory of the Peoples of the Yüeh River Valley], chap.
8, Shanghai.

Htin Aung
1962 *Folk Elements in Burmese Buddhism*, London, Oxford University Press.

Hu, Chang-tu et al.
1960 *China: Its People, Its Society, Its Culture*, New
Haven, HRAF Press.

Huard, P.
1941 "Les Portugais et l'Indochine," *IIEH*, 3, 47-65.

Huard, P. and A. Maurice
1939 "Les Mnong du plateau central indochinois," *IIEH*, 2, 27-148.
Hudspeth, William H.
1937 *Stone Gateway and the Flowery Miao*, London, Cargate Press.
Huke, Robert E.
1954 *Economic Geography of a North Burma Kachin Village*, Hanover, Dartmouth College Department of Geography (mimeographed).
1956a "Geography and Population," in *Burma*, ed. Frank N. Trager, HRAF Subcontractor's Monograph No. 37, New Haven (mimeographed).
1956b "The Kachins," in *Burma*, ed. Frank N. Trager, HRAF Subcontractor's Monograph No. 37, New Haven (mimeographed).
Hutchinson, E. W.
1934 "The Lawa in Northern Siam," *JSS*, 27, 153-82.
Hutton, J. H.
1921a *The Angami Nagas*, London, Macmillan.
1921b *The Sema Nagas*, London, Macmillan.
1922 Introduction to J. P. Mills, *The Lhota Nagas*, London, Macmillan.

IBRD (International Bank for Reconstruction and Development)
1955 *The Economic Development of Malaya*, Washington, D.C.
1959 *A Public Development Program for Thailand*, Baltimore, Johns Hopkins Press.
Imperial Gazetteer of India
1908 *Provincial Series, Burma*, 2 vols. Calcutta, Office of the Superintendent of Government Printing.
India. Census Commissioner
1912 *Census of India, 1911*, 9, Burma, Pt. I, Rangoon, Superintendent of Government Printing and Stationery.
1931-34 *Census of India, 1931*, 46 vols. Delhi, Manager of Publications.
India (Republic). Census Commissioner
1952-57 *Census of India, 1951*, 17 vols. Delhi, Manager of Publications.
Indochina, French. Service de la statistique générale
1936 *Annuaire statistique de l'Indochine*, Hanoi.
Ingram, James C.
1955 *Economic Change in Thailand since 1850*, Stanford, Stanford University Press.
Its, R. F.
*1960 "Miao: Istoriko-Etnograficheskii Ocherk [Miao: An Historical-Ethnographic Sketch]" in *Vostochno-Aziatskii Etnograficheskii Sbornik* [East-Asian Ethnographic Papers], ed. O. L. Vil'chevskii, Moskva, Trudy Institut Etnografii im. N. N. Miklukho-Maklaia, Akademii Nauk SSSR, n.s. 60, 1-118.
Iwata, Keiji
1961a *Ethnic Groups in the Valley of the Nam Song and Nam Lik*, Laos Project Paper No. 15, ed. Joel M. Halpern, Los Angeles, University of California (mimeographed).
1961b *Minority Groups in Northern Laos, Especially the Yao*, Laos Project Paper No. 16, ed. Joel M. Halpern, Los Angeles, University of California (mimeographed).
Izikowitz, Karl Gustav
1941 "Fastening the Soul: Some Religious Traits among the Lamet," *Göteborgs Högskolas Arsskrift*, 47, Pt. XIV, 1-32.
1943 "Quelques notes sur le costume des Puli-Akha," *Ethnos*, 8, 133-52.
1951 *Lamet: Hill Peasants in French Indochina*, Etnologiska Studier No. 17, Göteborg, Etnografiska Museet.

1962 "Notes about the Tai," *Bulletin of the Museum of Far Eastern Antiquities*, 34, 73-91.
1963 "Expansion," *Folk*, 5, 173-85.

Janlekha, Kamol O.
1955 *A Study of the Economy of a Rice-growing Village in Central Thailand*, Bangkok, Division of Agricultural Economics, Ministry of Agriculture.
Jones, Robert B., Jr.
1961 *Karen Linguistic Studies: Description, Comparison, and Texts*, University of California Publications in Linguistics, vol. 25, Berkeley and Los Angeles, University of California Press.
Jones, S. W.
1953 *Public Administration in Malaya*, London, Royal Institute of International Affairs.
Josselin de Jong, J. P. E. de
1951 *Minangkabau and Negri Sembilan: Socio-political Structure in Indonesia*, Leiden, Eduard Ijdo.
Jouin, Bernard
*1949 *La mort et la tombe: L'abandon de la tombe*, Paris, Institut d'Ethnologie.
1950a "Enquête démographique au Darlac, 1943-1944," *BSEI*, 25, 263-80.
1950b "Les traditions des Rhadé," *BSEI*, 25, 357-400.
1951a "Histoire légendaire du Sadet du Feu," *BSEI*, 26, 73-84.
1951b "Rituel prophylactique des Rhadé K'Drao," *BSEI*, 26, 85-88.

Kapadia, K. M.
1950 *The Matrilineal Social Organization of the Nagas of Assam*, Bombay, Popular Book Depot.
Kaufman, Howard K.
1960 *Bangkhuad: A Community Study in Thailand*, Locust Valley, N.Y., J. J. Augustin.
1961 *Village Life in Vientiane Province (1956-1957)*, Laos Project Paper No. 12, ed. Joel M. Halpern, Los Angeles, University of California (mimeographed).
Kemlin, J. E.
1917 "Alliances chez les Reungao," *BEFEO*, 17, 1-119.
Kennedy, Raymond
1935 "The Ethnology of the Greater Sunda Islands," unpublished Ph.D. dissertation, Yale University.
Kerrest, J.
1941 "La consultation du bâton," *IIEH*, 4, 216-23.
King, Frank H. H.
1957 *The New Malayan Nation: A Study of Communalism and Nationalism*, New York, Institute of Pacific Relations.
Kingshill, Konrad
1960 *Ku Daeng—The Red Tomb: A Village Study in Northern Thailand*, Chiengmai, Thailand, The Prince Royal's College.

Lafont, Pierre-Bernard
1953 Notes from Lai Chau (Viet Nam).
1955 "Notes sur les familles patronymiques Thai Noirs de Son La et de Nghia-Lo," *Anthropos*, 50, 797-807.
1959 "Pratiques médicales des Thai Noirs du Laos de l'ouest," *Anthropos*, 54, 819-40.
1960 Review of J. M. Halpern, *Aspects of Village Life and Culture Change in Laos*, *BEFEO*, 50, 184-90.
1961 Personal notes. (Specific notes from previous field experiences in Laos and Vietnam.)
1962a "Les écritures 'tay du Laos," *BEFEO*, 50, 367-94.
1962b Personal notes. (Specific notes from previous field experiences in Laos and Vietnam.)
1963 *Toloi Djuat: Coutumier de la tribu Jarai*, Ecole Française d'Extrême-Orient, Publications, Paris.

Lan, J.
  1919 "Le Riz: Législation, culte, croyances," *Bulletin des Amis du Vieux Hué, 6,* 389-451.

Langrand, G.
  *1945 *Vie sociale et religieuse en Annam: Monographie d'un village de la côte Sud-Annam,* Lille, Editions Univers.

Le Thanh Khoi
  1955 *Le Vietnam,* Paris, Editions du Minuit.

Leach, E. R.
  1954 *Political Systems of Highland Burma,* Cambridge, Harvard University Press.

LeBar, Frank M. and Adrienne Suddard, eds.
  1960 *Laos: Its People, Its Society, Its Culture,* New Haven, HRAF Press.

Le Boulanger, Paul
  *1931 *Histoire du Laos français,* Paris, Plon.

Leclère, Adhémard
  1890 *Recherches sur la législation cambodgienne (droit privé),* Paris, Challamel, Librairie Coloniale.
  1914 *Histoire du Cambodge,* Paris, Paul Geuthner.
  1917 *Cambodge: Fêtes civiles et religieuses,* Paris, Imprimerie Nationale.

Lehman, F. K.
  1963 *The Structure of Chin Society: A Tribal People of Burma Adapted to a Non-Western Civilization,* Illinois Studies in Anthropology, No. 3, Urbana, University of Illinois Press.

LeMay, Reginald
  1926 *An Asian Arcady: The Land and Peoples of Northern Siam,* Cambridge, Heffer and Sons.

Le Pichon, J.
  1938 "Les chasseurs de sang," *Bulletin des Amis du Vieux Hué, 25,* 357-409.

Leuba, J.
  *1923 *Les Chams et leur art,* Paris et Bruxelles, G. Van Oest.

Leuschner, Friedrich W.
  1911 "Die Yautse in Süd-China," *Mitteilungen der Deutschen Gesellschaft für Natur- und Völkerkunde Ostasiens, 13,* 237-84.

Lévy, Paul
  1959 "The Sacrifice of the Buffalo and the Forecast of the Weather in Vientiane," in *Kingdom of Laos,* ed. R. de Berval, Saigon, France-Asie.

Li, Fang-kuei
  1943 *Notes on the Mak Languages,* Academia Sinica, Institute of History and Philology, Monograph Series A, No. 20, Shanghai.
  1957 "The Jui Dialect of Po-ai and the Northern Tai," *Bulletin of the Institute of History and Philology, Academia Sinica, 29,* Pt. I, 315-21.
  1959 "Classification by Vocabulary: Tai Dialects," *Anthropological Linguistics, 1,* 15-21.

Liétard, Alfred
  1909 "Notes sur les dialectes Lo-lo," *BEFEO, 9,* 549-72.
  1913 *Au Yun-Nan: Les Lolo p'o: Une tribu des aborigènes de la Chine méridionale,* Münster, Aschendorff.

Lin, Yueh-hwa
  1940 "The Miao-Man Peoples of Kweichow," *HJAS, 5,* 261-345.
  1944 "Social Life of the Aboriginal Groups in and around Yunnan," *JWCS, 15,* 47-56.
  1946 "The Kinship System of the Lolo," *HJAS, 9,* 81-100.
  1961 *The Lolo of Liang Shan [Liang-shan I-chia],* Shanghai, Commercial Press, 1947 (translation by Ju-shu Pan published by HRAF Press, New Haven).

Ling, Shun-sheng and Ruey Yih-fu
  *1947 *Hsiang-hsi Miao-tsu Tiao-ch'a Pao-kao* [A Report on an Investigation of the Miao of Western Hunan],

Academia Sinica, Institute of History and Philology, Monograph Series A, No. 18, Shanghai.

Ling, Zeng-seng (Johnson Ling)
  1929 *Recherches ethnographiques sur les Yao dans la Chine du Sud,* Paris, Presses Universitaires de France.

Lo, Ch'ang-p'ei
  1944-45 "The Genealogical Patronymic Linkage System of the Tibeto-Burman-speaking Tribes," *HJAS, 8,* 349-63.

Löffler, Lorenz G.
  1959 "Die Khyang der Chittagong Hill Tracts (Marginalien zu neuem linguistischem Material von D. und L. Bernot)," *Zeitschrift für Ethnologie, 84,* 257-69.

Lombard, Sylvia
  1963 Personal communication, based on missionary work in Chiengrai, 1957-62.

Lorrain, J. Herbert and Fred. W. Savidge
  1898 *A Grammar and Dictionary of the Lushai Language (Dulien Dialect),* Shillong, Assam Secretariat Printing Office.

Lowis, Cecil C.
  1906 *A Note on the Palaungs of Hsipaw and Tawngpeng,* Ethnographical Survey of India, Burma, No. 1, Rangoon, Superintendent of Government Printing and Stationery.

Luce, G. H.
  1958 "The Early Syam in Burma's History," *JSS, 46,* Pt. II, 123-214.
  1959a "Introduction to the Comparative Study of Karen Languages," *JBRS, 42,* Pt. I, 1-18.
  1959b "Chin Hills—Linguistic Tour (Dec. 1954)—University Project," *JBRS, 42,* Pt. I, 19-31.
  1959c "Note on the Peoples of Burma in the 12th-13th Century A.D.," *JBRS, 42,* Pt. I, 52-74.
  1959d "Old Kyaukse and the Coming of the Burmans," *JBRS, 42,* Pt. I, 75-112.

Lunet de Lajonquière, E.
  1906 *Ethnographie du Tonkin septentrional,* Paris, Leroux.

Lyngdoh (Nonglait), U Homiwell
  1937 *Ka Niam Khasi* [The Khasi Religion], Shillong.
  1946 *Ka Pomblang Nongkrem bad Ka Thang Syiem Sohra* [The Nongkrem State Ceremony and the Cremation of the Sohra Chief], 2d ed. Shillong.
  1952 *Ki Syiem Khasi bad Synteng* [The Khasi and Jaintia Chiefs], 2d ed. Shillong.

McFarland, George Bradley
  1941 *Thai-English Dictionary,* Bangkok, Bangkok Times Press.

McGilvary, Daniel
  1912 *A Half Century among the Siamese and the Lao,* New York and London, Fleming Revell.

Madge, Thomas Charles
  1955 *Village Communities in North-east Thailand: Survey of the Thailand–UNESCO Education Center,* United Nations Technical Assistance Program Report, TAA/Tha/1.

Maitre, H.
  1912 *Les jungles Möi,* Paris, Larose.

Majumdar, Surendra N.
  1925 *Ao Nagas,* Calcutta, Sailen Majumdar of 93-1 J. Baitakhana Road.

Maneffe, H. and L. Bezacier
  1940 "Les groupes sanguins en Indochine du Nord," *IIEH, 3,* Pt. II, 57-100.

Marshall, Harry I.
  1922 *The Karen People of Burma: A Study in Anthropology and Ethnology,* Columbus, Ohio State University.

Maspéro, Georges
  1928 *Le royaume de Champa*, Paris et Bruxelles, G. Van Oest.
  1929-30 *Un empire colonial français: L'Indochine*, 2 vols. Paris, G. Van Oest.

Maurice, A.
  1941 "A propos des mutilations dentaires chez les Moi," *IIEH*, 4, 135-39.
  1942 "L'habitation Rhadé," *IIEH*, 5, 87-106.

Maurice, A. and G. Proux
  1954 "L'ame du riz," *BSEI*, 29, 129-258.

Maxwell, W. E.
  1884 "The Law and Custom of the Malays with Reference to the Tenure of Land," *JRASSB*, 13, 75-220.

Menetrier, E.
  1926 "Monographie de la circonscription résidentielle de Kampot," *Extrême-Asie*, Nos. 1-6.

Metford, Beatrix
  1935 *Where China Meets Burma: Life and Travel in the Burma-China Borderlands*, London and Glasgow, Blackie.

Mi Mi Khaing
  1946 *Burmese Family*, Bombay, Longmans, Green.

Mickey, Margaret P.
  1947 "The Cowrie Shell Miao of Kweichow," *PMAAE*, 32, 1-80.

Mills, J. P.
  n.d. "Some Recent Contact Problems in the Khasi Hills," in *Essays in Anthropology Presented to Rai Bahadur Sarat Chandra Roy*, eds. J. P. Mills, B. S. Guha, K. P. Chattopadhayay, D. N. Majumdar, and A. Aiyappan, Lucknow, Maxwell.
  1922 *The Lhota Nagas*, London, Macmillan.
  1926 *The Ao Nagas*, London, Macmillan.
  1935 "Notes on the Western Rengma Nagas, Northern Sangtam Nagas, Chang Nagas, Thendu Konyaks, Thenkoh Konyaks and on the Effect on some Tribes of Assam Districts of Contacts with Civilization," in *Census of India, 1931*, 1, India, Pt. III, Ethnographical, 130-32, 143-49, Delhi, Manager of Publications.
  1937 *The Rengma Nagas*, London, Macmillan.

Milne, Mary Lewis (Harper)
  1910 *Shans at Home*, by Mrs. Leslie Milne, London, John Murray.
  1921 *An Elementary Palaung Grammar*, by Mrs. Leslie Milne, with an Introduction by C. O. Blagden, Oxford, Clarendon Press.
  1924 *The Home of an Eastern Clan: A Study of the Palaungs of the Shan States*, by Mrs. Leslie Milne, Oxford, Clarendon Press.
  1931a *A Dictionary of English-Palaung and Palaung-English*, by Mrs. Leslie Milne, Rangoon, Superintendent of Government Printing and Stationery, 1st pagination.
  1931b *A Dictionary of English-Palaung and Palaung-English*, by Mrs. Leslie Milne, Rangoon, Superintendent of Government Printing and Stationery, 2d pagination.

Mitton, G. E.
  1936 *Scott of the Shan Hills*, London, John Murray.

Moerman, Michael
  1962 "Class and Culture in Northern Thailand," paper read at the Annual meeting of the American Anthropological Association, Chicago, November 1962 (mimeographed).
  1963 Personal communication and notes on the Lue of Chiengkham district, province of Chiengrai, northern Thailand.

Monfleur, G.
  1931 *Monographie de la province du Darlac*, Hanoi, Imprimerie d'Extrême-Orient.

Moninger, M. M.
  1921 "The Hainanese Miao," *JRASNCB*, 52, 40-50.
  1932 "The Hainanese Miao and Their Food Supply," *Lingnan Science Journal*, 11, 521-26.

Monod, G.
  *1931 *Le Cambodgien*, Paris, Larose.

Moorehead, F. J.
  1957 *A History of Malaya and Her Neighbors*, vol. 1, London, New York, and Toronto, Longmans, Green.

Morechand, G.
  1952 "Notes démographiques sur un canton Meo Blanc du pays tai," *BSEI*, 27, 354-61.
  1955a "Caractères économiques et sociaux d'une région de pêche maritime du Centre-Vietnam," *BEFEO*, 47, 291-354.
  1955b "Principaux traits du chamanisme Meo Blanc en Indochine," *BEFEO*, 47, 509-58.

Morizon, R.
  *1936 *La province cambodgienne du Pursat*, Paris, Les Editions internationales.

Morris, John Hughes
  1910 *The History of the Welsh Calvinistic Methodists' Foreign Mission, to the End of the Year 1904*, Carnarvon, C. M. Book Room.

Mosel, James
  1957 "Thai Administrative Behavior," in *Toward the Comparative Study of Public Administration*, ed. William J. Siffin, Bloomington, Indiana University, Department of Government.

Mukherjee, Ramkrishna et al.
  1941 *The Khasi Huts of Mawphlang*, University of Calcutta Anthropological Papers, n.s. 6, pp. 177-87.

Murdock, George P.
  1962 "Ethnographic Atlas," *Ethnology*, 1, 265-86.

Mus, P.
  1933 "Cultes indiens et indigènes au Champa (conférence faite au Musée Louis Finot)," *BEFEO*, 33, 367-410.

Musgrave, John K.
  1956 "The Languages of Burma," in *Burma*, ed. Frank N. Trager, HRAF Subcontractor's Monograph No. 37, New Haven (mimeographed).

NCTXH (Nha Cong-Tac Xa-Hoi Mien-Thuong) [Bureau of Social Action for the Highland Area]
  1960 *Tong-So Cac Sac Dan Thuong* [The Total Highland Population Figures], Saigon.

NNCDT (Nhom Nghien Cuu Dan Toc [Cua Uy-Ban Dan-Toc]) [Minority People's Study Group (of the Committee of Minority Peoples)]
  1959 *Cac Dan Toc Thieu So O Viet-Nam* [Minority Peoples of Viet Nam], Hanoi, Nha Xuat Ban Van Hoa.

Needham, Rodney
  1956 "Ethnographic Notes on the Siwang of Central Malaya," *JRASMB*, 29, Pt. I, 49-69.

Ner, M.
  1941 "Les musulmans de l'Indochine française," *BEFEO*, 41, 151-200.

Ngo Quy Son
  1940 "De quelques interdits chez les Annamites du Tonkin," *IIEH*, 3, 21-37.

Nguyen Thieu Lau
  1944 "La population Cham du Sud-Annam s'accroît-elle?" *IIEH*, 6, 213-23.

Nguyen Van Huyen
  1939 "De l'institution des castes dans la commune annamite," *IIEH*, 1, 59-70.
  1940 "A propos d'une carte de répartition des génies tutélaires dans la province de Bac-ninh (Tonkin)," *IIEH*, 3, 137-56.

1941 *Recueil des chants de mariage Tho de Lang-Son et Cao-Bang*, Ecole Française d'Extrême-Orient, Collection de textes et documents sur l'Indochine, vol. 5, Hanoi.

Nguyen Van Khoan
1930 "Essai sur le dinh et le culte du génie tutélaire des villages au Tonkin, *BEFEO*, 30, 107-39.
1938 "Croyances tonkinoises relatives à la protection de l'enfance," *IIEH*, 1, 75-78.

Noone, H. D.
1936 "Report on the Settlements and Welfare of the Ple-Temiar Senoi of the Perak-Kelantan Watershed," *Journal of the Federated Malay States Museum*, 19, Pt. I, 1-84.

Odaka, Kunio
1950 *Economic Organization of the Li Tribes of Hainan Island*, translated from the Japanese by Mikiso Hane, New Haven, Yale Southeast Asia Studies.

Olivier, G. and H. Chagnoux
1951 "Anthropologie physique des Chams," *BSEI*, 26, 271-318.

Ollone, Henri M. d'
1912 *In Forbidden China: The d'Ollone Mission, 1906-1909: China-Tibet-Mongolia*, translated from the French by B. Miall, Boston, Small Maynard.

Orléans, Henri Philippe Marie, d'
1898 *From Tonkin to India by the Source of the Irawadi, January '95–January '96*, translated from the French by Hamley Bent, London, Methuen.

Orleans, Leo
1957 "The 1953 Chinese Census in Perspective," *Journal of Asian Studies*, 16, 565-73.

P'ang, Hsin-min
*1932 "Kwang-tung Pei Chiang Yao-shan Tsa-chi [Miscellaneous Sketches of the Yao-shan of North Kwang-tung]," *Bulletin of the Institute of History and Philology, Academia Sinica*, 2, 473-514.

Paris, P.
1955 *Esquisse d'une ethnographie navale des peuples annamites*, Publicaties van het Museum voor Land-en Volkenkunde en Het Maritiem Museum "Prins Hendrik," Rotterdam.

Parkinson, C. N.
1960 *British Intervention in Malaya, 1867-1877*, Singapore, University of Malaya Press.

Parmentier, H.
1918 *Inventaire descriptif des monuments Čams de l'Annam*, 2 vols. Paris, Leroux.
1951 "La maison commune du village Bahnar de Kombraih," *BEFEO*, 45, 223-24.

Parry, Neville Edward
1932 *The Lakhers*, with an introduction and supplementary notes by J. H. Hutton, London, Macmillan.

Pasquier, P.
*1907 *L'Annam d'autrefois: Essai sur la constitution de l'Annam avant l'intervention française*, Paris, Challamel.

Pendleton, Robert L.
1943 "Land Use in Northeastern Thailand," *Geographical Review*, 33, 15-41.
1962 *Thailand: Aspects of Landscape and Life*, New York, Duell, Sloan, and Pearce.

Petit, R.
*1931 *La monarchie annamite*, Paris, Les Editions Domat-Monchrestien.

Phansomboon, Somsak
1957 "A Bioserological Consideration of the Migration of the Thai Race: A Preliminary Report of a New Concept," *JSS*, 45, Pt. II, 55-63.

Phillips, Richard
1961 "Here Are the Tribes," *Primitive Frontiers*.
1962 Unpublished map of ethnic groups in the highlands of South Vietnam.

Pinnow, Heinz-Jürgen
1959 *Versuch einer historischen Lautlehre der Kharia-Sprache*, Wiesbaden, Otto Harrassowitz.

Pitchford, V. C.
1937 "The Wild Wa States and Lake Nawngkhio," *Geographical Journal*, 90, 223-32.

Porée-Maspero, Eveline
*1950 *Cérémonies des douze mois: Fêtes annuelles cambodgiennes*, Phnom-Penh, Portail.
1958 *Cérémonies privées des Cambodgiens*, Phnom-Penh, Portail.

Pugh, Berkeley D.
1951 "The Religion of the Khasis," unpublished M.A. thesis, University of Chicago.

Purcell, Victor
1951 *The Chinese in Southeast Asia*, New York, Oxford University Press.

Queguiner, Dr.
1943 "Notes sur une peuplade moi de la chaîne annamitique sud: Les Cau S're," *IIEH*, 6, 395-402.

Rabel, Lili
1961 *Khasi: A Language of Assam*, Louisiana State University Studies, Humanities Series No. 10, Baton Rouge, Louisiana State University Press.

Rafy, K. U.
1920 *Folk-tales of the Khasis*, London, Macmillan.

Rajadhon, Anuman
1954a "Kingship in Siam," *JSS*, 42, Pt. I, 1-10.
1954b *The Story of Thai Marriage Custom*, Thailand Culture Series No. 13, Bangkok, National Culture Institute.
1955 "Me Posop, the Rice Mother," *JSS*, 43, Pt. I, 55-61.

Reeve, W. D.
1951 *Public Administration in Siam*, London, Royal Institute of International Affairs.

Reinach, Lucien de
*1901 *Le Laos*, 2 vols. Paris, A. Charles, Librairie-Editeur.

Rigby, J.
1929 *The Ninety-Nine Laws of Perak*, Papers on Malay Subjects, Law, Pt. II, Kuala Lumpur, The Government Printer.

Rispaud, Jean
1937 "Les noms à éléments numéraux des principautés tai," *JSS*, 29, Pt. II, 77-122.

Robequain, Charles
*1929 *Le Thanh Hoa: Etude géographique d'une province annamite*, 2 vols. Paris et Bruxelles, G. Van Oest.
1944 *The Economic Development of French Indo-China*, London, Oxford University Press.

Robert, R.
1941 *Notes sur les Tay Dèng de Lang Chánh*, Mémoire No. 1, Institut Indochinois pour l'Etude de l'Homme, Hanoi, Imprimerie d'Extrême-Orient.

Robinson, H. C.
1923 "Fauna: (1) Vertebrates," in *Malaya: The Straits Settlements and the Federated and Unfederated Malay States*, ed. R. O. Winstedt, London, Constable.

Rock, Joseph F.
1935 "The Story of the Flood in the Literature of the Mo-so (Na-khi) Tribe," *JWCS*, 7, 64-80.
1936a "Ha-la, or the Killing of the Soul as Practiced by Na-khi Sorcerers," *JWCS*, 8, 53-58.
1936b "The Origin of the Tso-la Books, or Books of Di-

vination of the Na-khi or Mo-so Tribe," *JWCS*, 8, 39-52.

1947 *The Ancient Na-Khi Kingdom of Southwest China*, 2 vols. Harvard-Yenching Institute Monograph Series, 8 and 9, Cambridge, Harvard University Press.

1952a "The Na-khi Naga Cult and Related Ceremonies, I-II," *Serie Orientale Roma*, 4, 1-800.

1952b "The Muan Bpo Ceremony, or the Sacrifice to Heaven as Practiced by the Na-khi," *Annali Lateranensi*, 16, 9-158.

1955 "The Zhi Ma Funeral Ceremony of the Na-khi of Southwest China," *Studia Instituti Anthropos*, 9, 1-229.

1963 "The Life and Culture of the Na-khi Tribe of the China-Tibet Borderland," *Verzeichnis der orientalischen Handschriften in Deutschland*, Supplementband 2, pp. 1-48, Wiesbaden, Franz Steiner Verlag.

Ropmay, D., ed.
1940 *Ka Centenary History Ka Balang Presbyterian ha Ri Khasi-Jaintia naduh 1841 haduh 1940* [Centenary History of the Presbyterian Church in Khasi-Jaintia Hills from 1841 to 1940], Shillong, Ka Literature Committee Ka Assembly.

Rose, Archibald and J. Coggin Brown
1911 "Lisu (Yawyin) Tribes of the Burma-China Frontier," *Memoirs of the Royal Asiatic Society of Bengal*, 3, 249-76.

Rouilly, M.
*1929 *La commune annamite*, Paris, Les Presses Modernes.

Roux, Henri
1924 "Deux tribus de la région de Phongsaly (Laos septentrional) I: A-Khas or Khas Kôs, II; P'u Noi," *BEFEO*, 24, 373-500.

Roux, Henri and Tran Van Chu
1954 "Quelques minorités ethniques du Nord-Indochine," *France-Asie*, 10, 135-419.

Roy, Jeebon
1897 *Ka Niam jong Ki Khasi* [The Religion of the Khasis], new ed. Shillong, Ri Khasi Press.

Roy, U Sib Charan
1914 *Ka Jingiapyni Ka Kmie bad Ki Khun* [Dialogue between a Mother and Her Sons], Shillong, Ri Khasi Press.

Ruey, Yih-fu
1960 "The Magpie Miao of South Szechwan," in *Social Structure in Southeast Asia*, ed. G. P. Murdock, New York, Viking Fund Publications in Anthropology No. 29.

Sabatier, L.
1940 *Recueil des coutumes Rhadées du Darlac*, Hanoi, Imprimerie d'Extrême-Orient.

Salzner, Richard
1960 *Sprachenatlas des Indopazifischen Raumes*, Wiesbaden, Otto Harrassowitz.

Savina, F. M.
1926 "Dictionnaire Français-Man, précédé d'une note sur les Man Kim-Di-Mun et leur langue," *BEFEO*, 26, 11-255.

1930 *Histoire des Miao*, 2d ed. Hongkong, Imprimerie de la Société des Missions-étrangères.

Schebesta, Paul
1927 *Among the Forest Dwarfs of Malaya*, London, Hutchinson.

1952 "Die Negrito Asiens," *Studia Instituti Anthropos*, vol. 6, I, Band. Geschichte, Geographie, Umwelt, Demographie, und Anthropologie der Negrito, Wien-Mödling, St. Gabriel Verlag.

*1954 "Die Negrito Asiens," *Studia Instituti Anthropos*, vol. 12, II, Band. Ethnographie der Negrito, 1.

Halbband, Wirtschaft und Soziologie, Wien-Mödling, St. Gabriel Verlag.

*1957 "Die Negrito Asiens," *Studia Instituti Anthropos*, vol. 13, II, Band. Ethnographie der Negrito, 2. Halbband, Religion und Mythologie, Wien-Mödling, St. Gabriel Verlag.

Scott, James George
1896 "The Wild Wa: A Headhunting Race," *Asiatic Quarterly Review*, 3d ser., 1, 138-52.

1910 *The Burman: His Life and Notions*, by Shway Yoe (pseudonym), London, Macmillan.

1921 *Burma: A Handbook of Practical Information*, 3d rev. ed. London, Alexander Moring, De La More Press.

1932 *Burma and Beyond*, London, Grayson and Grayson.

Scott, James George and J. P. Hardiman
1900 *Gazetteer of Upper Burma and the Shan States*, Pt. I, vol. 1, Rangoon, Superintendent of Government Printing and Stationery.

Seidenfaden, Erik
1958 *The Thai Peoples*, Bangkok, Siam Society.

Shafer, Robert
1955 "Classification of the Sino-Tibetan Languages," *Word*, 11, 94-111.

Shakespear, J.
1912 *The Lushei Kuki Clans*, London, Macmillan.

Shakespear, L. W.
1914 *History of Upper Assam, Upper Burma and the North-eastern Frontier*, London, Macmillan.

Sharp, Lauriston
1957 "Thai Social Structure," paper read at the Ninth Pacific Science Congress, Section on Anthropology and Social Science, Bangkok.

Sharp, Lauriston, Hazel M. Hauck, Kamol Janlekha, and Robert B. Textor
1953 *Siamese Rice Village: A Preliminary Study of Bang Chan 1948-1949*, Bangkok, Cornell Research Center.

Sharp, Lauriston, Frank J. Moore, and Walter F. Vella
1956 *Handbook on Thailand*, HRAF Subcontractor's Monograph No. 42, New Haven (mimeographed).

Shaw, G. E.
1926 *Rice Planting*, Papers on Malay Subjects, Malay Industries, Pt. III, Kuala Lumpur, The Government Printer.

Shaw, William
1929 *Notes on the Thadou Kukis*, edited with an introduction, notes, appendices, illustrations, and index by J. H. Hutton, Calcutta, published by the Asiatic Society of Bengal on behalf of the Government of Assam.

Shorto, H. L.
1962 *A Dictionary of Modern Spoken Mon*, London, Oxford University Press.

Siguret, J.
1937 *Territoires et populations des confins du Yunnan*, Peiping, Henri Vetch.

Silvestre, Captain
1918 "Les Thai Blancs de Phong-Tho," *BEFEO*, 18, 1-56.

Sinavong, Boun Than
1957 "Agrarian Rites in Laos," paper read at the Ninth Pacific Science Congress, Bangkok (mimeographed).

Singh, U Rabon
1950 *Ka Kitab Niam-Khein Ki Khasi, la Pyniasoh bad Ki Ain Ki Adong bad Ka Rukom Hiar Pateng* [A Book of the Important Religious Customs of the Khasis, Together with Customary Law and the Inheritance System], Shillong.

Sisawat, Bun Chuai
*1952 *Săm sip chāti nai Chĭang rǎi* [Thirty Nationalities in Chiengrai], Bangkok, Outhai Press.

Skeat, Walter William
1900 *Malay Magic, Being an Introduction to the Folklore and Popular Religion of the Malay Peninsula*, London, Macmillan.

Skeat, Walter William and Charles O. Blagden
1906 *Pagan Races of the Malay Peninsula*, 2 vols. London and New York, Macmillan.

Skinner, G. William
1957 *Chinese Society in Thailand: An Analytical History*, Ithaca, Cornell University Press.

Smalley, William A.
1956 "The Gospel and the Cultures of Laos," *Practical Anthropology, 3*, 47-57.
1960 "The Gospel and the Cultures of Laos," *Practical Anthropology*, Supplement, pp. 63-69 (reprinted from 3, 47-57).
1961 *Outline of Khmuʔ Structure*, New Haven, American Oriental Society.

Smith, Gordon
1959 Unpublished map of ethnic groups in the highlands of central Vietnam.

Smith, T. E.
1952 *Population Growth in Malaya: An Analysis of Recent Trends*, New York and London, Royal Institute of International Affairs.

Souvannavong, Oudom
1959 "Some Practices of Traditional Medicine," in *Kingdom of Laos*, ed. René de Berval, Saigon, France-Asie.

Stegmiller, P. F.
1924a "Das Marktleben der Khasi," in *Festschrift P. W. Schmidt*, ed. W. Koppers, Wien, Mechitharisten-Congregations-Buchdrückerei.
1924b "Opfer und Opferbräuche der Khasi," *Mitteilungen der Anthropologischen Gesellschaft in Wien, 54*, 211-31.
1925 "Pfeilschiessen und Jagdgebräuche der Khasi," *Anthropos, 20*, 607-23.

Steinberg, David J.
1959 *Cambodia: Its People, Its Society, Its Culture*, rev. ed. New Haven, HRAF Press.

Stevenson, H.
1943 *The Economics of the Central Chin Tribes*, published by order of the Government of Burma, Bombay, Times of India Press.

Stevenson, Paul H.
1932 "Notes on the Human Geography of the Chinese-Tibetan Borderland," *Geographical Review, 22*, 599-616.

Stübel, Hans
1937 *Die Li-Stämme der Insel Hainan: Ein Beitrag zur Volkskunde Südchinas*, Berlin, Klinkhart und Biermann.
1938 "The Yao of the Province of Kwangtung," *Monumenta Serica, 3*, 345-84.

Sukhabanij, Kachorn
1956 "Was Nam Thom the First King of Sukhodaya?" *JSS, 44*, Pt. II, 139-44.
1957 "The Thai Beach-head States in the 11th-12th Centuries," *Silapakon Journal, 1*, 1-22.

Swettenham, Frank
1929 *British Malaya: An Account of the Origin and Progress of British Influence in Malaya*, 2d rev. ed. London, Allen and Unwin.

Swift, M. G.
1956 "Village Socio-Economic Organization in Malaya," *Information* (Paris, International Social Science Council), 7, 1-16.

Taillard, P.
1942 "Les Saoch," *IIEH, 5*, 15-45.

T'ao, Yün-k'uei
*1936 "Kuan-yü Mossu chih Ming-ch'eng Fen-pu yü Chien-I [Notes on the Origin of the Tribal Name Moso and their Distribution and Migration]," *Bulletin of the Institute of History and Philology, Academia Sinica, 7*, 121-35.

Taylor, E. N.
1937 "Malay Family Law," *JRASMB, 15*, Pt. I, 1-78.

Telford, J. H.
1937 "Animism in Kengtung State," *JBRS, 27*, Pt. II, 86-238.

Textor, Robert Bayard
1960 "An Inventory of Non-Buddhist Supernatural Objects in a Central Thai Village," unpublished Ph.D. dissertation, Cornell University.

Thailand. Ministry of Agriculture
1953 *Thailand Economic Farm Survey, 1953*, Bangkok, Division of Agricultural Economics.
1957 *Agriculture in Thailand*, Bangkok.

Thomas, David
1961 "Classification of Southern Vietnamese Malayo-Polynesian Languages," Saigon (mimeographed).
1962 "Mon-Khmer Subgroupings in Vietnam," Summer Institute of Linguistics, University of North Dakota (mimeographed).
1963 Personal communication.

T'ien, Ju-k'ang
1949 "Pai Cults and Social Age in the Tai Tribes of the Yunnan-Burma Frontier," *AA, 51*, 46-57.

Tran Van Trai
*1942 *La famille patriarcale annamite*, Paris, P. Lapagesse.

Tregonning, K. G.
1961 "The History of Malaya: A New Interpretation," *Eastern Horizon, 1*, 13-18.

Tufo, M. V. Del
1949 *Malaya, Comprising the Federation of Malaya and the Colony of Singapore: A Report on the 1947 Census*, London, Crown Agents.

Tweedie, M. W. F.
1953 "The Stone Age in Malaya," Monographs on Malay Subjects No. 1, *JRASMB*, vol. 26, Pt. II.

United States. Central Intelligence Agency
1959 *China: Provisional Atlas of Administrative Units*, Washington, D.C.

Veyre, P.
1938 "Du tatouage chez les Annamites," *IIEH, 1*, 97-115.

Vu Van Hien
*1939 *La propriété communale au Tonkin (Contribution à l'étude historique, juridique et économique des Công Diên et Công Thô en pays d'Annam)*, doctoral thesis for the Faculty of Law, University of Paris, Paris, Les Presses Modernes.

Wales, G. H. Quaritch
1934 *Ancient Siamese Government and Administration*, London, Bernard Quaritch.

Wang, Hsing-jui
*1948 *Hai-nan Tao chih Miao-jen* [The Miao People of Hainan Island], Institute for Chinese Frontier Studies, Ser. B, No. 2, Canton, Chu-hai University.

Wang, T'ung-hui
*1936 *Hua-lan Yao She-hui Tsu-chih* [The Social Organization of the Hua-lan Yao], Shanghai, Special Government Research Publication.

Ward, F. Kingdon
1912 "Through the Lutzu Country to Menkong," *Geographical Review*, 39, 582-92.
1921 *In Farthest Burma*, London, Seeley, Service.
1924 *From China to Hkamti Long*, London, Arnold.

Warington Smyth, H.
1902 "Boats and Boat Building in the Malay Peninsula," *Journal of the Society of Arts*, 50, 570-86.

Weaver, Robert W.
1956 "Through Unknown Thailand," *Natural History*, 65, 289-95, 336.

Wells, Kenneth E.
1960 *Thai Buddhism: Its Rites and Activities*, Bangkok, The Christian Bookstore.

Wheatley, Paul
1962 *The Golden Khersonese: Studies in the Historical Geography of the Malay Peninsula before* A.D. *1500*, Oxford, Oxford University Press.

White, Walter G.
1922 *The Sea Gypsies of Malaya*, London, Seeley, Service.

Wiens, Herold J.
1954 *China's March toward the Tropics*, Hamden, Conn., Shoe String Press.

Wilkinson, R. J.
1920 *The Incidents of Malay Life*, Papers on Malay Subjects, Life and Customs, Pt. I, Singapore, Kelly and Walsh.
1926 *The Aboriginal Tribes*, Papers on Malay Subjects, Supplement, Kuala Lumpur, The Government Printer.

Williams-Hunt, P. D. R.
1952 *An Introduction to the Malayan Aborigines*, Kuala Lumpur, The Government Printer.

Wilson, David A.
1959 "Thailand," in *Governments and Politics of Southeast Asia*, ed. George McT. Kahin, Ithaca, Cornell University Press.

Wilson, David A. and Herbert P. Phillips
1958 "Elections and Parties in Thailand," *Far Eastern Survey*, 27, 113-19.

Wilson, T. B.
1958 *The Economics of Padi Production in North Malaya*, Pt. I, Department of Agriculture Bulletin No. 103, Kuala Lumpur.

Winnington, Alan
1959 *Slaves of the Cool Mountains*, London, Lawrence and Wishart.

Winstedt, R. O.
1925a *Arts and Crafts*, Papers on Malay Subjects, Malay Industries, Pt. I, Kuala Lumpur, The Government Printer.

1925b *The Kampong, The House, Furniture, Dress, Food*, Papers on Malay Subjects, Life and Customs, Pt. II, The Circumstances of Malay Life, Kuala Lumpur, The Government Printer.
1929 *Fishing, Hunting, and Trapping*, Papers on Malay Subjects, Malay Industries, Pt. II, Kuala Lumpur, The Government Printer.
1950 *The Malays: A Cultural History*, rev. ed. London, Routledge and Kegan Paul.
1951 *The Malay Magician, being Shaman, Saiva, and Sufi*, rev. ed. London, Routledge and Kegan Paul.

Wissmann, H. von
1943 *Süd-Yünnan als Teilraum Südostasiens*, Schriften zur Geopolitik No. 22, Heidelberg, Kurt Vowinckel.

Wist, Hans
1938 "Die Yao in Südchina; nach Berichten neuer Chinesischer Feldforschungen," *Baessler Archiv*, 21, 73-135.

Woodruff, L. W.
1960 *Report on the Study of a Vietnamese Rural Community: Administrative Activities*, 2 vols. Saigon, Michigan State University Viet Nam Advisory Group (mimeographed).

Wu, Che-lin
*1945 "Mossu Jen chih She-hui Tsu-che yü Tsung-chiao Hsin-yang [The Social Organization and Religious Beliefs of the Moso People]," *Frontier Affairs*, 4, 9-19, 28-32.

Wu, Che-lin and Ch'en Kuo-chün
*1942 *Kuei-chou Miao-I She-hui Yen-chiu* [Studies of Miao-I Societies in Kweichow], Kweiyang, Wen-t'ung Book Co.

Wulff, Kurt
1934 *Chinesisch und Tai: Sprachvergleichende Untersuchungen*, Det Kgl. Danske Videnskabernes Selskab, Historisk-filologiske Meddelelser 20, Pt. III, København, Levin, Munksgaard, Ejnar Munksgaard.

Young, O. Gordon
1961 *The Hilltribes of Northern Thailand*, Bangkok, United States Operations Mission to Thailand.

Zadrozny, Mitchell G., ed.
1955 *Area Handbook on Cambodia*, HRAF Subcontractor's Monograph No. 21, New Haven (mimeographed).

Zainal Abidin bin Ahmad
1949 "Malay Festivals and Some Aspects of Malay Religious Life," *JRASMB*, 22, Pt. I, 94.

Zelinsky, Wilber
1950 "The Indochinese Peninsula: A Demographic Anomaly," *Far Eastern Quarterly*, 9, 115-45.

INDEX OF NAMES

INDEX

COUNTRY-NAME CONCORDANCE

Each of the ethnic groups in the table of contents is listed below, first in alphabetical order, followed by the political entity or entities within which it is found. The political unit within which a group is most numerous is in each case capitalized. A second order of arrangement is by country or province, each group appearing once under the political unit within which it is most numerous—with secondary distribution indicated by names of countries or provinces in parentheses.

Achang—YUNNAN, Burma
Ahom—ASSAM
Akha—YUNNAN, Burma, Thailand, Laos
Alak—LAOS
Ataouat—LAOS

Bahnar—SOUTH VIETNAM
Bih—SOUTH VIETNAM
Black Tai—NORTH VIETNAM, Laos
Bout—SOUTH VIETNAM
Brao—LAOS, Thailand, Cambodia, South Vietnam
Bru—SOUTH VIETNAM
Burmese—BURMA
Burmese Shans—BURMA

Cao—SOUTH VIETNAM, Laos
Chams—SOUTH VIETNAM, Cambodia
Chaobon—THAILAND
Cheng—LAOS
Chinese Shans—YUNNAN, Burma
Chins—BURMA, Assam
Chong—CAMBODIA, Thailand
Chrau—SOUTH VIETNAM
Chuang—KWANGSI, Kwangtung
Chung-chia—KWEICHOW, Yunnan
Churu—SOUTH VIETNAM
Cua—SOUTH VIETNAM

Duane—SOUTH VIETNAM

Garos—ASSAM

Halang—SOUTH VIETNAM, Laos
Halang Doan—LAOS, South Vietnam
Haw—YUNNAN, Thailand, Laos
Hkamti Shans—BURMA, Assam
Hpon—BURMA
Hre—SOUTH VIETNAM
Hroy—SOUTH VIETNAM

Jakun—MALAYA
Jarai—SOUTH VIETNAM, Cambodia
Jeh—LAOS, South Vietnam

Kachins—BURMA, Yunnan, Assam
Kadu—BURMA
Kalo—SOUTH VIETNAM
Karens—BURMA, Thailand
Kasseng—LAOS
Katang—LAOS
Katu—SOUTH VIETNAM
Kayong—SOUTH VIETNAM

Kelao—KWEICHOW, Hunan, Yunnan, Kwangsi, North Vietnam
Khasis—ASSAM
Khmer—CAMBODIA, Thailand, South Vietnam
Khmu—LAOS, Thailand
Khorat Tai—THAILAND
Khua—NORTH VIETNAM
Khün—BURMA
Kil—SOUTH VIETNAM
Krung—SOUTH VIETNAM
Kui—THAILAND, Cambodia

Lahu—YUNNAN, Burma, Thailand, Laos
Lamet—LAOS
Lang Ya—SOUTH VIETNAM, Laos
Laotian Tai—LAOS, Thailand
Laqua—NORTH VIETNAM, Yunnan
Lat—SOUTH VIETNAM
Lati—NORTH VIETNAM, Yunnan
Lawa—THAILAND
Laya—SOUTH VIETNAM
Li—HAINAN
Lisu—YUNNAN, Burma, Thailand
Lolo—YUNNAN, Kweichow, Szechwan, Laos, North Vietnam
Loven—SOUTH VIETNAM, Laos
Lü—YUNNAN, Burma, Thailand, Laos, North Vietnam
Lutzu—YUNNAN

Ma—SOUTH VIETNAM
Malays—MALAYA, Thailand
May—NORTH VIETNAM
Menam—SOUTH VIETNAM, Laos
Miao—KWEICHOW, Hunan, Szechwan, Kwangsi, Yunnan, North Vietnam, Laos, Thailand
Minchia—YUNNAN
Mnong—SOUTH VIETNAM
Moken—BURMA, Thailand, Malaya
Monom—SOUTH VIETNAM
Mons—BURMA, Thailand
Muong—NORTH VIETNAM

Nagas—ASSAM, Burma
Nakhi—YUNNAN, Szechwan
Neua—LAOS, North Vietnam
Ngeh—LAOS, South Vietnam
Ngung Bo—LAOS
Nha Heun—LAOS
Nhang—NORTH VIETNAM, Yunnan

Noang—SOUTH VIETNAM
Noar—SOUTH VIETNAM, Laos
Nop—SOUTH VIETNAM
Nüa—YUNNAN
Nung—KWANGSI, North Vietnam

Oy—LAOS

Pacoh—SOUTH VIETNAM
Pak Tai—THAILAND
Palaungs—BURMA, Yunnan
Panthay—YUNNAN, Burma
Pa-y—NORTH VIETNAM, Yunnan
Pear—CAMBODIA
Phuan—LAOS
Phuong—SOUTH VIETNAM
Phuthai—LAOS, North Vietnam, Thailand
Pru—SOUTH VIETNAM
P'u Noi—LAOS

Raglai—SOUTH VIETNAM
Rai—SOUTH VIETNAM
Red Tai—NORTH VIETNAM, Laos
Rengao—SOUTH VIETNAM
Rhadé—SOUTH VIETNAM, Cambodia
Rien—SOUTH VIETNAM
Ruc—NORTH VIETNAM

Sach—NORTH VIETNAM
Saoch—CAMBODIA
Sapuan—LAOS
Sayan—SOUTH VIETNAM, Laos
Sedang—SOUTH VIETNAM
Sek—LAOS, Thailand
Semang—MALAYA, Thailand
Senoi—MALAYA
Siamese Tai—THAILAND, Malaya
So—LAOS, Thailand
Sop—SOUTH VIETNAM
Sork—LAOS
Sou—LAOS
Souei—LAOS
Sre—SOUTH VIETNAM
Stieng—SOUTH VIETNAM, Cambodia

Tau-Oi—LAOS, South Vietnam
Thap—LAOS
The—LAOS
Tho—NORTH VIETNAM, Kwangsi
T'in—THAILAND, Laos
T'ou Lao—NORTH VIETNAM
Tring—SOUTH VIETNAM

Trung-cha—NORTH VIETNAM, Kwangsi
Tung-chia—KWEICHOW, Hunan, Kwangsi

Ven—LAOS
Vietnamese—SOUTH VIETNAM, North Vietnam

Wa—BURMA, Yunnan
White Tai—NORTH VIETNAM

Yao—KWANGSI, Kwangtung, Hainan, North Vietnam, Laos, Thailand
Yuan—THAILAND, Laos
Yumbri—THAILAND

YUNNAN
Achang (Burma)
Akha (Burma, Thailand, Laos)
Chinese Shans (Burma)
Haw (Thailand, Laos)
Lahu (Burma, Thailand, Laos)
Lisu (Burma, Thailand)
Lolo (Kweichow, Szechwan, Laos)
Lü (Burma, Thailand, Laos, North Vietnam)
Lutzu
Minchia
Nakhi (Szechwan)
Nüa
Panthay (Burma)
KWEICHOW
Chung-chia (Yunnan)
Kelao (Hunan, Yunnan, Kwangsi, North Vietnam)
Miao (Hunan, Szechwan, Kwangsi, Yunnan, North Vietnam, Laos, Thailand)
Tung-chia (Hunan, Kwangsi)
KWANGSI
Chuang (Kwangtung)
Nung (North Vietnam)
Yao (Kwangtung, Hainan, North Vietnam, Laos, Thailand)
HAINAN
Li
BURMA
Burmese
Burmese Shans
Chins (Assam)
Hkamti Shans (Assam)
Hpon
Kachins (Yunnan, Assam)
Kadu
Karens (Thailand)
Khün
Moken (Thailand, Malaya)

Mons (Thailand)
Palaungs (Yunnan)
Wa (Yunnan)
ASSAM
Ahom
Garos
Khasis
Nagas (Burma)
THAILAND
Chaobon
Khorat Tai
Kui (Cambodia)
Lawa
Pak Tai
Siamese Tai (Malaya)
T'in (Laos)
Yuan (Laos)
Yumbri
LAOS
Alak
Ataouat
Brao (Thailand, Cambodia)
Cheng
Halang Doan (South Vietnam)
Jeh (South Vietnam)
Kasseng
Katang
Khmu (Thailand)
Lamet
Laotian Tai (Thailand)
Neua (North Vietnam)
Ngeh (South Vietnam)
Ngung Bo
Nha Heun
Oy
Phuan
Phuthai (North Vietnam, **Thailand**)
P'u Noi
Sapuan
Sek (Thailand)
So (Thailand)
Sork
Sou
Souei
Tau-Oi (South Vietnam)
Thap
The
Ven
NORTH VIETNAM
Black Tai (Laos)
Khua
Laqua (Yunnan)
Lati (Yunnan)
May
Muong
Nhang (Yunnan)
Pa-y (Yunnan)
Red Tai (Laos)
Ruc
Sach

Tho (Kwangsi)
T'ou Lao
Trung-cha (Kwangsi)
White Tai
SOUTH VIETNAM
Bahnar
Bih
Bout
Bru
Cao
Chams (Cambodia)
Chrau
Churu
Cua
Duane
Halang (Laos)
Hre
Hroy
Jarai (Cambodia)
Kalo
Katu
Kayong
Kil
Krung
Lang Ya (Laos)
Lat
Laya
Loven
Ma
Menam (Laos)
Mnong
Monom
Noang
Noar (Laos)
Nop
Pacoh
Phuong
Pru
Raglai
Rai
Rengao
Rhadé (Cambodia)
Rien
Sayan (Laos)
Sedang
Sop
Sre
Stieng (Cambodia)
Tring
Vietnamese (North Vietnam)
CAMBODIA
Chong (Thailand)
Khmer (Thailand, South Vietnam)
Pear
Saoch
MALAYA
Jakun
Malays (Thailand)
Semang (Thailand)
Senoi